THE LIFE OF
KENNETH
TYNAN

'Now we can read about [Ken] and in these grim times that is a great pleasure. It's like sitting in the gloomy monetarist and respectable 1840's and reading a life of Lord Byron, for Ken was a creature of his times . . . He was an artist who wept at sad endings, great performances and when one of his silk suits split across his bottom when he was courting his second wife . . . A full and carefully documented life of Ken Tynan is therefore heartily welcome . . . For the period covered by this most enjoyable book the time was Ken's, and he undoubtebly made the most of it.'

John Mortimer

'Posterity will find that it is not so much Tynan's craving to be noticed as the phenomenal vividness, authority and precision of his writing that will endure in reviews that gave the generation of actors lucky enough to be his contemporaries the kind of immortality Hazlitt gave Kean, something precious few critics have ever had to give in this or any century.'

Hilary Spurling

Novelist, journalist and screenwriter, Kathleen Tynan is the author of *The Summer Aeroplane* and *Agatha*. She lives in London with her children Roxana and Matthew.

Cover photos: copyright by H. J. Whitlock (front) and by Ida Kar/Monika Kinley/copyright Eileen Gray Estate (spine)

THE LIFE OF
KENNETH
TYNAN

Kathleen Tynan

Methuen · London

First published in paperback in this corrected edition in Great Britain
in 1988 by Methuen London,
Michelin House, 81 Fulham Road, London SW3 6RB
Originally published in Great Britain in 1987
by George Weidenfeld & Nicolson Limited, London.

Illustrations are from the author's archive
unless otherwise credited in the list of illustrations

Excerpts from letters by Louise Brooks are reprinted
by kind permission of the Estate of Louise Brooks

Printed in Great Britain
by Richard Clay Ltd, Bungay, Suffolk

British Library Cataloguing in Publication Data
Tynan, Kathleen
The life of Kenneth Tynan
1. Great Britain. Theatre. Directing
Tynan, Kenneth, 1927–1980
I. Title
792′.0233′0924

ISBN 0–413–18590–7

To Ken

Contents

	List of Illustrations	ix
	Prologue	I
I	Peacocks and Tynans	I2
2	Childhood	I9
3	The Young Dandy	28
4	*Quand Même*	37
5	Gangster in the Groves of Academe	49
6	The Marvellous Boy	62
7	A Leaping Salmon	80
8	Both Sides of the Footlights	91
9	Star Quality	97
I0	A Fleet Street Bishopric	I09
I I	New Blood	I17
I2	Involved, Committed, Engaged	I27
I3	Raised Voices	I37
I4	Rose Abandoned	I45
I5	The Toast of New York	I49
I6	Travellers' Tales	I56
I7	Back to Broadway	I68
I8	Theatrical Battles and Political Stages	I75
I9	Private Turmoil	I82
	Interlude	I92
20	The New Girl	I97
2I	Wooing	204
22	The Partnership with Olivier	2I5

CONTENTS

23 Living with Ken   230
24 Four-Letter Word   236
25 It Was Always Spring   243
26 *Soldiers*   249
27 Sex and Politics   256
28 End of the Decade   265
29 *Oh! Calcutta!*   277
30 Treading Water   286
31 Third Act: Curtain Up   290
32 Change   298
33 An Erotic Scenario   306
34 End of Summer   311
35 A Testing Time   321
36 Into the Labyrinth   326
37 Disaffection   338
38 Tynanosaur   350
39 Los Angeles   360
40 Louise Brooks   376
41 Endgame   390

    Epilogue   405
    Acknowledgements   409
    Books by Kenneth Tynan   413
    Source Notes   415
    Index   447

Illustrations

(*First section*)

Peter Peacock, 1912 (*Warrington Museum and Art Gallery*)

Peacock's Penny Bazaar, 1910 (*Mrs Ann Griffiths*)

Rose Tynan, Peter Peacock and Ken, 1927

The Mayor and Lady Peacock at a Christmas party for poor children

Sir Peter Peacock and Ken, 1934

Rose and May Tynan

Ken on holiday in Bournemouth

Peter Peacock and Ken

The schoolboy

Ken in fancy dress

The school prefects

Pauline Whittle and Ken, August 1945

A sixth-form conference, 1945

A letter from Orson Welles, 1943 (*Estate of the late Orson Welles*)

Ken as Hamlet, 1945

Oxford, 1945–48

Notes by Ken on his Oxford career

Cherwell front cover

Isis 'Idol' headline on Ken

Isis 'Idol' headline on Alan Beesley

Ken's production of *Samson Agonistes*

Ken directing *Winterset*, Paris, 1948

An Oxford revue

Ken as Holofernes in *Love's Labour's Lost*

Winterset: Ken as Judge Gaunt

Notes for Oxford Union speech by Ken

Essay by Ken on Ben Jonson

Jill Rowe-Dutton

Ken on the Committee of the Oxford Union, 1947

Ken's twenty-first birthday, Oxford, 6 April 1948 (*Keystone Press*)

Two photos of Ken directing *Man of the World*, 1950 (*Roger Wood*)

Eric Bentley and Ken at Salzburg, 1950 (*Eric Bentley*)

Directing Claire Bloom in *Martine*, 1952 (*BBC Hulton Picture Library*)

As the Player King with Alec Guinness in his *Hamlet* (*Trustees of the Theatre Museum, Victoria and Albert Museum*)

Ken directing *The Beaux' Stratagem*, 1949

(*Second section*)

Wedding of Ken and Elaine, 1951

Two photos of Ken and Elaine at bullfight school

Panorama magazine, Spring 1952

Theatre review by Ken

Ken and Peter Brook (*Bill Brandt*)

Ken, Elaine and Peter Ustinov

Two newspaper clippings

'The boy wonder', 1954 (*Peter Kneebone*)

Ken photographed by Cecil Beaton (*courtesy of Sotheby's, London*)

Programme for Foyle's Literary Luncheon, 21 November 1952

Article by Ken in the *Daily Sketch*

ix

Notes for Foyle's Literary Luncheon

Ken and Elaine at Mount Street

Rose and Tracy Tynan, 1953

Campaign for a national theatre, 1958 (*Michael Boys*)

Ken's first *Observer* theatre review, 5 September 1954

Aldermaston, 1958: Ken, Doris Lessing and Christopher Logue (*Roger Mayne*)

Ken and Tennessee Williams in Spain, 1955 (*Duncan Melvin*)

New York Post headline, 23 September 1960

Ken with Lenny Bruce, 1959

With Vivien Leigh at his New York farewell party, 1960

Lord Harewood being interviewed by Ken on *Tempo* (*ABC TV*)

Ken and Laurence Olivier with a model of Chichester Festival Theatre (*ABC TV*)

Groucho Marx, S. J. Perelman and Ken, London, 1964 (*Jane Bown, Observer*)

Ken's notes on the National Theatre production of *Othello*

National Theatre programmes (*Ken Briggs*)

Ken, Lord Chandos and Laurence Olivier

Ken outside the temporary National Theatre offices (*Stuart Heydinger, Observer*)

Interviewing Laurence Olivier on television, 1966 (*BBC Television*)

Ken with Helene Weigel

Ken and Kathleen lunching at the Etoile, 1964 (*Brian Seed*)

With Dominic Elwes in Ronda

Orson Welles and Ken in Madrid, 1964

Tracy with Ken in London

Ken and Kathleen in Valencia, 1968 (*D. D. Ryan*)

Antonio Ordóñez in Tarifa (*William Keating*)

(*Third section*)

Playboy cover (*Gerald Scarfe*)

Newspaper article on philology

Cartoon by Trog (*Trog, Daily Mirror*)

Oh! Calcutta! Calcutta! painted by Camille Clovis Trouille

A *Daily Mirror* headline

Joan Plowright, Rolf Hochhuth, Laurence Olivier and Ken, 1967

Marlene Dietrich with Ken and Kathleen at their wedding, 1967 (*Penelope Gilliatt*)

Roxana and Ken (*Frederick Ayer*)

Edna O'Brien and Roxana outside Thurloe Square, London

Kathleen, 1971

Tom Stoppard

Matthew with Ken

Mary McCarthy and Germaine Greer at Thurloe Square

Elia Kazan, Sam Spiegel, Budd Schulberg and Ken, 1972

Part of a poem for Roxana

Ken with Ratty

Ken by David Bailey (*copyright David Bailey*)

Ken in Italy, 1969

Roxana and Ken in Lucca, 1969

Laurence Olivier and Ken on television, 1975 (*BBC Television*)

Ken at Thurloe Square, 1976

Kathleen with Ken in Alsace in 1974

Ken as Louise Brooks (*Tim Jenkins*)

Matthew and Ken in Paris

Roxana with Ken in Puerto Vallarta in 1979

At home in Los Angeles (*Roddy McDowell*)

Ken in Havana

Michael White, Tracy and Jim McBride Tynans, Tony Richardson, Princess Margaret, Gore Vidal and Jack Nicholson in Bel Air (*Roddy McDowell*)

A sketch by Ken

Louise Brooks (*Jim Laragy*)

A letter to Adrian Mitchell

Burial service in Oxford, 1980 (*Angela Huth*)

Ken in Spain, 1978

Winter 1979 (*Roddy McDowell*)

Prologue

It is an odd business to turn sleuth on one's husband, to excavate and plunder a life, not just that married term to which a wife might lay claim, but the whole extravagant span. Yet it was a path I zealously wanted to pursue.

I had thought initially that I would have to choose between two avenues of access: that of the biographer or the route of the memoirist. The first was pressing in order to discover the Ken I never knew and to do justice to a man of interest to strangers: he was an important and influential figure in the theatre, in the evolution of mid-century *mores*, and as a man of letters. This approach would lead me to the archives and would require objectivity and distance.

But Ken was also important and influential in my life as my lover, my husband, my teacher, the father of my children, my scourge. Objectivity and distance would be difficult. The relationship indicated a memoir rather than a life, a book that would display the texture of lived experience, written not in the third person but in the first.

I balked at making a choice: I wanted to be outsider and insider, third person and first; a double vision, two voices, seemed the demand. Mine would be two books in one. The first part would be the more distant and impartial, while the second, after my arrival on the scene, would be more intimate. It would be necessary to distinguish where the one persona began and the other ended.

But as I began to examine Ken's life, and to lay out my thoughts and my research, this demarcation line broke. My two voices colluded, merged, went silent, clashed, argued, conflicted in *both* halves of this exercise in biography.

The road, quite clearly, wasn't going to be smooth. Nor would the conclusions reached at the end be shapely and definitive. My subject refused such treatment.

I lived with Ken for more than sixteen years. And through our courtship and married life, through his public battles and our private dramas, during halcyon days and black times, even during his long illness, I was forever astonished. I could not guess what would happen next, nor could I, loyalist and watchdog, much influence him, warn him of repercussions if the road were mined, direct him toward a more sanguine and mild course, because he would then accuse me of joining the tyrannous ranks that follow the middle way. Ken took violent sides but didn't join. He was *hors concours*, a solo performer. Still he did not care to be alone, which is why I was there with him, trying to fly with this bright plumed bird, trying to keep up, though I was much else as well: adoring, admiring, loving, entertained, angry, suicidal, and at many other stations of the cross of romantic love.

He was self-invented and brilliant, with a spontaneous capacity for expressing himself in an original way, particularly in his writing, where heart and head could be seamlessly conjoined. He thought he was a failure, yet even his most severe critics have called him the best drama critic since Bernard Shaw and one of the finest prose writers of our time. He knew well or had met many of the creative giants of the Western world, and thought that he was merely Boswell to the Johnsons. But, as Tom Stoppard proposed at Ken's memorial service, he was the 'product of his time but ... our time was of his making'.

In September 1979 Ken delivered a short letter to his agent about the autobiography he intended to write:

I've always been a talent snob – in other words, I've always wanted to meet and know and analyse the people I admire, whether they are actors, playwrights, directors, politicians, athletes, conversationalists, or what have you. A major theme of the book will be this quest for the best in all fields; and an allied theme will be my attempts – as journalist, propagandist, and impresario – to celebrate talent and make more room in the world for it to flourish.

He then provided a cast list: Laurence Olivier, Ernest Hemingway, Roman Polanski, Richard Burton, Marlon Brando, Lena Horne, Orson Welles, C. S. Lewis, John Lennon, James Thurber, Tennessee Williams – and so the list continued. I suspect this letter was more a flag to wave at publishers rather than a declaration of intent.

Ken died ten months later in a Santa Monica hospital without having started the book. He had wanted to write an autobiography before he was thirty, for he thought he'd be dead by then, having done everything there was to do, having lived to the hilt. Publishers frequently nudged and cajoled him to get on with the book; nor did he ever abandon the idea of writing a 'totally honest' account of his life. He would, from time to time, come up with a title: 'Tumbler Boneless' 'Independently Blue' and 'Sans Taste' were a few. He wrote to me in 1972, 'Byron has found me the title: "The Summer of a Dormouse".' What did I think? It did not sound quite apt.

'Rouse tempers, goad and lacerate, raise whirlwinds' – Ken had pinned these instructions above his desk and he followed them religiously. 'He was the sort of character every era needs to polarize its opinions and sort out its prejudices,' as a fellow critic, Alan Brien, put it. Ken would make people apoplectic with anger. After he had used the word 'fuck' on a television programme in 1965 to describe the sexual act, four motions attacking him were tabled in the House of Commons. One angry citizen wrote, 'Sir, I think it my duty to let you know that in my opinion you are a dirty dog. For God's sake shoot yourself and avoid further corruption.' The label 'controversial' was pinned to him like a hand grenade: too puritan, too left, too libertine, too hedonistic, too much.

It was not just his health that sent him out of England in 1976, but a true need for America, where he knew the carping would cease and the generosity begin. There is an entry in his journal which reads: 'Distaste, disdain, revulsion – the nouns of withdrawal, of contact rejected or scorned – these evoke the characteristic behaviour of only one country. They are the nouns of England.'

But he was very English, and he missed England. Self-exiled in Los Angeles, he had his secretary record and send him tapes of cricket matches. He read and re-read Dr Johnson, the prose writing of Byron and the works of P. G. Wodehouse. He particularly missed his favourite Indian restaurant, and Oxford in the summer, and the scale of the place (for he believed that no country of over 50 million people could function in a humane way). And he missed a few friends, odd circuitous conversations with strangers and passionate wasted hours on word games and anagrams. And he very much missed roast pheasant with bread sauce and a ready supply of Marmite. Not Johnny Carson, nor a brush with Fred Astaire, nor the everyday sun gave him much solace.

The autobiography he had hoped to write was never begun. However, Ken delivered, during those last few exiled years in California, five long profiles to *The New Yorker* magazine, written against awful odds because he was often hospitalized, panicked most hours of most days by his inability to breathe, with thoughts of death and talk of suicide, though he would never have managed it. It was not so much fear that stopped him from killing himself as rage. Rage at the emphysema, rage at the appalling and humiliating restrictions it imposed, a waking drowning. Sheer rage till the day he died.

I see him sitting on the edge of a bed attacking me, abusing God, shouting at some frightened nurse, his face blue from carbon dioxide poisoning, retching and hacking. Shortly before he died he told me, 'If you don't come down to the bottom with me, I don't want to go anywhere with you.' He knew for that journey I would desert.

In the time after his death I buried that picture and called up others of Ken well and buoyant. He was the blithest, best company you could wish for, and marvellously funny. Outings and pleasures were carefully planned (though he loved random incident) so that on good days, like Shakespeare's Master Fenton, he capered, he had eyes of youth, he spoke holiday.

Thin, tall, with a large bony English face and full lips, he dressed like a dandy with a blind eye for good taste. He always seemed to be leaning forward in anticipation, waiting to receive a new thought or sensation and to take hold of it as a dancer his partner, though soon to exhaust the partner and take off on a solo turn. When we first lived together I could not bear him to be out of sight. I would watch him from the window of our flat gusting down the street to catch a taxi, running for the cab, thin legs flying out frantically behind him, and I'd feel panic, as lovers do, at the thought that some fearful accident would befall him.

Electrically charged, though not properly earthed, that's how he seemed then. But there are other pictures more grounded and peaceful: Ken in Spain, near some cool water, by choice under an umbrella, concentrated in conversation, or in a book, or on one. He lived so completely in the present. Even when he was thinking I felt it was focused thinking, no little wispy daydreaming thoughts like mine.

There is a photograph of Ken addressing the Oxford Union debating society in 1948, 'grievously thin' as a witness put it. 'His head was so bereft of flesh that it could have played Yorick in an emergency, and it was crowned with a farouche thatch of butter-coloured hair.' And in the same photograph is a packed audience convulsed with laughter – for Ken could build a funny image or anecdote and stretch the invention beyond the conceivable limits, never letting the line snap.

Quite a few of those laughing Oxford contemporaries carried their Tynan-watching, or Tynan-baiting, into their postgraduate years. One of them, Alan Brien, wrote of him in 1954, at the time Ken became the drama critic for the *Observer* newspaper, that his whole ensemble recalled the young Aubrey Beardsley. 'What could a Beardsley from a middle-class Birmingham home do – except decide to be a genius or a freak.'

I have a photograph of that Birmingham boy, aged perhaps five. He wears a Christopher Robin hat and a trim little cotton outfit, but he has his lip hooked up in an expression which seems to cock a snook at his father, a florid middle-aged Edwardian.

More photographs as I open drawers and files ('clearing up' it is cheerfully called, this business of sorting through the ticking evidence of another's life). Here's a press snap of Ken, in London, with Marlene Dietrich. He's almost in the centre, and certainly in the light.

Ken with our three-year-old daughter, Roxana. He is grave and attentive. She is expansive. How could she not be under the beam of that attention? The secret, according to one of the many women who came under that beam – this one around 1959 – was Ken's 'marvellous concentration. With Ken somehow everything was possible. You felt the sentences could be finished, the ideas could germinate.' I remember nodding collusively as she talked, this stranger, one of my husband's onetime lovers. She said, 'No one was ever quite like him again,' after which I packed up my tape recorder and slunk off like an intruder.

A press photograph of Ken chairing a conference on drama at Edinburgh in 1963, steel-rimmed spectacles, hair cut short. A rigorous schoolmaster? Or the same exotic philanderer who had persuaded me to join him there for our first tryst (secret too, since I was but recently married to another man)? Ken's manner of wooing was showy, but it was brave. He took me rowing on a chilly lake outside the city. For this sporting event he wore a gold silk Italian suit. He struggled manfully with the oars, whereupon the silk suit tore across his backside. He wept.

I think he had hoped that the outdoors would win me over, for I was rather a conventional girl, much younger than he, who wore a tailored green coat and a silk equestrian headscarf of the royal sort. That weekend he said I ought to know about his political allegiances and his sexual tastes. He spelled them out very solemnly like a manifesto. (A month or so later he sent me a letter laying out his financial prospects, because he had marriage in mind.) The odd thing is that though I was not practised, I wasn't fazed by this eccentricity, and I loved him from that Edinburgh weekend.

I went on 'clearing up' in Los Angeles while the obituaries went on coming in. 'Did not live up to early promise' was a frequent comment. 'Ken killed himself,' friends would say in their friendly way. And I'd mumble about cigarettes and lungs and Ken's genetic predisposition to emphysema, and say it wasn't as simple as that. And they would go on, 'Ken dramatized death more than anyone else I've ever met.' Or they'd say, 'Ken was a cripple who soared.' Or, 'You see, every man is a fool with his own signature. Ken was not suicidal. He was a fool; he destroyed himself without being intimately aware.' Or, 'I think he thought, "Well, I'm riding very near the edge, but I'll get through."' 'I think he was enormously optimistic, ultimately, and it gave him audacity, and that's why he crashed.'

Early in 1982, two years after Ken's death, I returned to England to begin work on this book. I drove north to Warrington to find out about his father, Sir Peter Peacock. I came back to London and began interviews and research which went on for a year and a half and took me to the United States, France and Italy. I saw friends of Ken's, enemies, colleagues, school friends, tailors, doctors, lovers, performers he admired, critics he had influenced, opinion-mongers and politicians he had offended. I opened files and read letters. I copied out his notes from the margins of books and from theatre programmes.

I read his school reports, medical reports, references to him in other people's books, his own books. And my understanding of him became less simple as the contradictions multiplied.

Ken believed that he first found out that he was illegitimate on the death of his father in 1948. But there is evidence that he learned the truth as a child and then effectively repressed it.

Ken began his career as a director and became a critic by default. Was he a performer who happened to write? At Oxford University he had adored the 'theatre of fantasy and shock'. Some years later he became aware that 'art, ethics, politics, and economics were inseparable from each other'. There was in him a real and mortal battle, violently demonstrated, between the moralist and the pleasure-seeker. In sexual matters he veered dramatically from the romantic puritan to the sexual and aberrant obsessional. (When he could not reconcile Wilhelm Reich's healthy utopia with the world of de Sade, he would *in extremis* turn to C. S. Lewis and to God.) He believed he was dependent on the good opinion of women and not of men. But I would suggest that it was male authority, and male approval, that he needed. He was not particularly familial, though he adored his three children. He took part in most of the political debates of his time, but hated crowds, neighbours. He loathed the idea of self-denial, and would turn violent at the concept of duty, but he was impressed by the discipline required of a socialist revolution.

A failed creative writer, a writer without an important subject, or a creative artist? A man fascinated by unity, by wholeness, yet with a compulsive need to break up the established order. Confident and sophisticated; self-conscious and shy. Handsome and ugly. A truth-finder and a liar. Aesthete and vulgarian. Rational and irrational. Pragmatic and dogmatic. Physically robust though congenitally ill.

He was, I believe, an intellectual of imagination, though I would not presume to prove this, and he was rigorous too, though many intellectuals thought him a dilettante and an eccentric. He rarely followed trends; he often set them. He put up thousands of trial balloons, hated art snobs, could be superficial in his judgements, hectoring and cruel. He changed his opinion on a subject a dozen times but always returned to Brecht's view that 'truth is concrete'.

For a year and a half I invaded Ken's past and, of course, there were forfeits to be given, a price to be paid. By day I became an observer, an obsessive collector of data, a sleuth ready to spend long hours in the pursuit of some minor truth – the colour of a suit, the make of a typewriter, the birth date of some peripheral bit player in this bursting saga. But by night, tormented by dreams, I would pay the price of my unnatural objectivity.

An acute and evil loneliness.

I telephone a friend to complain. 'All this research, it's so difficult.' There's a silence on the long-distance line. Then my friend says, 'Don't forget the photograph of your wedding with you smiling at Ken. You've got to hang on to that.'

I sink my teeth in this stuff, this evidence, and I feel pain. I want it over and done. But who can easily 'cancel and pass on'?

Kierkegaard says only robbers and gypsies never revisit the past. He's wrong. I revisit the past. And I'm a robber – of Ken's life. And a gypsy: I live nowhere, a transatlantic migrant, happiest as a stranger in a Latin country. Robber, grave-robber, user, usurer, used. Colleague, friend, victim, victimizer. Analyst, microscopist. Lover, dislover. Wife, daughter, mother. Still bound by hoops of steel.

I went to Italy before starting to write and on a whim took a detour, turned inland from Viareggio on the airless valley road that leads to Florence and branches off to the walled mediaeval city of Lucca.

In 1969, when Ken and I came to live in a farm house near Lucca, we would drive down the hill to the town two or three times a week to lunch at the Buca di Sant'Antonio, or to sit in the café in the Piazza San Michele, alongside the pillared thirteenth-century church. And there we would order a Cinzano, read the newspapers, watch the pigeons sweep over the statue of the archangel Michael that crests the façade of the church.

I sat in the square for a while and then drove north out of the city on a now unfamiliar road packed with new crazy-paved villas, farm holdings and small factories, past the Villa Mansi with its fountains and water gardens, and further up into the vineyards to find the Fattoria Mansi – a seventeenth-century house, the colours of a white peach – where we had lived.

Memory had played no tricks. It looked as I remembered it when first we came in 1969, to retreat, for Ken to write, to replenish, to take stock – a constant factor, to be counted on, as unequivocal as the memory of my childhood house. Roxana, our daughter, was two. That summer she wore a lime-green cotton sundress, and ruled a lank stray dog (twice her size) called Serafino.

Ken reading under the umbrella on the terrace. Ken with drink in hand, Ken wearing turquoise sunglasses, cotton trousers and an orange shirt. And many other fragments of memory. Ken opening the shutters of his work room on the upper floor and calling down to me, reading out something he had just found. 'Listen to this: "The news from Tashkent was discouraging and for the rest of that day Chekhov was unable to write." ' A while after, 'Better still: "1858–1859 was a fallow period, during which Flaubert carried out the essential task of recharging his creative batteries." ' And two or three nights later, 'How about this? "The next decade was not a productive one for Swift." '

Ken proposing a trip. Let's go to Arezzo and see the Piero della Francescas. To Pisa. To San Gimignano. Well then, let's go to Lucca and buy ice-cream. His voice, my voice. Opening and closing of shutters. Smell of burning wood as October mornings grew sharper, the sun still hot enough to pull out the scent of the yellow rose that grew up the side of the front door. And at night the pungent smell of burning *spirali* to keep off mosquitoes.

We lived in that huge house with little more than beds, a few tables, and some cooking pots. The farmer brought in fresh produce every day, beans, sage, peppers, peaches and the local wine. His wife taught me how to make *zuppa di magro* with ham bones, vegetables and herbs.

In the grounds we had a carp pond fed by a mountain stream, and a grotto; inside the dank cave was a statue of a bagpiper, with a wine cask slung over one shoulder, his face worn away to a smile or a grimace – you could choose.

This period was a high-water mark in a marriage before the tide turned, before the past was explored to make sense of the present.

We had left London on 28 June 1969 to catch the air ferry from Lydd, eleven days after the New York opening of the erotic revue *Oh! Calcutta!*, and with Ken still badly bruised by its critical reception. By dusk we had reached Paris. At the restaurant Chez Denis we were joined by Derek Lindsay, an old and close friend of Ken's from Oxford, known at the university and ever after as 'Deacon', presumably because of his morose Italianate looks. I had been warned – for this was my first encounter – that he was deeply pessimistic and reclusive, and that he had spent much of his life in a cork-lined room. After leaving Oxford, he had written a highly praised novel called *The Rack*, set in a Swiss sanatorium.

Such was our dinner companion. He had re-entered Ken's life a few weeks before with a letter to beg Ken not to heed his enemies: 'You were always our marvellous boy, a dear post-war Cocteau, and you have vindicated all our hopes for you.'

Lindsay's enthusiasm did not extend to himself, nor to life in principle. And as Monsieur Denis served us *la religieuse de saumon*, Deacon began to examine his own 'intense and terribly destructive' character and to attack the questionable advantage of this long feast of life. 'Each of us a tube and not much more,' he began, to which we could do little but nod since our mouths were full. His old friend, who was also worried about the business of getting *au fond de lui-même*, interrupted. 'I quite simply seek enjoyment,' said Ken, 'because I remember about thirty times between waking and sleeping and always while I'm asleep that I'm going to die. And the more scared I am, the more pleasure and enlightenment I want to squeeze from every moment. But then I feel agonized about work left undone. So as a profoundly death-fearing man, I'm capable simultaneously of the highest delight and the deepest despair.'

I said he could stop despairing for a bit as we were on holiday. That reassured him, and he went on to tell his friend he now believed that only those activities which could be described as a form of play were worthy of his attention, that the next few months would be turned into a private playground, instead of the public battleground of the last few years. He said he was definitely going to have a nice time. There would be solitude *à deux*, since he and his wife were determined to meet as few people as possible. Recently, he explained, he had tended to lose interest in people as soon as they passed out of his life. Often he lost interest when they were simply not present; sometimes even when they went behind his chair for a moment. Some parts of his mind were muddy from intellectual self-abuse; others musty from disuse. He explained that his posture as a left-winger was held by many to be ambiguous. He concluded that a man with one foot in the past and the other in the future is peculiarly vulnerable to emasculation in the present.

At this point I joined in the philosophic exchange and announced without a great deal of sense that 'no wine should be drunk with champagne'. Then the evening more or less wound down, the bill was called for and paid, and the charming malcontent waved off in his taxi.

On the road: Auxerre to Avallon (for lunch at the Hostellerie de la Poste). Saulieu to Roanne (for dinner *chez* the *frères* Troisgros). We are testing the rhythm of a holiday, making concessions to the small discomforts. Ken notes: 'To ensure immediate arrival of breakfast in hotels: lock the door, remove your clothes and go to the lavatory.' I add, 'To ensure successful picnic get into car and close windows.'

Slow waking together after foolish holiday dreams. Ken dreams about going to the circus to see the little black dog. 'He is very small. About 3 inches high, but very confident. The ringmaster comes out and announces, "The little dog will now give his famous impersonation of Hamlet, Prince of Denmark." The little dog comes to attention, salutes with right paw and barks. The crowd goes mad. "He's a fine old Gaelic gentleman," a voice cries. "What else does he do?" "He doesn't do much," says the ringmaster, "but he's got some lovely costumes."'

Clever pronouncements noted down on napkins, in diaries, on the margins of holiday reading. Maxims that almost substitute for real, thoughtful work. On Milan cathedral: 'Too *pizzicato*,' Ken says. 'No calm passages. Every spire and gargoyle shrieks, "Look at me!" Secure cathedrals say, "I'm looking at you."'

Milan, Genoa, Portofino. Lunch with a famous actor and his tortured wife. 'What would the *Variety* headline be,' asks Ken as we drive away, 'if star slugged autograph collector? It would be: SHIT HITS FAN.'

Porto Ercole: snorkelling and sun. Sun worship. '*Soleil, soleil! . . . Faute éclatante!*' Ken says that sunworshippers tend to be animal, pagan, pantheistic, Manichean (since the sun is indifferent). Akhenaten's 'Hymn to the Sun'. But Akhenaten, according to C. S. Lewis, did not identify God with the sun; the latter was merely God's manifestation. Ken now proceeds to undermine his previous position: he has always admired the heretic pharaoh as the first individualist in history. Now he wonders whether what is truly original about Akhenaten is the fact that he was an early prophet of Christianity.

When we finally reached Lucca and settled into the Fattoria Mansi, we quite quickly discovered that there was no time for work.

I do not now recall why we left or what commitments Ken felt he had to keep. But at the end of November our daughter and her nanny were put on a plane for London, and by 1 December we were in Geneva. I remember dining there with the Marxist art critic, John Berger, who was busy licking his political wounds after Prague and Paris, and considering whether a retreat into self might not be on the cards. I remember the icy drive to Paris in my Mini Cooper, and arriving at the Hôtel Lutèce in the Rue Jules-Chaplain, off the Boulevard Montparnasse, idly thinking that it was the end of the sixties and that there was nothing merely fashionable or specious in bemoaning the end of that dazzling decade.

Well almost nothing, for my view of the sixties was severely tested, the next night, at a performance of Arrabal's *Orison* at Théâtre de l'Epée du Bois. To reach the auditorium we were forced down a dark tube, physically assaulted the while by actors for the dubious enlightenment, once we had reached the auditorium, of watching an emaciated Christ with dirty feet and green skin pee bountifully over us from the stage. Ken, who had regard for the rights of the audience, was outraged. He recalled Orson Welles' advice to a director: 'Gentlemen, many things are permitted to us in the theatre vis-à-vis the audience. We can throw bombs at them, we can turn flame-throwers on them. What we cannot do, gentlemen, is to unzip our flies and piss on them.'

We were glad to be back in Paris. Glad to be back at the Lutèce, this quiet little hotel that had been our Paris home since first I lived with Ken, and his Paris place for many a moon and love before me. Next door was a music conservatory and opposite a whore house, noted for La Comtesse, who worked only with feathers. On the corner was the O.K. Bar, across from Rodin's massive statue of Balzac at the top of the Boulevard Raspail. Many of the regulars at the Lutèce were circus performers and vaudevillians, though many were one-night lovers. Each room had a double and a single bed, and mirrors built into the wall. But the place was oddly chaste, and one June night I leaned out of our window over the back courtyard to listen to a nightingale.

Recently I found the following in the journals of Cyril Connolly. He wrote from Paris in September 1929: 'I am for the intricacy of Europe, the discreet and many folded strata of the old world, the past, the North, the world of ideas. I am for the Hôtel de la Louisiane.' I had only to substitute 'Lutèce' for 'Louisiane' for tears to spill.

When I went back to revisit, the hotel sign was down and the door firmly shut. I rang and was told by a hirsute woman that the place was now occupied by an order of nuns, '*un foyer pour les religieuses*,' she explained, for her sisters '*en passage*'.

So that's gone, though I hold hard to its memory as to all the others of that summer and autumn. Now, as I begin this book on Ken, I set them up like icons, those zestful images, for reassurance and for protection.

1

Peacocks and Tynans

> In any real sense of the word I was born at Oxford: I have
> no more connection with my early life and with Birming-
> ham than I have with Timbuctoo.

Ken took the view, which he never abandoned, that life started on his first day at Oxford. He came up to the university in 1945, and by the time he left in 1948 he had become a legend. This elegant Andrew Aguecheek was incontrovertibly original. 'It was the kind of originality', according to Ken's fellow undergraduate Derek Lindsay, 'that was not remotely laboured. I had the impression that his confidence was total, that it was soundly based upon a perfect appraisal of his most astonishing capacities, which came into life fully formed.'

'Those astonishing capacities', however, were not delivered raw to Oxford, but had been effectively nurtured and rehearsed in Birmingham, 'the ugliest city in Europe, that cemetery without walls', as Ken described his home town. He left the English provinces in 1945 – without accent or marks of class – and rarely returned, 'because [Birmingham] bored me, the people bored me'. The stories he subsequently told about his childhood were set pieces, casually inaccurate, recalled for the benefit of interviewers or to satisfy my avid curiosity; they were without resonance. If I prodded and pushed him, he would tell me of Uncle Bill's Delage, or his mother's potato cakes; of girls picked up in youth clubs; of seeing *Citizen Kane* for the first time, and playing the lead in *Hamlet*. Of cricket. Or of staying home on parade day to masturbate by courtesy of the *Sunday Pictorial* pin-ups. Though he felt affection for his mother, he had little to say about his father except that their relationship was not warm. 'We got on not badly but not closely.' His most fond and animated memory of Peter Peacock (alias Tynan) was that he had once shaken hands with a man whose father had shaken the hand of Samuel Johnson. It was Ken's sole claim to a link with the literary past.

Four times Ken's childhood erupted, and on each occasion he briefly dramatized the effect upon his psyche: in 1948, when he was told, on the death of his father, that he was illegitimate; in 1961, on the death of his mother in a mental home; in 1962, when he went into analysis to allow himself – so he put it – to leave his first marriage; and finally in the mid-1970s, his health destroyed and his second marriage under stress. After each of these eruptions settled, Ken passed on like an amnesiac.

Oxford was to blame, he argued. It had cut him off from his roots, performed 'heart-transplant surgery'. Occasionally the Oxford Ken would come up against the Birmingham Ken in a half-hearted, unresolved sort of class engagement. But the fight was only part of the story. The true and mortal conflict (never fully understood or examined) took place between this lovely, self-propelled freak of genetics and his innocently punitive parents.

Kenneth Peacock Tynan was born in the morning of 2 April 1927, in a small Birmingham nursing home, Glenhurst, 319 Shaftmoor Lane, Hall Green. A doctor and midwife were in attendance, and the baby was delivered by Caesarean section. The birth certificate lists the parents as Peter Tynan – occupation 'draper (shopkeeper)' – and Rose Tynan, both of 955 Stratford Road, Hall Green. The certificate is not devoutly accurate. Peter Tynan was in fact Sir Peter Peacock, a fifty-four-year-old justice of the peace and civic dignitary, six times Mayor of the north-country town of Warrington and a successful businessman.

The mother, 'Letitia Rose Tynan formerly Tynan', was a thirty-eight-year-old unmarried Lancashire woman of Irish origin. About the birth there was nothing shotgunnish for the parents had been living together as man and wife, and Ken was preceded by another love-child, a daughter, who had died at birth.

When Peter Peacock ran off to live in Birmingham with Rose, he abandoned his wife and five children for good. He did, however, return to Warrington two days of every week for the rest of his life in order to carry out his civic and business activities. To protect his secret he arranged a carefully orchestrated double life, one for Peter Tynan, another for Sir Peter Peacock. The reason for this elaborate charade is not clear. Was it to protect Rose, the Baptist working-class girl who thought that to be an unmarried mother was a sin? Or was it to protect *his* reputation since Maria Peacock had refused him a divorce? Perhaps his libido required some alternative life which the public and commercial role did not permit, a scenario familiar to the nineteenth century, and one which Robert Louis Stevenson took to its extreme conclusion with Dr Jekyll and Mr Hyde.

The Peacock saga has the authentic ring of a penny dreadful, but it is also Ken's history.

The working-class streets of Warrington where Peter Peacock was brought up, with their two-up, two-down rows of squat houses, now look less like slums and more like a model toy town – the brickwork painted red, the front steps waxed and polished. In the eighteenth-century town hall there is an oil portrait of Sir Peter Peacock, which presents a handsome moustachioed, thrusting man. One hand, surprisingly delicate and soft, holds on to his mayoral chain. Elsewhere in Warrington the name of Peacock is attached to a street and is inscribed on a plaque which commemorates the new bridge of 1915. Yet, despite this local celebration, he is buried in the municipal cemetery in an unmarked grave.

Who was Peter Peacock, Ken's improbable father? He was born on 13 April 1872, in the village of Clophill, near Bedford, in the Midlands, to Susan (née Grummitt) and Jesse Peacock, a shoemaker. Peter was the seventh child of the union. On the birth certificate of the next child, in 1874, Jesse is described as a farm labourer, which would suggest that he had lost his job as shoemaker. This may explain why, around 1875, the family decided to move to the industrial north, where Jesse worked as a 'drayman', driving a brewer's cart.

The eldest son, Albert, who had served a draper's apprenticeship in Hampshire, eventually took effective charge of the ten children, since his father suffered from epilepsy and from what his death certificate, in 1893, described as 'cerebral softening'. Albert had his brothers and sisters selling matches, and when they left school he set them up in apprenticeships. In 1891 he rented four stalls in the covered market in Warrington and sold candles, shoe polish and toys at a penny an item.

By the turn of the century the Peacocks had set up twelve penny bazaars and two drapery stalls in Warrington, and were beginning to expand in the neighbourhood. Like Marks and Spencer they started in market trading, with goods supplied from their own warehouses, and then set up their own cheap and garish multiple-goods stores in the new fangled American style. Peacocks flourished in England and Wales in the 1920s and 1930s, and declined in the 1950s.

Peter Peacock used to say that he had known hard times during his childhood in Warrington. 'I had bare feet and a snotty nose,' he would tell his housekeeper. At fourteen he left school to enter the service of the railway company in Cheshire as a five-shillings-a-week office boy. At sixteen he joined the Fellowship of Foresters, to which his father and grandfather had belonged. It was the beginning of a lifelong association with the friendly societies – those organizations begun in the seventeenth century to provide working men with sick benefits and insurance, the ancestors of the trade union movement.

In 1890 Peter, now a railway clerk, married Annie Timmins, the daughter of an iron puddler. Both were nineteen. In October of that year Annie died in childbirth, having produced a son, Peter. She is buried in the municipal cemetery under a handsome Gothic headstone decorated with convolvulus.

Below a delicate hand with a finger pointing towards heaven are the words, 'Meet Me Here'. Years later Peter said, 'I worked hard for that stone, but she deserved it.'

Maria Timmins, three years younger than her sister Annie, took charge of the baby, and evidently moved in upon the widower, for in July 1893 she married him, and eventually produced five sons, two of whom died young. The last child was a girl, Marian, born in 1916.

Photographs of Maria show a dumpy, predatory person. It is hard to find anyone with a good word to say for her. Bertha Peacock, who married into the family, recalls Maria's bad temper, how she would throw a tantrum and refuse to show up at a civic function. 'Why did I marry Maria?' was a self-contained joke Peter liked to tell after he had left his wife.

Around 1896 Peter became a sub-agent for the Great Northern Railway. Two years later he went into business as a coal merchant, then as a stone-mason and contractor. He also set up an accounting firm. By 1899 he had joined the soap works of Joseph Crosfield and Sons, for which he later became traffic manager. And in 1903, standing as 'the working man's friend and a progressive reformer', he was elected Liberal councillor for Bewsey Ward.

In 1912 Peter won a huge majority over the Tory candidate at Whitecross Ward. And a year later he was Mayor of Warrington. He told his council that he thought of himself in his new role as chairman of a board of directors – an apt description of the way he would handle the job. Chairman of boards was more or less his role for the rest of his career, and he brought to it patience, a high boredom threshold and an ability to take charge. Behind Peter was the family business and extensive interests in land and housing; he could afford to devote himself to civic duties and charitable causes.

As mayor, he was fully engaged in the war effort, 'the work of our great Empire', and campaigning for Lord Derby's recruiting appeal. 'When I walk down the streets', he said, 'and see the young men, it makes my blood boil when I think that they ought to be in the firing line helping their comrades.'

In 1918 he received the freedom of Warrington, became Master of the masonic Lodge of Lights, and on 3 June he was knighted along with fifteen other provincial mayors and justices of the peace. In Warrington, flags were hoisted, bells pealed, and at Peacock's Bazaar warehouse in West Street the whole neighbourhood came out to celebrate.

In the same year he was elected mayor for a sixth term, and was unanimously selected as Liberal parliamentary candidate. He never had much of a chance and lost by a wide margin. His great hero, Lloyd George, had given his support to the Coalition candidate, Harold Smith, a Tory and a much tougher and more sophisticated campaigner. Sir Peter said he would not 'get soured'. 'I have been fighting all my life, first to get a living, and then for the community'.

On 20 August 1919, a garden party was given to bid Sir Peter farewell as mayor, and as a consolation prize he was given the honorary post of deputy mayor.

Towards the end of the Great War a young voluntary postal worker called Rose Tynan met Peter Peacock at a whist drive. The date, never established by the protagonists, may well have been 14 November 1917, for on that day the Warrington postal staff went to Parr Hall, for Mayor's Sunday, and the centrepiece of the event was a whist drive.

That the Mayor, upon meeting Rose, rushed her off to Switzerland (Ken's version of the story) seems unlikely. Nor does family record tell us how the courtship developed. All that is certain is that Peter would visit Rose Tynan and her family, turning up quite openly in his chauffeur-driven mayoral limousine, and that by 1921 Peter and Rose were living together in Birmingham, as man and wife.

Rose was short, bandy-legged and plain. In photographs of the early 1920s she is almost indistinguishable from her equally plain sisters May and Georgina, though Rose's smile is sweeter and her nose longer. 'She was one of the fey people,' according to May's daughter Ruth Cashmore. 'Very sweet, a little bit simple. I mean when she was baptized she took a hanky with her to dry her eyes.' A woman who knew Rose when she worked at Crosfield's packing perfumed toilet soaps, says, 'She didn't run after the boys. She wasn't a showy or common girl. I always remember her carrying books under her arm.' A nephew, Bill Tynan, said of her, 'She wasn't comely, but light and love and beauty shone in her eyes.'

Letitia Rose Tynan was born on 19 September 1888, in Warrington, to Samuel Tynan of a Protestant family from Abbeyleix, Ireland, and to Anne Rebecca, née Mitchell. Rebecca worked as housekeeper to a major, and it was most probably through this military connection that she met Samuel Tynan (an army private who had served as a batman in India). They were married, and produced four daughters and a son.

Samuel drank himself into the grave: acute alcoholism is recorded as the cause of his death, at the age of sixty-four, in 1915, one year after his wife's demise.

Rebecca had brought up her children as teetotallers and Christians, and she passed on to them the finesse she had acquired in service. When she was dying of bronchitis and of what was probably severe emphysema, she called in her daughter May. She sat up in bed, wrapped in several shawls because the room was so cold, and she spoke with effort. 'You're going to have to look after Rosie and Georgie for the rest of your life because they'll never manage on their own.'

After her death at the age of fifty-seven, her three unmarried daughters moved into a house at 4 Arthur Street. Rose took in hand laundry, May worked as a seamstress, and Georgina as a cashier. By 1915 May had left to marry George Wooldridge. Five years later Georgina married William Rafter. As for Rose, the least dare-devilish of the sisters, she stayed on in Arthur Street for a few months and then took off with Peter Peacock and a life in sin.

The story was kept muted in Warrington, though you can still find old ladies there who will whisper disapprovingly about Peter Peacock's affair. His old family, and the new, conspired to keep things quiet.

Peter Peacock took with him to Birmingham a large entourage of Peacock, and Tynan relatives. He helped set up Rose's brothers-in-law in small shops. And he went into the drapery business with his brother Albert, already established in Birmingham. When Albert left in 1926, he put his own son George in charge of the wholesale warehouse in West Bromwich and of Peacock stores. Peter remained overseer, godfather of the enterprise and financial adviser.

On Monday of each week Peter would return to Warrington, by train or in his chauffeur-driven Daimler. There another chauffeur in another car (first a Wolseley, many years later a Chrysler Airflow) would take over. He would stay at 62 West Street, looked after by his sister Annie, and by his housekeeper Nellie Fairbrother, and leave on Wednesday morning. He continued an active association with the town council which ended only with the election of the Labour government of 1945. Each Tuesday he sat on the magistrates' bench. He worked for the local Liberal Party (becoming president many years later in 1938). He bought and developed more land, suburban housing and holiday resorts. He built up a chemical works, as well as brick, transport and aluminium firms. His interests spread far beyond Warrington. In short, his was the story of a successful self-made man.

His sons, Ken's half-brothers, on the other hand, had undistinguished careers. Peter liked to gamble. Douglas ran a wholesale tobacconist's. Stanley was a publican and Reginald worked in insurance. His daughter, Marian, was closest to her father, and he delighted in spoiling her when she came to visit him on his trips to Warrington. Today she lives in North Wales, and is an active supporter of the Liberal Party. Ken met his half-sister once, in 1965, during negotiations to liquidate a family trust. He said she was a tall, rather severe woman with whom he got on amiably but with whom he had no rapport. He never met any of his half-brothers. Nor did he wish to. He once explained, 'I'd have nothing to say to them.'

As for Lady Peacock, she continued to live in Warrington in a series of comfortable houses, as if nothing had changed. Sometimes she would stay at her bungalow in Fairbourne, North Wales, where Peter and Rose also had a house. One Peacock relative recalls that Peter used to order smoked salmon and other goods in Warrington and despatch his chauffeur to pick up the order and deliver it to Wales. If Maria heard that Peter had been in the shop, she would send her own chauffeur along to requisition the goods.

Peter Peacock was an even-tempered man, despite the provocation of Maria. His housekeeper says that he was always smiling and that if he were miserable he would never say so. Peter would come back from the courts and tell Nellie and her family about the day's business; he would have them in stitches.

He wore a swallowtail coat, a top-hat or a bowler, grey spats and very soft boots with buttons and laces. All his shirts were handmade, of Lavista silk. He had a beautiful diamond ring, his nails were always manicured and he carried a cane.

'I'd make him green pea soup,' Mrs Fairbrother recalls. 'He liked it thick so that the spoon would stand up. He used to say, "I think these peas have gone through on bloody stilts." He kept very good champagne and, although he was a teetotaller, called for it whenever there was a child born.' He normally drank nothing but Vichy water, and he would say, 'It's what Frenchmen wash their feet in.'

By all accounts Peter adored Rose. He took her to Ascot races, to holidays at the seaside and to the music hall. Rose's sisters even maintained that he turned down a baronetcy because of his liaison, though other members of the family claim that he turned down the honour because he did not think his eldest son deserved to inherit.

2

Childhood

From 1921 Rose and Peter Tynan lived in Birmingham, at Hillcrest, 955 Stratford Road, an ugly three-storey terraced house of the turn of the century, maintained by a cook-general; there was also a gardener.

After a number of miscarriages, Rose bore Ken. He was dedicated at the Hall Green Baptist chapel. Neighbours and relatives attest to the fact that he was adored and cosseted, 'the apple of his mother's eye'.

Ken's view, recorded on scraps of paper and theatre programmes during a nine-month period of analysis that he undertook in 1962, is drastically different. 'A caesarean and a bastard and a contemptible object,' he wrote: 'A bedwetter, I soiled my mother and she punished me by refusing to feed me.' The proclamations sound as violent as bursts of machine-gun fire on a pastoral morning. How had Ken come by this information? Or had it been planted by his therapist? Had he as an infant been affected by Rose's sense of shame? ('I wasn't really wicked, you know,' she used to tell her Methodist friends, many years later, as if to seek reassurance.) Is Orson Welles' fanciful explanation more to the point, that every English, or even Anglo-American, child must have some side of his memory touched with the idea of some terrible sin – 'It's part of the culture'? The questions beg answers which are not easily forthcoming. Ken had no continuing interest in these incendiary scraps of information. I recall that he told me to keep the notes but to put them away in the souvenir file. There they lie today along with mementos of the 1960s, used bullfight tickets, and drawings made by our children.

Ken's Aunt May used to say of him when he was a baby, 'You'd have thought he was half-witted. He didn't talk till he was nearly three.' When Ken did begin to talk, he also began to stammer. He was sent to a speech therapist and, according to his cousins, 'fought tooth and nail' to overcome his impediment. As he got older his stammer lessened, and he never stammered when acting or delivering a prepared speech or in a relaxed one-to-one conversation. But from time to time, usually when under stress, words would get locked. Then his lips would be forced back as by an invisible bit, leaving teeth and gums bare; as the journalist Godfrey Smith described the effect, 'At these moments onlookers had the disquieting sense that something awful was going to happen.'

The medical profession has come up with no very scientific explanation for the cause of stammering, but almost all the suppositions put forward apply to Ken. He was overprotected by an anxious and demanding mother. He was left-handed and forced to be right-handed. He was both dependent on the approval of his mother and possibly hostile towards her for that dependency. He felt his relationship with his father was distant. He had a bronchial condition. 'It must have felt like swimming in a vast vat of yeast,' is Ken's cousin Ruth Cashmore's description of the atmosphere of his early years. 'It's a wonder he didn't become a homosexual. If they could be made, that was the background to do it.'

In an article on stammering written in 1976, Ken observed that 'When I was about six I had a rather sadistic teacher who said to me "If you don't shut up, Tynan, I will cut your tongue out." That was a pretty ghastly moment, and may have started me stuttering.' This casual, unconsidered and possibly invented explanation exactly illustrates how hard it is to interpret those distress signals now stored in a souvenir file.

One possible effect of the stammer was to make Ken's natural eloquence more extravagant; and if anyone tried to inhibit that extravagance of opinion or expression he would push it even further. Throughout his life he refused to be moderate or merely reasonable.

The first school Ken attended was a state institution in College Road, Birmingham. Aged five, he was the King of Hearts in the school play. He wore white trousers, a jerkin with a big red heart back and front, and a crown. His Peacock cousin Betty Lawley, almost the same age, remembers him at this age as 'very sensitive and kind. Anything to do with blood was distasteful. He was also very pro-American.' By six he was keeping a journal and writing and performing in plays for solo performer.

Holidays were spent in a house called Kenrose, at Bournemouth on the south coast. From here the family would take off for picnics in the New Forest, under the benevolent dictatorship of Peter Peacock. They would meet at the Balmer Lawn Hotel at Brockenhurst amid the rhododendrons and the wild ponies, and play cricket on the lawn. They would form a ring and sing 'Under the Spreading Chestnut Tree', and if anybody missed a gesture or lost track of the words he'd be thrown out in disgrace.

The great puppet master was Peter Peacock. 'He was a showman, really,' Ruth says, 'because he would set a scene and get everybody where he wanted them. Then he would sit back and laugh while people got themselves in a mess. He would take all the children on a mystery tour and throw pennies out of the car to encourage the children to open the gates. He'd challenge members of the family to smuggle themselves through toll gates by covering themselves in a blanket or hiding in the boot of the car.'

Peter once bought a set of cut-glass champagne goblets, and gave the one with the eight little holes around the rim to Auntie Annie. As she tipped it up, the champagne trickled out, and she kept saying, 'Ooh dear, I am a dirty girl, aren't I?', and Peter kept saying, 'Yes, Annie, and it's all that that's going in making it worse.' And he would wheeze when he laughed because of his bad chest and clear his throat with a 'rrum' and smile, looking like an amiable walrus. Ken, emulating his father, tested his family with bouncing plates, drip teacups, suspended window tappers and sewn-up pyjama legs. Many decades later Ken became obsessed with the kind of man who could dominate his environment, able to impose his own terms. The model of such a man was Sir Peter Peacock.

From an early age Ken's family were in awe of him, of his astonishing intelligence. Realizing how unusual he was, his parents allowed him to try anything he wanted. He was not so much spoiled as encouraged to satisfy his huge curiosity ('He used to *read* the dictionary,' his cousin Betty reports). They gave him money to buy books, records and subscriptions to magazines, money to go to the movies once or twice a week, and money to buy a monc :le. Whatever this mysteriously gifted child took up he had to be perfect at it, whether it was sailing model boats, playing the piano or rowing. If he felt he had failed he would give up the endeavour. He took dancing lessons but when he slipped and fell during a demonstration foxtrot he was so mortified that he decided to abandon the dance floor there and then.

His cousin Alan Jackson Mee found it very difficult to keep up. 'Ken would say, "Aren't you following me? Aren't you with me?" I'd have to be a valet and he'd be a count with a French accent.' Ken would drag his cousin off to cricket matches by bus or car because – and this was true of him throughout his life – he did not care to walk. 'If you said, "Let's walk," ' Alan recalls, 'he'd have a punch-up with you on the spot.' Nor was it because he got out of breath, as in later years. He was not then especially asthmatic. (The only health problem was a series of ear infections, which led to a mastoid operation.)

At the age of eight, in 1935, Ken transferred from the College Road School to the George Dixon Elementary School, and there he stayed for three years. His extra-mural activities consisted of swapping boys' magazines, writing and performing in his own plays, and getting pregnant. He became pregnant after reading A. J. Cronin's *Hatter's Castle*, a popular fiction about a Victorian girl who looks in the bathroom mirror, sees her stomach swelling and feels the man-child growing within her. Ken was a plump little boy and he too looked in the bathroom mirror. He was going to have to go to the headmaster and say, 'There's something I think you should know.' One evening he contemplated suicide. Should he, like the girl in the book, throw himself in the river and end it all? An American boy at his school told him the facts of life: that either he'd be responsible for the Second Coming or he'd be all right.

Ken had enrolled at the George Dixon School in the same year that his parents moved from Hall Green to another ugly suburb of Birmingham, to Portland Road, Edgbaston, where the family employed a maid, cleaning woman and chauffeur. The newly built house was detached, with red brick and white stucco. In the front were stained-glass windows of castles, windmills and sailing boats. A conservatory and a large garden backed on to recreation grounds. It was a house full of walnut furniture from Maples store, cut-glass vases and oil paintings of cows in fields. When Ken was a teenager and no longer his mother's vassal, he would turn all these paintings of cows to the wall. Rose would come into the living room and say, 'Oh Kenneth, you shouldn't do that.'

Ken and his cousins would draw stools up to the kitchen hatch and pretend it was a milk bar, because milk bars were American and very much in fashion. Rose would make milkshakes in her Horlicks mixer. Nothing was too much for her. She would play endless games of rummy and patience with the children, watch their magic tricks and listen to them recite. She allowed Ruth to dress up in her furs and jewellery.

On rare occasions she showed signs of childish spitefulness, but she could hardly be blamed, for the sisters never quite let her forget that she was living in sin. Thus conscience-stricken she compensated by protecting and indulging Ken. He in turn adored her. When she went away for a month in 1939, he wrote in his diary: 'Mother is going away. I would rather not live than miss her. She doesn't realise. "Kenrose" is being parted.'

Rose found it difficult to discipline her son, though she kept a fly-swatter with which to chastise him. Ken, who at twelve was as tall as she, would pick her up and stand her on a chair. 'There now, you can reach much better.' When his father tried to impose restrictions, he would play him off against his mother. And she in turn would never want Peter to find out that Ken had done anything wrong.

By this time Peter's relationship with Rose was more paternal than sexual. When she had a tantrum, he would just chuckle or go off into his study. Rose and Kenneth were his hobbies; the rest of the family were satellites, if not parasites. Ken's cousin Betty says that it was like two worlds, Peacocks and Tynans in armed truce.

Sixty years later the scandal remains alive. Elderly Peacock relatives, when questioned about Ken, will answer: 'He is one of the skeletons in the cupboard we prefer not to discuss.'

When Ken and his cousins were young, they would ask Peter what he had done as a young man and he would say, 'I worked in a broken-biscuit factory.' Then they would ask where he worked before he had Peacock stores, and he would say, 'Oh, I worked down a chip potato mine.' He never said where he came from. When Ken once asked him why he bore the same name as his mother, he was told that they were distant cousins.

Rose became frantic when she was asked about the family. On one occasion Ken said to his mother, 'Come on, Lilian Rose,' and Ruth piped up, 'Her name's Letitia.' Rose was furious because she disliked the name and had told Ken it was Lilian. There were numerous of these small deceptions. Cousin Betty would ask, 'Who is Auntie Rose, and who is Auntie Maria?' and her mother would answer, 'Well, when you're old enough, I'll tell you.' When she was eleven she told her mother, 'I know that Uncle Peter is Sir Peter Peacock when he's there and he's Mr Tynan when he's here.' Ruth found out by reading an article about Sir Peter in a local Birmingham paper. Alan found out. So how come Ken never guessed, with the coming and going of cousins and hangers-on, the whispering and conniving, the intrusiveness of the lie? Betty believes that by the time he was eleven he did know. She recalls very clearly that, 'Alan said something a bit out of line. I saw Ken withdraw in that sensitive way of his. So I turned the conversation and shut it off. Then I went home to mother and said, "He knows."'

Whatever the truth of the story, Ken managed to excise the information very effectively through secondary school and university.

He did, however, provoke fights with his father, symptomatic of his frustration and anxiety. He would try to draw him, to better him. By the time he reached his early teens 'the old campaigner', as Ken's friends described Sir Peter, was suffering from phlebitis and from the effects of a primitive prostate operation which required the attendance of a nurse. Ken would argue with the semi-invalid, working himself into rages so that the veins stood out on his face. The cousins remember that at such times Ken looked as if he were going to have a fit. And his father would just laugh. No response could have been more provocative than Peter Peacock's amiable refusal to engage, to inform and to explain, but it was not for lack of concern. He worried about his son's affluent upbringing and felt that Ken was cocooned from reality. He wanted particularly to send him away to boarding school, to Rugby, and for him to become a lawyer. But he bowed to Rose, who feared that if Ken left home he would find out their dreadful secret.

Ken's best friend at George Dixon's and in his early years at King Edward's School was a long-nosed Birmingham boy called Geoffrey Hackett. Hackett, less well off than Ken, lived very close to 'the Smethwick frontier'; nor was Ken so very distant from that centre of industrial philistine England. The only effective protection from it, and from the world of their parents, was to become intellectual snobs.

On rainy days they played in the Tynans' loft, which was reached by a ladder, or in Ken's spacious bedroom with its huge glass-fronted bookcase and its photographs of Humphrey Bogart, Peter Lorre and Peggy Cummins. Here Ken kept his collection of the Jane cartoon strip, in folders with brass fasteners. (Jane was a sexual Eurydice for half the boys of wartime Britain.) Here they played board games like GHQ and draughts. Their favourite was Stumpz, based on cricket, which required a knowledge of the players and of the championship tables.

In September 1938, at the age of eleven, Ken entered King Edward's School as a Foundation Scholar. A partly kept diary for 1939 and a full one for 1941 exist. They are lively, informative, confident and not especially stylish chronicles of a happy child. They show the formation of tastes and habits to which he remained faithful for the rest of his life: late mornings, shopping expeditions for records and books, careful planning of pleasures – such as visits to the theatre, the cinema or restaurants:

18 April 1939: Stayed in bed as usual late, reading Wodehouse and the *Film Pictorial*.
19 April: Went to Theatre Royal to see Stanley Lupino's show *Fleet's Lit Up*. It was jolly good, and I'm trying to get his autograph as soon as poss.
21 April: Got up. . . . after good breakfast only just in time to go to Stratford with Dad. Mother came too. Touched 56 going, and stopped at Henley-in-Arden for one of their world famed ices. . . . Took mother for $1\frac{1}{2}$ mile rowing trip up the river. She considers my rowing as 'safe as a row of houses'.

On 3 September 1939 Ken and two of his cousins, Alan and Ruth, were up on Hengistbury Head, a windy bluff west of Bournemouth. There they heard on the coastguard's radio Chamberlain's declaration of war. Their mothers went shopping for blackout material. For the next two terms Ken was transferred as a safety precaution from King Edward's in Birmingham to the Bournemouth Boys School. But in the spring of 1940 the family returned to Birmingham.

The city endured seven major air raids between 1940 and 1943, and the deaths of several thousand of its citizens. But apart from visits to the shelter, mild damage to their house from a nearby land-mine, and some compulsory drilling as a member of the school Air Training Corps, Ken's war was relatively unfearsome.

His diaries are full of mouthwatering descriptions of his mother's cooking: of bread sauce, baked beans on toast, cornish pasties, potato cakes, mulligatawny soup, thick gravy and chicken curry – 'the strongest, most savoury, and undoubtedly the most delicious imaginable'. To all these tastes he remained loyal, even after his seduction, many years later, by *haute cuisine.*

The diaries also reveal that he took piano lessons, received 2s 9d pocket money a week, and attended the Baptist Sunday School. He usually went twice a week to the cinema and kept a record of his favourite films (*The Big*

Store, The Devil and Miss Jones and *The Road to Zanzibar* all made the top category). Laurence Olivier and Vivien Leigh were described as 'rotten' in *Lady Hamilton*. The test for films, he insisted, was this: 'Can you remember that you enjoyed them.' Actors who impressed him included Mary Martin 'because of her way of putting over a song', Oscar Levant because of his 'piano playing' and 'wise cracking', and Charlie Chaplin: 'A much more subtle comedian than many people think.' Brenda Joyce was also included 'because she can take a spanking better than any other woman on the screen'.

He bought books by Oscar Wilde, James Thurber ('really great'), Damon Runyon and Edith Sitwell. And he kept up his subscriptions to *Film Pictorial*, *Picturegoer*, the *Dandy*, *Illustrated*, *Picture Post*, *Lilliput*, *Melody Maker* – with which he regularly corresponded – and *London Life*. This last magazine, eagerly awaited by the teenage Ken, sported a twenty-page letters column from such as Shoe-Shop-Suzie, Strict Aunt, Lucky Slave and Wrestling Freda. (Many years later, in honour of these obsessional pen pals, Ken wrote a sketch for *Oh! Calcutta!* called 'Suite for Five Letters'.)

Like most children from a puritanical background, his sexual formation was influenced by theatre, film, magazines and cartoons rather than by his family. In 1966 in a eulogy to the female bottom called 'Meditations on Basic Baroque', he wrote: 'At the age of twelve I saw a trio of adagio dancers in a Christmas pantomime at the Prince of Wales Theatre, Birmingham ... The girl in the act', Ken claimed, 'was nude except for a G-string and a coat of green paint that covered the rest of her body. Her whole get-up transfixed me, but when she turned her back I was hypnotised. In memory, I still am. It was a moment of traumatic pleasure.'

At eleven – so he declared – he masturbated for the first time, and he remembered very clearly that the thought passing through his head when he came was, 'I own this girl!' So he set out without apology to own girls for the rest of his life. If feminist friends attacked him for male chauvinism or for following a double standard, he would become exceedingly angry. He could deal with the contradictions but found self-scrutiny heavy going.

At no time did it seem to him worth noting that his view of sexual ownership might possibly have been inherited from his patriarchal father. The idea would probably have shocked him, for he was very anti-authoritarian and claimed to have no interest in power of any kind.

If Peter Peacock's influence on his son's sexual attitude to women is merely supposition, there is plenty of evidence for his theatrical influence. There were the practical jokes and the elaborately designed scenarios. Once in 1941 Peter challenged his son, for eightpence, to dress in drag and take a letter to the post office. Ken describes in his diary putting on his mother's dress, gloves and silk stockings ('rolled down'), brogues, rouge, powder and padding. And this first dare led to other experiments in dressing up. At Christmas that year

Ken produced for the family, and performed with his cousins, a two-hour extravaganza of music, poetry and jazz called 'The Unilateral Triangle'.

His mother was responsible for introducing him to music hall, taking him to London to see Leslie Henson and Lupino Lane, Ivor Novello, the Crazy Gang and Gilbert and Sullivan operettas.

She also took him, in November 1938, to see Donald Wolfit in *Macbeth*. Ken recalled that he was 'scared to death for days afterwards'. In his 1941 diary he records going to *Rookery Nook*, starring Ralph Lynn and Robertson Hare, and *The Man Who Came to Dinner*, with Robert Morley ('The greatest play written'). He saw John Gielgud in *Dear Brutus*, for which the actor was awarded 96 points out of 100.

But the full beam of Ken's critical attention was on the music hall. Here he learned from comics, jugglers and acrobats about what he termed, many years later, 'high definition performance'. At the Birmingham Hippodrome, the Aston Hippodrome and the Theatre Royal, Ken saw Jewell and Warriss ('In my opinion the best comedy team who ever drew breath'), Murray and Mooney, Jimmy James ('magnificent') and the great Sid Field. The notes he made as a schoolboy were developed in critical journalism as an under-graduate at Oxford, which in turn he polished and reprinted for his first book, *He That Plays the King*. Here is a description of Sid Field from that first book published in 1950:

He would incline, with earnest benignity, to the members of the pit orchestra, and inquire politely: 'And how are yooo to-day? R-r-r-reasonably well, I hoop?' The incongruity of all this, proceeding from those stolid peasant lips, was irresistible. He always revelled in these elocutionary achievements. I once heard him successfully pronounce that formidable word 'Shostakovitch'. At first the magnitude of what he had done escaped him; he passed on and would have finished the sentence. But all at once glorious consciousness of it overtook him and he stopped, enthralled in recollection. After a moment's rapture, slow irradiation broke across his face, until it became a huge, blushing, beaming rose. Impulsively he turned towards the wings, and sang out: 'Did you heah *me*, Whittaker?' I do not know who Whittaker was.

If his critical style was unpolished in 1941 his confidence in his judgement was fully developed. 'Have decided to keep a list of pretty well unknowns in whom I have great faith,' he wrote, 'it includes Nat Jackley, Jewell & Warriss, Harold Berens, Freddy Bamburger.... Of course I ignore established favourites such as Gillie Potter [his favourite comedian, a straw-hatted sham-Harrovian eccentric], Jessie Matthews ... Kenway & Young, Flanagan & Allen.' If you missed them live, the same comics could be heard on radio programmes like *Hi, Gang!*, *Music Hall* and *Bandwagon*. The radio introduced Ken to American comics like Bob Hope and Jack Benny, to American writers like Alexander Woollcott, and to American jazz. Ken would comb Dale Forty's or Priestley's record store and the junk shops of Smethwick, for Duke Ellington and Bud Freeman.

His other major hobby was autograph collecting. Between 1938 and 1941 he indiscriminately hounded the famous to secure their signatures. Here was the beginning of a lifelong passion for stars. As a correspondent Ken was both persistent and impressive. The comedian Tommy Handley thanked Ken for his charming letter, which he had read out to the cast of his radio programme: 'You haven't missed a single point of the whole show,' and he added, 'My only hope is that we can keep up the standard.'

The political world also had its pen poised for Master Tynan. Winston Churchill's private secretary sent Churchill's autograph in May 1939. The Prime Minister, Neville Chamberlain, and his wife signed in May 1939. The following year the War Cabinet was bagged. Lord Beaverbrook at the Ministry of Aircraft Production thanked Ken for his £1 contribution to a Spitfire and added, 'I am most grateful to you for helping us in this way to drive Nazis from our skies.' Joseph Kennedy, the United States Ambassador to Britain, wrote in April 1940 that it was 'heartening to know that one's sincere efforts in difficult times are not misunderstood. May I add that if you write such a graceful letter when you are twelve, you should be of diplomatic calibre when you reach man's estate.'

By the autumn of 1941 this celebrity seeker *par excellence* has reversed roles. We learn from his diary of November that on the bus home, 'A chap [from school] sat down next to me, asked me if I was Kenneth Tynan and said he had read a letter of mine in the MM [*Melody Maker*]. Was delighted to hear he is a "fan".' By December the bird is on the wing. His first contribution – probably his first-ever published piece – was accepted by his school magazine, the *King Edward's School Chronicle*. The title, 'Insignificance', spoke a cautionary tale: 'In every community there exists a certain element of the insignificant. This is a deplorable fact, but an undoubtedly correct one. The undistinguished person; the person who never argues, never shouts, and whose presence is not immediately noticed. ...' The homily concludes: 'As I watch the useless lives of these people, so foolish, so wasted and so ordinary, I become afraid, and try desperately to forget them.'

In the same month that his first published prose piece appeared, Ken took part in a school debate. He argued against the motion that 'This House Thinks the Present Generation Has Lost the Ability to Entertain Itself' by praising the joys of masturbation. After the debate he wrote in his diary, 'I spoke about sex and turned the tide.'

'He had to take your breath away, he just couldn't resist it,' his friend Geoff Hackett recalls. 'And it went right through his life.'

3

The Young Dandy

Should you drive through the suburbs of Birmingham in search of the heart of the town, you will eventually arrive at a soul-annihilating prank called the Bull Ring, a post-war reconstruction of stores, causeways and pedestrian tunnels, only marginally less awful than the centre as it was during Ken's schooldays in the 1940s – empty by six in the evening, street lights off, the people under siege. The effect of this midlands conurbation on sensitive and intellectual children was to make them want to leave as soon as possible. 'We were coiled springs,' recalls Maurice Shock, now Vice-Chancellor of Leicester University, who was at school with Ken, 'absolutely determined to break out of that claustrophobic provincial atmosphere.'

While waiting to get out, what could a brilliant changeling do but create a rebarbative beauty out of a shocking presentation of self? To be flamboyant and a dandy were Ken's initial tactics; in some situations only a Dada gesture would do. At sixteen he wrote to his school friend Julian Holland:

Nice bit of surrealism I practised: whilst waiting for the bus Joe and I went into the entrance hall of Queen's College Chambers. I threw my glove into the middle of the floor, in the centre of the restricted splash of light. Soon the liftman walked through and picked up the glove. I told him it was mine, and he returned it to me. I immediately threw it back into the light. He looked at me for a long moment. 'What's up with you?' he said. 'I like to look at it there,' I said – and I did – it looked extraordinarily moving, one finger pointing at the gentlemen's bogs. He departed bemused.

In that same winter of the gauntlet-throwing, Ken went to a Rugby football match in a black and white check lady's raincoat ('my stock garment') and a pair of plus-fours. When not sucking on *two* red and yellow lollipops, he sported a foot-long 'wine-dark' cigarette-holder in which he smoked 'abominable Brazilian cigarettes'. A month or two later he bought a pink satin tie. He took to carrying a black silk umbrella with a red silk ribbon wound spirally round it, and he would sweep down the main street of Birmingham, his cousin Ruth remembers, 'like the Peacock he didn't know he was'.

James Dawson, a wry Scots boy, noted in his diary the appearance of the red-ribboned umbrella. 'I saw KPT today in Selly Oak, from my tram. There he was – tall, angular, cynical, with a long arm at right angles to his body. In his hand he held his umbrella menacingly – pressing a shop's door-bell!' Dawson was already a seasoned Tynan observer. He had met Ken when, aged eleven, they first joined King Edward's School, and remembers being impressed by his extraordinary brilliance of speech and thought. One afternoon coming back from school, Ken said, 'You'd better hang around with me, Jimmy, because I want you to be my Boswell.' Five years later, in January 1944, Dawson recorded in his diary that his benefactor had abandoned the idea of 'giving me that highly honoured position' with a 'You may go now, Dawson. I have done with you.' 'This is terribly depressing news,' wrote Dawson,

for I have an extremely high opinion of KPT which amounts to hero worship. I have got beyond the bounds of the two main schools of thought regarding him as i) A Bohemian lunatic ii) A stuck-up prude. I have also got beyond the jealousy of ii) ... thro' sheer resignation. A great and likeable fellow, with the inhumanity, sometimes of Olaf Stapledon's 'Odd John'. I stake all my hopes on his becoming a great literary character, for his is the stuff geniuses are made of. He has however been born in an age where the great individual is not so admired or so important. It is not past him to stage a counter-movement for his own sake!

'As long as I'm not ignored,' Ken wrote to Julian Holland, 'you know quite well I'm perfectly happy.' Holland, two years Ken's senior, had now taken on Dawson's job, though he performed a far more complex service than that of a mere Boswell. He was audience and friend (to whom Ken could unbutton without fear of humiliation). He was teacher and, more often, prepared to be taught, an equal who knew about Eisenstein and silent movies, American comics such as Danny Kaye, and *New Yorker* writers. (So impressed were the two of them by that magazine that they tried to launch a copy called *The Midlander*, but translating the New York scene to Birmingham was beyond the hubris even of the Holland–Tynan team.)

For Julian, a bright, sceptical, precise boy who demanded that Ken should astonish him, Ken could show off his style and ideas, experiment with fiction and criticism, try out his jokes, show off his clothes, his girls – and do so by post!

Julian had made it to London, where he worked for the BBC. And Julian's floor was there to sleep on, when in the winter holidays of 1943 Ken, aged fifteen, made his first major assault on metropolitan theatre, cramming in twenty plays in the space of two weeks, and then writing up his reviews. He told Holland not only what to think about London's theatre but how best to enjoy the capital.

... if you go to ealing studios and mention my name they'll show you round the place....

... scour the continental bookstalls in leicester sq for american and french mags.

... try the pam-pam restaurant opp the Empire leic sq.

... try the threepenny slotmachines ... in the amusement arcades (or as i call them, sex tunnels) on the strand if you feel that old urge.

... go to the windmill and give my regards to huia cooper, that girls got skin like velvety copper.

Ken had always to be first, explaining what was worthy of attention and how to respond. Yet, despite the knowingness, this correspondence is always sweet-toned and sometimes touching. About the time that he dismissed Dawson, he wrote to Holland, 'I am wondering whether I am really a repulsive character – whether my pose is exorcising the real Me.'

And a few weeks later he signs off:

> In tears, I am,
> perhaps too insincerely,
> the boy upon whom
> so little depends
> and so much is
> weighing.

The sacred bond between Tynan and Holland was Orson Welles. Ken had first heard of *Citizen Kane* in *Time* magazine when the film came out in 1941. On 4 March 1942, the day *Kane* opened in Birmingham at the Gaumont Cinema, the fourteen-year-old Ken was there. He came away, as he later wrote, 'dazzled by its narrative virtuosity, its shocking but always relevant cuts ... its brilliantly orchestrated dialogue, and its use of deep focus in sound as well as vision'. By the end of the week he had seen the film five times, once with his mother, once with his eyes shut in order to prove that the sound track was expressive enough to be listened to in its own right. Like the protagonist, Ken intended to live on his own terms, 'the only terms anybody knows': 'Disappointed in the world', as Jed Leland says, '[Kane] built one of his own.'

Holland got hold of the script, and the two boys devoured it line by line. It was the acting, according to his friend, that most excited Ken. 'He couldn't get over the cheek of Welles taking his company of theatre actors to Hollywood and showing the locals how to make films.'

Ken wrote in his journal, thirty years later, that *Kane* was the biggest cultural event of his early life. 'Believing all I read (and Welles said) about it, I thought it was a one-man show, conceived, produced, written, directed and predominantly played by Orson. This notion of a work of art as a solo performance affected all my attitudes towards theatre, cinema and my own career for many years.' (With the appearance of Pauline Kael's *The Citizen Kane*

Book in 1971, in which she attributes the script to Herman J. Mankiewicz, and much of the visual bravura to the cameraman Gregg Toland, Ken's notion of single authorship was undermined, though he rushed to Welles' defence.)

The Magnificent Ambersons came to Birmingham a year after *Kane*, and Ken wrote off eagerly to Holland: 'the opening sequences are good with their jangled odds of conversation winging out of the highly atmospheric gloom. ... i like the ending too the mike swinging up and into a ray of light and orson welles out of the void. ... of course the real star is agnes moorehead that performance is the finest I have ever seen. ...'

It is not greatly surprising that he was now in correspondence with his hero. In the only letter from Welles to Ken that survives from the period (on Mercury Productions paper) dated 29 April 1943, the director wrote that he was mightily cheered and heartened by what his correspondent had to say about *Ambersons*, and went on to explain that the studio had cut it without his consent. 'The picture suffered from all this meddling, but your letter makes me feel the result perhaps wasn't as disastrous as I'd feared.'

By the end of that year Ken published, in the school magazine, his first article on Welles, entitled 'The New Playboy of the Western World'. He wrote:

... Orson Welles is a self-made man and how he loves his Maker. ... He plays the piano with a new harshness; he is a writer of the most brittle poetry, shot with the superficial majesty of sorcery; he moulds art out of radio, the scourge of art; he is a wit as only Americans can be wits; and he is a dandy among impromptu speakers. He is a producer of plays in kingly fashion, independent as a signpost in all he does; and he has carved out of a face of massy granite the subtle likeness of a great actor. He is a gross and glorious director of motion pictures, the like of which we have not seen since the great days of the German cinema; he reproduces life as it is sometimes seen in winged dreams.

Then the young fan added a proviso (a criticism which in later years made him wince): 'One perquisite of greatness he lacks: artistic integrity. Perhaps he has burgeoned too early and too wildly. ... But it will come with praise and age. ... Until then – watch him, watch him well, for he is a major prophet, with the hopes of a generation clinging to his heels.'

Here was the perfect model with whom Ken could identify: precocious, original and 'independent as a signpost'. 'I like whores,' he wrote to Julian, 'especially Whoreson Welles.' And, 'I have a new pose: arrogance, bass voice, hanging lower lip. Which reads O-R-S-O-N.' In March 1944 Ken wrote to Holland, 'Entered Gaumont Cinema, and found confronting me a vast picture of a Man, in a tall coat, with a floppy fur hat enveloping his head. His hands were clasped behind his back, and he regarded me. Brilliantly to parody a line of Victor Hugo (how brilliantly you'll never know): "L'oeil était dans la caverne, et regardait Ken." '

Many years later Ken asked Welles why it was that his films had no fathers.

'I am thinking not so much of *Macbeth* and *Othello* as of George in *The Magnificent Ambersons*, who ruins the life of his widowed mother; and especially of Charles Foster Kane, whose father never appears.' Welles replied that there was no reason at all, and that he had adored his father. Nor did he see fit to point out that Kane's father does appear in the film. (Welles loved his father and, to confuse the issue, he claimed he was the natural son of another man.)

Ken did not love his father. Instead he looked to Welles as his 'daddy figure', and sought him out over the years across the globe. For his part Welles was immensely fond of Ken but did not much wish to play the patriarch. Speaking of his relationship with Ken, he explained that he himself was:

a total chameleon and hypocrite. If I like somebody, I pretend to be what I think they want me to be. I have no integrity in that respect. There was almost nothing Ken said to me on any subject that I didn't think, 'That's absolutely untrue. You're a nut.' So if he was a Boswell, he was a Boswell to a fellow who was always trimming himself to please. And why? Because I liked him.

Ken pulled himself out of a hat, and he did it all before the age of eighteen. But the trick had one all-important assistant, the ancient King Edward VI grammar school, known for turning out scholarship boys in competition with public schools like Eton and Winchester. In Ken's time the headmaster Charles Morris ran the upper school like an Oxford college, creating a meritocracy where eccentricity was admired and encouraged. Students whose fathers were clerks or working men received an elitist classical education which tended to cut them off from their backgrounds for good.

King Edward's also provided the ethos of an upper-class institution without the snobbery or the emphasis on character-building. And as a day school it never succumbed to the suffocating sexual arrangements of boarding school. Of the one overtly homosexual master at King Edward's Ken said, 'Of few others can one truly say "Ecce homo".' His own experience never included the homosexual. 'Never even a mild grope', he would say without pride, for he felt it a failing.

Ken had arrived at King Edward's a 'quiet and astonishingly polite boy', as his Latin master recalls. 'But when he was dealing with matters near his heart he soon switched to an abrasive and ruthless exposition of his ideas. ... He was almost obsessed with accuracy of idea and expression, a semantic enthusiast.'

By the time he left, in 1945, it was King Edward's School for Tynan and his Friends and Acolytes. His demanding standards provoked his contemporaries to measure up to him. He always questioned the orthodox: 'Write heresy, pure heresy,' he advised a friend who was required to turn in a history essay.

Ken did not seem to find anything particularly taxing; like an animal he could not put a foot wrong. After school he would often read for up to six hours in the Birmingham Reference Library. In the evening he would write up his journal, turn out a theatre review, and the following day produce immaculate school work, which he had completed in the early hours of the morning. It was not all showmanship, as his brilliant academic record testifies.

His name first appears in the minutes of the Literary Society in February 1943, where it is recorded that he proposed a reading of Alexander Woollcott's *Hands Across the Sea*. (In an obituary of Woollcott written around this time, Ken wrote of 'the platinum, the ruby-encrusted joy of dramatic criticism from the gilding pen of Alec Woollcott'.) By October he was Secretary of the Society and keeping elegant minutes. He wrote to Julian Holland asking him to come and lecture on art in the cinema, 'Otherwise I shall have to do it; and as I'm also speaking on "The Impressionists and Surrealism", "Modern Lyric Poetry", and "American Drama" – you see what I mean.'

On 16 February Ken delivered a lecture (in lieu of Holland and heavily attended) on 'Film as Graphic Art'. He first showed a reel of Pudovkin's *The End of St Petersburg*, another from Robert Wiene's *The Cabinet of Dr Caligari*, then the third reel of Pudovkin's *Mother*. His biggest coup was acquiring Eisenstein's *Battleship Potemkin*, from the Workers' Film Association, and exhibiting it at the Literary Society with his own comments. Further Russian masterpieces from the same source were postponed because the headmaster was 'unwilling to provoke a Communist outbreak so early in his administration'.

In May Holland received a letter which read as follows: 'TRY AND BE HOME FOR JUNE 9TH. I am lecturing to the Literary Society on "ART AND I" – an autobiography of an eclectic. My publicity campaign has already begun. ... It will be a grand affair – a history of the Influences that have Gone to the Making of KPT.'

At the Debating Society Ken had already begun to break down those 'inhibitions of speech', as a master tactfully recalls, 'which led to his later verbal sensationalism'. At the joint debate with the King Edward's girls' school Ken proposed the motion, that 'This House considers Happiness to be the Supreme Aim in Life'. His schoolfriend Geoffrey Darby's minutes tell us that he spoke of 'Pagan love, said that life was very sweet. ... He revelled in the luxury of sensual pleasure. ... There was no divine purpose in life, only a human one. ... It was better to have loafed and lost, than never to have loafed at all.' Maurice Shock, opposing the motion, then argued that the proposer, stood or fell by selfish pleasure, to which Ken replied that he was there to make the House *think*. Dawson rushed to his journal to record the event: 'Tynan was at his very best today; brilliantly wrong.' And Ken wrote to Holland: 'I made certainly the best speech of my life, and dominated the debate like a patriarch.'

But for most of the rest of his life dominating any situation like a patriarch was precisely what he felt he could never achieve. What he did was to dominate the Debating Society (as he later dominated the Oxford Union) like a clever vaudevillian, promoting suitably provocative subjects of his own choice.

Early in March 1944 Ken had stood as an 'Independent Confucian' for a Civics Society mock election against a Liberal, a Conservative and a socialist. He offered five general principles – which included the abolition of organized religion and conventional morality – and the introduction of 'Contemplative Leisure' as the highest aim of man. He also evolved a 'Fourteen-Point Charter for Rationalists' which included the repeal of laws against divorce, unnatural vice and abortion. He then sent himself telegrams from Mahatma Gandhi and Chiang Kai-shek and held an inflammatory first meeting in the school lavatories, hoisting himself up to address his audience over the top of a partition. Here is Ken's account of the subsequent events:

JDC [the history master] spotted my fourteen points, and immediately violated all privilege as well as courtesy by tearing them down. ... He said they were disgusting and a mockery; I offered him the chance of taking up the challenge ... to convince any member of the school or staff of their reasonableness within thirty minutes. He replied by taking the matter to REG (chairman, Civics Society). REG agreed with JDC, and asked me to retract the points or withdraw. I was proudly forced to withdraw. ...

Next morning Shock told me that REG was refusing to let me re-enter the lists, since that would mean his having to admit that he had CHANGED HIS MIND. ... I hurtled to REG and argued vehemently with him for an hour. He remained calm and quite firm. So I acted – quite unscrupulously, I fear, but another great journalist once did it: I published a vast denunciation in green ink on our noticeboard headed: 'J'ACCUSE'. ...

And now the entire business is off, because the other three candidates ... withdrew in sympathy.

He had given his school fellows an idea of potential freedom, and to that shocking manifesto Ken remained broadly loyal. He did not make a serious political commitment until the mid-1950s, when he gave his vote to the socialists, and espoused a kind of romantic Marxism. At school he merely tried on different political costumes – anarchism, Fabian socialism, Koestler-style 'Western revolutionary humanism' – over his central credo: that sex was the supreme mystical emotion (cribbed from D. H. Lawrence); that good and evil are words, meaningless in the presence of the ideal, which is beauty (out of Mallarmé); that the life of sensation came first. Politics was a game he could afford to play, sheltered by an affluent background and at a time of full employment.

Ken used words to delight, to provoke and to wound. 'Whipwords', as he described them, could demolish enemies or boring relatives. (A cousin recalls that Ken let it be known that he kept a 'black book' of derogatory comments on his family.) But words were not mere weapons. 'Worry about words,' Ken counselled Holland, 'they are the only consistent elements in your life. as rémy de gourmont said "ideas are well enough until you are twenty; after that only words will do." ' This deeply felt lecture came after Ken had attended a youth forum meeting at which a postwar reconstruction report was presented. 'I read the thing, saw how hideously written it was, overgrown with jungle english, journalese and (worse) official jargon, so i rose on saturday to intervene in the great cause of words, with 88 grammatical and syntactical amendments, excising unnecessary verbiage and pompous periphrasis wherever they were flourishing. . . . we do not fight in vain.' This teenage allegiance to 'the great cause of words' lasted passionately and consistently until the day Ken died.

Two years before his stand at the youth forum he had sent Holland an 'excellent' quotation from Nietzsche: 'What is the characteristic of all literary *décadence?* It is that life no longer resides in the whole. The word gets the upper hand and jumps out of the sentence, the sentence stretches too far and obscures the meaning of the page, the page acquires life at the expense of the whole.' Here was a useful maxim. Ken taught himself to write with clarity and tightness, and he managed to do so *before* he reached Oxford. Penelope Houston, required to edit Ken's theatre reviews for the university magazine *Isis*, recalls that 'Ken wrote so you couldn't cut. Every paragraph linked. So one used to sit for an hour, thinking how in hell do I lose five lines of this copy without spoiling it?' His other editors were to have the same problem.

In the mid-1940s the schoolboy was trying on literary hats. First there was the literary fan, filling up occasional books with the words of the masters and some of his own: 'Beware of half-tones', he wrote, 'in literature as in everything else; they too often tell of an inability to give the full tone.' There was the aphorist: 'Johnson is marvellous. He delves into the obvious and brings forth truth; your modern writer delves into the subtle and brings forth the super-subtle.' Then the diarist, anecdotal rather than analytic: 'Dreamt of a KPT clad in insecure porridge-stained pyjamas insulting Ivor Novello and Noël Coward simultaneously and undefeatedly, and finally beating Dame Lilian Braithwaite with a metaphorical umbrella. I know it was metaphorical because there was a large card attached to it reading "This umbrella is metaphorical. By Order".' A novel about a paranoiac, parodies, limericks and clerihews followed. He sent Julian a literary quiz with fifteen short pieces of prose criticism: 'Who wrote the following and of whom?' All fifteen turned out to be by KPT.

Then Ken tried a play. Messrs Tynan and Holland had, in the summer of 1943, devised and performed for the school a zany comedy based on the film *Hellzapoppin.* Their next project, developed by post, was another play, but of portentous dimensions, featuring God and the Devil, and wrestling with the nature of good and evil. In December Ken wrote to Holland with disturbing news. The idea they had worked on was not original. He signed off: 'With spirit gum on my chops, I am, having seen *King's Row* (go-o-od) an unrepentant, KPT'.

Drama, Ken concluded, was an even more difficult art form than the novel. Meanwhile, with true prodigality, Ken the critic was recording his views on literature, theatre, sports and music.

On jazz, he wrote: 'OOOOOH! Listen to Geraldo playing a BEEYOOOTIFUL burlesque of the danceband style of the twenties. Corny, smirking, twisting alto solos, scraping, dusty drums, trombone swipes, sweeping violins, "comments" by vocal quartet, masculine vocal chorus by Carless – the tune "When the midnight Choo-Choo leaves for Alabam – ALABAM, ALABAM, ALABAM!"'

He wrote also on cricket, another life-long passion. (As a summer sportsman and member of the school First XI, he was a left-handed batsman and a slow spin, left arm bowler.) 'Read Edmund Blunden's "Cricket Country" and learn to love my game,' he tells Holland. And in August 1944: 'You may have guessed my life has been cricket for the last week – watching ... cricket festival at the county ground and composing lovely clerihews about the players:

> l j todd
> should not be confused with god.
> todd bowls at the festival;
> god bowls at mephistofel.'

4

Quand Même

Birmingham is the home of Sir Barry Jackson's famous repertory company, founded in 1913, the training ground for such actors as Ralph Richardson, Laurence Olivier, Paul Scofield and Albert Finney. In this intimate and practical theatre Ken served his critical apprenticeship. There he saw H. K. Ayliff's 1943 modern-dress production of *The Taming of the Shrew*. In the late summer of 1945 he saw the young Peter Brook's *Man and Superman* at the rep, and wrote to Julian Holland: 'Shaw's plays make one long for the interval; so that one can discuss them with one's neighbours.'

At that other local theatre, Stratford-on-Avon, to which he would bicycle from Birmingham in the blackout, he saw the three wartime Hamlets, those of Basil Langton, George Hayes and John Byron. He told Julian that he had written some 7,500 words in essays and criticism on the Stratford productions of 1944 alone, and he added: 'Incidentally plays about ideas are not good without genius.'

The third great local inspiration was the touring company of the great baroque actor Donald Wolfit, which, between 1941 and 1945, sent Ken running for pen and paper to record his impressions. He saw Wolfit's *Macbeth* for the second time in 1944 and wrote, 'this is the greatest piece of shakespearean acting i have ever seen'.

Of *Richard III* he wrote: 'Agate always regarded this as one of his best: though, as Wolfit would be the first to admit, the moon-like face he possesses, shroud it though he may in whiskers and bedizen it with lines, is, like Garrick's, essentially a comic face, a comic mask. ... Richard III is a Renaissance villain, a wonderful development of Iago, and, to me at least, one of the most fascinating in a wonderful gallery of rogues.'

'hazlitt would have loved this performance,' he said of the actor's Volpone, 'how he impressed ... with the hissing delivery of his triumphant "i am volpone, and thisssss my sssslave." ... i bravoed at the last curtain – the first time i have ever done so.'

But Ken could not reconcile himself to Wolfit's 'stubby dane': 'one felt that here was comprehension rather than concentration. ... all of hamlet was there, but not a whole hamlet. ... wolfits curtains were, as ever, gorgeously theatrical. irvings cannot have been far different.'

Shortly after the great feast of Wolfit in the winter of 1944, Ken wrote to Julian Holland asking him to get tickets for Richardson in *Peer Gynt* and Olivier in *Richard III* in their season at the New Theatre; also seats for Gielgud in *Hamlet* at the Haymarket. His reviews of these great performances were worked up at school, and polished and delivered in *He That Plays the King*. Here is Ken's description of Olivier's Richard III:

From a sombre and uninventive production this brooding, withdrawn player leapt into life, using the circumambient gloom as his springboard. Olivier's Richard eats into the memory like acid into metal, but the total impression is one of lightness and deftness ... he acts chiefly with his voice. In Richard, it is slick, taunting, and curiously casual; nearly impersonal, 'smooth as sleek-stone', patting and pushing each line into shape. Occasionally he tips his animal head back and lets out a gurgling avuncular cackle, a good-humoured snarl; and then we see the over-riding mephitic good humour of the man, the vulgar joy he takes in being a clever upstart.

He had begun, early in childhood, to record his theatregoing. He never declared, however, his intention of becoming a professional drama critic. His schoolfriends presumed he would stay close to the theatre, but as an actor or director. They did not expect him to become a playwright, or a novelist; Ken had firmly declared that he had no ability for that kind of writing.

His first big acting part at school was the lead in Jules Romain's *Doctor Knock*, performed on a new school stage which he had helped to design. Ken thought the production fell wetly, 'like a dirty penny into mud'. He next played Shylock in the trial scene in a deliberately underplayed performance. This was followed in December of 1944 by John Drinkwater's *Abraham Lincoln*. The local drama critic on the *Birmingham Post* recorded that Ken's performance in the title role showed unusual promise. And he went on to suggest that 'should destiny take him to Oxford', King Edward's School would be well represented in the Oxford University Dramatic Society (OUDS).

Perhaps this particular critic knew that Ken had already been accepted at that university for the autumn term of 1945. He had been interviewed by the great English scholar C. S. Lewis. After what Ken recalled as 'a half hour of controversy with the benign man', he was accepted into the bosom of Magdalen and offered a demy scholarship of £50 a year. This, with his City of Birmingham and state scholarship, would more than cover his tuition. Dawson wrote in his diary, 'So he's done it again, the cunning dog.'

Early in 1945 Ken began his battle to avoid military service. He took the Higher School Certificate examination for the second time, thereby gaining a longer exemption. In May, now eighteen years old, he wrote to Magdalen pointing out that the Minister of Labour, Ernest Bevin, had announced that a limited number of scholarship-holders would be deferred from military service. This loophole kept him out of the army for the duration of his Oxford career.

He masterminded his future without the aid of his father. Friends like James Dawson recall that when they visited his house Ken never introduced his parents. The old man would sit wrapped up in his armchair 'like the ageing Citizen Kane', Dawson says, 'and allow this extraordinary youngster to go on with his life'. His mother would stay in the background like a solicitous maid. Very occasionally Ken mentions them in a letter to Holland: 'Mother found your last but one letter in a coat that was going to be cleaned and there was an almighty fuss. She threatened to stop my allowance ... and made me promise I hadn't had intercourse.' (This in December 1943.) A few weeks later he writes that his parents have opposed his visit to London.

My father has become extremely traditional about it: he chooses to see a sinister design behind your taking a flat just before I arrive. ... My visiting aunts, uncles, and firemen have been enlisted to help ... plead. ... I have had to insult them all, severally; to one weeping relation I actually said 'Get the hell out of here, you bore me.' A family split is imminent; my mother feels the rest of the gang are laughing at her lack of control over me.

One of these cousins believes that Ken never had a normal relationship with any of them. 'He was never brought up to be considerate, or to know how to deal with emotion. Of course he never intended to hurt and he had a charming manner if he did.' 'My Tynans', Ken wrote to friends, 'spend their time and other people's money hectically profiteering in drapery.'

Ken was proud of his middle name (though hardly of his aged parents, who turned up at school functions as Mr and Mrs Tynan), and often appended to his correspondence the Blakean tag: 'The pride of the peacock is the bounty [sic] of God.' Neither schoolmasters nor schoolmates ever confronted him with his illegitimacy; and they confirm that he had no conscious idea of it until his father's death.

He did, however, express an ambivalence towards authority which lasted throughout his life. By April 1944 the headmaster Charles Morris discussed with Ken the possibility of his becoming a prefect. He said that if Ken misbehaved or indulged any of his more provocative habits, he would be expelled. On the other hand, Morris cunningly proposed, if Ken were to remain a freelance, allowances would be made. 'Now here is my great dilemma,' Ken wrote to Holland (and it remained a dilemma). 'Shall I shackle myself, become continent, self-disciplined and virtuous? or shall I carry freely on, and let the prefects go hang?'

In this instance he joined and carried out his duties correctly, though he also managed to turn the prefects' meetings into a series of mildly lewd entertainments. He proposed a swear box and a complicated scheme which differentiated between words denoting sexual and other functions. He dismissed a retiring school captain with the advice that 'All you need in the armed forces is a pair of sheep's legs down your gaiters.'

Ken was pied piper as a ladies' man, more adventurous than the other virgins among the prefects, constantly picking up pretty girls in the street, and making extravagant verbal play to win their attention. To Julian Holland, in the autumn of 1943, aged sixteen, he had announced, 'I have become engaged to Pat Martin' (probably the first in his exceedingly long line of fiancées). A week or two later he has found 'the Girl of a Lifetime' in a park. 'She is intensely mystic, considers me a "brilliant creature". We were closer together than good and evil.' A week or two later he meets a girl at a bus-stop in Paradise Street: 'first time in reprobate life i ever used word love to a woman. ... says she wants to go to the ends of the earth with me little does she guess that what I want from her i can get at the top of the road. ...' Next comes a 'brash little filly' named Joy, and another with breasts 'as firm as belltents in a light breeze'. In the botanical gardens he meets Kathleen: 'A gorgeous young light-heavyweight' who 'kisses like a kick from Whirlaway'.

At the end of 1944 Dawson recorded in his diary that he had just left Ken picking up another girl. 'When in their presence he becomes sticky, and can rarely emerge with less than two or three clinging to him. But one might as well expect humanity from him, as honey from a wasp.'

One of these girls, called Irene, informed Ken that he was a miserable sinner, 'if only *you'd* be miserable'. But Irene, according to Dawson, was on the way out. Early in February 1945 Ken announced that he intended to lose his virginity. It was time he knew about sex, and the partner was to be an intense, nervy blonde called Enid, 'very hard and artificial' and a well-known robber of virginity. Ken wrote to Holland: 'I am now within a pebble's flip of a sordid physical affair with [a] petite, enigmatic, intellectual, 24-year-old. ... She bites when she kisses. Hard. And I love it.'

A few weeks later he returned to the business of Enid. He wrote to Julian that 'she stripped stark naked and leapt and lunged at me. ... she is a ruinous cobra and a despicable hoyden; but she fascinates.' He added, however, that on this first occasion, 'vibrate as she might, I was impotent'. The deed was finally accomplished on the night of 28 February 1945 in a shop doorway on the Bristol Road. The next day Ken lunched with Dawson to tell him the news. He declared that it was the last time he would perform in a doorway, and spent the rest of the luncheon reading aloud from Max Beerbohm's *A Christmas Garland*.

By the end of March Ken had decided that he could not stand Enid and was in love with Joy. 'Only she can give me that salmon-spawning leap in the belly. ... Jules, write and TELL HER TO LOVE ME. PLEASE.'

In Birmingham, a young person of panache was bound to frequent the Kardomah. This was a coffee shop in New Street which Ken and his friends turned into a private club. The entrance fee for a day was the price of a cup of coffee (threepence) and the habitués gathered on the first floor and took over the window benches, from where they could see everyone they knew going up and down New Street. Ken used to take his typewriter there and work among a bevy of Kardomah haunters.

One boring afternoon, everything quiet at the Kardomah, Joe Simon, a KES boy, discovered some spare cash, and Ken and he and a group of friends hired a car and went off to a country pub to drink champagne. On that occasion Simon remembers Ken using the phrase 'beyond the angels Ken' – in lieu of his signature – on the champagne bottle. He would also use Sarah Bernhardt's motto *'Quand Même'* ('Despite the consequences') to sign off.

It was at the Kardomah that King met two King Edward's girls Hazel Young and Barbara Siggs, who decided to write a novel about him – though they had been warned by the history mistress that he had an 'unsavoury reputation'. They loved Ken's clothes, and his ostentation, and they thought him very kind. When Hazel won a scholarship to Cambridge she rushed out and found Ken: 'He lifted me off my feet and whirled me around and we waltzed all the way up New Street. He knew how important it was.'

Ken took their education in hand, sent them a series of complicated intellectual quizzes with obscure quotations and pastiches of his own. And he tested them – as he did all his friends all his life – with Consequences or the Truth Game: who would be shoved off a Russian sleigh and in what order?

In answer to one of their questionnaires for the proposed novel, he wrote, 'I shall never write a sustained novel or critical essay; my collected works will bulk small but precious.' He told them that he liked cricket, rowing, fives, table tennis, at all of which he was moderately good. His eccentricities included odd pets to be toted around on pieces of string, such as mockingbirds, grey rats, dragonflies; he liked cigarette-holders, large signet rings and Eton crops. 'Eccentricity,' he added, 'like all forms of surreal art, must come from within, and must be creatively egoistic.' His preference for clothes included dark-green bowties with red spots. He had no views on capital punishment, but 'my views on corporal punishment are pronounced. i believe, with mr coward, that women should be beaten regularly, like gongs.'

One spring day at the Kardomah in 1944, while Hazel and Barbara worked at their Tynan novel, a burly twenty-three-year-old amateur actor was chatting with a group of friends. Suddenly a lank young man with hair like flax on a distaff knelt before him, kissed his hand and said, 'You're talking about Ibsen. You're talking about my god,' which is how Ken introduced himself to Hugh Manning, whom he described – several decades later – as 'the man responsible for my career'. Manning introduced Ken to Harry James, one of the leading lights of the New Dramatic Company. This was an amateur group which performed revues in the parks and local halls as part of a wartime entertainment called 'Holidays at Home'. Ken burst into the group like a bombshell. He proposed bringing enough young men from King Edward's to fill the minor parts of the company's first major productions, if the company in turn would allow him to play the lead in *Hamlet*; and he engineered a reading of the play at his house. At the meeting was the lead actress of the company, a girl called Pauline Whittle, two years older than Ken, with the modest manner of a D. W. Griffith heroine. She was a white-skinned and dark-haired beauty, and according to Ken liked people who had 'preserved their poetic souls in the industrial heart of an empire'. She in turn remembers Ken standing in front of the fireplace: 'Aesthetic, tall, appealing. I was riveted, because you simply didn't see people like that in Birmingham.'

In January 1945 the NDC opened its first big production, a fantasy called *Berkeley Square* in which Ken played a small part. In the next production he played the Russian ballet master Kolenkhov in *You Can't Take It With You*. Behind the scenes he was fighting for the Holland–Tynan adaptation of *Hamlet* (cut to the bone – excising Rosencrantz and Guildenstern – to make the action move with speed and logic), which Hugh Manning now proposed to direct. The text had been the subject of argument between Holland and Ken for well over a year. In March 1944 Ken had written to rebut Holland's view that Hamlet should be undecided in his actions. 'Only in his actions is he decisive. It is when he calls into play that awful intelligence of his, and begins arguing with himself (as when he fails to kill the praying King) that he lapses into dubiety.'

On 9 January 1945 he told Holland that the outlook was bleak, that the committee members seemed scared 'since they knew next to nothing of the proposed protagonist', and were offended 'by our presumption in seizing Pauline' for the part of Ophelia. He told Manning that it was up to his conscience to persuade the committee to go ahead. On 19 January, to press his case, he gave a lecture to the school Literary Society called 'Towards a New *Hamlet*', beginning with a survey of all the critical opinions on the play, from Samuel Richardson on. Then he underlined his main theme, that Shakespeare was '[not] a psychologist', that he was not concerned with making consistent characters, that he was busy merely with making appearances seem real.

At the end of January the NDC decided to give the production the go-ahead, and rehearsals began in March. Theatrical circles in Birmingham, Ken reported, buzzed with the news. And Hugh Manning went to work on his prompt copy, on the cover of which was written 'The *Hamlet* that was of William Shakespeare . . . sacrificed in a great cause'. They rehearsed all hours into the middle of the night, lived on bread, jam and tea, and crawled home on foot in the pitch-dark city, torches in hand, for there were still sandbags and blackouts.

Ken, dallying with the girls of the company, would ask them after rehearsal, 'which of you is coming downstairs with me tonight?' Often there was a competition for the honour. He was physically fearless, balancing on a ledge over a sixty-foot stairwell, or taking a panicky girl across a roof.

When *Hamlet* finally opened at the Midland Institute, the local Birmingham critic, T. C. Kemp, gave the production a favourable review. Of the lead he wrote, 'Throughout he tends to argue too much, and seldom shows us the man caught up in great gusts of emotion. Yet Mr. Tynan always holds the attention.' Another critic pleased Ken by describing his performance as 'neurotic'. For the part Ken wore black velvet and five pairs of tights to flesh out his skinny legs. At the close he was carried off horizontal and stiff, long hair hanging down (achieving apparently instant *rigor mortis*) over the heads of six bearers.

In the spring of 1945 a group from the New Dramatic Company including Ken, Hugh Manning and Pauline Whittle went up to London to see John Gielgud's *Hamlet*, Hermione Gingold's *Sweet and Low* and Noël Coward's *Sigh No More*. Ken hosted a lunch at Kettner's restaurant and they stayed up all of one night visiting Fleet Street and watching the dawn from the Embankment. Back in Birmingham he called Pauline, put the telephone on the piano, and sang and played for her 'Sigh No More'. (Almost four decades later, when he was ill and dying in California, she wrote to remind him of the song. 'I wept then, and I weep again remembering the happiness you gave me.')

Pauline had offered her heart, but Ken was not quite ready to take it. There was still the matter of Joy.

On Monday, 7 May, the European war ended, and that night Ken and his friend Geoff Darby, with Joy and another girl, celebrated in a local pub and drank whisky for the first time. The man next to them bit into his half-pint glass tankard and chewed it down. 'Is it the whisky', Darby asked, 'or are we seeing what we're seeing?' – which is how he remembers the end of Hitler. For Ken the next two nights, during victory celebrations, were less amusing. They were 'the most terrible of my life', he wrote to Julian. 'This is about the end. I cannot go on very much longer.'

On Tuesday Ken's party, led by Hugh Manning acting as MC, went out to buy drinks for different branches of the Allied Services.

We then congo'd up and down and around town until about 1 a.m., full of cherry brandy and champagne.

So far so very good. ... I had noticed with increasing distress Joy's habit of going [off] for periods of 10 minutes or so with David Bird ... [then] without saying goodnight, the girl whom I had dated and fêted walked off home with this Bird creature. I followed, fighting drunk ... and we almost came to blows. ...

Wednesday night capped everything. I have never felt nearer to murder than I did then and do now. As before we met at the St. James. ...

43

Then I noticed something. Joy, who would never let me kiss her in public, was kissing Bernard ... all over the place in public....

At first I didn't mind. I told myself that, as before, everyone was kissing everyone else. ...

The horrible rasping sore throat I had was getting rapidly worse. ... We walked along in a colossal line spread out across Bristol Road – all except Joy and Bernard, who walked ecstatically in front, embracing each other every few yards. Then I got mad. I went completely berserk and walked bang into the headlights of a car approaching along Priory Rd. I was utterly, utterly despondent. ... Hugh brought me down into the gutter by a flying tackle as the car passed. I dashed off after Joy. ... They stopped, *laughed at me* (O Christ) and proceeded to neck in front of me. ...

It took eight of them to stop me from strangling the filthy bitch and that low bastard. ... That night I invited Pat Brewer to stop the night with me, as Hugh was running me home in the car anyway. She came. But mother *refused* to entertain her, and made her leave to walk 8 miles home. I was completely humiliated, and had to drag her back in tears. Mother was still nagging and shouting, and swearing not to give her any breakfast. I managed to smuggle her into a bed at about 3.30 am., but she had gone by 7. Julian, I just can't stand any more humiliation. I want to kill Joy, and to kill my mother. ... This is not madness that I have uttered.

In all of Ken's correspondence to Julian there is nothing quite like this desperate cry from the unmasked provincial sophisticate, betrayed by a girl and humiliated by his narrow-minded mother.

Two weeks later, after a day rehearsing *Hamlet*, and the exchange of a kiss, Ken rang up Pauline Whittle to ask her out. She said no. When he called again and protested his affection, she burst into tears and said, 'Ken, for the last six months I've been worshipping the ground you walked on.' Ken sent her a note the following day to say that he had just spent the happiest twenty-four hours of his life. 'I am so instinct with joy', he declared with the Joy episode behind him, 'that I could wish life to cease.' That evening, however, he went off to the school Joint Hop and indulged in some heavy necking with a 'fast, loose, sophisticated bitch'. It was a gesture, he later explained to Julian: 'I had a reputation as a libertine to keep up; and I had to keep it up until I had *seen* Pauline to make quite sure that it was not merely infatuation with my surface and my pose. I was not going to be hurt again as Joy so brilliantly hurt me.'

The day after the libertinage Ken took his new love to lunch at the Lantern restaurant in Corporation Street. Pauline recalls, 'I was quite overcome with emotion and my hands were shaking so that I couldn't keep the soup in the spoon.'

Ken wrote to Holland to announce that Pauline and he were in love and intended to become engaged: 'Believe me, J, this Pauline episode is going to grow into a common autobiography. I think I mean it this time. Reciprocity from the desirable is now my recipe for love.'

To Pauline he wrote: 'The tousled, haggard figure who dashed home in a series of jerky, rocket-like spurts would never have been recognised as the cultural "petit maître" he aspires to be.' He told her he was reading Peter Quennell's portraits of Boswell, Gibbon, Sterne, and Wilkes – 'Inhabitants all of that priceless century, the eighteenth. A period of cynical modishness, darling, – my exact spiritual atmosphere.' And he went on to reassure her that he still loved her incredibly (after the passage of a full ten days): 'Spiritually I have already loved you twenty times the length of my life.' He asked if she had yet spoken to 'Parental Authority'. 'Mother and father are distantly amused, but I think they know as positively as I do that this is real and perdurable. Psychologically,' the eighteen-year-old added with a touch of caution, 'I have discovered that long engagements are excellent.'

Despite the demands of true love, and of the New Dramatic Company, Ken was still deeply engaged at King Edward's. As long ago as December 1943 he had decided, should he ever be asked to edit the school magazine, to write all the original contributions himself, and to append to his editorial a quotation from the Jacobean dramatist John Webster: 'You are your own chronicle too much, and grossly flatter yourself.' The plan was carried out in the 1945 summer edition of the *Chronicle*. His original contribution was a lush, perfumed piece called 'Little Poem in Prose: L'Art pour l'art', an excitable homage to the 'art for art's sake' movement. Half a dozen other contributions by Ken included an announcement of a sixth-form conference at which all the schools in the King Edward's foundation could participate.

For this event the 'impresario', and 'ringmaster-cum-connoisseur' (in the Peacock tradition), K. P. Tynan, was made president. And, with Geoff Darby as second in command, he set to planning the three-day bonanza, which would include his own performance (with the New Dramatic Company) of *Hamlet*, a concert of chamber music to include Mozart's Clarinet Quintet, a showing of *Citizen Kane* (with an introductory speech by KPT), a cricket match and a dance. He persuaded the headmaster to invite the leading drama critic of the day, James Agate, and the distinguished editor of the *New Statesman*, Kingsley Martin, to come and talk. Both accepted.

A provincial theatre lover who wanted to know what it was like to be in a London theatre on a particular night followed James Agate each week in the *Sunday Times*. Ken knew his writing well enough to make friendly fun of it for the entertainment of his friends, and he relished the idea of a confrontation. Shortly before the conference Ken asked the headmaster for permission to meet the great critic at the station. A Lancashire man, from a background of trade, Agate looked like a red-faced farmer, which belied a life spent a curtain's throw from Sarah Bernhardt, Henry Irving or Marie Tempest. He wrote wonderfully observed, robust and opinionated theatre criticism (in the style, as Ken wrote, of 'a butcher boy hypnotised by Beerbohm'), and a diary eventually published in nine volumes. He wore rakishly tipped hats, carried a silver-knobbed cane and lived an active homosexual life.

On 19 July 1945, at the station in Birmingham, Ken met the sixty-eight-year-old critic, who was wearing a tropical suit and a Panama hat. Into a taxi they climbed and, after a short exchange on the matter of the conference, the critic placed a hand on his host's knee and asked, 'Are you a homosexual, my boy?' 'I'm af-f-fraid not,' said Ken. 'Ah well,' Agate replied, 'I thought we'd get that out of the way.' Agate spoke that morning on English drama and literature and the need for a national theatre. He was introduced by his boy-chairman, who delivered seven minutes of verbal fireworks in which he managed to quote twenty or more authors. At the end there was a pause in which the audience wondered whether it was in order to clap. Agate stood up, smiled and said, 'Far be it for me to contradict such an intellectual dustman as Mr Tynan.' That evening Ken performed for the second time (and before James Agate) in the NDC's production of *Hamlet*.

Agate took back to London Ken's prose poem on 'L'Art pour l'art', and responded:

My Dear Hamlet,

Of course you you can write. You write damned well. You write better than I have ever attempted to write. The mistake you make is the old one of trying to do too much. ... Why, when you are in full spate of discussion about Huysmans, lug in Voltaire? ... And I conjure you, now and forever, to put a stop to your punning. Say, if you must, of Guillaume Apollinaire that 'devout and donnish, here was Phoebus Apollinaire turned fasting friar'. But to say that 'Verlaine was always chasing Rimbauds' is just *common*.

Ken wired back: 'I shall in all my best obey you, madam. Hamlet.' A few days later he wrote at length, admitting he had not read everything he claimed in his prose poem. 'I have, as you must know, never read de Sade (the nearest approach to him I have made is that best of bedside books, *Psychopathia Sexualis*); I have only seen the glow of Balzac refracted and dimmed by upstart crows of critics.' He then argued that there are no rules. 'Art laughs at locksmiths. My quid-pro-quoem is irritatingly derivative and allusive because the Symbolists were.' A further letter from Agate, who now signed himself Polonius, offered illustrations from Shaw, Walkley, Beerbohm and Montague on the correct use of quotation. 'I do not want you to write like any of those four great [drama] critics. ... I want you to make for yourself a style – which can be done only out of your own bowels and nobody else's – that will make readers say, "That's Tynan," just as people say, "That's Hazlitt" or "That's Lewes".'

Hamlet replied:

> I believe in artifice for art's sake.
> I do not believe in sincerity or profundity.
> I believe in superficiality. I believe in shallowness.

In fact, *quand même*, I believe in
Kenneth P. Tynan

On 4 August they met at the Café Royal in London, after which Agate wrote in his diary: 'Lunch with Hamlet, who says, "I would give all literature for one rare meal a day. I wouldn't swap the aural and visual arts, which I rate higher than the literary." ... An amusing hour ends with the following dialogue: Hamlet: "May I introduce you to a friend who insists that the best art of the twentieth century has come out of the trumpet of a jazz-musician called Bix Beiderbecke?" J.A.: "No." '

But Hamlet would not take no for an answer and the following day he took Hugh Manning and Julian Holland (the admirer of Beiderbecke) to lunch with Agate at the Imperial Hotel. Agate drank double whiskies and afterwards took the boys to his place in Grape Street for coffee. His pianist friend Leo Pavia played pastiche of the great composers.

Ken stayed on in London for a week and then, with Pauline, caught a train crowded with servicemen to Bournemouth. There they holidayed at the family bungalow with Rose in attendance. Ken would ask his mother what the menu was, and if he didn't fancy it, he would take his girl out to a restaurant. 'I must have a choice,' he'd tell Rose (and with choice in mind, he would always after prefer restaurants to eating at home).

He bought a black and white cigarette-holder and a red lighter, and started smoking long, gold-trimmed Balkan Sobranie black Russian cigarettes. He tried to get Pauline to dye her hair black. Buried in her trunk of memorabilia are photographs of the two of them walking along the promenade, raincoats slung over shoulders, both wearing bow ties, Ken with his cigarette-holder: it was always his dream to make love to an idealized twin sister.

Back in Birmingham the lovers would sit on the swing seat in the garden of the Edgbaston house, and Rose would bake lemon cakes for them. Ken was very fond of her, Pauline remembers, but he told her off frequently and indulged in tantrums. He had nothing in common with either of his parents. 'His father looked just like a lord mayor, a complete northerner, and not particularly polished. My impression was that he was always angry with Ken. I can see him standing with his back to the fireplace, a big man, big face. "If you're going to make a noise like that coughing, go outside in the hall," he'd say, because Ken was always coughing.'

Late in August Ken went up to London with Pauline to help her get a temporary acting job with Donald Wolfit. At the same time he was preparing for Oxford. He wrote off to Magdalen College to say he knew almost nothing about the details of residence and very little about university life in general. He asked if they could supply him with information. The college wrote back to advise him to get a reading list from his future tutor, Mr C.S. Lewis, and reassured him that he would acquire information about university life gradually during his first term.

On 11 October Ken, his mother and Pauline set off for Oxford in Peter Peacock's chauffeur-driven Daimler. They brought along with them Ken's trunk and one of Rose's lemon cakes. 'It was a sad farewell,' Pauline recalls, 'and tears were shed by the three of us, It was a new life for Ken, and I knew I could not be part of it.'

So ended Ken's life in the 'cemetery without walls'.

5

Gangster in the Groves of Academe

For the merest pause Oxford upstaged him before he took off and took possession of Oxford. Two weeks after his arrival at Magdalen College, and settled into rooms on Kitchen Staircase, above the set of rooms once occupied by Oscar Wilde, Ken wrote to Julian Holland: 'Your extroverted KPT is become a morbid, Palinural introvert. He is mentally in extreme anguish.' Many years later he described being a little lost that first term, 'worried about knives and forks, and not having eaten an oyster before.'

By the third week of the university term he was almost back on form, writing to Julian of 'my clique', of reading Sartre's *Huis Clos* ('Everyone is talking about it'), taking the actress Hermione Baddeley to dinner at his favourite restaurant, the Taj Mahal, and reporting that the Oxford Union was only slightly higher in quality than his school debating society. He described being found by a classmate from King Edward's, 'lying flat on the floor in my dressinggown with all the lights out, suffering terribly from neuralgia.' 'Go on!' screamed the visiting provincial, 'Talk ardently about God and sex.' 'Up here,' said Ken stiffly, 'we tend to identify them.'

Early in that Michaelmas term of 1945, he joined the Experimental Theatre Club, which was supervised by the don Robert Levens and his wife Daphne. Mrs Levens was taking down names and particulars of applicants, when a lanky youth of eighteen, flamboyantly clothed, with hair hanging round one side of his face, presented himself and gave his name as Kenneth Tynan, stammering in an agonizing manner, his whole face split from mouth to ear. Daphne Levens waited patiently as he gave her details of his age and college, and then she asked him what kind of parts he liked to play. 'Neuuurrotic young men,' he said.

In November he played Iago in an ETC acting contest; the play won second prize. *Isis* described Ken's performance as good, 'except for his voice which seems to quiver most unnaturally'. That was the only show of nerves before an entirely confident three-year performance. According to the girl he most

49

loved at Oxford, Gillian Rowe-Dutton, Ken 'took a deep breath and said, "Here I am! I've arrived, and this is what I am!" None of the rest of us knew. I never thought that he faltered at all. He seemed to be totally happy.'

'I don't think there is anybody who was a legend in his own undergraduate lifetime. But Ken was a legend,' says Daphne Levens, who had recorded the stammering particulars of the very odd young man.

'It's typical of Oxford ... to start the new year in autumn,' said the narrator of *Brideshead Revisited*, which came out five months before Ken went up to the university. 'In the college gardens the smoke of the bonfires joined the wet river mist, drifting across the grey walls ... new figures in new gowns wandered through the twilight under the arches and the familiar bells now spoke of a year's memories.'

Waugh's novel celebrated wit, class and nostalgia in the figures of Sebastian Flyte and Anthony Blanche. The Tynan persona also appeared effete, a celebrant of art for art's sake and decadent languor. But he was only distantly related to either of those earlier Oxford fashionables Brian Howard and Harold Acton, who had inspired *Brideshead*. He had rather more in common with Oscar Wilde. They were both scholars at Magdalen and both were of Irish blood. Wilde as an undergraduate was larger than life and hard-working; he almost reformed fashion, fended off the attacks of the Philistine hearties, reportedly got a girl pregnant. And in all these respects Ken followed suit. But Ken was less robust, less 'virile' as he put it, and his funniness was more a branch of vaudeville than of Wildean epigram.

'We could pass our lives in Oxford without having or wanting any other idea,' wrote William Hazlitt. 'We are in the sanctuary, on holy ground.'

Oxford was Arcadia and Parnassus and Elysium; twenty years after he had left the place, Ken wrote that he had spent most of his adult life 'trying to live with the knowledge that nothing can ever top the sense of privileged exhilaration I felt then'. He was perennially absorbed with the Oxford ethos, forever forcing a comparison between the Oxford Cavalier and the Cambridge Roundhead: 'I never liked that university of dark blue suits and dark blue veins,' he wrote of Cambridge, 'where to laugh is a judgement passed rather than a moment fulfilled – a place rigorous and extreme, like the east wind that buffets it, as against the gentle miasmic swamps of Oxford.... Cam is the home of austerity and certainty, Oxford, of indulgence and doubt.'

He would say that he was a creation of Oxford – that, like a stick of seaside rock, he was stamped Oxford all the way through. But none of his contemporaries quite agreed. Because for all of them Ken made Oxford in his own image. As Alan Brien put it, 'He was the epitome of the Oxford spirit, yet entirely un-Oxonian – a cosmopolitan provincial, a Brummagem bohemian, a shy poseur, a hard-working time-waster.... the cry was always: "He's gone too far this time." ' And to go too far is very un-Oxonian.

Post-war Oxford, like the rest of the country, was austere, rationed, cramped, cold and hungry. Into this city of golden stone, unbombed by the Germans, poured a seven-year backlog of raw material, so that by 1946 90 per cent of the freshmen were ex-servicemen, most of them on government grants. There were colonels who had fought at El Alamein, war-wounded, ex-prisoners of war, and girls with missions to readjust them all to civilian life. There were also the teenagers out of school, for whom the world had been made safe, able to enjoy a relatively carefree respite before the 'H-bomb and Korea. The guests at this party, more crowded than it should be, with standing room only for people, talent and ideas, included future politicians like Anthony Wedgwood Benn, Shirley (Catlin) Williams, Edward Boyle; future media figures like Paul Johnson, William Rees-Mogg, Godfrey Smith, Alan Brien, Robin Day and Ludovic Kennedy; the novelists Kingsley Amis and John Wain; directors-in-the-making like John Schlesinger, Lindsay Anderson and Tony Richardson; and athletes like Roger Bannister and Christopher Chataway.

The eighteen-year-old Ken realized quite smartly that he had to be extremely professional if he were going to impress this group, many of whom had been through the Italian landings or D-Day. He could not just walk down the High Street with a lily in hand and expect them to fall at his feet. He had to be original. So he set about imposing his own present tense, creating his own elite, repudiating nostalgia and pre-war upper-class values. And in so doing he became something of an intellectual pirate, 'a gangster in the groves of academe', as he put it, unrationed, extravagant, funny, exhibitionist, always intelligent, passionately determined to introduce gaiety and release, and everywhere at once – as writer, actor, director, debater, lover, scholar, dandy, party-giver and pleasure-seeker.

During his first term he had made to order a purple doeskin suit, waisted over the hips, which he wore with gold satin shirts that cost £2 15s from the famous Oxford tailor Hall Brothers. Later there was a cloak with a blood-red lining, and a bottle-green suit, reputedly made of billiard baize and worn with creamy silk shirts. There were broad gold velvet ties, bowties – changed frequently during the course of a day – and soft green suede shoes. Sometimes Ken wore make-up or so the story went: his girlfriends would say, 'Don't wear make-up, Ken,' and he would answer, 'Just a little crimson lake on the mouth.'

But it was the purple suit in fine doeskin flannel that took the fancy of his admirers, while it enraged the hearties and the puritans. And, as with all totems, nobody quite saw the suit the same way: lavender, wine-red, plum, claret, pink, brilliant maroon, crimson, heather-coloured, the colour of darkest African violets; made of gaberdine, corduroy, velvet, serge, suede – so they claim.

The rest of the world wore their army greatcoats and uniforms with the insignia ripped off. If you bought a new coat on ration, it was old by the time you had saved up enough coupons to get a pair of shoes. The girls knitted wool stockings, since nylon stockings were hard to come by, and wore navy-blue serge knickers, unless they were fortunate enough to become one of Ken's peahens and were presented with blue crêpe camiknickers with mink trim, or black silk with lace.

He liked extravagance. He went to expensive restaurants and, when he was ready to leave, he would ask the waiter to order him a taxi ('Fiat Luxicar,' he would quip), but he rarely had the cash to pay for the fare, and usually had to borrow. He liked notes and hated loose change. He would stand at the top of St Giles' by the taxi rank, pull the pennies out of his pocket and throw them down the street, because he couldn't bear the rattle of money. The scholarship boy had no bank account, but £20 in fresh notes would arrive once a fortnight from his father. (It was a modest income by comparison with the very rich students, but generous by the standards of an ex-serviceman who might have to support a family on an allowance of £7 a week.) Creditors would rush round to claim their debts. The money would soon be spent, for Ken was generous as a host, and when it was gone the borrowing would start again.

He was out to be noticed from the start. During his first term a girlfriend recalls meeting him for the first time at an Oxford club. He was telling a story to a crowded room, 'a story which had a rape as the chief feature, and I could see heads turning as he pitched his voice so most could hear'.

At the end of that first term Ken went back to shock Birmingham, where his cousin Ruth Cashmore saw him prance down the main street in his new purple suit. His local love Pauline was away on tour with Donald Wolfit's company, and Ken was evidently jealous, because he wrote to tell her that the idea of sexual contact on his part with any other than the beloved was 'unalterably foreign'; and he warned, 'When, even momentarily, you cease to love me, I cease to exist.'

A few months later he bought her an opal engagement ring in a setting of diamond chips, but on several occasions the ring had to be pawned. 'Ken never had any money,' Pauline says. 'He came to visit me in Cambridge and he couldn't get back to Oxford. I remember going through my wardrobe and getting a couple of dresses, going to a friend to sell them for £5 and rushing back to Ken. I can see him now, legs over the chair, fallen asleep, and I woke him up and said, "Here you are, here's the money for the fare." He was quite nonchalant about the matter. Things came quite easily to him.'

He could behave like a child, but he was already writing with the authority of an adult. During that first Oxford vacation Ken went to London to see the Old Vic productions of *Oedipus Rex*, *The Critic* and *Henry IV, Parts I and II*, and the reviews he wrote at the time may be found in *He That Plays the King*. Here is his description of Ralph Richardson as Falstaff: 'Richardson never rollicked or slobbered or staggered: it was not a sweaty fat man, but a dry and dignified one. As the great belly moved, step following step with great finesse lest it overtopple, the arms flapped fussily at the sides as if to paddle the body's bulk along.'

Of the naturalistic scenes in Justice Shallow's orchard: 'There was a sharp scent of plucked crab-apples, and of pork in the larder: one got the sense of life-going-on-in-the-background, of rustling twigs underfoot and the large accusing eyes of cows, staring through the twilight.'

And of Olivier's Shallow he wrote: 'This Shallow . . . is a crapulous, paltering scarecrow of a man, withered up like the slough of a snake; but he has quick, commiserating eyes and the kind of delight in dispensing food and drink that one associates with a favourite aunt.'

After seeing those performances, he wrote to the literary editor of *Isis*, Kenneth Harris, applying for one of the two posts as drama critic. It was typical of Ken to know what job he wanted and to set out to get it. The letter was followed by a visit in person. The editor was not pleased at being hounded to his digs, 'But at the same time,' Harris recalls, 'one had to give him credit for keenness.'

Ken's first review (of Ronald Millar's *Frieda*) appeared in February 1946, and in no time at all he had made a considerable impact. He sent his first piece to Julian Holland along with the news that he was writing a 'mordant burlesque of the Koestler style' for 'a glossy Oxford miscellany' called *Mandrake*, that he was playing Granillo in *Rope*; and that he was 'inconstant consort to a tired but brilliant sewing-circle of pseudo-débutantes . . , and still sodden in cheap gin and hip deep in broken glass from a party I flung last Friday night. My scout said it was the worst mess he'd had to clean up since the Prince of Wales had these rooms.'

Having assaulted university drama and journalism, Ken next took on the Union debating society. Opposing the motion that 'This House Deplores the Tyranny of Convention', he deplored extravagance in what the *Oxford Magazine* described as 'a superbly extravagant maiden speech' (one in which he managed to fit a plea for Augustan prose and Augustan tranquillity). The late Sir Edward Boyle called this performance 'an absolute masterpiece', though it was hardly an impromptu one. As at school, Ken had written out the whole speech in his elegant hand, without any marks of emphasis. So skilful was his manner of delivery that even his stammer seemed to be used with calculated effect. Thereafter the Union was full whenever he spoke, the gallery often crowded with women (not at that time allowed to be members). He became a 'licensed shocker', according to Robin Day, 'expected to go slightly beyond the accepted bounds'.

Behind the showmanship, however, there was a discreetly hard-working academic. His tutor C. S. Lewis said of Ken's early essays in English literature that if Lamb and Gibbon had been the same person, Ken's were the kind of essays they would have produced at prep school. This praise became much more fulsome after the first public examinations, when Ken received distinctions for his essays on Milton and Shakespeare.

Lewis was already well known, not just as a literary critic and author but as a Christian thinker. He lived in the eighteenth-century New Buildings at Magdalen, in rooms that looked to the deer park on one side and towards the tower on the other, and he could be seen around the college grounds, walking-stick in hand, a ruddy-complexioned man in Norfolk tweeds, looking like a country farmer.

During cold, fuel-less winter months, Lewis would receive his students in a woollen cardigan with an old dressing-gown on top. 'Occasionally,' Ken recalled, 'he would quite unceremoniously get up and go to the next room to relieve himself in a chamber pot, and then come back and continue the tutorial. And he would always puff on his pipe to make marvellous debating points. . . . He could take you into the mediaeval mind and the mind of a classical writer. . . . As a teacher he was just incomparable.'

While other undergraduates found Lewis bullying, Ken thought him exceptionally kind. Because of his stammer Lewis would volunteer to read aloud his pupil's essays for him. 'It became quite a test writing essays that could survive being read in that wonderfully resonant voice.' Ken learned how to respect a correct choice of word, verbal structure and rhythm. On one of Ken's essays about early English drama, Lewis wrote, 'Keep a strict eye on eulogistic & dyslogistic adjectives – They shd *diagnose* (not merely blame) & distinguish (not merely praise).' Lewis also demonstrated how to argue in a vein of outrageous paradox to the point where Ken realized that 'too many of his arguments depend on crafty analogy'.

Just before his death Ken compared his old tutor to Dr Johnson: '[Lewis] had the same swiftness to grasp the heart of a problem and the same sort of pouncing intelligence to follow it through to the conclusion.' Here was the most impressive mind that Ken had seen in action; and this improbable guru – a Tory and a High Churchman – affected and haunted him throughout his life.

Early in the Hilary term of 1946 Ken attended the second meeting of the Author–Critic Club, the brainchild of an undergraduate from Pembroke called Alan Beesley. The goal of the club was to cut through the old, turgid undergrowth of literature and present something new and shining. But very quickly, according to Derek Lindsay,

It became a figment of fun, as far as Alan, Ken and I were concerned.
At the second meeting I remember there were about twenty people there, and my eyes lighted on Ken and I was immediately astonished and delighted by what I saw. He was very thin, unlike anyone I had ever met before or subsequently. He had a

54

charm bracelet on his left hand. I was delighted by his manner, his appearance and his way of speaking, and then of course by the instant realization of the degree of his talent, and ability. This was what I thought Oxford was all about, without grasping that Ken was totally unique. I admired his hands; I think that was my first reference, speaking to him, and he replied, "Yes, they're very tenuous." We were meeting to read our modest contributions, and Ken rather surprisingly asked me to read his for him, because of his stammer. So that was the beginning and it was quite clear to me that a new person had come into my life.

Alan [Beesley] was a considerable curiosity but he had none of Ken's intense panache, which was intrinsic rather than assumed. Ken was just Ken. Alan was a sort of acquired taste.

But Alan was a taste that Ken acquired and kept, addicted to the pungency and valour of this personality, which was unmodish, with a Cagney-like resilience. The son of a schoolteacher, Alan had served in the RAF in Canada, had attempted suicide there and had come up to the university in 1945. In an *Isis* 'Idol', under a photograph of Alan's dark, piratical face, Ken wrote:

He was born in 1923 ... small, compactly tough, and urgent.... He smokes continuously with dazed nonchalance, and carries his shoulders in an aggressive defensive bunch about his neck....

He is probably the only genuine neurotic in Oxford. You get a sense of rapport with the Life-Force.... In a sense he *is* the disease of this generation; in much the same sense, a pearl is a disease of the oyster. This modern world, given luck and frequent solace, may be Alan's oyster.

Many years later Ken compared Beesley to John Osborne's outsider, Jimmy Porter, to which Alan replied, 'For Christ's sake, I wouldn't have a sweet stall, now would I? A betting agency, perhaps.' He was like 'a tightly packed case of dynamite', as one friend put it, clinically insane, yet wise and intelligent, unattached to any kind of dogma. 'Nothing can give such relief as the complete failure,' he wrote at Oxford. So he gambled as a way of failing with honour. He loved to gamble, and if he won he would throw his money on to a bar and say, 'Let everybody drink! Get rid of the fucking stuff!' And everybody – for friends stuck to him like honey – drank until there was nothing left.

At Oxford Alan would from time to time threaten to kill himself, to throw himself under a bus; it seemed to his friends the most normal thing in the world. 'Because who wouldn't have the impulse to throw himself under a bus?' Derek Lindsay explains. 'It was the temper of the times, and how we all were, with the difference that for myself it was deadly serious, and I thought that it was a tremendous joke for everybody else.'

Deacon Lindsay, whom Ken described as 'an expensive limited edition of a curious object' was several years older than Ken. He had a housekeeper, a private income and a mysterious, tortured private life. (He told one girl at

Oxford, 'It's not really that I want you – it's this terrible libido.') Deacon was quite evidently an excellent writer of fiction. 'He was going to be the great man,' the novelist Kingsley Amis recalls, 'greater than all of us.' But apart from his one great novel, *The Rack*, Deacon's life has been fiercely non-eventful. Life, he claims, started at Oxford and 'virtually nothing has ever happened subsequently'.

In the summer term of 1946 Beesley and Ken, bored with the Author–Critic Club, decided to buy the moribund university magazine, *Cherwell*, and to reanimate it. The Beesley–Tynan–Lindsay philosophy would inform the magazine. Sartre's *Les Chemins de la Liberté* had been skimmed and they knew they were condemned to be free. But not free enough, according to Alan. He feared a third world war; he despised the constrictions of the welfare state. Both, he thought, were evil. He required that his friends share his degree of despair and it was the quality of the despair that mattered rather than the *reason* for the despair.

Ken respected the authenticity of his two deeply pessimistic friends, but he felt with Byron that 'The great object of life is sensation – to feel that we exist, though in pain.' Out of Mario Praz's *The Romantic Agony* and Senecan drama, Ken formulated his own stoical philosophy, and peopled it with heroes. To Pauline he quoted more Byron, ' "Eat, drink, toil, tremble, laugh, weep, sleep, and die." I saw with terrific clarity that I had done all those things – except die. I suddenly knew that I would have to die soon … that an old, fitful joy in life I once took was slipping irrevocably from me.' In another letter to her in the autumn of 1946 he wrote: 'To my plans for next term you can add a *new Philosophy* we of the *Cherwell* have cooked up. It will be, we hope, as fashionable as Existentialism, and we shall publicise it every week in the paper, as well as making it the basis of our speeches when we invade the Union. It has no name as yet; vaguely we call it "a Philosophy of Transience".… it has quite set fire to me and my whole life will be run accordingly.' His letter closed: 'Aren't dance tunes of the early '30s wonderfully nostalgic? I have spent this morning weeping copiously over an Ambrose record of "Smoke Gets in Your Eyes".'

The first post-war Labour government did not register much on the *Cherwell* set. While undergraduates like Anthony Crosland, Peter Parker or Tony Wedgwood Benn were entertaining Labour Cabinet ministers at Oxford meetings, full of high hopes for the country's socialist future, Ken chose to be, as the industrialist Peter Parker puts it, 'a brilliant illuminated margin. I would never have thought of talking seriously of politics to him.'

Both at school and at Oxford Ken's political schemes were of the Aldous Huxley type, island idylls and certainly elitist, but with an un-Huxleyan tendency to authoritarianism. When confronted by the Oxford University Liberal magazine about his fragile political commitment as a Union man, Ken replied: 'I will tell you about my politics. A century ago I should have been a feudal Tory; a century hence, an Anarchist. At the present I am a Liberal, with Confucian leanings.' Thereafter he was known to this particular journalist as 'Ken Ty Nan, the Confucian Liberal'.

Ken tried hard to play the nihilist and to embrace Alan's view of betrayal as a heroic duty, but he found it impossible to suppress a radiant enthusiasm for his writing, for the theatre and particularly for his two friends. He would drink with them through the night and then go back to his rooms and write an essay or plan a production. So productive and successful was he that Alan and Deacon formed an Inner Betrayal Circle for the express purpose of plotting the downfall of their young friend, whose life was all too ordered and fruitful.

Ken's by-line was in almost any undergraduate journal you picked up – on Orson Welles, on Arthur Koestler, on *The Man Who Came to Dinner*: 'And here I had better come right out and say that in my view the nonchalant, exquisitely turned vulgarity of the American comic stage is one of the finest, neatest things that has ever happened to the drama.' By the end of the term 'objectionable Kenneth Tynan' was said to be Oxford's best journalist. He also played the lead in Maeterlinck's *Pelléas and Mélisande*, and directed his first Oxford production for an ETC acting competition, a 'vivid interpretation' of T. S. Eliot's *Sweeney Agonistes*, for which he won first prize.

At 11 a.m. Ken's day would start with coffee at the Playhouse Theatre. He would then move on, with his friends, to the bar at the Randolph Hotel. Avoiding the long lines at the cheaper restaurants, or a dull meal in college, he would usually lunch at Whites, a lush establishment that offered a cocktail bar on the ground floor and a restaurant upstairs which had carpets and flattering pink lighting. The French menu, written in silver on white, offered a wide choice of what was thought to be black-market fare, and an excellent wine list. This 'pink sink of impotent iniquity' was exactly what Oxford needed.

It was nice to be asked to Whites by Ken, and good for your social reputation to have him as a guest. He usually managed to be an hour late at a party, so that by the time he got there someone had already announced, 'Tynan's coming.' 'I remember him standing outside the door,' Peter Parker recalls, 'checking his suit and then going *in*, which was how he directed a play. It was a matter of attack!' Usually Ken would arrive at a party with a story, something that had happened to him, or that he had heard, and he would embellish the anecdote as he found the incongruities. Sometimes he would pick up a new person and invent for him or her a whole history. He was marvellous company, marvellous fun.

He soon discovered that he could use his effete appearance to deflect the attention of male competition. He even encouraged the rumour that he was homosexual. In a period of sexual inhibition, or at least of sexual hypocrisy, Ken was a great proselytizer for permissiveness. He would take a girl to tea and say, 'The trouble with you is that you're a virgin and nobody notices you. You must break out of your cage.' To an old Birmingham friend who came to visit, he said, 'The trouble with you is you won't admit to being homosexual. The sooner you make up your mind what you are, the happier you'll be.' His whole attitude to sex was a liberated one.

His critics felt he did unpardonable hurt. A don's wife explained: 'He would run two or three girls at the same time (to be in the magic circle of Ken Tynan held a tremendous cachet), making each of them believe that she was the one that mattered, and then just turn on his heel and walk away. He was not a kindly man.' A girlfriend said: 'He would pick people up, play them along for a while until he drained them.' If he were not interested in 'draining' someone, he was inclined to be opaque, indifferent and cold. Having an ordinary conversation with him was unusual, for he had no small talk or social oil.

The part of Ken that liked to make wounding or shocking remarks was deeply resented. Deacon Lindsay remembers a group of friends cooing over a baby: 'When it came Ken's turn to coo, he said, "I think it looks as if it's expecting to be hanged." I always thought he was intrinsically interested in what the reaction would be.' He would make a cruel remark quite suddenly with nothing in the context to account for it. It was a habit he did not grow out of: to a neurotic male friend he once said, 'If you keep crossing and uncrossing your legs like that you'll set yourself alight.'

Although he could be wounding, he was in turn easily wounded. It hurt him to be criticized, and he was frightened of rejection. If hurt he could re-taliate in a spiteful way. 'He was vain and childish,' one girlfriend claims, 'but he could be very good, which is an odd thing to say. He was a good person.' 'He was a wonderfully loyal and generous friend,' says Elisabeth Zaiman.

Elisabeth Zaiman was the first of several Jewish girls at Oxford whom Ken courted. She was a medical student with large eyes in a pale face, surrounded by curly black hair. And she was a theatre lover: there was hardly an Oxford production that she was not part of – as actress or wardrobe mistress. 'Did you know that all smooth things meet in you? that you are the cynosure of all light curves? that you are a pure wave of limb? Of course you didn't. I can tell you of these things', Ken wrote to her in May 1946, 'given half a chance.' He followed this letter with another. 'I have received: item, a tin of corned beef; item, a bottle of pickles; item, three jars of jam; item, 2 lbs. of sugar; item, a tin of condensed milk ... and I want you to come to tea.' The next letter read, 'All right. I cry off.' Which he did. They became friends, exchanged jokes and played word games, and met regularly no matter to whom he was engaged. In the summer of 1946 Ken was still engaged to Pauline, and still living in college, which presented a problem since women had to be off the premises by 7 p.m. The solution was to keep a girl with you overnight and then, with the connivance of the college servants, to smuggle her out through the kitchen yard in a laundry basket.

From time to time Ken's sexual confidence would collapse. He wrote a poem to the effect that 'no vitalizing juice would flow', and asked a friend whether his temporary impotence might be due to his stammer. 'I thought that underneath he was a rather tearful boy,' says an older male friend, 'a good deal younger than his years but loaded with this extraordinary theatricality, talent and wit, and it became too great a burden for him. One could see the small boy – not suffering, not skulking, but wincing, I think, underneath.'

During that summer he toured the cathedral cities of southern England, playing Sir Covetous in *The Castle of Perseverance* among a cast of undergraduates which included Lindsay Anderson and Timothy Bateson. They hired a van with a loudspeaker and toured each town before the performance, roaring out, 'Come to the cathedral at night and hear the voice of death weighing God's justice in balance.'

The following month Ken used the same publicity device in Birmingham to promote his New Dramatic Company production of Euripides' *Medea*. Several committee members had tried to tone down their director's extravagant ideas (to which he had responded, loud and clear, for the first – though not the last – time: 'Bugger the committee'). Ken wrote to Holland that, despite setbacks, the production was 'brilliant and atmospherical'. He played Chorus with his hair Marcel-waved, and in pink tights. And he acted the part of the Messenger, who relates the news of Medea's slaughters, against a background of trumpet solos from Duke Ellington's 'Black and Tan Fantasy'. 'I used a balletic mimed prologue (very dirty) to introduce the play ([backed by] Ravel's "La Valse").... I designed the set and executed it myself: a pink palace, with an 18-ft. silver sword draped across it; a wild, Blake-esque sky, two pillars on a rostrum; and a jet black house for Medea. The *Despatch* critic spoke of the production as having "the genuine creative energy, the life force" and compared me with Peter Brook.'

With a sprawling, a 'conglomeration of opinions, new evidences of adulthood, things seen and digested, things read and relished', Ken returned to Oxford.

The lodge at Magdalen was more than usually crowded at the beginning of the Michaelmas term 1946, with a huge influx of ex-servicemen – 'A rather elderly hardened bunch', according to a teenage freshman called Paul Johnson.

Suddenly in the midst of that throng came this tall, epicene figure wearing a plum-coloured suit and a lavender tie, followed by what appeared to be a cortège of porters carrying trunks. He turned to one of his bearers and said, 'Have a care with that trunk, my man. It is freighted with golden shirts.' And he swept past, followed by all our goggling faces. There was Ken Tynan, fighting a little lone war all on his own, to bring glamour back to Oxford.

Two weeks later on 18 October the first issue of the new fortnightly _Cherwell_ appeared. Ken was literary editor, soon to become co-editor with Alan Beesley. There were stories by Derek Lindsay and John Wain, and a contribution from Robert Graves. From Ken there was a review of Laurence Olivier's _King Lear_, his first published criticism of the actor. He opened with a slap for the 'ingenuous claqueurs' who nightly fed the Richardson–Olivier company with nothing but eulogy. Then he offered a cool appraisal of Olivier himself: 'He is our model Richard III, and his Hotspur is unique. But he has no intrinsic majesty ... and he cannot play old men without letting his jaw sag and his eye wander archly.... the performance told us nothing new of either Lear or Mr. Olivier; it merely showed us a few wholly unexpected facets of the private life of Mr. Justice Shallow.'

In the next issues Alan Beesley pronounced the magazine to be schizophrenic and insane: 'For until the bores, the illiterates, the yahoos, the trolls, the Group Men and the bigots have been silenced, CHERWELL's personality must remain split.'

Ken represented the sober and intelligent part of the split personality, with contributions on Coleridge, eighteenth-century Bath and the splendour of Ralph Richardson's performance as Cyrano de Bergerac. Dame Edith Evans's performance as Cleopatra, on the other hand, he described as 'a drunken Gingold at large on a viola', 'as hostile as a glacier'.

In unsigned columns Ken wrote of Sacher-Masoch, Sid Field, biblical art and his horror of 'the grey evil': 'the old, blind, rooting Evil, that is damp, groping, lonely. It is the hard core of inadequacy, of indifference to being.' He added as if he were still a prisoner of Birmingham, of insignificance and of his parents: 'It is emptiness, sterility.... The certainty of the complete isolation of a personality.'

Outside the _Cherwell_ office Ken prepared a production of _The Song of Songs_, and appeared in yet another ETC acting competition, as Oswald in Ibsen's _Ghosts_, 'an exquisitely bored youth in raspberry and lemon yellow', a part that gave him the opportunity of hinting to his friends that he too, like Oswald, was a hereditary syphilitic. He also directed _A Toy in Blood_ for the ETC, his own modern-dress adaptation of the Hamlet–Ophelia scenes. The curtain went up on the Danish court waltzing slowly around the stage. A blackout and a pistol shot fired into the audience (a trick borrowed from Peter Brook) pronounced Polonius dead; and the nunnery scene was played with Hamlet in bed in the company of a whore, and Ophelia drunkenly talking to him from a telephone kiosk. The music was by Artie Shaw.

On 19 January 1947, the first Sunday of the Hilary term, the Great Frost set in and the country froze up, with sub-zero temperatures and snow-storms made intolerable by the fuel crisis and the ban on the use of electricity for five hours of the day. At the beginning of March milder temperatures brought on a concert of burst pipes, followed by the worst blizzard of the year.

At Magdalen the college scouts burned anything combustible, while the undergraduates went into hibernation. At eleven o'clock in the morning hooded figures would emerge from their rooms, with mugs in hand, wearing gloves. They would help themselves to coffee and then go back to their rooms. The atmosphere could not have been more grim.

For Ken it was the most festive period of his life, and the beginning of a golden year of achievement and delight. *Cherwell* came out on 23 January with its best issue to date, and with the first of two pieces by Ken on the magazine's philosophy. ' "Cervillism" [from the Latin for Cherwell] means acquiescence in the fact of mortality, acceptance and reconciliation with death,' he wrote buoyantly, and proceeded to define its attitude as 'the key to pleasure', cousin to Taoist detachment, favouring civilized organization in 'small groups'. The word 'why', he argued, was to be expunged from the vocabulary. 'The only indisputable facts are (a) the moment, and (b) our existence in it.'

The second part of this manifesto never appeared, for the magazine was banned: 1000 copies of a sex questionnaire had been sent out by *Cherwell* to women undergraduates, and one or two of these had fallen into the hands of women dons, who reacted poorly to questions like 'If unmarried, have you experienced sexual intercourse?'

Ken wrote his flamboyant *Isis* 'Idol' of Alan Beesley, and moved on to other platforms. He took part in his first official Union debate, on the notion that 'There Is No Hope for the Modern Novel', and concluded that there were no more novels to be written: 'Yet I myself am surely the stuff, cheap, flimsy, suggestive, of which modern novels are made. They hymn my panicky pride.' The *Oxford Magazine* listed his debating skills as '(1) The wild, appealing, distracted stare at the gallery. (2) The clutching of the text of the speech (fully written out on mauve scented paper ...) to the heart with sinuously twisted fingers. (3) the body curved backwards like a bow ... convulsively jerked into a vertical position for the ejection of a word. ...'

A few days after this debate Ken played his first major part at Oxford, Bishop Nicholas in Ibsen's *The Pretenders*. His extravagant performance as the dying Bishop Nicholas in this dire production was praised by *The Times* and politely labelled 'Irvingesque' in Oxford. 'Ken wasn't one of your Stanislavsky boys who stand in the shadows and murmur into their chests,' Daphne Levens explains. 'He liked theatre theatrical. There was the voice, and the hand and the flashing eye, and the terrifying burst of energy when the bony old man rose in his night shirt and sank back groaning on the pillows. Nobody could stop him once he was dying, and he took as long over it as he liked.'

6

The Marvellous Boy

One morning outside the Playhouse Theatre, Ken saw a tall girl with dark hair and a long equine face like a Chardin – her nose slightly upturned, suggesting wit rather than pertness. He discovered that her name was Gillian Rowe-Dutton and that she was a medical student at St Anne's. He sent her a note saying that he would be at her rooms at four o'clock to take her to tea. A presumptuous note, for he no doubt knew of Jill's reputation in Oxford as a travelled sophisticate, daughter of a diplomat, considered a *femme fatale*, with a string of aspiring lovers.

Jill Rowe-Dutton, on the other hand, thought of herself as a family-oriented country girl.

I felt there was nothing about the country in Ken at all, not a blade of grass. So I thought of *him* as the sophisticate, and I was rather flattered by his instant approach. I looked around Oxford and thought who is the mostest. It wasn't necessarily the best or most of anything particular, just the most outstanding. And there was no question: he was young, startlingly funny, unconscionably arrogant, and lived extravagantly on five bob a week.... he could switch on intellectual brilliance like a floodlight.

You didn't just go and sit on the top of a bus and wait till you'd reached your destination. You sat on top of the bus and everyone was falling about, either absolutely shocked, or roaring with laughter. It was very exciting, and of course he was wonderful looking.

And so she fell in love. As indeed did Ken.

Alan Beesley first saw Marie Woolf cycling down the High Street in green stockings and a red coat, introduced himself, spent the next twelve hours in her company and married her six weeks later. Like Jill Rowe-Dutton, who happened to be her best friend, Marie was a medical student. She was small, with soft fair hair, high cheekbones, blue eyes and a fugitive shyness. She was the niece of Virginia Woolf and spoke in a Bloomsbury drawl. Marie and Jill shared digs at 82A St Aldate's, behind the original of the Sheep Shop of

Alice in Wonderland. And there the four friends gathered during the ice-cold winter, drew the curtains by two in the afternoon, lit the candles, stoked up a fire, drank cheap wine or Ovaltine or apricot brandy, and talked, pairing off only for sleep.

On one occasion Jill Rowe-Dutton's discarded lover, John Godley, came drunkenly in search of her and lay in the snow below the window, weeping loudly. 'I went out to comfort him,' Marie recalls, 'while Ken remained upstairs in a state. Jill abolutely shattered her boyfriends.'

When Deacon Lindsay first came to the rooms in St Aldate's, he was already enamoured of Ken, and was soon to fall for Jill and Marie. 'They were absolutely lovely. Marie was wearing a rather tweedy jacket. God knows who it had belonged to, perhaps her father. No one was very particular about clothes except Ken. Marie was eating, music was playing very loudly, and she spilled some food on her jacket. Jill suddenly started licking it off, sweetly and charmingly. And Marie sat there allowing this strange thing to happen. Immediately an intimacy between all of us was established – between Ken, Jill, Marie, Alan and myself, in this little flat to which one was to return over and over again.'

Alan played his 78 r.p.m. Coleman Hawkins recording of 'Blue Moon', with Joe Thomas hitting high c on trumpet. He was obsessed with it. There were always a few phrases he had to hear over and over again, and he played it at every speed on the wind-up gramophone. He would say, 'Put it on again. I've got to hear it again. Put it slow – Oh Christ it's stopped! No, no, get it turning. Now let's have it fast.' 'This would go on all night,' Deacon explains. 'Ken would sit brooding and talking to Jill, rather clinically, about what was going to come of all this, and whether it would really be better for Alan to kill himself there and then.'

'Deacon was our magic person,' says Jill Rowe-Dutton. He would tell stories of being chased by wolves down St Aldate's, or a saga that began: "I am a costing clerk in a clay-pot corporation," stories that became depraved and appalling, nasty fairy stories for these children on their way to bed. And when they accused him of telling tales that were too depressing he would promise, "From now on the corpses will *dance*!" '

At three or four in the morning, during the cold spell, wearing his army greatcoat and boots, this melancholic jester would trudge off under a crystalline moon to his secret life in North Oxford.

At one of the parties in the St Aldate's digs Deacon caught his first glimpse of Stanley Parker, a misshapen figure who danced alone, as if he were a very sexy young man, suddenly dropping to his knees, making extraordinary motions with his tongue and propelling himself across the room. Stanley Parker, the son of an Australian sheep farmer, had invented for himself a benign persona, a comic hybrid of Noël Coward and the Baron de Charlus. He was around thirty, not very tall, his plump figure corseted, his face framed in dark ringlets. He lived on the fringes of university life, off a reputation as a minor journalist and draughtsman. He had met everybody, including Pavlova, Melba, George Bernard Shaw and Marlene Dietrich. He had met everybody at Oxford – Lord David Cecil, Max Beerbohm. But he had not met *the* undergraduate, until Ken was brought to him, in his famous suit with a cigarette dripping from between his third and his fourth finger.

'He was, of course, quite obviously, dead,' Parker wrote about this first encounter. 'He had been drowned, I think, for a lot of green seaweed was dripping down his livid face, and trickling over his magenta suit which, with the saffron shirt and cloth-of-gold tie, was intensified by being completely sodden. His feet were, quite frankly, crushed bananas.' 'Who is that charming cadaver over there?' Stanley asked. The charming cadaver, they told him, was Kenneth Peacock Tynan.

'Will you', I asked the Undergraduate, 'play John the Baptist in a *completely* realistic production of Oscar Wilde's *Salome*? You are obviously the only man in the world who could play more than one performance.' 'You don't think I would look odd,' [Ken] suggested, dilating his nostrils, shimmying his shoulders ... and giving that Disdainful Look we all know and love so well, and They all hate, 'on the Second Night, with no head at all?'

'I don't,' I told him honestly. 'I think, if anything, you would look *less* odd.'

And then it happened. All his poise went to the winds, and I saw that agonized orgasm of the spirit that I have come to treasure, because it means that I have struck gold. The eyes, the whites *above* the pupils, dart right into the farthest recesses of your psyche, the hollow cheeks crease into the shape of a stylised gargoyle, and more fangs than one had believed possible fight like maenads to jockey themselves to the front. It doesn't last long. It is over in a flash. But in that flash you have seen Tynan. You have seen him whole. You have seen him naked. You have seen his soul. And you suddenly know – quite out of context, for the spasm is what is commonly held to be laughter – that it is lit, by possibly only a spark (but a spark that might well start a world conflagration), of that frightening, wonderful, awesome thing called Genius.

The lime-green English spring arrived and Ken bought up a whole stall of daffodils, showered them on his friends, and took them to the Bear at Woodstock for celebration. Alan and Marie were soon married and moved into a flat in North Oxford, so Ken applied to the university authorities to live at 82A St Aldate's, but was refused.

In the vacation he broke his engagement to Pauline, asked for his letters back and cruelly showed her a photograph of Jill. His fiancée put on a brave face. 'He took me home, looked around my mother's attractive drawing-room which he had always described as a "stage set" and said, "I shall never see this room again." I was broken-hearted.'

His new fiancée was staying meanwhile with Marie Beesley and writing to Ken: 'My thoughts are just lazy pictures and dreams about the future. A vision of you coiling round a punt pole and looking down at me. Or you and me walking down the High holding hands, into the sun so hot that one wears practically nothing. . . . Us having breakfast – dancing – waiting for an evening to end – walking out of Whites in disgust (going back next day) enthusing our way down the Corn with the Beezles. And then later perhaps people will say, "My dear, *have* you heard? The Tynans –" '

On 21 April a document consenting to the marriage of Gillian Rowe-Dutton to a minor was signed by Peter and Rose Tynan, and witnessed by Marie. The minor and his future bride were installed at 31 Park Town along with some black and gold china, but very little else. And from that address Ken wrote to Julian Holland: 'I'm living with Jill – an expensive business – and saving up to get married.'

Their engagement was announced in the *Isis* on 7 May, and a week later Ken was featured as an *Isis* 'Idol'. Of his future the magazine declared:

He will go apart, taking a few with him, to an unmapped island: write short criticisms and produce long plays. Jill will be with him, of course, and the expensive German record of Marlene Dietrich.

Meanwhile the roof is to be taken from St. Mary's for his appearance as God in *Faust*.

The play was Milton's *Samson Agonistes* – not *Faust*, but Milton's text with a few additions from the Book of Judges. Ken also added a character called the Angel of the Lord, gave him some of the best lines belonging to the Chorus, and played the part himself, strung up high on the wall of St Mary's Church, his arms stretched out under ten-foot purple velvet wings. Nothing quite like it had been seen before in Oxford, let alone in a church.

Ken's programme note announced that he had in mind 'the idea of imprisonment . . . in the dungeon of selfhood . . . [of Samson] trying unsuccessfully to escape *upwards* towards self-annihilation and God; and thus denying his real vocation, which is to come down and perform God's work *on earth*. Hence I have made the Chorus his fellow-prisoners, with the difference that they are resigned to their chains, and to the restrictive doctrine that "To The Public Good Private Respects Must Yield", and Samson is not.' (Samson, he told his tutor, was 'the authentic, treasurable, Nietzschean Super-Man', and therefore a fitting subject for heroic drama.)

In a long article on his production of the play, Ken delivered a highly personal manifesto on his working relation with the theatre: 'This sad age needs to be dazzled, shaped and spurred by the spectacle of heroism. I believe not that the theatre reflects life, but that life reflects theatre.' That 'life reflects the theatre' was not merely a clever notion, but a confession of his circumstances. In the theatre as a performer in the lighted area, or as a passionate critic in the audience who watched and became part of what he watched, Ken was sure of his identity, released from his stammer and given a bountiful sense of freedom and distinction. Outside that area, away from its aura of clarity and light, he was less sure who he was.

The manifesto proceeds: 'All that my being can comprehend is the importance of devoting itself to one little end: to investigating, by curious squints, what combinations of aural and visual attacks, performed on a lighted stage before a dark auditorium, can cause the great white mottle of watching faces simultaneously to flush, blench, gasp, shriek, recoil, or stare in awe.... I am interested in immediacy, the sudden start of here and now.'

Having declared his theatrical intention (already rehearsed in his productions of Medea, Sweeney Agonistes and A Toy in Blood), he developed his theory of shock:

Regular visual shocks are ... important to prod the audience into expectancy (examples: a house falling down, a thug dressed in white satin, a thick green fog).... Shock is the denial of what is expected....

[The audience] must be made aware that emotions are being evoked on the stage before them of a quality *enviably* finer than any they have shared, much less experienced. They must be rendered green-eyed with the desire to participate; and with passionate humility, which is another name for awe.

The production would unleash an 'Asiatic pageant' in St Mary's, dramatically opposed to Stanislavsky's method, since Ken believed in starting with externals and working inwards.

Stealing an idea from William Poel's production of the play – that it should be performed on the vertical plane, with Samson at the apex of a pyramid – Ken found a thirty-foot wooden tower used for repairing overhead tram wires, and installed it in the church. He placed his Samson on the top of this edifice – where the audience could barely seen him. He had Delilah, her skirts slashed to the waist, wearing gold platform shoes from Portugal, climb precariously rung by rung up the tower.

He installed elaborate loudspeaker equipment. Balinese gongs clashed for the catastrophe; Tunisian cymbals whispered for Delilah, whose 'tiny negro maid' was required to scatter cheap scent on the audience. The Chorus was represented by a chain-gang of prisoners, and the Messenger coughed gallons of blood over the wounded survivors of Gaza. A vast crimson curtain was fastened to the vaulting of the church roof. At the moment when the gongs announced the fall of Gaza, the slip knots were loosed, and the great bulk came sweeping down.

Nevill Coghill, the don from Exeter who had produced the play in 1930, wrote to Ken praising the adaptation but adding, 'Even with the resources of Cecil B. de Mille no stage spectacle could equal the force of Milton's words.... You have so much talent that what you need is not to force your fancy, but to control it.... you have a fatal streak of cleverness that is out of place, shatteringly, when vision is called for.'

On 30 May there appeared the first issue of *Oxford Viewpoint*, a highly professional undergraduate literary magazine run by George Scott. Ken submitted a review of Frederick Valk's performance as Othello opposite Wolfit's Iago. His manuscript, in mauve ink under his printed signature, needed no editing. He also provided on request a short biographical note, which included his ambitions: 'To be a talker, hack, feuilletoniste, dramatic critic, and actor–producer'.

Valk was a bulky German who spoke imperfect English – the ideal actor to execute Ken's theory, developed during his production of *Samson*, that 'It is, after all, the physical things which go to make good theatre.' Ken had first seen Valk as Othello the previous September. 'I nearly had a heart attack during III iii,' he wrote to Julian Holland after viewing the play; 'My heart was leaping and thudding about as I have never known it before. I was breathless and beautifully exhausted at each curtain. I experienced full catharsis last Monday night.' He wrote a review of the play without any plan for publication and sent the piece to James Agate. On 2 January 1947 Agate quoted an excerpt in his diary. It began, 'I have seen a public event of enormous, constellated magnitude and radiance.' With a need to be consumed by the experience, Ken continued: 'I have watched and become part of a transfusion of bubbling hot blood into the invalid frame of our drama.... I have lived for three hours on the red brink of a volcano, and the crust of lava crumbles still from my feet....' After several pages of quotation Agate commented: 'Anybody reading this in a hundred years' time should know what these two actors had been like in these two great rôles. And that, and nothing else, in my view is dramatic criticism. In other words, here is a great dramatic critic in the making.'

In Oxford the young usurper was seen to burn one of Agate's letters in order to light a cigarette.

On 18 June 1947 Ken played his last part of the term, as Holofernes in an OUDS production of *Love's Labour's Lost*. 'Doddering, precious, mouthing his words with relish, superbly and strangely transformed by his make-up,' so *Isis* described the quirky pedant of the mediaeval school. Ken would deliver an alliterative poem full of wordplay, in the guise of Holofernes, and step forward to explain: 'This is a gift that I have; simple, simple; a foolish extravagant spirit, full of forms, figures, shapes, objects, ideas, apprehensions, motions, revolutions.' Then with a distinctive movement, he would turn to the audience and conclude, 'But the gift is good in those in whom it is acute, and I am thankful for it.' He had left the schoolmaster and was talking about himself – a sudden moment of self-declaration, of allegiance to 'the great cause of words' – and the audience roared and applauded there and then.

Sensing that their daughter was unsure about marriage, Jill Rowe-Dutton's family had sent her and Ken that summer vacation to Donegal. In the wilds of Donegal Ken was completely out of his element. On one occasion he disappeared to the cellar, surfacing some time later with marks on his neck. He said he had been trying to hang himself. 'You have *not* been trying to hang yourself,' said Jill, 'because you want to marry me.'

On 24 September Ken wrote to Holland from Oxford: 'Jill has left me. I thought several times of writing or coming to see you, because I think you know about that ache and that hunger and that waste and loss. I crumpled pretty completely.... I am learning to aspire to that wonderful loneliness they talk about, and to solace myself with Shaw when he said, "God is alone".'

Jill Rowe-Dutton returned to the arms of her former lover John Godley. Ken wrote an anguished letter to her: 'Please SEE me ... with my face drenched with tears and my eyes red and nearly invisible. And see, too, my ANGUISH at your cool, bloody, hateful betrayal.... Where O Chum is the vestige of CONSCIENCE?' Several pages later he declared with astonishing presumption: 'Oh how could you do it? You chum. The you I *created* in February and shared through March, April, May, June, July, August.' That letter was not delivered, but a more spiteful one was sent to Jill's father, describing his daughter as a loose woman. 'We had a great row,' Jill remembers, 'and he slapped my face very hard. I went home in floods to my parents.' Ken's angry letter was opened, more tears shed. But the family closed ranks and Jill decided not to see Ken again.

Meanwhile, John Godley made a raid on Ken's rooms in St John Street to recover Jill's best pair of camiknickers trimmed with black lace, which had been hung on the wall over a whip. Ken then rushed off to the police, to report the loss, and to answer questions:

'What do you seem to be missing?'

'A pair of c-c-camiknickers.'

'And where did you last see them?'

'Hanging on my wall.'

During the autumn term Ken became engaged again, and then again: to Ruth Cropper, a charming Politics, Philosophy and Economics student (for whom he ordered yet another pair of camiknickers, this time in blue crêpe de chine with ermine trim), and then to Gillian Staynes, a girl with Pre-Raphaelite hair and theatrical clothes. He gave a dinner in Oscar Wilde's old rooms in Magdalen to celebrate their engagement, presented his fiancée with a collection of Charles Addams cartoons, and told her about bullfighting. 'He cavorted round ... demonstrating *véronicas*,' Miss Staynes recalls – thus providing the earliest evidence of Ken's lifelong passion for the *corrida*. (His rooms were decorated with bullfight posters and Bosch's *Garden of Earthly Delights*.)

Miss Staynes, however, developed doubts on the matter of marriage. Entering a restaurant one evening, the two of them paused to check their appearance in front of a mirror before making their entrance. 'Without noticing, [Ken] blocked my reflection in raising his hands to adjust his bowtie. This seemed to me symbolic and I told him at dinner that I couldn't marry a man who was first at a mirror before me, which amused him, and we parted on the best of terms.'

Getting engaged was a game with roots that went deep into his unsure and unresolved past. To his great friend Lis Zaiman he would say, 'Let's get engaged,' and she would answer, 'Yes, Ken, often.'

During the Michaelmas term of 1947 Ken established himself as a host who could command celebrity. At a party for the all-black cast of *Anna Lucasta* (playing at the New Theatre), the lead actress shimmied, the lead actor read a long poem about the American black and another guest, Dylan Thomas, constantly interrupted.

A few weeks before the party Ken had found the Welsh poet weaving drunkenly down the middle of the High Street, had led him to the pavement and asked: 'Is there anything I can do for you?' 'Get me some more bloody crème de menthe, you fucking idiot,' said Mr Thomas. So Ken got him some crème de menthe, and took him back to St John Street. He later reported to Holland that Thomas was 'a surly little pug, but a master of pastiche and invective. Thinks himself the biggest and best phoney of all time, and may be right.'

The next celebrity bagged was the actor Trevor Howard, who was playing at the New Theatre in a production of *The Taming of the Shrew*. Before the performance one evening, Howard was chased to the stage door by an 'incredible creature looking like the Négresco Hotel in Nice'. The creature said, 'Come to a wine party,' and he added, 'You gave the laziest performance I've ever seen'. Howard, who had been 'belting it out' as Petruchio, found the compliment dubious, but he agreed to turn up at the party. Undergraduates were charged an entrance fee of ten shillings, complained loudly and paid up.

Two weeks after the *Taming of the Shrew* party, on 1 November, Mary Bolté, the wife of Charles Bolté, who was an American Rhodes scholar, recorded in her diary the details of another extravaganza:

Ken Tynan ... arrived at our door in a taxi bearing another man and three girls. We then drove ten miles to 'The Bear', an inn at Woodstock, where, to put it plainly, we made a night of it.

Of the three girls the wildest and most bewitching was a little black-haired black-eyed Austrian [called Maria].... She has no money, no home, and starts Monday as a bus conductor....

The party was wild, Maria being the center of it all, sitting on Ken's lap, crawling under the table with him, weaving to the john and shouting 'I will go slowly, from pillow to pillow.' ...

> We came back in a taxi ... went on to Ken's black negligée draped apartment for coffee and old jazz records. Everybody violently ill but me and Chass.

Chass was a one-legged veteran of El Alamein whose stomach was stoutly lined from years of drinking old fashioneds. He introduced Ken, around that time, to a young American writer called Truman Capote, who happened at their first encounter to be sitting on an inverted bath tub. When asked if he knew Orson Welles and Rita Hayworth, the novelist from the Deep South replied: 'Oh Orson, yes – lazy boy – whenever I see those two together I ask myself one question; what do they do? What can they conceivably do? I do not know but I believe they have invented a new vice. In what it consists I dare not guess, but I believe it has something to do with frogs, and fire hydrants and incantations to the moon.'

At the end of the term Alan Beesley and Ken gave an Interminable Party which celebrated their recent victory over the hearties: on Guy Fawkes' Night a bunch of Tynan-baiting rowdies had hoisted an effigy of Ken near the Martyrs' Memorial and set light to it. Alan's response was to commandeer a car and, with Ken at his side, drive straight through the flames.

Ken's star turn at the Union that term was defending the motion that 'This House Believes Sincerity to Be the Refuge of Fools'. He flounced to the despatch box, and announced that he was an enthusiast ('In a very real sense, Mr President, I am the zeal of thy house, and I do mean the performing zeal').

His other major role that term was playing Hieronimo in Nevill Coghill's truncated production of *The Spanish Tragedy*, a performance which Peter Wildeblood described scathingly in *Isis*. A week later in the same journal Ken retaliated:

I want to protest against a school of critics which has its middle-age in the Sunday papers, and its squalling youth in *The Isis*; a dangerous, sapping school which is sucking the heart out of our drama.... They are the boozed eulogists, the starved, fasting mockers. They are drawn from the long and once respectable ranks of the almost-brilliant, and they address themselves to the huge, bristling Behemoth of semi-culture.

He concluded: 'Your critic must be capable of awe, of hate, enthusiasm and rapture.... The Malignant Sciolist's joy lies in killing the same man over and over again, and in the end he will discover it is himself.'

Somewhere in this short but violent piece, Ken attacked the style of Harold Hobson and the 'silk-purse-out-of-a-sow's-ear tradition of Maxolatry' practised by such as Ivor Brown. Harold Hobson, drama critic of the *Sunday Times*, read the piece and said to himself, 'This young man is dangerous. I do hope he doesn't come to London.'

By the beginning of his third and last year at Oxford, Ken had demonstrated that he could write about performance and personality. His attack on the malignant sciolists had proved his skill at invective. Early in 1948 he published two long articles on tragic drama, called 'The Invincible Must', in *Oxford Viewpoint*, which persuaded his Oxford contemporaries that he had stopped 'frisking around the surface' and 'gone deep' with some hard thinking. 'The Invincible Must' was an extension (as applied to theatre) of Ken's philosophy of transience, fleshed out with his interpretation of Senecan stoicism.

Ken later abandoned his glorification of heroic drama, of graceful and memorable death under pressure, a fanciful theory which also reflected his own visceral concern with mortality. He announced that he would be dead by thirty, and his consumptive looks and poor health – he suffered frequent colds and bouts of bronchitis – seemed to confirm his fears. There is an odd reference in the second of the two articles on drama, which reads, 'Catarrh can strike awe into you if you realize, as Flamineo does in *The White Devil*, that what you have caught is "an everlasting cold".' This was what Ken suffered from, by genetic disposition, though he had no knowledge of it at the time.

During the Hilary term of 1948, Ken wrote to C. S. Lewis requesting permission to postpone his final examinations until the following December because of chest x-rays and 'anxiety'. Lewis told the Senior Common Room at Magdalen that it was possible to argue both for and against the request, yet he effectively persuaded them to allow Ken to postpone.

Thereupon Ken expanded his extra-curricular activities. He appeared in another of Sandy Wilson's ETC revues, *Ritzy, Regal and Super*, to which he contributed his own sketch, 'Production Number'. For this wildly successful monologue, he wore a snappy lambswool jacket and mimicked a very camp county theatre director: 'Now Roger you old emptyhead I want you to plant this speech: wrap it up warm and safe and shove it home, as Ellen Terry used to say. And for all our nice sakes, keep your hair out of your mouth. I know it tastes nice, you know it tastes nice, but there are going to be chaps out there who just won't care vitally.'

This was followed by what a local magazine described as a 'breath-taking pot-pourri of all we have felt most uneasy about in the productions of the Old Vic', a travesty of trumpets and battle scenes and all the clichés from hackneyed Shakespearean productions. He ended by throwing his profile towards his shoulder, looking like an aghast replica of Robert Helpmann, and crying out, 'My God, there's an owl on my shoulder.'

He next took on his most demanding Oxford production to date, Maxwell Anderson's *Winterset*, a verse drama of the thirties, set in a tenement building near Brooklyn Bridge and dealing with a miscarriage of justice in the wake of the Sacco–Vanzetti case. Ken loved everything American and particularly the gangster genre, which may explain why he fell upon this impenetrable moral tale, played the part of Judge Gaunt and turned the play into a successful piece of theatre. One of the effects was to build a bridge jutting out over the audience. Ken's sound man then rigged up a series of lights and loudspeakers with volume controls, to simulate a moving train.

Halfway through the Oxford run, two rich French undergraduates saw *Winterset* and arranged for the whole production to be shipped to Paris, to the Comédie des Champs Élysées, for one performance on 15 March. Ken was described by *Le Monde*, on his first trip abroad, as the latest disciple of Wilde and Ruskin.

Early in April some 200 of Ken's friends received silver-on-red invitations to his twenty-first birthday party. Ken ordered fairy lights, champagne, beer and whisky at his disapproving father's expense, and on the 6th the party set out by river boat from Westminster Pier. The cast of *Anna Lucasta* came aboard. The Oxford jazz group, The Bandits, provided the music. Stanley Parker brought his mother and performed his famous jitterbug. The girls bared their flesh in New Look dresses; with the war all but forgotten, some of the men put on their uniforms and medals as if they were costumes. The host wore black tie with an orchid in his buttonhole. As they sailed past the House of Commons, they gave a few defiant hoots to the Chancellor of the Exchequer, Sir Stafford Cripps, who that very afternoon was delivering his Malvolian austerity Budget.

A month later the Peacock received the first effectively wounding stab to his reputation. It came in the form of an attack by Alan Brien in the pages of *Isis*, a response to an article Ken had written for *Vogue* called 'Oxford Now'. He had run down Oxford's worthy ex-servicemen and the chastening effect of the Labour Government upon the university: 'What sets Oxford apart is ... a savour of gaiety ... a tang of flair ... a golden satin shirt.... There are fewer titles amongst us; there is much less money; but there is a fiercer, more *piratical* and less *wanton* adventurousness.' Brien replied: 'Few of us have the arrogance to dismiss anyone who does not fit our personal pattern. Even so unique a person as Mr. Tynan has a place in our scheme of things – every society has its buffoon.'

According to Brien, Ken was delighted: 'He knew that nothing so polishes up a star as an occasional vicious scratch on the chrome and he sought me out in my beer-drinking, hairy-jacketed, old sweats *New Statesman* reading lair. "Where have you been?" he said. "Everybody wants to meet you." '

In December 1946 a group called the Corporate Club had entertained Oswald Mosley in Oxford. They did so without proctorial recognition and under attack from left-wing undergraduates like Tony Wedgwood Benn. The moving light of the club was Desmond Stewart, a Roman Catholic, a homosexual and a reputed Nazi sympathizer. He could be found, elegantly turned out on a Sunday morning after mass, at Whites.

Ken was amused by Stewart's personality; but when Stewart asked him to a tea in honour of Mosley, during the summer term of 1948, Ken had serious qualms. He discussed the invitation with his Jewish girlfriend Elly Horowitz. Not surprisingly, Miss Horowitz, whose family were Austrian refugees, advised against accepting. But Ken had very little understanding of what had gone on during the war, and he was attracted to the idea of an elite. 'It was no more than a flirtation,' Elly Horowitz explains, 'but he went to the tea.' By way of apology Ken took with him Ruth Cropper, and together they decided to behave badly: 'We spent a lot of time sharpening knives,' she recalled, 'just to tease the Fascist spirit.'

During the summer term of 1948 Ken took Elly Horowitz dancing. 'A one-man writhe and wriggle to the rhythm, stretching out his arms,' she remembers, 'which suited him very well.' One night during Eights Week the two of them were strolling along when a gang of rowing men closed in on them, grabbed hold of Ken, and tried to debag him. He fell to the ground with a piercing cry. 'My hip, my hip, it's gone again!' he wailed, and the crowd fell away and dispersed. Ken was seen to hobble to the sanctuary of the Union, but the victim was not hurt at all: with a brilliant ruse the actor had saved himself. Inside the Union the 'virilescent member from Magdalen' pilloried Oxford to roars of applause in the Eights Weeks debate, that 'This House Deserves Its Doubtful Reputation'. Shortly after, the Union elected him their secretary.

As the term drew to an end, he began to prepare his last and most ambitious Oxford production, that of the First Quarto Hamlet. He announced that the familiar version of Hamlet, 'a judicious blending of the Second Quarto and the First Folio, compares, dramatically and psychologically, very ill with the brief and unpolished First Quarto'. And with this contentious view in mind he set to casting the 1603 text. He would present the play as 'a political tragedy of assassination, espionage and fear', and dress the production for an eighteenth-century European court. 'I watched Ken seduce people to give them confidence,' says Peter Parker, who played Hamlet. 'He was very assured, and he'd wind you in on his reel.' Lindsay Anderson, who was made to play Horatio as a middle-aged German professor, was less impressed by Ken as a director. He found him eccentric and showy, and likens him to the young Tony Richardson, who was just starting his meteoric and flamboyant directorial career at Oxford.

To the opening at the Civic Playhouse, Cheltenham (where the Oxford company was housed), on 7 August, came three distinguished Hamlets: Donald Wolfit, Paul Scofield and Robert Helpmann. Wolfit reviewed the production for a local paper and called it a 'solid achievement'.

On 22 July Ken had received word at his hotel in Stratford, where he had been staying for a few days, that his father had died that morning. He took the train back to Birmingham, and arrived at 229 Edgbaston Road as the top-hatted morticians were removing Sir Peter Peacock's body from the house.

Peter had died that morning of uraemia, complicated by bronchitis. He was seventy-six. Rose Tynan immediately telephoned Gladys Bebbington, a Peacock relative, to give her the news. She said, 'Now he's yours,' Bertha Peacock recalls. 'Rose knew she couldn't have anything to do with the funeral.' So a few hours after his death Sir Peter Peacock, alias Peter Tynan, was driven back to Warrington into the bosom of the family he had deserted a quarter of a century before.

Meanwhile the ugly 1930s house in Edgbaston Road, with the stained-glass windows and mahogany furniture, was crowded with Tynans and Peacocks who normally kept well apart. There was George Peacock, Peter's nephew, who managed the Birmingham stores, to whom Peter had entrusted the financial arrangements for his much loved Rose. 'Look after her,' he had said. 'She's looked after me.' There were also the solicitor and the family doctor, and one of these three took Ken into his father's study and told him the family secret. Ken ran upstairs to his old bedroom and locked himself in. When he came out, his cousin Ruth saw that he had a wet face and puffy eyes, and that he was angry. 'He threw up his arms, sending the hanging lamp in the dining room flying, and he told me, "If only I'd known, because I could have learned so much from him and I always thought he was a fool."'

He went to his mother and attacked her bitterly for not revealing the secret, and Rose wept, apologized and said, 'We thought you'd be ashamed.' Back in his bedroom, Ken wrote to his first love, Pauline. He told her he had been sorting through his cupboards, 'uprooting toy soldiers, contraceptives, evil-smelling sandwiches and bits of typewriters', and had come across a picture of a 'pouting plump thing with raving round calves and goodness if it wasn't you'. In a style of strained enthusiasm, he told her he'd been thriving in strange, colourful ways, and he concluded his letter: 'At 10.45 a.m. this morning my father died. Ever, Ken.'

While the national and local press reviewed Sir Peter's career as distinguished Liberal, magistrate, civic dignitary and successful businessman, and revealed that he had left £120,615 5s 1d to ten family beneficiaries including his widow, his body lay in a downstairs room of Maria Peacock's house in Warrington. She removed the roses that one member of the family had placed on his coffin.

On the following Monday the amiable ex-Mayor was given a grand farewell. There was a service at a Methodist church, after which a long procession of family, local politicians, members of the friendly societies and business associates accompanied the hearse to the Warrington municipal cemetery. There he is anonymously buried in the same plot as his first wife, Annie: his nieces offered to pay for a headstone, but Maria would not allow it. Rose Tynan did not presume to attend the funeral.

Two days after his father's death Ken was in Cheltenham preparing his production of *Hamlet*. He spoke about his father's death compulsively to the girl with whom he was now living, Eileen Rabbinowitz. 'I think he felt a lot of anger towards his mother, which was unexpressed.' Ken was shaken, but the more he considered his illegitimacy, the more he cared for the proposition. At last his childhood was interesting, confirmation that he was different, and quite soon he began to brag that his father had been financial adviser to Lloyd George. He liked the romantic notion that Sir Peter had sacrificed a larger career to run off with his mother.

His old Birmingham friends remember that he went 'dead' on them, closed his mind to his home town for good. When he encountered Julian Holland in London at first nights, 'He never wanted to talk about the old days.' His father's death was the cut-off point, and thereafter he dropped the 'Peacock' from his name.

Back in Oxford after his production of *Hamlet*, Ken walked into the Randolph and announced that he was the bastard son of a knight, 'just like Faulconbridge'. He told his friends that 'the old master had turned out to be a man of importance'. But the bravura was not all that assured: after coming down from Oxford Ken attended an informal club of fellow graduates whose aim was to infiltrate the London job market. At the first meeting a dispute broke out over which of them came from the most deprived family. Alan Brien pointed out that Ken received an allowance of £500 a year from his mother, whereas he was paid £600 a year and had to support a wife. John Wain said that he did not come from a 'posh' background since his father was a dentist. Kingsley Amis reported that his father was a minor civil servant. Brien jumped in to say that his father was a genuine working man, a fitter who had never earned more than £2 10s a week in his life, and that he demonstrably was from the lowest social category. Ken then interrupted: 'No, no, no, I am lower, because I'm a b-b-bastard.' That silenced everybody.

As the years went by Ken found his illegitimacy of diminishing interest. 'Do you have a block about it?' the journalist Susan Barnes asked him in 1972. 'There is nothing of interest I could have said on the subject,' he told her. 'There are two sorts of illegitimacy: you think people are your parents and you discover they're not; that must be traumatic, terrifying. Or you find that your parents aren't married; that is not traumatic.'

But he paid for the phenomenal mismanagement of this relatively simple issue in complex and diverse ways. He paid for the pathetic lie from his cradle until his death. The past both crippled and animated him, forced him on to a tightrope of insecurity without which his life might have had less flavour. Despite and because of the handicap, he soared. Where might he have flown had he been free?

Ken returned to Birmingham after the Cheltenham production of *Hamlet* and began a pornographic correspondence with Eileen Rabbinowitz, the tone of which is comradely rather than passionate, and quite unguilty. 'I was a very hung-up little Jewish girl still living with my rabbi father,' she explains, 'and Ken was my first lover. I suspect he sensed my innate masochism. His was the schoolgirl-type fantasy, never the master–slave type. There was no bondage, no need to immobilize the woman, as there is with so many. It had to be free will. He wanted people to know about it because at that point he didn't have a lot of hang-ups about it.'

Ken wrote to Eileen: 'I like your slant eyes, your mellow-mushroom voice, your *beeg* mouth.... Let's often (I mean all the time) read the same books ... let there always be something *going on* between us – feuds, and suspicions and sudden meetings and visits to Bognor Regis or Sierra Leone and roars of laughter.' He gave her a sexual questionnaire to answer, told her that he liked the word 'chastise', which 'has a good Victorian ring of retribution'. He said a 'smack' should be 'administered in the drawingroom of one's aunt', and that the word 'spank' was 'very potent', had the 'correct school girlishness'. He told her that 'Sex means spank and beautiful means bottom and always will.'

Together they went to the Edinburgh Festival despite the problems of ration cards, morality and short funds. They stayed at the North British Hotel and Ken kept a journal of the visit which he published in a university magazine. He saw and dismissed Olivier's film of *Hamlet*, and Gielgud's production of *Medea*; he liked Cocteau's *La Belle et la bête*, and admired Jean-Louis Barrault (his first stage appearance in England) in *Les Fausses confidences* by Marivaux.

He borrowed money from Dylan Thomas, and spent whatever time that was left with Eileen Rabbinowitz. 'I had the feeling', she recalls, 'that he was a man in a hurry, that he was going to get places and he didn't have a great deal of time to get there, which meant that he would brush things aside, he would roar through things, he would devour experiences and then move on to the next one. It was too hectic, and he was whirling too fast.'

On 26 September Ken went to London to appear at the Playhouse Theatre in Sandy Wilson's *Oxford Circus* – a compilation of the best of the post-war Oxford revues. In the audience were such celebrities of the day as Hermione Gingold, Hermione Baddeley and Max Adrian.

Ken took over Peter Wildeblood's 'Ballet Shame' (the first line went, 'I wish my mum 'ad never seen Pavlova') and he came on at the end of the show with his own 'Production Number', which the London critics called the 'hit of the evening'.

He had already tried it out for Hermione Gingold, then appearing at the Ambassador Theatre in her own revue, *Sweetest and Lowest*. She had heard about this marvellous boy from her son Stephen, and had agreed to try him out. 'It was the funniest audition I've ever sat through and the longest,' Miss Gingold recalled. 'He was entirely unique. I had said, "Have you got something that runs for about five minutes?" His wonderful monologue went on for nearly an hour. It was the new sort of humour that I did – which was satirical, not gags – and the one thing I longed to use, but the show only ran two hours and a half, and I was not about to give an hour over to Mr Tynan.'

Ken was now exploring career possibilities in every direction. When told by a friend that he could become the new Danny Kaye, he replied, 'Is *that* all?' He was planning to put together a collection of his theatre pieces. He was writing to the drama critics on national newspapers asking for their jobs. A letter along these lines arrived on the desk of Harold Hobson. Quite soon after this Hobson met the young upstart at the Playhouse in Oxford. 'He seemed to me a very handsome, very tall and very prescient young man. What I would like to be in appearance is Jack Buchanan, and Kenneth struck me as favourably resembling Jack Buchanan – very graceful.'

This generous man read some of Ken's reviews and was impressed by his capacity as a writer, by his being totally different from any of his fellow critics. 'It never struck me that he was really influenced by anybody at all, unless one goes back to historic figures like Hazlitt.' Harold Hobson introduced the young rival to his own publisher, Mark Longman.

Ken's most passionate wish was to direct. He would tell his friends, 'Peter Brook is twenty-three, and he's a famous director already. I have so little time left to make it.' To that end he tried to lease a London theatre and to start the New Commercial Club, under the artistic control of its directors, which would produce plays and revues, make and show films, print books, papers and magazines, and provide a new architectural unit, 'for lack of which the theatre has been marking time for fifty years'. But the company never materialized.

There was one obstacle before him, and that was the recurrent threat of military service. Hoping for deferment, he had applied for a university scholarship in the United States. He sought to be a conscientious objector. Finally he devised a stratagem for his army medical examination: he selected a bizarre homosexual case history from Krafft-Ebing, covered himself with Eileen Rabbinowitz's new bottle of Yardley scent and presented himself at the office of the army psychiatrist, Dr Edward Glover. In a performance that went way overboard, he said he could not have sexual relations without the aid of spurs, and stammered outrageously. The doctor came to the conclusion that anyone who had taken so many pains to avoid serving his country should be excused. A few days after his interview, Ken received a copy of the psychiatric certificate for the recruiting authorities which declared: 'His general psychological state is such that he can only function [under] specially protective conditions of life, removal from which seems almost inevitably to provoke breakdowns of varying degrees of severity.'

Back in Oxford Ken had himself wheeled into the Union in a dustman's cart, and gave a party for Gertrude Lawrence, for which he charged his usual ten-shilling entrance fee and installed a giant bouncer, called Tiny, to keep out undesirables. On 25 November he began his final examinations in English.

The result was a second-class honours degree, rather than the expected first class. It was the worst thing, Ken felt, that had ever befallen him. C. S. Lewis wrote to offer comfort and good sense. He explained that the 'authorities of the castle' had found the language papers inadequate. 'All this, I imagine, is much what you expected – i.e. that you had the troops on the dash but in the excitement of the battle did not manoeuvre as well as we hoped. Don't let it become a trauma!' he cautioned, with foresight. 'It signifies comparatively little.'

The term, and Ken's Oxford career, came to a climax at the Farewell Union Debate, with the motion, moved by the Hon. A. N. Wedgwood Benn, ex-president, that 'This House Would Like to Have It Both Ways' and opposed by the outgoing secretary, Mr Kenneth P. Tynan. The latter argued that there were at least forty or fifty ways of having it. As the laughter became uncontrollable, he added, glancing up towards the gallery which was packed with a posse of his girlfriends, 'Not excluding the one on the grand piano,' whereupon he was bombarded with violets and balloons.

The party was over. Ken packed up his manner of life and took it with him to London. A tearful Oxford muse mourned his departure in *Isis*:

> The Golden Age is finished, gone the grace,
> Who now so fit to fill KEN TYNAN'S place?

From time to time the famous undergraduate, now called a 'legend', and 'prophet' to a new generation, returned. (He said he was not a legend but 'more of an exploded myth'.) He talked and wrote about Oxford, planned a book about it to be called 'Now at Last Demolished'. Somewhere he wrote that his sweetest memory was of 82A St Aldate's, 'with all those gramophone records nailed to the ceiling', and wisely he left it at that, for the golden band had broken up.

Jill Rowe-Dutton fell in love with Peter Parker, and later married him. Deacon Lindsay took his pitted lungs to a sanatorium in Switzerland, and nearly died. Alan Beesley went to visit him in hospital to borrow some money for a smuggling venture; and Ken sent the dying man an ecstatic account of his thriving career (Deacon wrote back inviting Ken to his funeral and asking to be spared another letter with Ken's printed initials all over. He suggested that Ken write them instead on tablecloths, walls and absolutely any material which lay to hand).

Marie and Alan Beesley had a child, and eventually separated. As Alan became more paranoiac and suicidal (he would say to Marie, 'I'm going to prove I love you by jumping in front of that car'), their kindergarten lost its euphoria. Years later he explained, 'Oxford *was*, and then suddenly it wasn't anymore. One never notices these things at the time. But the rug went out from under, and I've been deliberately smashing things up ever since.'

Ken remembered it as a superb parenthesis in his life, and 'Like all the best parentheses, they mean more than all the rest of the sentence: e.g. "Patriotism, social service, technological progress and godliness are (except for *living*) the most important activities of mankind." '

Once or twice, however, he cast a shadow of doubt over that enchanted interregnum. Twenty years after coming down from the university he wrote that Oxford 'removed something from me – something connected with my origins – and replaced it with a Rolls-Royce spare part. I gained speed and sophistication. I doubt if I shall ever know what I lost.'

7

A Leaping Salmon

The move from Oxford to London was neatly made with the transfer of his undergraduate production of the First Quarto *Hamlet* to the Rudolf Steiner Hall. Ken Tynan – as he now billed himself – had arrived and he was welcomed. *The Times* commented on the production's gushing fountain of ideas, 'some very good, some very bad'. Michael Redgrave wrote to say that he had made a tiny but tidy mark with his recent production. 'You are clearly the next casting for the *enfant terrible* of the English theatre.'

Thus encouraged, Ken made the practical decision to join a provincial repertory theatre and to learn his job. But before taking off for the provinces, he signed a contract with Longmans on 25 February 1949 to write a book on drama, £100 payable on publication; he was not hedging his professional bets but working as always on the pluralist principle.

He had agreed to run the David Garrick, at Lichfield in Staffordshire, a repertory theatre recently renovated by an enamelled and ambitious local lady called Joan Cowlishaw. As part of the deal he would be allowed to do one classic or serious play out of four. His first production, as the youngest professional director in the country, was of J. B. Priestley's *The Linden Tree*, the first of twenty-four plays in twenty-four weeks. At the end of this gruelling span Ken announced, 'I now pretend to know only about 60% of what there is to know.'

To the partially formed resident cast, Ken added a young *ingénue* called Diana Mahoney (who was married to the actor Donald Sinden). Miss Mahony remembers her first meeting with the young director, his face twisted in his effort to overcome his stammer. 'He had enormous charm and made me feel that I was one of the most marvellous creatures he'd ever seen. And so I was engaged.' But she soon discovered that another marvellous creature, Patricia Brewer, was getting all the best parts and sharing the director's bed.

Miss Brewer was a handsome, Junoesque, dark-haired girl, a friend of Ken's since Birmingham days. He went down on his knees before her mother in the Green Room of the theatre, and said, 'May I take your daughter's hand in marriage?' To which Mrs Brewer replied, 'Well, I suppose so, dear.'

'Of course we had an affair,' Pat Brewer says, 'and of course he had another girlfriend. I think I was sensible enough to realize that while the wit, the generous side of him, was fun, there was nothing particularly stable. The moment you left him, you were out of his mind. It was as simple as that.'

On a Friday night, after the show, Ken and Pat Brewer would entertain the cast in their flea-infested digs, providing cheap wine and what little food they could scrounge. Ken, who loved games, would insist they play charades, which after a concentrated week of acting must have seemed demanding.

At work he was also demanding but the actors give him high marks as a director. He would show them how to do something with a quick thumbnail sketch; he was very good at getting straight to what mattered. And he was an enthusiastist who never missed a performance.

His first major production was of George Farquhar's *The Beaux' Stratagem*, for which he dressed each couple to represent a different era: the young lovers were Victorian, Lady Bountiful was in the uniform of the Women's Voluntary Service, and Hounslow was played by a black actor as a contemporary gangster. The *Illustrated London News* came up to cover this 'Lichfield All-sorts'.

Ken's next major play was Eugene O'Neill's *Anna Christie*, for which he managed to persuade Frederick Valk to come north and play Chris Christopherson (opposite Patricia Brewer's Anna). The director deferred to Valk, who would declare in his none-too-perfect English, 'Here I make a powse.' And the 'powse' would last for five minutes. Ken allowed his star frequent rests, knowing how unaccustomed Valk was to learning his lines in a week. His directorial attention focused on Anna, the prostitute, and he told Pat Brewer to shave her armpits on stage as a signal of her trade, a piece of business which shocked the Lichfield audience.

Anna Christie was followed by such repertory favourites as Joseph Kesselring's *Arsenic and Old Lace*, and Coward's *Present Laughter*. At the end of the Coward play the lead actor, John Grant, as was the custom, came forward to make a curtain speech. He said that the night was a historic occasion since it was their director's first appearance (as the poet Roland Maule) on the professional stage. Grant recalls that Ken wagged a finger at him in the manner of Noël Coward and said, 'D-d-don't you e-e-ver do that again.'

Ken evidently felt unhappy about *Present Laughter*, for he wrote to his old friend Harry James of the Birmingham New Dramatic Company, who had not liked the production:

Instead of becoming a *nice* uncle (which was what I expected), you've become a *nasty* one. You see, I am now in a profession where one pays attention only to people with *proven skills*. . . . This is all an oblique way of saying that I have no time for what you said of *Present Laughter*, and that when I pay you the £6-2-5 [which he owed] it will be in the form of a strange and possibly embarrassing present: if I can find an armadillo costing £6-2-5, it shall be yours. . . . the Lichfield Khan is outraged.

Ken went on to explain that weekly rep was the 'Golgotha of drama'. 'In twenty weeks here I have been responsible for twenty productions. I soon realized that the only plan which would save me would be to do two goodish productions, one bad production, and one *good* production each month.... you saw a bad production ... we put on plays with an average of 18 hours rehearsal, and we nearly starve doing it.'

His major productions during this taxing period were *Juno and the Paycock*, *Six Characters in Search of an Author* and *Pygmalion*. His last was Ben Travers' *Rookery Nook*. Halfway through Garrick's adaptation of *The Taming of the Shrew*, which was set in the American south, he fell out with his boss. Mrs Cowlishaw decided she had had enough of his ambitious concepts, and dismissed him.

Ken moved into a ground-floor room in St John's Wood, North London, and brought with him his books and his silk cushions with tassels. His landlady recalls that he wrote with great concentration, day and night; that he used up the precious bath water; that after a cache of pornography was found in his cupboard she told him to leave. He responded by kneeling at the front door and begging to be allowed back.

Pat Brewer, meanwhile, was left in the Lichfield lurch. Ken wrote to tell her that he missed her scent and 'the smell of your neck and your gurgle and the bat-eyed gleam behind the glasses', and that he still wished to marry her. He told her that he was trying for a job at Bromley, Greenwich or the Tavistock Little Theatre.

But none of these positions was confirmed and during that autumn of 1949 Ken auditioned for a semi-nude revue at the Windmill Theatre. He sang and danced a camp piece about a restaurant opening which ran:

> Say Si Si
> Chez Chi Chi
> We serve brandy out of jerry cans
> To visiting Americans.

He then gave the audience of stunned chorus girls his true-and-tried Oxford cabaret piece, 'Production Number'. The theatre's owner, Vivian Van Damm, called up from the stalls, 'Thank you, no! You're much too queer for our audience.'

Ken next approached Oscar Quitak, who, with Caris Monde and Hazel Vincent Wallace, had formed a Sunday-night play-producing society called the Under-Thirty Theatre Group. Quitak offered Ken a new play, called *A Citizen of the World* by C. E. Webber, an ambitious work, expressionist in manner and told in flashbacks, about an international financier with plans for world unity.

'Who do you see in the leading part?' Quitak asked.

'Orson Welles,' Ken replied.

'What makes you think Orson Welles would do it for us?'

'Leave it to me.' He wired Welles, who politely declined.

'If I were casting the lead part for the West End I'd like Paul Muni,' said Quitak.

'Well, ring him up and ask him,' Ken told him. 'Always go to the top.'

Paul Muni was doing *Death of a Salesman*, and although he was unavailable he helped secure the Phoenix Theatre for a Sunday night performance of the Webber play. It was put on under Ken's direction on 11 December – so successfully that he received five offers to transfer to the West End. After a try-out at Stratford, the play opened with the Company of Four under the management of H. M. Tennent, at the Lyric, Hammersmith. Roger Livesey played the lead opposite Ursula Jeans, and a seventeen-year-old J. Arthur Rank starlet called Diana Dors won the part of the millionaire's poppet, Carmen. For her first West End appearance she wore long blonde hair page-boy style, and little more than a man's pyjama top.

Ken juggled with complicated lighting and a multi-dimensional stage and, according to Peter Brook, brought to the production 'a bit of Kafka, a shadow of Orson Welles, a flavour of French films'. Harold Hobson reported that the production had speed and fire, and hoped that the name of Mr Ken Tynan would soon be familiar.

Mr Tynan's name was not exactly unfamiliar. 'He behaved like somebody whose mark had already been made for him by his reputation,' according to Peter Ustinov, 'but he didn't know quite how to fill it.' Ken dashed around London zealously promoting his career and his contacts; planning a production of Picasso's *Desire Caught by the Tail* and a *Macbeth* with Peter Ustinov (in which Lady Macbeth would appear naked in the sleepwalking scene); writing an adaptation of Dumas' *Kean*, a film scenario and a play; delivering a progress report to *Isis* a year after he had flopped breathless out of the little pool of the university and 'leapt salmonwise upwards into the big one'. He listed his productions, his engagements, his encounters with Orson Welles and Tennessee Williams, Louis MacNeice and Mai Zetterling. He wrote: 'I have learnt from the lips of Henry Hathaway the new word for wolf: M.T.F., meaning Must Touch Flesh. I have written eighty-six thousand words. I have not been idle.'

A London magazine, *Contact*, concluded: 'It is difficult to know exactly what he takes seriously besides his own career. All geniuses, true or suspected, have to be egotists – often egomaniacs – until they are quite sure of their own genius. Tynan is a solo performer, and this for a producer has its great dangers.' This prescient journalist continued: 'I hope he will become a journalist and theatre critic.... [But] the clown wants to play Hamlet, and the born journalist is possessed with an urgent desire to produce a mother-fixated Macbeth. It will probably sort itself out.'

Ken had been 'hotly pressed', so he claimed, to invest with Pat Nye and John Penrose in the formation of a new theatre company at the Bedford

Theatre, Camden Town. His request for the job of resident director of the club theatre was turned down, but he was offered several plays in return for a huge investment of £2000. Miss Nye recalls that Rose Tynan and a male relative – most probably George Peacock – came to the theatre to put up Ken's share.

His first production, *Craven House*, a comedy set in a boarding-house, was not much liked. His next production was the Victorian melodrama, *The Bells*, Frederick Valk playing the part with which Irving had taken London by storm in 1871. On opening night Ken swept into the theatre surrounded by his entourage and wearing a burgundy velvet dinner jacket ('the first of its kind', according to the theatre archivists, Joe Mitchenson and Raymond Mander, 'though Noël had a brown one').

Pat Nye thought everything overdressed and overdone. She felt that Ken could not handle people very well, on stage or off. He wanted to take on more plays but she told him that he did not have enough professional experience, and that she doubted that directing was his *métier*.

The setback can hardly have made much difference professionally. Ken was working on a production of *Winterset* for the Arts Theatre Club, on an adaptation of *Cold Comfort Farm* with Peter Wildeblood, on his collection of theatre pieces, on a revue with Peter Myers, and on speeches for both the Oxford and Cambridge debating societies.

Nor was he negligent socially. He gave a party and provided twenty-four bottles of gin, a record player and 'everybody'. At another party the playwright Alun Owen saw Ken walk into a squalid, candlelit flat wearing a pink and white striped shirt with a tiny little blue bowtie. 'He greeted a new arrival across the room, and as the shortest distance between two points is a straight line, he walked over bodies and furniture, jam jar full of gin in one hand and a cigarette-holder in the other, mounting a settee and turning it upside down, to reach his friend.'

He was, of course, intolerable. A French diplomat met him *chez* Louis MacNeice, during the spring of 1950, and asked him where he would be going for the holiday. 'He looked at me [and] languidly drawled, "I'm toying with the idea of going to Baghdad to give back a book, borrowed from a friend who lives there."'

He was as broke as ever, borrowing against his Post Office savings account book, which he claimed held £800 – but never accepting gifts. People would always be prepared to pay for him, and he had a string of admirers, not only girls but also young men whom he bossed around. Rose Tynan would bail him out, and occasionally he would ask her to London and introduce the nervous woman to his friends, declaring that any success he achieved he wanted for his mother.

He went on asking girls to marry him. He even asked his old flame Pauline, now living in London, if she would reconsider his first proposal. Sensing this to be a flippant enquiry she declined. 'In that case,' said Ken, 'I have to go to see a girl in Purley.'

In the summer of 1950 Ken travelled with a group of young British actors to Salzburg to take part in a Harvard-sponsored seminar in American studies. (He was asked by a handsome American Rhodes scholar called William Becker.) Ken co-opted Oscar Quitak, from the Under-Thirty Group, two other actor friends, Harold Lang and Derek Prouse, along with his devoted girlfriend of the moment, a young actress called Elizabeth Thorndike. The group gathered at Schloss Leopoldskron, a rococo eighteenth-century castle once owned by Max Reinhardt and recently vacated by the Nazis. Here on 28 and 29 June, under the direction of the critic Eric Bentley, they performed e.e. cummings' *him*, with Ken playing the lead. In this obscure play about a failed marriage he was said to have been excellent, performing with great tenderness and sensitivity.

Eric Bentley recalls that he and Ken were very touchy about each other, very competitive. 'Ken was a fearsome phenomenon, forging ahead at twenty-three, carrying under his arm the galley proofs of his first book.'

Bentley lectured the group on Bertolt Brecht and played the *Dreigroschenoper* for them. His point of view was very Brechtian – he had even worked with the great playwright – and Ken's book expressed a very different attitude. Bentley was deeply shocked by it, because it echoed 1890s' aestheticism and an elite view of things which was not political. 'I was certainly the first person to talk to Ken about Brecht in any detail and I told him he should go to Berlin to see the company.'

On his return to London Ken began to put together a touring production of *Othello* under the auspices of the newly formed Arts Council. Tyrone Guthrie saw the production in an ice-bound Liverpool teachers' training college and wrote to a friend at the Arts Council to say that he thought Ken Tynan decidedly impressive. 'There was much that was technically and imaginatively brilliant; and I for one *liked* him for the things that to me were outrageous breaches of taste – after all taste is entirely subjective, and the thoroughly offensive is at least positive.'

Ken had, some months previously, examined the directorial work of Tyrone Guthrie and placed him with Peter Brook (who had already made his mark with *Measure for Measure*, *Huis Clos* and *Ring Round the Moon*) and Michael Benthall. However excellent, no one of these three maestri, he concluded, was the Messiah. The best production he had seen since the war was Elia Kazan's *Death of a Salesman*, but Kazan was American. Should the English produce a Kazan, 'Let us pray that someone will buy him a theatre, give him a company of 20 actors and two other producers under long-term contracts, a permanent staff of playwrights, and a free hand. Only by such benefactions are styles born and developed.'

He had paid tribute to Olivier and Gielgud as established directors. He had also taken a passing swipe at Olivier's treatment of *A Streetcar Named Desire*. Vivien Leigh as Blanche, he wrote, was a 'posturing butterfly, with no depth, no sorrow, no room for development and, above all, no trace of Blanche's crushed ideals'.

In a further article, entitled 'Where Are the Playwrights?', Ken claimed that England had no tradition of playcraft, no established rules. There were vignettists around, like Christopher Fry, but no Jonsonians, like George Kaufman and Moss Hart, or Aeschyleans, like Eugene O'Neill. Germany had Brecht, 'a new tradition of sorts', and France had Giraudoux and Anouilh. The immediate answer was to translate good foreign plays.

He pursued his thoughts on styles and producers for the BBC Third Programme, arguing that while the English had produced their Keans, Irvings and Oliviers, 'we have produced no Diaghilev, no Copeau, no Stanislavsky, no Meyerhold'. And he concluded that one had to have total authority to create a style, a quality 'nourished chiefly by a passionate belief in absolute standards of aesthetics'.

This argument in favour of theatrical dictatorship and aesthetic standards was developed in *He That Plays the King*. This was a collection of enthusiasms (published in October 1950) written out of an 'almost limitless capacity for admiration'. The frontispiece was of the epicene Egyptian pharaoh Akhenaten, and the introduction was written by Orson Welles.

The previous December Ken had gone to Paris and spent a fruitless half hour on the telephone trying to persuade a corn salesman from Iowa named Finlay Welles to write a preface to his book. He finally tracked down the real Mr Welles at the Lancaster Hotel and, materializing out of the foggiest Paris day Orson Welles could remember, handed over his manuscript. 'If you don't write the preface,' said the intruder, 'I can't get it published.' So Welles agreed. 'The fog and the stammer helped,' he explained. 'This unknown Oxford fellow seemed to have gone to such a great deal of effort and to be so intelligent that I instantly found him very likeable. I didn't need to read the manuscript, and I said yes rather the way one sometimes casts without asking anybody to read; you're absolutely certain that they're right.'

When the collection came out, Ken was compared to Hazlitt and to Shaw. Michael Redgrave advised theatre addicts to get hold of 'this witty, scholarly ... infuriating book before the young author becomes an old hand and the book a collector's piece'. Roy Walker, however, in the excellent *Theatre Newsletter*, attacked Ken's 'devastated susceptibility to dominant impassioned big men', and his criticism of many well-known actresses. But he conceded that 'Tynan has a genuine claim to blood royal in dramatic criticism.'

Ken moved to a new apartment at 19 Upper Berkeley Street near Marble Arch. And he sent out his Christmas card. It read:

> Dear chum, be gay
> (Hooray! Hooray!)
> Be comic and divine. On
> This as every other day
> I love you. Kenneth Tynan

Because of the crippling censorship of plays by the Lord Chamberlain, the restrictions of commercial management, and – most important – the licensing laws, experimental theatre developed during these years in clubs. A large amount of Ken's social life, and some of his work life, took place in theatres like the New Lindsay, the Boltons, the Gateway. At the Watergate, off the Strand, which seated 150 people, Ken directed a Cockney comedy called *Nothing Up My Sleeve*, by Ronald Duncan. Here he planned to direct his adaptation of *Cold Comfort Farm* and Firbank's *The Princess Zoubaroff*. And to the Watergate he introduced his friend from Oxford revue, Sandy Wilson. At the Player's Club a year or two later Sandy Wilson launched *The Boy Friend*.

Ken was, throughout his life, without envy, and he was exceptionally generous in helping people whom he considered deserving. When an unknown Yorkshireman called John Braine sent him a verse play in 1951, Ken wrote to say that he had a talent comparable to Arnold Bennett's, and should apply it to the novel. Braine took this advice to heart and wrote *Room at the Top*. There are many other instances of this kind.

Ken's friend Stella Richman recognized his entrepreneurial side, for which, she believed, his writing was a substitute. Ken would take her to the jazz clubs in Charing Cross basements. There he would look at the dancers jitterbugging and say, with wonder, 'They're dancing six feet apart!' He was always restless, always on the move, finding entertainment that no one else knew about. After a time his 'spinning-top thing' was too much for Miss Richman. When he asked her to marry him, one moonlit night on Westminster Bridge, she refused. He slapped her face. He said, 'Do you realize how many months of my life I've wasted?'

Their chief meeting place during all these wasted months had been the Buckstone Club, a grey, unadorned cellar in Suffolk Street behind the Haymarket Theatre, and the cockpit of the young theatre world. It was an offshoot of the Under-Thirty Group and was run by an actor called Gerald Campion, a bossy, bouncy, shrewd person, who cooked good cheap food and served his friends well beyond official licensing hours. Peter Finch came, along with Stanley Baker and Maxine Audley. An out-of-work actor called Sean Connery would collect his dole money and spend it on a pint or two at the club. Eventually more established actors like Emlyn Williams began to frequent the Buckstone. When Wendy Hiller was playing in *The Heiress* at the Haymarket, she would cross the road for a hard-to-come-by boiled egg. Peter Wildeblood would drop in to pick up gossip for his *Daily Mail* column. Harold Lang was another regular: a flamboyant homosexual, a teacher of theatre, a self-educated intellectual and by many accounts – certainly Ken's – a mimic and comic fantasist of genius.

And Ken was king of the place. He wore his purple suit with pink feathers in the buttonhole, and a new dove-grey suit with a yellow shirt.

I saw a tall, dark, graceful erect young man seated on the sofa. He wore a pale grey suit, a pale yellow shirt, pale grey suede shoes and his tie of peacock-blue was part of a silk bathrobe-cord, at least that's what it looked like. A heady mixture, but somehow he brought it off. He looked gay and disarming. He looked like a dandy.

That is a description of the romantic hero, Max, who shows up towards the end of Elaine Dundy's novel *The Dud Avocado* and sweeps its daffy heroine into marriage.

The real story was not so very different.

Elaine Rita Brimberg was born on 2 August 1921, in Great Neck, Long Island, the second daughter of a Polish-born Jewish immigrant who worked as a tailor and then went into the metal-shelving business. Her mother Florence, a pretty and cultivated woman, was the daughter of Heyman Rosenberg, who made a fortune as the inventor of certain types of industrial screw. From 1936 the Brimbergs lived at 1185 Park Avenue, a big, dark overfurnished apartment.

The rooms of their three daughters, however, were bright and something of a shock, as indeed were the three girls. Shirley, the eldest, was the most impressive. She went on to study dance with Martha Graham and, as Shirley Clarke, became a successful experimental film-maker; Elaine grew up powerfully influenced by her older sister; Betty, the youngest and prettiest, became a social activist.

All three of them had been sent to the progressive Lincoln School, attached to Columbia University, which placed a high value on academic standards and mixed children of the rich with scholarship students. Elaine, a petite girl with round brown eyes and a pretty figure, entered the school in the ninth grade. She is described during her high school years as bright, bubbly and keen on boys. She appears not to have been greatly interested in school work. She liked to listen to Frank Sinatra and would go to hear Benny Goodman play at the Manhattan Room of the Hotel Pennsylvania, hanging around till the chairs were put on the tables.

After graduating in 1939, she spent a year at Mills College in California before carrying on with her liberal arts studies at Sweet Briar, a southern college with the airs of a finishing school. Though she was regarded as a nervous person and an incessant talker, she seems to have been happy there. According to one of her classmates who had preceded her to Sweet Briar, Elaine fell in love with learning. She also had a crush on Terence Anderson, the son of the playwright Maxwell Anderson, whom she had first met at the

Lincoln School. She would come up to New York to visit him, unconvincingly disguised in a blonde wig, in case she should bump into her parents.

For Elaine had to contend with Sam Brimberg. He was a short, bald man who smoked cigars and was an authoritarian father. According to classmates, Elaine did not get on with him. 'He was a terror,' Terence Anderson recalls. 'The first man I ever knew who played the radio over dinner and said "shush" if anyone talked over it.'

Between July 1943 and the end of 1946 Elaine worked as a civilian in the US Army Signal Corps and the Signal Security Agency in Arlington, Virginia. She then spent several years in and around New York painting, studying theatre and playing small parts, before taking off, in 1949, for nine months in Paris.

She was evidently not one of those young Americans who hung around outside American Express in crisp clean seersucker. She went native, or as native as a questing, spontaneous and in some ways still rather proper New York girl would go. Judy Feiffer remembers meeting Elaine one morning at Patrick's Bar. 'She was not sophisticated in today's sense, but she had read Isherwood and was trying to be an actress. I gave her a leopard rug for her room at the Hôtel des États Unis, and we corresponded about Stanislavsky.'

In the summer of 1950, Elaine Dundy (she had now changed her surname) went to London to stay with Hazel Vincent Wallace, who had known her as 'a little kooky juvenile' from the White Barn Theater in Connecticut. Elaine still wanted to act, and soon found her way to the Buckstone.

She had read Ken's book, and went up to him at the club to say that she loved *He That Plays the King*, and that she had been dying to meet him. He said, 'Have lunch with me next Thursday.' He wrote down in his engagement book for Thursday, 14 December, '1 – Yank girl Buckstone.' Stella Richman, who had witnessed the introduction, and who thought Elaine forward and Ken in no way interested in her, reckoned that it would lead nowhere. Two days after the luncheon and within the blink of an enamoured eye he was engaged to the Yank. They went to see the Marx Brothers in *Monkey Business*, and preferred W. C. Fields in *It's a Gift*; and they drank champagne in various afternoon clubs. Many years later Elaine Dundy told the BBC, 'At one of these [clubs] he suddenly said to me, "I'm the illegitimate son of Sir Peter Peacock. I have x amount of pounds a year. I will either kill myself or die at the age of thirty, because I will have said everything there is to say. Will you marry me?" Well, I thought, I just might.'

They went to Paris for a few days, and on their return Ken took his fiancée to visit a young American friend, Hjalmar Boyesen. Peggy Brooks, then married to Boyesen, remembers that the romantic glow surrounding the engaged couple that evening was 'scary'. Elaine appeared to embody everything Ken loved about American theatre and films. 'She looked happy but frightened, and kept looking at Ken as if she wanted to believe the romance was real, as if she weren't sure of her lines. He wanted to tell us what he felt about her, and he didn't want to go home.'

On 25 January 1951 they were married at the Marylebone Registry Office. In attendance were Tessa Prendergast, a handsome Jamaican girl, and Peter Wildeblood, Ken's droll Oxford friend. Ken wore his grey suit with a green carnation in his lapel, and Elaine a smoked-grey nylon organdie dress, with feathers in her short hair. They went to Wildeblood's flat afterwards to be photographed for the press while Tessa Prendergast sang a wedding calypso. Then, according to Wildeblood, they rushed off to Peter Ustinov's. Ken said, 'I've just got married and I want you to be the last to know.' Elaine's grandparents cabled their congratulations from Hollywood, Florida, and her parents from Long Island City, New York. In Birmingham, England, Rose Tynan, who had had the news by telegram, went to meet her sister May, told her that 'our Kenneth' was married, and tried to bottle up her tears.

The couple honeymooned in Oxford for a weekend, and returned to 19 Upper Berkeley Street. The new Mrs Tynan lipsticked the mirrors with hearts and the words, 'I Love Ken', and fell readily into her husband's way of life. 'If you hadn't existed I would have had to invent you,' says *The Dud Avocado*'s Sally Jay Gorce of the man she loved.

She pursued her career as an actress, working in television plays. But she was not chafing about her career, Peggy Brooks recalls. 'It was great fun for her to be with Ken and he opened doors for her.' Peter Wildeblood had liked her immediately, when he first met her in the Buckstone. 'She was self-centred, but she was funny about herself, more impulsive and more reckless than Ken.'

Ken told a friend that he discovered Elaine's father was a millionaire only a week after he was married. He was always very candid about Elaine's contribution from her small private income to their household. He also continued to call for financial help from his mother.

Ken was now writing regularly in *Sight and Sound* about the American screen heroes he had worshipped during his childhood. He described W. C. Fields: 'He would screw up his lips to one side and purse his eyes before committing himself to speech; and then he would roll vowels around his palate as if it were a sieve with which he was prospecting for nuggets.' He praised James Cagney with his 'spring-heeled walk', and he wrote of the Tracy–Hepburn team, of their American sophistication, very different from the European sort: 'It unbends, it wears sneakers about the house.' This beloved couple delivered 'the comedy of marriage, not flirtation', and their antagonisms were intellectual rather than 'sheerly sexual'.

Here was the duo to be emulated, and it may well have been that in those early days of marriage Elaine Dundy felt a little overwhelmed by the role in which Ken had cast her. She told an old New York schoolfriend that she felt inadequate among Ken's circle of friends.

8

Both Sides of the Footlights

In the month of his marriage, Ken was commissioned by Alec Clunes, who ran the Arts Theatre Club, to direct Cocteau's *Les Parents Terribles*. A translation, retitled *Intimate Relations*, was made. And a theatre *grande dame*, Fay Compton, agreed to play the mother.

Ken went to work on the text, making elaborate notes for himself. 'The characters', he wrote, 'are not good or evil. Each thinks himself *right*.' The nervous but determined young director started work with his distinguished cast, and after several rehearsals he arranged a screening for them of Cocteau's film of the play. The cast felt that some of Ken's good ideas had come straight out of the film. Fay Compton declared that she needed confidence in her director, turned against Ken and asked for his dismissal. Alec Clunes agreed he should go.

Ken took this as a major defeat, and concluded that he could not work with anyone over thirty again. So humiliated was he that he felt he no longer had a future as a director of theatre. Twenty years later he wrote in his journal:

When Clunes fired me from the Arts production – I had a chance between hanging back as an onlooker and plunging in as a participant – i.e. continuing as a director. I took the safer course and became a full time critic. That is why, today, I am everybody's adviser – Roman's [Polanski], Larry's [Olivier], Michael White's – and nobody's boss, not even my own.

Ken's claim that the traumatic event at the Arts Theatre changed the course of his life is belied by the direction he had already set for it. He was already writing regular drama criticism for the *Spectator*, film criticism for *Sight and Sound*, and occasional pieces for such periodicals as *Lilliput*, *Panorama* and *Bandwagon*. Between the beginning of 1951 and the end of 1953, he wrote hundreds of thousands of published words of criticism and journalism, as well as two books. In addition he worked on dozens of projects that never came off. For television, co-adaptations of *Antony and Cleopatra* and *The Taming of the Shrew*, and a script based on the life of Bix Beiderbecke; for radio, an adaptation of *Nineteen Eighty-four*; outlines for a book on Oxford and another on Sid Field; and an original stage play set in America.

Nor did he abandon acting. In 1951 Alec Guinness was at a peak of his professional career, with films such as *Kind Hearts and Coronets* and *The Lavender Hill Mob* to his credit. As a contribution to the Festival of Britain, he decided to direct and perform a very full version of *Hamlet* which would be neither overly heroic nor too Freudian and naturalistic. Alan Webb was cast as Polonius, Michael Gough as Laertes, Stanley Holloway as the First Grave-digger, and the young Robert Shaw as Rosencrantz. Guinness now consoles himself for the subsequent disaster of the production by pointing out that 'almost every member of the cast became a star of some sort'.

Guinness had had a dream of Ken as the Player King. He had also seen him play the Second Actor in the Rudolf Steiner production and thought his acting striking, if perverse. He asked the young man out to lunch and Ken showed up at the White Tower restaurant 'dressed in bright green from top to toe'. He was offered the part and accepted, although he knew that the Player King should be a middle-aged man with a voice of brass, and that he himself was 'as skinny as a willow', and had a voice of tin.

Guinness hired a young BBC radio director called Frank Hauser to help him direct. Cumbersome and all too authentic Elizabethan costumes were designed. Ken held up a great cage of a doublet on top of his spindly legs, and wore a beard, a huge hat and heavy jewellery. By the time he was fully dressed he had disappeared.

At the first dress rehearsal he played the part in broad Irish. The next morning Guiness said, 'About the Player King ... ' and Ken stammered and said, 'It was a mental aberration, Alec.' But it was more a *cri de coeur*.

Almost from the beginning of the first night, on 17 May, the newly installed lighting system, in the hands of a panicky operator, went berserk. The lights went down in the court scene so that the Swiss Guard, dressed with one leg black and one orange, looked merely one-legged. The Ghost appeared in broad daylight. Hamlet, wearing a little goatee and a moustache, ran from one light to another calling out, 'Remember me.' When Gertrude announces that Ophelia is drowned, Laertes has to say, 'Oh where?', not the easiest line for any actor. With the stage lighting switching madly on and off as if handled by Frankenstein in an electric storm, this Laertes got a huge laugh.

It would seem that technical matters were in hand for the climax of the play scene. This took place after Ken had taken leave of his Player Queen, and dropped off to sleep. 'As the murderer crept up to slip him the potion there was a slow black-out,' Ken recalled, 'except for a single spotlight on Claudius' face. Phosphorescent paint had been applied to the crown, the vial of poison and a great plastic left ear which I wore over my own: these glowed in the darkness, and the tableau as the poison was poured took on the aspect of an advertisement for a proprietary brand of run.' Feeling remarkably like Van Gogh, he was required at the end of the performance to hand in his ear to the stage manager.

Ken's performance – by some accounts delivered in a muffled sing-song voice, his fingers stuck desperately together – was not a success. The *Evening Standard* critic, Beverley Baxter, in a review entitled 'The Worst Hamlet I Have Ever Seen', singled out the performance of the Player King: 'I am a man of a kindly nature who takes no joy in hurting those who are without defence, but Mr. Ken Tynan ... would not get a chance in a village hall unless he were related to the vicar. His performance was quite dreadful.'

Peter Brook, with whom Ken was on very friendly terms at the time, knew how vulnerable he was to criticism, 'to the way he was received by the outside world', and was impressed that Ken countered with lightness and attack. Ken discovered that a clever pseudonymous article in *Panorama* attacking contemporary theatre criticism, in particular Baxter's 'merciless volubility', had been read by Baxter some short time before the first night of *Hamlet* and attributed by him to Tynan. He wrote an open letter to the *Standard*, and it was headlined 'Baxter's Dreadful Man Bites Back', explaining that, although he was the drama critic of *Panorama*, he had not in fact written the offending article. 'But I am quite a good enough critic to know that my performance in *Hamlet* is not "quite dreadful"; it is, in fact, only slightly less than mediocre. I do not actually exit through the scenery or wave at friends in the audience.' Baxter replied unconvincingly that he had never heard of Mr Tynan.

A week later Ken's first article appeared in the paper. Five months later he was writing drama criticism. A year later the *Standard*'s proprietor Lord Beaverbrook had dismissed Baxter and replaced him with 'the dreadful man'.

The explanation, of course, is more complex than a cheeky letter. The real author of the pseudonymous attack on critics, Gavin Lambert, did nothing to prevent the rumour that Ken was behind it. The successful film critic of the *Evening Standard*, Milton Shulman, had read one or two things by Ken, and thought the *Panorama* attack on critics was typical Tynan. He took it to the features editor of the paper, Charles Curran, and said, 'If you want to read the work of a really bright young man, read this – a great attack on Baxter.' Curran knew about Ken, and had the previous year tried unsuccessfully to get him on to the *Standard*. On 17 May, the very day of the *Hamlet* opening, he lunched with Ken at the Savoy to discuss a series of freelance articles. On the 18th, the paper's editor, Percy Elland, wrote to Beaverbrook about the affair, and added: 'I have invited Tynan to write an article for us on the Danny Kaye myth. I think his sharp pen may do well in the *Standard*.' The contretemps delighted Beaverbrook, who had at one time been close friends with Baxter but had recently resented his missing first nights because of his duties as a Member of Parliament.

On 29 May, the *Standard* published Ken's first article, 'Is He Great? I Say No!', a showy reputation-bashing look at Danny Kaye, who was then immensely popular, and ripe – in the *Standard*'s view of things – for a fall. Elland wrote to Beaverbrook to say that the article had created quite a stir:

It has particularly upset Beverley Baxter.

Baxter telephoned me: 'Is the rumour true that the *Evening Standard* is getting a new editor?'

I said: 'Very likely. Who is the man?'

He said: 'Ken Tynan. They say he is first to be the *Standard*'s theatre critic and then editor.'

We laughed, and Baxter said: 'This must be the biggest reward for a bad performance that any actor has ever received.'

Elland proceeded to ask Ken to write another article 'putting Vivien Leigh in her proper perspective'. He also asked Beaverbrook if they should employ Tynan as a stand-in theatre critic during Baxter's holiday.

Vivien Leigh and Laurence Olivier were at the time playing to capacity at St James's Theatre in Shaw's *Caesar and Cleopatra* and Shakespeare's *Antony and Cleopatra*. Ken's article on Leigh began uncharitably:

Overpraise, in the end, is the most damaging kind of praise, especially if you are an actress, approaching forty, who has already reached the height of her powers....

Fondly, we recall her recent peak: when, in 1945, she held together the shaky structure of Thornton Wilder's play, *The Skin of Our Teeth*. She used her soul in this display; and was sweet.

Ken went on to argue that Miss Leigh was nothing more than 'sweet' in the two great roles she had assumed. As Shakespeare's Cleopatra, he said, she picked at the part 'with the daintiness of a debutante called upon to dismember a stag'. And of Olivier he wrote: 'Blunting his iron precision, levelling away his towering authority, he meets her half-way.... A cat, in fact, can do more than look at a king: she can hypnotise him.'

This cruel, if accurate piece (which deeply distressed Vivien Leigh) was an attention-seeking device, as Ken confessed to his friends. But he believed what he wrote.

The hard work Ken put in as a journalist paid for an exceptionally full social life, much of which took place in the French Club off St James's Street, where you could get a meal for five shillings, where you would find artists, documentary film-makers, writers and straggling members of the Free French. Ken also ate at the Asiatic and the French Pub in Soho, as well as at the more expensive places like the Savoy Grill, the Ivy and the Caprice.

The Caprice was a showcase for the theatrical elite, where the clientele wore off-the-shoulder cocktail dresses, black tie, jewels and furs. Into the restaurant one night swept Marlene Dietrich on the arm of Alfred Hitchcock and 'suddenly everyone went silent', the Canadian actress Barbara Kelly recalls. 'The fifties had glamour and Ken was very much at the centre of things.' Barbara Kelly and her actor husband, Bernard Braden, would dine with the Tynans and the Richard Burtons at the Caprice, or at the Stork Room, where Ken would mischievously persuade Burton to get up and sing, which he loved to do.

Burton had recently appeared in *Henry IV* at Stratford and Ken wrote: 'His Hal was no jovial roisterer, catching as catch can. He sat transfixed, often hunched or sprawled, with dark, unwinking, continent eyes, mildly staring ahead into the time when he must steady himself for the crown.' Later he praised Burton's honest-looking Iago. He also wrote about the actor with a kind of objectivity that made friendship edgy. 'The trouble is', Burton would say, 'Ken wants it both ways.'

Burton's then wife, Sybil, remembers that Ken's sharp criticisms bothered Elaine, while at the same time she loved the excitement of the life. Sybil Burton also recalls that after a trip to Spain Elaine's small figure could be seen at first nights encased in a bullfighter's pink cape which was as stiff as cardboard. The Tynans and the Burtons were introduced, in August 1951, to John Huston and to the Humphrey Bogarts. 'After supper,' Peggy Brooks recorded in her diary, 'came home with by now exceedingly drunk Elaine.... Ken embarrassed.'

Ken's social life embraced stars, actors, eccentrics, and almost any American he could find. With Hjalmar Boyesen, he would eat, drink, read aloud from Sherlock Holmes, and talk about *The Catcher in the Rye*, which had just been published.

He went with the Boyesens, along with Tennessee Williams, a young White Russian actress Maria Britneva (who, as Maria St Just, became a good friend of the Tynans), Laurence Harvey and Hermione Baddeley to a polo party given by the Maharajah of Cooch Behar, a singularly fraught afternoon at Cowdray during which Tennessee Williams, noting his host to be a man of colour, politely observed, 'I – er – I expect you know the Aly Khan.'

Laurence Harvey was stung on the lip by a wasp. 'Christ fuck it, I'm *filming* tomorrow,' he said, 'and what happens to the fucking close-ups if my lip's swollen up like a fucking balloon?' According to Ken's report:

Miss Baddeley smoothed him, procured a bottle of brandy and retired with him into one of the cars, closing doors and windows and pulling blinds behind them. Outside the car conversation remained becalmed in the heat. Occasionally men on horses thundered by and were lost to sight in the distance.... Tennessee became silently drunk. No one had any idea why they were there. My wife and I joined Baddeley and Harvey in the car for some brandy. Harvey was moaning, Baddeley philosophically drinking. Emptying the bottle, she peered through the window and said memorably: 'I think I'll pop out for a mouthful of fresh wasp.' ... Harvey's lip had, in fact, as he predicted, begun to swell up exactly like a little pink balloon. We climbed back into the cars.

... As we were purring ... past the Albert Hall the leading Rolls drew up at the kerb and Miss Britneva flew out. She ran back to our jeep, weeping hysterically. Opening the door, she said: 'Get me out of here, Tennessee. That shit Harvey has just spat in my face.' It turned out that she had interrupted a monologue by Harvey on the subject of his film career to deliver herself of an incisive opinion on the effect of narcissism and megalomania on talent (if any). Whereupon Mr. H, who was facing her on a jump seat, had leant forward and let fly.

In November 1951, at the small Irving Theatre near Leicester Square, Ken co-directed with Ellen Pollock a programme of Grand Guignol of which the centrepiece was an abridged version – cut by Ken and Peter Myers – of *Titus Andronicus*. The presence of the St John Ambulance men, Ken assured his critics, was not superfluous attention-seeking. 'An average of two people, in an audience of just over a hundred, have fainted at each performance. And last Sunday, to everyone's astonishment, one of the Ambulance men fainted himself.'

Here were the kind of dramatic shocks which Ken had tried out at Oxford in his production of *Samson Agonistes*. But his *Titus* was a lark rather than a serious endeavour. It was also the last time he directed in the live theatre.

9

Star Quality

Ken's writing was now being widely read and its quality, along with his personal flamboyance, opened doors to the stars. For the next couple of years he wrote profiles, pen portraits and sketches of most of the cultural grandees of his time. One of the first to be captured was Noël Coward, who, after first meeting Ken, wrote in his diary that he found him 'a curious young man, very intelligent and with a certain integrity'. Coward had plied Ken with questions. What was he doing and for whom and for how much? In between the questions he told Ken that his writing sounded genuine and affectionate, important assets in a critic.

The two discussed their mutual grail, star quality. 'I don't know what it is,' said the Master, 'but I know I've got it.' It was Ken's passion to define this quality. In Coward's case it was 'the ability to project, without effort, the shape and essence of a unique personality, which had never existed before him in print or paint. Even the youngest of us', he wrote in 1952, 'will know, in fifty years' time, precisely what is meant by a 'very Noël Coward sort of person'.

It was Coward's triumph, Ken felt, to have been born into his own era, and he belonged to it as ineradicably 'as the five-piece jazz band and the electric razor'. Here is Ken's description of seeing him in cabaret: 'Benign, yet flustered, as a cardinal might be at some particularly dismaying tribal rite; exuberant, replete to the brim with a burning, bright nostalgie de la boo-hoo, taut, facially, as an appalled monolith; gracious, socially, as a royal bastard; tart, vocally, as a hollowed lemon – so he appeared for us at the Café de Paris.'

As a solo performer Ken wrote of him thus:

The head tilts back, the eyes narrow confidingly; they will flash white only when an 'r' is to be rolled, as in words like 'Frrrrantic' or 'Digby-Frrrrrrobisher! Baffled and amused by his own frolicsomeness, he sways as he sings from side to side, occasionally wagging a finger if our attention wanders.... Baring his teeth as if unveiling a grotesque memorial, and cooing like a baritone dove, he displays his two weapons – wit and sentimentality.

After this performance in print, Coward shook a reproving finger at Ken and said, 'Of the two of us, Mr T, I thought that *you* came out of it exceedingly well.'

Loyalty never clouded Ken's judgements; admiration, and even love, would be withdrawn if the star failed to live up to his or her best. Coward's *Quadrille* (which appeared in the autumn of 1952) was 'comedy gone flabby, swollen with sentiment and tugging at heartstrings that have slackened long ago with tedium.'

On 19 October Ken turned on another hero, Orson Welles, as *Othello*: 'No doubt about it, Orson Welles has the courage of his restrictions.... Welles's own performance was a huge shrug.... His bodily relaxation frequently verged on sloth.... He positively waded through the great speeches, pausing before the stronger words like a landing craft breasting a swell.... Welles's Othello is the lordly and mannered performance we saw in *Citizen Kane*, we have adapted to read 'Citizen Coon.'

Quite soon after this notice, Ken and Elaine went backstage at the St James's Theatre to ask Welles if he would care to do a few magic tricks at the Café de Paris. Welles cried, 'Out! Out!' Ken was always surprised when his friends resented criticism.

Welles found the 'Citizen Coon' tag unworthy of Ken, and he responded with pure anger to a Tynan profile in the *Sketch* where he is described as 'hunching his blubber shoulders in laughter. The shoulders rise like boiling milk, and he chokes over his own good humour, fuming like an awakened volcano.' 'That made me a permanently fat man,' Welles claimed years later, roaring with laughter. 'I'd been in training, I ate nothing. I thought if I have "blubber shoulders" after what I've been going through, to hell with it!'

Other actors and actresses whose physical attributes Ken lit for inspection never forgave him. He, in turn, was always genuinely surprised to have caused offence; since he believed he bore no malice, he assumed his sharp word pictures would not be taken personally. He wrote of his friend Maxine Audley that there was nothing wrong with her performance (in *Tobias and the Angel*) 'that three months' fasting would not cure'. He said of Claire Bloom's 'inexpert' performance as Virgilia in *Coriolanus* that she 'yearns so hungrily that I longed to throw her a fish'. Richard Burton, who was enamoured of Miss Bloom at the time, threw a punch at him at a party (and missed).

Ken could be cruel, and disingenuous about the cruelty. Yet in a time of social cravenness his attack on established theatre was bold. He was tired of writing about old actors and playwrights and 'their steady marble successes'. But he could be as tough on the vulgar end of the entertainment world, when it showed no talent. Of the singer Frankie Laine's performance at the Palladium, he wrote: 'He spreads his arms out like a wrestler, and then hits a mad, toneless head-note, holding it so long that you expect him to drop like a stone at the end of it. Seizing a bull-whip, and grinning intimately, he can even get passionately excited over mules – a rare thing in the modern theatre, or any other, for that matter.'

There was a gusto about Ken's criticism, even when he hated: when he loved, he wanted it known. The next-best thing to being on a stage was to be a passionate participant, on the 'necessary side of the curtain', as Orson Welles had put it.

When he loved, he could occasionally go overboard. His review of Mary Martin in *South Pacific* began: 'I wept, and there is nothing in criticism harder than to convey one's gratitude.' To a large degree he found Mary Martin responsible. 'Skipping and roaming round the stage on diminutive flat feet, she had poured her voice directly into that funnel to the heart which is sealed off from all but the rarest performers.' *South Pacific* opened at Drury Lane in November 1951, and Miss Martin remembers it as the most exciting first night of her career. Then the reviews appeared and they were all bad, with the one exception.

Ken became friendly with Mary Martin, and with Joshua Logan, who had directed the show. He had already met the theatre critic of the *New York Post*, Richard Watts Jr, and the great teacher, critic and director Harold Clurman, and they heralded his arrival in New York.

On 8 December 1951, with his pregnant wife, Ken set sail on the *Liberté* for the country he had loved since childhood. On the voyage, he propped up the bar, which heaved every few seconds 'like a matron's bosom', and tried to find entertainment for Elaine, who, he wrote to a friend, 'niggles about the lack of amusements'.

No sooner had they docked than the amusements began. Elaine's sister Betty and a group of friends met them and whisked them off to a party in Greenwich Village. Shana Alexander, who was part of the group, noted what appeared to be a green iridescent suit and Ken's fearful stammer, and thought, 'Holy Christ, wait till Sam Brimberg gets a look at his son-in-law.' Sam Brimberg and his wife Florence soon got a look at their odd son-in-law, as did the Rosenberg grandparents and Uncle Louis and Cousin Bob.

Ken also met friends of Elaine's, like the composer Richard Adler, and he was entertained by the Joshua Logans, Hermione Gingold and Harold Clurman. He called upon editors at *Holiday*, *Mademoiselle*, *Vogue* and the *New York Times*, and ensnared the legendary Carmel Snow at *Harper's Bazaar*. He went to the Russian Tea Room, to Sardi's, to the Copacabana. Of the ice-cold winter city, he wrote for the *Spectator*: 'To the visitor all doors are unlocked... and more women remove their shoes within the first half-hour of a cocktail party than one would have thought possible.' There was 'vagrant electricity' everywhere, except in the theatre (George Jean Nathan assured Ken it was the worst season since 1932). He found it hard to find a straight play that did not depend on music of some sort, or on a star. In all but one of the eleven straight plays he saw, there was an English actor in the lead or in a featured role; and the eleventh play was about Englishmen.

He did however catch one 'clear masterpiece', *Guys and Dolls*, the finest musical he had ever seen and the most 'lovably stylish' thing he had encountered in America. He was almost as enthusiastic about *Pal Joey*, the 'cornet clarity' of Ethel Merman's voice, and the 'vividly fast and funny' performance of Phil Silvers in *Top Banana*.

He was impressed as well by the number of good young actresses working on Broadway, and the number of good parts that playwrights like Tennessee Williams and Thornton Wilder served up. In his first article for the *New York Times* he saluted Julie Harris in *I Am a Camera*, writing of her 'aura of frank disintegration, of moths and flames ... of butts stubbed out in pots of cold cream'. And he praised Uta Hagen, Lee Grant, Maureen Stapleton, Judy Holliday and a new girl, called Audrey Hepburn, who had come to New York to play *Gigi*.

Back in London in the New Year, Ken and Elaine moved to Bayswater, 29 Hyde Park Gardens, to a top-floor flat in a Regency building with a view of the park. Elaine organized the decoration of the five rooms, putting up purple striped wallpaper and papering Ken's study in bullfighter posters. Despite her reputation for hating domesticity, she appears to have entered into wifely life with gusto, celebrating her marriage anniversary and Ken's birthday, laying in nightgowns, bonnets, blankets and gripe water in readiness for a baby, and entertaining friends with a lavish amount of drink, though rarely with food. They were a generous couple on not a large amount of money. Ken worked prolifically, earning as little as £10 an article from a highbrow journal, and as much as £90 from an American glossy, but his life-style was expensive. Elaine had her own funds, and an inheritance of about $10,000 after her grandfather's death that February.

Observers regard loving couples with a mixture of ignorance and arrogance, for they judge where they can never know. In the case of Ken and Elaine they saw a young man on a meteoric course with a lively wife who yet remained in his shadow and who was for some years happy to be his appendage. Friends liked Elaine's oddball face, her kind laugh and her capacity for friendship. She was always generous with her time; anyone could call up and come around. She liked to talk, to find the centre of the action. She wasn't ambitious in the sense of being on the make, though she was still trying to be an actress. 'I think she really did absolutely adore Ken,' says the journalist Drusilla Beyfus. 'She'd found the complete answer to her life – brother, father, lover, husband, and she was tremendously romantic. I think she fantasized her love for him in a way that was almost novelettish.'

Yet so fragile was Ken's sense of himself that he needed allegiance to be demonstrated. Just before the birth of their child he made a list in his engagement book of instructions for his wife: '1) Expose yourself more 2) Accept wholeheartedly my fixations 3) Worship me much more plainly.'

Early in 1952 Ken had completed a BBC Television trainee programme and had become one of the first freelance directors employed by the Corporation. On 11 May, while Ken struggled with the complicated cues for a live television transmission of *Martine* by Jean-Jacques Bernard, Elaine went into labour. At 9.20 on the morning of 12 May Tracy Peacock Tynan was born. Two weeks later Elaine was 'sprung', as she put it, from Westminster Hospital and shortly afterwards godparents were chosen. They were Cecil Beaton, Vera Lindsay (then married to Sir Gerald Barry, who had run the Festival of Britain), Richard Watts Jr, the gentlemanly and conservative drama critic, and Katharine Hepburn – a predictably stellar group.

In June Miss Hepburn opened in London in Shaw's *The Millionairess*, and Ken – who had caught the performance on tour – rushed into print ahead of his fellow critics to evangelize. Having first dismembered the didactic farce, with its hateful heroine, he wrote how Hepburn 'glittered like a bracelet thrown up at the sun; she was metallic, yet reminded us that metals shine and can also melt ... Miss Hepburn is not versatile; she is simply unique ... she reached a high point in her brazen retort to somebody who enquires, in the second act, whether she throws temperaments merely to make herself interesting. "*Make* myself interesting!" she flings at him. "Man: I *am* interesting."'

Ken believed that, like most stars, Hepburn as an actress could do one or two of the hardest things supremely well, and he was in her thrall. He had met her the previous year on the set of *The African Queen*. After seeing her in *The Millionairess* he engineered a meeting at the house of novelist Rosamond Lehmann. It was there that he asked the star to be godmother to his daughter – named Tracy, after the heroine of *The Philadelphia Story*. 'He had gall,' Miss Hepburn remembers.

Ken had been writing theatre criticism for the *Evening Standard* on an irregular basis. But from 25 April he stepped permanently into Beverley Baxter's shoes. A crisp note from Lord Beaverbrook had reached the paper's editor on 15 April. 'I hope in future when Baxter sends you those fill-in articles, that you will refuse to print them.... [He] must write about the current theatre.' Here was the go-ahead to release Baxter. For the next fifteen months Ken wrote for the *Standard*, for a weekly fee of thirty-five guineas, and ten guineas expenses.

He was now firmly established on the London scene. At a Foyle's literary luncheon in November 1952, in the presence of Christopher Fry, Peter Ustinov and the London critics, Ken delivered from notes his thoughts on drama criticism. 'The critic must not attempt to teach playwright and actor their jobs. Drama criticism is essentially a fallible verbal reflexion of how a particular entertainment struck a unique mind on one special evening.... The last thing a critic ought to be concerned with is the people who read him first. He should write for posterity.'

The idea of the bullfight had first intrigued Ken at Oxford. In *He That Plays the King* he wrote in a passage, embarrassingly purple, that the matador was the only symbol left in Europe that might compare to the exploits and deaths of Shakespeare's kings. For this Orson Welles, in his introduction, rapped Ken over the knuckles: 'It is not the man who is the hero of the tragedy.... The bull is the protagonist. It is his nobility ... which raises the festival above mere sport and pageantry.' Ken had clearly been to the library; he had not been to Spain.

But in March 1951, shortly after his marriage, he had bought linen trousers and sandals, and gone south to see his first bullfight. In July he went back to Spain, to Valencia. On his return to England he was sure that he had found more 'nobility, more grace, more passion and more exhilaration in the Spanish bullrings' that year (and particularly in the torero Miguel Baez Litri) than he had seen on the English stage – barring a few performances by Olivier and Valk. In the ring honour could be pursued through risk. The following July he took his wife to the festival of Pamplona, to Madrid and to the July feria of San Jaime in Valencia. Thereafter he went regularly to Spain for the bulls and in 1955 he published *Bull Fever*, an account of a dozen corridas seen in the space of three weeks in Spain during the summer of 1952. It is still regarded by aficionados as one of the best books on the bulls in English since *Death in the Afternoon*. It is both a guide, a play on philosophic notions, a series of sketches of the toreros and of their fans, and a journal of Spain.

Ken introduced himself to his reader by acknowledging the contradiction for an Englishman and a believer in the abolition of capital punishment of succumbing to bull fever. 'But now the bullfight seems to me a logical extension of all the impulses my temperament holds – love of grace and valour, of poise and pride; and, beyond these, the capacity to be exhilarated by mastery of technique.'

In January 1953 Ken made his second visit to New York for another feast of playgoing and people. He saw George Axelrod's hit, *The Seven Year Itch*, *An Evening with Beatrice Lillie*, Rosalind Russell in *Wonderful Town* with lyrics by Comden and Green, and the crooner, Johnnie Ray, famous for 'Cry'. The pit of his stomach dipped and surged with *Cinerama*, and steadied for an interview in which Ken declared once again that the job of the critic is to write for posterity.

He went to see Cecil Beaton, whose penthouse at the Sherry Netherland was decorated with Cocteau drawings and blown-up playing cards, and there they worked on a book of 100 pen-portraits and photographs of people they admired. Ken wanted to include John Gielgud, whom he had recently met.

'What a possession for any theatre! It is irrelevant to say that he was fair in this part, good in that, brilliant in that: Gielgud is more important than the sum of his parts.'

A month later he met Rebecca West and wanted to include her too. 'She bristled and barked staccato orders at me,' he told Beaton, 'and threw gauntlets in all directions. How can a woman contrive to be a non-smoker and yet look all the time as if she were chewing a cheroot? She seems to be Kensington's reply to Colonel Blimp: and yet the best journalist of our time.'

Cecil Beaton later reported to Ken that he had 'got some honies of Abe Burrows.... I'll try to get Judy Garland.... She is looking like a sugar pig, but is miraculous with lips vibrating with emotion at the microphone. Sugar Ray [Robinson] was a pet.'

Tynan and Beaton were also trying to bag Adlai Stevenson, whom Ken admired. The biographer Charles Higham recalls visiting the Tynans during the middle of the Stevenson–Eisenhower campaign. Ken was playing a record of *Top Banana* to Sandy Wilson. Tracy was crawling around on the floor inside a small playpen. Elaine came in. 'She was very upset and turned Phil Silvers off, saying that the guests could not be heard; [Ken] became furious and the pair... had a fantastic spat right in front of us. Soon after that the radio went on: a broadcast about Adlai Stevenson.... [They] both suddenly joined hands and began chanting, "Madly for Adlai", and we had to join in.' Ken now supported the liberal left and actively fought censorship and apartheid.

In 1953, Coronation year, Ken looked around the English theatre and found no dramatist in the league of Tennessee Williams, Arthur Miller, Jean Anouilh or Jean-Paul Sartre. To the second rank he assigned Terence Rattigan, whose *The Deep Blue Sea* he had admired, and the poetic drama of T. S. Eliot and Christopher Fry. He argued that their use of verse was hostile to complex ideas. He gave a bouquet to Claire Bloom for her Juliet at the Old Vic, and another to Peter Brook for his production of Otway's *Venice Preserv'd*, with John Gielgud.

But it was in the demolition field that he excelled, executing a hatchet job comparable to Shaw's of the 1890s. He was appalled at the English public's 'incorrigible loyalty to anything twenty years out of date and performed by a popular married couple'. And he went to town on Anna Neagle's Coronation offering, *The Glorious Days*.

First, she acts in a fashion so devoid of personality as to be practically incognito; second, she sings, shaking her voice at the audience like a tiny fist....

... The curtain is no sooner up, disclosing a war-time pub, than news arrives that Miss Neagle has been decorated for gallantry; and her entrance is the cue for the opening number, a ragged chorus of 'For She's a Jolly Good Fellow', vivaciously led by a Chelsea Pensioner.

On leaving the pub, Miss Neagle is maliciously greeted by a bomb and the rest of the entertainment tells in its own illimitable way, the story of her concussion.

Its prevailing tone, to sum up, is a mixture of cynicism (they'll lap it up) and joviality (God bless them). *The Glorious Days* demonstrates once and for all that the gap between knowing what the public wants and having the skill to provide it is infinitely wider than most English producers ever dream.

A month later he found the same flat, mediocre and dated style in a revival of *The Wandering Jew*. The part of the Jew (who had insulted Christ and was doomed to live until the Messiah should return) was played by that old carthorse of touring theatre, Donald Wolfit. Wolfit wore a burnous and his usual make-up, a 'thick white line down the bridge of his nose', and 'roared like an avalanche of gravel'.

After reading Ken's review, the actor issued a writ for libel against the *Evening Standard* and its drama critic. Much to Ken's anger the paper did not spring to his defence, and battle was never engaged (the *Standard* eventually paid Wolfit's costs). Ken had made another rabid enemy in the profession. At London parties actors would either keep frigidly out of Ken's way or hang on to his every word. Hermione Gingold would have him over to her house in Limerston Street where he would lean on the mantelpiece, wearing a string tie and his fake leopard-skin trousers with matching shirt, and hold forth, according to his hostess, 'as if he were going to leap right up into the air and land on you and eat you all up'.

Lord Beaverbrook's reaction to his drama critic's notoriety was to ask him to dine. And the response of the editor was to create controversy. The *Standard* touted Ken as the most-talked-of theatre critic in London.

One woman reader, in defence of Anna Neagle, wrote to the paper demanding, 'When, oh when can we have Mr. Baxter back as your drama critic? I can no longer stomach Mr. Tynan's impertinences.' This inspired the paper to print a whole page of letters headed 'Who's for Baxter and Who's for Tynan?'

Letters questioning Ken's fitness to be a critic continued to appear into July, as he was negotiating a new contract with the paper. When Elaine Dundy received a call from the features editor, Charles Curran, complaining that Ken's copy was delivered late, she replied that the critical letters – letters which she was sure were written inside the paper – were making life difficult for him.

In mid-July Ken could take no more, and wrote to the paper threatening to sue them for libel if they published a proposed page of letters headlined 'Should Actors Be Critics?' 'Since I'd made only one appearance as a professional actor in my life, I resented being cast as the punching-bag in this debate.' Several days later the editor wrote back to say that Ken was fired.

On 24 July Ken called up Percy Elland to say that he had written in a fit of anger. He said that he could not believe that one letter could mean a final breach after such a happy relationship, and that he would withdraw his threats. Elland would not relent.

The story, however, was not quite so simple. The *Standard*'s film critic, Milton Shulman, had been called in by Lord Beaverbrook and told that Tynan had threatened to sue the paper for libel. He asked what the outcome would be and Beaverbrook said, 'I've fired him. We can't have a fellow who threatens to sue his own paper for libel.' Beaverbrook then offered the job to Shulman.

Charles Curran, whom Ken admired and liked, wrote to say that he had done everything he could but that there was no going back on Ken's letter. 'If you want to have a row with someone do it by word of mouth,' he advised, 'never, never, never in writing.'

'This is not a disaster, and you must not imagine that it is,' he wrote – in the same consoling and wise manner that C. S. Lewis had written to Ken after he had failed to get a first-class degree. 'These last 12 months have put you firmly on the map, and made you the most discussed theatre critic in London. No other critic – not Agate or Shaw or Walkley or Archer or Beerbohm – has ever established himself at so early an age. The dismissal', insisted the kindly editor, 'is just a piece of anecdotage, material for one chapter of autobiography.'

On 7 August, Ken's last column appeared in the *Evening Standard*. Believing that 'the comparable Bax' was on his way back, Ken ended his piece with an announcement of his own departure. 'The older generation', he explained, 'is knocking at the door.' But that final paragraph was not printed.

On 6 August Rose Tynan came up to London to fetch Tracy and take her to Bournemouth and the following day Elaine and Ken set off for Spain. It was no doubt a welcome escape from the drama of the *Evening Standard*, and from the drama of Ken's first extra-marital fling. The girl in question was the beautiful, dark-haired wife of the Labour MP Woodrow Wyatt. Elaine soon found out. 'Since when have you been using Alix's scent?' she asked Ken. She called up Alix Wyatt offering her husband: 'Would you like him? You can have him.' Mrs Wyatt was speechless. She had not yet quite fallen for Ken, but she liked the way he could light up a room.

A few weeks later Ken telephoned Alix and asked her to lunch at the Café Royal. He said, 'If I leave Elaine after the holidays, would you come and live with me?'

'At that moment I fell in love,' she recalls. 'I said, "Of course I will." "What holidays?" a sceptical friend asked when told of the offer. "It has to happen now."

Having heard nothing from Ken for four days, Alix called him and they met in a drinking club in Curzon Street. He told her that the three most important things in his life were Tracy, Elaine and herself in that order; he was very sorry, but the deal was off.

'I was very bitter,' she recalls. 'I said, all we need to hear is that damned theme music from *Limelight*, the film of the moment, and on cue the music began.'

Ken and Elaine set off for Biarritz and Bilbao for the bulls, and dropped in at St Jean de Luz where Eileen and Larry Adler and Irwin and Marion Shaw had taken houses for the summer. The region was then very unspoiled and ideal for children, with fine beaches and mild weather.

A young American writer, George Plimpton, saw Ken crossing the street in St Jean, wearing a seersucker suit. He recognized the legend from Oxford who had recently, it was rumoured, blown a smoke ring into Lord Beaverbrook's face and he introduced himself. Another American writer, a gentlemanly Yankee wit called John Marquand Jr, connected with the *Paris Review* and Plimpton, was dining that summer with his future wife Sue in a seafood restaurant in Bilbao when somebody pointed out the young English critic. It was explained that the frantic tousled girl, who at that moment was shrieking at him from the other end of the long communal table at which they all sat, was his wife. 'Then we saw her stand, empty a dripping platter of paella upon her husband's head and storm out of the place. Poom! And that was my first sight of the Tynans,' John Marquand recalls. 'The next day at the bullfight, I was introduced to Kenneth, who simply said, "I believe you were there last night. A curious evening."'

The Marquands and the Tynans became fast friends. John remembers Ken's exuberance in those early days: 'This sort of boyish thing underneath a great veneer of cynicism and sophistication. Going to the theatre, he'd rush, you know. He was always in a hurry to get there before everybody else. I remember him walking down Sixth Avenue taking coins and throwing them way up in the air, and catching them with delight, like a child playing, just out of *joie de vivre* to be in New York, to be going to the theatre.'

It was the spring of 1954 and Ken had just signed a contract with the *Observer* to become their drama critic. It was by far the most important thing that had happened in his career, and it did not come out of the blue.

Ken's goal for some time had been to write drama criticism for one of the distinguished Sunday weekly papers. Three months before being fired from the *Standard* he had made a note in his diary to write to Ivor Brown, the theatre critic of the *Observer*, and this note was followed by other reminders to contact the paper's editor, David Astor. But it was not till after the *Standard* had dismissed him that he took up his pen and wrote, on 30 July 1953, to Astor. He said that they had not met, but that his daughter's godmother, Lady Barry (Vera Lindsay), had often been on the point of introducing him. He explained that he had no fixed plans, that he was wondering whether 'there might be any possibility of my acting as second or third string critic to Ivor Brown', and he added that he had written to Mr Brown on the same subject.

Now this letter struck the editor of the *Observer* very forcibly, partly because of its modesty (Astor had never met Ken, but he had just read *He That Plays the King* and had been enormously impressed by it), and partly because he had for some time been dissatisfied with the work of Ivor Brown – who had been the paper's drama critic since 1928. He had Ken in mind to replace him. In this he was strongly encouraged by his new arts and literary editor, Terence Kilmartin. There remained the tough job of removing the dinosaur. (Astor had taken over from Brown as editor of the paper, and now he intended to deprive him of another job.) On receiving Ken's letter he had his secretary telephone to say that he would indeed like to discuss the matter.

In early September Ken went to see David Astor, and they exchanged compliments and agreed that he would write some freelance articles. The first of these, 'A Bunch of Comics', which appeared in the newspaper on 20 September, was a homage to Ken's favourite clowns: old favourites, like Sid Field and W. C. Fields, originals like Frankie Howerd and Tommy Cooper, and newest to Ken's pantheon, Jacques Tati.

Ken continued to work unhappily for the *Daily Sketch*, which he had joined as drama critic in October 1953. He told his readers that he would like to see Olivier as *Macbeth*; the great French actress Edwige Feuillère in *Camille*; an English musical by Terence Rattigan; the work of a director as dynamic as Elia Kazan or Harold Clurman; a stage designer with a sense of architecture, no sense of period and no sense of humour; an American-style burlesque show; a production of *Pal Joey*; a new play by Angus Wilson, Ivy Compton-Burnett, Nancy Mitford or Henry Green. In fact, a new play by a novelist. In fact, a new play.

He did not find what he wanted in the London theatre and set about brutally disposing of the shoddy stuff on view. The Society of West End Theatre Managers complained to the *Sketch*, which in turn whipped up a front-page controversy. On this occasion the critic under fire seemed unconcerned.

That autumn two of his books came out: *Persona Grata*, his fan club of portraits illustrated by Cecil Beaton, and a study of the work of the actor Alec Guinness. Both were well received. He was also writing humorous pieces for *Punch*, which was then under the editorship of Malcolm Muggeridge.

Meanwhile David Astor had paid a call on Ivor Brown to tell him that the paper needed a change and to ask if he had any ideas about a successor. Brown came up with several names and then added, 'There is, of course, Mr Ty-nan,' as he called Ken. Astor then said that he had come to the conclusion that Mr Ty-nan would be the brightest.

Quite soon after this meeting Ivor Brown began to mind very much about leaving. His wife, a theatre producer called Irene Hentschel, mobilized the theatre establishment to lobby both Astor and the paper's chairman Dingle Foot. Brown's defenders argued that he stood for certain standards, and that Tynan would damage the theatre.

Astor knew he had one of the few real bishoprics on offer. He knew Ken was in disgrace with the *Standard* and would probably not get on with any employer. On the other hand, he admired him. So he made his decision: 'the bravest thing I did, and one of the most important'.

On 16 December 1953, the editor wrote to Ken to confirm his appointment as the *Observer*'s drama critic, starting the following summer for a period of three years. He would be paid an annual salary of £1500 for a weekly column and occasional special articles.

Ken wrote back to say that he was resigning from the *Sketch* in March and was looking forward, 'with a decent amount of professional rapture, to the prospect of working for you. It will, I expect, be not unlike moving from a brewery into a vineyard.'

10

A Fleet Street Bishopric

Between the announcement of Ken's new job as drama critic of the *Observer* – one which fulfilled all his ambitions – and his stepping, aged twenty-seven, into Ivor Brown's ill-fitting shoes, the press turned their attention on him.

The London tabloids sneered at the 'new Bernard Shaw' tag attached to him, and laughed at his fake leopard-skin trousers. *Time* magazine, more kindly disposed, described his velvet-lapelled jackets with turned-back Edwardian cuffs, and his mink tie. 'It looks like a raccoon at my jugular,' Ken told them. 'People ask me, "Who's your friend?" '

Peter Brook gave the insider's view. He described how, night after night, at cocktail parties and dinners Ken would be discussed and condemned; and he quoted John Gielgud's comment on the criticism: 'It's-wonderful-when-it-isn't-you.' Brook concluded that the gadfly, now a pundit, would have to change his ways. 'The theatre has imposed on him a deep responsibility. He has not really asked for it, but it is there, unavoidable. For the theatre has paid him its greatest compliment. After every first night it is asking: "What has Tynan said?" ' Not everyone, however, took him so seriously. Alan Brien's critical piece, 'The Boy Wonder', produced a hurt letter from Ken congratulating its author on his portrait of a stammering effeminate.

He could be wounded, but he did not lack courage. On 9 January 1954, a little more than a week after the new appointment was announced, his old Oxford friend Peter Wildeblood was arrested for homosexual offences and asked Ken to stand bail. Whatever qualms he might have had, he immediately agreed. An 'exclusive' photograph in a London tabloid shows Wildeblood hiding his face behind a hat as he is driven away from the Hampshire courthouse while Ken is seen gesticulating to the driver with delicate hands, 'like exiguous ivory, Japanese fans', as Alan Brien would describe them.

Wildeblood, with Lord Montagu of Beaulieu and Michael Pitt-Rivers, went on trial accused of indecency and conspiracy to commit certain sexual offences, and was sent to gaol. The press embellished the modest incident with stories of orgies and high living, gloating over the fate of these 'evil men'. In a letter to Lord Beaverbrook, the *Evening Standard*'s editor wrote that Scotland Yard was stepping up its action against homosexuals, that Benjamin Britten had been interviewed, and that Cecil Beaton was on the list. He told his boss that 'There was a great roar of laughter in Fleet Street at the news that Kenneth Tynan had stood bail.'

While in gaol Wildeblood can hardly have been comforted to hear from Ken that he and Richard Burton were going cruising, hoping to be caught. What did help was the knowledge that he could now 'discard the mask which had been such a burden to me all my life'.

Many years later, a newspaper photograph of Edward Montagu reminded Ken how much life had been improved and civilized by the abolition of the law against homosexuals. He recalled the snide attacks on 'theatrical bachelors', and how the critic James Agate had been blackmailed for decades by a vicious guardsman. 'In retrospect, I don't think I ever did anything for which I'm prouder than having stood bail for Peter Wildeblood.'

In the theatre the breakthrough was made in 1956: John Osborne's *Look Back in Anger* 'lanced a boil', as Ken put it. Middle-class taste and understatement were replaced by the voice of 'a sophisticated, articulate lower-class'.

Ken joined battle both inside and outside the theatre; on occasion – determined to 'discard the mask' – he was the vanguard. Unlike Jimmy Porter, he found lots of brave causes worth fighting for. As a critic he wrote about what was wrong with the British theatre and about what was missing. He championed the English Stage Company, the home of new playwrights like John Osborne, N. F. Simpson, Arnold Wesker, John Arden; Joan Littlewood and her people's drama at Theatre Workshop; Brecht's Berliner Ensemble from Germany; and Beckett and Ionesco (about whom he was less fulsome) from France. By the end of the decade he concluded that the strongest and most unmistakable influence on the English theatre – not all of it admirable – had been that of Hollywood and Broadway, of Welles, Wyler, Wilder and Kazan, and of the plays of Arthur Miller and Tennessee Williams. 'If latter-day English drama is serious in intent, contemporary in theme, and written in rasping prose, Broadway and Hollywood are part of the reason.'

Writing of the 1953–4 London season, Ken had noted that twenty-two of the twenty-six straight plays were concerned with life in the upper or upper-middle classes, and that the other four were broad farces. The Depression may have forced American playwrights to face the bleaker facts of contemporary life, but impoverished post-war Britain was busy turning out plays about Ruritanian principalities. Ken advised that British playwrights should not ape the Americans, but that they should at least learn from them. In the powerful wake of a visit to New York, at the beginning of 1954, he wrote

about Arthur Miller and Tennessee Williams for a newly established intellectual monthly called *Encounter*.

He saw that both these seemingly opposed playwrights were united against
commercialization – the killer of values – and full of love for the 'bruised
individual soul'. Their characters came to self-knowledge through desperation, Ken concluded, a notion that may have been triggered by the following
exchange in *Camino Real*. Lady Mulligan complains to Gutman, the proprietor
of her hotel, that he has chosen to shelter some highly undesirable guests
whereupon:

Gutman: They pay the price of admission, the same as you.
Lady M: What price is that?
Gutman: Desperation!

The recipe for drama – self-knowledge through desperation, as practised'
by ordinary people and not exclusively by heroes – became the cornerstone
of Ken's critical theory. He would continue to quarrel with what he regarded
as Williams' embarrassing pseudo-simplicities and with Miller's political sim-
plifications (for Ken was still wary of political propaganda), but he could find
no fault with American drama that dealt with humiliated ordinary men,
'ignoble in the sight of all but the compassionate'.

'Flew out of New York with light valise containing wispy dacron-orlon suit,
savage looking Hawaiian shirt and opaque, blue glasses, which am assured
are standard cocktail garb in Hollywood.' So wrote Ken about his first trip to
Los Angeles, in March 1954. He and Elaine were put up for the first part of
a two-week stay (for their dollar supply was severely limited) in the guest
house of Pamela and James Mason in Beverly Hills. There, one day, Buster
Keaton, a former owner of the main house, knocked on the door and asked,
deferentially, if he might show his new wife around. Ken was shattered to
see his hero so down at heel and to hear that he was doing a mime act three
times nightly at a sleazy saloon in Las Vegas.

He met Oscar Levant, the pianist, radio star and sword-throwing wit, who
declared, 'People either dislike me or detest me.' Ken noted, 'His face awake
bears an expression of utter disgust most men wear asleep.' He was the guest
of Peter Ustinov, 'playing one-eyed Egyptian in epic'; cavorted with his New
York friends Adolph Green and Betty Comden; and interviewed Stewart
Granger and the columnist Sheilah Graham. The latter recalled her life with
Scott Fitzgerald, how one afternoon he had a craving for candy, how he put
a handful in his mouth, licked his fingers, then stiffened and fell. 'He was very
considerate,' she told Ken. 'He died in the afternoon.'

He went to dine at George Cukor's, where he watched Senator Joseph
McCarthy being demolished by Edward R. Murrow on television. Ken noted

the 'thunderous face' and poverty of vocabulary of the Senator from Wiscon-
sin. At the conclusion of the programme he cheered Murrow. 'Jesus Christ,
I'm surrounded by a bunch of pinkoes,' said Cukor. He was smiling, the guest
recalled, 'but my God he was also nervous'. In those days of the Blacklist,
stars were confessing past leftist allegiances and losing their jobs, while others
more dimly pinkish were suffering from the guilt disease known locally as
'subpoena envy'.

At Gene Kelly's house on Rodeo Drive in the flats of Beverly Hills, the
company was politically more convivial than at Cukor's, and more 'dismayingly intellectual'. 'No guest lolls naked on leopard-skin divan.'

The Kellys' house was animated by the Pittsburgh-Irish host's competitive
intelligence and charm, and his then wife Betsy Blair's active support for left
causes. Their front door was never locked, and through it poured a talented
bunch (most of them from New York) who would make their way straight to
the bar. There was lively political talk, and noisy charades, and endless word
games. There was usually someone at the piano, Leonard Bernstein or Oscar
Levant – who would call out, 'What'll it be, kids? A Stabat Mater or a blues?'
Judy Garland and Lena Horne sang. Marilyn Monroe made hotdogs.

'Ken loved our gang,' recalled Gene Kelly and, when Elaine had to leave
Los Angeles, he moved in, wrote there in the mornings in the front room,
looking out to black acacia trees and milky skies before the sun broke.

One night Ken joined friends at the Beachcomber, a popular Hawaiian-
style restaurant near Grauman's Chinese Theater. He saw a very white-
skinned, blue-eyed Dresden doll in the group and asked her name. Adolph
Green said she was Carol Saroyan, an altogether brilliant, crazy and funny
person, and Ken said, 'That's all I wanted to know.' He was placed beside
her.

He spoke not one word to Carol Saroyan during dinner until the party
broke up. Then he asked her, 'Will you come to England and marry me?' And
she answered, 'I can't get to the drugstore.'

This 'darling little flibbertigibbet', as her friend Garson Kanin describes her,
'pretty as can be, and unreal', was just divorced for the second time from the
playwright William Saroyan, and living with her two children in Pacific
Palisades.

Ken asked if he might go home with her for a drink. The drinks and the
conversation lasted until six in the morning. Ken talked about his marriage
and his life; and he fell in love with Carol Saroyan's *faux-naïf* wit and blonde
beauty. She in turn was 'enamored with his consumptive elegance and in
awe of his courage. I'm very interested in valor, because I have none, and I
thought he had it. He wasn't *careful*.'

The next day Ken flew back to England.

On his return to England Ken sent recordings of Dylan Thomas's radio play

Under Milk Wood to his Hollywood hosts, paid his rent and his debts, and settled down to journalism. He made a note in his engagement book to write his autobiography, no doubt reminded on his twenty-seventh birthday that there were but three more years before his declared death.

His private life was somewhat upset. He took a woman friend to lunch to confess his feelings for Carol Saroyan, and he made a note to see a psychiatrist. There is no evidence that he carried out the plan until the following year. Ken demonstrated an extraordinary recovery capacity in his personal relations. He could throw off a domestic row with the ease of a strict devotee of the present tense. In May he took Elaine on holiday to Rome, and then to Madrid, for the feria of San Isidro, ending with a visit to Seville.

He wrote exotic letters to Carol Saroyan, but when she came to London in July, having sold her jewellery to pay for the trip, he could not, or would not, 'get out'. Later in the summer they met again at San Sebastian, in the company of the Irwin Shaws. In a restaurant Ken asked her, 'Will you get up and leave with me now?' But this time Carol would not and she went unhappily back to the States.

Ken was simply not very reliable about romance and he was now reverting to his undergraduate habits. To one woman he complained that he was unhappy, that Elaine was the eternal Peter Pan who would not grow up. In public the two of them would quarrel in front of distressed onlookers.

He began to flirt with another American woman, an intelligent, pretty girl with Broadway connections called Betsy Holland, whom he had met in London early that summer. With a friend, she visited the Tynans' flat for drinks, and spent a nervous, chatty hour. 'I found Elaine snappish and extremely edgy. But I'm sure she couldn't understand why she was expected to entertain us. The door closed behind us and then was flung open again. Ken came chasing after us stammering, "You've forgotten your umbrella." "But I didn't bring one." "I know," he said. "I want to see you again." '

They met and began a musical adaptation of S. J. Perelman's story, *All-Girl Elephant Hunt.* (Ken's treatment reads, 'On the plane the girls explain in song their reasons for going to Africa. Possible Helen Hokinson ballet, revealing the ghastly dreams entertained by normal bridge-playing women.') Early in 1955, when Ken and Elaine were in New York, Miss Holland brought S. J. Perelman to drinks. Ken danced with delight as he told Perelman about turning his short story into a musical. 'Sounds terrific,' said the famous man, 'what the hell do I need you two for? I can write it myself.' He followed up with a legal letter, and so ended, more or less, the unconsummated romance.

During the first half of 1954, Ken engaged in two major platonic love affairs: with Garbo and with Dietrich. He had met Garbo in the company of Cecil Beaton, to whom she was strongly attached. He half expected a female impersonator, but the 'fabrication was demolished within seconds of her entering the room; sidelong, a little tentative, like an animal thrust under a searchlight, she advanced, put out a hand in greeting ... and then gashing her mouth into a grin, expunged all doubt. This was a girl, all right.' He saw that her lipstick was badly applied, that her skin was porous and unwrinkled except for vertical laughter lines, that she tipped her head back when she laughed, that her eyes were large and blue, and her hair mole-dark. She was a hungry listener and a defenceless talker. Had he been to Westminster Abbey? she asked. Did he know the pine trees near Bournemouth? 'Like a Martian guest, she questions you about your everyday life, infecting you with her eagerness, shaming you into a heightened sensitivity.'

But it was the screen Garbo who enslaved him. 'What, when drunk, one sees in other women, one sees in Garbo sober. ... Most actresses in action live only to look at men, but Garbo looks at flowers, clouds and furniture with the same admiring compassion, like Eve on the morning of creation.' He noted how she kissed, 'cupping her man's head in both hands and seeming very nearly to drink from it'. Of her decade in the talkies he wrote that often 'she gave signs that she was on the side of life against darkness; they seeped through a series of banal, barrel-scraping scripts like code messages borne through enemy lines'. But he was unable to give the final accolade to this actress who had never attempted any of the great parts. He compared her to Marlene Dietrich, claiming that both women were all things to all men, women and children. But Dietrich's masculinity appealed to women, and her sexuality to men. 'She has sex, but no particular gender.'

Miss Dietrich came upon this description of herself, and liked it. 'There were all these people trying to guess me out, and he understood the whole thing.' When she arrived in London in June 1954, to appear in a nightclub act at the Café de Paris, she told her friend Noël Coward that the only person she wanted to meet was a man called Ken Tynan. A few days before her opening, he arrived at her suite in the Dorchester Hotel.

'Who are you?' she asked.

'I'm Kenneth Tynan. You said you wanted to meet me,' said the young man who looked to Dietrich no older than nineteen.

'*You* are the one!' she cried.

From then on they were friends. Shortly after midnight on 21 June the dance floor at the Café de Paris was cleared. Noël Coward made his introduction and down the stairs, dressed in a pink light and a rhinestone sheath, came Dietrich. She sang 'Lazy Afternoon', 'See What the Boys in the Back Room Will Have' and 'Falling in Love Again'.

After the first night, she was seen leaving the theatre in a white ermine coat and white 'toreador' trousers. Behind her, wearing a white dinner jacket, followed Ken. 'For three days he simply disappeared,' a friend recalls. 'Elaine was very good-natured about the whole thing.' He would go backstage after her performance, and Dietrich would shoot out a hand from her dressing-room and drag him inside, spurning other suitors. Inside he would discreetly watch her bathe and dress, and then take her to dine. He wrote about her 'curled up like a sated lioness in the back seat of a car, suddenly dissolving into laughter ... raising her eyebrows and gnawing her lips in self derision', after which he went overboard and told his readers that Dietrich listened to 'late Beethoven quartets, early Stravinsky and middle-period Lena Horne'.

After Ken's death, when I asked Dietrich, who was alone and partly bed-ridden, for her memories of him, she replied that she had never, nor would ever, meet anyone like him. 'I adored him. Flowers and presents of cigarette lighters, sweetheart, I don't remember. But I *do* remember him every day and night.' She added, 'What a world without him to tell us what the outcome will be!!'

As a preamble to his job as drama critic at the *Observer*, Ken reviewed television for that newspaper and sorted out his views on criticism. He declared, with tongue in cheek, that applause in a darkened theatre was one of the few altruistic activities of man, and he developed his view, first expressed two years before, that the critic's job was to give permanence to something impermanent. He argued that the critic had no obligation to be constructive or impersonal but should act rather as a lock to the playwright's key. 'If the key fits his temperament, the complex of opinions, biases and preferences which make up an individual soul, he rejoices.'

The burden of Ken's first few thoughtful and unshowy theatre reviews for the *Observer* was that the playwright should be sent back to the locksmith, the more speedily if he were to reclaim the intellectuals from the movie house. He suggested that the critic should not apply a double standard when reviewing the second-rate, and he bemoaned the fact that there were only three straight plays among the twenty-seven current West End shows. Finding little to like in contemporary theatre (though he thought Rattigan's *Separate Tables* was 'as good a handling of sexual abnormality as English playgoers will tolerate') he wrote about Ibsen, Shakespeare and Shaw, small essays which were practical about stagecraft, pointing out, for example, how actors performing in minor Elizabethan plays become masters of two 'arid' skills: 'that of making bad verse sound poetic, and that of making dead puns sound funny'. He was also scholarly about text, and passionate where he was moved.

Ken's first few *Observer* pieces were coolly received in some quarters. It was felt that if he became too responsible he might turn into a dullard. Harold Hobson thought the work pedantic, and was momentarily reassured that he had nothing to fear by way of competition. Even Ken's own editor, Terence Kilmartin, expecting fireworks and showmanship, was disconcerted.

Then, on 31 October 1954, he delivered a full broadside at the London theatre, where, apart from revivals and imports, he could find nothing worthy of discussion with an intelligent person for more than five minutes. In London, theatre lovers pinned their tenuous hopes on the work of John Whiting (whose *Saint's Day*, Ken reminded readers, had given new linguistic life to the Arts Theatre Club some three years before). In Paris they complained of decline apart from Sartre, Anouilh, Camus, Cocteau, Aymé, Claudel and Beckett.

'Survey the peculiar nullity of our drama's prevalent genre,' Ken wrote, 'the Loamshire play. Its setting is a country house in what used to be called Loamshire but is now, as a heroic tribute to realism, sometimes called Berkshire.' This 'glibly codified fairy tale world', peopled by the playwright's vision of the leisured life, had engulfed theatre. Ken argued that there were more playwrights at work than ever before but that they were all writing the same play, while English actors were playing the same part; that Loamshire's greatest triumph was the crippling of directors and designers. He concluded that if the theatre were to lure an audience with 'passionate intellectual appetites', it must 'widen its scope, broaden its horizon. ... We need plays about cabmen and demi-gods, plays about warriors, politicians and grocers – I care not, so Loamshire be invaded and subdued.'

A month later, in the *Atlantic Monthly*, Ken widened his attack on apathy in the West End theatre to include the arts in general. He wrote of the 'swelling suspicion on the part of British youth that their country is culturally out of touch, somehow shrunken and inhibited, desperately behind the times', a place fearful of bad taste, obsessed by the monarchy and the past, by Regency stripes, curly brimmed bowlers and Queen Anne cottages; a place where novelists were expected to have the right accent and a proper disdain for the lower orders (he cited Evelyn Waugh, Nancy Mitford and Ivy Compton-Burnett), but he admitted a small resistance movement led by Kingsley Amis, who had made rudeness genuinely funny.

The darkest cloud over the cultural landscape, he noted, was that of 'steadily increasing xenophobia': fear of America, fear of the advent of commercial television (which Ken welcomed), fear of criticism; fear enforced by a film censor who discouraged political attacks on the Establishment, and by a theatre censor, the Lord Chamberlain (a former Governor of Bombay), who refused licences to plays which parodied politicians or which alluded to sexual deviation. 'The truth is that in hiding so much of life from the public's eye the censors are carrying out the public's wishes' – a public, Ken suspected, that was happy to see books banned and homosexuals prosecuted.

At the *Observer*, he continued to attack what was damaging to theatre and to point out what was missing. He argued that the English had not produced an acknowledged dramatic masterpiece since the third decade of the seventeenth century, and that their dramatic reputation was based on Shakespeare and the Irish – that conspiracy which had produced Farquhar, Goldsmith, Sheridan, Shaw, Wilde, Synge and O'Casey. He suggested that foreign directors be hired to stimulate British actors, and he admonished playwrights to use the living language and to make words 'put on flesh, throng the streets and bellow through the buses'.

11

New Blood

In Paris in the winter of 1954–5 Ken discovered that the theatre was discussed as if it were as vital as politics, and he paid homage to those three temples of theatre, 'international in scope as only truly national theatres can be', Jean-Louis Barrault's Compagnie Renaud-Barrault, and the two subsidized companies – the Comédie Française, where he found the best acting on earth, and Jean Vilar's Théâtre National Populaire. At the TNP he admired Gérard Philippe in Corneille's *Cid* (despite his antipathy to French classics).

Then, on the afternoon of 1 January 1955, he saw a production of Brecht's *Mother Courage*. Though he had seen only one other production of Brecht before – the New York version of *Threepenny Opera* – he wrote knowingly of this epic of the Thirty Years War. It was 'a glorious performance of a contemporary classic'. He pointed out that it had played everywhere in Europe except in London, a city devoid of a style, let alone a national theatre, and that the performance, with Germaine Montero as Mother Courage, had the huge audience cheering and weeping. A note in his engagement book reads: 'one feels an idiot recommending Brecht 20 years after everyone'.

After the performance, according to Elaine Dundy, Ken returned to his hotel and declared, 'I have seen *Mother Courage* and I am a Marxist.'

Determined to correct his parochialism, and that of his readers, Ken returned to Paris in June for the International Theatre Festival to see the Peking Opera and its distant relative, Brecht's Berliner Ensemble. He saw that the ancient company and the post-war German group, formed in 1949, mixed dance, mime, speech and song in the service of narrative. Brecht, he found, had discovered a new way of telling a story, which emphasized how events happen rather than the emotions of the people they affect. Of *The Caucasian Chalk Circle* he reported that he was unmoved by what Brecht had to say, but overwhelmed by the way in which he said it, by the beauty and precision of the stagecraft, which showed the influence of Brueghel and the Orient. Here was the perfect method for presenting *Henry* IV, *Tamburlaine* or *Peer Gynt*.

During that Paris visit, Ken met Brecht for the first and only time. He described him as 'ovally built, and blinking behind iron-rimmed glasses', conversing in 'wry, smiling obliquities, puffing on a damp little cigar'. According to the critic Eric Bentley, Brecht was very keen to recruit impressive supporters and knew all about Ken. Many years later Ken wrongly surmised that he was probably Brecht's only political convert. But his conversion, as reflected in his criticism, developed slowly out of his admiration for the craft and the poetry.

On his return from Paris, Ken reviewed the English première of *Mother Courage*, produced by Joan Littlewood's Theatre Workshop. He was awed to discover that, despite Brecht's leftist sympathies, he showed no sentimentality towards his downtrodden protagonist, a bawdy cynic who is in the war for her own profit. He concluded that this epic tale of endurance, made of earthy language that took 'frequent flight into song', was dismally handled by Theatre Workshop, which had made do with fourteen players instead of Brecht's prescribed fifty. 'The result is a production in which discourtesy to a masterpiece borders on insult.' He counselled Miss Littlewood (whose company he had applauded in the past for its 'absolute, unquestionable dedication') to take heed that it was on artistic rather than on ideological grounds that the West End had, to date, shunned her players.

He did not see another production of Brecht for eight months, but by that time he had argued himself into a position powerfully sympathetic to the playwright's point of view.

In the spring of 1955, Ken's book on Spain, *Bull Fever*, was published, and praised. Other books were planned, though not executed: one for Mark Longman on 'genius-watching', a subject for which Ken considered himself perfectly suited; and a short monograph for Rockcliff on the brilliant if eccentric actor Eric Portman.

He had met Michael Simon Bessie of Harper's in New York in 1954, and had discussed with him the ideas he had explored with Longmans. So began an instructive and sometimes fruitful working friendship, which led to the publication of Ken's first major collection of theatre pieces by way of other plans – a book on the theatres of four countries and an autobiographical book pinned to a portrait of Ken's generation.

During the first half of 1955, Ken returned to the subject of his perennial father-figure, Orson Welles. He approvingly described Welles's production of Melville's *Moby Dick*, which he adapted, directed and starred in, as 'pure theatrical megalomània'. Later in the year he wrote: 'The final decision may well be that Welles is a superb bravura director, a fair bravura actor, and a limited bravura writer; but an incomparable bravura personality.' In the spring of 1956, Welles replied without bravura to Ken's request that he write about the impresario in the cinema.

It is said, and not seldom, that I am before anything, a showman. But the number of times I've managed to set up my pitch and actually lure customers into a tent of my own boils down to a fairly gloomy statistic. The rest of my career as an impresario is the merest drumbeating. ...

You I follow weekly to my profit and think of much more often than that with personal fondness.

Laurence Olivier was also following Ken each week. During the Stratford-on-Avon season of 1955, he played Malvolio in *Twelfth Night* and the leads in *Titus Andronicus* and *Macbeth*. About the latter performance Ken wrote: 'Last Tuesday Sir Laurence shook hands with greatness, and within a week or so the performance will have ripened into a masterpiece ... a structure of perfect forethought and proportion, lit by flashes of intuitive lightning.'

Olivier had recently met Ken at a party given by Noël Coward. Despite the animosity he felt towards the young critic because of his tough reviews of Vivien Leigh, Olivier was on this occasion friendly. 'At a party you don't say, "Would you kindly remove your coat and your spectacles?" Not in England you don't,' Olivier explained. 'Vivien was really remarkable with him, "I'm so sorry, Ken," she'd say, "this can't interest you. You're much too young."' The meeting passed off well enough for the Oliviers to offer Ken a lift home. 'I remember him leaving the taxi and us both watching him,' Olivier continued. 'He didn't turn around and wave or anything like that, and marched straight up with the key and disappeared. He didn't want to be too pally. He felt Vivien was an interloper between myself and my fucking genius. He said her Lady Macbeth was "more niminy-piminy than thundery-blundery".'

Ken was yet more dismissive about Miss Leigh's performance as Lavinia in *Titus Andronicus*. He wrote that she 'receives the news that she is about to be ravished on her husband's corpse with little more than the mild annoyance of one who would have preferred foam-rubber'. Olivier was, at the time, terrified of the effect the criticism might have on her, since she was subject to extreme nervous depression. 'But she took it very pluckily, with extreme bravery and gallantry.'

Maxine Audley, who played Lady Macduff, recalls how Ken got to know the Oliviers that season at Stratford, and how Vivien Leigh was fascinated by him. She recalls too that Elaine Tynan was suffering. 'I remember an evening with Elaine and Vivien, and Elaine saying, "Where has love gone?"' Love had not flown so much as been tested.

In January 1955 Ken had signed up with John Pratt, an analyst of the independent school. He made visits twice a week for a couple of months and then abandoned the therapy. He was suffering at the time from his habitual winter bronchial attacks, and from sinus problems which forced him into hospital for an operation. His constitution was, in other respects, robust. He ate the hottest sauces, took the amphetamine Dexamyl (with his doctor's permission) several times a week, and drank heavily with his wife. Strangely, he almost never appeared drunk.

But during this heady first year at the *Observer* he felt the first seeds of self-doubt. He wrote in his diary:

Those minds which I do not despise, I fear. At the same time, however, I know this and dislike myself for it. . . . Sheer laziness has stultified my mind. It must be reawakened. . . . The need to defy. . . . Is my egotism showing? And what a worthless ego! Plus a basic unwillingness to do anything which does not give me positive pleasure . . . an arid creaking brain. Working in spasms, in convulsive hops rather than in a steady stride.

It is not clear when this complaint was made, nor when he entered a note for a letter to be sent to his friend the actress Jill Bennett, with whom he had a strong platonic flirtation. It read: 'Save me – which is the last thing you want to do. . . . Save me, revive me, shape me, reform me: for I am yours in the deepest ways. Not in the sexual way: but in the other larger way.'

The letter, which was not delivered, resembles the self-confession of the diary: one can smell some truth in a strong wind of self-dramatization. Ken's self-criticism may well have been prompted by sexual guilt over infidelities in a marriage for which he was not ready. 'Do not marry before the age of thirty,' he would often counsel his friends. Marriage meant encroachment which he courted and would then reject. Late in 1954 he had contributed an article to *Picture Post* on men's hates, in which he complained that 'women wished to have you surrender all your secrets'. He wrote: 'A love affair nowadays is a tableau of two wild animals, each with its teeth sunk in the other's neck, each scared to let go in case it bleeds to death'. Women, he added, 'should drop gloves, not fling gauntlets', an attitude which was clearly not acceptable to his free-spirited wife. Ken made another entry in his diary, 'Discovered that [Elaine's] *only* aim is to assert herself independently of me. Q: Why not leave me???' This was the kind of provocative note Ken would enter after a hurtful confrontation (just as, when he was a child and a relative displeased him, he would write in his 'black book', in full view of the offender).

In Cannes that summer Elaine scribbled a note into Ken's same engagement book declaring that she loved him so and that she kept trying to make him unhappy because she could not make him happy; she signed herself 'Skippy'.

Ken reached Barcelona on 16 July 1955, independently of Elaine and Peter Wildeblood, and there joined Tennessee Williams, already fed up with the bulls but enjoying the friendship of a Spanish drama critic who liked to slip into beaded gowns of the 1920s and perform the Charleston. Williams had also been to the Bohemia (Ken's favourite Barcelona nightclub), where a very large lady would sing Puccini arias half a tone flat, while her emaciated companion sang hearty songs of rowing and mountain climbing.

The Tynan party, which included Williams and Lewis and Jay Presson

Allen, moved on to Valencia to stay at the Excelsior Hotel, and to attend the feria of San Jaime (at which Ken's hero Litri fought). In a profile of the soft-fleshed, cat-like playwright Ken described how he hung out in the bars of the ugly coastal town: 'Mostly he is silent ... a vague smile painted on his face, while his mind swats flies in outer space. He says nothing that is not candid and little that is not trite. A mental deafness seems to permeate him, so that he will laugh spasmodically in the wrong places, tell you the time if you ask him the date, or suddenly reopen conversations left for dead three days before.' A photograph of Ken and Williams under an exploding firework shows up two sensitive boyish faces, both marked by a look of wounded innocence.

The playwright did not last the feria: the water supply had been mysteriously cut off and shortly after the power went. Baths had to be taken by candlelight, in mineral water laced with eau de cologne. By the fourth day there came a rumour that a plague of some sort was raging in the docks. The following day Williams packed and left.

Through Arthur Miller's work Ken had received an education in social responsibility, in how to make the present work; this playwright believed in progress towards an attainable summit. From Tennessee Williams, that twin master of the contemporary stage, Ken learned compassion for social untouchables, for incomplete people 'with ideals too large for life to accommodate'.

Suffering from his own growing sense of self-consciousness – shame over his sex life made worse by a surprising shyness and low self-esteem – Ken himself felt like one of Williams's untouchables. But he could not accept the playwright's view that flesh and spirit were irreconcilable. He was always antipathetic to the dualist notion that separated the heights of emotion from the basest physical behaviour. In Aldous Huxley he found support for the view that, however exalted, love is always accompanied by events in the nerve endings, and that words are needed to express the natural togetherness of things. Brecht confirmed these sympathies, and provided an excellent maxim, that 'truth is concrete'. In Brecht's work, as in Arthur Miller's, Ken found that 'passionate desire to improve the human condition' which so appealed to his own essentially hopeful nature.

Ken's 'Valentine to Tennessee' came out in February 1956. Williams was delighted with the profile, although he had asked Ken to soften his remarks about Kazan (who had changed the third act of Cat on a Hot Tin Roof). 'We just don't have another director over here with his way of bringing a script to violent, brilliant life,' he pointed out, and he argued that the theatre was after all an impure art. 'Only in Waiting for Godot have I ever seen a totally pure exercise of the dramatic art.'

Ken had seen the same production at the Arts Theatre Club, directed by Peter Hall, two days after returning from Spain. He wrote that Beckett's Waiting for Godot:

frankly jettisons everything by which we recognise theatre. It arrives at the custom-house, as it were, with no luggage, no passport and nothing to declare; yet it gets through, as might a pilgrim from Mars. It does this, I believe, by appealing to a definition of drama much more fundamental than any in the books. A play, it asserts and proves, is basically a means of spending two hours in the dark without being bored.

His two tramps pass the time of day just as we, the audiences, are passing the time of night. Were we not in the theatre, we should, like them, be clowning and quarrelling, aimlessly bickering and aimlessly making up – all, as one of them says, 'to give us the impression that we exist'.

The play was summed up for him by the line from *Crime and Punishment*, 'Man is a vile creature! and vile is he who calls him vile for that!'

Having been forced to re-examine the rules which govern drama, he declared himself a '*godotista*'.

Ken spent the autumn on the attack, demanding new contemporary plays, plays which recognised sex and religion as serious subjects for the stage. Off duty, he experimented with the drug mescaline. He had read Huxley's *The Doors of Perception*, and persuaded his friend Digby Wolfe, then working as a comic at Harry Green's club, to take the drug with him. One Sunday morning, they nervously began the experiment, while Elaine looked on. Soon they were giggling hopelessly. While Wolfe put his thoughts on paper, Ken lay down in the bedroom, decorated with pink cabbage roses, and watched them turn into the many faces of Charles Laughton. He too made notes. '*Not* visionary. *Not* spiritual', he wrote. But he admitted he could not utterly let go: 'Strong feeling of relief at nothing having happened very much out of the ordinary. ... Lots of green. But *no* repeat *no* new insight.'

On 16 November, Ken set off for Moscow, to see Peter Brook's production of *Hamlet* with Paul Scofield – the first English theatre troupe to visit the Soviet Union since the Revolution. He took a good look at the Moscow theatre and came away with respect for the large choice of 150 plays and for the securely employed (and often ancient) actors in the established companies like the Moscow Arts. The city reminded him of America without the neon, and he bemoaned the lack of it, 'symbol of salesmanship and hence of ingratiation'. On the whole he found he missed the '*pizzicato* of the spirit, the relaxed gaiety which makes work worth while'.

Yet, back in London, he complimented Sartre on his political comedy *Nekrassov*, and added that the play could only come out of a country 'where extremism is not yet a term of abuse'. A week later, he took a further step towards political commitment. In a critical review of Jean-Louis Barrault's performance as a horse in *Les suites d'une course*, Ken pointed out that Brecht, like Barrault, favoured a stylized drama: 'But [Brecht] has a point of view bursting with life and purpose.'

With admonitions for a point of view, and counsel against negativity, Ken proceeded to announce his major commitment to 'art for our sake'. He noted how *Nekrassov* had been condemned by his colleagues as propaganda, and he admitted that he used to share that bias. 'Now ... I begin to wonder whether I was right. In demanding an end to propaganda, was I not depriving the drama of one of its most ancient sources of energy?' One that had animated the Greeks, *Everyman*, *Henry v*, *An Enemy of the People* and all of Brecht. Should not propaganda at least be allowed a place in the hierarchy of theatre? 'Its aim is to "start you talking", and though I agree that the effect of the greatest plays is to *stop* you talking, to present an action so complete that only silence can succeed it in the heart, I cannot understand by what logic this rules out the theatre of parable, polemic and pamphlet.'

Sam Wanamaker's production of *The Threepenny Opera* opened in London, and Ken was eager to ally himself with its point of view, 'that it is useless to talk morality to the poor until you have fed them'. Here was his first commitment to a socialist principle. He might have said, with the critic John Berger, 'far from dragging politics into art, art has dragged me into politics'. (Or as Brecht said, 'When I read Marx's *Kapital* I understood my plays.')

A production in London of *A View from the Bridge* gave Ken occasion to discuss Miller's essay 'On Social Plays'. Here was no cry for 1930s-type tracts, 'hoarse with rage and hungry for martyrdom'. If ancient tragedy had put the question, 'How are *we* to live?', modern tragedy had asked, 'How am *I* to live?' – its first protagonist, Hamlet, had 'despised and rejected' every value on which his society hung. Arthur Miller was now arguing that he could no longer take with seriousness 'drama of individual psychology written for its own sake'. To this Ken added, 'I shall continue to applaud all plays that are honestly frivolous, devoutly disengaged; but I shall reserve my cheers for the play in which man among men, not man against men, is the well-spring of tragedy.'

The English Stage Company was the result of a fortuitous conjunction of two like-minded groups, that of the Earl of Harewood, from the Royal Opera House, and his playwright friend Ronald Duncan; and that of the teacher and director George Devine (who had worked at the Old Vic) and a young television director called Tony Richardson. The new company set up shop in a 400-seat theatre run by Oscar Lewenstein in Sloane Square called the Royal Court, and they advertised in *The Stage* for new playwrights. Only one of the several hundred plays submitted caught the interest of George Devine and his associate. It was called *Look Back in Anger*. The company meanwhile had opened its doors on 2 April 1956 to Angus Wilson's *The Mulberry Bush*, a piece about the reaction of a famous progressive family to the news that its prize scion, lately dead, was something of a cad. Ken found the play improved by rewriting since its première in Bristol, but 'marred by recasting'. 'The

English Stage Company embarks with this production on a repertory season of new plays. I wish their enterprise too well to embarrass it with further criticism.'

The response from the theatre was jaundiced, for the company had been expecting support from this particular critic. Lindsay Anderson, soon to join the Court but at the time writing for the film magazine *Sight and Sound*, and developing strong views on committed art, wrote to Ken complaining about his review. Here, he argued, was a young troupe of promise, 'and a play attempting to tackle a subject of social, moral and human importance. 'It seems to me nothing less than criminal to dwarf their debut.' But Ken's peculiar integrity forbade that kind of assistance. He had already told Tony Richardson, who had asked him to help, that he was not a salesman, and that his responsibility was to his readers.

His review of the second Court production, Miller's *The Crucible*, was also double-edged. On reviewing the play the previous year, he had felt the author imprisoned by his convictions, which allowed the enemy no appeal. Now he found the play had gained in emotional power, and could be judged as a study of mass hysteria, not just as an attack by association on the witch hunts of Senator McCarthy. The performances, however, he roundly condemned.

Then on 13 May 1956, in a review entitled 'The Voice of the Young', the Royal Court managed to please the critic extravagantly. It began: ' "They are scum" was Mr. Maugham's famous verdict on the class of State-aided University students.' And Ken went on to say that anyone who shared this opinion should stay well away from *Look Back in Anger*. Its hero, Jimmy Porter, 'with his flair for introspection, his gift for ribald parody, his excoriating candour, his contempt for "phoneyness" ... and his desperate conviction that the time is out of joint ... is the completest young pup in our literature since Hamlet, Prince of Denmark.'

Here was the familiar malcontent Ken had first come upon and applauded at Oxford, and here was a recognizable young couple 'engaged in competitive martyrdom, each with its teeth sunk deep in the other's neck'.

Is Jimmy's anger justified? Why doesn't he do something? seemed to Ken irrelevant questions. 'There will be time enough to debate Mr. Osborne's moral position when he has written a few more plays.' But already Ken had spotted in Jimmy some of the qualities he had despaired of finding in English plays, 'the drift towards anarchy, the instinctive leftishness, the automatic rejection of "official" attitudes, the surrealist sense of humour ... the casual promiscuity, the sense of lacking a crusade worth fighting for and, underlying all these, the determination that no one who dies shall go unmourned'. For these classless and leaderless Jimmy Porters, John Osborne was now the first spokesman in the London theatre. Ken praised the actors and the direction, expressed certain reservations about the length of the play, and concluded that it was the best young play of its decade.

He also thought that the play would remain a minority taste. 'What matters, however, is the size of the minority. I estimate it at roughly 6,733,000 which is the number of people in this country between the ages of twenty and thirty.' He then made an outrageous gesture of solidarity: 'I doubt if I could love anyone who did not wish to see *Look Back in Anger.*'

Harold Hobson also gave the play a good review, although he admitted Ken's was more courageous and personal. The rest of the press was mixed. Those critics who did not like it found the play 'exasperating', 'vulgar', 'self-pitying snivel'. One critic thought this 'back-street Hamlet' should be 'ducked in a horse pond or sentenced to a lifetime of cleaning latrines'.

The box office remained indifferent and the play did not pick up until a television excerpt some nine weeks after the opening. The theatre, in search of a new kind of audience, needed time to build one. Within two years *Look Back in Anger* had played Broadway, the West End, much of Europe and almost every repertory company in Britain. The effect of Ken's review was to alert young intellectuals, particularly those in the provinces who had never set foot in a theatre, to its seriousness. Arnold Wesker saw *Look Back in Anger* and went straight home to start writing *Chicken Soup with Barley.*

Only one subsequent play of John Osborne's was set in the provinces. Out there, Jimmy Porter was as isolated as Kenneth Tynan in Birmingham, with whom he shared a fastidious loathing of vulgarity, the vulgarity of entrenched values and shoddy feeling. Like Jimmy Porter, Ken collected grievances to animate and dignify his lonely condition. And like Porter, a political liberal but a sexual despot, he demanded unquestioning allegiance from his women. Osborne's women appear 'wearing his colours', as Mary McCarthy put it; 'both girls, while they *are* his, are seen wearing one of his old shirts over their regular clothes'.

With the author Ken shared several other, more curious traits: both men felt shame about their working-class mothers. In Ken's case this attitude turned to guilt, and in Osborne's – if one is to judge from his autobiography – to anger ('I am ashamed of her,' he wrote, 'as part of myself that can't be cast out'). Both had an older sister who died young; both could cut out women who had once been close to them, like a ritual blood-letting. In most other respects they were very different: Ken, an enthusiast and university wit, John Osborne, a demolition expert and an intuitive artist. Nor were they particularly close.

When Ken first met Osborne he described him as lean and driven, and something of a peacock in dress. Osborne knew Ken by his Oxford reputation, and admired him for being the 'devil king' to 'the so-called lilac Establishment'. He was grateful for the good review, although he later described it as 'the most hedging rave ever written' because of the 'best *young* play of its decade'. Over the years their barbed friendship was occasionally chilly. After Ken's death, however, Osborne described him as the best critic since Shaw with a remarkable inside feeling for the theatre.

Ken formed a much closer friendship with Kenneth Haigh, *Look Back in Anger*'s trumpet-playing Jimmy Porter. Shortly after the première, Haigh received a telephone call from the *Observer*'s drama critic, who asked him over and announced, 'I'm taking trumpet lessons.'

By July, and at the end of the 1956 theatre season, Ken was feeling, for a change, distinctly optimistic. Apart from the Royal Court, there were other good things in London: a new play by Michael Hastings about James Dean, and *The Quare Fellow*, Brendan Behan's Irish masterpiece set in an Ulster prison, where one of its inmates is about to be hanged. Here he found language 'out on a spree, ribald, dauntless and spoiling for a fight'. It was the best advertisement for Joan Littlewood's group that he had so far found.

What Ken saw in these wildly disparate dramatists was a similar attitude to life. 'Their mistrust of authority is coupled with a passionate respect for the sanctity of the individual.'

12

Involved, Committed, Engaged

In October 1955, Ken had advertised for a 'large flat near the West End, rent around £500 p.a.'. He found exactly what he wanted and, with financial help from his mother, moved into 120 Mount Street, Mayfair. This was a high-ceilinged Edwardian apartment laid out around a circular lift-well. 'Two enormous rooms for parties', as Elaine Dundy described it, 'then a long sort of passageway where Tracy could sleep so that we wouldn't disturb her so much.' Somewhere down that passageway was an au pair, and a kitchen which was rarely used.

One book-filled room was painted an evil black, furnished with a record player and a good deal of fifties furniture of the spindly-legged sort, the type that prompted one guest to say, 'My God, look at that chair! It looks as if it just refused that coffee table.'

On one wall of the adjacent living-room was a large blow-up of Hieronymus Bosch's *Garden of Earthly Delights*, which Tracy Tynan (a well-mannered, grave little girl, with dark-brown eyes and a fringe) described to guests as 'a weekend in paradise'.

In between the two large rooms was a small study, with an opaque glass window, where Ken worked at a typewriter on a 'utility' wood table. Two eighteenth-century bullfighting prints hung on one side of the desk, and a caricature of Henry Irving, in *The Bells*, on the other. On the back wall was a mysterious black and white blow-up which Ken would challenge his friends to identify. Was it spiral nebulae, a shaved cunt, a honeycomb, a thumbprint, or a carpet? Answer: it was the cleft of the buttocks of La Goulue.

In this study, he kept a small blue metal box of pornography. His wife one day came upon it when he was out. She found photographs of 'schoolgirls' about to be spanked by disembodied male hands, and the stuff evidently shocked her for it produced from Ken the following:

> Dear Mrs. T
> You tied to me
> The knot that never loosens
> How sad that I
> Turned out to be
> Yours truly Eugene Goossens

(The limerick referred to the recent arrest of the musician on a charge of smuggling pornography into Australia.)

Into this study Ken would go on a Friday to write his *Observer* column of 1000 to 1200 words, expanding the few notes – thoughts caught on the wing – that he had jotted on his programme during the performance. He would work through the day and into the evening – on several bottles of white wine – first on a single-spaced draft, before his finished version.

Here, after the excitement of the Royal Court's debut, Ken retired to write about critics. 'What counts is not their opinion,' whether absolutist or relativist, 'but the art with which it is expressed. They differ from the novelist', he wrote with more than a little cheek, 'only in that they take as their subject-matter life rehearsed, instead of life unrehearsed.' This comment provoked several cross readers' letters, to which Ken replied that there was no such thing as an impersonal critic.

A few weeks later, on George Bernard Shaw's centennial, he offered his thoughts on that master of righteous indignation, whose capacity for outrage was equalled by none, 'who cleared the English stage of humbug, and the English mind of cant', but who only made Ken 'qualmish' when he voiced approval. He was an Irish aunt, Ken claimed, but 'gorgeously drunk with wit'.

Each week, after he turned in his piece there would be celebration. He might buy himself a small 'Saturday present', a tie or a book, and take a friend to lunch. Very often on Sunday evenings the Tynans held open house. Elaine would look kittenish and animated, and would sometimes be dressed in leopard-skin trousers to match her husband's. Both – actors *manqués* – would be at their best. Elaine would deliver fast New Yorkish one-liners and welcome newcomers, like the young Cambridge graduate Julian Jebb, with kindness and curiosity. As the two became very friendly she began to introduce him to the world of Freud, about whom he was ignorant. 'Come on, Jebby,' Elaine said, 'get it right. There's sex and death. That's it.'

Ken loved to bring together surprising guests, to entertain them with his stories, to introduce them to new books or new records – a New York musical, or flamenco, or jazz. He used to play the album *Twisted* sung by the scat jazz singer Annie Ross, a chamber musician with a distaste for flamboyance whom he worshipped; or Bix Beiderbecke's 'Ostrich Walk'; or Paul Dessau's 'Chanson de Mère Courage'. He described his taste in music as 'eccentric, extremely bad, but highly personal'.

Elaine did not cook, so the Tynans ate out most of the time, and if guests joined them Ken usually picked up the tab. He insisted on the best restaurants, the best tickets and was rashly generous.

To Mount Street came Christopher Isherwood, who brought his young lover, Don Bachardy, to introduce him to this exemplar of cultural life. (Bachardy chiefly remembers Ken's black Italian silk suit.) Isherwood was impressed by his courage as a critic. 'Hasn't anybody ever hit you?' he asked.

To Mount Street came Derek Prouse and Harold Lang, where they would work on a continuing fantasy about a card-carrying lesbian writer modelled on Naomi Jacobs. The real Miss Jacobs spoke in a deep ruminative Yorkshire baritone, '*slairtly* spoiled by gentility', as Ken described it. She had first been sighted on a troop ship by Lang. More precisely he had heard her voice booming: 'Steward, steward, where's my shaving water?'

There was no nonsense about Mic, as she was called. 'Went to see this play by a man called Ibsen. *Wild Duck*. Seemed to be about a little girl who falls in love with a dead duck. Couldn't make head or tail of it.' The Tynan gang would take off from there, improvising wild and lewd fantasies on the theme of Mic Jacobs. They were all the more astonished when, on asking her to play herself for a radio version, she readily and quite innocently accepted. *The Quest for Corbett* by Ken and Harold Lang was broadcast in 1956 and published in 1960.

In the early summer of 1956, while Elaine was away in America, Ken had an affair with a successful young writer called Elizabeth Jane Howard, whose novel *The Long View* had just appeared. She was statuesque, blonde and liked to cook; and she was perfectly amenable to ending the relationship on Elaine's return. Though she loved Ken, she was not in love with him, nor he with her. 'I felt he'd probably never been in love, but liked to play with ideas of what it might be.'

During that hot summer Miss Howard frequently wore a white dress, the only decent dress she had. Ken told her, 'You *would* wear white.' He explained that she wore it 'to attract attention to us'.

She felt about her lover that he *designed* his life (an arrangement which his schoolfriends had noted many years before), knowing exactly what he was going to do and with whom he was going to be. 'We stayed in his frightfully uncomfortable flat, all pitch black and meant for living at night, as though fit for a bat in a cave. It seemed he'd had an intricate idea as a child of what being a grown-up would be like and had jolly well stuck to it.'

Ken did not seem to Elizabeth Jane Howard to have reached maturity. She surmised that growing old would be hard for him, that 'the compensations which other people discover, or collect, would not be his. He'd just fight it all the way, hate it.' Though she found him immensely attractive, she also thought he was sexually insecure, guilty about things that he enjoyed or wanted, as if he felt there was something wrong with him. 'I could never quite see why he needed to feel that way.'

Ken never talked about his past, nor about Elaine. He had none of the novelist's preoccupation with looking back or wondering what was going to happen next. He lived in the present. 'I remember him dancing about with nothing on doing "The Rain in Spain", from *My Fair Lady*, which had recently opened. And I can never hear that music without thinking of Ken.'

On Elaine's return from the States, the affair ended, and the married couple took off for Barcelona and the bulls. They stayed with John and Sue Marquand in a rented house on the Costa Brava where the Marquands, and Elaine, had to listen to Ken's plans for leaving home and striking out. They knew he was not going to do it. Sue Marquand would say, 'You're not going to break up. It's ridiculous. Let's talk about something else.'

And so they would go in search of entertainment. Living nearby was the novelist Robert Ruark, much influenced by Hemingway, and a big-game hunter. He had lions, elephants and other trophies on display and he would take guests on a tour of his house, always ending up before a minute antelope that looked like an overgrown rodent. This creature had horns about as big as a fingernail, and the host would say, 'That's the prize, that's the prize dik-dik. These are record horns.' He'd add, 'It was something I had to shoot.'

'Ken had a way with people like that,' John Marquand explains. 'He had to go back and have the tour over and over just so he could hear about the dik-dik. He would say, "Ruark!" The very name sounds like a goose rising from the marsh at dawn.'

That summer, while Ken and John Marquand were on their own in Valencia, Ken found a nightclub whose sign read 'Uninterrupted Dancing'. They went in and picked up two whores, paid off the Guardia Civil and took the girls back to the hotel. The next morning Ken told John he had ended up doing nothing, because his girl had had a tragic family life, and anyway he 'couldn't make it with whores'.

Quite soon afterwards the Tynans departed for Málaga on the south coast. There they visited, for the first time, Bill and Annie Davis at La Cónsula in Churriana. American expatriates of considerable means, this civilized couple entertained at their colonnaded marble house. Cyril Connolly was the house writer and master of ceremonies, who would take charge of the table placements and see to it that certain guests were asked only for a swim before lunch, whereas others would qualify for lunch as well. He had been responsible for inviting the Tynans.

Ken had been quoting Connolly's melancholic and pleasure-loving maxims since he had read *The Unquiet Grave* while at school, and he had been suitably awed by the dictum that 'the true function of a writer is to produce a masterpiece, and that no other task is of any consequence'. Two years earlier he had written a profile of the literary mandarin in which he described his 'pink child's face', 'slack jowls' and 'somewhat sour, blank eyes'.

More recently Ken had become friendly with Connolly and after a missed luncheon had sent a letter of apology blaming a heavy hangover and an evening out with Ava Gardner and six enthusiastic flamenco players. 'Miss Gardner,' Ken wrote by way of excuse, 'whom I hardly know, is a convivial girl and not easily discouraged when she gets the smell of riot in her nostrils, and I allowed myself to be swept in an open car twice across London with her engaging entourage, which was joined at odd times by a policeman and a rich swimmer ... on whose presence Miss Gardner insisted, saying that a party wasn't a party without a drunken bitch lying in a pool of tears.'

At La Consula in 1956 Connolly could be found, very fat and wearing an unbecoming fake leopard-skin bathing suit. He hated bullfighting and when the houseguests returned from the *corrida* he once raised his head from his newspaper and enquired, 'Did you read about the bull in Barcelona yesterday? Didn't want to die. *Wouldn't take his medicine.* They had to give him black banderillas.'

On 27 August 1956 the Berliner Ensemble began a three-week season in London. A few weeks before this first British tour, Brecht died of a stroke. His last instructions, pinned to the noticeboard of his theatre in East Berlin, were a warning to his company about the language barrier and the fact that the English would expect of German art something heavy and pedestrian. 'So our playing needs to be quick, light, strong. This is not a question of hurry, but of speed, not simply of quick playing, but of quick thinking.... The audience has to see that here are a number of artists working together as a collective in order to convey stories, ideas, virtuoso feats to the spectator by a common effort.'

'There speaks the practical Brecht, whom actors loved,' Ken wrote. He read the plays in translation, where they were available, and in German where not. On 2 September his review of *The Caucasian Chalk Circle*, *Mother Courage* and *Trumpets and Drums* (the Ensemble's adaptation of Farquhar's *The Recruiting Officer*) appeared in the *Observer*. 'Brecht's actors do not behave like Western actors,' he decided. 'They neither bludgeon us with personality nor woo us with charm; they look shockingly like people, real potato-faced people such as one might meet in a bus queue. Humanity itself, not the exceptional eccentric, is what their theatre exists to explore.' This from an 'exceptional eccentric' comes as something of a surprise. But the reader soon discovers that it was Brecht's skill in the theatre that had won Ken, the 'snow-white glow' of the impartial lighting, and the grouping. 'The beauty of Brechtian settings is not of the dazzling kind that begs for applause,' Ken explained. 'It is the more durable beauty of *use*.' He examined the alienation effect, designed to counter-balance the rhetoric of German classical acting, and he admitted that Brecht's 'rejection of false emotions sometimes means that the baby is poured out with the bath-water: the tight-wire of tension slackens so much that the actors fall off.' But the method was invaluable as a corrective, bringing 'the wide canvas and the eagle's-eye view back to a theatre hypnotised by keyhole impressionism and worm's-eye foreshortening'.

Of Helene Weigel's performance as Mother Courage he wrote, 'We are to observe but not to embrace her.' But,

Twice, and agonisingly, she moves us: once by the soundless cry which doubles her up when she hears her son being executed and again when, to avoid incriminating herself, she must pretend not to recognise his body. She walks towards it, wearing a feigned, frozen smile that does not budge from her lips until she has stared at the body, shaken her head and returned to her seat. Then her head slumps and we see, collapsed and petrified, the sad stone face of grief.

Ken felt nothing but contempt for the majority of his fellow critics, who were bored and annoyed by the Ensemble, or who wrote it off as old-hat Expressionism. He gave a party for the troupe at Mount Street, and came to know Weigel, Brecht's widow, who was director of the theatre and chief keeper of the flame. He liked her gaunt face, nut brown and high cheek-boned like a Spanish peasant, and he found her seductive and uncompromising. She in turn, according to her daughter, 'had a flirt on with Ken you wouldn't believe'.

In September 1956 Ken went to Berlin for the first time, where he discovered that theatrical freedom went hand in hand with subsidy – both in the East and the West. In West Berlin he witnessed 'the most drastic experience the theatre has ever given me': the German première of *The Diary of Anne Frank*. In New York he had felt the play smacked of exploitation, but in Berlin the stricken and silent audience redeemed it. At its finish there was no applause, and no curtain calls. With Ken was Helene Weigel, herself a Jew. After the performance she wept. Lee Strasberg, of the Actors' Studio, also in the audience, asked her if it was not encouraging that such a play could be done in Germany. But she shook her head and said firmly, 'I know my dear Germans. They would do this again. Tomorrow.'

In November Ken went to see the Royal Court production, directed by George Devine, of Brecht's *The Good Woman of Setzuan*, and tried to grapple with the complicated business of ends and means. He now changed his view of Brecht's alienation effect: 'At every turn emotion floods through. More and more one sees Brecht as a man whose feelings were so violent that he needed a theory to curb them' – a comment which aptly described Ken's own temperament: he needed a scheme by which he could analyse the world. To those of his readers interested in fundamental human problems he recommended the play. Though the problems with which it was concerned might appear irrelevant in the prosperous West, 'they are still cruelly relevant to more than half the inhabited world'.

In January 1957 Ken was back in Berlin for *The Life of Galileo*, the first new production of the Ensemble since the death of its leader. In this study of the social responsibility of the intellectual, Galileo defines knowledge as 'the product of doubt', and the 'art of doubt' as the only progressive art. But the protagonist muffles his doubts and compromises with authority, in this case with the Church (as Brecht compromised – Ken pointed out – with the East German Communists): 'By allying himself to one falsehood, Galileo implicitly allies himself to a hundred.' In the second half of the play Brecht develops the view that all living thought is sooner or later social thought, and the critic explained how the playwright puts theatrical flesh on this idea.

With that review, the first phase of Ken's education in Brecht ended. A passionate convert to his theatre, and a fellow traveller alongside his socialism, Ken became the most effective publicist for the German writer in the English-speaking world, a role which he was to refine and develop for twenty years.

The work of another playwright with a social conscience had been on show in London in the autumn of 1956 – Arthur Miller's *A View from the Bridge*. In a profile for the *Observer*, Ken wrote about Miller's 'stern, Ibsenite heritage' and his lack of patience for the split between psychology and politics. 'Miller's theatre has one aim, strict, firm and simple: to present, in his own words "Man as the creature of society, and at the same time as its creator."'

A month after the play's opening Miller took part in a symposium called 'Cause Without a Rebel', chaired by Ken, on the state of English drama. (His wife, Marilyn Monroe, sat intently in the audience.) Miller said that British drama seemed to be 'hermetically sealed against the way the society moves', but he praised *Look Back in Anger* for throwing light on life, and for being involved.

'Involved', 'committed' and 'engaged' were now words on every young intellectual's lips. These concepts were inextricably connected to radical protest, which was all the sharper because of the political events of that autumn. In July President Nasser of Egypt had nationalized the Suez Canal. In November an Anglo-French force launched its disastrous invasion (it was in the same month that the Russians successfully crushed the uprising in Budapest).

The *Observer* came out with a strong attack on the Suez adventure and a call for the resignation of the Prime Minister, Sir Anthony Eden. A huge political demonstration against the government, the first of its kind since before the war, marched from Trafalgar Square to Downing Street. The angry young men had at last found a brave cause to fight for, and were out *en masse*. The poet Christopher Logue came upon an outraged Ken pinioned by a mounted policeman in Whitehall, and complaining loudly that 'This horse is *still* on my foot!'

In the pages of the *New Statesman, Tribune, Universities and Left Review, Sight and Sound* and the theatre monthly *Encore*, these protesters could be heard. John Berger gathered together a group of them (including Ken) to form the Geneva Club in an attempt to work out ideas for a New Left alliance in the wake of Hungary. *Sight and Sound* interviewed Ken, Osborne, Amis, Iris Murdoch and Berger, to find out whether 'the artist can ignore the social conditions of his time'. Now committed to socialism (however subjectively interpreted) Ken answered surprisingly moderately: 'Art that turns its back on life is uncivilised in the exact meaning of the word. Whether the artist should have a fixed political attitude depends entirely on his ability to prevent it from impairing his vision. If it excludes pity and irony I should say it was evil; if not, not.'

Across the Channel could be found, in the early months of 1957, a season of interesting international drama, including a fortnight of Brecht. While in Paris, Ken pounced on Brecht's illustration of the difference between the drama of the past and the drama of the future. The playwright had noticed in a news picture of the great Tokyo earthquake that most of the houses were smashed, but a few modern buildings remained. The caption read, 'Steel stood.' 'If you compare that', said Brecht, 'with the elder Pliny's description of the eruption of Etna, you will grasp what I mean. To reflect calamity is nowadays not enough for drama. Its task is to show how to survive it.' Ken picked up this dictum and called it loudly through his next reviews (still insisting that the *critic's* concern should be with his art rather than with his opinions, yet making other demands upon the dramatist).

Then, for the first time in his career on the *Observer*, a new notion seemed to cloud his vision, rather than to light it. He described the world première of Samuel Beckett's *Fin de partie* (at the Royal Court) as a work of despair. Where he had found human affirmation in *Waiting for Godot*, he now could find only mean-spirited solipsism. 'There, says Beckett, stamping on the face of mankind; there, that is how life is. And when protest is absent,' Ken added, 'the step from "how life is" to "how life should be" is horrifyingly short.' In the thirty-odd years since *Endgame* first played, audiences have found it to be a stoical, sometimes funny and often moving play about making do with very little, about survival in a disrupted and rootless world. Ken, on the other hand, thought the play was an 'allegory about authority, an attempt to dramatise the neurosis that makes men love power', a view as off-centre as the idea that *King Lear* is a mere 'allegory of authority'.

Sounding more like a cultural commissar than his usual self, he accused Beckett's *Acte sans paroles* (which accompanied the première of *Fin de partie*) of 'facile pessimism' and described it as 'the projection of a personal sickness'. His lock, to use his own conceit, did not match the key.

His next review of a play by Beckett was a parody of *Krapp's Last Tape*; he called it 'Slamm's Last Knock', and Beckett fared even worse.

Peacock's Penny Bazaar, 1910

The Mayor and Lady Peacock at a Christmas party for poor children

...e, Peter and Ken, 1927

...Peter Peacock and Ken, ...4

...e and May Tynan

Ken on holiday in Bournemouth

With his father in Bournemouth

Peter and Ken

The schoolboy

Ken (front row, first left)

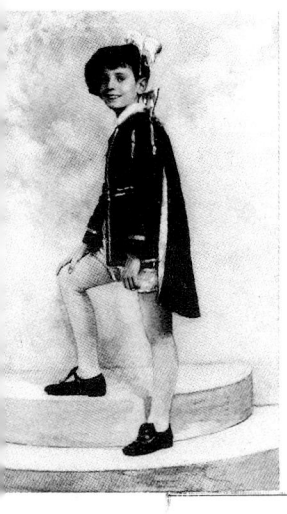

K.E. SIXTH-FORMERS SEE THE WORLD IN AN AGATE SETTING

TELLING' POINT FOR STUDENTS

Critic Agate puts over a telling point in his address to sixth formers of the King Edward Foundation at Birmingham to-day.

Wife said t
her hus
al

line and Ken, August
5

Mercury Productions, Inc.

ORSON WELLES   JACK MOSS

April 29, 1943

Mr. Kenneth P. Tynan,
229, Portland Road
Edgbaston
Birmingham, 17
England

Dear Mr. Tynan:

It is difficult for me to tell you how mightily cheered and heartened I was by your kind letter, and what you said about "The Magnificent Ambersons" particularly made me happy. While I was away in South America, the studio cut it without my knowledge or consent, and released it before I could work on it. The picture suffered from all this meddling, but your letter makes me feel the result perhaps wasn't as disastrous as I'd feared.

Again, many thanks, and all good wishes.

Sincerely,

Orson Welles

er from Orson Welles,
3

Ken as Hamlet, 1945

While at Oxford (1945-48) Tynan: ———

produced "Sweeney Agonistes" (T.S. Eliot), winning the Experimental Theatre Club
   Contest and the British Drama League Regional Competition (Summer 1946)
was Dramatic Critic of the "Isis" (1946)
restarted and co-edited "The Cherwell" (1946-47)
produced "A Toy in Blood" (his own adaptation of "Hamlet") (Autumn 1946)
produced the "Medea" of Euripides (Autumn 1946)
contributed regularly to "The Isis" and "Oxford Viewpoint" (1946-48)
played Bishop Nicholas in [................................] by Ibsen (Spring 1947)
played Pelléas in Experime[...................................] "Mélisande" (1947)
produced "Samson Agonistes" [.........................] Church (Summer 1947)
played Holofernes in O.U. [...................................] mmer 1947)
contributed to "The Oxford [..............................]
was President of O.U. Ex[..........................] 47)
wrote material for and ap[.....................] (1947-8)
served on Oxford Union [.................]
served on Oxford Union [.................]
was elected Secretary of [.................]
produced and played Tu[.................] C.' "Winterset" by Max
   Anderson, by both [.................] 1948)
produced and played the Ghost in Oxford University Players' First Quarto "Ham"
   at Cheltenham and London. (1948)
played, at various times, Iago in "Othello", Granillo in "Rope", Fear in
   O.U.D.S. "Masque of Hope" presented for Princess Elizabeth, Courtsnoss in
   "The Castle of Perseverance" in Oxford, London, Bath, and Exeter.
spoke at the Cambridge Union; appeared in revues presented at the
   Cambridge Footlights Club and at the Playhouse, London.
contributed to "Mandrake", "Autumn Harvest" and other periodicals.
edited "Avant-garde", an Oxford broadsheet.
threw parties for the Old Vic Company, "Anna Lucasta", Gertrude Lawrence,
   and himself.
got a second in the Honours School of English Language and Literature.

14 May 1947

THE ISIS

ISIS

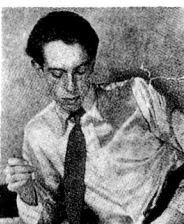

Photo.]   [*Linton Westmoreland.*
Kenneth Peacock Tynan

IDOL

12th February, 1947

THE ISIS

11

HE was born in 1923, but isn't sure where. Somewhere in London, he ... 1945 he ... F., and ... o Pen... her facts ... re swal... he pun... ality. It ... at him; ... dealist; ... t who ... ror and ... sy; but ... ed into ... was like ... t othe...

Photo]   [*Linton Westmoreland.*
ALAN BEESLEY

hour, and are then renewed. **Alan wears** things out quickly, including himself. He lights his candle at both ends: tremulous, hypnotic flames which he snuffs regretfully, always just before both ends meet. While it burns, and you are with the subjective, not the objective Alan, you are mesmerized by that relentless personality—so shaming and humiliating that it might be tangible. You even put out a wary hand. But then the reverie ends, and you see that Alan is yards away from you, staring past the fire into his thoughts.

To his confusion, he finds himself constantly attended by friends, willing and hoping to help him through the imbrangl...

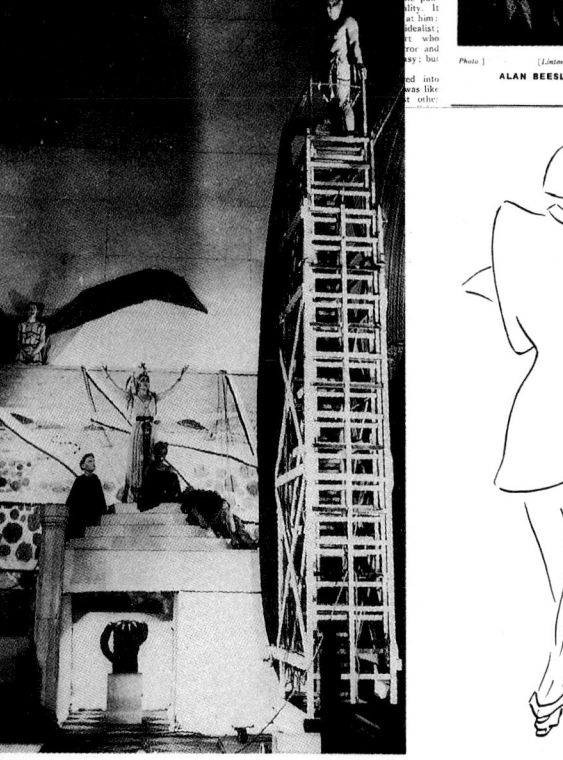

Le Chef de la troupe.
Winterset.

(Left) Oxford revue

Revue Review

"R ITZY, Regal and Super" hardly describes the standard of what Wardour Street would call the "montaj" of the E.T.C.'s latest frolic, for the revue was above all else "intimate" in the most interestingly suggestive sense of the word. The mixture was, to be sure, colourful enough and sufficiently sweet to appeal to the unitiated spiced with a new tartness which may particular to Sandy Wilson and his c but which we like to think is an integr ant of contemporary Oxford's sense of

Not much escapes Sandy Wilson eye. The dilatory Oxford waitress, th in-the-guts school of film drama, the hot-house exoticism of Oxford's most expensive stamping-ground (the title of which sketch, by the way, seemed more than vaguely familiar, not to mention some of the obvious of hem-line, th were parodi of the incon humour, and our toes in the "Oklah standard of which we d while straw

In an g vidual perfo persistent p an irresis innuendo ; (which dese Bottom at breath-takin uneasy abo Robert Hel shoulder!") and our fairy god-fathers in Drury Lane, all of which was very funny indeed. So far as personal allusions are concerned, Cherwell suf fered no more knocks than did Auntie if that "tributary" crack did smart m and we are convinced that Tony School of our only suit and favourite tie in Marriage" was the purest of coinciden

For the rest, from the delicious Corinne Hunt to Robin Bishop's mortises and tenons, we can find

(Right) Ken (centre) as Holofernes in *Love's Labours Lost*

(Bottom) *Winterset*: Ken as Judge Gaunt (centre)

Paris: Thirty members of the E.T.C. will give one performance of 'Winterset' on 15 March.

Disengagement: 'Any altar I might lead you to would be purely sacrificial.'

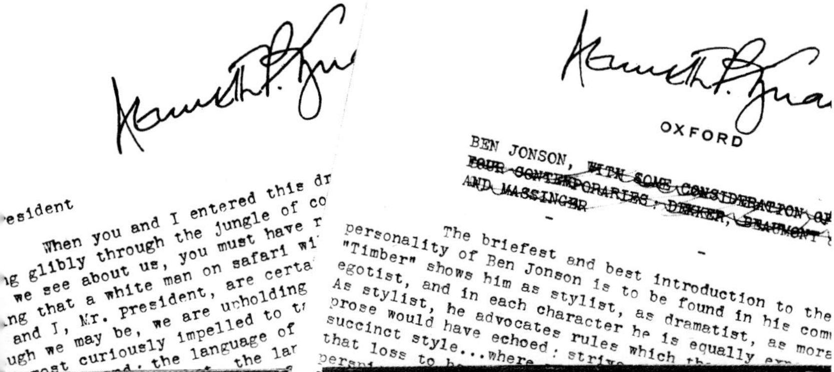

~~BEN JONSON, WITH SOME CONSIDERATION OF FOUR CONTEMPORARIES: DEKKER, BEAUMONT AND MASSINGER~~

When you and I entered this dr
g glibly through the jungle of co
we see about us, you must have r
ng that a white man on safari wi
and I, Mr. President, are certa
ugh we may be, we are upholding
ost curiously impelled to t
d; the language of the lar

The briefest and best introduction to the
personality of Ben Jonson is to be found in his com
"Timber" shows him as stylist, as dramatist, as more
egotist, and in each character he is equally ex
As stylist, he advocates rules which th
prose would have echoed; striv
succinct style...where
that loss to h

Jill Rowe-Dutton (Centre right) Committee of the Ken's twenty-first birthday. 2
Oxford Union. 1947 April 1948

(Top row) Ken directing *Man of the World*, 1950

(Centre) Eric Bentley and Ken at Salzburg, 1950, and directing Claire Bloom in *Martine*, 1952

(Bottom) As the Player King with Alec Guinness in his *Hamlet*, 1951, and directing *The Beaux' Stratagem*, 1949

Ken's critics began to accuse him of being doctrinaire, of taking a theoretical line on sex or economics. Yet, with the exception of Beckett, when reviewing plays worthy of his attention – as opposed to talking on platforms or writing outside the theatre – Ken almost always had a strong enough sense of the uniqueness of the experience not to overload it with ideology. He wrote that the shortest way to bad playwriting was to start with 'a grand purpose'. He understood that the genesis of good plays was rarely ever abstract but something as 'concrete and casual as a glance intercepted, a remark over-heard or an insignificant news item buried at the bottom of page three'.

The week after the opening of *Fin de partie* in April 1957, the Royal Court delivered another première, Osborne's *The Entertainer*, set during Suez and featuring a family of run-down vaudevillians as a microcosm of contemporary England. Within the limits of the play, which Ken considered to be Osborne's failure to explain and account for its protagonist's desperation, was 'one of the great acting parts of our age', a part which Laurence Olivier, with his canny sense of survival, had magnificently taken on.

A month later Ken was in New York, to welcome José Quintero's production of Eugene O'Neill's *Long Day's Journey into Night*, the posthumously received experiment in autobiography written out of 'a terrible need to forgive his parents, his elder brother and even, perhaps, himself for the pain they inflicted on each other'.

It was the more disappointing to return to England and discover that directors as excellent as Peter Brook and Peter Hall were busy resurrecting minor Shakespeare. Repudiating his youthful enthusiasm for sensationalism, Ken wished that Laurence Olivier (as Titus Andronicus) had set himself a larger task than 'a versified atrocity report'.

But the theatre season overall had been exciting, and Ken had 'performed well', as the literary editor Terence Kilmartin would declare on a particularly good week. David Astor was delighted. He had already told Ken how terribly proud he was that he had associated the *Observer* with Brecht so prominently. In August 1957 he persuaded his drama critic to take up the contract for a further three years. 'Apart from lending a great brilliance and integrity to the paper, you have also been a wonderfully helpful colleague.' Ken wrote back to say that he had often felt as if he were walking on eggshells, so that it was encouraging to discover that 'in spite of my fears none got broken'.

Astor thought it wise to keep his distance from his volatile young critic, though often, over the years, he regretted this self-imposed deprivation. On one occasion, passionately disagreeing with Ken's point of view, he wrote a pseudonymous letter of complaint to his own paper. He would never have openly censored one of his staff.

Ken would sweep in once a week to deliver his copy, and the next morning he would come in to make corrections on the 'stone'. Kilmartin rarely tampered with the piece. 'You could quarrel with his views, but his prose was so beautiful.' One Saturday, struggling to caption a review of Ken's on *The Wild Duck*, due out on a Christmas day, he asked for help. 'Christmas Quacker!' shouted Ken over his shoulder, without a moment's pause, as he rushed off for a Saturday lunch, or in search of his 'Saturday present'.

13

Raised Voices

With Ken's career thriving, and his wife's writing career not yet launched, the marriage became more acrimonious. The Tynan rows became famous in London, embarrassing everybody except the principal players. Ken's secretary would never know, on arrival in the morning, whether she would find a broken window or some other sign of violence, although her employers, by that time, might well be behaving like a couple of honeymooners. One of these women, Ann Head, concluded that 'ordinary life was not Ken's thing'. The secretary was expected to bring her boss coffee in the late morning, to take dictation, to keep his diary of coming events and to deal with bills (mostly paid by Ken, though Elaine made generous contributions). No secretary ever found him less than thoughtful and kind. The au pairs, however, would leave regularly, unable to tolerate the domestic dramas; on each occasion Tracy would feel that she was responsible and mourn the loss of the friendship.

At the back of Ken's diary for 1957 is a list of some twenty women whom he would call upon to accompany him to the theatre when Elaine could not, or would not, go with him. One of these was a young American called Sally Belfrage, very blonde and very bright, whose father Cedric Belfrage, a left-wing victim of McCarthy, had recently been deported. Sally was 'collected' by both Ken and Elaine, and she became one of Ken's theatre-going second-stringers, intrigued by his unflagging wit and perceptiveness. Inevitably the following morning Elaine would telephone to invite her to lunch to find out what had happened. But Sally never slept with Ken. She would meet Elaine in the late morning at the French Club or the Colony and from there they would move on, 'drinking, drinking drinking, picking up people and dis-carding them', until the late afternoon. They would take up with the steady daily drunks, and the fly-by-night day people who had 'come in and out and been sort of wrung out for their amusement value and then discarded as if they were yesterday's newspapers'. Elaine was always very generous about introducing people, making contact. 'She would be full of wisecracks, and she'd keep the ball up in the air. It never fell down, not for a long while. When it fell, some years later, oh boy.' They would go back to Mount Street late in the afternoon, and then out to dinner with Ken, until three or four in the morning.

It would take me about a week to rest up. But Ken and Elaine were at it again the next day. There was this frenzied, feverish activity all the time, and there was never any pause to allow anyone to think, to reflect what it was about. The essential thing was to keep moving in as many crowds of amusing people as possible. For me being with them was thrilling, like a very fast tennis match.

A typical scene would be to arrive at the door of the Mount Street apartment, where the locks had usually just been changed by one or other of the Tynans. There were locks from floor to ceiling on the front door. Ring the bell, sounds of screams and smashing crockery, and tiny Tracy opening the door, trying to find which lock was working. Ken shouting, 'I'll kill you, you bitch.' Smash, smash, and whimpers from the nanny, and Tracy absolutely poised and calm, saying 'Hello, how nice to see you. Come in. Can I take your coat?' And taking one into the living-room, and pouring drinks and sitting down, looking very interested. She was such an extraordinary child. She made everyone feel as if this pandemonium in the background was supposed to be going on.

When Elaine drank too much, Ken would be embarrassed and protective, sometimes putting her in a taxi to get her home, sometimes trying to ignore it. One night Elaine showed up at Sandy Wilson's after a row, shortly followed by Ken, and Wilson wrote in his diary, 'Nothing like a visit from the Tynans to bolster up one's own security.'

Close friends of the Tynans would be called by one party or the other to listen to their grievances. One day Elaine arrived with Tracy at the house of their friend Lady St Just, declaring that she couldn't stand things. Then the doorbell rang and there was Ken, recalled Lady St Just, 'absolutely livid, in a mackintosh. "I've been next door to the police, and I'm having you arrested for abducting my wife and child. Where are they?" And I said, "Don't be so stupid, Ken, they're in the kitchen. Why don't you come in and have some tea?" So he took his mackintosh off, rather gloomily, and came in and had some cake. In about five minutes we were all having a lovely time.'

So why did they stay together? 'I think they stayed together because they got used to it,' says Maria St Just, 'the same way you get used to any kind of love relationship. I don't think Elaine has ever got over it.'

Another visitor, the screenwriter Jay Presson Allen, who had travelled in Spain with the Tynans, found their rows both depressing and stimulating. 'Both of them seemed to be looking for some abstract legitimacy that they could never find in one another. Elaine had this inchoate ambition, which really had to do with a kind of frenzy. She'd get up real close to you and say,

"I think Tyrone Power is the most attractive man in the world, don't you?", all in one breath, without context, and you'd say, "No." '

Sometimes at Mount Street guests would find she had scrawled angry words with her lipstick on the bathroom mirror, and they would remember that in the early years of the marriage she had lipsticked on other mirrors 'I love Ken'.

Sally Belfrage remembers one night at Mount Street: 'All the guests weaving in and out, and Elaine trying to take her clothes off, which she tended to do. And Ken wandering around like a ghost saying, "The trouble is I don't love her. The trouble is I don't love her." '

On 20 July 1957, Ken left Elaine to meet Carol Saroyan in Spain. He told her that he had asked Elaine for a divorce. In London the following day Elaine gave an impromptu party to announce the end of the marriage, and sent detectives in hot pursuit of her husband.

After a few days spent at the Palace Hotel in Madrid, the couple moved on to the feria of Valencia, where Ken began to feel pangs of guilt. Fearful that his wife would instigate divorce proceedings and that his career would suffer, he telephoned Elaine to say he would be coming home. One night as he and Carol Saroyan lay talking in the dark, she said, 'Someone burly just came in.' Ken shot up like a bolt, and the burly person who had just come in said, 'I'm very sorry but I'm Mr O'Sullivan representing Mrs Tynan.' So ended the romance. Ken took Carol by bus to Barcelona and said, 'Please don't let this ruin it.' Years later he recorded the event in his journal and added: 'And so I went back to seven more years of the inferno with Elaine.'

Carol Saroyan sent a cable to her best friend, Gloria Vanderbilt, which read, 'The pain in Spain comes mainly from Elaine,' and then she flew off to Geneva to take refuge with her other best friend, Oona Chaplin.

Ken was reconciled with Elaine at the Davises' house in the south of Spain. One night in the early hours, he was in the kitchen of La Cónsula with his hostess when Elaine stormed in stark naked and angry. Ken said, 'I was just making you some supper,' and he presented her with a plate of eggs and bacon. 'She took the plate and threw it on the floor,' Annie Davis recalled, 'and she stomped off. Ken drew himself up and said, "Of course, we will leave tomorrow." It was Ken who surprised me, and not Elaine coming in naked.'

Elaine had begun to write, spurred on by Ken, and she would leave Mount Street and go and work on her novel in the Grill and Cheese, which was part of Lyons Corner House in Coventry Street. Her friend Cyril Connolly told her she was incapable of developing her characters, that they were one-dimensional. And when people asked him if her book would be any good he would say, 'Oh I shouldn't think so, just another wife trying to prove she exists.' But he was wrong.

In January 1958 *The Dud Avocado* came out, its title inspired by Sandy

Wilson's effort to grow avocados from stones. He had complained that one of these was a dud and Ken told Elaine, 'There's the title for your novel.'

The reviews of the novel were excellent – 'as delightful and delicate an examination of how it is to be twenty and in love and in Paris as I've read'. 'Witty', 'brilliant' and 'scandalous' wrote the critics. The book became a bestseller; the balance in the marriage was somewhat altered. 'She was no longer Kenneth Tynan's American wife, Whatsername,' observes Gore Vidal, a great admirer of Elaine.

Vidal was in England at the time, writing scripts for MGM, and since Ken was script-editor on an adjacent lot, at Ealing Studios, the two would drive out to Elstree together. Ken was deeply impressed by Vidal's ability to deliver perfect paragraphs, with exemplary phrasing, at eight in the morning.

Ken's job had come about as a result of an article he had written, in the summer of 1955, on Ealing, that breeding ground of *The Lavender Hill Mob*, *The Man in the White Suit* – comedies, many of them set in bomb sites and in pubs, whose style Ken labelled 'patriotic neo-realism'. The studio was run by a benevolent patriarch called Sir Michael Balcon, who read Ken's piece, and in the spring of 1956 took him on as script adviser for £2000 a year. Ken hoped to be able 'to act as a pipeline for the sort of blood transfusion I thought the British cinema needed'. He had no way of knowing, as director Sandy Mackendrick recalls, 'the very subtle way Balcon would frustrate him'.

Two years later Ken resigned from Ealing in bitterness. The studio had, in its last dying years, turned out a bunch of mummified films. The pictures they had *not* made, suggested by Ken, included the following: Cecil Woodham-Smith's devastating study of the Crimean War, *The Reason Why* (*The Charge of the Light Brigade*); Joyce Carey's *The Horse's Mouth*; William Golding's *Lord of the Flies*; an original script by Lindsay Anderson about life in a casualty ward of a London hospital. These projects, sometimes in an advanced state of production, were dropped by Ealing and were eventually made by different studios and other directors.

All his projects were abandoned except for *Nowhere to Go*. This was an adaptation, by Ken and Seth Holt, of a crime novel about betrayal. George Nader played the confidence man, Maggie Smith made her film début, and Holt directed this 'least Ealing film ever made', as Charles Barr described it in a recent study of Ealing. He writes that *Nowhere to Go* 'offers a crime story which is neither police-centered nor moralistic ... made with the creative enjoyment of film as a medium which, apart from Mackendrick ... 'fifties Ealing entirely lacks'.

Ealing gave Ken his first major chance to explore his talents as an impresario and screenwriter, and his first taste of the awful frustration that comes when you are not your own boss.

During the summer of 1957 Ken supervised the final arrangements for the *Observer* play competition to encourage new work. Then he returned to the business of current theatrical ills. He complained about cloakrooms, programmes and having to stand for the National Anthem. He complained that the Arts Council annual theatre grant of £71,000 was but one-fifth of the French government grant to the Comédie Française alone. He told Benn Levy, at the Arts Council, to go and see Joan Littlewood's actors, 'who look and behave like unobserved, uninhibited human beings'. He was photographed, dressed in mourning, at the National Theatre site in a mock service of remembrance for that non-existent building.

Ken developed this theme and others in a long hotchpotch of a personal essay, part of a collection of position papers by young writers (among them Doris Lessing and John Osborne) on their work in relation to contemporary society. The publisher presented *Declaration* as the voice of the angry young men (stealing the famous tag used by the Royal Court's press officer), though the group was not of one mind.

Ken's piece was rather clumsy but influential. He argued that dramatists who want to change the world 'seldom write very subtly. Subtlety operates best in a *status quo*.... In a stormy sea only waves are visible; and we who live in imminent danger of the hydrogen tempest, need plays that are waves.... If all art is a gesture against death, it must not stand by while Cypriots are hanged, and Hungarians machine-gunned and the greater holocaust prepared. It must go on record; it must commit itself.' He wrote that healthful sex must be free of guilt and repression. Socialism ought to mean progress towards pleasure, 'a gay international affirmation'. He compared the rapturous morning exhilaration of socialist enlightenment to C. S. Lewis's description of an early Protestant's conversion: 'He feels that he has done nothing, and never could have done anything, to deserve such astonishing happiness.' Here was a religion to nurture a sense of wellbeing and self-respect.

The only other valid religion he knew was that of love, not the neurotic kind 'whereby a man spends his life seeking a partner with a wound that matches his teeth', nor the surrendering kind, nor yet *égoisme à deux*, 'where two frightened lovers build a protective wall to keep out the hostile world. ... To know yourself is the first step. To love what you know is the second. To love others as much is the third. To love one other person is the fourth and last,' he wrote. 'So ends the lesson, and we had better get back to the theatre.'

The very personal tone of this manifesto might explain why Robert Knittel at Jonathan Cape hounded Ken to write his autobiography. He wrote to say that he could think of no one else of Ken's age in England to whom he 'would or could make such a suggestion'. He offered an advance of £500, and as a possible title: 'One Score and Ten'. But Ken held back.

The disparate band of young people labelled 'angries' had one thing in common: they had come of age around the time that the grown-ups invented the hydrogen bomb. On 17 February 1958, an unexpectedly large crowd of 5000 people, which included Ken, went to the Central Hall, Westminster, for the first meeting of the Campaign for Nuclear Disarmament, constituted a month before.

The inaugural meeting prompted Ken to pen his first political letter to a newspaper, an ironic complaint addressed to the left-wing *Tribune*. The government, he maintained, had volunteered for annihilation. 'We shall go to our graves in quiet heart, secure in the knowledge that by our sacrifice we shall have made our island uninhabitable to the invading hordes.' He went on to suggest that the Royal family should be evacuated without delay. 'We would all, I feel sure, rest easier in our graves if we knew that somewhere in the world a British family survived to carry on the British traditions of civilised decency and respect for human life.'

On Good Friday Ken showed up in Trafalgar Square for the first day of the march to Aldermaston (the weapons research station forty-six miles away in Berkshire) but he did not accompany the small band of several hundred, in their duffle-coats and plastic macs, who set out on foot in the rain and snow, for the first time holding up the banner with its now famous insignia. On the Monday the weather cleared, and the small nucleus swelled to some 4000 persons for the last lap to the site. At 12.30 p.m., a taxi deposited Ken, smartly coated in tweed, at the head of the march. He stepped out with a 'Hello, hello, hello', and joined Christopher Logue and Doris Lessing for a picnic.

Ken told the politician Wayland Young that the march was not just about nuclear disarmament. 'It's about everything. It's about destroying and changing the whole structure of society.' Young did not agree at all. But CND did become the focus of many new political and social ideas and explorations; and the marches and demonstrations became platforms for the performance of beat poetry, jazz and rock music.

In the late spring of 1958, the Moscow Arts Theatre brought four productions to London, including *Uncle Vanya* and *The Cherry Orchard*. As always with seasoned masterpieces, Ken was at his best. He wrote that the English had made *The Cherry Orchard* in their own image, 'as drastically as the Germans have remade *Hamlet* in theirs'. He argued that the English had invested the play with a nostalgia for the past alien to Chekhov's world, turned his country gentry into aristocrats and falsely romanticized them. The Moscow Arts production restored the 'calm, genial sanity of the play', so that it became, as its author intended, a comedy not about 'freaks trapped in a tragic impasse' but about 'recognisable human beings in a mess'. Applying his favourite theory of comedy to this play about estrangement, he wrote that the characters are 'deaf and blind to the world outside them: which is why they are funny and also why they are appalling'. He found a Vanya who looked capable of tragedy yet 'his tragedy is that he is capable only of comedy'. And he found not verbal acting, but total acting; he reminded his readers that Konstantin Stanislavsky often made his players rehearse without words, 'to make sure that their faces and bodies were performing as well'. Ken was reassured to be told by Harold Clurman, founder of the Group Theater, that the great Russian, unlike his disciple Lee Strasberg at the Actors' Studio, was as concerned with artifice in the theatre as with affective memory and subtext.

On 22 June 1958, in a piece for the *Observer* entitled 'Ionesco: Man of Destiny', in response to the Royal Court's production of *The Chairs* and *The Lesson*, Ken let fly a warning salvo about the Romanian playwright who wrote in French, 'Founder and headmaster of "*l'école du strip-tease intellectuel, moral et social*".' Ever since the Fry–Eliot poetic revival had caved in, Ken wrote, 'the ostriches of our theatrical intelligentsia have been seeking another faith', whose enemy was realism. Here was Eugene Ionesco come along to declare that communication between human beings was impossible, and to dismiss words, 'the magic innovation of our species', as useless and fraudulent. He admitted that Ionesco could be hilarious, and even evocative, but on a second viewing profoundly tiresome. It was a theatre that led up a blind alley. What really disturbed Ken were the 'anti-humanists' who held up this type of theatre as the gateway to the future.

The following week Ionesco came to his own defence, arguing that 'a work of art has nothing to do with doctrine'. Tynan's idea of reality seemed limited to the social plane, the most superficial. Sartre, Osborne, Miller, Brecht, he claimed, were merely the new '*auteurs du boulevard*'. True society, 'the authentic human community', he wrote, is 'revealed by our common anxieties, our desires, our secret nostalgias. . . . no political system can deliver us from the pain of living, from our fear of death.' The critic's job, he insisted, was to look at a work of art and decide 'whether it is true to its own nature'.

Back came Ken to deny that he wanted drama to echo a particular creed, and to insist that all human activity had social and political repercussions. He regretted that a man so capable of stating 'a positive attitude towards art' should deny that there was any positive attitude worth taking towards life or even ('which is crucial') that there was an umbilical connection between the two. He felt that Ionesco (as he felt about Beckett) was in danger of locking himself up in that hall of mirrors known as solipsism. Both art and ideology, Ken counselled, must 'stand guard for us against chaos', and endeavour to free us from 'the rusty hegemony of Angst'.

Ken ended by rebutting Cyril Connolly's statement that 'from now on an artist will be judged only by the resonance of his solitude or the quality of his despair'. 'Not by me he won't. I shall, I hope, respond to the honesty of such testimonies; but I shall be looking for something more, something harder: for evidence of the artist who ... concerns himself from time to time, with such things as healing.'

Anxiety and healing were twin concerns of Ken – not so very removed from Ionesco's need for lightness and freedom, nor so opposed to Beckett's stubborn search, in a modern wasteland, for signs of compassion and continuity.

But no one who took part in the ensuing fuss which filled the pages of the *Observer*'s letter column and arts pages pointed this out. Philip Toynbee came forward to defend Arthur Miller against Ionesco's charge that he was an '*auteur du boulevard*', and an exemplar of left-wing conformism. Letters flowed in defending Brecht, Miller *et al.*, and advising Ionesco to study these playwrights for the 'roots of non-conventional language' and for a poetic imagination that worked on 'real patterns of individual human emotions'. George Devine, at the Royal Court, defended Ionesco's 'broader, more balanced conception of theatre as an art', while John Berger defined a political system as a means of delivering man from poverty and death.

Orson Welles entered on Ken's side to remind everyone that the critic was not telling the playwright what to do, but was attacking Ionesco's fan club. He added that 'an artist must confirm the values of his society; as he must challenge them'.

Into the fray sprang Lindsay Anderson, with a cry for art related to moral, spiritual, social and political life. N. F. Simpson, Ann Jellicoe and others weighed in. And back came Ionesco with another go at his 'courteous enemy', to defend himself against accusations of anti-realism and to beg Ken not to try to improve the lot of man.

In subsequent years the playwright has talked of the meaninglessness of things, of a 'higher order', of 'pure good and pure evil'. In other words he has been thoroughly inconsistent; but then so was Ken. In an interview with Richard Roud for *Encounter*, around the time of the great intellectual spat, he was asked why indeed he *liked* Ionesco's work, and he answered: 'Being as schizophrenic as everyone else, I am partly drawn towards the ideals of Zen Buddhism (i.e. non-thought) and partly its antithesis: i.e. progressive social thought .... It explains why I like Ionesco, and it explains why I like Brecht. I think that Brecht and Zen meet full circle ... both have tangible, concrete views of life.'

But Ken's liking of Ionesco rather paled. *Rhinoceros* turned out to be an ideological protest against totalitarianism (despite all Ionesco's strictures against political tracts), and a poor one. 'There is nothing worse than a bad social play,' Ken wrote. Later plays persuaded the critic that Ionesco was feeding him the same diet as in the early days. He wondered, off duty, whether if you had seen one Ionesco, you had seen them all; or rather if you had seen them all, you had seen one.

14

Rose Abandoned

In 1948 Ken had written about the mother in *The Glass Menagerie*: 'We despise and kneel before her, love and detest her, as her whim dictates. She swings us alternately into admiration for her devotion, pity for her clumsiness, shame at her middle-class unscrupulousness, and anger at her insensitiveness.'

As a child he had felt much the same about his own mother. But after Peter Peacock's death, he more or less turned his back on Rose and cut her out. There were class reasons, of course, and career reasons. But he always held it against her that she had failed to tell him the truth.

After Peter Peacock's death in 1948, Rose had moved into a smaller house in Pages Lane, Great Barr, white-plastered and beamed, nicely furnished with her favourite Maples mahogany and with cut-glass bowls. She was well provided for outside Sir Peter's will, and received, from interest on shares and property alone, an annual income before tax of around £1800.

Across the road in Pages Lane lived a Methodist minister and his wife, Frank and Edna Thewlis. Rose became friendly with this kind and intelligent couple, and she became an active member of their church. Frank Thewlis knew Rose's secret, was not the least bit shocked and tried to reassure her that Peter Peacock would have married her if he had been able. He found her a lovely, generous person, well spoken and nicely dressed.

The only time she was invited to London was to help take charge of Tracy when Ken and Elaine were abroad. 'She didn't understand Elaine,' according to Ken's cousin Ruth Cashmore, and thought she was responsible for keeping Ken away. Elaine, in turn, took no great interest in Ken's family.

According to the Reverend Thewlis, Rose was 'right as rain' until around 1955, when extreme loneliness and self-effacing shyness began to take its toll.

One day Ruth and her husband went to visit. 'Shush!' Rose said. 'They've got the football on. Come into the kitchen.' In the front room Ruth discovered that her aunt had set up photographs of all her family to face the television set. She would tell neighbours, while out shopping, that she had to get back 'because I've got to get their dinner on', or she'd address a photograph of Ken and say, 'Go and get your hair cut, and take that cigarette out of your mouth.' Rose would sit next to strangers in the park and complain, 'Nobody wants me, nobody cares about me.' She would offer them £50 to come home with her and allow her to make them a cup of tea.

Frank Thewlis used to go up to London to confront Ken with his lack of responsibility. Ken would feel badly and, when he saw his mother, treat her with kindness and affection.

In 1956 Thewlis moved from Birmingham to Keighley, in Yorkshire, where Rose would visit. In the spring of 1958 the police telephoned to tell the minister that they had picked up a very unkempt woman at a local station, asking for him. She was carrying a large case with a sign on it which read, 'I don't know where I'm going, but I'm going to those who love me.'

For a short period she was put into a local mental home in Birmingham. Meanwhile Ken arranged for her to be transferred as a voluntary patient to the best psychiatric hospital he could find, St Andrew's, outside Northampton. Her condition was diagnosed as organic dementia, which today, with further evidence at hand, would be described as senile dementia, Alzheimer type.

On 7 October 1958 Ken accompanied his seventy-year-old mother to the hospital. He filled out a questionnaire for the medical staff, telling them that Rose was docile, helpful, pious, though sometimes obstinate; that her tastes were '*very* simple', that she never drank, had no hobbies, other than giving parties for local children, that she was estranged from her relatives because she was the only one of them with wealth. When asked, 'Do you know of any possible causes for her mental illness?' he answered, 'Loneliness.'

To these notes the hospital added their own comments on the witness, that he was aged thirty-one, a drama critic, 'above average intelligence' with 'marked stammer and facial tic'.

Many years later Ken wrote: 'If she had come to London and lived with me in the '50s, she could have been sustained by human contact ... lacking it she degenerated. I could have postponed her death at the expense of my own absorption in self advancement. I chose not to.' He had no way of knowing that his mother's illness was caused by genetic factors.

During the summer of 1958, while he was dealing with the painful business of his mother's illness, Ken's career took a new direction. In mid-August, Wolcott Gibbs, the drama critic of the *New Yorker* magazine, died unexpectedly, and with this very desirable position vacant a number of critics looked to serve. Truman Capote called Alan Brien's wife, Nancy, and told her, 'Old Gibbs has cooled, baby. Why doesn't your beau write to Shawn?' Thereupon he promised to put in a good word with that very editor.

A few days later Brien, with his wife, went to Edinburgh to write about the festival. Late at night on 1 September, he found himself at the George Hotel in the company of Ken and Elaine, when a hotel servant announced a telephone call from New York. Elaine said, 'That'll be for me.' 'No, it's for Mr Tynan,' said the porter. Ken asked, 'Who can it be?' To which Brien answered, 'It's the *New Yorker* asking you to take over from Wolcott Gibbs.' 'I said that', Brien explains, 'because it was the very last thing I wanted to happen, and I felt the gods would never be cruel enough to allow it.' Ken went to the telephone, and he came back and said, 'It's the *New Yorker*, and they want me to go across and see them.'

The group sat around for a while talking about this offer. Elaine wondered whether Ken would go, and he said he wasn't sure. She wanted to know which of his friends in England he might miss, and he couldn't think of anybody. 'Not even Christopher Logue?' 'Well, I'd miss him,' Ken said absently; 'there won't be anybody like Christopher in New York.' 'You see,' says Brien, 'on his way back from the telephone we had all been erased. He was already in New York.'

On 9 September, Ken flew to New York, checked in at the Algonquin Hotel, and on the following day lunched at the Carlton House with William Shawn, 'a small, round, dormouse-like man in his early 50s'. Ken knew about Shawn's devotion to good writing and about his literary taste, like that of a singer born with perfect pitch; and Shawn admired Ken, whose reputation was already well established in America, and suspected that the offer had not entirely surprised him. Although Ken had, in previous years, told his agent Edith Haggard how much he liked the idea of writing for the *New Yorker*, and although – even before the death of Wolcott Gibbs – his agent (and his publisher Mike Bessie) had suggested to the magazine that he write for them, the call from Shawn was prompted independently.

It was agreed that Ken take up the post in November, for a theatre season, and that he write a column more or less as short or long as he wished, and be paid $1540 a month.

Ken's plane to London left that afternoon, at 5 p.m., and he took off from the airport rather like Bolingbroke on entering London in triumph: he 'did feel his blood within salute his state'. He found himself in the first-class compartment alongside an attractive dark-haired girl in her mid-twenties. 'I longed to introduce myself, and celebrate my new appointment with her, but it was a night flight, which means a truncated sleep; and the girl soon covered herself with a blanket, turned towards the window and switched off the light.' Ken removed the detachable chair-arm which stood between them, covered himself in a blanket and, in a euphoria of success and aeroplane champagne, decided to make love to his neighbour. 'I let my left hand rest lightly on her left hip. She did not stir. After a short pause I let my hand travel down to the hem of her skirt. Still no reaction: I paused again as the stewardess passed. . . . Now for stage three. . . . (This was before the great counter-revolution against gropers took place, imprisoning women from the waist down in the impregnable puritanism of tights.) As my fingers moved higher, I came up against the armadillo-like casing of a girdle', and he withdrew. Suddenly the girl sat bolt upright, and pushed past him. He could see the headlines: 'Indecent Assault on Plane: Critic Charged'. 'Girl Goosed Over Gander'. But she returned and took up the same position. The girdle had been removed, allowing for adventure.

In the morning Ken discovered that the girl's father was a diplomat. At London airport he offered her a lift to her hotel. Would she care to dine with him that evening? 'It's very kind of you,' said the lady, but 'my parents don't like me to go out with people I haven't been introduced to.' And that is how Ken described the day of his accession to the *New Yorker*.

On 1 November he and his family set sail for New York. He would work there until May, and then there would be the Paris theatre in June, Málaga for the bulls in August, Berlin at the end of that month, and then, perhaps, back to New York. 'Jazz, beat, Mort Sahl, *Mad*, Salinger, H'wood 10, Dissent, Zen.' Those were the notes he made in his diary as he crossed the Atlantic, and those were some of the subjects, apart from the theatre, which he pursued during two exuberant years in America.

15

The Toast of New York

Ken liked to travel to New York by air, to fly in on a clear day, with the sun's reflection shooting through the lakes and rivers of New England, leading the traveller to the 'carnival of concrete'. But on the occasion of his joining the *New Yorker* magazine as drama critic in November 1958, he brought Elaine, Tracy, a nanny and their luggage by boat. He moved his family into an ugly, down-at-heel, five-room apartment on East 89th Street, set his typewriter up on the dining-room table, and went off to Broadway to catch his first play.

'They say the *New Yorker* is the bland leading the bland,' he told a journalist before leaving England. 'I don't know if I'm bland enough.' It was probably the only flippant remark he ever made about the magazine, despite the fact that he was an unlikely loyalist to that prim institution. He had been a regular reader since his schoolboy days, having tried, aged sixteen, to produce a replica for provincial England. Although the *Midlander* was stillborn, Ken's admiration for the *New Yorker*, for its 'bright, blind devotion to accuracy, directness and unwounding wit', was life-long.

While on the staff, he went so far as to criticize his friend James Thurber's biography of the *New Yorker*'s first editor, Harold Ross, who had founded the magazine in 1925. Ken thought that Thurber gave a picture of an ignorant, eccentric pedant, in charge of an enchanted madhouse. He argued to the contrary that Ross had 'loathed the legend of haphazardness that had grown up around him', and had passed on to his successor, William Shawn, 'a highly efficient organisation'. The criticism only momentarily upset Thurber. He had written Ken a fan letter out of the blue some years before, and had welcomed him to the magazine. He wrote: 'I don't have to tell anybody who can read that you have brought a new and special brilliance, style, wit, and learning to the theatre page.'

'What I want to say is Olé. I'm glad you've come,' announced another *New Yorker* writer, John Steinbeck. And he challenged Ken to stir up the other critics from whom 'a good notice is an insult'.

Ken's first review appeared on 22 November, a homage to Robert Dhéry's *La Plume de Ma Tante*, in which he explained why and how the Parisian comic – as dead-pan as Jacques Tati in the face of calamity and as fertile with visual gags – made him laugh. Then he looked at a misconceived Method interpretation of Sean O'Casey's *The Shadow of a Gunman*. In his third week, he performed a demolition job on Rodgers and Hammerstein's *Flower Drum Song*, a musical set in San Francisco's Chinatown and peopled with Orientals of a 'primitive, childlike sweetness', who conversed with more than a 'smidgen of pidgin'. He ended his review: 'Perhaps as a riposte to Joshua Logan's *The World of Suzie Wong*, Rodgers and Hammerstein have given us what, if I had any self-control at all, I would refrain from describing as a world of woozy song.'

The following week he developed some sober thoughts on the preoccupation of post-war American drama with personal autobiography, with 'strolls down memory lane, that broad highway leading from the wrong side of the tracks to the anteroom of Perry and Pulitzer'.

He then turned on another genre, the religious–metaphysical play, specifically Archibald MacLeish's *J. B.* and Tennessee Williams' *Sweet Bird of Youth*. If God dominated *J. B.*, Freud was the culprit behind *Sweet Bird of Youth*. In both cases, Ken argued, the playwrights gave their alienated characters 'no hope of shaping the circumstances in which they lived'. The director of both plays was Elia Kazan, the only 'trend' in the Broadway theatre, Ken claimed – a director whom he admired but felt had 'come to worship energy for its own sake'.

Much to the distress of the *Observer*, whose editors were willing to offer close to any terms to keep him, Ken decided to stay in New York for another season and not to return as their permanent drama critic until the late spring of 1960. He explained to David Astor that his decision was influenced by his and Elaine's tax positions, rather than by the seductiveness of Broadway. He suggested that Harold Clurman would make an excellent stand-in during his absence.

The New York season of 1959 continued on its dull and undistinguished course, while Ken at least changed his particular column. It was no longer blasé and detached, and it reached, according to Eric Bentley, a 'high intellectual level somewhat left-orientated'.

Once a week he would spend an hour or so editing his piece under the scrutiny of William Shawn. They would sit in the editor's large sober corner office, Ken recalled, like a pair of mediaeval scholars at a holy text, a text which already bore 'loops and whorls and scribbled marginalia from half a dozen editorial advisers', including a mysterious figure known as 'the Comma Man'. In Ken's first review appeared the word *'pissoir'*, which the courtly but intransigent editor insisted should be altered. Together they settled on 'a circular kerbside construction'. At the *Observer* and later working for Laurence Olivier as dramaturg for the National Theatre, Ken would sooner commit hara-kiri than submit to verbal restriction; for Shawn he allowed himself to be censored.

Shawn had worried initially that there might be problems on politics or that Ken might want to use language of which the *New Yorker* did not approve since they were 'squeamish,' he explained, 'prudish about obscenities. But I never had any trouble with him. He was so quick to understand anything to do with clarity, syntax, accuracy.'

A couple of times Ken was late with his copy. On one such occasion the devoted editor appeared at the Tynan apartment in a snowstorm, wearing his galoshes, and went through to the bedroom where Ken was working, in order to remove the copy and take it off to the printer.

Shawn disapproved of his drama critic's elaborate social life. He felt that he did not allow himself time to think, and that his writing, 'as fine as it was', had not reached its limits. As brilliant as he was in style, wit and originality, 'comparable to Max Beerbohm and Shaw yet altogether different', he could still have done more. Why, Shawn wonders, did Ken not take the Shavian route and write plays?

There are notes to himself in Ken's engagement book, during 1959, which read, 'Write play. Write autobiography', and also 'Write pornographic book'. But though none of these projects was accomplished, much else – besides the merely·social – kept him busy. He wrote a monthly cultural column for the *Observer*, a number of long articles for American magazines other than the *New Yorker*, and he made elaborate preparations for an English television programme on American nonconformity.

But this solid side of Ken's life was not evident to the group of writers – Burton Bernstein, Donald Ogden Stewart Jr, Niccolo Tucci – who shared with him a large windowless area, up on the twentieth floor of the *New Yorker*. Ken would use the office several times a week, to pick up his messages and to confirm social arrangements. He would arrive at his desk in the airless room, which, like the rest of the magazine, resembled a federal agency on its way out of business, and there he would open a large loose-leaf address book and set to the business of his social life. His telephone never stopped ringing, according to Burt Bernstein: he was the toast of New York, 'the hottest thing going'. To his pile of messages from New York hostesses, his fellow writers would add the odd fake invitation such as 'Jean Stein wants you for tea with Greta Garbo and Adlai Stevenson.' All a lonely guest had to do at a New York party to attract attention, according to Ken's friend and fellow critic Richard Watts Jr, 'was say loudly "Kenneth Tynan" and excited men and women would start arguing violently'.

Writing about the newest hit, with its seasonal 'built-in obsolescence', was a fairly thankless task. Nor was he permitted to write about Off-Broadway, since the *New Yorker* had parcelled it off unreasonably to another critic. Genet, Beckett and new plays by Edward Albee, Arthur Kopit, Jack Richardson and Jack Gelber were all outside Ken's parish, so that his only redress was to town-cry, and to write extra-murally. He told the readers of the *Observer* about Mort Sahl, whose political nightclub banter was 'unlikely in the US but impossible in Britain', and he quoted Sahl's line about the GIs rehabilitating some Far East islanders. 'We'd taught the people to live off each other instead of the land.'

Sahl recognized that the real purpose of the House Un-American Activities Committee's operation was 'not to go for the Communists, but to drive dissent out of the country. They were after the liberals, and they wanted to drive them underground.'

He had started in San Francisco at the hungry i night club in 1953, and he was followed there by Lenny Bruce, a stand-up comic who had first been discovered by jazz musicians in a Los Angeles strip joint. 'They thought he was very funny,' Sahl explains, 'because, like the musicians and hipsters, he was looking at society and exposing social hypocrisy.'

Ken first saw Bruce's act in New York at the Duane Hotel in the spring of 1959:

Lean and pallid, with close-cropped black hair, he talked about Religions, Inc., a soft-selling ecumenical group on Madison Avenue whose main purpose was to render the image of Billy Graham indistinguishable from that of Pope John, ('Listen, Johnny, when you come out to the Coast, *wear the big ring.*') Clutching a hand mike, he slouched around a tiny dais, free-associating like mad; grinning as he improvised, caring as he grinned, seldom repeating in the second show what he said in the first, and often conducting what amounted to a rush job of psychoanalysis on the audience he was addressing. He used words as a jazz musician uses notes, going off into fantastic private cadenzas and digressions, and returning to his theme just when you thought he had lost track of it forever.

'Where's Lenny Bruce?' 'Down the Duane,' ran a popular tag. And down the Duane Ken went, on four different occasions, introducing friends like Terry Southern (who had just published *The Magic Christian*) to the still unknown comic who, the critic felt, was more acutely conscious of what was happening to his generation than anyone else.

During his first spring in New York Ken also applauded Professor Irwin Corey, the zany comedian whose voice 'would veer alarmingly from Oxford English to the Bronx'. And he heard for the first time, and fell in love with, Mike Nichols and Elaine May. With his passion for putting together those whom he admired, he introduced Nichols to the English comic Peter Sellers, but on that occasion no magic was made. 'Nothing that Peter said amused Mike; nothing that Mike said amused Peter. The sly, pragmatic, New York Jewish sense of humour meant nothing to Peter; and the giggly facetious, whimsical fantastic Goon-jokes of Sellers seemed merely embarrassing to Mike. I've never been more conscious of the abyss that separates British humour from the specialised world of Jewish Manhattan.'

Another specialist in New York humour, taken up and admired by Ken, was Jules Feiffer. His cartoons of Madison Avenue advertising men, Greenwich Village Bohemians and pseuds, college boys and Zen beatniks, had first started appearing in the *Village Voice* in 1956. When the British edition of his collected cartoons, *Sick Sick Sick*, appeared Ken provided a preface. Here was dialogue, Ken wrote, 'as acute as any that is being written in America today ... dialogue aimed at sophisticated minds, usually with the purpose of shaking them out of sophistication into real awareness'.

Quite soon after Ken's arrival in New York, he made friends with Feiffer and drew him into his circle. 'I met everyone through Ken and on the same night,' Feiffer recalls. And among the 'everyone' was Judy Sheftel (the model for Judy in Elaine Dundy's *Dud Avocado*). The Tynans told the real Judy, 'We want you to meet this very attractive cartoonist.' The meeting led to their marriage.

At George Plimpton's East River apartment, the headquarters of the *Paris Review*, could be found the core of the 'quality lit set', often drunk, usually noisy, sometimes merely childish. Here Ken first got to know Norman Mailer. According to Mailer, they got off to a poor start. 'Whatever it was I did, I always seemed to irritate him enormously. At a certain point that first evening, he just lashed out at me: I was opinionated. He had that marvellous authority of seizing the moment, and dictating what you were going to think.'

By his own testimony Ken liked and admired Mailer, thought his mental emotional spectrum 'wider than any of his American coevals', and praised him in a review for the *Village Voice* of *Advertisements for Myself*, for setting out to make 'a revolution in the consciousness of our time'.

At Plimpton's Ken and Elaine would bump into other friends, such as James Baldwin, Allen Ginsberg and Terry Southern (with whom Ken set about inventing a musical on the life of Byron to be called 'Funny Foot'). There was never any knowing how safe these confrontations would be. Ken tended to proselytize about his socialist principles. On one occasion William Phillips of *Partisan Review* refused to engage in political discussion. He told Ken that his arguments were so old that he, Phillips, could no longer remember the answers. Jules Feiffer, on the other hand, liked to talk to Ken about what was wrong with America. 'It was pre-radical chic and it was fun. But in those post-McCarthy days many people still shied away from radical politics.'

Mailer admired Ken for his 'extraordinary ability to get what he wanted out of the Establishment without ever compromising himself fatally with them. He was their darling, but he never gave them two bits if he didn't want to. And I never met anyone else who could do it at that level.'

Friends of the Tynans remember Elaine Dundy saying that New York was wonderful. 'Everything is so lively and great and it's open all night.' She was good company, 'very bright and rather bitchy', Plimpton recalls. 'I never knew what the relationship was between the two of them. They didn't appear to be affectionate. They both seemed to work out of their own individual fortresses.' Another friend, Gloria Vanderbilt, then married to Sidney Lumet, remembers that 'Elaine and Ken were time bombs with each other.' She concluded that they stayed together because 'when people drink excessively, it's hard for them to make decisions.'

Ken's secretary, a studious, modest girl called Nydia Leaf, believed that their habits held the Tynans together in a rootless sort of existence. Twice a week at least she would be privy to a row, provoked by Ken, perhaps over a shirt, or by Elaine just before Ken's deadline.

Tracy Tynan, six years old, had entered the Brearley School. For her birthday her parents bought her an expensive battery-operated soda fountain. When they did focus on her, according to Kenneth Haigh, 'It was so concentrated that it would last for a while. Ken would do to her what he did to all of us. He would say, "Tracy, you mean you haven't seen this? We're going!" Tracy was actually running that madhouse,' he adds. 'She was the chairman.' Tracy loved Ken Haigh, and his girlfriend Jean Marsh. At Christmas in 1958, Jean came to cook the dinner. 'I can still see Tracy looking at Jean basting that goose.'

Jean Marsh would often be drawn into the rows; no less hateful to her were the games the Tynans played, like the Andrea Doria, in which you had to choose which member of the group would be abandoned first; or the Truth Game, in which Ken would ask, 'Would I be better without Elaine?' On 9 January 1959 Ken flew to Mexico City with Jean Marsh and Ken Haigh, and a thermos of iced martinis. Jean knew that both Kens loved her dearly, one of them from the vantage point of her bed, and the other as a suitor, so she was fairly miffed that on this wonderful holiday the two Kens spent all their time inventing Shakespearean blank verse and talking 'constantly, brilliantly to each other'. Occasionally Ken (Tynan) would crawl unwillingly into the full blare of the noonday sun, 'damply and hotly and redly', and say, 'Leave Ken [Haigh] in the pool, and come with me.' And Jean would refuse. Finally Ken asked Elaine to join them.

He took his group exploring, to bad nightclubs, the Zócalo – a bar where they met the American bullfighter Sidney Franklin – the murals of Diego Rivera, the university, which Ken described as 'functionalism rabid with colour', and the pyramids, which he judged the dullest architectural form since the sand castle.

'Ken was a genius friend and he did things to set out to please you,' Haigh says. 'One day I had to go back to New York to rehearse a play, but life was Mexico and Ken Tynan, as far as I was concerned.'

The trip inspired Elaine to write a fine, if perversely wishful, short story called 'The Sound of a Marriage', about two couples sipping planter's punch in Acapulco, passing the time of day. The narrator of the story, peaceably attached to one man, regards the volatile behaviour of the other couple with growing envy. She records their rows and their screaming matches, the shrieks of 'Sadist!' and the peals of sarcastic laughter, the cries of 'Get out of my life'. 'We laughed at them ... but we pitied them as well, locked forever in their horrible unending struggle for co-existence.' Then the narrator's love affair comes apart while the other couple are back 'laughing, cooing, gurgling, shrieking at each other.... Now I understood. All those words, rivers of angry words pouring themselves out over one another, they were only *sounds* to them – like their gurglings and cooings and shriekings right now.' And the narrator concludes, 'The sound of a marriage was not the sound that we would ever make.'

16

Travellers' Tales

'We should be back in Cuba before the end of this month,' wrote Ernest Hemingway to Ken on 1 March 1959. 'And I will be happy to do anything to be of use to you.'

Three weeks later Ken arrived in Havana, eager to take up Hemingway's offer, and curious to witness the romantic revolution of Fidel Castro and his youthful followers, installed but three months before.

Of Havana Ken wrote that he was reminded not so much of a national capital as of an international zone. 'Its brisk winds, its driving seas, its whispers of vice, its rich novelties and ancient poverties, all combine to suggest that this may be Tangier transplanted to Latin America.' But this impression was soon to be jolted by the revolutionary *barbudos*: during one night-club act a drunken member of the audience pulled up a couple of *barbudos* on to the stage and proposed a collection in aid of agrarian reform. At another a 'Castro guerrilla' crooned a romantic song with one hand resting on the butt of a loaded revolver. As for 'vice', Ken discovered that the whore houses were nearly all shut down, Superman and Superboy – stars of the porn scene – already departed, and the casinos barely functioning.

On Ken's third day in Havana he drove out to San Francisco de Paula to lunch with Hemingway and his wife Mary. They had met first in 1954, in Madrid, and again briefly in New York. Hemingway admired Ken's *New Yorker* writing, and kept a copy of *Bull Fever* at the Finca Vigia. But those close to him always felt that his admiration was ambivalent: not only was *Bull Fever* highly regarded, but the young Englishman had had the audacity to move in on Hemingway's turf.

Ken found the *finca* spare and white, with books everywhere, and trophies on the wall. In the study were more books, more trophies, a brass bedstead and a high narrow desk, at which Hemingway worked standing up. 'In manner and appearance', Ken wrote of his host, 'he suggests an enormous boy. A giant child made gruff by shyness. . . . His eyes are curiously innocent.

In moments of anger they grow baleful, but in fits of enthusiasm they gleam with a delightful eagerness, the lips part in a sharklike grin, and the whole heavy head nods with pleasure.'

Hemingway tended to deliver judgements rather than opinions, and Ken concluded that he had 'the humility that comes of absolute certainty'. F. Scott Fitzgerald was 'soft', and 'dissolved at the least touch of alcohol'. William Faulkner could not *rematar* – a taurine verb meaning to finish a series of passes with the bull. A particular Catholic writer was 'going pretty good there for a while, but now he's a whore with a crucifix up his ass'.

So passed the first lunch. Their next encounter was at the Floridita, the famous Havana bar and restaurant decorated in Colonial Empire style, kept almost pitch dark and as cold as a deep freeze. At the bar Hemingway had his particular seat, under a bronze bust of himself ('We cover it during Lent,' he explained). He would order for himself, and his friends, double frozen daiquiris called Papadobles. And here, on Ken's first visit, as a guest of the Floridita's king, a black trio sang a song they had composed for 'Ernesto', about an apologetic lesbian who cannot – no matter how hard she tries – be as Papa would desire her. Later that afternoon Ken found Hemingway sparring with the men's-room attendant. 'When you gonna grow old, Papa?' asked the attendant.

Two days later, in early April, Ken stage-managed a bizarre meeting at the Floridita between Hemingway and Tennessee Williams, who had recently arrived in town and claimed to be awaiting the arrival of 'a banana millionairess from Key West'. Williams expressed a guarded wish to meet the novelist. 'But won't he kick me?' he asked Ken. 'They tell me that Mr Hemingway usually kicks people like me in the crotch.' Ken assured him that that would not be the case, and, having ascertained that Hemingway would welcome the meeting, he set the time and turned up, as arranged, at the Floridita. Shortly afterwards Hemingway arrived wearing a baseball cap, a white T-shirt and tropical trousers. Considerably late, Williams appeared, having 'tanked up' on martinis, and wearing a yachting jacket with silver buttons, 'as if to persuade Hemingway', Ken later noted, 'that although he might be a decadent, he was at least an *outdoor* decadent'.

The final version of the meeting, only slightly bent towards poetic effect, Ken told as follows. The two figures, Hemingway, aged fifty-nine, and Williams, forty-eight, were introduced. Drinks were ordered and silence fell.

Hemingway gazed at the bar. Tennessee beamed at the ceiling. Suddenly: 'What I've always admired about your work, Mr. Hemingway,' said Tennessee bravely, 'is that you care about honour among men. And there is no quest more desperate than that.' Hemingway swivelled his leonine head. 'What kind of men, Mr. Williams,' he said, 'did you have in mind?' Tennessee started to shrug, but Hemingway continued: 'People who have honour never talk about it. They know it, and they confer immortality on each other.'

... By now the bar was filling up, and so were we. Tennessee was once again making the running. 'I was in Spain last year for the bullfights,' he said. 'Last summer I met one of the matadors on the beach, a lovely boy, very friendly, very accessible. Named Antònio Ordóñez.' Ordóñez was not only the greatest bullfighter in Spain, but one of Hemingway's closest friends. Tennessee continued, 'He was utterly charming to me, a most enchanting boy. He even showed me his cogidas.'

'He showed you his *what*, Mr. Williams?' said Hemingway, furrowing his brow and feigning incomprehension.

'His cogidas,' Tennessee rattled on, 'his horn wounds. The scars on his thighs. Of course he was wearing a bathing suit.'

'Do you think he would talk to us and show us his cogidas?' said Hemingway, all deadpan innocence.

'Oh, I'm certain he would,' Tennessee assured him. 'As I say, he's a most accessible boy.'

... More drinks ... and Tennessee plunged in again. 'I used to know your second wife, Mr. Hemingway,' he said. 'I believe her name was Pauline.... She was very kind to me when I was poor – a lovely lady, a most hospitable lady. I often wondered what happened to her. They tell me she died. Did she die in great pain?'

Hemingway, who was profoundly attached to his second wife, replied with a stoical sentence that deliberately verged on self-parody...: 'She died like everybody else,' he said, leaning portentously across the bar, 'and after that she was dead.'

I went to the lavatory, and found when I returned, that the meeting of minds for which I had hoped had taken place in my absence. The two writers were brow to brow, urgently debating the relative importance of the kidneys and the liver.... I disrupted their communion by announcing that I had a date with Castro and would have to leave at once. To my slight alarm, Tennessee insisted on accompanying me. He and Hemingway shook hands warmly, linked at last by medicine and mortality.

Just on time, Tennessee and I passed through the gates of the Presidential Palace. Instead of frisking us, the sentry drew our attention to a collection of butterflies owned by one of his colleagues. We admired it, and we were escorted to a leather couch outside Castro's anteroom. Here we spent two-and-a-half hours, while soldiers, pregnant women, and men in ice-cream coloured suits strolled in and out of the leader's presence. Tennessee, growing restive, focused his gaze on a teenage boy in olive-green battle dress who was standing guard at the door. 'Have you noticed,' he mused, 'how everybody touches that boy before they go in? Do you suppose it's for luck? I wonder would he like some American cigarettes...'

Before I could answer his questions, someone identified Tennessee as the famous Yankee playwright, and we were whisked through the anteroom into Castro's sanctum, where a vital cabinet meeting was in session.... Because of Tennessee, the meeting was suspended and Castro strode over to greet us. In clumsy but clearhearted English, he told Tennessee how much he had admired his plays, above all the one about the cat that was upon the burning roof. He hoped that Mr. Williams would come to live in Cuba, and write about the revolution. He said he was also grateful to Mr. Hemingway. 'We took *For Whom the Bell Tolls* to the hills with us and it taught us about guerrilla warfare. But why does not Señor Hemingway write and speak more about our revolution?' I improvised something to the effect that I did not think Hemingway wanted to be involved in politics. Castro and his whole group laughed.

'We are not political,' he said. 'We make our revolt to get the politicians out. We are social people. This is a social revolution.'

Meanwhile Williams, smiling noncommittally, asked Ken out of the corner of his mouth whether the boy with that moustache on his left would be willing to run across the square and bring him a hot tamale. Ken replied that he doubted it, because the boy in question was the Minister of Education.

And so they took their leave. But it was not the last of Ken's adventures with Tennessee Williams in Cuba. The storytelling, however, must pass to George Plimpton, who set it all down in his autobiographical book *Shadow Box*. One afternoon a group was gathered around a table at the Floridita eating club sandwiches: Ken and Elaine, Tennessee Williams with his United Fruit Company millionairess and George Plimpton. An American soldier of fortune called Captain Marks joined the group. He said he had fought with Castro in the hills. He said he now had a job up at the Morro castle in charge of execution squads. 'That very evening', in Plimpton's words,

there was going to be quite a lot of activity over in the fortress and he'd be just delighted if we would consider joining him as his guests at what he referred to as 'the festivities'.... At this point there was a sudden eruption from Tynan. He had been sitting, rocking back and forth in his chair; he came out of it almost as if propelled.

... At first, I don't think Captain Marks was aware that these curious honked explosions of indignation from this gaunt arm-flapping man in a seersucker suit were directed at him, but then Tynan got his voice under control, and Captain Marks could see his opened eyes now, pale and furious, staring at him and the words became discernible – shouts that it was sickening to stay in the same room with such a frightful specimen as an executioner of men ('l-l-l-loathsome!'), and as for the invitation, yes he was going to turn up all right, but in order to throw himself in front of the guns of the firing squad! He was going to stop the 'festivities' – the word sprayed from him in rage – and with this he pulled his wife up out of her chair ... and rushed for the exit.

Plimpton, to his own shame, wanted to attend that execution, and he went over to Hemingway's *finca* that afternoon to get some advice and to tell him about Ken, how Ken had stunned the man Marks and steamed with rage. Hemingway felt that it had been a mistake to ask Ken to an execution since his emotional make-up was just not suited to such things, that he would give the revolution a bad name. But he encouraged Plimpton to go.

Thus armed, Plimpton set off to meet Williams for the event. Tennessee had discovered from Captain Marks that a young German mercenary was scheduled to be shot that evening and he felt that if he had the chance to do so he would get close enough to give him a small encouraging smile.

I wasn't sure that a 'small encouraging smile' from Tennessee was what one hoped for as one's last view on earth....

Captain Marks arrived. We all stood up and looked at him.

'It's been called off,' he said. We hardly listened to him. 'Circumstances ... difficulties ... postponement....'

Frankly, I have no idea whether Tynan was actually responsible for the evening's 'festivities' being canceled. I like to think that he was; that the officials had got wind of his outraged reaction to Captain Marks in the Floridita ... that he was going to throw himself in front of the guns. No, it was best to let things cool down; to let this weird fanatic clear off the island. At least they would not have to worry that just as everything was going along smoothly, the blindfolds nicely in place, not too tight, just right, Tynan's roar of rage would peal out of the darkness ('St-st-stop this in-in-infamous be-be-behaviour!'), and he would flap out at them across the courtyard, puffs of dirt issuing from his footfalls as he came at them like a berserk crane.

A month after this event Ken received a letter marked 'T. Williams, in transit, El Minzah Hotel Tangier.' The writer Paul Bowles, it would seem, had passed on a story from Gore Vidal, who had reported that Ken had called Williams a sadist because he wanted to witness an execution in Havana. 'Please don't try to brand me as a brutal person!' wrote the playwright. 'If I had witnessed an execution, a real one, I doubt that anyone present would have found it more painful to witness.'

And that more or less was the end of Ken's Havana episode.

The feebleness of the 1959 Broadway season, from which Arthur Miller had decided to withhold his next play, helped focus Ken's attention on what was missing. The non-profit-making Lincoln Center for the Performing Arts was under construction. Here was a possible solution to a commercial theatre 'distorted by economics and ideology'. Since the early 1950s, Ken had campaigned for a British national theatre. Now he hoped that Lincoln Center would provide the American equivalent, with a 'full spectrum' of the riches of American drama.

A respected Broadway manager, Robert Whitehead, was the chairman of the theatre committee, with a plan for assembling around twenty actors to perform six productions a season. Both in print and among theatre people Ken constantly asked where the actors, authors and directors for such a theatre would be found, and how the theatre could properly function if it were required to make a profit. He proposed his friend Harold Clurman, that 'stubby, volcanic sage', as a contender for artistic director; he would very much have liked the job himself.

Three times, on his regular beat, he was able to muster genuine enthusiasm. There was Lorraine Hansberry's *A Raisin in the Sun*, the first Broadway production by a black writer, with an all-black cast which included Sidney Poitier, staged by a black director, Lloyd Richards. The piece is set in Chicago and concerns the reactions of a poor black family to a windfall of insurance money. Ken praised the 'proud, joyous proximity to its source, which is life as the dramatist has lived it'.

Before presentation of the annual New York Drama Critics Circle awards, Ken lobbied his nineteen comrades to vote in its favour, declaring it to be the best American play of the season. Once the 'infant Dalai Lama of the European theatre had spoken,' Alistair Cooke wrote in the *Guardian*, 'there was nothing much the resident prophets could do but go along with him'. And although Brooks Atkinson of the *New York Times* voted for Archibald MacLeish's *J.B.*, and Walter Kerr of the New York *Herald Tribune* for Tennessee Williams's *Sweet Bird of Youth*, *A Raisin in the Sun* was the winner.

In early April Ken devoted his weekly column to Pearl Buck's *Desert Incident*, which addressed the problems of developing nuclear power whether for peaceful or for military purposes, and whether the scientist was morally bound to withhold information from his government. Although the play was clumsily written, and poorly constructed and reasoned, its author won Ken's praise for choosing to write about 'the most important subject in the world'. Having stated his allegiance, Ken set out on a lengthy detour – in the form of a conversation with an arch-conservative who would rather be dead than red, and who would readily sacrifice mankind itself to preserve the freedom of mankind.

More of a political argument than a theatre review, the piece prompted hundreds of *New Yorker* readers, members of the Committee for a Sane Nuclear Policy, academics, religious leaders and politicians to write to Ken in passionate support of his stand.

The third time Ken allowed his enthusiasm full rein, during that dowdy Broadway season, was for *Gypsy*. Jule Styne's music, Stephen Sondheim's lyrics, Jerome Robbins' direction and choreography, and the voice of Ethel Merman – 'the most relaxed brass section on earth' – produced a rave review for 'an effortless coalition of all the arts of the American musical stage at their highest point of development'.

In May 1959, almost at the end of the theatre season, Ken wrote to William Shawn to tell him that, though a trip to England would cost him £1275 in UK taxes, he had decided to 'succumb to nostalgia and go'.

On 25 May he packed some books for work in progress on Cuba, and on Brecht, along with the *Goncourt Journals*, and the following day he flew to Paris. Elaine, in the meantime, planned to spend her summer on Martha's Vineyard, and to take Tracy to meet Ken in Spain for the Málaga feria in August.

Several nights after Ken's arrival, he went for drinks with Thomas Quinn Curtiss, who was then, and still is, a cultural reporter for the *Herald Tribune*. At Tom's Ken was introduced by James and Gloria Jones to Addie Herder, an American painter with short cropped hair, a small, curvaceous figure and a look not dissimilar to Elaine's. And that very night he began an affair with her. She had recently left her husband to explore the world, but the world came to be defined by Ken. 'Why he picked on me that night, I don't know. Perhaps because I had a good wardrobe or that I had one of the greatest bottoms of all time.'

That night Addie more or less moved into Ken's hotel, the Lutèce, in the Rue Jules-Chaplain, and for the next few weeks she was never out of Ken's sight, except for a swift daily visit to the flat of her friend Monique, where she kept her clothes.

I would leave the Lutèce for Monique's and walk down the street with the water in the gutter and the sound of the music school next door, and of course it was June, and the morning sun shone on Paris, and that music, and falling in love, so that it was the most glorious thing that could happen. I had known many intelligent people and I'd had wonderful sex, but Ken had a combination of more things than any one person I had ever known. His presence, his own body of information, and quick-wittedness, brought out everything in me that was possible at that time (though he was not a man I could come to with my troubles).

I was leaving a marriage of eighteen years. I was older than he. He described us as both having trial separations, but I didn't believe that. He was just in Europe, and his wife wasn't there. The rules didn't apply to him, and I felt that he could change the rules any time he wanted. I don't know what his standards were. Probably they were not to be bored.

'He had an intellectual approach to sex,' Addie Herder noted, 'a belief that ritual is what makes things interesting.' Like many other observers, she saw that Ken had a preconception of how he wanted life to be arranged. 'He didn't want to talk about his family, and that was the only time I ever heard anything sharp from him toward me. "You're asking all the wrong questions," he would say. The only other thing that troubled him was not working.'

In Paris they dined with Jean-Louis Barrault at Le Grand Vefour, and drank with Janet Flanner, the *New Yorker's* Paris outpost, the playwright Arthur Adamov and the newly successful novelist Françoise Sagan.

On 11 June Ken took his new girlfriend, with the James Joneses, to Germany. They flew to Frankfurt, where Ken had his hair cut, or rather 'butchered' as Addie Herder recalls.

It was ridiculous and he was very upset. He said, 'How can they take me seriously as a critic with a haircut like this?' I don't think he believed he was good-looking. I was crazy about his looks, but it was only because they gave him a certain fallibility from perfection. His face – that quick, responsive face – would immediately assume sympathy or shock, or whatever. I don't know if they were real emotions, but he expressed himself very freely and in superlatives.

By 26 June Ken had seen thirty-two plays in five cities during twenty-eight days. His *New Yorker* piece on Paris was already delivered: an account of the inner workings of the established theatre in tandem with an interview with the Minister of Culture, André Malraux, on how state-subsidized institutions might be invigorated. The review of the German theatre was on its way. He found that there was no theatre in Europe to match the 'versatility, consistency and extensiveness' of the 121 subsidized theatres in West Germany and 86 in East Germany. The European classics were the backbone of these repertory companies, but they also housed modern Russian, Chinese, East European, French, English and American work.

He went for the first time to Hamburg, unprepared for the city's 'green, water-girt beauty', and saw Schiller's *Mary Stuart* at the Schauspielhaus (run by the veteran Gustav Gründgens), the first part of Goethe's *Faust*, and Brecht's *St Joan of the Stockyards* – 'a bitter attempt to illustrate the interdependence of capitalism and religion'.

But the theatre company that most affected him was Brecht's Ensemble at the Shiffbauerdamm, in East Berlin. Ken devoted the rest of his long essay to making admiring reference to John Willett's *The Theatre of Bertolt Brecht* and Martin Esslin's *Brecht: A Choice of Evils*. He watched a rehearsal of *The Threepenny Opera* and saw two established productions, *The Life of Galileo* and *The Mother*, Brecht's version of the Gorky novel. He also saw the company's newest production, *The Resistible Rise of Arturo Ui*, written in 1941, a raucous parody of Hitler's rise to power told against a background of Chicago in the twenties. Arturo Ui was played by Ekkehard Schall, and Ken described his performance as

one of the most transfixing human experiments I have ever seen on a stage, and a perfect image of Brechtian acting. Schall, who is under thirty ... invests the part with all the deadpan gymnastic agility of the young Chaplin: clambering onto the back of a hotel armchair and toppling abruptly out of sight; biting his knuckles, and almost his whole fist, when momentarily frustrated; indulging, when left alone with women, in displays of ghastly skittishness; and learning, from a hired ham actor, that the golden rule of public speaking is to preserve one's chastity by shielding – as Hitler always did – the lower part of one's belly. Yet Schall can change gears without warning, switching from pure knockabout to sudden gloom of fearful intensity; the virtue of Brechtian training, as of Brechtian thinking, is that it teaches the infinite flexibility of mankind. The play itself is rowdy and Chaplinesque. What the production – and Schall, above all – had added to it is a fever, a venom, and a fury that make laughter freeze like cold sweat, on one's lips.

The description of Schall's performance was no more than a parenthesis in Ken's world picture of Brecht.

Tennessee Williams read this and wrote to Ken (this time from the Repulse Bay Hotel, Hong Kong) to tell him: 'Now and then I feel like paying homage to those who do great writing.... Your piece about the theatre of Brecht ... [was] way beyond what Capote calls "reportage": It's a piece of literature.'

On 23 June Ken flew alone to London to prepare the third of his *New Yorker* articles, and Addie Herder was left with her dreams. They met again in New York but the affair was never again so concentrated nor so delightful.

In London Ken led a gypsy life, staying at a friend's house in St John's Wood or at hotels, cared for and entertained by his closest woman friend, the writer Penelope Gilliatt, and her neurologist husband Roger Gilliatt.

At the Royal Court he saw Willis Hall's *The Long and the Short and the Tall*, directed by Lindsay Anderson. Out of nowhere – or perhaps out of everywhere – had emerged an ambitiously talented bunch of young provincial actors, among them Robert Shaw, Bryan Pringle and Peter O'Toole.

He reviewed Arnold Wesker's *Roots* – which had opened at the Royal Court in June and had since transferred to the West End – about an ignorant daughter of an agricultural labourer who discovers there is a bolder world to explore, and with her first sense of self-identity cries, 'I'm beginning, *I'm beginning*!' At that point – it is the end of the play – Ken stumbled out of the theatre into the hot July night 'in a haze of emotion'.

It seemed that the dead land of West End London theatre was flowering. There were two productions with working-class characters from the maverick outsider Joan Littlewood; Shelagh Delaney's *A Taste of Honey* and Brendan Behan's *The Hostage* were both playing there. Meanwhile the Royal Court was thriving; Bernard Miles had opened an experimental theatre, the Mermaid; and the greatest actor of them all, Laurence Olivier, was playing Coriolanus at Stratford-on-Avon under Peter Hall's direction. Here were the 'wagging head, the soaring index finger, and the sly, roaming eyes of one of the world's cleverest comic actors, plus the desperate, exhausted moans of one of the world's masters of pathos. But we also confront the nonpareil of heroic tragedians, as athletically lissome as when he played Oedipus a dozen years ago.... the voice ... sounds distinct and barbaric, across the valley of many centuries, like a horn calling to the hunt, or the neigh of a battle-maddened charger.'

And so Ken ended his exile's report from England. 'Olivier's was a performance', he wrote to Shawn, 'worth being double-taxed for.'

On 17 August Ken returned to New York to begin his second season as drama critic for the *New Yorker*. In the preceding seventeen days he had been in Málaga, and the time had been memorable. He wrote to William Shawn suggesting an article about that dangerous summer and the rivalry between the two toreros, Luis Miguel Dominguín and Antonio Ordóñez, which had culminated in the legendary *mano a mano* on 14 August, with Ordóñez receiving six ears, two tails and two hooves by way of trophies, and Dominguín walking away with five ears, two tails and one hoof.

Ken had arrived in Málaga on 1 August. He settled in at the Miramar, a grandiose Edwardian hotel set back from the ocean, where the bullfight crowd and the foreign *afición* would meet after the corrida to deliver opinions. On one such night early in August, and early in the feria, Ken found himself at a large table with a group of friends which included Ernest Hemingway (living at the Davises' and in attendance on Ordóñez, about whose contest with Dominguín he intended to write). Though Ken had been generously welcomed by Hemingway in Havana, he was well aware that the great novelist, when surrounded by a circle of sycophants, could be brutally curt and even boorish, traits exaggerated by ill heath, growing paranoia and the threat of competition.

The writer A. E. Hotchner recalls that 'Ernest was sitting directly opposite Ken; everybody was talking and there was a band playing. But Ernest had this incredible ability of being able to pick up any part of the conversation in a crowd.' Hemingway was holding forth on the afternoon's *corrida*, while across the table Ken was giving his account of a particular kill by Jaime Ostos. The older man called out, 'Tynan, are you holding yourself out as the authority on this afternoon's fight?' Ken answered him mildly, not wishing to provoke. Hemingway pursued: 'You know, just because you wrote one skinny book doesn't make you an authority. On what authority do you make those statements?'

To which Ken replied, 'On the authority of my eyes.'

'Fuck your eyes. You need glasses,' roared the literary lion.

Whereupon the cub sprang up and declared, 'There's no point to my staying at this table any longer.'

'Maybe you'll stay long enough to pick up the check.'

'I'll make arrangements for that,' said Ken over his shoulder and headed out.

He passed Bill Davis in the bar. 'Ken was white and beside himself with rage,' Hotchner says. He told the barman to put the drinks for Hemingway's table on his bill. Davis, malicious as always, said, "Why Ken, you look disturbed." And he answered, "I have just been insulted by a man with a white beard who doesn't have the wisdom to go with it." Then he left.'

Although Hemingway apologized to Ken the following day, he often referred to the incident. At a *corrida*, he might say of a bad performance, 'Tynan would like that *faena*,' or if a bull bumped a torero in the backside, 'Tynan would have approved that pass.'

When Penelope Gilliatt came to join Ken and his family in Málaga, and in Torremolinos, the resort west of Málaga, talk was still of the Hemingway fracas. She had never seen a bullfight before, and her first was particularly gory. Ken was horribly upset that it had not been better for her, and blamed the poor performance on the overcast sky.

It was not merely the bullfight that distressed Mrs Gilliatt, but the fights between the Tynans. Elaine had that summer begun an affair with William Becker, a tall, wiry man who worked in the theatre and in real estate, an acquaintance of Ken's since Oxford and part of the *Paris Review* crowd. She had also been briefly embroiled with Terry Southern. But the affair with

Becker was more serious. Becker, who had met Elaine in Paris and bumped into her again at a Plimpton party, found her bright and sharp with a wicked, witty view of things.

Becker's wife, the choreographer Patricia Birch, knew of the affair, so that when Ken telephoned her to discuss the matter she was perfectly unfazed. Then Ken called Becker himself, interrupting a property transaction, to tell him, 'I just felt you'd like to know that I'm naming you as co-respondent.' Becker said, 'You don't want to make me famous on several continents.' After that Ken calmed down. He'd got it off his chest. (When sexually betrayed, Ken reacted with spite and jealousy while applying other standards to his own infidelities.) The affair went on after the Tynans returned to London in 1960, but Becker felt throughout that Elaine, despite her complaints, was obsessed by Ken.

Ken noted in his engagement book that Elaine had attacked him on his 'inability to make love to her'. He also noted that she was sending Tracy to a 'snob dance school' against his wishes, that she accused him of mistreating her and complained about his infidelities. Friends, as usual, tried to work out why the Tynans stayed together. For Tracy certainly. In honour of the good times? Out of habit, out of some residue of passion? Because the marriage was socially convenient? Or because of Ken's theory that their teeth were so deeply buried in each other's wounds they could not separate for fear of bleeding to death?

Norman Mailer believed that Elaine and Ken wounded each other profoundly. 'They'd hit each other shots that you'd just sit there and applaud like you would at a prize fight. If you didn't see it, you heard about it the next day, and usually you heard about it horizontally. Everybody was so intimate with everybody else in that *Paris Review* gang. It was the nearest thing we ever had to Bloomsbury.'

Mailer recognized in Ken, during that time at the end of the 1950s, another warrior in a battle of which neither, at the time, could name the cause, each travelling very fast 'cutting through the crust of the old snow' and laying down tracks for others. The repercussions could be quite severe for the women attached to these dangerous trail-blazers – for Mailer's then wife Adèle or for Elaine Dundy, who despite her competitiveness wanted above all to be her husband's wife. When Carol Saroyan, with whom Ken had run away in 1957, finally met Elaine, she found not the bitchy and mean woman Ken had described, but a wounded woman unhappily in love.

In the meantime there were other women in Ken's life. On his return to the States in the autumn, a tall, dark, intelligent woman called Marion Capron and Ken began a friendship that lasted on and off for several years.

He also met a beautiful café-au-lait actress called Ellen Holly, who combined genteel middle-class ways and a militant sense of rage about black injustice.

She would not allow Ken to sleep with her, but kept his friendship until his death.

In New York, during those two theatre seasons, Ken drew many other admirers, actresses who wanted his good opinion – for whom he had little time – old friends, like Jean Marsh, whom he had still not managed to seduce, though he continued to try. 'He would take me to the theatre. Beforehand he had looked up every single reference book. We went to see *Redhead*, and he had all sorts of quotes ready for "redhead". He was armed, which he didn't need to be because his own thoughts were always so much funnier and more original than anyone else's.'

Ken's flirtations were not always light-hearted. A woman whom Ken met at the end of his New York sojourn and whom he continued to see in London attempted suicide because of him. On another macabre occasion, he discovered that the woman he was sleeping with had a hole in her heart, whereupon, terrified of some accident, he refused to make love to her again. He could very swiftly pull women into his thrall and, if having done so he uncovered a heavy sexual neurotic, he would get out fast, ignoring the consequences.

17

Back to Broadway

In August 1959, shortly after returning to the States from Spain, Ken set off to San Francisco for a week. In March the following year he spent a further week there. Poets, freaks and union leaders who remember his visit swear he was there for at least six months.

He went to the city with the view that the beatniks – whether hipsters, white Negroes or mystics – were a last late flowering of romanticism, and that they were discouragingly anti-intellectual. San Francisco did not alter this view, but he nonetheless fell for the tolerant city, with its temperate climate which cherished such extremes of feeling and opinion. He met the old guard, like the poet–critic Kenneth Rexroth, who had once championed the beats but had come to reject them as artistic loafers. He met the writer and lover of the bullfight Barnaby Conrad. He found Paul Desmond, the alto sax player and exponent of West Coast jazz, and Alan Watts, who had first led him to Eastern philosophy with *The Art of Zen*.

In jazz and Zen he applauded the 'direct elliptical communication' beyond the spoken or written word. But he took up Zen Buddhism more as an appealing and contrary idea than as a practical discipline. Nor did Eastern philosophy much invade the content of what he wrote, though his words could reach the page as effortlessly as 'snow from a bamboo leaf' – the image by which Zen masters teach their pupils artless art.

He turned his attention to the beatniks (already well established at North Beach), a colony of maverick, communal, weirdly selfless rejectors of status, non-militant enemies of the military, many of them teenagers from the East Coast. But the founding fathers like Jack Kerouac, Allen Ginsberg, Gregory Corso and William Burroughs had left, and already the beat underground was developing in other parts of the world. Of Burroughs Ken wrote, after reading *The Naked Lunch*, that he had a command of prose 'more precise and wittily sepulchral than any of his disciples have yet achieved'.

At the Bread and Wine Mission Ken found Philip Lamantia reciting a poem about 'junkies, tricks, dummy poets, mads ... beat Jews, spade trumpet players, pot heads, Zen nuts ... black supremacy, white supremacy, and Red Indian-supremacy, wild ones'. At the Bagel Shop, somebody mused, 'Kant is to Hegel as hole is to bagel.' He met the soft-spoken poet Lawrence Ferlinghetti, who had started the City Lights Bookshop in 1954 and published Ginsberg's *Howl* in 1956. Finally he went to San Quentin Prison to meet Neal Cassady, the handsome original of Dean Moriarty in Kerouac's *On the Road*, who was serving a term for possession and sale of marijuana.

Ken sent a note to Shawn to say that he was now too busy to write about the summer feria in Spain, and he signed off with uncharacteristic informality: 'What a city! What a roller-coaster!' Then he went back to New York to write about San Francisco for the *Observer*, and later for *Holiday* magazine.

Back at his job monitoring Broadway, Ken was dispirited once again to hear New York audiences ask of a new play, 'Do you think it will go?' rather than 'Are you enjoying it?'

He headed his review of Rodgers' and Hammerstein's *The Sound of Music* 'The Case for Trappism', but was momentarily pleased by the musical *Fiorello*. He was cast down again by William Inge's *A Loss of Roses*, a play, Ken wrote, which takes place 'in the cycle of Freudian Mysteries that formed the religious core of the winter theatre festivals held annually on the island of Manhattan for the benefit of the United Hospital Fund'.

Plays about people and glorified biography would not do. He wanted plays about ideas. And, with these strong feelings bearing down, he chose in November to write a highly critical review of the established Broadway writer Moss Hart's autobiography, *Act One*. 'For him, a success is a success is a success,' wrote Ken. 'and any price is worth paying to ensure it.' And he went on, 'Apart from its evocation of the Borscht Circuit, its glimpses of Mr. [George] Kaufman, and its unabashed glee at the prospect of money, the main value of the book will probably be as an anthology of autobiographical clichés.'

The response to this review was extremely poor. The agent Irving Lazar considers it a vicious thing to this day. Hart's wife, Kitty Carlisle, the beautiful actress who had played with the Marx Brothers in *A Night at the Opera*, was deeply hurt, and even Ken's loyal friends Comden and Green were offended. 'Moss was an absolute charmer,' Betty Comden says, 'and he had very high standards.'

Ken's offence was all the more heinous since he had, several weeks before the publication of the review, gatecrashed Moss Hart's fiftieth birthday party for several hundred show business celebrities, held at a Broadway restaurant called Mamma Leone's.

Many of the guests had worked up sketches in honour of the birthday. 'It

was a *rehearsed* party,' Kitty Hart explains. Phil Silvers was master of ceremonies. Comden and Green did a sketch on how *Act One* might be adapted
for the screen. Howard Dietz and Arthur Schwartz wrote a twenty-minute
musical based on the book. And somewhere in the middle of the evening a
not very celebrated thirty-three-year-old television writer called Mel Brooks
improvised a routine, with his partner Mel Tolkin, in which he played Moss
Hart's puritan analyst. Some of it went like this:

Q: Could you tell us, sir, what Mr Hart talks about during your analytic sessions?
A: He talks smut. He talks dirty, he talks filthy, he talks pure, unadulterated smut.
It makes me want to puke.
Q: What are Mr Hart's major problems? Does he have an Oedipus complex?
A: What is that?
Q: You're an analyst, sir, and you never heard of an Oedipus complex?
A: Never in my life.
Q: Well, sir, it's when a man has a passionate desire to make love to his own
mother.
A: [after a pause] That's the dirtiest thing I ever heard. Where do you get that filth?
Q: It comes from a famous play by Sophocles.
A: Was he Jewish?
Q: No, sir, he was Greek.
A: With a Greek, who knows? But, with a Jew, you don't do a thing like that even
to your wife, let alone your mother.... Moss Hart is a nice Jewish boy. Maybe on a
Saturday night he takes the mother to the movies, maybe on the way home he gives
her a little peck in the back of the cab, but going to bed with the mother – get out of
here!

When the sketch finally came to an end the guest of honour proclaimed
that it was the funniest fourteen minutes he could remember. The gatecrasher
felt much the same and became a lifelong fan of Mel Brooks.

From time to time, forbidden to review Off-Broadway, Ken checked in to
see what he was missing. On his return from Spain in August 1959, he went
to see *The Connection*. This was the first play of a young poet and short-story
writer called Jack Gelber, and it had opened in July at the experimental Living
Theater, recently opened by Judith Molina and Julian Beck. Ken thought it
'the most memorable theatrical experience in New York' and he explained
that it dealt with 'the mystique of dope addiction'.

He found the play to be a work of such startling novelty that he wrote to
William Shawn to suggest that the *New Yorker* record its arrival in its Off-
Broadway listings. He explained that it took place in a beat pad, and that 'the
action – or rather, the neurotic inaction – is accompanied by a lively cool
jazz group on stage'. He wrote about it in *Harpers* magazine, and told all his
friends to go and see it. 'If any one person made *The Connection*,' Mailer
declares, 'it was Ken.'

Over Christmas 1959, Ken was in London editing *We Dissent*, his television documentary on American nonconformism. The ninety-minute programme was broadcast in January 1960 late at night on Associated Television and was touted as the first television programme of Americans publicly questioning the values of their civilization. Ken's view was that the standard image of an affluent country, bursting with abundance and 'organization men', gave by no means the whole picture; and that fifteen months in the States, and thousands of miles of travel, had revealed to him people and pockets of nonconformity.

Twenty-five dissenters were interviewed, including Alger Hiss, who talked moderately about the United States legal system as one which had benefited from dissent. The socialist Norman Thomas said that the country was governed by the four bureaucracies – government, military, big business and labour. The beat poet Allen Ginsberg talked about American prosody that explored the rhythm of American – rather than English – speech. Along with Lawrence Ferlinghetti, they spoke about the horrors of nuclear war – the theme of the programme. There was also the voice of Norman Cousins, spokesman for the Committee for a Sane Nuclear Policy; the black satirist Nipsey Russell on desegregation; Norman Mailer on hipsterism and psychopathology (living in the present and turning morality inside out). The sociologist C. Wright Mills confirmed that there was no organized dissent in the United States. 'I think it is confined to small groups of intellectuals in and out of universities and I think even there it tends to dry up very quickly.'

Jules Feiffer attacked political apathy. David Wesley, the journalist, said that the affluent society produced 'a vast accumulation of junk ... freedom of speech with nothing very meaningful to say', and the economist Kenneth Galbraith argued for a large public sector to build acceptable capitalism. The programme was reported extensively in the American press. The well-known red-baiter, George E. Sokolsky of the *Washington Post* and *Times Herald*, asked, 'Why provide these particular Americans with a shop window in England?' The FBI read Sokolsky's column and looked into their files. There they found that during the previous summer and autumn they had already begun to monitor Tynan's preparations for his programme, which intended, they noted, to 'discredit the American way of life'. At that time they considered 'putting the spotlight of publicity' on Ken, and had contacted the 'appropriate congressional committees'. Their research revealed that Ken had been known at Oxford University 'for his eccentric behavior', and having turned up this dire bit of information, an agent carefully underlined it.

Senator Dodd, a conservative Democrat, ex-FBI special agent and vice-chairman of the Senate Internal Security Subcommittee, formed in 1951 and companion to the House Un-American Activities Committee, told his subcommittee in great detail about *We Dissent*, claiming that the malicious and irresponsible criticism of America voiced in the programme simply played into the hands of the Communist enemy. He concluded that it was 'a sacred duty to combat divisive influences within the Western alliance and to promote its spiritual unity'.

Meanwhile Ken found himself involved in more political trouble, this time on American turf. A CBS newsman called Robert Taber, who had interviewed Fidel Castro in the Sierra Maestra, appeared in the *Nation* in January 1960 with a pro-Cuba article. This was read by a New Jersey civil libertarian called Alan Sagner, who contacted Taber and suggested forming the Fair Play for Cuba Committee, which would solicit prominent people to question and counter the deluge of anti-Castro 'propaganda' in the press.

On 6 April 1960 the Committee went public with an advertisement in the *New York Times* to combat what were deemed false press reports about Cuba; the advertisement quoted Fidel Castro as saying, 'Our revolution is not Communist but humanist.' The signatories included James Baldwin, Simone de Beauvoir, Truman Capote, Jean-Paul Sartre, Norman Mailer and Kenneth Tynan.

On the evening of 27 April Ken was handed a subpoena from the Senate Internal Security Subcommittee commanding him to be in Washington D.C., a few days later. But the section of the document designated to reveal what the investigation would be about was blank. 'My first response was bewilderment,' Ken later wrote, 'and my second dread – the kind of nebulous chill that besets all of us when the finger of officialdom points straight in our direction. Economic fears welled up; supposing I was publicly smeared, would my American earnings be jeopardized?' He discovered that he was evidently the first foreign journalist (and first Englishman) to be summoned.

On the morning of 5 May, he made his first trip to Washington. Shortly afterwards, Ken presented himself to the silver-haired Senator Dodd from Connecticut and to the subcommittee's chief counsel and inquisitor, the 'florid and genial' (according to Ken) J. G. Sourwine; and began to answer questions, having decided not to take advantage of the Fifth Amendment. Sourwine, a one-time Nevada newspaperman, had made his name, during his spell with the Senate committee, as the Capitol's outstanding red-hunter, earning the title – in the wake of Joe McCarthy – of the '97th Senator'.

Ken told the subcommittee he was not a member of the Communist Party, nor a member of the Fair Play for Cuba Committee, and that he had approved the content of the committee's advertisement, though he had not contributed funds. 'How did it happen', Sourwine asked, 'that you took the action of signing a statement in support of Castro in defiance of the views of President Eisenhower?' Now openly contemptuous of the committee, Ken replied that he wondered if, as an Englishman, his opinion should be formed by 'whether or not I am contradicting the opinions of the President of this country'.

At that point the subcommittee moved on to quiz Ken about *We Dissent*, about his associates at A T V, and how he had contacted the various unsavoury Americans interviewed. The subcommittee eventually agreed to enter into the record Ken's statement. He declared that the only organizations to which he paid dues were the Royal Society of Literature, the New York Drama Critics Circle and the Diners Club. 'I respectfully suggest there may be better ways of demonstrating to the world this country's traditional and splendid regard for freedom of speech. . . . I merely submit that governmental grilling of foreign newspapermen is not a practice that one instinctively associates with the workings of Western democracy.'

At the end of the hearing Ken signed the form that entitled him to a $12 witness fee, and returned to New York. He checked out his visa status and paid his lawyer Leonard Boudin $1500. His friends remember that Ken was distinctly shaken. His great love affair with the United States had been somewhat undermined.

Ken's commitment was clear: *We Dissent*, the Fair Play for Cuba advertisement, his senatorial engagement, the Committee for a Sane Nuclear Policy rally on 19 May, in which he took an active part, and the civil rights movement, which he passionately supported. With Harry Belafonte, Ken met Martin Luther King Jr and asked him why he did not make the point that it was economic exploitation rather than racial prejudice which kept the blacks down. 'If I say that,' King told him, 'they would call me a Communist. Christianity is safer.' At a time when black separatism was developing, under the leadership of Malcolm X, Ken would argue with his black friends, like James Baldwin, that their battles for integration and equal opportunity would not be effective until they decided that they were part of a world-wide revolt against ownership and profit. It was the Marxist line, and at that time Baldwin did not find it acceptable. But there was nothing particularly orthodox about Ken's 'romantic Marxism', which he buttressed with the views of the sexual libertarian Wilhelm Reich.

On 22 May he gave a grand farewell to New York at a party in the Forum of the Twelve Caesars, and was photographed in a pale blue dinner jacket happily embracing Vivien Leigh. Others among the 200 guests at the supper party – more uptown than downtown – included Gore Vidal, Lauren Bacall, Bea Lillie, Richard Avedon, Harry Belafonte, Charles Addams, Dwight Macdonald, Lillian Hellman, Sidney Lumet and James Thurber – who got very drunk, as was his habit in those last sad days before his death.

Edmund Wilson was one of the guests who could not attend the party. But he wrote to say that he was relieved Ken was going back to England because, although he would be missed, he could write with greater latitude at the *Observer* than on the *New Yorker*. He hoped Ken would publish a collection of his articles, 'the best writing of the kind since George Nathan, if not since Beerbohm and Shaw'.

Two days later, on 24 May, Ken flew home to London, leaving behind Broadway's 'intricate, stunningly resourceful and brilliantly manned machine for the large-scale utterance of carefully garnished banalities'.

He had gained weight and now looked a little jowly, after his two seasons in New York. He had joined the ranks of the pundits, and become even more of a celebrity. He had packed his life full, crammed those little black engagement books to the point where he cannot have had time for any quiet reflection. He had not resolved his marriage; and he was returning to the *Observer*, to the job he had relinquished two years earlier.

18

Theatrical Battles and Political Stages

In the late spring of 1960 Ken returned to London and began his second
term with the *Observer*, and his last as a full-time drama critic. By the
summer of 1963 he had given up weekly theatre reviewing, crossed the
footlights and gone into service as dramaturg to Laurence Olivier and the
newly formed National Theatre, a move which more or less answered the
question he had casually posed some years before: what happens to boy
critics?

He made the change not just because his enthusiasm for weekly journalism
was exhausted (as Shaw had exhausted his in 1898 and moved impatiently
on to more playwriting), but because he wanted the active role, to explore
his skills as an impresario, to engage in the wider political issues, to get back
on the inside, and at the same time to have a job which would allow him
time to write at greater length and under less pressure. The move, however,
did not please those admirers who would never have thought about directing
or writing or becoming drama critics had it not been for Ken – acolytes
who as undergraduates had read him during the mid-1950s and had been
persuaded by him that the theatre was not a dull backwater, but rather a
cockpit of intellectual and political excitement.

He helped inspire John McGrath, Roger Smith, Bamber Gascoigne, Trevor
Griffiths and Tom Stoppard to become playwrights. Sheridan Morley, as an
undergraduate at Oxford, used to cross the High Street barefoot and in his
pyjamas at eight in the morning to buy the *Observer*. 'If it hadn't been for
Ken I don't think I, or Michael Billington, or Robert Cushman would have
thought of being critics. He made us believe it was something worth doing,
and he taught us that there was a way of attacking the theatre from a position
of love.'

At the *Observer* during the early sixties was another young critic, Irving
Wardle, acting as Ken's second string.

I'd been terrified of him. He was extremely glamorous and reputed not to be very friendly to anyone who was boring, or belonged to the world of bicycle clips. But when we met in the local pub he was very direct and friendly. At the same time sort of bubbling over with show business stories about Vivien Leigh in some terrible state, and her clasping her hands on his cock. This extraordinary closeness to the top figures in the profession in their most private moments rather contrasted with the Baynard Castle half-pint drinkers.

One thing I remember being struck by when I first joined the paper was looking at proofs of Tynan hanging up, from which a paragraph had been cut. Cut Tynan? Impossible, I thought. He'd have gone to Leatherhead to see a revival of something rare, like *Magda*, and written fifty words of very honest, direct prose – the working journalist side of Ken – and I was impressed that such a race horse, such a performer, could have the professional integrity and affection for the theatre he was serving to do a kind of carthorse job too.

Wardle also admired the way Ken could pick up some small event in the West End the previous week, or a forgotten classic, and use it as a platform for making a resonant statement about human life.

Ken drew his ideas from everywhere, from the classical and the popular, from a sound knowledge of the European tradition, and sometimes, less reliably, from whatever he happened to be reading that week. His manner of embracing an intellectual idea with an extreme point of view could be very un-English, though his genius for making connections in his criticism, for cross-fertilizing all aspects of theatre, was characteristic of the post-war generation.

Brecht, for whom Ken had campaigned so passionately, was by the early 1960s in the theatre's bloodstream, and Ken now began to attack his imitators, Robert Bolt for example, whose *A Man for All Seasons* was an 'attempt to do for Sir Thomas More what Brecht did for Galileo. Bolt looks at history exclusively through the eyes of his saintly hero – Brecht's vision is broader: he looks at Galileo through the eyes of history.'

Another playwright influenced by Brecht fared better. Ken found Sartre's *Altona*, set in Germany – though its subject was inspired by the Algerian war – and not yet seen in Paris, 'a rich, cold, brain-twisting play' with a message that 'beliefs count for nothing compared with acts'.

It was on the Continent rather than in England that Ken found the best theatre. He went to East Berlin to see Helene Weigel's four-hundredth performance as Mother Courage, and to Stockholm to see another magnificent state-subsidized company, Ingmar Bergman's Royal Dramatic Theatre, 'homogeneous in personnel, flexible in technique, contemporary in outlook and international in scope'.

In Warsaw he found state-subsidized theatres as technically superb as the best German *Stadttheater*; and a choice of established plays (from Sophocles to Beckett) incomparably larger than in London.

At home his enthusiasm was yet again for European artists, for Franco Zeffirelli's revolutionary production of *Romeo and Juliet* (at the Old Vic). 'Nobody on stage seems to be aware that he is appearing in an immortal tragedy ... instead the actors behave like ordinary human beings, trapped in a quandary whose outcome they cannot foretell.'

On 1 October 1961, a year and a half after he had returned to London, Ken's weekly review was entitled 'The Breakthrough That Broke Down'. So little in ten years, he wrote, seemed to have changed. The Royal Court had made a beachhead for the new wave. But the majority of theatres were still inhabited by the kind of play Ken had roundly condemned in the early fifties. Joan Littlewood (whose apathetic production of *Fings Ain't Wot They Used T'Be* was running in the West End) had left Theatre Workshop; Brendan Behan had been silent since *The Hostage*; and Shelagh Delaney had not, according to Ken, lived up to the promise of *A Taste of Honey*.

Ken went on to argue that:

Too many of our younger playwrights have forgotten, in their passion for novelty of content, the ancient disciplines of style. .... In the battle for content, form has been sacrificed.

What I look for in working-class drama is the sort of play that is not ashamed to assimilate and acknowledge the bourgeois tradition.

But without a National Theatre, London had no playhouse in which the best of world drama was accessible.

There was, however, one exceptional stylist: Harold Pinter. Ken had reviewed *The Caretaker* the previous year and not recanted his first impression of *The Birthday Party*: 'a clever fragment grown dropsical with symbolic content', a piece 'full of those familiar paranoid overtones that seem to be inseparable from much of "*avant-garde*" drama'. In *The Caretaker* he found the same symptoms of paranoia, but the symbols had retired to the background. 'What remains is a play about people.' And he praised Pinter's bizarre dramatic technique, 'his skill in evoking atmosphere and his encyclopaedic command of contemporary idiom', his 'miraculous ear for colloquial eccentricities'. *A Slight Ache* transmitted 'a genuine theatrical chill'. *A Night Out*, performed in October 1961, combined 'colloquial authenticity with a sense of imminent dread'. But he deplored the 'Pinteretti', 'a whole school of dramatists speaking in his very accents; his is the new small-talk, and very small, on lips stiffer than his, it can sound'. Anyway had it not all been started by Eliot with 'Prufrock'?

In the early 1960s Ken devoted more and more time to political action. He wrote letters to the press; fought for sexual freedom and for an end to theatre censorship; and campaigned for nuclear disarmament and Castro's Cuba.

In November 1960, the six-day trial of *Lady Chatterley's Lover* caught his fancy. The proceedings at the Old Bailey had ingredients guaranteed to excite him: sexual bigotry, class warfare, the Establishment set against the forces of light, and all these elements dramatized by a trial. (He loved trials and might well have made an excellent advocate if he had followed the career his father preferred for him.) The Crown had decided to prosecute Penguin Books for their publication of the unexpurgated version of Lawrence's novel, in order to test the 1959 Obscene Publications Act. This allowed that a book deemed likely to 'deprave and corrupt' its readers could not be condemned if it could be demonstrated that the work was 'for the public good on the ground that it is in the interests of science, literature, art or learning'. Thirty-five expert witnesses were called.

Ken highlighted the confrontation between Lawrence's England and Sir Clifford Chatterley's England; between contact and separation; between love and death; between the defence counsel Gerald Gardiner, 'that rock among silks', and Mervyn Griffith-Jones, counsel for the prosecution, 'a voice barbed with a rabid belief in convention and discipline'. And he recorded the sociologist Richard Hoggart's testimony, pointing out how Lawrence had 'striven to cleanse [the word] of its furtive, contemptuous and expletive connotations, and to use it in the most simple, neutral way: one fucks'.

And there the word appeared for the first time in a Sunday newspaper, for Ken had persuaded his editor that if the hearing was about whether the word could be printed, and if the *Observer* was in favour, then they must follow through and use it. 'Ken knew that public opinion was ready,' David Astor recalls. 'He slid it in and there was no fuss.'

In June 1961, so concerned was Ken about the East-West confrontation over Berlin that he switched, halfway through a review of *Hamlet* – carried by a tenuous connecting quotation from 'How all occasions' – and pounced on a recent article in the *Guardian* by Lord Altrincham which had declared that, unless Krushchev agreed to an honourable settlement before the end of 1961, 'we must get ready to die'. 'The hero nowadays', Ken argued, 'is the man who elected to live under the new regime, hoping to change it; and the coward would be the man who preferred, like Lord Altrincham, to lie down and die.'

Altrincham wrote to the *Observer* the following week: 'If we are not prepared to risk our lives we do not deserve to be free.' Nuclear war, Ken retorted, would mean the total destruction of everything one prizes. 'Lord Altrincham is thus in the position of saying: "For the sake of democracy, let democracy perish."'

In August he developed his thoughts on the theme of 'better red than dead', and on the Berlin crisis, in *Time and Tide*.

Suppose that our choice was life: we would still have sunlight in the streets, and talk, and sex, and work, and food, and laughter. I will settle for these; but then I am the kind of coward who respects people more than the system under which they live; and the kind of fool who believes that the eventual survival of democracy can best be assured by the continued existence of the people who created it.

His engagement book reflects this preoccupation: 'I think a little alarm and even despondency shd. be spread. Time is past when one can say that to give in isn't manly. ... People who aren't frightened by H. bomb must be mad.' A year or so later Noël Coward bumped into Ken in the White Elephant Club, and found him still 'gibberingly scared' about the 'atom bomb'. ('It seems to me far too vast a nightmare to be frightened of,' wrote Coward testily in his diary.)

During the spring of 1961 Ken was also deeply engaged in drawing public attention to the mobilization of the United States against Cuba. On 14 April he wrote to the *New Statesman*, urging that the time to protest was 'now'. But 'now' was too late, and after the invasion of the Bay of Pigs, on 17 April, he organized a letter to *The Times* condemning the armed aggression. His fellow signatories included Anthony Wedgwood Benn, John Freeman, Michael Foot, E. J. Hobsbawm, Doris Lessing and Penelope Gilliatt.

Ken helped organize a demonstration in Hyde Park, memorable for the large number of pretty girls who took part, and at the end of April he was the guiding light in the formation of the British Cuba Committee.

His reaction to the Cuban missile crisis was less public spirited. According to his friend Peter Wildeblood, Ken panicked and 'thought the world was coming to an end. He concluded that the only sensible thing to do was to go to Australia, and he booked *one* seat one way. Did I know where was Qantas? He thought it was a place in Australia, and that's where he was going to sit out the apocalypse. I said, "You'll hate it. Nothing to do there but shoot crocodile and make handbags." Fortunately, the crisis blew over.'

Ken had from time to time during the fifties bemoaned the lack of political cabaret. In October 1960 he had suggested in the *Observer* that 'the theatre as a whole has been infected, and injured, by our weakness in the tiny, ancillary department of satirical cabaret' which could 'pierce to the quick of the ulcer', and speak freely on any subject. Lively cabaret was the cause of satire in other theatrical forms. Brecht and Weill had been influenced by Berlin cabaret of the twenties. Adolph Green and Betty Comden came out of the clubs of Greenwich Village; Abe Burrows was a cabaret parodist. America had Nichols and May, Mort Sahl, Lenny Bruce. What was there in England? And would not the actor Harold Lang or the blues singer George Melly thrive if there were somewhere to develop their skills?

The following May, *Beyond the Fringe* opened in London (having tried out in Edinburgh the previous summer), and Ken declared that English comedy had taken its first decisive step into the second half of the twentieth century. Messrs Cook, Miller, Bennett and Moore were taunting the accents and values of John Betjeman's suburbia; they were wonderfully funny anti-reactionaries. They did not go as far as Ken hoped, 'but immeasurably further than one had any right to expect'. Jonathan Miller recalls that although the four of them knew their show was funny, they did not think they were revolutionary until 'Kenneth Tynan shoved his banner into our hands'.

Six months after the opening of *Beyond the Fringe* Peter Cook and Nicholas Luard opened The Establishment, the first serious satirical club. The cabaret dealt glancing blows at political figures. But such teeth as the script had, according to Ken, were 'engaged more in nibbling than in biting'. 'Whether the nominal target is the Church, the Tory Party, Civil Defence, linguistic philosophy or the BBC, the real target is nearly always the same: namely, the cloying, paternal tone traditionally adopted by top people when addressing the rest of us. This is the show's strength; but also its limitation.' Ken told the proprietors that no political cabaret can be accounted a success unless at least a quarter of the audience walks out in the course of the performance.

When Lenny Bruce appeared at the Establishment, people *did* walk out – thereby proving to Ken the effectiveness of his satire. Sometimes, Ken felt, 'Mr. Bruce drawls and mumbles too privately.' He wished that this 'impromptu prose poet' were better read. But if *Beyond the Fringe* was a pinprick, Bruce was a bloodbath. Ken pointed out that 'in didactic moments Bruce liked to remind his audience that "Thou shalt not kill" *means just that'*. Bruce was also extremely funny, but seldom so without an ulterior motive.

Several weeks after Bruce's appearance at The Establishment Ken echoed in another context his ever present concern with mortality. 'Satire is protest, couched in wit, against the notion that there is anything more important than the fact that all men must die.'

In October 1961 he reviewed George Steiner's *The Death of Tragedy*, which had appeared earlier in the year. If serious plays like *The Life of Galileo* or *Luther* were based on the assumption that man is capable of moulding his destiny, comedy had meanwhile occupied the territory that tragedy had vacated: the clowning in Beckett and Ionesco, the sick humour of Lenny Bruce. 'Comedy on one level or another', Ken wrote,

has distinguished all the productions I best remember from Theatre Workshop and the Royal Court: Behan, Frank Norman, Nigel Dennis, N.F. Simpson and the early Osbornes.

What with Harold Pinter, Keith Waterhouse and Willis Hall on the sidelines, I think it safe to predict that satire, irony, gallows-humour and other mutations of the comic spirit will be the guiding forces of our theatre in the coming years. Tragedy, with its traditional respect for hierarchies and its passion for bloody *dénouements*, has little to say to a rebellious generation obsessed by the danger of imminent megadeaths.

A week or so later he referred to the Polish critic Jan Kott's now famous comparative study of *King Lear* and Beckett's *Endgame* in a review of *Heartbreak*

House: 'the last scene of Shaw's play is a harbinger; it is part of the great process that has since ... transformed our century's drama – the steady annexation by comedy of territories that formerly belonged to the empire of tragedy'.

Kott argued that, in an era which repudiates absolutes, tragedy cannot exist: 'When accepted values are overthrown and there is no appeal from the "tortures of the cruel world" to God, nature or history, the Fool becomes the central figure in the theatre.'

'Here we are already close to the anarchic latitudes of *Heartbreak House*,' Ken wrote,

that rudderless ship of fools with its clownish, rum-soaked skipper. It may not be too fanciful to picture Captain Shotover as a missing link between Lear and Beckett's Hamm, a halfway halt on Lear's journey to the absurd. He is a prophet of disaster, whose ruling desire is to invent a device capable of blowing up an unsatisfactory world; like Lear, he will register his protest in deeds that shall be 'the terrors of the earth'. By the time we reach Beckett's play he has presumably succeeded; the outside world has been abolished, as if by nuclear intervention, and Hamm sits enthroned in a claustrophobic dungeon, monarch of nothingness.

On 3 June 1962, Ken took up the case of Martin Esslin's *The Theatre of the Absurd*, on the work of, among others, Beckett, Ionesco, Adamov and Genet. He recognized that the dramatists of the Absurd, 'by their repudiations of verbal logic, psychological consistency and any kind of ideological commitment', were attempting to shock the audience into an awareness of their plight in a godless, purposeless universe; that they wanted a return to the original religious function of the theatre, 'the confrontation of man with the spheres of myth and religious reality', as Esslin put it.

But how was their work to be judged? According to Esslin, by whether it 'springs from deep layers of profoundly experienced emotion' and 'mirrors real obsessions, dreams and valid images in the subconscious mind of its author'. 'But what does "valid" mean?' Ken asked. 'The man who reacts to the universe with a cry of impotent anguish is acceptable as an artist only if he can persuade us that he has sanely considered the other possible reactions and found them inadequate.' He was impressed by Arthur Adamov, who had recently espoused Marxism, 'not in order to make men equally happy, but to give them equality of opportunity to contemplate their unhappiness'. This attitude seemed for Ken 'to get the priorities exactly right. What irks one most about Absurdists is their pervasive tone of privileged despair.'

He also wrote a few weeks later in a review of *Love's Labour's Lost*: 'Nature has chastised the presumptions of those who, denying her demands, have sought to live as hermits. The messenger's announcement forcibly reminds them that life itself imposes on all who live it a final, inescapable deprivation: there is no need to invent others.'

19

Private Turmoil

The Tynans had returned to Mount Street, to the curious study, the incongruous floral wall-papered bedroom, and the almost derelict kitchen, next to which slept the nine-year-old Tracy and, nearby, the au pair. There was a cat called Geranium, a cantankerous Cockney cleaning lady, and from the autumn of 1960 a charming Australian secretary called Su Dalgleish. There were also the two lead characters, who seemed to regard the flat as a base from which to operate – separately. Elaine started a second novel; Ken was theatre critic for the *Observer*, political activist, town herald, often herald to the Western world, and, in the autumn of 1961, in charge of a television arts programme.

He went on jaunts to Venice, to Málaga, overnight to New York, as surprise guest to Mike Nichols' birthday party given by Richard Avedon, bursting in to the Chinese restaurant Foo Chow, where the party was held, and casting armfuls of red roses before the guests. He went to Berlin, to Vienna, to Paris, to Madrid, taking with him different women, and combining in all these travels missions of work and pleasure. But so much was crammed into so short a space, putting his physical and mental health under such strain that in the autumn of 1961, aged thirty-four, he suffered a temporary breakdown. He described himself in his first journal as 'aggressive, contemptuous and breaking to pieces with anxiety' and exhausted by the war with Elaine.

He noted:

One effect of intense marriage: erosion of the ego. I am left with a super-ego of enormous (though sporadically exercised) power, in the form of a bitterly remonstrating conscience that enforces periodic bouts of self-punishing work, and an equally powerful Id, seeking immediate and constant sensual gratification. But my ego has been ground away to the vanishing point – dust between the two major opponents. ... Hence my weak sense of normal identity. Ask me who I am when working all night, and when making love or eating, but with the cessation of these pursuits, I vanish. . . . Any kind of compromise is alien to me, but not because I am brave or principled. It is simply that I am too guilty to be corruptible.

The 'intense marriage' was now a feature of London life, for neither abroad nor at home did the Tynans modify their high-decibel fights. At the end of 1961 Ken asked his secretary Su Dalgleish whether he should stay with Elaine. 'By that time I was so appalled by the pointlessness·of it all, that I answered, "Well, to be quite honest with you, Ken, I do feel that if you are intending to grow emotionally, then you'd better check out. But if you intend to stay at the stage that you're at at the moment, then the marriage is made in heaven."'

Elaine and Ken were sophisticated provocateurs of the other's neurotic and emotional past. Ken would tell his wife that her father had always wanted a boy and that was what he had got. She in turn would claim that to be married for ten years was to know complete isolation, that there was no rest in his love, that it was her father all over again.

Su Dalgleish observed how, in collision with each other, they would lose control. Tumblers, among other things, would be thrown, narrowly missing the hapless secretary, who felt there must be something sexual in those physical assaults, 'a way of their getting back together again. But it was like flogging something that was dying. Meanwhile Tracy was a little girl and needed a home, and preferably one which was not flying apart all the time.'

Elaine was quick to tell Ken that she was now making more money than he. (Ken's income was in the region of £6000 a year, which included his salary from the *Observer* and income from American magazines.) In 1963 Elaine's father died leaving over $2 million, of which she was the beneficiary of a trust worth in the region of $200,000. At one point Elaine had bitterly asked her friend Maria St Just if Ken had married her for her money. But the question seemed merely provocative. As in all bad marriages money became the subject of dispute, but it was always a peripheral issue.

The Tynans could not let go. There were more Mount Street parties, though one or other of them might be living elsewhere. And there were the annual trips to Spain. In May 1961 they went to the festival of San Isidro, and there they joined Orson Welles, about whom Ken was writing yet another profile.

That summer they also went to Málaga for the *feria* to watch Ordóñez, 'the courteous young maestro of Ronda', fight on six consecutive days. In Málaga they met up with the actress Georgia Brown, who recalls the craziness between the Tynans. 'Their fights became the entertainment for the evening. And about what? Nothing. Power. Whose conversation was more interesting.'

In early October Ken's collection of theatre reviews and profiles, *Curtains*, came out and was highly praised. Across the Atlantic it was – from Harold Clurman to Alfred Kazin – admiringly welcomed.

However, there were those at home who carped. In the *Observer* itself, Mary

McCarthy argued that Ken was a facile parodist, though she liked some of his parody. She next suggested that 'rational discourse is not Tynan's strong point'. He provided a performance, not an analysis. But she did not see fit to justify this claim.

Several years before, Ken had unfavourably reviewed a collection of Miss McCarthy's called *Sights and Spectacles*. The literary editor of the *Observer* felt that whether McCarthy had a grudge against Ken or not, her review was terribly wounding, and he commissioned another, entitled 'Contrary Mary', to appear on the same day. This was penned by Alan Pryce-Jones, who took McCarthy to task.

In the *New Statesman*, the writer A. Alvarez delivered a further attack, comparing Ken's work to Edmund Wilson's *Classics and Commercials*: 'Where Tynan merely records or asserts, Wilson works out his perceptions gradually, subtly and without any flagrant parti pris.' But the root of the problem, for Alvarez, was that there was no 'mature, developing intellectual life' in the English *theatre*.

From the other side of the footlights John Whiting wrote: 'God knows, it is almost insulting to ask a playwright to get *pleasure* from reading a volume of dramatic criticism, yet that is what I felt when reading this book. ... Not since Bernard Shaw has any man done more. Like Shaw, Mr. Tynan has wonderful prejudices. What Ibsen was to Shaw, Brecht is to Mr. Tynan.' The playwright recognized in Ken a man of the theatre, as much so as 'our best actors and directors'. He complimented him for his honesty and admired the way he pricked the balloons of any writer merely hitched to a good cause.

Through the summer of 1961 and into the autumn, Ken was working for the *Observer* as well as preparing *Tempo* for commercial television. He set up his office in a panelled suite at the Piccadilly Hotel in the centre of London, and went to work. He crammed his engagement book with meetings to explore ideas. Orson Welles for a film on bullfighting; Kingsley Amis on pop culture; Douglas Cooper on Picasso; Gore Vidal on the art of conversation; Louis MacNeice on art and war; the Oxbridge 'octopus'; Roger Vadim and Norman Mailer on erotic art (alongside this idea Ken wrote: 'Distinguish erotic art from pornographic, then ask if it's desirable'); John Osborne on the new British cinema.

In October the first of the fifty-minute fortnightly programmes made its début, with the Earl of Harewood interviewing Laurence Olivier about the new Chichester Festival, followed by irreverent comment from the stars of *Beyond the Fringe* – Jonathan Miller, Peter Cook, Dudley Moore and Alan Bennett.

Of the fifteen editions, Ken was most pleased with an idiosyncratic interview with Gordon Craig on his ninetieth birthday (Craig said off-camera that Ken's face was that of a 'blooming martyr'); a programme in which Françoise Sagan, Nathalie Sarraute and others were interviewed in Paris about the artist's responsibility during a political crisis, such as the Algerian war; the first performance in England of Isaac Stern's trio; Jill Craigie's filmed critique of contemporary British architecture; an essay on Christ in art, written by John Whiting; Graham Sutherland at work; and John McGrath on psychotic art.

Ken ran the show like a 'brilliantly eclectic maverick', its originàtor, Brian Tesler, recalls. But he ran it against impossible odds: a shoestring budget, poor technical facilities and an actors' strike.

Rose Tynan had remained, since the autumn of 1958, at St Andrew's Psychiatric Hospital, an imposing Georgian building set in large grounds. Having found the best possible place for his mother, Ken put her affairs, and the cost of the hospital, which was eighteen guineas a week, into the hands of the Court of Protection, while he himself paid to transport his mother's sister May to the hospital to visit.

Early in her stay, the hospital noted that Rose was confused and disoriented, that she tended to wander, partly dressed, 'as though setting out on a shopping expedition. She has put herself to bed in other patients' rooms, discarded her clothing inappropriately, and been found standing on her bed pulling vaguely at the curtains for no apparent reason.' But the patient was 'pleasant and affable, friendly and cooperative'. In May 1959, six months after her arrival, she was reported to be 'more confused', her 'health failing'; a year later she was 'incontinent and frail, profoundly demented and no conversational coherent contact can be made with her'.

Ken's engagement book, on his return to England from New York, is full of reminders to write to Rose and to see her. He may have gone to Northampton in October 1960. Most certainly he visited on 11 February 1961. Two days later he wrote to the hospital to say, 'I am sending a parcel of fruit and confectionery off to her today; it is obvious from her condition that she will be unable to consume the contents unaided, and I should like to feel sure that somebody would be assisting her. If you could let me know the name of the nurse who looks after her, I would be most grateful.'

Subsequently, he wrote to check on the number of visits paid to Rose by her sister May. Ken's contact appears to have ended there until the following November when he received a letter from the hospital telling him that Rose was in serious decline, her condition complicated by broncho-pneumonia. On Monday, 13 November Ken visited the hospital and saw his mother during the afternoon. She was 'appallingly emaciated', he later wrote. At 12.15 a.m. the next day she died. Three days later she was cremated and buried at the Northampton Crematorium.

To the funeral came Ken, 'pole-axed by emotion', according to his cousin Ruth, and with him Elaine, loyally trying to protect him from his relatives.

Five red rose bushes and a bronze memorial plaque costing £101 14s were ordered and paid for with Sir Peter's money. The plaque reads: 'In loving remembrance of Letitia Rose Tynan 1888–1961'.

Rose left everything to Ken: an estate valued before death duties at £25,387 7s. By 1965 the value of the estate was closer to £40,000 (though by that time Ken had reduced the total capital). It was always an embarrassment to him that he had inherited stocks and shares, and he set about disposing of his inheritance carelessly and at speed.

The day after Rose's funeral, Ken flew to Berlin on a cultural mission for his television programme, taking with him his wife (with whom he had a violent quarrel). He returned on 21 November to his habitually packed timetable. On the 22nd there are eighteen entries in his engagement book. They include a film, a play, and six work appointments. On the morning of the 23rd, Ken went early to the *Tempo* office in the Piccadilly Hotel, followed by a literary luncheon in honour of Bertrand Russell. After a dental appointment, he began to write his weekly *Observer* piece.

The following morning the article was delivered by taxi. It started quite sensibly with a review of Eugene O'Neill's *Mourning Becomes Electra*, then went into the tensions in the making of *Tempo*, and finished with 'Next week Orson Welles will be in this space, outrageously correct.' It was a kind of mind blitz, according to those who read it at the *Observer*, and Ken, when confronted, seemed unaware of what had happened. The second string was sent to cover the week's theatre.

Two days later, Ken made a note to call his friend Jonathan Miller for the name of a psychiatrist, and by 12 December he was in Hampstead on the couch of an independent Freudian called Paul Senft. The analysis, consisting of two or three sessions a week and lasting until the following September, appeared on the surface to have achieved its aim, which was to help him leave his marriage. By September he had drawn up a draft separation agreement, though even then Ken was not sure that he wanted a divorce, and it took a further two years finally to break the strong emotional ties of that relationship.

As for the deeper issues exposed by Dr Senft, many appear to have been recognized, committed to scraps of paper, and eventually put away in a drawer: 'With Elaine as with Jill [Rowe-Dutton, his first Oxford love] I engineer a situation where I am humiliated,' Ken jotted down. 'E and I – 2 injured narcissists (healthy narcissists live thru 1st year of life and find their own identity, injured ones are punished, rejected during that year – and thereafter are uncertain which part of reality is themselves and which is hostile and outside them)'. He continued: 'My desire to buy a Jaguar: a desire to kill myself – I let my mother die and now I will kill myself with the dead Baron's legacy. I have two moods – puritan tension, followed by sadistic exhibitionism etc. No sense of reality (my own reality)'.

There are more of these incomplete illuminations. Ken wrote on a *School for Scandal* programme of 29 March 1962: 'I have introjected my parents – especially my father.' And he noted:

1. His legs were bad – I don't dance or play games
2. He didn't drive – nor do I
3. He had bronchitis – so have I
4. He kept 2 houses – so do I [Ken had taken a separate apartment to live with a girlfriend]
5. He was out of his class – so I am

Dr Senft was clearly a good sleuth and Ken for once an enthusiastic witness. If introjection is correctly defined as the unconscious incorporation of external ideas into one's own mind, then Ken – with his therapist's help – was surely on to some important revelation. Around the same time he drafted a letter to Elaine, which reads most movingly: 'I was illegitimate and I was made to know it by my father and my family – I was the boy who tied up his boots, at whom everyone smiled knowingly and despisingly, and I have pretended ever since to be somebody – anybody – else.'

To his friends George and Patricia Harewood, some two years later, Ken said of their illegitimate son Mark: 'He must know exactly who he is. You must make sure this child knows who he is.' He was obsessive on the matter.

Another theatre programme, for the evening of 2 April 1962, Ken's thirty-fifth birthday, carries more revealing notes. 'You are creative,' the analyst is quoted as saying. 'You have brought out things – a social historical change. Remember the Greeks thought the Spokesman was the greatest man – the public truth-teller.'

Ken never allowed this material to resonate, never appropriated it, reinvented it or made connections with it. When asked by a friend, during those early months of analysis, 'Why don't you write a novel?' he replied, 'What about? I have nothing to say.' And although for many years he had considered writing a play, on one occasion only did he ground the wish in a subject close to himself – his mother. In July 1958, just before Rose was committed to hospital, he had made a note in his engagement book to write a play about her. 'Mind your eyes. Scarborough, Lemon sole. Husband a sponger. Are you going to kill me?' These are the rich and tantalizing *aides-mémoire* – his mother's deranged words perhaps – that he jotted down.

Ken was clearly not a 'failed creative writer', as so many of his friends and enemies maintain. He was an exceptionally creative writer, and entirely original. The process of recapturing his past, of investigating the everyday, whether in autobiography or fiction, might have allowed him rather to make a quantum leap from those intuitions and half-realized thoughts provoked by an analyst. He might have explored the broad and deep realm of memory and therein seen himself in the context of his past rather than condemning himself as a victim turned victimizer. He might have broken the neurotic pattern which would not allow him to trust his own authority, and cracked the silly secret of his childhood wide open. ('A neurosis', he wrote around this time, 'is a secret you don't know you're keeping.') Then surely he might have forgiven himself.

'Mind your eyes. . . . Husband a sponger. Are you going to kill me?' What might he have made of them?

There is, of course, a corollary to the notion that Ken needed to unlock his past as a writer. He was a great essayist and critic in some measure because of the odd circumstances of his birth and of his self-invention. It is no coincidence that he frequently used the metaphor of the pearl as the disease of the oyster. If Ken had made the journey into the past, he would not necessarily have written great or even good prose. He might, however, have made some discoveries for his peace of mind. But he still found the ordinary uninteresting, and he passed on. The visits to Senft, after all, were only to allow him to break with Elaine, and Senft told him, to Ken's great relief: 'The sexual thing is bosh.' But Senft also suggested that he kept on bringing up his sexual proclivities like 'the burglar who is concealing a murder – the murder of your talent'.

During 1962 Ken and Elaine were in and out of each other's lives, moving to separate flats, coming together again, only to split once again in their usual dramatic manner. On 13 February Elaine's play, *My Place*, opened in the West End, a stage dressing-room comedy, with Diane Cilento playing the actress from an East End Jewish background (thought to have been loosely modelled on that of Georgia Brown). John Dexter directed. The play received mixed notices and ran for five months. Both at the time and subsequently the author gave generous thanks to Ken for his advice. Elaine gave this description of her play: '[It's] about the tensions between two selfish and talented people who are very much in love with each other. Both are actors.'

Ken had taken a dismal flat in Groom Place sw1, and there he spent time with a very pretty, blue-eyed, blonde portrait-painter called Brenda Bury. He decided to leave Elaine.

Miss Bury found Ken sweet-tempered and mild – except during Elaine's visits:

I saw this man whom I adored, gibbering in front of her. He became a child. And I wondered if she replaced his mother. She'd complain about his philandering. She'd turn to me and say, 'He'll never be faithful to you either,' and Ken would stammer and shake, and be destroyed.

I could not imagine [such a relationship] but he would say, 'Then you've never been in love.' What he had to lose was everything he had built up for himself, and Elaine was part of that. And there were financial reasons. I don't think he knew what marriage was like, and I don't really think he'd been in love with anyone.

When he came down with a particularly severe bronchial attack and cold, he looked around the wretched, damp flat and announced to Brenda Bury, 'This is how I began.' 'He was looking for an excuse to go back to Mount Street, which was home.'

One of Ken's secretaries, Judy Scott-Fox, recalls that when he was in residence in Mount Street 'Ladies used to drift up with suitcases. They looked as if they'd come for months. Then you found out they were just between plays.' Miss Scott-Fox did not care to arrive in the morning to the sight of two nude bodies and some empty tins of mulligatawny soup. 'I didn't think this was in the line of duty. In the end we evolved a scheme that if there were two glasses in the living-room, there would be somebody in his bed and I would stay clear.'

One of the girls whom Ken saw much of during 1962 and 1963 was a Chinese actress called Tsai Chin. She was impressed by how generous he was about the talent of other writers, perhaps because he was so secure in his own talent. But she felt he had never built up any self-discipline. Miss Chin, like others of Ken's girlfriends, found that he was helpful in some ways, yet unsympathetic to her career problems in other ways. Perhaps it was a matter of generation, that nothing in his childhood would have prepared him for women bursting out and wishing to succeed. Nor was he very practised at ordinary everyday problems. He would be generous and affectionate but he did not always know how to give moral support to a friend in deep distress.

Once or twice Elaine appeared at Tsai Chin's place. 'I think she was very lonely or upset. And then I would leave them alone ... so neurotic with each other.'

On 22 March 1962 Elaine served Ken with a divorce petition, and demanded that, notwithstanding her adultery during the marriage, she be granted custody of Tracy, alimony and child support. On to this document Ken scribbled notes for his defence. But it also seemed that he wanted a legal separation and, unless Elaine agreed, he would bring a countersuit. A deed of separation was not drafted until the following September – one in which Ken demanded custody of Tracy, and that Elaine should support herself.

On 28 July Ken had set off for the Málaga feria and the Miramar Hotel on his own. Elaine came to stay at the Miramar with Georgia Brown. At some point, while Elaine was asleep in her room, Ken burst in having persuaded the concierge to give him a key, and the result of the confrontation was that Elaine suffered a broken nose. She went rushing off to the house of Orson and Paula Welles, who applied cold compresses, gave her a drink and sent her away. 'They were obviously having a terrible time together,' Welles said, 'the nature of which we weren't interested in looking into because Ken didn't want to talk about it, and Elaine did.'

During the first part of 1963 they were separated for longer periods, and after a short holiday together in the summer of 1963 the Tynans more or less parted for good – though not without the aftermath of pain, regret and sadness that haunts any true if fierce marriage.

Ken moved on and recovered. Elaine's journey of return to the living took a longer and more painful course. Perhaps with all the excitement and expense of spirit she had grown tired, and had begun to wonder, like her heroine in *The Dud Avocado*, 'What happens when your curiosity just suddenly gives out? When the will and the energy snap and it all seems so once-over-again? What's going to happen to me five years from now, when I wake in the night . . . take a deep breath to start all over again, and find that I've no breath left?'

Having for years belittled Beckett, Ken saw *Happy Days* at the Royal Court in November 1962 and described him as that 'prophet who cannot help seeing beyond creature comforts to the engulfing grave'. He was moved by its main character, Winnie, buried up to her waist in earth, yet 'grateful for the mercy of survival', hailing each new day 'as another free gift of happiness'. Winnie gazes straight at the audience and asks: 'And you, she says, what's the idea of you, she says, what are you meant to mean?' and Ken counsels, 'Only those who are sure of the answer can afford to miss the play.'

A week later Peter Brook's great production of *King Lear* opened at Stratford-on-Avon, with Paul Scofield as Lear, and a rough-hewn setting combining Brecht and Oriental theatre. 'Instead of assuming that Lear is right, and therefore pitiable, we are forced to make judgements – to decide between his claims and those of his kin.' A week or two later Ken once again examined this position of 'moral neutrality'. 'For [Brook] the play is a mighty philosophic farce, in which the leading figures enact their roles on a gradually denuded stage that resembles, at the end, a desert graveyard or unpeopled planet . . . for the first time in tragedy a world without gods, with no possibility of hopeful resolution.'

The theatre, in particular the European theatre, was drawn up in battle formation: on the one hand Sartre and Brecht, on the other Beckett and Ionesco. Though Ken favoured the views of the first group, he recognized the legitimacy of the second.

In September 1962 Peter Hall and John Barton triumphed with their Brechtian reinterpretation of Shakespeare's history plays – the three parts of *Henry VI* and *Richard III*, called *The Wars of the Roses*. There was also Clifford Williams' production of *The Comedy of Errors*, which Ken described as 'unmistakably a Royal Shakespeare Company production. The statement is momentous; it means that Peter Hall's troupe has developed, uniquely in Britain, a classical style of its own. How is it to be recognized? By solid Brechtian settings that emphasize wood and metal instead of paint and canvas; and by cogent deliberate verse-speaking, that discards melodic cadenzas in favour of meaning and motivation.'

At Stratford's main home in London was Peter Brook's production of Friedrich Dürrenmatt's *The Physicists*. David Rudkin's striking début *Afore Night Come* was staged at their smaller house, the Arts Theatre. And at Stratford East Joan Littlewood made her celebrated return to Theatre Work-shop, with *Oh What a Lovely War*, 'revolutionary alike in content and form', her company sharing a vision 'that extends to life in general; it is thus, rather than by any rehearsal method or technique of staging that true theatrical style is born'.

Across the Atlantic were Edward Albee's *Who's Afraid of Virginia Woolf?*; Eugene O'Neill's *Strange Interlude*; Zero Mostel in *A Funny Thing Happened on the Way to the Forum*; and Jerome Robbins' *Mother Courage* – actually mounted on Broadway. In addition there was the fragile promise of Elia Kazan and Robert Whitehead's Repertory Theater at Lincoln Center.

Meanwhile, and despite this rich time, the critic was not content. The theatre in Europe was still superior to the British. The battle still to be fought and won was for a National Theatre.

Interlude

A year and a half after I began to write, the first part of a manuscript lay before me, bulky with evidence of Ken's avid, urgent life. Though I had in my uncensored search opened myself up to all and any discoveries, I had begun to feel numb. As Ken would have jauntily put it, I was writhing in apathy: it was inhuman.

In willed hope I pinned up over my desk a stanza of a Rilke poem recently torn out of a magazine:

> Work of seeing is done,
> now practice heart-work
> upon those images captive within
> you; for you overpowered them only: but now
> do not know them.

Heart-work, of course, would be better practised with my first-hand participation. I would have to step forward, declare myself, come clean, or as clean as I dared or knew how. If Ken had become a stranger to me, the girl whom he married was no more than a shadow.

Away from the dead matter of filing cabinets and other people's recollections, I began to pull out memories of Ken, odd, sweet, jolting, unfamiliar intimacies. And many of these memories were of Ken in Spain.

I don't think he was ever happier than in that southern corner of Europe (with the possible exception of Oxford), for there, as at Oxford, he could create his own world against a sympathetic background. If he had been Spanish in the 1930s I imagine he would have belonged to the Anarchists, with their belief that freedom and moral self-realization are interdependent.

This English provincial liked the summer heat in Spain, and the solemn beauty of the country. He claimed that all adjectives ending in '-id' applied, like arid, morbid, lurid, torpid, squalid, intrepid, sordid and vivid. He rejoiced in the great post-war Spanish plot to confine foreign tourists largely to the coastline, thereby protecting most of the peninsula from spoliation.

Ken loved the sight of bulky castles, and golden prairie viewed from the cool of a high-beamed room. He liked the cold piquant soup, spicy sausage called *chorizo*, and he would scan a menu in search of quail or partridge, ideally marinated and served in a brown gelid sauce; and he liked the light sherry called *fino*, which is acrid dry.

When first he went to Spain in 1951, the streets were full of beggars, whom he did not find at all picturesque or amusing. Yet he was not quite at ease with post-Franco Spain, and part of him resented modernization and the encroachment of Europe. He used to say that you should bring your own Band-Aids to Spain because you never knew when you were going to sprout your own stigmata. But he also responded respectfully to the Spanish pre-occupation with death.

I do not believe that there was anything particularly sensational or sadistic – not unfamiliar Tynan characteristics – in Ken's love of the bullfight (which he never defended on moral grounds). He once wrote: 'Bullfighting is the difficult craft of facing a charging bull with stillness, grace and rhythmic control; of slowing its pace to fit your tempo, of forcing it to follow the course you prescribe.' He felt that if as a spectator you felt anxious, as one might at a gladiatorial spectacle, fearful and over-excited, then the matador was not performing properly. In Antonio Ordóñez of the magic cape, whom Ken first saw fight in Pamplona in 1952 and last in Tarifa in 1972, he found the perfect exponent of classical fighting. Eventually he modified his view of the fight to match that of Ordóñez, who believed that it was a question not of dominating the bull but of coinciding with him.

Ken also recognized in Ordóñez the quality which the Spanish call *garbo*, once translated for him as 'the flaunting of an assured natural charm, poise infected by *joie de vivre* ... the essentially female attribute (even in bullfighters).' He understood that the *macho* bullfighter who has not the feminine qualities of grace and sweetness is offensive. And he responded to the female part of the male torero, dressed in his showy suit of lights, for it was close to his own make-up. I remembered, by distant association, Ken dressing in drag for a fancy-dress ball, preparing with deadly, nervous seriousness, for he wanted to know what it felt like to be a woman. And I recall telling him that he had the makings of a good lesbian, though not of a homosexual.

When Antonio Ordóñez was in the ring and working well, whilst at close quarters with death, Ken – a supremely anxious man – felt consoled, 'as though it had all become beautiful and simple to everyone', as Hemingway wrote of the same torero.

But most of my memories of Ken in Spain have nothing to do with death, or sexual fragility, or solemnity of any kind. I see him at the Ritz in Madrid, that ideal of Edwardian hotels, cheap enough in the mid-sixties for us to afford to stay. I see him dressing for the evening. The suit is banana cream, the shirt a sea-green and aquamarine water print. The tie is blue grosgrain. Socks are striped pink, shoes a pale dove-grey. He has managed to make this popinjay's outfit of his own design look beautiful. Naked, his shoulders are overly slim, the hips too wide above long thin legs, so that he looks like his favourite pharaoh, Akhenaten; dressed, he is in proper proportion. He regards the finished result in the mirror, pulling his upper lip down to disguise the length of the teeth in that long equine face. Only in mental concentration does he lose his physical self-consciousness. But his own vanity pales beside his admiration for the love object, and I am endlessly regarded, photographed, applauded.

Dressed for the evening we sail into the lift, held open by a boy with white gloves. Chin jauntily up, Ken saunters across the marble lobby to the cool, though never ice-cool salon, and there he orders champagne cocktails. He sits next to me, elegant ankles crossed, one hand examining his pocket diary in which are the tentative plans for the evening, the thumb and index finger of the other hand thoughtfully rubbing his left ear-lobe, a familiar gesture. He is at ease, in charge and, in my eyes, awesomely distinguished. He smiles in anticipation.

I see him on a beach in Palma de Majorca during our first summer of 1964, long and tubular, wearing a vile pair of mustard-coloured swim-shorts, and trying to avoid the heat of the sun under a wide-brimmed hat. He is reading aloud from the letters of Scott Fitzgerald: 'Gertrude Stein ... said that we struggle against most of our exceptional qualities until we're about forty and then, too late, find out that they compose the real *us*. They were the most intimate self which we should have cherished and nourished.' I watch him scribbling a note in the margin, then tearing out a strip of paper to clean his teeth.

He always used books in this way, and he always read out the good bits, told you the plot if it was a novel or a play. He was compulsive in this matter. On a journey he liked to tell you what you would see next and how it would be, and for years I was happy to be told until time crept up and irritation set in.

I used to have a strong recurring fantasy of Ken on a pilgrimage. He would not be part of the group but always ahead, harbinger of things to come, or galloping back on some flea-bitten Rosinante to report what was over the next hill, and to make his discovery exciting in the telling, to stop the Wife of Bath – a great communicator in her own right – in mid-sentence.

Ken in the garden restaurant of the Ritz in Madrid. With us is Ava Gardner, wearing a pretty hat with artificial cherries. After the afternoon bullfight she asks us back to her apartment. Ken whispers that it will be a disaster, that she'll drink too much. When we arrive with George and Patricia Harewood,

Miss Gardner's shoes are off, and she is dancing around to the music of a gypsy band. About the only other guest is her sister. But I know that all is not lost, for afterwards Ken will reinvent the sad evening and make it unforgettable.

Driving south from Puerto de Santa María on the inland road, this time with an English friend, Nicholas Luard. Our lights have failed, but Nick continues at the wheel, with me in the back and Ken in the front singing to keep the driver awake: songs in German, French and English from the music hall and cabaret, Marie Lloyd, Edith Piaf and Kurt Weill. He sang all through the night until, at dawn, we reached our valley.

Driving through Andalucia on another occasion, in 1972, through rolling ranch country dotted with olive groves, to visit a ruined house called La Consolación, which we wanted to buy, for Ken intended to give up city life and to breed bulls. Long before, in 1954, he had written to his publisher to tell him, 'My ultimate ambition is to buy a half-interest in a bull ranch and retire there, but at present I don't know nearly enough about strains and breeding to contemplate that.' Thus was a critic saved.

Movie stars and grandees were peripheral to Ken's Spanish life, unless of course they were hard-core members of the bull crowd. By the early sixties the hard core was already out of general fashion, an odd fanatic group. The reigning queen was an elderly spinster schoolteacher called Alice Hall, from Georgia. There was Duff Bigger, a Texan poet who disappeared into the hills to live like a Spanish gypsy. There were the wit and bounder Dominic Elwes, whom Ken loved, and the gentleman–adventurer Hugh Millais. There was our friend Michael Wigram, a London banker with immense knowledge of the bloodlines of the *ganaderias*. And there was Conrad Janis, the actor and jazz musician, who understood, as we all did, how unseemly it was to discuss, among ourselves, anything outside Spain and the bulls. Year after year, and often several times a year, the steel threads of responsibility loose, we would meet and move from one feria to the next.

The essential summer feria was Valencia's. This ugly industrial city on the south-eastern shore of Spain's Mediterranean coast was Ken's Mecca – and mine too, though only after I had been put through its hoops, and proved myself able to endure its horrors gallantly, even joyously.

Valencia, 'the wart on the Mediterranean lip', as Ken described it, fetid, steamy, a bastion of banking, neon and small industry, famous only for noise and fireworks, its people, according to one American expert, the most stupid in Spain, barring the Murcians. 'Here we can loaf,' Ken wrote, 'not so much solitary as truly alone.' And he continued: 'Some people go on vacation in order to meet strangers. Others go to meet themselves. For this group, Valencia, world hub of anti-tourism, is the predestined haven and hiding place.'

This 'obsessively unsmart' city was a place where, he felt, you could create your own private myths, and live in your own emotional climate. He insisted that 'If a relationship can survive Valencia, it can survive anything.'

To Valencia in the middle of the feria of San Jaime, I went to meet Ken on 23 July 1964, leaving behind me my old life to start anew. I remember the next day, around lunchtime, standing in the blazing sun in the Plaza del Caudillo (now, in post-Franco days, called the Plaza de Valencia) for the daytime fireworks known as the *mascletas*. The noise was so bad you felt Valencia had just declared war on the world, while each barrage of explosives set off tracers of violet, primrose and royal blue into the sky. Not long ago I heard that the city had put an end to the business because one of the giant noise-makers blew somebody's head off.

I remember lunch at the beach, followed by a siesta. Changing for the bullfight, the fight. And afterwards, tired or elated, the walk from the ring to the bar at the Astoria Palace, a short walk down the street with all the bars, through the *corrida* crowd, air full of the smell of cigars and cheap cologne. In the bar of the hotel the taste of gin fizz, and the knowing talk. Or, if it had been a good afternoon, the self-congratulation of the fans, as if each one of them had been out there in the ring.

After dinner during the fiesta, we would separate from the group, and go off to the tree-lined fairground alongside the river. The fair always had dance bands and flamenco singers, the Great Carnivorous Dragon, and a shooting range where you never won a Serrano ham. Always Ken would wind the string of a helium-filled balloon around one ear, and this tall Englishman, trying to keep a solemn face for the benefit of the Spaniards and their children, would take my hand and walk me to a position where we could best see the 1.00 a.m. fireworks.

At that hour Valencia would come unarguably into its own, because the city makes the best *fuegos artificiales* in Spain, and perhaps in the world. Of a 'prolonged spasm of organized fire', Ken wrote:

There are the solo heavyweight missiles, blown into the air from mortars and descending in quintuple tiers of expanding colour ... salvos of elemental noise ... and always the rockets in their regiments, thrown into battle regardless of casualties, rushing upward to reenact in multiple form the big-bang theory of cosmogony – initial flash, bright centrifugal spray, and final decline into darkness. They are images, on the way up, of individual birth, so many spermatozoa squirming for survival; on the way down, of cosmic death, so many cooling stars. You realize that an art superficially childish can be emotionally overwhelming, touching some resonant chords indeed.

And this childish art would move me to tears, and Ken too of course, mixed with thanksgiving to be one another's best.

20

The New Girl

The room where I worked alongside the arts editor, at the old Tudor Street premises of the *Observer*, furnished with mahogany tables and huge leather armchairs, had the look not so much of a newspaper office as of a seedy Edwardian club. Through this room, during the course of a week, would pass the poet and critic Philip Toynbee, shaggy and gap-toothed, a man both comical and dangerous. Someone or other would be told to keep an eye on him, make sure he didn't go on a drinking binge, and get him back to his wife in the country. The film critic Penelope Gilliatt, a redhead with a sharp face and generous heart, came in on a Friday. Nigel Gosling, who reviewed art and ballet, elfin and elegant, both to look at and to read. And there was the critic Maurice Richardson, who liked to imitate an ape – letting his arms hang out – or to walk up and down reciting bits from Soviet pamphlets of the 1920s.

At the centre of this group was the literary editor, Terence Kilmartin, whose handsome face would frequently set into a sceptical grimace. 'Now really, don't you think ... I mean' (wince) 'haven't you gone a little far this time?' But what he really liked was when his writers went too far, and took intellectual risks.

If you were lucky enough to be a fledgling reporter in your twenties (in my case for a column on arts news) and to be taken up a bit by this gang, asked to the pub or out to lunch, then you were very fortunate, for there was never a moment without surprises, jokes, altercations and enlightenment. And I, eager and incongruous, liked nothing better than the company of these middle-aged delinquents.

On a Friday evening mid-way through December 1962, just after I had moved to this particular section of the paper, Ken Tynan walked in to deliver his weekly theatre review. With him, so I saw as I sat at my desk pretending not to see, was a pretty Chinese girl, and while he corrected his proof this blackbird perched on the arm of his chair, nestled close to him and twittered.

'And *who* are you?' he asked me as he left. The next Friday, Ken came in alone and later joined our group at the White Swan pub. There he stood out, even among these convivial renegades from the pedestrian, because of his wit, his charm and his confidence. As he sat on a pub banquette, holding a glass of gin and ginger ale, cigarette between the third and fourth finger of his hand, he obviously felt pleased. He had sighted me the week before, and now he considered me with smiling, pale-blue eyes, not making any effort to disguise his curiosity, while the rest of our group noticed with mild concern – no doubt on my account, because I was not much more than six months married, and they knew Ken's reputation as a swift seducer. He came into the office again on the following Friday, and then he was gone – to Berlin, I was told, and a few weeks later I read his report from that city.

When first he took me out to lunch, on 25 January 1963, he talked a lot, rather nervously, as we sat in the Étoile restaurant in Soho and drank Alsatian wine. He told me about a girl he knew, a golden hobo, whom he had met in the Costa del Sol. He said that within the space of three days she had caught fire, bees had nested in her suitcase, she had lost her passport and her hair had begun to fall out, that none of these disasters fazed her, not even the hair loss, since she'd discovered the remedy for baldness – a mixture, in equal parts, of lard and gunpowder.

Then he began to question me: who was I, and what were my tastes and preferences, and would I agree to play a psychological game, which involved dropping keys in bottles or choosing one's ideal house, garden and wall? And this test I took, slightly surprised the while that this very clever man should be so contrived in his effort at intimacy. And then he asked me to marry him. I smiled, ran my hands through my hair for something to do, and wondered whether this precipitate invitation was part of his usual routine.

But I got it wrong, because Ken went on taking me out to lunch, and asking me to live with him, to run away with him, and always to marry him. Shortly after our first lunch he told an *Observer* pub regular, 'I intend to marry that girl.' He made a note in his engagement book to introduce me to the father-figure, Orson Welles. And as often, with a new horizon in sight, he reminded himself: 'Start autobiography.' He took me to lunch, to the Savoy, to Boulestin's (where he kissed me for the first time, as we climbed up the staircase of the restaurant), to the White Tower, and always back to the Étoile.

He wrote to me, spelling out his proposal in practical detail, exhorting me to leave my husband, and to move in with him, ending with a quotation from *Camino Real*: 'Make voyages! Attempt them! – there's nothing else....'

He asked me to Paris, and I did not dare go. He went to New York around Easter 1963, and brought me back two Easter chicks from Saks. He persuaded me to interview Terry Southern, Harry Kurnitz and whoever of his visiting

American friends were passing through. He gave me sharp funny portraits of these people. He talked about the Berliner Ensemble, and told me to read Firbank's 'elegant romp', *The Princess Zoubaroff*.

These weekly lunches were delightful to me, so I learned very quickly that time with Ken raced the pulse and opened my eyes. But I also thought that he was nice, and decent too. He would say to me, 'I like the way you flick your hair, the way you push it back.' He would say, 'You look like the young Garbo,' for Ken could flatter outrageously; but he could also pick out certain qualities you liked to think were yours, and deserving of attention. He could see ahead for you – if you were in his beam. He saw what you might become and set up the signposts, though as easily, I discovered, he could foretell an ugly future, and cut you down and spit you out.

Eight months after I first lunched with Ken I fell in love with him. Eleven months after that I ran away to live with him. Three years after moving in with him, both of us at last divorced from our previous partners, we married. For a man who evidently liked instant gratification this long wooing looks exceedingly flattering. But I was attractive to Ken, according to his friends, precisely because he had to work so hard to win me.

So who was I?

From Ken's point of view I was quintessentially English, from the upper class, without ties to the world of the theatre, and therefore a girl out of his ordinary. I was in fact Canadian, by virtue of my parents, and middle class, brought up – I am reminded by mildewed childhood diaries, opened now for the first time in decades – on an intensive diet of theatre. My father, Matthew Halton, was a journalist and correspondent for the Canadian Broadcasting Corporation, who became something of a figure during the Second World War because of his brilliant despatches from the front. He was slenderly built, fine and fair, of sweet and courageous character. Born and brought up in the foothills of the Rocky Mountains, he was one of many sons of a poor Lancashire couple who had gone to Canada at the turn of the century and crossed country by covered wagon, on the track of other members of their family, Mormons and missionaries.

My mother, Jean Joslin Campbell, was the handsome daughter of a well-to-do Canadian landowner and entrepreneur who was of Scottish origin, from a line of engineers, clergymen and civil servants. Her mother came from an English family whose first members had settled in Canada in the mid-eighteenth century.

In 1929 my parents moved to Europe, where my father was one of the first journalists to write about the dangers of Nazism. In 1936 he went to Spain to report and to support the Republican side. 'Idealism', he would say with unabashed enthusiasm, 'is the only realism.'

I was born in London and was evacuated with my brother to Vancouver during the war. Thereafter I spent holidays in Canada, fishing and riding in the foothills of southern Alberta, where my father had gone haymaking and duck-shooting as a child, and where he is now buried.

In London we lived in a neo-Georgian Hampstead house, and I attended a local private school. At fourteen, I went to the oldest girls' school in London, Queen's College in Harley Street; this entailed a long daily bus ride to get 'down there', as my mother would describe central London – a place where the air was noxious, as opposed to the healthy heights of suburban Hampstead.

From my father, when I was eight, I had received a letter which read: 'I would love to take you to La Mère Catherine for dinner tonight. Will you come? You shall have snails, poularde de Bresse and ananas au kirsh.' And quite soon after this invitation arrived, on 25 August 1946, he did take me to Paris, where I made my first diary entry.

Skipping idly through these pedestrian but enthusiastic journals, kept up into my university years, I find to my surprise a tangential experience with Ken's, and on three occasions they record that we actually met, evidence which perhaps suggests that we cannot have been such an odd couple after all.

On 29 April 1947: 'Daddy took me to the Savoy Theatre to see *Hamlet*. It was wonderful. Specially when Ofillia goes mad.' This I realize is the same production, by Donald Wolfit, that Ken first saw three years before and described as 'coarse-grained'.

Unlike my future mate, I am a poor speller: 'Mother and Daddy and I spent the evening listening to music and talking about the vast Eunaverse.... No hot water. Pipe burst.... Very sad about lack of Pasion in my life and no adventure and wished I had different character.' Like Ken, however, I am impressed by celebrity. At the end of the above entry I record: 'Daddy went out in the evening to a party for Philip Mountbatten. I was very lonely.'

In 1951 I am confirmed at St Paul's Cathedral, love the Oliviers in *Caesar and Cleopatra*, and conclude that *A Winter's Tale* is not one of Shakespeare's best. (Of the same production Ken wrote that it would 'probably establish once and for all that the play is unactable'.)

On 12 November 1954, at a bottle party in the mews flat of an ex-débutante called Virginia Pope, I have 'Long talk with Kenneth Tynan – *Observer*'s Dramatic Critic'. The diary alas leaves it at that. I test my memory and see a tall, thin man in black, wearing a string tie, and standing, polite and unsmiling, in the hall of the flat, surrounded by admirers. He had barely started writing for the *Observer*.

Early in 1956 I went to Vienna and eventually to Paris to take up residence as a student. I registered for the Cours de Civilisation Française at the Sorbonne but attended rarely, preferring to walk, to explore and to record in rich and dreadful prose my self-examination: where were the limits, could I continue to be free, how could I curb my headlong rush at things, and when would I begin to concentrate?

In Paris I learned from my schoolfriend Marion how to read music, and how to dress, for she knew about seams and cut and what went with what, and kept her underwear in a hand-sewn silk case (all under the influence of a Swiss mother). When our allowance arrived we would go straight to the shops for cork-heeled mules, white leather gloves and angora sweaters. Under her supervision I bought a little black dress, which required several fittings, and a black wide-brimmed hat from Jean Barthet which, with Italian shoes and long pink gloves, I wore to a party looking as though I had raided my mother's wardrobe.

I went back to London, back to my old room with the faded chintz curtains, but now I was almost never at home. I saw *Look Back in Anger*, which I judged to be for 'my generation', and Brecht's *Mother Courage*, during the first visit of the Berliner Ensemble but 'didn't understand a word', according to the diary, 'So no opinions on what the critics are raving about'.

In the autumn of 1956 I went up to St Clare's Hall at Oxford, an establishment on probation as a possible new addition to the women's colleges, and there I read English. A small group of us joined the university on the most favourable terms, having the benefit of the best tutors and all other privileges. After three raffish years, we took external London University honours degrees.

At the end of my first term at St Clare's, my father died of a brain tumour, and part of me closed down. It was not until Ken entered my life that I allowed myself to feel strongly again. After my father's death I threw myself into Oxford life with even less discrimination than usual, and having discarded my first invitation, which read: 'Can you come to tea and a discussion on religious things afterwards?', I accepted almost everything. My friend Dinah Brooke, with whom I shared rooms, who had been educated at Cheltenham Ladies' College, and Hated Life, used to see me pedalling furiously after a Greek god who would be racing ahead of me on his own second-hand bicycle. 'How can you be so happy?' she would say to me contemptuously. But I was.

I didn't want to miss any of it. I joined the Experimental Theatre Club and helped on a production of Tennessee Williams' *Summer and Smoke*. I took part in a forum on sex and the theatre. I was production secretary to Nevill Coghill's OUDS staging of *Dr Faustus*. I entertained Maurice Bowra to tea. I followed the Oxford Beagles. I danced with Dudley Moore. Dined out with a defrocked priest. Made friends with a group of Balliol intellectuals. Sought the company of a handsome dandy. Discovered sex. Translated *Beowulf*, wrote essays on the Romantic poets for the Wordsworthian scholar J. B. Leishman. Was photographed by Tony Armstrong-Jones. Saw Antonio Ordóñez fight at the Seville feria during vacation. Drove to the South of France during another vacation, to stay with the Aga Khan. Talked to Kenneth Tynan (the third encounter; the second was at the opening of *Under Milk Wood*) at the Oxford première of John Osborne's *Epitaph for George Dillon*.

The tempo was too fast, I noted in the diary. ('It would be disastrous if everything really mattered.') I had become avidly superficial. Marion, my Paris friend, wrote to me reprovingly, noting the change. 'Who would have thought that you of all people would have given up fighting? What has turned you into this almost aimless, negative person, whose strong, sometimes *too* hard-outlined character is blurring at the edges?' Oxford had done the damage, she concluded. In Oxford, after visiting me there, she wrote, 'I frankly disliked you.'

In my last year I was told by the historian Raymond Carr that a certain Oliver Gates of New College was the nicest and cleverest undergraduate he had recently come across. When I met Oliver, this recommendation fortified the appeal of his beaky Cornish good looks, while he very speedily took a shine to me. He introduced me to his mother, Pauline, a wayward beauty, and told me that she had had many lovers, including the novelist Henry Green. He introduced me to his father, Sylvester Gates, a brilliant academic and lawyer, who had served as a clerk to Felix Frankfurter, but whose taste for money had eventually directed him to industry and banking. He introduced me to his cousin by marriage, Cyril Connolly, and to his uncle Robert Newton, or more precisely to the urn which held the actor's ashes, and which rested in the wine cellar of Manningford Abbas, the Gateses' country house in Wiltshire. Oliver took me to the White City to bet on the greyhounds, to the Milroy nightclub, to a college ball.

Then Oxford was over, though not my attachment to Oliver Gates. Early in 1960, I took off for New York, found myself a job as a trainee at *Newsweek* magazine, and graduated some months later to the foreign department, where I worked as a researcher. Out of office hours I threw myself into New York life. I met Norman Mailer, Norman Podhoretz, A. J. Liebling, Joseph Heller, Senator John Fitzgerald Kennedy, and a great many feckless Europeans. An Oxford friend remembers me as a tough little snob. 'Nobody could drop more names than you could. What made your name-dropping very innocent was that to you Lumumba and Isaiah Berlin were more or less on the same level.'

In the autumn of 1960, I went to Washington with Oliver, now working in the States, to stay with Felix Frankfurter. Justice Frankfurter had looked after Oliver during the war, and loved him as a son. His black maids, Matilda and Ellen, cooked us roast duck and wild rice; and his bed-ridden and seductively malicious wife Marion made us laugh. Frankfurter declared in his sprightly manner that Bernard Baruch was 'undoubtedly a fraud', that Walter Lippmann was 'pretentious', and that Senator Kennedy – about to win the presidency – was 'a potential hazard in the White House'. Eight months later he was just as wary of the incumbent. Too much use of the telephone, too many snap decisions. The Bay of Pigs débâcle was the result of not thinking things through by means of the best intellectual process, Felix told us, whereupon he took a book from his library shelf and read from a speech by Pericles on the necessity for discussion in government.

When Oliver returned to England to work for Du Pont's, I would from time to time visit the Frankfurters, and from time to time a precious letter, signed 'F.F.', would come my way. One day I was immeasurably pleased to get a letter from him complimenting me on my 'drive toward honest thought and speech in areas where honesty, even with oneself, is not easy'.

I had in November 1960 become unofficially engaged to Oliver, and had sent my mother a cable which read: 'UNOFFICIAL ENGAGEMENT TO OLIVER STOP IF APPROVE PLEASE TELL HIM STOP I INSIST YOU DONT MENTION OR EVEN SUGGEST ENGAGEMENT TO ANYONE UNTIL RETURN ENGLAND ALL LOVE.' I was quite evidently unsure, and had told Oliver as much. Was he not too young and too green? He wrote asking me to communicate more enthusiastically, to loathe the world and to love him: he grew older hourly by reading *Encounter*. But in March 1961 I broke off the engagement.

By autumn 1961 I was back in England and soon after was employed at the *Observer* by Anthony Sampson, to work on a new magazine-style page called Daylight.

I became re-engaged to Oliver Gates in the spring of 1962, seduced more by his family, where lovers were taken and rejected, where one's dinner companion was likely to be an intellectual heavy, where food was French, swags were silk and walls were dragged in the manner of Colefax and Fowler, than I was by the luckless young man who had asked for my hand. We had very little in common, but I was of the generation that believed marriage to be the goal, though I knew all the time that marriage without love would be a terrible self-betrayal.

Two wise suitors counselled against, while the banns were published and the announcement placed in *The Times*. On 18 May 1962 my godfather, Rache Lovat Dickson, gave me away in Hampstead parish church and my mother fêted the family party.

We set up house with our parents' help, and pooled our resources. Oliver was happy, for I was his possession and his way out of the family. I was not.

21

Wooing

Through the spring and into the summer of 1963, the secret meetings between Ken and me continued. Meanwhile Elaine came and went, her place taken by theatre companions, sexual partners, confidantes. The eleven-year-old Tracy settled into boarding school at Dartington Hall. And all the time Ken was helping prepare for the opening of the National Theatre. The *aides–mémoire* in his engagement book include 'Write Zeffirelli, Jan Kott, Giorgio Strehler, Wole Soyinka, Arthur Miller.'

In June I signed a contract with the *Sunday Times*, and changed jobs. In July Ken went on a gastronomic tour of France with Elaine and Gore Vidal. The holiday was sealed with bad memories. He went on with her to Pamplona to meet James and Gloria Jones, and recorded the fights over his sexual infidelities. Though he had planned to meet me in Cannes – where I had managed to escape – he cancelled. 'At the last moment I backed down,' he wrote years later, 'postponing the amputation.'

On his return Ken made a note to write to Elaine: 'Say we've twice tried. No good; confess adultery. No condoning.'

The publisher John Calder had in 1962 organized a writers' conference as part of the Edinburgh Festival. In its aftermath, he began to organize a drama conference for the following summer; and Lord Harewood, who was in charge of the festival, proposed that Ken should chair the proceedings.

On 18 August 1963, Ken went north to prepare the six-day jamboree. Calder felt that the purpose of the discussions was 'to fill in the background' for the audience, to let the artists 'speak for themselves and explain themselves'. Ken, on the other hand, knew all along that he had to deliver an entertainment and that the point of gathering together over 100 of the most distinguished people in world theatre, including Laurence Olivier, Peter Brook and Joan Littlewood, was to set them loose on each other, outside the conference hall.

On 23 August, I flew to Edinburgh to begin my researches for a *Sunday Times* article on 'the world of music'. No doubt I had suggested to my editor that the festival, with its concentration of musicians and orchestras, was the perfect place to get cracking. In any event that is what I told my husband. But my real intent was to take the jump into Ken's arms.

I have a clear picture of meeting him, I in a silk headscarf and my green flared 'going away' coat, Ken in a pale mackintosh. It was raining, of course, in this charming, dark, northern city, as we drove first to the Caledonian Hotel, falsely to register my presence, and then to the annex of the George, into which you could smuggle a girl, a feat impossible in the main building.

Once undressed in our room, Ken talked, and I listened. He talked about how we should share our lives, and what he believed in. He cut up an empty packet of Player's cigarettes, for want of paper, and wrote on it: '*Communist Manifesto, The Necessity of Art* – Ernst Fischer, *Letters of Marx and Engels*, and *Studies of a Dying Culture* – Christopher Caudwell'. He said this was vital reading (though I still have his list, I've not yet managed to work my way through it). Then he told me, with the utmost seriousness, that his sexual tastes were unusual, that he liked to spank girls, and was I terribly shocked? I said I wasn't, whereupon we chastely made love. I was, despite my innocence, undisturbed by Ken's curious declarations, sensing that they masked a tender man.

I remember little of the week. I dimly recall some of the more exotic delegates, as they began to pour into the city, Andrzej Wajda and the great Polish actor Zbigniew Cybulski. Arthur Adamov turned up from Paris, and Jack Gelber labelled him the 'heterosexual Genet'. He looked utterly loath-some, but he turned out to be wise and funny. I remember George Harewood struggling to meet the demands of Judith Anderson and Lillian Hellman, saying that they were the two women in the world he most disliked. I distantly remember Ken's battle with the Home Secretary, who had refused entry visas to the Berliner Ensemble.

But mostly I remember Ken, walking down the street with him, holding his hand. He took me to lunch at John Calder's country house, thirty miles outside Edinburgh. And it was there that we went boating on the loch, and there that Ken tore his gold suit. Our hostess, Bettina Jonic, noticed the L-shaped rip with the leg showing through and how embarrassed by it Ken was in front of me. She had heard that I was a cool, ambitious, English journalist, that I might be using Ken, but she saw that we adored each other, that we were perhaps soulmates.

On 30 August I flew back to London alone. I had fallen in love, and my identity felt as sharp as the morning. Needless to say I kept all this from my husband. Deflected for a few days by my editor from the 'World of Music' to the 'World of Gardening', I found out about tubers and landscaping, and why roses are the lowest form of horticultural life.

In Edinburgh, on 2 September, the conference opened with a dull discussion before a 2000-strong audience on who dominates the theatre – actor, director or playwright.

On the second day Ken insisted that he liked plays which taught him how to survive with a certain amount of grace and dignity. The playwright should not indulge in the luxury of 'privileged despair', he argued. Outside the conference hall Harold Pinter buttonholed Ken in a bar to ask what exactly he meant by 'privileged despair'. He picked up an ashtray and said he could write a perfectly valid play about it without referring to social or economic conditions.

On Saturday, 7 September, the last day of the conference, the subject for debate at the McEwan Hall was the future of the theatre. After a short interval there began an elaborate Happening, or demonstration (planned beforehand, with Ken's collusion). Charles Marowitz asked the audience to come up with an official interpretation of *Waiting for Godot*; a planted heckler rebuked him. There followed organ music, and taped excerpts from the week's discussions. Then a nude girl, on a BBC camera trolley, was wheeled across the balcony above the speakers' platform. A woman with a baby dashed across the stage. A piper played, a curtain dropped behind the speakers' platform to reveal rows of shelves on which were sculpted heads. Uproar ensued.

When things calmed down, Ken dismissed the event as a clumsy echo of *Hellzapoppin*. He said art should impose order on chaos, that the point of being alive was to achieve some control over our circumstances, and he challenged the creator of the Happening, Kenneth Dewey, a young man from San Francisco, to explain if his demonstration were a development of drama or an alternative to it. 'We are trying to give back to you, the audience, the responsibility of theatre,' said Dewey, 'performing your own thoughts, building your own aesthetics.' But Ken was not impressed. 'Totalitarian and apocalyptic,' he decreed. Later on he claimed that the East Europeans, who had come 'to discuss experimental theatre on a serious level', called it 'nonsense', and that even Ionesco was dismayed. Outside the hall, the conferees were invited by Allan Kaprow – in charge of another Happening – to walk over a pile of tyres.

The townsfolk, meanwhile, having heard about the nude, were up in arms. 'Degrading' and 'anti-Christian', cried the city elders; and how could the Queen's cousin, the Earl of Harewood, have become involved? Lady McChatterley (as Bernard Levin dubbed the naked girl) was charged with 'acting in a shameless and indecent manner', and acquitted, but not before the Moral Rearmament fanatics had had a field day.

On the evening of the infamous event, John Calder threw a farewell party for the conferees at his Victorian shooting lodge outside Edinburgh. Jack Gelber arrived early to find a pack of local gentry in moth-eaten dinner jackets, waiting for the entertainment. And entertainment they were given. Out of the evening, so it was surmised, came two marriages and three divorces. A Dutch novelist lost his wife, and an Edinburgh doctor found her. Joan Littlewood was seen roaming about the woods. Zbigniew Cybulski sang the blues, while Monica Vitti wandered around aimlessly. At dawn a drunken bus driver took off for Edinburgh, but his terrified passengers persuaded him to stop, and they set off back to Calder's house on foot in the rain. Another bus got through, the one with Ken and me aboard, wrapped up in each other, 'canoodling' as one observer quaintly recalls, and oblivious of the mayhem of the night.

The following afternoon we boarded a special plane for London. 'What's the delay?' someone asked. 'They're waiting for John Calder to bring a drunken pilot,' said Ken. Once in the air, I was approached by Arthur Kopit and asked for a lunch date. I declined. Back in his seat Jack Gelber said to Kopit, 'Do you know what you just did?' Then Ken loomed up. He said, 'Arthur, if you'd really like to take Kathleen out to lunch, it might be a good idea. You see she's married and. . . .' Thereafter Kopit became my beard. We left the plane together, and we met my husband together, and if it had not been for my awful euphoria I doubt that the young man whom I was treating so shabbily would have been at all suspicious.

In London my lunches with Ken became more frequent, and we began to meet for early evening drinks. It was a hot September, and I remember going bare-legged and wearing sleeveless dresses well into the month. On the 27th, I flew to Paris, telling Oliver that I was off to Wales to investigate some rare trees. Ken and I booked in at the Lancaster Hotel in the Rue de Berri, and we took off for the clubs, to hear Mabel Mercer at the piano, followed by Chet Baker on trumpet at the Blue Note, singing his reedy plaintive version of 'My Funny Valentine'. By dawn my lover was drunk, or as drunk as I ever saw him, and girlishly romantic.

The next day he took me to meet James and Gloria Jones, whose apartment on the Quai d'Orléans was a clearing house for American expatriates. Ken knew that Jim was gruff but gentle, and he described him in his journal as such: 'Big chin and bashful smile, shorter than he would have chosen to be, and perhaps less belligerent, too; uxurious towards his busty and beloved Gloria as few husbands I have known have been towards their wives. . . . Not the greatest of writers, but a great friend and companion, full of classless curiosity.' After that weekend, the Joneses' place became for me, as for Ken, an essential Paris port.

On the Sunday we went to the country for lunch, and somewhere along the way I picked up a chestnut, for luck. Now cracked and weightless, it sits in a jewel box along with buttons and badges left over from the sixties, a blue bead against the evil eye, which Ken gave me in Turkey, and a gold Valentine's Day heart in a box marked 'From K to K'.

Ken chose his presents carefully. He once gave me a silver compact inscribed with a quotation from Congreve; a bright sweater painted as by Mondrian; an almost backless bathing-suit. (He wanted me out of my pastel wools and tasteful tailoring and into clothes which spoke his signature on his girl.)

Through the autumn of 1963, we continued to see each other in secret. One day a letter arrived, from which I quote:

This is after calling you, and sadness isn't the word. I can't stop talking to you. With you I have that rarest feeling – a sort of passionate peace.... Believe it or not, as you like, but I cannot imagine the future without you .... I can doubtless survive, and even put on a show of sporadic energy, but I shall have no sense of where I am going, because where I am going is you.

He then listed the problems he thought might hold me back, that I did not trust him, that he would tire of me. But he claimed to be certain: 'We fit; we mix; we blend.' He thought that perhaps I might mind losing my world and told me that we would make one of our own, 'not so sequestered, not so rich, but travelled and raffish ... an international network of nice unguarded people who live by their wits in the arts'. 'Occasionally', he continued, 'we allow the inhabitants of your present world to entertain us, but we keep our distance, because we prize our independence; also because we suffocate in private gardens.'

He believed I might have qualms about living with a man I could not marry for a year and a half: 'One possibility: change your name and take mine until you can quietly divorce. If we had a child late next year the hubbub of your bolting would have died down and nobody would raise an eyebrow.' He thought, too, that I might be worrying about his divorce: 'Let me reassure you. With or without you, I intend to go through with it.' He thought I might be concerned about money: 'In an average year I earn around six thousand pounds, and there's a little capital to fall back on. After the divorce I shall pay for my daughter's upbringing, but my wife has money in America and has promised to ask for no support.'

'You hate to hurt Oliver,' he concluded. 'This is a real problem and I cannot solve it for you. All I know is that the longer you postpone leaving him, the greater the injury will be when you finally do so; and if you don't leave him at all, the injury to yourself will be irreparable. Not to mention me.'

On 4 October he wrote again: 'It's midnight of a bad night. You promised you would see me once last week; by a mighty effort you saw me twice; but it was a close thing. In fact you kept your bargain, forgetting that the whole **point of my life is to cause you to break it forever.**'

On the following day he added:

Morning of devastating introspection and reluctance to get up; spirits not notably raised by morning mail including (a) letter from American magazine indicating polite disappointment with article I wrote a fortnight ago and (b) letter from Tracy passing on news that Elaine has sold the screen rights of her forthcoming novel to Hollywood for gigantic sum.... I am not overwhelmingly fond of myself at this moment; petty envy and self-pity make a sour mixture.... I toy with the idea of watching the racing at Windsor on television. Beryl the lecherous lodgerette puts her head round the door to say that Professor Potts called from Leeds University wanting to discuss his new translation of Rumbo (Rimbaud, presumably. But why me?) Almost call him up to discuss it; anything would be better than aimless scab-picking like this, and melancholy speculation about what you are doing *and who with*.'

A third bulletin follows:

THIS CANNOT GO ON MY DARLING: I CAN'T BEAR THE SILENCES: I SHALL SETTLE FOR ANYTHING, ROWS AND VIOLENCE AND BROKEN GLASS, RATHER THAN SOLITUDE.

I lunched today with the Ogden Stewarts ... in Hampstead; their son, who works for the *New Yorker*, was there with his beautiful new wife ... all fun, and plans and family. Unbearable. The son asked me whether you and I could dine with them this week (I'd talked about you endlessly): foolishly, stupidly, shamefully, blushingly, I had to say that we didn't dine together, we just lunched. But you're in love with her? they said. Yes, I said. And she's in love with you? She says so, I said.... Please try to see that I cannot go on getting the worst of both worlds – a marriage without love and *in absentia*, and love without contact and *in absentia*.... I feel you must decide soon, and move. I promise that Elaine will not cite you: why should she, since she already has evidence?

What do these letters reveal? Ken's sweetness, a different voice, Ken's terror of solitude, a solemn approach to marriage and divorce typical of the times. They also reflect my guilt in my turning him down. Yet one thing was clear: I loved Ken.

On 18 October, and with no one firmly in his life, Ken drafted a letter to Elaine in Hollywood, a version of which he may or may not have sent. He wrote:

Today *Private Eye* has a cartoon of me called Hall of Fame. I am sitting in a dingy bureaucrat's office with pipe, bowler hat and pinstripe trousers. The door is labelled National Theatre. I am staring at the reader with a look of blank misery. Before me are trays labelled 'In', 'Out' and 'With it'; all are empty. Behind me an empty filing cabinet with one drawer labelled 'Brecht'. On my desk is a German dictionary. They cannot know how true the picture is.

'Tracy's half-term is soon,' he continued. 'If you leave me you will not see her again, because we belong together.... Come and save me; come and you will be saved. I have got the pills and if you don't I will truly take them, not to hurt you but quite simply and practically to stop feeling any more pain.'

And so the melancholy autumn continued. But of course Ken was by no means always melancholy; it was not in his exuberant nature, and indeed he enjoyed his new post at the theatre. With wife and mistress in absentia both, he took the Chinese actress Tsai Chin to the opening of the National.

At the end of October, Elaine returned to England for Tracy's half-term. But the marital reunion cannot have worked out, because a week later Ken was again making notes to himself on the subject of a Mexican divorce.

My problem was simple: I loved Ken but could not leave my marriage, while Ken's telegrams continued to come to the Sunday Times: 'DARLING WHAT HAVE THEY DONE TO YOU STOP DO NOT LET THEM BRAIN WASH YOU STOP DO NOT DESTROY US.'

Meanwhile Ken felt that if he couldn't be happy with Elaine, he might remember what happiness was like. Early in January he wrote to tell her of a poem he had dreamed, about a faithful dog, Tom, who is dying because he cannot love just one of the two of them. With it he included an invitation to the Canary Islands. Elaine replied that she had received the poem, and was more moved by it than by anything she had ever read. She also wrote that she could not endure the violence of their life, Ken's hatred for her. And she reminded him that she wanted equal partnership, not the third-class citizenship which, she claimed, he had accorded her and her work.

Ken made one last despondent effort to persuade me to leave my marriage. On 12 January we flew to West Berlin, and that evening drove across Checkpoint Charlie to East Berlin. While we travelled through the ice-cold dusk, Ken translated the text of the play we would see at the Berliner Ensemble, The Messingkauf Dialogues, a conversation piece by Brecht between a dramaturg, two actors, a philosopher and a worker. 'In the very nature of acting . . .' he read in a light and winning voice, 'there is an essential gaiety. . . . No matter how fearful the problems they handle, plays should always be playful.' And he quoted further from 'the philosopher': 'Tomorrow our corpses may be pulverized and scattered. But here, today, we busy ourselves with the theatre, because we want to evaluate our lives with its help.' (These words and the manner of their delivery were exciting to me, and I recall very clearly the sensation of boundless and beautiful horizons opening up.)

The next day in West Berlin we lunched with Erwin Piscator, the founder of epic theatre, who had recently directed The Merchant of Venice as a parable of anti-Semitism. In the evening we were back in the Theater am Schiffbauerdamm to see Brecht's Mahagonny.

In Hamburg, the next night, we checked into the Vier Jahreszeiten Hotel. And in Hamburg, this rich, instructive time came to an abrupt end. My husband called from London, having tracked me down, and for reasons now mysterious to me I got out of the bed with the man I loved, packed my suitcase, and flew that very night to London.

The period ahead was a painful testing, but one in which Ken was able to rid himself of some of his separation trauma, and I to prove to myself that there was no way to live with Oliver.

Since being on his own was never Ken's strong point, he sought company and diversion. And around this time he bumped into his first love, Pauline Whittle. 'He was very depressed,' Pauline recalls.

He showed me the padlock on the front door of his flat. He talked a great deal about this girl he was in love with. He said you were always appearing out of the mist to meet him, at train stations and airports. And he went on about Elaine, how she talked relentlessly about her work, and how he had no home life. He said, 'I'm thirty-six years old and I'm frightened of my wife.'

He was jaded, he said. He felt worn out and he didn't know which way to turn. He was having trouble with his breathing. Life had made too many demands on him – his work, the need to make money, to keep the flat; and Elaine, not draining him of money, draining him of the joy of living.

He asked me why he couldn't live like everyone else, in a semi-detached in the suburbs. 'Why do I think I'm superior?' 'Because you are superior,' I told him. 'No,' he said, 'Oxford gave me a superiority complex. I think it ruined me.'

In extremis – as on the therapist's couch two years before – Ken asked himself some searching questions, and instinctively turned to his childhood for the answers. But having opened the door an inch, and glimpsed the ordinary, he then shut it firmly and changed the subject.

In March Ken embarked on a brief affair with the American actress Rita Moreno. And in March Elaine wrote to him, after a meeting, to say that she had never meant things to be as they were, that she'd meant them to have a happy, loving life. She wrote that she felt wonder that Ken existed at all, and that she loved him. Yet something was all wrong.

Early in April divorce was again in the air. One morning Ken telephoned Pauline from the Green Park Hotel, where he was staying, to announce: 'I've got her at last!' He described how he had walked into the Mount Street flat to find Elaine in the kitchen in the company of a man naked but for his necktie. The intruder turned out to be a poet and BBC producer. Ken took the man's clothes out of the bedroom and threw them down the lift shaft. But he allowed the poet to leave in a borrowed mac. (In Ken's version of the story the man then returned to borrow some money for a cab.)

Shortly after these lively events, I called Ken to tell him that if he still wanted me I was his, that I had made my decision.

With the help of the man-in-the-mac evidence, Ken visited his lawyer to see if Elaine could be persuaded to instigate divorce proceedings. And in mid-May Elaine went to Juárez to obtain a Mexican divorce on the ground of incompatibility.

At last we were on the same course. We met in Paris to celebrate, walked the springtime streets and lunched one day at the Tour d'Argent, a restaurant undervalued by the French, Ken explained to me as we sat in the corner window looking over the buttresses of Notre Dame. That same weekend Ken took me to see his Parisian *patronne*, Janet Flanner. The famous *New Yorker* correspondent, with short-cropped hair and sparkling blue eyes, wore a mannish suit and badly flung-on red lipstick. She urged Ken to visit as many ageing celebrities as he could and to question them before they died. 'Tax their brains,' she instructed. 'It's like lobsters. Go for the head – there's tasty chewing there.' She was preaching to the converted.

Shortly after I bolted, my husband stormed in through Ken's front door, looking for me. But I was not there and his rival cowered behind the sofa. Then he struck again. One night, Ken returned me to my mother's house in Hampstead, where I was in temporary residence, and as we approached the front door, Oliver jumped from the rhododendron bushes, clutching the garden hoe. While the two men fought, I squealed, whereupon my mother, wearing a dressing-gown and a furious face, arrived on the scene. Down the drive, another scuffle was taking place, this between Ken's waiting cab driver and a hefty ex-boxer from across the road who, hearing the noise, had rushed to my mother's aid. He was wearing striped pyjamas. By the time the ex-boxer realized his error, apologized to the taxi driver and turned on Oliver, Ken was missing a few handfuls of hair and was bleeding from the knee. The hoe, however, had rebounded on Oliver, who was complaining loudly of a broken wrist, thereby allowing us to make our escape inside.

For a time Ken and I managed to hold out in my mother's house. Then we crept into the night. Some distance down the road, Ken swore we were being followed, and climbed into a nearby dustbin. I lurked near him, not terribly impressed by the love of my life, and unable, once he had finally crawled out of his lair, to find the right words of sympathy.

Oliver's visit to Oakhill Avenue was followed by a more dignified one by his father, who arrived by Rolls-Royce. 'Kathleen cannot leave Oliver,' he told my mother. 'I think she will probably leave,' came the reply. 'Then I shall see her in the gutter!' he said. My mother then rose to her feet to announce, 'Now I'm convinced she should go.'

And so the sad little soap opera continued.

On the weekend of 11 and 12 July Ken organized one of his Mayfair home film festivals. In the black library with the ugly furniture and Mexican masks, we showed Louis Malle's *Zazie dans le Métro*, the British première of a Soviet film called *Nine Days of the Year*, and Judy Garland in *Strike Up the Band*. Several of Ken's old girlfriends, including Tsai Chin and Rita Moreno, turned up and regulars like Clive Goodwin and the poet Christopher Logue.

Princess Margaret came with Tony Snowdon (with whom I had been working at the *Sunday Times*). I remember that she gamely sat through an eight-minute short on pores, called *Geography of the Body*, but made small squeaking noises of disapproval during a film on bullfighting. For years Ken was attacked for his friendship with royalty. How could he demand its abolition while consorting with one of its members? He saw no particular contradiction: he liked Princess Margaret's appetite for the theatre, her wit and her loyalty to friends.

That July before finally settling in with Ken, I went by request to see my husband's parents in their Eaton Square flat. 'Won't you stay with Oliver?' Sylvester Gates asked. I answered no. He cared deeply for his son, and I believe he thought he owned me, by association, as he owned his wife – though not her gypsy heart. It was a quiet little meeting, full of pain, and I never saw either of those volatile, brilliant, troubled people again.

I had caused a good deal of grief, but I'd broken loose. With Ken I was back in my mainstream, where I had been before the Gates family temporarily seduced me.

'This time you must be sure,' said my mother. And I was.

The plan was to meet Ken in Spain. He had gone ahead to the Valencia feria of San Jaime, in order to prepare an article on El Cordobés. (Cordobés was the meteoric star of the corrida, who wore a Beatle haircut and whose unclassical and vulgar style of fighting bulls had shocked the taurine world.) At 2.30 a.m. on 24 July, I arrived at the old Valencia airport to be met by Ken. 'You've done it!' he said. From then on we were together.

We flew to Palma de Majorca, where Ken had rented a small apartment on the outskirts of the town. From there we drove to Deyá, to spend the day with Robert Graves and his wife. The poet was charming and skittish, and he impressed us by diving into the sea from the highest rock. If one queried his astonishing, not to say fantastical stories of ancient times, he would answer loftily: 'Even the Cretans knew that!', and we would be silenced.

On 8 August we were in Madrid to complete the second part of Ken's mission: after our union, my introduction to Orson Welles. He was working at the time on *Chimes at Midnight*, his film adaptation of Shakespeare's history plays, and was installed in a villa on the outskirts of the city. There, one bright morning, we found him by his pool, dressed in a white guayabera shirt and white trousers, with a macaw perched on one shoulder. He told Ken he had decided not to go to the Valencia feria, having had enough of Litri and Cordobés – 'two generations of *tremendismo*'; besides which he didn't share Ken's passion for the place. He did not think it the town with which to inoculate a newcomer to the *corrida*, because it was so rough. 'The way to begin, of course,' said Welles, 'is Sevilla.'

I was fairly frightened of our host, and very silent during the introduction, but I could see how happy Ken was, and how eagerly he listened, when Welles began to talk about the *Henry* plays (which were Ken's favourites), to expand his ideas on the theme of authority, and to propose that Falstaff is the only great character in literature who is also good. 'He is Prince Hal's real father, the one who gives him affection and love, as opposed to the king who offers him nothing but power.'

Drinks were served and the conversation changed. Summoning my courage, I asked Welles (his parrot still in position) if he liked *Treasure Island*, and might it not be filmed. He swivelled an intimidating pair of fiercely startled, wide-apart eyes in my direction, and for a second I thought he would devour me. Instead he said, 'I love it! *How* did you know? I'm planning to film it and to play Long John Silver.' This announcement set off a deep belly laugh, which built till his shoulders shook, sending the bird scuttling from its perch.

That night the three of us dined at Horcher's, and I watched the fat man and the thin man tuck into a rich marinated dish of game, for which the restaurant is famous.

Ken was forever in search of Orson, or so it seemed to me, and though we saw quite a bit of him during those early years, he became more and more elusive: the promise of a meeting in Paris would be followed by a call from Rome, cancelling the arrangements, while the waiting and disappointment would make Ken frantic with anxiety. Once we tracked him down in Split. 'What are you doing in Split?' Ken asked over the long-distance telephone. 'I was hoping you could tell me that,' Orson boomed.

The older man was very fond of the younger, but he did not wish to be hero-worshipped. To be reminded of success was corrupting, he once explained, 'and nothing is more vulgar than to worry about posterity'.

Years later, when it seemed that Welles had become all our fathers rolled into one child, he told me that he tried not to think of his life and fate, 'because I think of myself as a failure, and I don't want to study what it is'. But none of this did I understand during those early years, and I too felt anxious, by sympathetic association, whenever we failed to hunt down and capture the great man.

After that holiday in Spain we returned to London, and the first thing Ken did was to show me a print of *Citizen Kane*. That accomplished, we settled into life at 120 Mount Street, and began the lovely though land-mined business of getting to know each other.

22

The Partnership with Olivier

In January 1954 Ken had noted that the British public was no nearer demanding 'what other European countries demanded and got years ago: a first-rate theatre where the state pays to preserve and foster the best in theatrical art'. So began his long campaign for a national theatre.

The idea had first been proposed in 1848 by a radical London publisher called Effingham Wilson. In 1880, Matthew Arnold pleaded for a Comédie Anglaise and for the start of state patronage in a country with none: 'The theatre is irresistible; organize the theatre!' This battle cry was taken up in different quarters, and most effectively in a detailed scheme published in 1907 by the critic William Archer, in collaboration with the actor–director–author, Harley Granville Barker.

But it was not until after the Second World War that the movement gathered practical momentum. In 1949 the National Theatre Bill was enacted, and £1 million was promised for the construction of a theatre on the South Bank. Seven years later Ken wondered whether the theatre 'had forgotten the long passion that brought its dream to the brink of fact'. And he pointed out that since 1949 one foundation stone had been laid, and in the wrong place. The grant, he insisted in the pages of the *Observer*, must be raised, and an artistic director, such as Anthony Quayle or Laurence Olivier, appointed. (Shortly after this call to arms, he wrote to Quayle – perhaps prompted by other independent campaigners – suggesting that he might make a fitting choice as Artistic Director, to which the actor replied that he did not believe the timing right, 'not for the Theatre, but for me'.)

Laurence Olivier had also been sounded out in 1956 for the job of Artistic Director by Lord Chandos and Lord Esher, representing the Joint Council of the National Theatre and the Old Vic. They told him condescendingly, 'What we want from you is a glamourpuss.' Although he believed he might not be the best man for the job, Olivier conceded that he 'was probably the only one'. Several years later, at the government's prompting and with the help of the distinguished lawyer Arnold Goodman, talks took place with the Shakespeare Memorial Theatre Company to explore the idea of a merger with the National Theatre group. In March 1962 Stratford withdrew. Never a supporter of such a scheme (believing that 'nothing is more likely to get the best out of a National Theatre than a subsidised competitor'), Ken endorsed the idea that Olivier now be put in control of the main venture, which would work out of the Old Vic Theatre until the new building on the South Bank was up. Olivier's appointment as Artistic Director was confirmed on 9 August 1962.

He was at the time directing a festival season at the open-stage Chichester Theatre. The response to his first production, Beaumont and Fletcher's *The Chances*, from his greatest and perhaps most worthy fan was negative. 'If Laurence Olivier was determined to open his exciting new playhouse with a forgotten comedy,' Ken wrote, 'he might better have chosen something by Wycherley, or Farquhar.'

No one had admired Olivier's art more lavishly nor more memorably; no other critic stood guard so ferociously over the actor's talent. Now that he was going to lead the National Theatre, Ken became even more vigilant. On 15 July he reviewed the second of Chichester's offerings, *The Broken Heart*, which he considered John Ford's best tragedy (and which he had previously recommended to Olivier). In an article headed 'Open Letter to an Open Stager' and addressed to Sir Laurence, he condemned the production roundly, including Olivier's performance as Bassanes: 'You played him from the first as a sombre old victim bound for the slaughter, too noble and too tragic even to be funny. Ford's tragedy was thus robbed of its essential comedy. Most remarkable of all, you were indistinct.' He went on: 'Tomorrow *Uncle Vanya* opens. Within a fortnight you will have directed three plays and appeared in two leading parts. It is too much.'

In the interval on the first night of *Uncle Vanya*, Ken's fellow critics greeted him, according to the press officer, with a chorus of raspberries and boos. 'Undaunted, he bowed, acknowledging their reception.' His review of the Chekhov was extremely favourable, but he was not at that moment deeply loved by the future director of the National Theatre. In August Olivier received a short letter from Ken congratulating him on the appointment, and explaining that despite recent hostility the critic's admiration for Olivier was intact and his enthusiasm for the National Theatre, with Olivier at the head, unbounded. Should a National Theatre be launched, that theatre would need someone to recommend plays, supervise translations and commission new work, and he now proposed himself for the job of dramaturg.

Astonished and angry, Olivier showed the letter to his wife, the actress Joan Plowright. 'How shall we slaughter the little bastard?' he asked. He was ready to reply in the most dismissive terms, when Miss Plowright stayed his hand. She told him not to be outraged, and reminded him that Ken had helped to save the Royal Court, that despite what he could do to an actor he was compulsively readable, a critic who travelled widely and knew world theatre. And she warned that if Olivier planned to surround himself with his old cronies, like Alan Dent, she would have no part of it. To take on Ken would be a feather in his hat and, she added, young audiences would be 'thrilled with the mixture of you and Ken'.

'It didn't take me very many minutes to see that,' Olivier recalls. 'So I wrote quite a different letter from the one I was boiling up to.'

His letter read: 'It will probably not surprise you to know that I think your suggestion is an admirable one, a most welcome one and one that I'd thought of myself already.' Whereupon he added a postscript: 'GOD ANYthing to get you off that *Observer*!'

Ken's appointment was passed by the theatre's board only after Olivier had refused to reconsider it. Its Chairman, Lord Chandos, would later explain Ken away as the 'Anti-Fuddy-Duddy' element.

Pursuing a policy, insistently encouraged by Joan Plowright, of surrounding himself with a young, talented and up-to-date team, Olivier appointed John Dexter and William Gaskill from the Royal Court as his two Associate Directors.

Ken was already at work. A contract was typed up which stated that he would be employed for a year, and thereafter three months' notice would be required on either side; and that he would remain free to continue freelance writing and authorship. During his decade with the theatre, he earned on average £46 net a week; when away on non-theatre business he insisted on going off salary.

Nineteen-sixty-three had begun auspiciously with the following letter from Olivier, penned in his own peculiar style: '*Everything* imaginably obstructive, poltergeists Gremlins Leprechauns, mysterious phone calls, odd callers on desperate business, objects inanimate sleep and that Saville engagement have kept me from writing to you this long while, and even before our last meeting, (breath) TO SAY how pleased and happy and prideful I am that you are so welcomely in on The Thing.' For 'The Thing', Ken settled on the title of Literary Manager (borrowed from Archer and Granville Barker) rather than the German 'dramaturg'. He would be house critic and chooser of plays, a job invented by the playwright and critic Gotthold Ephraim Lessing in 1767, when a group of Hamburg businessmen first tried to start a national theatre.

Throughout 1963 Ken and Olivier discussed everything from casting to the logo of the theatre's writing paper. At the National's first press conference in 1963, Olivier announced that the theatre would aim to perform, in repertory, the whole 'spectrum of world drama' (a phrase borrowed from Ken, who had, in 1959, wished a 'spectrum' upon the planned American national theatre at Lincoln Center).

On 22 October, in the refurbished Old Vic, the National Theatre opened its doors. The production was of *Hamlet*, starring Peter O'Toole and directed by Olivier. It was not the most distinguished of débuts, but it was warmly received nonetheless; and it was to be followed, without a great deal of fanfare, by four years of memorable theatre while the company was cohesive and sure of purpose. No other British theatre ever established itself so speedily or so effectively, nor offered such a multifarious and constelled repertory. No other theatre was so international in scope. Eight out of the eleven productions during the first year were, as Ken put it, 'copper-bottomed successes', and that year included work as diverse as Farquhar's *The Recruiting Officer*, under William Gaskill's stylish though socially sharp direction; the British première of Samuel Beckett's *Play*, in tandem with Sophocles'· *Philoctetes*, and a new play by Peter Shaffer, *The Royal Hunt of the Sun*.

During the first four years plays proposed by Ken included *Othello* (for which he persuaded Olivier to play the lead), *Much Ado About Nothing* (for which he cast Zeffirelli as director), Tom Stoppard's *Rosencrantz and Guildenstern Are Dead*, *Mother Courage*, Max Frisch's *Andorra*, Feydeau's *A Flea in Her Ear* (Ken suggested that it should be directed by Jacques Charon from the Comédie Française, and adapted by John Mortimer), and *As You Like It*, for which Ken put forward Jan Kott's idea of an all-male cast. He also suggested Noël Coward to direct his own revival of *Hay Fever*.

In the late sixties the quality of the company slumped, though it revived brilliantly at the end of Olivier's reign, in the early seventies, with Eugene O'Neill's *Long Day's Journey into Night*, Tom Stoppard's *Jumpers*, Ben Hecht and Charles MacArthur's *The Front Page*, Eduardo de Filippo's *Saturday, Sunday, Monday* and Trevor Griffiths' *The Party*.

There were of course failures. Over the decade, the theatre did not develop enough young directors. Ken failed to bring in sufficient unorthodox and experimental work, though he had a partial excuse: the great flowering of the fringe did not come about until after the demise of the Lord Chamberlain in 1968.

Whatever its limitations, it could be fairly demonstrated that of the seventy-nine plays staged by the National between October 1963 and December 1973 more than half were undisputed critical and box-office hits, as compared with a ratio in the commercial theatre of one success in twelve. Thirty-two of these productions were Ken's ideas; twenty were chosen with his collaboration. People who worked at that theatre remember it as a golden period, subsequently unmatched. Leading members of the British theatre – directors, writers, actors, critics, impresarios – wonder why the first decade of the National's history remains mysteriously unrecorded and unsung. Those of them who closely observed its operation point particularly to Ken's largely unrecognized contribution. Olivier has said that he could not have done the job without Ken, that it was a 'highly successful partnership'.

Although several of his fellow critics believe that Ken wasted his time at the National, his former editor at the *Observer*, David Astor, considers his contribution to the theatre 'even greater than what he did for us'. Martin Esslin maintains Ken's was a 'historic achievement'.

Despite its accomplishments, the two most important creators of that early regime – Olivier first, of course, much more than a mere actor–manager, and Ken second, much more than a mere architect of the repertory – were both dismissed from the theatre in the early 1970s, and left in a kind of despair. Olivier suffered a near nervous breakdown, and Ken's already damaged health was exacerbated by his departure from the National. Only now, after years of complaining about how unhappy was his time there, does Olivier agree that he produced a more successful theatre troupe than any other in the world. At the time, both men felt the new man had been unfairly imposed on them from outside, that they had been usurped, and that the company created was deprived of its proper continuity.

The story of the regime's success and of its unhappy end is a complicated one, very much to do with the dispositions of Olivier and Ken, and with their odd, uncomfortable relationship to each other. 'We were never Mick and Mack,' as Olivier says.

As architect and spokesman, Ken had, in 1964, tried to lay down the guidelines:

Good repertory theatres fall into two main categories. One is the kind that is founded by a great director or playwright with a novel, and often revolutionary, approach to dramatic art.... The other category consists of theatres with a broader, less personal *raison d'être* whose function – more basic though not more valuable – is simply to present to the public the widest possible selection of good plays from all periods and places. In this group, you can place the Schiller Theatre in West Berlin; the Royal Dramatic Theatre in Stockholm; and the National Theatre in Waterloo Road. Their aim is to present each play in the style appropriate to it.

Years later he wrote in his journal that his policy of having no policy 'was partly tailored to the limitations (and strengths) of Larry's temperament – pragmatic, empirical, wary of grand designs or distant goals'.

Nonetheless there *was* a blueprint and it was Ken's: to put on the best of world drama, a spectrum which would cover, as the Archer–Granville Barker scheme had proposed, new and modern plays, revivals of English classics, including Shakespeare, and new, modern and classic foreign plays; to create an international company which would seek out new playwrights, and make imaginative adaptations of foreign classics; to build a permanent repertory of about forty plays, which would eventually fill the two main theatres and the workshop theatre, planned for the South Bank; to form a company of around fifty, elastic and versatile, 'a company that can do anything', as Ken put it, not confined to one particular house style, a growing organism, ideally, with a shared attitude to life.

Ken prodded the company to follow these policies, while he became their public spokesman. He lectured, he spoke on television, he gave interviews to journalists from all over the world, and he continually proselytized in favour of state subsidy: subsidy offered 'what commercialism negates: the idea of continuity, the guarantee of permanence. If a new production fails on first showing, it need not be lost forever.... Subsidy also enables the theatre to build a durable bridge between the past and the present. We are not selling a product, we are providing a service.' With subsidy, Ken argued, criticism need not be feared. 'We can learn from it without rancour, since we do not depend – as the commercial theatre must – on rave reviews for survival.'

A magnetic director, who wished to impose his own style, would not be right for the National, Ken had argued. But it was from the opposite position that Olivier initially approached the job. His ambition was to be 'the English Stanislavsky', he says. Joan Plowright elaborates: 'There was Brecht and Barrault and Stanislavsky. Larry hadn't had the kind of far-reaching influence that those men of vision had, except in the acting. He had not yet put his stamp on a theatre.'

In the event Olivier did not impose himself but aimed to provide the best theatre in the world, and a company with 'the hot breath of unity'. The result was that he sacrificed some of his own choice of plays and his wish to direct more often than he did (he directed only eight productions out of seventy-nine) to a concept of the theatre proposed by Ken.

Adored by his company, which included such fine actors as Maggie Smith, Robert Stephens, Colin Blakeley and Anthony Hopkins, very much the king of the castle, Olivier yet ran the National very democratically. In the early days he made artistic policy with John Dexter, William Gaskill and Ken. If two of them were for a play, one neutral and himself against, he would bow to the majority and not impose a veto. He listened, 'because I would have been very bloody stupid not to'. He listened so intently, Dexter recalls, that 'you could almost smell the way he was going to jump'. And above all he listened to Ken. 'I wanted to have the means of helping me get there,' Olivier recalls, and Ken's 'wise and experienced advice was matchless. I think I only made three decisions against his opinion.'

As a leader Olivier mixed with each member of his company (whereas Ken's shyness kept him at bay). As a performer his 'sheer physical exuberance', as Gaskill describes it, spilled over to the company. He would say, 'Never show your last ten per cent,' that the imagination of the audience would supply the rest. And though a young actor knew he could not emulate Olivier, he would at least be inspired. As Joan Plowright explains, 'Larry never actually developed anybody beyond himself, because no one could beat him.' Some-times spiteful and ungenerous in little things, he was magnanimous in the big decisions. Jealous of other stars, he nonetheless brought them into the company. Though accused of minding deeply only about himself, he dismissed anything to do with personal considerations when running the theatre.

His attention to detail was single-minded, as is evidenced by hundreds of painstaking letters and memos circulated to members of his staff. An example is one sent to Ken. When George Devine came to the National in 1964 to direct Samuel Beckett's *Play*, Ken complained that it was being done 'in a breakneck monotone with no inflections'. 'We are not putting on *Play* to satisfy Beckett alone,' Ken wrote to Devine. 'It may not matter to him that lines are lost in laughs or that essential bits of exposition are blurred; but it surely matters to us.' George Devine sent an understandably angry response. Back came Ken with a letter in defence of 'a theatre of intelligent *audiences*. . . . I thought we had outgrown the idea of theatre as a mystic rite born of secret communion between author, director, actors and an empty auditorium.'

Quite soon after this cheeky communication, which had enraged Devine, Olivier wrote a long and admonitory letter to Ken. 'It is obvious to me', he explained,

that you do not quite appreciate the livid state of inflamation [*sic*] that the nerve ends have arrived at in all the people who have to live through a pre-production period. . . . I like you, I like having you with me, apart from it rather tickling me to have you with me, but you can be too fucking tactless for words. It may be that such criticism as you received when you were young did not hurt you much, or it may be that you've had so much of your own back since, that it has all got obliterated, but you should realise your gifts for what they are and your position for what it is and like a wise jockey not always let these things have their head.

This authoritative tone was rare in their communications. On occasion the roles would be switched, and Ken would sound like a reproving conscience. On others he would be fan to star (though never kowtowing), Iago to Othello, or merely flirtatious.

Ken described his own job self-effacingly. He was 'Sir Laurence's right-hand man', 'a built-in early-warning system', 'house critic', 'backseat driver', 'not a competitor'. He explained that no government would ever engage someone as unpredictable and provocative as himself to run a state organization.

For several years Ken's excitement in being part of the theatre made up for all the diligent, unrecognized backroom work he put in. But the limitations of the post and the unnatural subservience self-imposed on a flamboyant personality eventually took their toll. A certain lack of confidence prevented him from asking for promotion, or for more institutionalized responsibility, and from trying his hand at directing. He was also unaware of just how unwelcome in the profession was a former critic.

Olivier was always very suspicious of critics. From his point of view you did not learn from them, and he feared Ken's capacity to hurt. Ken made him feel stupid. Joan Plowright recalls: 'Larry was forever suspecting there was some devious political message one hadn't seen in a play Ken would propose.' He suspected Ken of manipulating him sometimes, and he was jealous of his intelligence and education, and he said so. He was also aware that Ken adored him, even though he fought him. Knowing that Ken respected him, yet was superior to him in certain areas, could be irritating.

'With steady people not brighter than he, Larry is extremely good-tempered,' Miss Plowright explains, but during meetings with Dexter, Gaskill and Ken there was an edge to everything and a difficulty in keeping up. 'When alone with Ken he found it a bit exhausting. Endless chat, and making of points, and Larry likes to have a break and a vulgar joke. When Ken recognized the need for relaxation and tried to talk about sex or something, they weren't on the same wavelength. Ken's jokes were highly intellectual and literary. Larry's were fairly low, or theatrical. He hadn't read Kafka or whoever.'

Both men had in common a need for intimacy and a talent for occasion, for adventure. But there was no recognition of these shared qualities between them. Olivier would say that he was a hollow man, or cold, or self-detesting, but he would usually be repeating someone else's words. In fact, he admits, he does not know what he is like. Ken once took Terry Southern to meet the actor and explained beforehand: 'Now, what you've got to realize about Olivier is that he's like a blank page and he'll be whatever you want him to be. He'll wait for you to give him a cue, and then he'll try to be that sort of person.' Ken too, on occasion, would describe himself as cold, hollow and self-detesting. But, unlike Olivier, the more he dramatized his self-criticism the more sure he was that he knew exactly who he was.

Ken's interest in Olivier's personality was usually subsidiary to interest in his acting, and beyond that the good of the National. He had once surmised that, because of his mother's early death, Olivier had 'a pipeline to some tremendous childhood pain inside him that we can only guess at'. But he was only interested in how the pain was used in performance. He viewed the actor – a conservative and a fatalist – as king of the jungle (both in life and in his best parts: Richard III, Macbeth, Coriolanus), exemplar of the territorial imperative (he chose to give Ken Robert Ardrey's *African Genesis* one Christmas). He also noted the 'passive feminine' side of Olivier, and the overly humble aspect. He thought his behaviour towards authority – to the National Theatre Board, for example – was obsequious (thereby misjudging his boss, as it turned out, who is not much interested in the Establishment; happiest rather in the Green Room, with working actors).

'Technical things obsess LO,' Ken wrote convincingly in his diary of 1964 during *Othello* rehearsals. 'I have worked quite closely with him, but have no idea of his general ideas on any subject but theatre – I have no idea what he believes.' Fourteen years later, Ken added a further bulletin:

[He is a] man who never had an abstract idea in his life.... His great parts a vast gallery of frustrations, of ambitions unfulfilled, of heroic projects foiled – with the shining simplistic exception of Henry v. An imposer; a wielder; a manipulator – but did he have any clear idea of *why* he wanted to be a great actor? Of what the purpose might be that could justify such enormous exertion? Or was it an end in itself? Or to say: 'How clever I am!' while at the same time demonstrating 'How imperfect we are!'?

I'm glad, on the whole, that he lacked the governing idea. It would probably have been banal; it would certainly have been confining. He leaves behind few images of beauty; many of cruel compassion; none that fit into a conventional preconception of what mankind is or ought to be.

Ken felt that Olivier would be bound to avoid anything involved with an intimate relationship.

Olivier, in turn, felt that Ken was responsible for the distance between them, and would have liked their relationship to be warmer. He believed that 'Ken had an absolute dread of any hint of homosexuality. I greeted him tremendously warmly, I remember, and I found him very reserved, as if to say, "Keep your place, just in case you think I'm a sucker."' Wrong though Olivier was on this score, Ken was obtuse in understanding that Olivier, on occasion, needed his hand held, and that it was inhuman to act solely as the keeper of the flame.

'Intolerant of the normal conceptions of classic theatre' and a 'born revolutionary', Olivier says of Ken.

I knew what I was buying when I bought him. He was very naughty. I remember him telling me that when he was at school, he would be caught out by the boys. They'd say, 'You don't want to masturbate because it grows hair on the inside of your hands.' He'd be caught looking at his palms and he'd be horrified that he'd given himself away. I remember thinking, 'Kenneth does take things terribly seriously.' I couldn't imagine myself, when a boy, minding if someone said, 'You shouldn't toss yourself off because it grows hair on the hands.' I'd say, 'Oh, fuck off,' you know. But Ken felt he'd given himself away. I thought, 'What a funny character you are, Ken, you really are strange.'

I've never met anyone like him. He was an absolute gem as a writer.

At this point, as if to prove Ken's view that he is almost exclusively interested in technical detail, the great actor tried to figure out the nature and ramifications of Ken's stammer.

As for the company's attitude to Ken, 'They didn't talk about him much,' Olivier recalls. 'They didn't know much about him.' He adds, 'I think, because he was such an intellectual, a basic kind of actor would despise him.'

Joan Plowright says that the company felt a certain aloofness on Ken's part. And John Stride recalls, 'One was always terribly aware of his critical ability. But there was no personal gossip about him, we felt great respect. Nobody thought of him as an outsider. But from his position of authority, he had to make the first move.' According to Derek Jacobi, 'Ken didn't invite our friendship.'

Ken would work at home in the morning, though not exclusively on National Theatre business, and then wander into his squat white office in the early afternoon. His assistant, Rozina Adler, had a little box of a room next to Ken's, full of tea-stained lists and bits of knitting, and they would shout instructions and gossip to each other through the paper-thin walls. She recalls that Ken could shut the door and in the space of a few hours 'read about three plays with immense concentration and perception'.

During the first few years he would give an interview almost daily. He would then get down to the business of orchestrating a repertoire, drawing up complex lists (including a booklet of some 400 of the world's best plays) and charting the course of a future season with regard to availability of actor, director or designer, audience response, cost and all-round balance. His memos, letters and critical notes are not merely practical, they make good reading even to an outsider.

Here is how he would proceed. The theatre needed a new one-act play. Over lunch, in March 1965, Peter Shaffer told Ken he had been thinking of the Peking Opera, where two men fight a duel in the dark, only all the stage lights are on, and it had occurred to him to apply this to a modern situation. With an idea, and a title – Black Comedy – the National announced the new play. Shaffer, John Dexter (who eventually directed it) and Ken spent hours debating possibilities and inventing plot. 'It is agreed', Ken wrote, '. . . that all the laughs must be directly connected with the light–darkness convention. . . . Hence the notion of an artist showing his sculpture to a potential buyer, and a former mistress returning unseen to disrupt the occasion.' They also agreed that there should be no hero or heroine in the usual sense: all parts in farce are character parts. Also that every twist of the plot should be designed to increase the desperation of the central character.

After several revisions, and input from Ken and the cast, the play opened on 27 July – four months later. 'A home-grown addition to the play catalogues', Ken described it, 'and the kind of risk that only a permanent company could have taken in such high hopes of making it pay off.' The play was also part of the theatre's organic growth. As the critic Ronald Bryden has pointed out, 'Without the lessons of split-second farce timing learned from Black Comedy, would it have been possible a year later to tackle Feydeau?'

Ken would summarize the meetings of the artistic directorate in order to clarify the various proposals and plans. If John Dexter, for example, was occupied at Chichester directing John Osborne's A Bond Honoured, should Krejča of Prague, Strehler of Milan or Orson Welles be called in to do a production at the Old Vic of The Voysey Inheritance, or The Castle, or Alan Sillitoe's translation of Lope de Vega's Fuenteovejuna? If Mother Courage couldn't be performed for contractual reasons, should the documentary on the General Strike, which Ken had commissioned, be put in that slot? Meanwhile questions were fired off from his desk: What was the state of the company for the next season, and should a lead actor be recruited? What was the future of Gaskill's workshop idea? What about the proposed American–Japanese trip at the end of 1965?

He asked for more money for a publications department. He wondered whether the seat prices should be reduced for non-commercial productions like Beckett's *Play*. He pointed out that the first season had revealed gaps in the company's strength: the lack of a really strong *jeune premier*, a good *ingénue* and a leading man aged between thirty-five and fifty. He criticized the 'relentless dullness' of some of the supporting players. He admitted the immense difficulty of creating a permanent ensemble when the terms of reference were so wide, and suggested that the 'guest performer' principle might have to be a permanent part of policy.

He was critical of the guest directors during the first year, and in a most un-Tynanlike vein wrote: 'I think our guest directors should be tactfully made to realize that every time we open a production, national prestige (not just *our* prestige) is at stake. I believe we would be more than justified in keeping an eye on all guest productions.'

In October 1965, in a memo to Olivier and Dexter, he proposed midnight readings – emulating the Royal Shakespeare's similar enterprise – to pull in students and Royal Court supporters, and suggested that Václav Havel's *The Memorandum* might fit the bill. In the same memo he suggested that the great Czech designer Josef Svoboda should work on Büchner's *Danton's Death*, that 'LO should play Danton to Gielgud's Robespierre'. (He had already suggested that Olivier alternate Lear and Gloucester with Gielgud.) And as a frivolous afterthought he proposed Bob Dylan for Peter Pan, with Joan Baez as Wendy, and the Rolling Stones as the Lost Boys.

In 1966 Ken put forward Tyrone Guthrie to direct Ben Jonson's *Volpone*, and Roger Planchon to direct Molière's *Tartuffe*. Planned in 1967 were the Seneca *Oedipus*, adapted by Ted Hughes and directed by Peter Brook, and a production of Euripides's *The Bacchae* to be directed by Jerome Robbins.

Ken would put together packages, and then he would start to manoeuvre and manipulate. His colleagues used to find his politicking excessive and even hurtful. 'He was so transparent,' John Dexter says, 'you always knew what he was up to.' It was also recognized that his object was to do the very best he could for the theatre.

At regular planning meetings, Ken played a crucial part, and Olivier relied on him. Michael Halifax, the Company Manager, remembers Ken coming up with Strindberg's *The Dance of Death* and suggesting that Olivier play Edgar.

'A blank look came over Sir's face and you knew he was thinking, "Have I read that play?" '

Years later, when Ken's position at the National was less powerful, he was still influential at artistic policy meetings. His colleague Derek Granger recalls that he was absolutely passionate in his advocacy of certain plays. It was very much like his notice of *Look Back in Anger*, in which he doubted he could love anyone who didn't wish to see this play:

'These things were resoundingly said and he became daunting. He had great power, very theatrical. Sometimes a little exaggerated. He used to absolutely quell opposition and people were left speechless. Before the last and clinching phrase there would be the hesitant rattle of his stammer and then crash, 'I doubt if I could love anyone etc.' I remember him putting up a terrific case for Giraudoux's *Amphitryon 38*. There was no stopping him, he was obviously moved by his own words, a quaver in his voice: 'There are very few plays in the rep which put so beautifully the virtues, and spirit, and charm, of love in the married state.' People were rather silenced by this. He spoke at times almost as well as he wrote.

Granger saw that Ken was a 'producer in the fullest sense of the word', and probably a frustrated director ('though I think there was a slight hesitancy, as if he liked to direct at one remove'). 'What made his expertise so doubly valuable was the sense that he never just picked a play because it was good, or hadn't been done for a length of time, or would give the members of the cast good parts. He picked a play because he could actually see it done in a particular way, like *Flea in Her Ear*. Ken would start from what do we want to do. Larry was always bound by expediency, "Who shall we give a part to?" '

As a play doctor, Jonathan Miller found Ken's influence particularly strong at run-throughs and dress rehearsals (though, as other directors point out, he was less helpful in the early, formative stages of production). 'He was so much a creature of the theatre itself – the grease paint and the noise and the stars – that he came into his own on the floor, as it were, of a production, and particularly when it was in trouble. I think the one thing that really is never discussed enough about Ken is his curiously practical sense of what would work, what was good showbiz in the crudest and perhaps the best sense. He was almost always right about something which was slack or badly thought out. And if one went back and tried to rebolt the thing according to his instructions, you almost invariably profited. And it was that which I found most valuable as a director.'

Tom Stoppard respected Ken's claim to have an inhuman capacity for objectivity. He saw that Ken believed that the theatre consisted of a lot of people working towards a common artistic end. And as a critic he did not consider himself outside this world.

In another role, as theatre historian, Ken published rehearsal logbooks of two National productions, and both records give a backstage account of Olivier at work. During the first week's rehearsal of *The Recruiting Officer* Ken wrote: 'Olivier's conception of Captain Brazen is too foppish and perky – a sort of Mr Puff in uniform. Guiding him towards the right tone of boorishness and sleazy vulgarity, Gaskill [the director] points out that the world of *The Recruiting Officer* [first performed in 1706] is quite different from Congreve's: small-town realism is the keynote, with no urban airs and graces. Olivier responds and his lines begin to take on the elephantine loquacity of the pub bore.'

Ken's logbook on the nine-week making of *Othello* is a guide to a great actor at work. He had sat in from the first dress rehearsal and nudged the director to work on Frank Finlay's weak Iago – 'his inability to match up to the enormous passion that Larry releases'. 'If they were not the notes you agreed with,' John Dexter recalls, 'they pointed you to an area where maybe there was something you'd overlooked.'

In addition to Othello, Ken persuaded Olivier to play, among other parts, Shylock in *The Merchant of Venice* and James Tyrone in *Long Day's Journey into Night*. He wanted him to play Prospero, and he even suggested at one point that he play Falstaff, not as a fat buffoon but as a thin, syphilitic, unfunny courtier.

One part of Ken's job was to select writers to adapt foreign classics: John Osborne produced a controversial adaptation of a Lope de Vega play called *A Bond Honoured*. Doris Lessing was given Ostrovsky's *The Storm*. Robert Graves took on Shakespeare's *Much Ado About Nothing*, and was asked to replace 'dead similes, archaisms and words of changed meaning with *living* Elizabethan words and images'. Ibsen's *The Master Builder* was adapted by Emlyn Williams (a decision which drew fire from those who disapproved of foreign plays being adapted by writers not conversant with the original language).

There were other duties: new plays of worth sent in and rejected with long critiques; journeys abroad and subsequent negotiations. Profligate entertainment of theatre people in London. Dutiful appearance at the British Council, or the Arts Council, to argue and defend the case of the National Theatre.

He initiated scholarly and elegant programmes, and helped to write and design them. For these he commissioned articles from theatre people as diverse as Eric Bentley, Thornton Wilder and Noël Coward – cunningly influential brochures which often directed a critic (who received his programme in advance of the production) to a 'right' way of thinking.

As part of his wide parish, he also, during the years 1964–66, attended meetings of the Building Committee set up to aid the architect Denys Lasdun in the design of the new theatre. Ken was in favour of two auditoriums and a small research studio. He believed that the most revolutionary contribution the architect could make would be 'a perfectly designed proscenium theatre'.

He also attended the National's Board meetings (under the patriarchal chairmanship of Lord Chandos), and here he fought for the autonomy of the artistic directorate led by Olivier. Like any other theatre, the National had to submit each play it wished to perform to the censor. The Lord Chamberlain's authority, established in 1737 and extended by the Theatres Act of 1843, allowed him to trim or ban 'whenever he shall be of the opinion that it is fitting for the Preservation of Good Manners, Decorum, or of the Public Peace'.

In his correspondence and meetings with the Lord Chamberlain and his officers, on behalf of the theatre, Ken would negotiate patiently to restore cuts in a classic like Brecht's *Mother Courage*. (Meanwhile, he campaigned, outside the theatre, for the Lord Chamberlain's demise.) *Mother Courage* was eventually performed. From *Dingo*, a new anti-war play by Charles Wood, the Lord Chamberlain wanted the deletion of all four-letter words, all blasphemy, *lèse-majesté* ('the L.C. doesn't like the reference ... to George VI not wanting to be King'), and impersonations of living persons. The play was not done.

A more serious reversal attended the plan, in autumn 1964, to mount Frank Wedekind's classic, *Spring Awakening*. Written in 1891, it deals with the danger of repressing adolescent sexuality. In one scene, two boys tentatively kiss; in another a group of boys in a reformatory engage in an inexplicit game representing masturbation.

After certain concessions, the Lord Chamberlain came to an accommodation with Ken. There was however a further censor to reckon with: the Board of the National Theatre, whose members included Henry Moore and Sir Kenneth Clark, unanimously decided to ban the play. As one member, Lord Chandos, put it to a theatre critic, 'If this is a masterpiece, my name's Rosenbaum.' Ken immediately cabled John Dexter that the play had been banned outright and without consultation with Olivier (who was out of the country at the time). 'BOARD FURTHER SAID IT INTENDED HENCEFORTH TO SUPERVISE ALL REPERTOIRE DECISIONS STOP LARRY BILL AND I FEEL THAT AS LONG AS THEATRE HAS CONFIDENCE OF PUBLIC WE MUST INSIST ON ARTISTIC CONTROL AS MINIMUM REQUIREMENT FOR SELF RESPECT'.

Dexter cabled back from New York, 'BOARD CENSORSHIP INTOLERABLE', and offered his resignation. Olivier complained strongly. But the situation was to a large extent of Olivier's making. On his appointment he had asked the Board for a subcommittee to help choose 'a balanced repertory'. A drama committee was set up and met for the first time on 11 December 1962.

After the *Spring Awakening* dispute it was agreed that if there were differences of opinion about a play between the drama panel and the executive the matter should be settled between Olivier and the Chairman, Lord Chandos. When the next big confrontation took place, in 1967, over Rolf Hochhuth's play *Soldiers*, that arrangement was ignored by the Board.

Had Olivier insisted, from the beginning, on a clearer separation of powers his term at the National might have ended differently. It was left to Ken to fight the good fight. At huge cost to himself and his career, almost single-handedly he fought (inside the theatre in confrontation with the Board; outside, lobbying at the Arts Council, in government circles and vociferously in the press) for the director's right to artistic autonomy. When Peter Hall was appointed to succeed Olivier, he did so on the condition – unofficially extracted – that his Board Chairman would not veto a play nor interfere in artistic decisions. (He also inherited from the Olivier regime a tried model from which to draw ideas.)

Ken was accused of being a romantic and a dilettante, with little practical experience of daily political effort. His term at the National surely tells a different story. He believed in joining the Establishment to change it from within. And beyond that he believed that the point of a revolution was to succeed, 'to become the establishment and still remain fluid and experimental.... I see no point in an avant-garde which has no ambitions beyond a tiny minority.'

That view informed his work, his commitments and his ideology through-out the decade of the drop-out.

23

Living with Ken

During our first years together, Ken worked phenomenally hard, yet he never gave the impression of so doing. Work and play were one, or so it felt to me because we were rarely out of each other's company. In addition to film criticism, and *ex officio* work for the National, and the research required for his journalism, he took an active part in various causes and committees (the quirkiest of which was the 'Who Killed Kennedy Committee'). He wrote a vast number of letters to the newspapers and to friends. In a spare moment he would polish up a satirical sketch for the BBC's *Not So Much a Programme More a Way of Life*. Because of his astonishing energy, and because the days were full, he would write at night and into the early hours of the morning (while I slept).

He always woke in a smiling good humour, for he had a strong head, a sturdy stomach and a sweet disposition. A tea-making machine with built-in alarm would wake him; shortly afterwards he would reach for the Marmite jar, kept beside his bed, and spoon out some of the dark salty paste. This *bonne bouche* would be followed by a cup of tea from the bedside machine and, a little later, by a can of Heinz mulligatawny soup. One of my first innovations was to introduce cooked breakfast to his life, bacon and fried tomatoes, which he liked so much that he'd postpone the pleasure of mulligatawny until later in the day.

Into our bedroom with its floral wallpaper and four-poster bed – quite out of keeping with the shabby–satanic look of the rest of the flat – would enter, around 10 a.m., a secretary to take dictation.

Somehow, in the mornings, there was time for chat and the making of plans and word games. Or Ken would add items to his invented arts festival – whose theme was boredom – at Charleroi in Belgium's industrial belt: indigenous folkloric manifestations would include Walloon liturgical drama, the traditional game of Fall Down Farmhouses, played annually to mark the

Wedding of Elaine and Ken, 1951

Bullfight school

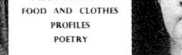
CITIZEN COON

WELLES DOES IT ALL WITH A SHRUG

THEATRE . . . by KENNETH TYNAN

NO doubt about it, Orson Welles has the courage of his restrictions. In last night's boldly staged OTHELLO at the St. James's he gave a performance brave and glorious to the eye; but it was the performance of a magnificent amateur.

I say this carefully, for I am young enough to have been brought up on rumour of his name and I sat in my stall conscious that, in a sense, a whole generation was on trial. If Welles was wrong, if a contemporary approach to Shakespeare in his thunderbolt

Waggonload o' Monkeys

In Queen Elizabeth Slept Here, Jimmy Hanley and Rosalyn Boulter played husband and wife. In Waggonload o' Monkeys they do not.

Above the Crowd in England

• Several years
drama critic and
conspicuous figur
long hair, he was
ness and real ach
duced scores of p
Heath and *Man*

Ken, Elaine and Peter Ustinov

(Far right) Ken, and Peter Brook

INTRODUCING

KENNETH TYNAN
the liveliest writer of the day

DOWN WITH
scarecrows snobs and sniggers !

'—Only ma...
are nev...
bored . .

THE first thing any critic ought to make clear is his capacity for boredom. The man who never yawns in the theatre is a menace to it, as callow and gullible as he is insensitive. Only maniacs are never bored.

The extreme total pleasure a critic gets out of a work of art is so elating that, in its absence, he resembles nothing so much as an addict who has lost his hypodermic.

Painful

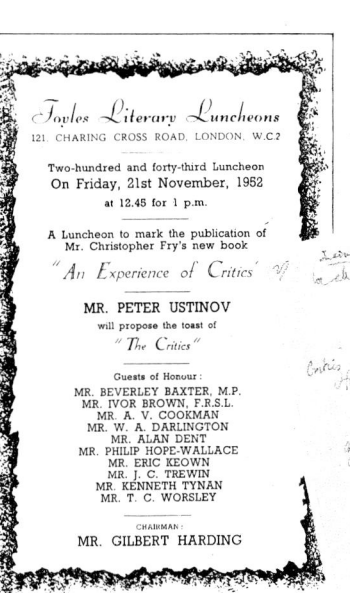

Foyles Literary Luncheons

121, CHARING CROSS ROAD, LONDON, W.C.2

Two-hundred and forty-third Luncheon
On Friday, 21st November, 1952
at 12.45 for 1 p.m.

A Luncheon to mark the publication of
Mr. Christopher Fry's new book

"An Experience of Critics"

MR. PETER USTINOV
will propose the toast of
"The Critics"

Guests of Honour :
MR. BEVERLEY BAXTER, M.P.
MR. IVOR BROWN, F.R.S.L.
MR. A. V. COOKMAN
MR. W. A. DARLINGTON
MR. ALAN DENT
MR. PHILIP HOPE-WALLACE
MR. ERIC KEOWN
MR. J. C. TREWIN
MR. KENNETH TYNAN
MR. T. C. WORSLEY

CHAIRMAN :
MR. GILBERT HARDING

THE DORCHESTER HOTEL, PARK LANE
TICKETS 17/6 EACH (including luncheon)

(Top left) 'The boy wonder',
1954

Ken by Cecil Beaton

Notes for Foyle's Literary
Luncheon

Ken and Elaine at Mount Street

Rose and Tracy, 1953

(Centre) Campaign for a national theatre, 1958

At the Theatre
INS AND OUTS
By KENNETH TYNAN

First *Observer* theatre review, 5 September 1954

Aldermaston, 1958: Ken, Doris Lessing and Christopher Logue

Senators Quiz a Drama Critic (British)

The Committee Calls Kenneth Tynan'

By ...'H WERSHBA

...ted British drama critic
...ed an American news-
...ent calling for ...
...ba has ...

voking any of the amendments
to the Constitution.

"I should like, however, to express my regret that the committee should have seen fit to
employ its authority to sub-
...na a visiting journalist. It
...done so before, to the ...
... knowledge, ...st there

that President Eisenhower had
made a speech in which he
stated that the Castro regime
was a menace to the stability
of the Western Hemisphere?

"No, I was not.

"And did I think myself justified in holding opinions that
openly defied those of the President of the United States? I
brooded over this for a long,
...inious moment, and then
... I was forming opin-
...orry

British Embassy in Washington,
and asked whether a Senate
committee was entitled to subpena a visiting foreign journalist; I was told that anyone—of
whatever nationality—could be
summoned to Washington as
soon as he set foot on American
soil. It was just my bad luck,
I gathered, that I happened to
be the first non-resident alien
ever to have been Congression-
ally subpena'd."

Brought before the committee
on May 5, Tynan was first
interrogated about a TV film
...he had prepared for
...The program ...
...dis-

calls. "It had not occurred to
me that the authority of an
American committee might extend to England. I replied that
I had discussed it with the production staff that had been assigned to me by Associated
Television."

"But what were their names?"
the committee persisted.

"Their names," Tynan pointed
out, "were listed on the credit
titles. In consequence, every one
of them was entered into the
record; even the cutter of the
show may have some very routine
questions to answer before he
ever apply for an Ameri-
...visa."

Immigration Dept. Acts

...similarly suspec...
...road
...subs
...Imme...
...connec...
...in ...
...pearar...
...tion a...
...a tech...
...ssport
...the Ur...
...ly beer
...here w...
...might ...
...ot of ...
...d legal...
...to lea...
...n term...
...ion. I ...
...y law...
...d to cl...
...e cred...
...plus w...
...acqui...
...rom th...
...it sure...
...he qu...
...of in...
...any ...
...tion w...

(opposite) Ken and Tennessee
Williams, Spain, 1955

With Lenny Bruce, 1959

New York farewell party: Ken
and Vivien Leigh, 1960

Tempo: Lord Harewood and Ken

Ken and Laurence Olivier with a model of Chichester Festival Theatre

Groucho Marx, S. J. Perelman and Ken,
London, 1964

THE NATIONAL THEATRE

22, Duchy Street, London, S.E.1.

WATerloo 2626

Chairman:
The Rt. Hon. Viscount Chandos, D.S.O., M.C.
Secretary:
Kenneth Rae.

Director:
Sir Laurence Olivier.
Administrative Director:
Stephen Arlen.

Othello: DR One Thoughts

1. Orange tights and orange backcloth.
2. Please make the cuts I suggested or some similar ones.
3. Frank's Beatle wig. Frank's capering and hamming. His playing of
so many lines "as to idiot children" protesting too much.
His way of giving all lines equal emphasis
being too light, too vince Othello
match of total inability
dis His releases
in separa ction it pr
Deta Othello scen
NCO.

love or
glad
in Bis
s line
llo's

The National Theatre

The Recruiting Officer

George Farquhar

The National Theatre

Rosencrantz and Guildenstern are Dead
Tom Stoppard

Three Sisters

(Top) Lunch at the Etoile, Ken and Kathleen, 1964, and Ken with Dominic Elwes, Ronda

(Centre) Orson Welles and Ken, Madrid, 1964, and Tracy with Ken, London

(Bottom) Ken and Kathleen Valencia, 1968, and Antonio Ordóñez, Tarifa

beginning of the open-cast mining season, and a Pudding Bee for local chefs.

Once out of his mustard-yellow robe and dressed for the day, Ken would choose a favourite record, Phil Silvers in *Top Banana*, or Groucho Marx singing 'Only a Rose', or Mel Brooks as the 2001-Year-Old Man, and he would try to explain to me why these men were talented and funny. Not having much sense of humour, at a loss with the Jewish joke, I usually failed to get the point.

Since Ken didn't believe in getting up early in the morning, he insisted that I leave my regular job at the *Sunday Times* and work from home, on a retainer basis. This I willingly went along with, for I had no strong ambitions other than to earn enough for my personal needs. When momentarily out of Ken's sight I interviewed members of the 'New Class' – hairdressers and working-class actors – before everyone knew we were in the middle of the swinging sixties.

Ken hated big parties; what he liked best was to get his friends – Duke Ellington or Norman Mailer or Albert Finney or Peter Brook – back to Mount Street on their own, so there could be controlled talk. Rapidly exhausted by this diet of Great Persons, and feeling inadequate, I would wait patiently for our guests to leave, after which Ken would still have energy for more music and talk, before we finally went to bed, where the evening, according to his plan, would begin.

He would get me to repeat some dialogue from a Bogart–Bacall film, and if I messed up, he would say with a degree of irritation, 'You're not a showbiz person.' How often I'd be dismissed and feel cast down, though accepting stoically the truth of what he said.

It was not merely the problem of my deficiency as a showbiz person, nor the decade age-difference. There were other tests to be met, particularly during the first six months, before our life together truly meshed. If Ken had fought hard to win me, it was now my turn to do battle for us. As a fierce practitioner of romantic love, I was entirely committed to him, and determined to ride the waves.

Our first declared confrontation was over sex. As part of my new-broom policy at Mount Street, I systematically invaded cupboards and drawers, throwing out old make-up bottles, other women's clothes, and objects that could only have been there for sexual use: a cork on a long string attached to a hot-water bottle, a pair of Victorian knickers and a single black stocking. On one of these raids I came across a metal box in which I found a large number of black and white pornographic photographs. The theme of almost every study was of a woman in some stage of undress being spanked by a fully dressed spanker, usually a man. They were period pieces, all shot well before the sixties gave us the male porno star – muscled, moustachioed and broadly smiling.

In the autumn of 1964, this Pandora's box (the very same, no doubt, that had upset the first Mrs Tynan) was strange and shocking to me and I recall closing it up, leaving the flat and walking twice around Berkeley Square to get my breath back.

That evening I told Ken of my discovery. He was visibly affected. We must part, he said. There was nothing else for it. Then he retired to the spare room for the night. That was the first of many occasions during my life with Ken when I learned, by trial and error, using all the common sense I had – of which he had not a whit – how to soothe his sense of personal humiliation, to calm him down and woo him back. In the final analysis I never really succeeded, because I never understood how deep-seated was his wish to think entirely well of himself and how impossible for him it was to achieve that state of ease.

As for his sexual quirks, they only shocked me in the abstract or by association. Like many a prudish person, I was not prudish in bed. Nor, on the other hand, was our sexual theatre very advanced. By the end of our first year together I was firmly convinced that the great passion between us, both emotional and physical, had ironed out all the odd little wrinkles on our sexual map.

Even with more advanced partners, Ken's experiments had never included the more dramatic demonstrations, like bondage; he never went to an orgy, never slept with a whore – all of which I set down with some sureness, since he did not lie about these things. He wanted to tell the world about his nursery garden of sexual habits, whether the world wished to hear or not, to have people say, 'That's all right, it's permitted, you may.' He would argue that the testing by means of theatrical fantasies of one partner by the other was the only democratic kind of sex, since each partner ideally wished to submit to the other in equal degree. He knew also that sado-masochism had not yet made what he described as 'an acceptable public breakthrough'. What he did not seem to know was how easily he could shock himself.

Ken's voluble public campaign for sexual liberty, fought through the sixties and early seventies, was partly aimed at persuading the world to demystify sex, to treat it as something ordinary, even a game for pleasure, and thereby to reduce the guilt. One result was that some Tynan-watchers confused his sexual evangelism with that of the health and efficiency brigade. Ken certainly didn't belong there.

In theory he was against monogamy, but in practice he watched the great dance of changing partners during that period from a distance: throughout the decade and into the seventies Ken and I were entirely monogamous. While constant, we both felt only respect and gratitude for the act of making love: 'the religious act of fucking', Ken would say. But that was one view he kept strictly private.

In those early years Ken looked after me with immense care, sending me to a doctor at the slightest sneeze, placing my writing with his American agent, taking charge of my taxes. He looked after me with the same attention to detail with which he looked after his daughter Tracy, keeping a close eye on her progress at the Devon boarding school, visiting her there, checking the state of her room or her spending when she was home with us, firing off letters to lawyers when he thought that Elaine – then living in America – might be trying to have her educated in New York, contrary to the terms of their separation agreement.

Not for a year and a half after moving in with Ken would Oliver Gates consent to start divorce proceedings. In this matter, too, Ken was very solicitous, knowing how affected by the situation, made thin and anxious, I was, and he tried to reassure me with the promise of babies and nests – taking me house-hunting each weekend. On 19 November 1965 Ken was finally served with a divorce petition, from Oliver Gates, along with a request for £5000 in damages. I was finally 'bought' a year later for a paltry £500 and costs, and the divorce became absolute on 15 May 1967.

The closest observer of our life together was our secretary Maggie Abbott. She would observe me in my dowdy Harrods-type clothes and Ken in his yellow dressing-gown, of a morning, and hear:

those 'darlings' ring through the flat, rather like a Noël Coward play. You were terribly in love, and the atmosphere was very high.

Ken liked bossing you. I remember thinking how clever you were to let him. You were very strong – strong in your innocence. There was no competitiveness. By just being yourself you tapped into what Ken needed. There'd be great discussions about shopping, and what you would eat. And lists would be made for parties, at the bottom of which Ken would add, 'And Maggie to serve drinks.' On Fridays, when the work had been done, I'd book a table for two at the Étoile.

I had begun slowly, but comprehensively, to take over Mount Street, to install an au pair, and to liven up the kitchen, so that we could eat at home. Tracy's room was repainted, and the drawing-room repapered in an all-too-tasteful dragged-à-la-Fowler green. In came a marble chimneypiece, off-white curtains, and lamps from the newly fashionable Spanish shop, Casa Pupo. But the blow-up of *The Garden of Earthly Delights* and the bullfight prints remained, so the room was a collision of tastes.

In this room we put the slow loris (our first pet), a grey lemur who came out at night and peed slowly across the newly dyed prune carpet. Everything about the animal was slow and mournful, suggesting retreat or escape. One day our friend Leo Lerman looked out of his window in Mount Street opposite our flat and said to his companion: 'There's Ken Tynan trying to hang himself.' But Ken was only trying to rescue the loris from the balcony. When Robert Graves came to visit us, he immediately sensed our disenchantment and asked his wife Beryl to take the creature. In due course the furry gloomster was shipped to Majorca, from whence Mrs Graves sent him to the Barcelona zoo.

Our next pet was a small-boned white and black kitten, brought to us from Devon by Tracy, and called Little. We loved her obsessively and childishly. I believe she was Tracy's official Christmas present to us in 1964. At any rate, Tracy was with us during the holiday.

That year we used to go across the street to the Connaught Hotel, which served as the local store, for butter or eggs and at Christmas for chicken wire to help secure our first tree. From then on Christmas became institutionalized as a time of serious entertainment.

Hard-core regulars at our Christmas Eve dinners were our hard-core friends: Christopher Logue, rouser of drawing-room rabble, the writer George Melly, the screenwriter Donald Ogden Stewart, and his wife, Ella Winter, another rabble-rouser. Through their famous drawing-room in Hampstead passed most of the Hollywood Ten. No one was more élitist than Ella, for all her leftist views. She loved stars – and entertained Dr Spock, Ingrid Bergman and Katharine Hepburn. When Charlie Chaplin came to visit she kept him upstairs and allowed only the very select up to meet him. What, we asked Don, would he write on the gravestone of his beloved Ella? 'She was awful, but she was worth it,' he replied.

Another good friend was the songwriter Steve Vinaver, a plump, sweet, manic young man. He could set Ken off for hours working on a limerick. He once wrote to us from Marseille with thoughts of King Kong and Fay Wray. Could Ken get any further? He could. Here is one of the half-a-dozen limericks he came up with:

> There was a young man of Marseille
> Who got into bed with Feille Wreille
> She said, 'Don't get me wrong,
> But after King Kong
> You can keep your Quatorze Juillet.'

On other people's turf, Ken was less predictable than at home, and less friendly, sometimes explosively angry if he got into a political argument. Women in particular felt they did not want to talk to him for long for fear of boring him. 'He was the most difficult person I ever met', says my novelist friend Angela Huth, 'to know what he was actually feeling at the moment.' He didn't enjoy the social dance.

Among Ken's many wild transatlantic friends who passed through Mount Street during those early years was H.L. ('Doc') Humes from the *Paris Review* crowd. A genius or merely an eccentric – nobody was quite sure. After the Kennedy assassination, Humes began to have fears of being assassinated himself, and brought his wife and children to live in London. One night, around 3 a.m., Doc showed up to warn us – since he claimed the CIA was bugging the flat – against an organization called Universal Aunts (from which we hired our cleaning ladies). He told us that the CIA used it as a front to gain access to people under surveillance. Ken said, 'Doc, do you realize you're talking like a paranoid schizophrenic?' 'I *am* a paranoid schizophrenic,' said Doc, smiling brightly. Ken's solution was to introduce him to Dr R. D. Laing, guru for the decade and already famous for his view that most schizophrenics were fundamentally healthier than you or I.

The friend of Ken's who seemed archetypal, who was everything he liked best and who opened more doors to my imagination than anyone else, was Pauline Boty. She was a beautiful, bold girl who lived with Clive Goodwin (then editing *Encore* magazine and working for television). She wore eight-foot feather boas and early miniskirts. She had studied at the Royal College of Art. She acted. Under the tutelage of Peter Blake she became one of the painters of the Pop movement. She came from a suburban background, and was classless. She married Clive, and was not possessive. She liked women, and was unguilty about sex.

She enjoyed smoking marijuana, and said so. She was committed to her work without being particularly ambitious. She had no interest in housework. In the flat she shared with Clive, we met rock musicians, drug-users, writers, directors and boutique owners – long before they had begun to mix with each other. I had simply never come across anyone like her, and she shook up my view of things. In July 1966, Pauline died of glandular cancer, aged twenty-eight.

The response to me among Ken's friends was mixed. One American friend of Ken's saw how much in love he was, and observed no reciprocal demonstration from me. Did I love him? Was I cold? Another woman recalls that 'You'd come into a party tossing that mane, but not pay much attention if they weren't your particular friends.' 'As for Ken,' recalls one observer, 'the costumes were fewer and he seemed to have more or less settled down into the right suit.' Or 'He had a solidity then which he didn't have before. Maybe it was just a healthier life, but he no longer had the pale bluish–greenish look of the early years.'

In turn, Ken changed and educated me. 'You had an enquiring mind,' Angela Huth says,

and Ken answered all your enquiries. You were eager – you know how new wives are. And for eight years or so you were very much the wife. I saw you together first in the winter of 1964, at the BBC. And I just have the impression of you both – I think you were arm in arm – coming through a door and gusting along the corridor, as if driven by wind. You were wearing a cloak or something which was billowing out behind you, and together you looked like a sort of winged object, absolutely at one – these two people, smiling, and an extraordinary feeling of zest, of oneness, about you.

24

A Four-Letter Word

On 13 November 1965, on a late-night live satire programme called *BBC-3*, Ken said 'fuck'. It was the first time the word had been used on television. The result was to set off an explosion, to produce a national fit of apoplexy.

Forever after Ken was known as the 'Man Who Said Fuck'. His obituaries referred to this event (and to his production of *Oh! Calcutta!*) more often than to his criticism, writing or theatre work: 'Is *that* how I'm going to be remembered?' he had asked.

The producer of the programme, Ned Sherrin, had heard that there was a long-standing feud between Ken and Mary McCarthy, set off by unfavourable reviews of each other's theatre criticism, and he decided to bring them together to create a little controversy. They met, before the show, with the moderator Robert Robinson, in order to find a subject for discussion. 'It turned out', Mary McCarthy remembers, 'that we were in complete agreement about everything, except possibly each other.'

In the end the only area on which they could agree to disagree was censorship. Ken was against it absolutely, Sherrin reports, and 'McCarthy could visualize a case for censorship in some circumstances.' Two days later they met on the air.

Robinson told the viewers that Ken and McCarthy both agreed that censorship should be abolished. He then asked Ken whether he would, thereafter, allow a play in which sexual intercourse took place to be put on at the National Theatre. Ken answered: 'Oh I think so, certainly. I doubt if there are very many rational people in this world to whom the word "fuck" is particularly diabolical or revolting or totally forbidden.'

It will be seen from this quotation that Ken slipped in the word slightly out of context – as if he had already planned to use it (though he had not warned Sherrin in advance). He then went on to defend the more questionable subject of sex on the stage. (In subsequent years he said that he personally would not find such a demonstration stimulating to watch, though he would oppose banning it.) He had also squeezed in two other points on the programme: that there should be no distinction between high and low art; and that, after the abolition of the censor, a play should be subject only to the law of the land.

The programme continued in an orderly fashion, ending with Ken's view that he was not exclusively concerned with the sexual aspect of censorship. He rather wanted to rule out the 'damaging and horrendous things [the Lord Chamberlain] does to free speech and politics and the church'.

These were points ignored, it would seem, by the great British public, who had heard *that word* and rapidly jammed the BBC's switchboard in their indignation. Ken's press service during the next few weeks delivered well over a thousand newspaper cuttings. *L'affaire du 'mot'*, as the French called it, managed for a few days to eclipse all other news, including the Unilateral Declaration of Independence in Rhodesia and the war in Vietnam; and to provoke a barrage of headlines and stories like 'That Word On TV: Millions of viewers were shocked last night when the naughtiest of all four-letter words was used on TV'; 'Insult to Womanhood'; 'Is This Moral?'; 'The War on BBCnity'; 'Sack 4-letter Tynan'. The top brass of the BBC issued not an apology but 'an expression of regret', recognizing that Ken had used the word in a serious discussion as part of a straightforward statement of his views. 'This is not a word that should be used on the air,' they stated. Huw Weldon, then in charge of programming, and Ned Sherrin, took a dissenting view and defended Ken. From Mount Street the corrupter of public morals issued the following statement: 'I used an old English word in a completely neutral way to illustrate a serious point, just as I would have used it in similar conversation with any group of grown-up people. To have censored myself would, in my view, have been an insult to the viewers' intelligence.' Then, feeling a little shaky, but rather enjoying things, he kept his counsel.

The *Daily Express* political correspondent, William Barkley, did not keep his. He wrote that Tynan's use of the word was 'the bloodiest outrage I have ever known'.

Mrs Mary Whitehouse, co-founder in 1964 of the Clean Up TV Campaign, said that Kenneth Tynan needed his bottom smacked, that there must be no more filth on television. She announced that she had written to the Queen, asking her to use her influence with the governors of the BBC. (The Queen sent the letter on to the Postmaster-General.)

Churchmen devoted their sermons to the scandal. Education authorities were voluble. Cartoons, limericks and philological discussions filled the columns. Stanley Reynolds, in the *Guardian*, wondered why 'that one simple word of four letters can provoke a greater reaction inside us than long and complex words like apartheid, rebellion, illegal, police state, and treason'. The explanation was simple, according to the *Sunday Times*, quoting from *A*

History of Modern Colloquial English: the word 'chills the blood and raises gooseflesh'.

In the House of Commons four motions were set down, supported by 133 Labour and Tory backbenchers, attacking Ken and the BBC. The first motion asked the Home Secretary to refer Ken's remarks to the Director of Public Prosecutions on the ground that he had used obscene language in public. Another called for Ken's dismissal as Literary Manager of the National Theatre. A third requested that the Postmaster-General set up a viewers' and listeners' council to protect the public. A fourth called for the dismissal from their jobs of both Ken and Sir Hugh Carleton Greene, the Director-General of the BBC.

Amendments were tabled by Ken's supporters, who included Tom Driberg, Michael Foot and Hugh Jenkins. Anthony Wedgwood Benn, the Postmaster-General, said it was not his job to interfere with the BBC. Sir Elwyn Jones, the Attorney-General, rejected the suggestions that obscene libel proceedings should be instituted since he did not believe that the use of a single word in a discussion on censorship had depraved or corrupted the public. The Prime Minister, Harold Wilson, jocularly promised not to use four-letter words in any of *his* television performances.

Meanwhile the liberal newspaper pundits sat heavily on the fence. They were glad that Ken had breached the taboo. But was it altogether polite to use the word at all – let alone on television? Should language not be a seduction, rather than a rape? And so on.

In Mount Street we kept a 'fuck file'. In it Ken put the thirty-eight letters he received on the subject. His attackers wrote that he was not to use that word should he ever attend a show at an officers' mess where there were ladies present; that his stammer no doubt covered 'an obvious repression'; that a similar disregard for moral standards produced Nazi Germany; that one correspondent or another would be coming to kill him with rusty scythes and red-hot pokers.

Ken's favourite defender was an 'ordinary Housewife and Grandmother', who attacked the 'maniac prudes who would seek to make every aspect of individual freedom (which *is* the individual life) either psychologically unbalanced or criminal, or both'. Support from this woman, who wrote that she liked 'the sweet word fuck', made Ken cry.

Asked to explain why he had bitten so deeply into the national consciousness he uncharacteristically replied that he did not want to comment. He said he did not believe in moral generalizations. 'The only generalization that I would ever permit myself', he stated ingenuously, 'is that all acts that one wants to perform one ought to perform, so long as they do not involve injury to others.' He was also coy about whether he had or had not intended to use the word. And over the years he never let on publicly whether he had planned to drop 'fuck'. I asked Mary McCarthy if she knew the answer, and she said she did. 'After the broadcast, we went into the hospitality room, and the feeling was rather gay about the whole thing, Ken claiming he hadn't prepared it. Then he asked Jim and me to come to your flat, where you were waiting. You came to the door and said, "Oh darling, you did it!" It was "My hero, welcome!", so we knew. We came in for drinks, and from then on we were friends.'

So ended a so-called literary feud.

On the night after the four-letter incident, Ken and Mary McCarthy again shared a platform, this time at the Royal Court Theatre, where Ken chaired a panel of critics friendly and hostile to Edward Bond's play *Saved*. Banned by the censor, it had been playing at the Court, a club theatre, and unsettling the audience. The scene which caused the most trouble was the stoning to death of a baby by a gang of thugs. Ken found the episode hair-raising, but did not think it should be banned. Mary McCarthy praised the author's concern with 'limit and decorum'.

A week later, Laurence Olivier wrote an impassioned plea to the *Observer* against censorship, and, in turn, Ken wrote to the *New Statesman*: 'What the image of violence can do is to confront us with our own complicity, to make us face the fact that something in us responds to it, to force us to admit that violence is not foreign to our nature. Would I ban a pro-lynching play? No, because I am as free to attack it in print as the author is to stage it. Better freedom for both of us than merely for me.'

It was not merely the theatre that seemed to matter acutely at that time. The health of the arts mattered as a whole, and the interaction of arts and politics was endlessly debated.

On 7 January Ken attended a discussion at the Mahatma Gandhi Hall on the arts and socialism. Taking part was the art critic John Berger and the director Lindsay Anderson, who had played a key part in the New Left of the fifties. Evidently Ken thought Anderson behaved irresponsibly, for he wrote to him complaining that his attitude had been patronizing and trimming by dismissing Berger's socialist views as 'rubbish'. Anderson replied, attacking Ken's 'rational cohesive social optimism' and accusing him of being a safety valve of the Establishment – 'Your characteristic has always been schizoid rather than organic.'

Ken did not need to be warned. He knew perfectly well how the Establishment forces operated, how you could win only limited battles when fighting them from within. He did not believe, during this period of revolutionary ferment, that Western capitalism would crumble, or that the class structure was ever seriously threatened. Yet he continued to fight, refusing Lindsay Anderson's pessimism.

As Noel Annan suggests, he was 'the forerunner and leader of the liberation of taste'. He proselytized for permissiveness, and hated the phrase 'permissive society' – 'because it implies one has to ask permission in the first place', he once explained. In the English antinomian tradition, he questioned the existing rules and wished to liberate the instincts. But that was not the end of it. He had his own solutions for the good life, and in their defence he could sound positively bigoted. (On occasion he would write about sex, as John Mortimer has pointed out, 'with the sort of apostolic zeal with which the Early Fathers of the Church discussed the Immaculate Conception'.)

There was nothing *laissez-faire* about Ken. When the pragmatists attacked him, he would counter that there was nothing so extreme as the 'tyranny of the middle way'. Typical of this tyranny, he argued, was Lord Goodman, the *éminence grise* behind many a reform movement of the period, and a 'fanatical compromiser'. Of this portly do-gooder and fixer, Ken wrote in 1972: 'When it actually seems as if real democracy might be about to exert some genuine influence on the nation's life, the ruling class produces an antibody to counter it. The antibody in our time is Lord Goodman. A man who has never held elective office, he has wielded more power than anyone in the country, except for the Prime Minister, during the last decade.'

From my perspective – as perhaps from Lord Goodman's – Ken was often unnecessarily provocative, when he might well have achieved the same ends by gentler methods. As the decade wore on, and he enlisted in more and more contentious causes, I felt that he was rash not only in his refusal to protect his own interests but also that he sometimes seemed to invite disaster. In taking on the Establishment, whether in a committee room or in the media or with his pen, he never realized how seriously *he* was taken. He did not play by the rules, he played on the enemy's turf; he wrote cleverly; he knew how to manipulate the press; he dared to be rude. He frightened them.

In subsequent years Ken paid the price for the opposition's displeasure. Many maintained that he was a gullible and enthusiastic victim of the period's excess, and they speculated on his psychological make-up. He liked to know where was the barrier of transgression; the real moment of excitement came when he reached that barrier. Having crossed it and forced a reaction, he would then establish a new set of rules, a new construct, which in time he would again put to the test.

It is not surprising that while Ken needed to transgress, he also loved and needed to play games, and play 'creates order', as Johan Huizinga wrote in *Homo Ludens* – a book Ken admired. 'Play demands order absolute and supreme. The least deviation from it "spoils the game", robs it of its character and makes it worthless.'

Recently I questioned Christopher Logue on the matter of inviting disaster, for I knew that the poet had on one occasion, while in the army, deliberately invited arrest for a trivial crime, and had thereafter claimed to have been discharged from the army with ignominy. He believes his boast had something to do with wanting to be known at any price. 'But that's not the whole thing.

You need some mint clues. It's very difficult.' He took out his notebook and read: 'A threat to authority – queue jumping.... Overwhelming sense of self-importance. No sense of the importance of oneself at the same time. The two together..... Disbelieving in one's importance unless that importance existed for others, but at the same time having no special respect for others or for their opinions.... A search for someone you can trust. Someone who does not condone but does not condemn. It is hard to find that person inside yourself.'

These thoughts and others, to do with identity, with the release of anxiety, teased my mind. But I had to step back and remind myself of two things: that the impetus behind Ken's attacks on entrenched positions was essentially rational, humane, radical and courageous; and that he also liked to provoke, because it was fun.

Shortly after the four-letter-word scandal, Ken appeared with the playwright Alun Owen at an arts symposium in Liverpool. Owen recalls:

Every time he hesitated the audience would tense and wait for a word. Would he say 'cunt' this time? Would he say 'asshole'. But no, he wouldn't. He said, Really, one wasn't there to play that game. Much too obvious. The next day we returned to London by train. The first-class compartment was crowded. Ken looked through his newspaper, then he produced a magazine with a title like *Spanking Times*, and began to read it quite nonchalantly. I looked, and everybody in the compartment was looking as well. Eventually I said, 'Well what's that then, Ken?' He said, 'It's an Am-me-me-rican publication, rapidly gaining ground in the old country.' I broke my ass laughing, and the other people in the compartment buried themselves in their newspapers.

Ken's post at the National Theatre allowed him time out for 'freelance writing', which included a full-time job as film critic for the *Observer*, begun in 1964, as well as regular commitments to articles for American magazines.

On average he had more fun in a movie house than he did in the theatre. Here he was exposed to the best in European culture, to Jean-Luc Godard, to the new Czech cinema, and to the work of Antonioni, Fellini, Bergman, Truffaut and Visconti. After seeing Godard's *Bande à Part*, he told his readers that 'no one speaks to me more intimately than Godard'. When he saw *Pierrot le Fou*, he found it 'wilful, aimless, anarchic ... but also an act of revelry, dedicated to the art of astonishing us'. He wished that Godard would admit that 'this flighty, haphazard film was really a toy, an unserious playwith' – a view which reflected Ken's current obsession with art as play, and in turn a step towards his abandoning of the word 'art' as a useful description of certain highly skilled activities which could delight and instruct. At the Cannes Festival of 1966 he saw *Masculin–Féminin*, and sympathized with Godard's view that it is man's social existence that determines his conscience. 'No other director', he wrote, 'has Godard's gift for posing the right questions.'

In Prague during February 1965 and again in the autumn of 1966, Ken discovered that the Czechs had 'the richest factory for cinema in the world'.

He wrote after his first visit that he had seen 'more serious criticism of the political Establishment in a week than he had seen in London in a year'. Evald Schorm's *Courage for Everyday* explored how a devotion to Marxism can alienate one from fellow human beings. Elmar Klos and Jan Kadár's *The Shop on Main Street* and Jan Němec's *A Report on the Party and the Guests* also dealt with the theme of how much of a man belongs to authority and how much to himself: 'What demands can society legitimately make of a man without requiring him to sacrifice his selfhood?'

It was an argument Ken relished, yet he believed that the real masterpiece to emerge from this explosion of history, one that far transcended a mere political argument, was Schorm's *The Return of the Prodigal Son*, about a successful young architect who tries to kill himself, and enters a mental home in search of the answer. 'From time to time he leaves the institution, but always he returns, shattered by some violation or other of human dignity, and unable to decide whether he or society is at fault.'

Apart from Kafkaesque parables and wartime sagas, the Czechs also delivered fun: Milos Forman's *Black Peter* and *A Blonde in Love* – intimate, sometimes improvised studies of adolescence, hilarious and unsentimental.

Elsewhere there were isolated pleasures, Roman Polanski's *Repulsion* and *Cul de Sac*; Richard Lester's 'shiny forgettable toy' *Help!*, 'an ideal playwith'. And Peter Watkins' 1966 *The War Game* about post-holocaust Britain: 'it may be the most important film ever made,' Ken wrote in one of his regular bouts of excess.

For someone with a considerable knowledge of movies, he wrote on the subject with a certain casualness. Passion flared when the subject was nuclear annihilation, as with *The War Game*, but was not so readily provoked by cinematic style. He did, however, take up arms against the director cult. He argued that the final shape of most films is 'dictated more by the combined skills of the writer, the composer and the cameramen'. Several times he returned to this theme, pointing out that directors were 'spared the basic creative pain of evocation out of nothing'.

Ken mustered a few other generalizations. He suggested that given a reasonable budget, it was difficult to make a totally boring film. 'Yet the cinema's advantage is also its pitfall. Where tedium is so easily avoided, there is a terrible temptation to settle for the negative virtue of not being boring.'

His film criticism does not compare with his theatre reviews. The real problem was that he knew he could have no impact on the outcome of a movie, as he could on a play. He missed, too, the sense of active participation. How could there be 'consensus without applause'? About his comrades he was particularly snide. There were more female critics of cinema, he wrote, than of any other art, and this female aspect was reflected in the men, in their 'reluctance to endorse ideas and attitudes (such as Godard's, for example) that might be thought unbecoming in a properly brought-up girl'.

25

It Was Always Spring

By the beginning of 1966 the famous party was well under way. 'It was always spring,' a friend of mine says of that time. 'It was always a Saturday afternoon.' The Queen had already made the Beatles MBES. Poets had already commandeered the Albert Hall with hash and flowers. Skirts were up, princesses were 'mod', and the accents of the working class were fashionable. I now shopped at Quorum, Granny Takes a Trip, and Biba, rather than Harrods, and Ken bought a pair of transparent plastic shoes that used to mist over, until we punctured them with little holes. He also had a Japanese 'happi' coat which he wore over a green satin shirt at our first big party.

This we gave on 31 March 1966, in honour of election night. Two television sets were installed to record the Labour victory, and were then all but ignored. Ken had recently come across the erotic paintings of an elderly French Sunday painter called Camille Clovis Trouille. For the party he hired a bunch of fibreglass models and dressed them as the creatures of Trouille's imagination. In one room we positioned a girl in picture hat, suspender belt and black stockings, with a bat spreading its wings between her legs. Across our bed lay a figure swathed in Indian silk. Sitting on the edge of the bath was a girl in nun's habit, which was hitched up to reveal stockings with red garters. (One of our guests, with a phobia about mannequins, ran screaming from the flat.) The woman who had hired out the models told John Mortimer that her 'girls' didn't accept invitations to just any old party.

And any old party it was not. It was bursting and explosive and fun, stuffed full with actors, writers, politicians and oddballs, and Ken in the middle of things, like a maypole. Gore Vidal was there. Richard Harris and Marlon Brando arrived drunk. At one point Brando led Ken into the bathroom and dared him to kiss him full on the lips as a proof of friendship. Ken did. I got in a fight with several gatecrashers and burst into tears. Michelangelo

243

Antonioni, who had called that morning to make sure he was invited – though he knew neither of us – turned up in a dark suit and lurked in doorways, 'looking grave and stricken', as Ken remembered, 'rather like Paul Lukas as a decent liberal in an anti-Nazi film'. From this party, the director later announced, came his image of 'swinging London', one he hoped to capture in *Blow-Up*.

On reflection the party was hardly decadent: no orgies, and no drugs that I was aware of. I remember sitting on Ken's knee, in his little study in the early hours of the morning, the flat still bulging with noisy guests, and wishing they would all go home so that we could be alone – together.

In his engagement book, around the time of our election party, Ken wrote: 'I write to become sexually desirable: now I have what I desire, why write?' He liked to provoke himself, as much as he liked to challenge others. He continued, of course, to write, believing the writing to be the central part of his career. He would do long pieces of journalism without the pressure of a deadline, and eventually he would write books.

When, in the autumn of 1965, the *New York Times* offered him the post of drama critic, he turned it down. He had no wish to be tied to daily journalism. When the *New Yorker* offered, that autumn, to pay him $10,000 to write four articles on world theatre – French, Czech, Italian and English, as it turned out – he jumped. By the end of May 1966, he had given up his job as film critic for the *Observer*, to make room for the *New Yorker*.

Ken had already signed an agreement, two years before, with *Playboy* magazine, to write three pieces of 3000 to 5000 words for an annual fee of $7000. In 1965 the annual fee went up to $8200. By March 1968 he owed *Playboy* $10,533.33. In the interim he had provided two interviews – with Peter O'Toole and Orson Welles; contributed to a panel on homosexuality and another on the future of the arts. He had also written about theatre censorship, Humphrey Bogart and stoicism, film festivals and Vietnam.

Playboy accepted Ken's radical views on politics, but turned down his three contributions on sex. The first was a scholarly homage to the female bottom entitled 'Meditations on Basic Baroque'. 'It seems to us', wrote *Playboy*, 'to have an archness which is middle-aged.' The second turn-down was Ken's defence of hard-core pornography. Hugh Hefner, the magazine's staff reported, was troubled by the emphasis on masturbation.

In December 1967, Ken wrote to his agent Emilie Jacobson at Curtis Brown to tell her he was embarked on 'a fairly light-hearted history of what you call panties and we call knickers. (I say "fairly light-hearted" because I take them moderately seriously.)' *Playboy*'s reaction was unanimously negative. An editor wrote, 'We hoped that Ken's insightful irreverence would relieve this somewhat squeamish subject of its fetishistic overtones, but I'm afraid that his more or less documentary approach – coupled with his declaration that bloomers "have exercised a powerful hold on the male imagination" from the Victorian era onwards – have substantiated rather than disarmed our reservations.' Reader interest, he felt, would not be aroused in 'this now-arcane preoccupation'. The result was 'an essay that comes off not only as a little bent but boring to boot'.

The magazine's reaction by this time did not surprise Ken, who had told his agent that the *Playboy* editors were 'scared stiff of anything that might go against their healthy open-air attitude towards sex'. And he added, 'If they don't want it, they don't want me as a writer. My suspicion is that it was too erotic for them. Which is a pity: I'd just begun to believe that *Playboy* really approved of sex and wasn't the titillating fraud that everyone says it is.'

Shortly before Ken delivered to the *Observer*, in March 1966, a long, critical review of Truman Capote's *In Cold Blood*, the author showed up at Mount Street. I had not met the diminutive charmer before and was struck by his deferential and effusive manner towards Ken. On the following day, since Ken was suffering from a cold, he sent a plant, and a note which read: 'Something to scent the sickroom (and how's *that* for alliterative horror?)'. That was the last time we saw Capote for many a year.

At the time of the original sentencing of the two murderer–heroes of Capote's 'non-fiction novel', Ken had confronted him at a New York party. Was he not exploiting the two young men; and if they were insane, as it appeared, should he not at least provide them with the best psychiatric and legal aid in an effort to save their lives? The argument between the two continued on other occasions. When the murderers were finally hanged, in April 1965, Capote, according to Ken's story, jumped up and down and declared, 'I'm beside myself, beside myself, beside myself with joy!'

When Ken came to review *In Cold Blood*, he suggested that, despite Capote's claim that he had legal releases, the book might have been different had the young men lived. His view was corroborated by a 'prominent Manhattan lawyer'. 'We are talking', Ken wrote,

about responsibility.... For the first time, an influential writer of the front rank has been placed in a position of privileged intimacy with criminals about to die, and – in my view – done less than he might have to save them.... An attempt to help (by supplying new psychiatric testimony) might easily have failed: what one misses is any sign that it was ever contemplated.... Where lives are threatened, observers and recorders who shrink from participation may be said to betray their species: no piece of prose, however deathless, is worth a human life.

Capote delivered a violent rebuttal to the *Observer*, accusing Ken of having 'the morals of a baboon and the guts of a butterfly'. He wrote that no one who worked on the case 'ever thought that a successful appeal could be made in Kansas courts (which abide by the M'Naghten Rule) on the basis of insanity or "diminished responsibility" '. He doubted whether the 'prominent Manhattan lawyer' existed, and he offered to pay a cheque of $500 to Ken's favourite charity should the lawyer produce an affidavit. Joseph P. Jenkins, who had represented the two murderers, Richard Hickock and Perry Smith, wrote in defence of Capote.

By mid-April Ken, Tracy and I had retired to Seville for a dose of the spring feria, a holiday made edgy by Ken's preoccupation with the Capote business – now taken up by the US press – and by the arrival and despatch of legal and editorial telegrams. On 5 May Ken's 'prominent Manhattan lawyer', Aaron R. Frosch, sent an affidavit to the effect that he had advised Ken that, although he had not read *In Cold Blood*, on the evidence he had he did not believe the book would have been released had the accused still been alive.

On 20 May, Truman Capote signed a cheque made out for $500 to the Howard League for Penal Reform, a copy of which Ken triumphantly pinned to his study wall.

Capote, in turn, put Ken on his most-hated-men list, and devised, as a party piece, an elaborate fantasy in which the scourge Tynan is slowly and luxuriously dismembered. Several years later we bumped into him in the huge corridors of the United Nations Plaza. As we passed each other, Capote dropped a pettish and eccentric little curtsy, and moved swiftly on.

We had made our first visit to Czechoslovakia in February 1965, in time to witness the burgeoning of post-Stalin freedoms, a process begun belatedly in 1961. It was explained to us that the lively connection between culture and politics had an organic and historical basis. Having visited some of the eighteen legitimate theatres, on that first trip and in the autumn of 1966, Ken concluded that Prague had 'a strong claim to be regarded as the theatre capital of Europe'. It had several steadily producing young playwrights of the first rank, Josef Topol and Václav Havel included; a number of world-class directors, among them Otomar Krejča and Jan Grossman; an army of gifted young actors; a flourishing trio of experimental theatres like the Divadlo Na Zábradlí; and the most influential stage designers in Europe.

'Temporarily uninhibited by economic and ideological pressures,' Ken wrote (that is, subsidized and largely left alone), 'the performing arts have had time to consider why they exist and what human purpose they should serve.'

But even the new permissiveness was free to be mocked. In Havel's *The Garden Party* a new-style bureaucrat declares, 'I'm glad you have contrary opinions – everyone should have from one to three contrary opinions.' Havel showed in a subsequent play, *The Memorandum*, how small compromises lead to greater ones, how a man who once betrays his convictions must go on betraying them.

The tension between individual choice and state restriction was exhilarating. In addition Ken was a prize guest in this ancient and beautiful city, fêted in taverns with wine and scented beer, taken to jazz clubs, like Reduta or Viola.

That year Allen Ginsberg was made King of the Carnival for a students' May Day demonstration; pop groups like Hell's Devils and the Bad Intentions sprang out of nowhere, and young men sang 'It's All Over Now', in English, hands pressed to their sides, stiffly twitching in poor imitation of the Rolling Stones.

Ken wrote that the artists could now raise their voices, 'secure in the knowledge that the days were past when retributive Russian tanks might rumble through the streets of Prague'.

Our friend the journalist Antonin Liehm was more cautious. 'First', he told us, 'we must institutionalize the process of democracy.'

Two aspects of the Czech experiment outside the artistic world impressed Ken: worker participation in the melting down of the great centralized system, and student participation. For a certain time, no country seemed to offer more freedom for the individual, although the Communist Party was still nominally in charge. The Czechs had passed from an advanced capitalist economy to a socialist economy of common ownership with a human face. Here – but for the Russians – was the model for the revolutionary future in Western Europe, or so Ken believed, until hindsight made a fool of him. In August 1968, ten days before the meeting of the Congress which would have legitimized many of the Dubček reforms, won during seven years of liberalization, the Russians moved in.

By the end of 1966 we were thoroughly settled into our happy Mount Street world. My divorce was granted, and we had merely to wait a further six months for it to be made final. The previous May, I had found a Victorian corner-house in Thurloe Square, South Kensington. It cost only £11,500 but the lease was a mere seventeen years. We were advised not to buy, but we had fallen in love with the huge rooms, stone staircase and leafy surrounds. With part of Ken's Peacock inheritance, and with money borrowed from my mother and friends, we went ahead.

December already had its routine for us – the visit to the National Cat Show, the foray for cheeses at Paxton and Whitfield, the Paris weekend, and Christmas itself. And this year I was pregnant.

We were, at that time, as lovers are, attuned to each other's slightest frown. One of these frowns may have impelled Ken to pen a letter to me from his office at the National Theatre. It read: 'When you are troubled, I feel it from heart to fingertips; I ache to help and comfort, and everything else turns grey and ashen until you light up again. I have never felt at peace except with you, never understood all the happy meanings of loving-kindness except through you, never known such a constant desire and a constant tenderness as I feel with you. Please be sure of me always.' And the letter ended: 'To think we have hardly finished the first chapter! *It is all such a privilege.* Every day of it – and always, and especially, tomorrow.' This was also how I felt about Ken.

26

Soldiers

By the end of 1966 the two subjects on which Ken had evangelized most passionately, sex and politics, became embodied in two theatrical ideas: an erotic revue to be called *Oh! Calcutta!*, which he would 'devise'; and Rolf Hochhuth's play *Soldiers*.

Both projects were part of his increasing need to be engaged inside the theatre, to express his impresarial talent. Both projects drew upon him international notoriety. For both he paid a savage price in energy, reputation and expense of spirit. Nor did either properly establish him on the right side of the footlights. In the case of *Oh! Calcutta!* the practical demonstration turned out to be other than the elegant ideal Ken had imagined. With *Soldiers*, the central idea was obscured by the notoriety of the play's secondary theme, the association of Winston Churchill with the death of General Wladyslaw Sikorski. In each case Ken had wanted to change existing attitudes. With what result? he wondered after the event. 'More sustained and virulent abuse than anyone in the theatre has received in the press for decades, and probably they changed nothing.'

In the autumn of 1958 Ken had welcomed a documentary play on Hungary, *Shadow of Heroes*, by Robert Ardrey. Here was revived the old idea of drama as living newspaper, and he counselled those who might wish to follow Ardrey's example to make sure their dialogue rang true, 'as true as the dates and facts on to which it is pinned'. But he conceded that all lively documentary plays involved selection and ended up as propaganda. What was wrong with 'honest propaganda'? Such plays urged us to find out for ourselves. 'Fiction dictates its own terms. Fact must meet us on ours.'

It was hardly surprising that early in Ken's career at the National Theatre he commissioned two docudramas, one on the General Strike and another on the Cuban missile crisis (scripted by Clancy Segal and Roger Smith). In

August 1966 he wrote to Olivier complaining that the authors of the Cuban piece were being kept in the waiting-room 'like Victorian hacks'. If the project were dropped, the decision would confirm not only the authors' worst fears but Ken's own fears 'about the seriousness of our intentions to make the theatre a place of contemporary excitement'.

But neither script came up to Ken's expectations. Meanwhile, in autumn 1966, the Royal Shakespeare Company under Peter Brook's direction made their contribution to the Theatre of Fact with a piece about the Vietnam war called *US* (a project which Lord Chandos had attacked on the ground that its anti-American tone 'might endanger the special relationship with our allies'). At the end of the first night the actors stood in line and silently confronted the audience. After some minutes Ken asked loudly from the stalls, 'Are we keeping you waiting or are you keeping us?'

The piece had offended him: as a passionate opponent of the Vietnam war, Ken felt that *US* belittled its serious subject by focusing on liberal guilt. He was all the keener that the National should deliver a worthy docudrama about recent history and was confident that he had the project.

The previous spring he had read that the German playwright Rolf Hochhuth, well known for *The Representative*, in which he accused Pope Pius XII of not intervening with Hitler on behalf of the Jews, was at work on *Soldiers*. Ken declared his interest, and on 5 July, the translator, Robert David MacDonald, gave him an outline.

By November Ken had been given the prologue, set in the ruins of Coventry Cathedral, and the first act of the play within a play, set in 1943, whose leading characters are Churchill, General Sir Alan Brooke and Lord Cherwell – the latter presented as the architect of saturation bombing. Ken felt on this evidence that the play was going to be marvellous.

'Our own deaths,' Hochhuth wrote, 'or those of our grandchildren, may possibly be brought about because the large-scale bombardment of population centres, the specific invention of the years 1940–45, which was never condemned by any court.' Having decided to write a play about the bombing war, he fell upon David Irving's book on the saturation bombing of Dresden. Later he engaged the figure of Bishop Bell of Chichester to argue with Churchill as a vehement opponent of area bombing. The playwright's own position is one of sympathy for Churchill, whom he felt had no other recourse at the time but to launch the bombing over Germany. In retrospect, Hochhuth told a journalist, Churchill may have been wrong:

Once it had been demonstrated that the sacrifice of 700,000 civilians, 56,000 British pilots, not to mention 44,000 American pilots, was in no way decisive in the Second World War, then no air strategist can any longer believe that the bombardment, say, of Vietnamese villages today can bring a decision on the battlefield.

If the main theme of *Soldiers* is Churchill's 'necessary' sanction of a large number of indiscriminate deaths, the secondary one is his implied collusion in the assassination of an individual who happened to be a friend and ally – General Sikorski, head of the Polish government-in-exile. On 4 July 1943, his plane crashed shortly after take-off from Gibraltar, and everyone aboard died except the pilot, who was injured.

Hochhuth's argument for the assassination theory was as follows. The British had gone to war to safeguard the independence of Poland; yet to win the war and protect the vital alliance with Stalin, Churchill knew that he would have to break faith with the Poles and hand over half their territory to the Soviets. He had in addition to turn a blind eye to the mass murder of Polish officers at Katyn, for which the Poles blamed the Russians. Sikorski, an international figure, was a constant reminder that victory would have to be achieved at the cost of dishonour.

The problem was the Sikorski plot: neither the reasons for it, nor the evidence produced in its favour, nor Hochhuth's claim that he had definitive proof from three British secret servicemen, proof conveniently locked away in three banks to be opened after fifty years, were sufficiently authoritative. Moreover, from the political viewpoint, Sikorski was dependent on the British for everything, including the pay of his troops. His complaints might have embarrassed Churchill but they could never have threatened him. And Sikorski exerted a moderating influence on the extremist Poles – he was more valuable to Churchill alive than dead. As for the circumstantial evidence of foul play, none of it stands up in the light of hindsight.

By Christmas 1966 a text of the play weighing six pounds had arrived at the National Theatre. Ken wrote a memo to Olivier which read: 'I don't know whether this is a great *play*; but I think it's one of the most extraordinary things that has happened to British theatre in my lifetime. For once, the theatre will occupy its true place – at the very heart of public life.'

Olivier, who had his doubts, nonetheless told his wife that the portrait of Churchill was marvellous and that there was a very good part there. He listened to Ken's persistent argument, which ran: 'Subsidy gives us the chance – denied to movies and TV – of taking a line of our own, with no commercial pressures and without the neutralizing necessity of being "impartial". In a way, I think Hochhuth is the test of our maturity – the test of our willingness to take a central position in the limelight of public affairs.'

John Dexter read *Soldiers* and found it completely engrossing. 'The same decisions are still being made all over the world,' he wrote, 'and the question of innocence or guilt is unimportant.' He knew that Ken had already canvassed Richard Burton for the part, but felt that a good actor, rather than a star, would direct the attention of the audience more effectively towards the ideas.

Meanwhile Ken began a campaign of persuasion. He sent the play to Lord Goodman at the Arts Council, who expressed the view that the play was an eccentric choice for the National, but that the Council would not interfere with the Board's decision. He submitted the script to the National's lawyers, who gave it a relatively clean bill of health, since the dead cannot be libelled, and the play appeared to them to make a serious contribution to historical record.

While maintaining that it was the playwright's prerogative to interpret history, and that he was under no obligation to be historically accurate (had not Shakespeare and Schiller taken extreme liberties with history?), Ken felt obliged to prove that the playwright's conjectures about the events of the war were within the bounds of possibility.

He corresponded with Air Marshal Sir Robert Saundby, Deputy Chief of Bomber Command, on matters of technical accuracy. He consulted the Ministry of Defence. He sent the play to Sir Arthur Harris, Chief of Bomber Command, who thought it a smear on Churchill, the War Cabinet *and* Bomber Command. He quizzed Hochhuth on his sources in a lengthy correspondence, and wondered whether he and Sir Laurence should not be told the nature of the playwright's private information (source-books Hochhuth would give, but not the name of his informants). As a result of Ken's pressure, Hochhuth decided to leave open 'how much or how little' Churchill knew about the so called plot.

To prepare for the crucial meeting of the National's Board and to give Olivier ammunition, Ken consulted a number of historians and military advisers. What he wanted to establish was whether or not the Sikorski assassination was 'a hypothesis that a rational man could entertain'. In a memo to the Board dated 7 January 1967, Ken claimed that the Sikorski assassination was a reasonable conjecture, and was 'very much an open verdict', by which he meant not that there were equal numbers on both sides, but that there was reasonable doubt.

In the same memo he wrote provocatively, 'It seems likely that if the play is presented by the National Theatre, Lord Chandos will resign.... As a former colleague of Sir Winston Churchill's, he feels that he cannot associate himself with Hochhuth's views.' He went on to argue that 'to suppress a serious work on a subject of national (and international) concern is an act that the Board should not lightly undertake.... The Voltairean cliché – about disliking what a man says but defending to the death his right to say it – should surely be what distinguishes the conduct of affairs at the Old Vic from "state theatre" in the bad sense.'

At the Board meeting on 9 January it was decided to postpone decision until the full text of the play was available and until the next Board meeting in April. Chandos, however, was against proceeding with any further rewriting, since the author 'had been guilty of so grotesque and grievous a libel'.

With this stay of execution the contending parties retrenched, and the Director went back to the real business of running his theatre. Olivier was also preparing to star in *The Dance of Death*.

The Strindberg play, a realistic study of a marriage red in tooth and claw, ends when the Captain dies of a heart attack. Of Olivier's performance Ken wrote, 'Crew-cut and jackbooted ... he grants us naked glimpses – thrown off like dewdrops from the lion's mane – of destructive impulses that we instantly recognize in ourselves. ... In this mood, Olivier makes his own rules. He doesn't care how far he goes, or whose derision he risks.'

After the opening night we had supper with Joan and Larry at their flat, along with the actor John Clements and his wife, Kay Hammond – the latter confined to a wheelchair after a serious stroke. Olivier told us that the part of the Captain was the easiest he had ever played, 'because it's me. It's my life with Vivien.' Our host was intent on explaining how he had executed a ramrod fall on stage, and in so doing he would prod Miss Hammond to check how authentic was his simulated stroke. 'Now darling, was that how it was? And which elbow did you use?' And Miss Hammond would grunt her replies. It seemed brutal, yet it was kind because it was terribly open.

Several times during this contentious period we visited Olivier in Brighton. Always a good and thoughtful host, he would serve us vintage champagne in the Regency drawing-room of the house. Jacket off, braces straining, he would carve the roast of beef at lunch, and on a Saturday afternoon he would take off with Joan's father, a north-country newspaper editor, to a football match. He looked as ordinary as his father-in-law, and wore the same kind of broad tweed suits. I suspect he felt happier in that comfortable seaside world with Joan and the children than he ever had playing the squire in the elegant surrounds of Notley Abbey, which he had shared with Vivien Leigh. Ken, on the other hand, was never relaxed on these visits. He seemed always to be pressing Olivier to some new task, some new challenge.

However, for a short period during the spring of 1967 this odd couple drew closer, not in their appraisal of *Soldiers*, but in their opposition to Lord Chandos. Olivier knew that Chandos had tremendous influence in lobbying and raising money, but he came to hate his 'arrogant ultra-Tory' Chairman. He was outraged that the Chairman expected the play to be turned down as a matter of good manners – because Chandos (as Oliver Lyttelton) had been a member of the War Cabinet and a close friend of Churchill. Olivier was even more outraged when Chandos said he could not countenance the play's production even *without* the Sikorski incident; as a member of Churchill's War Cabinet Chandos had sanctioned the area bombing of Dresden.

'I remember saying to Larry one might, "Well, what do you actually, honestly feel about the play?"' Joan Plowright recalls. 'And he said, "I don't like the bloody thing. But I expect it'll get near to grounds for divorce if you think I'm frightened of doing new stuff. You'll despise me, won't you?"' But it was not so much his wife's support of the play as his Chairman's hostility that decided Olivier to take up arms in the real struggle, which was for the supremacy of the Director and artistic control.

In preparation for the April meeting of the National's Board Ken made some notes for Olivier on the separation of powers: 'the doctrine that should operate in any non-profit-making theatre if it is to claim artistic integrity.' He explained, 'What the doctrine means is that an appointed board of governors should administer the theatre's affairs, fix its budget, decide the broad outlines of its policy and appoint its artistic director.' The Director is then in charge of all matters artistic until such time as he 'loses the confidence of the public and the critics', at which point the Board is entitled to dismiss him. Ken cited the Arts Council report on subsidized theatres, which had suggested that theatre boards should be 'trustees of the grants they receive, and represent the public element in the enterprise. But the real going must be made by the professional people in charge of the theatres concerned.' Would not Olivier wish to be remembered as a man who bequeathed an idea, Ken argued, 'the principle that our National Theatre is artistically ruled not by politicians or bureaucrats but by artists'?

Before the crucial meeting the parties, pro- and anti-*Soldiers*, prepared their positions. To a historian friend, Lord Chandos wrote: 'Nothing would induce *me* to allow the National Theatre to produce such a play.... you would have thought that anyone with ... even common loyalty or good manners, would have refrained from putting up a play to a Board whose Chairman was a very close friend of Winston and the Prof, who knows that all the so-called facts are phoney.' He need not have worried: both the Lord Chamberlain and the nine members of the theatre's Board lined up – after a certain amount of pressure – behind him.

Meanwhile the Lord Chamberlain, Lord Cobbold, having been asked by Ken to license the play, instead contacted Chandos for a 'private and informal word'. On 19 January 1967, the Lord Chamberlain's office told Ken that they were not prepared to comment until the final script was submitted by the Board.

On 16 April Ken lunched with Peter Hall in Stratford and told him he was thinking of resigning if *Soldiers* were turned down. Hall's advice was 'Never resign.' But so serious was Ken about leaving the theatre that he wrote to his agent to enquire about foundation grants that might enable him to write a book about the Mediterranean coastline, or perhaps the Oxford book he had considered writing about himself and his generation.

The Board met on 24 April and Olivier asked them to give him more time to work on the play – in effect to give him a vote of confidence. They refused, and a press release was prepared noting that 'the Board unanimously considered that the play was unsuitable for production at the National Theatre'. Ken looked across accusingly at Olivier. Olivier said he would like to add a comment. Chandos replied, 'I don't think that's necessary.' 'I'd like to say that I'm unhappy', Olivier said, 'about the decision.' Here a member of the Board, Sir Kenneth Clark, cut in with, 'Oh let him be unhappy if he wants to.' Thus Olivier was allowed to add his dissent to the bulletin.

Olivier and Ken next announced that they intended to mount the play independently in the West End with a company whose directors would include Peter Hall of the RSC and William Gaskill of the Royal Court. Chandos told the press that he thought it very odd that Ken should conduct a campaign against his Chairman and Board while retaining his salary, to which Ken replied: 'It would indeed be odd if the National Theatre were an industrial concern in which the chairman and board were majority shareholders. Happily, it is nothing of the sort. My first loyalty is to the National Theatre, not to its Board.' Then he fired off letter after letter in defence of the separation of powers, a campaign taken up with varying degrees of public support a year later.

As for *Soldiers*, Ken's involvement had only just begun.

27

Sex and Politics

The *Soldiers* fracas, noisy as it was, seems on the evidence of Ken's engagement book to have been a minor theme during 1967. On 24 January he appeared before a joint parliamentary committee on theatre censorship. He proposed that, once the Lord Chamberlain's jurisdiction were removed, theatre prosecutions should be filtered through the office of the Attorney-General, to safeguard managements against frivolous attack. He also suggested that production of a play should not be suspended while awaiting trial.

On 24 July, he signed an advertisement in *The Times* in favour of the legalization of marijuana. He made token and not very enthusiastic appearances at various 'psychedelic' rave-ins and be-ins for underground magazines like *International Times*. He greeted cult figures like Mick Jagger or Terence Stamp or Jean Shrimpton; attacked George Harrison for joining forces with the Maharishi; decided not to appear in Yoko Ono's bottom film, *Number 4*; and tried to persuade Paul McCartney to write the music for an all-male production, at the National, of *As You Like It*. McCartney turned him down because he did not '*really* like words by Shakespeare'.

In February he was in Italy to write about the theatre for the *New Yorker*. Also for that magazine he was making notes on the London theatre, and on the new work of Joe Orton, Harold Pinter, Peter Nichols, Charles Wood and the subsidized companies. (Neither in print nor in his journals did he ever give up being a drama critic, though he had abandoned weekly reviewing.)

Such energy and activism were in some respects counter to the fashion of the time. He was not 'laid back', he did not like hard rock music, nor did he experiment with sex and psychedelics. Yet no one was a better celebrant in London, during the middle of the decade, when every aspect of life seemed electric, when class mattered less, and a sense of freedom and confidence (along with the advantage of an elastic currency) made many of us feel heady.

As a couple we went our way, with a certain panache, for which we were recognized, written about and mocked. Our large, semi-furnished house in Thurloe Square resembled at its best a stage set, at its worst an uncomfortable barn (for we spent less than £5000 on the whole decorative venture). I stripped the stone and the pine, painted the walls white, or covered them in dark felt. I brought in chrome and vinyl, steel and perspex; and lamps and chairs from Italy. William McCarty turned the dining-room into a Mondrian-like red-panelled box. Angela Conner improvised a bathroom with silver-painted corrugated paper, wicker, cork, sea shells and pieces of her sculpture. The theatre lighting expert, Richard Pilbrow, came in to install spotlights and rheostats. From our artist friends we bought mobiles, opticals, painted geometric boxes, while we combed the galleries and art colleges for poor man's pop art and posters.

In the spring of 1967 Ken made his main contribution to this set: he designed the K/K Self-Regarder, a mirror made of light Melinex sheeting, the width of our bed and held aloft on two arced metal arms. When tired of self-regarding, you could swivel the mirror to the blind eye of the opposite side. Sharing the sad fate of most married couples, we eventually ignored the Self-Regarder, but our friends still speak of it with a mixture of awe and prurient concern.

Ken made one other contribution that spring to domestic life. Since I was pregnant, he decided he must learn to drive. He would be one up on his father he said, tongue half in cheek.

On 17 June we flew to Montreal where Ken made a speech on the National Theatre at the world fair Expo '67, and where he met Marlene Dietrich, who would soon join us in New York. She told us that the sex of our child would be dictated by the parent less interested in sex. She went on, more convincingly, to explain that she was bored by sex and always had been. She had been taught to pretend to like it. Was she a lesbian? No, but the rumour was a useful diversionary tactic.

What interested Dietrich, outside herself, was honour and friendship (viewed through a prism of her own self-invented style), and she worked hard at both. When Ken wrote about her, in the autumn of 1967, with uncharacteristic lushness, she was wounded. She wrote to tell him that not only had he failed to guard their intimacy, but worse, he had managed to write about her in a banal way. That he'd brought her the article meant that he 'did *not know* it would shock me... In my idea of you you *know things*, particularly about me who had opened the shirt of her heart and brain for you to see. But you as you – not you as a relay racer between me and strangers.'

Many years later Dietrich quoted in her autobiography from the very same flattering article, which was worthy neither of her nor of Ken.

From Canada we flew to Chicago, to stay at the Playboy Mansion as guests of Hugh Hefner. We were put up in a drably furnished set of rooms amply supplied with internal telephones and bells – none of which worked. But I was famished, being now six months pregnant. I finally made an outside call and asked my contact to telephone into the Hefner pad and beg for some food. About ten minutes later a servant arrived with a sandwich.

We discovered that life here did not start until after midnight, when the boss came out of his cave into the panelled baronial main hall and the girls appeared from the attic. Inscrutable black servants in black silk Italian suits were everywhere, three or four of them watching over Hefner. Ken formed the theory that the black revolution had taken place, that Hefner was a mere puppet mouthing whatever words these suave and menacing men instructed him to utter.

The object of Ken's visit was to meet A. C. Spectorsky, the magazine's elegant editor in charge of writers. With the Spectorskys we discovered Chicago and the modernist movement in architecture, met Bertrand Goldberg and visited his Marina City, and sailed on the lake.

From New York Ken wrote to thank Spectorsky and to say that New York was fetid by comparison with Chicago – 'Everything (and nearly everybody) seems rusty and polluted. The old theory is true: civilization really does move westward.' Meanwhile he set down some ideas for future work, one on the sexual revolution (for he had been re-reading Wilhelm Reich): 'Can you change society without first changing sexual mores? Does the paternalistic, authoritarian state depend on the survival of its microcosm – the paternalistic family hierarchy?'

However, in New York our thoughts were neither of rust nor of Reich, but of getting married, though it was Ken alone who put our plan into action and orchestrated the event. On 26 June, four days before my marriage, Jule Styne and his wife gave a large party at Sardi's in our honour attended by New York's theatre grandees. I remember wearing a green pleated tent dress and clinging to my one friend there, the songwriter Steve Vinaver.

A couple of days before the wedding we discovered that guilty parties in divorce cases cannot remarry in New York State until three years have elapsed. So on the rainy morning of Saturday the 30th we set off by rented Cadillac for Englewood, New Jersey. With us were Steve Vinaver, Penelope Gilliatt, ever loyal friend, camera at hand, and Marlene Dietrich, our matron of honour, dressed for service in navy blue, every hair of her ash-blonde head in place from shoulder to strawberry root, self-cast for practical matronly service, eye protectively on the portly bride, who was wearing a coat of many colours.

In Englewood, we were met by an impatient young judge, who led us to a little office full of golf trophies. He asked, 'You sure you want to go through all this marriage baloney?' We said we were. It had only taken years of legal struggle to get to the long-desired goal. The judge asked Ken for his address. 'In New York or London?' 'Whichever is quicker,' he snapped. As he filled in the form he said, 'I had another marriage an hour ago and there's one after lunch, so there's my weekend down the drain.' He was elaborately unimpressed by Dietrich and asked how to spell her name. Then he led us over to the fireplace, explaining that 'It's more dignified over there.' As he began to recite the service, Marlene, to cut out the noise of typewriters from the next room, edged backwards towards the sliding door and tried to close it behind her. The judge interrupted himself with no pause or change of tone: 'And do you, Kenneth, take Kathleen for your lawful wedded – I wouldn't stand with your ass to an open door in *this* office, lady – wife, to have and to hold . . .' But the awesome words seemed to check even the golfer–judge, who eventually bound us together with some solemnity.

We drove back to New York for lunch, and later regrouped at a 6 p.m. cocktail party in Mike Nichols' apartment at the Beresford.

Some time later in the evening, Dietrich – still playing the role of maternal *commandante* – told Mailer to go around the room and tell the guests that Kathleen would like them to leave. Mailer thought she was a blonde from White Plains, until she came up close. 'If you're a nice boy,' Marlene said, 'I'll go to dinner with you.' But he felt offended: he could see that the hostess was having a perfectly good time and did not want the party to end, and he wasn't going to be bribed to go out to dinner with Marlene Dietrich. It was not the way to his heart. So he didn't do what she said but hung around and got drunk. Joseph Heller did not please our glamorous guardian either. He told her, 'My wife would love to meet you.'

Eventually the guests trailed off; my friend Otto Friedrich took Dietrich home, and Ken and I were at last alone – except for Norman Mailer. He then took us to Frankie and Johnnie's, off Eighth Avenue, for a steak. And there he and Ken tanked up on red wine, while I, the mother-to-be, drank water, perfectly content, and tried not to fall asleep. The celebration, it seemed, was between the two men, both drunk, both mellow, Ken declaring, with tears in his eyes (they had not been dry all day), that his old friend was a charmer who could not hurt a flea, to which Norman, apparently moved, agreed.

Thus the wedding – a thrillingly happy day, we both felt, for all its eccentricities.

Two days later we flew up to Martha's Vineyard to stay with Sue and John Marquand. Ken played 'A Day in the Life' over and over again – the *Sgt Pepper* album had just come out. He suffered a vicious sunburn and, told that tannic acid was the cure, drew a bath and had the Marquands' six-year-old son, James, fill it with tea-bags. 'He's an Englishman,' John explained to the child, who, pointing at the naked, moaning figure in the tub, asked, 'Is *that* an Englishman?'

My chief memory of these golden few days was of hunger. One night we dined out at Lillian Hellman's and I stuffed myself. She must have felt sorry for the poor pregnant girl, because the next day she sent over a pail of lobsters.

Another night Rose and William Styron had us to dine and I remember how balmy the night was as we sat outside by candlelight at a long table under the trees. Styron had recently come across the US Surgeon-General's latest bulletin on cigarette-smoking. A sure test for emphysema, he explained to us, was whether you could blow out a candle or a match from a short distance. Without pursing the lips, everybody at the table could blow out a candle except for Ken. Somebody said, it may have been Styron, 'You probably have emphysema.' Ken, though momentarily shaken, quickly put that grim shadow from his mind.

Back in New York we dropped in on the Café Cino, and on the Electric Circus in the East Village to stare at the multiple projections. A few blocks away we were entertained by the Fugs singing 'Kill for Peace' and 'I Got the Clap'. Ken liked the hairy group but missed the sense of occasion he had felt when going to hear Lenny Bruce. 'Now', he noted, 'you go to relish atmosphere, not talent.'

Around this time he began to put together his thoughts on the all-fashionable and all-too-accurate soothsayer Marshall McLuhan, whom he described as 'a Catholic spy in the intellectual camp, plotting the destruction of reason'. McLuhan sought to destroy epeolatry, and Ken, a worshipper of words, was epeolatrous. Here was a scholar who had 'a single brilliant insight into the relationship between the invention of printed books and the rise of individualism, then was popularised and had to extend his theories to cover *everything* – all human activities'. Madison Avenue, television and the business world adored him because 'he distracts attention from *what* is being said or done, to the *way* in *which* it is said. He discourages criticism and value judgements.'

We settled into London for the rest of the summer, Ken into his web of work and plans, I to await our baby and to write the odd, sedate interview. The drawing-room windows of Thurloe Square were open to the summer smells of sticky lime trees and honeysuckle while inside the room was noisy with friends and the sounds of the Beatles, or Dylan, or The Incredible String Band. Ken and I were not much out of each other's company, even lunching together, often at Chez Victor's, in Soho, talking about practical intimacies or short-range plans: the abundant sharing of ordinariness.

On 14 September I gave painless birth to a girl at Westminster Hospital. Roxana Nell weighed 7 lb 15 oz and comported herself very well from the beginning. I filled my diary with gushing superlatives. She looked like 'a thoughtful Bardot', I wrote. Ken came to visit with roses, with champagne, with my mother, with Tracy. He told a newspaper that Roxana shared the Lord Chamberlain's birthday. 'In the years to come if ever she asks me who he was, I shall take great pleasure in explaining that she was on her way in as he was on his way out.'

Godparents were canvassed: Gore Vidal stoically consented with the words 'Always a godfather, never a god'; Diana Phipps, our witty and generous Bohemian friend, accepted and sent choice gifts.

A few days after delivery, in brilliant autumn sunshine, Ken brought us home. The Virginia creeper on the house had already changed colour but the air was still warm. In the kitchen, fish mousse and Jerusalem melons on the pine table, a neighbour's gift. Upstairs a maternity nurse with red cheeks and lace cap. Ken in the living-room, breathing easy. The baby sleeping. Details in a still life.

In October Ken's second major collection of criticism and articles, largely selected from the previous decade, was published in London and shortly after in New York under the title *Tynan Right and Left*. In the introduction he described the pieces as the 'work of a drama critic at large not only in theatres but in cinemas, books, cities and the lives of other people'.

What, if anything, had this forty-year-old critic learned? 'What, if anything, has he changed?'

'Occupation,' he wrote:

Opinion-monger, observer of artistic phenomena, amateur ideologue. Latterly, Literary Manager of the National Theatre....

Political beliefs. Socialism – always provided (a) that it leaves room for the gay, irreverent spontaneity of Zen, and (b) that it takes into account the basic doctrines of Lorenz: namely, that human beings are animals in whom love is inseparable from aggression, and territorial (not class) allegiances are ultimately paramount.

Moral beliefs. Is on record as having said: 'If the artist is to give the chaos of events any meaning, he must place them in a structure of ideology, which implies a morality. This is true of all works of narrative art.' Explains that he is too guilt-ridden to be corruptible: he cannot permit himself the moral leeway that more innocent hearts could survive untainted.

Psychological diagnosis. Possesses a Super-Ego of tremendous ... power, in the form of reproving conscience that drives him to periodic bouts of self-punishing work; and an equally powerful Id, which insists on immediate sensual rewards.

Literary diagnosis. Regarded by many fellow-journalists as a snob, and by many academic critics as a charlatan.... Not very artistic, except perhaps in temperament. Probably best summed up as a student of craftsmanship, with a special passion for imaginative craftsmen who put their skills to the service of human ideas.

Conclusion. Still unreached.

The conclusion arrived at by his critics was almost unanimously complimentary. 'The size and quality of the achievement', wrote John Raymond in the *Sunday Times*, 'still intimidate. Like Shaw, his master, Mr Tynan has the natural stance of a creative critic.'

Richard Boston in the *New York Times* wrote that 'Like George Orwell he has the ability always to pick up on the important issue.' John Mortimer cited the following as one of Ken's best pronouncements, a caution attached by Ken on his own instructions to the artist to work out an ideological position: 'The people who exalt abstractions, concepts, dogmas, ideals and ideologies above the five great human imperatives of birth, food, shelter, love making and death – these are and always have been the satirist's raison d'être and his perpetual target.'

And Mortimer was the first of Ken's critics to ask after the boy: 'It would be interesting to meet the distant, lonely Tynan who had never heard of *Citizen Kane* or the Berliner Ensemble.' 'Tynan's Doppelgänger,' wrote Harold Clurman, 'the man hidden in the motley, has been and still is a youth of tender susceptibilities and compassion.'

I used to put a note outside our bedroom at night with breakfast instructions for the au pair. Ken found that regular note reassuring, because it promised continuity. Our bedroom filled up, that autumn, with the toing and froing of the baby to be nursed; with the German au pair; with two new kittens. There was Rosemary Nibbs, Ken's new secretary, who might be given something rather academic and quite hard to follow up on, or sent in our stead to grapple with the bank manager, told to squeeze out of him what she could, for we always had an overdraft.

Outside the bedroom, which was the command post, Ken would keep aloof from the household's operations and he rarely made it to the nursery: we came to him. Sometimes Penelope Gilliatt or Tom Stoppard would turn up of a morning and perch on the end of the bed for a cup of coffee, immediately lifting Ken out of his panic over money and into a light, inventive mood – a mood so pleasant that before finally getting up he would order some extravagant wine from a vintner willing to extend him credit.

That same autumn Laurence Olivier, who had recently suffered cancer of the prostate, and had had a heavy touring schedule, decided to back out of producing *Soldiers*. He felt that the play needed a full-time producer. Since Ken had stuck his neck out and 'championed the thing', he should continue on his own.

If Ken felt a little let down at the time, he might have been more understanding if he had known what Olivier had been through on his behalf. After the rancorous private and public dispute between Ken and the Chairman over *Soldiers*, Chandos had drafted a letter to Ken demanding a written guarantee of no further printed attacks on his Board. Olivier was shown the draft and implored Chandos not to send it. It would lead, in his opinion, to Ken's immediate resignation, and this he could not face. Would Chandos leave the matter for him to come to a personal understanding with Tynan, to secure a six-month truce? Chandos wrote back agreeing to leave Tynan alone. He added, 'You should, however, realize what this means, to me in particular. He is a man completely lacking in probity and loyalty, and is unscrupulous and untruthful.... This is the man whom we are to keep, temporarily, at your request.'

Though fed up with the whole affair and already ill, Olivier was determined to stand up to Chandos. It was his wife, however, who conducted the negotiations. She explained to the Chairman that Ken was a 'necessary irritant' in the administration, that his record was impressive. If Ken were sacked, she argued, the press would be extremely hostile. Joan Plowright recalls: 'Chandos was an astute old bird, he took that in, and he struck up the most dreadful bargain.' If she could get 'that chap' to swear on oath that he would write not one more word about the business, Chandos would reconsider. 'Then I rang Ken. I thought if I put it like that he'll go straightaway and write the most vitriolic piece, and say "fuck you" to everybody. I just said, "Ken, are you writing any more about this?" And Ken actually was in a depressed and resigned state, fed up with the whole business too, and agreed not to write another word.'

Ken's own battle to put on *Soldiers* continued. With the rights in hand, and Michael White behind him, he approached actors for the lead. Orson Welles said he had the right cigar, but was otherwise busy. Richard Burton said he was interested in playing the part and thought he would like to co-direct with Ken. Elizabeth Taylor was against. Her godfather, Victor Cazalet, Sikorski's political liaison officer, had been killed on the famous take-off from Gibraltar. She told her husband that he would accept the part 'over my dead body'. Some weeks later Burton cabled to say that he still thought the play remarkable but couldn't figure out a way to play 'the old man'.

On 9 October the play had its world première in Berlin, at which the author was booed and the play condemned. But Berlin was followed by more successful productions elsewhere in Europe. In Britain the Lord Chamberlain still held up production. He refused to consider licensing the play until he had permissions from the surviving members of the families of the historical characters. Nor would he say whether or not there was a risk if Ken proceeded with a theatre club production.

With no immediate hope of a London production, Ken (who held an option) gave Clifford Williams permission to mount the play in Toronto. It opened on 28 February 1968, and was highly praised. 'Hochhuth', wrote one critic, 'makes Churchill guilty of greatness.'

At the first night was the pilot of the Sikorski plane, Edward Prchal, a quiet, friendly man who lived in the States. He did not see fit to sue for libel either in Canada or when, a few months later, the play opened in New York. Nor did Ken and Clifford Williams ever consider that the play implicated Prchal, as the only survivor of the Sikorski crash, in any wrongdoing.

With the demise of the Lord Chamberlain as censor in September 1968, Ken and Michael White were able to mount *Soldiers* in London. The play opened at the New Theatre on 12 December (its twenty-first presentation) in a shortened version of Clifford Williams' original Toronto production, and with a fine cast led by John Colicos, Alec Clunes and Raymond Huntley. Michael White, who had received bomb threats and hate mail against the 'Churchill smear play', had placed guards at every door. But all passed smoothly, the performance ending with an ovation for the actors. The reviews were almost uniformly excellent. On opening night, with the successful conclusion of his two-year campaign, Ken wept with relief.

But that was not the end of it. On 7 January the pilot of Sikorski's plane issued a writ of libel against the producers, theatre owners, directors and Ken. A separate writ went out against Hochhuth, and another against the publishers of the play.

On 6 March the producers of *Soldiers* announced that the play was coming off. The scandal, mixed with the feeling that they had already seen the play because of the extensive publicity, kept the public away.

28

End of the Decade

In January 1968, Ken had rejoined the *Observer* to write a weekly column on the arts, called 'Shouts and Murmurs'. For forty annual pieces of 1000 words, he would be paid £4000. Here was a platform on which to vent his views and explore the jottings in his newly started journal. Some columns were 'marvellous', as his editor Richard Findlater remembered. Others fell 'flat as a pancake'. In one Ken defined the idea of 'high definition performance' as 'supreme professional polish, hard-edged technical skill, the effortless precision without which no artistic enterprise – however strongly we may sympathise with its aims or ideas – can inscribe itself on our memory ... the hypnotic saving grace of high and low art alike, the common denominator that unites tragedy, ballroom dancing, conversation and cricket'.

If, during the late fifties, Ken had developed an aesthetic of drama as 'an extension and an illumination of our experience, not something different and "artistic"', he now appeared to be on another – though not exactly contradictory – course. He had repudiated 'art' in its lofty, exclusive application. Now he appeared to be returning at least to 'artfulness'. Though he would say that the quality of high definition performance was the necessary partner of substantive ideas, that it should 'instruct and delight', it was also desirable in itself, when demonstrated in games or light entertainment.

He conceded that when strong views ('persuasive exhortations') needed expression 'cool' might have to be sacrificed. None the less 'cool' was the essence of high definition. (Bix Beiderbecke – a man 'in supreme command of his instrument and his environment' – or the cricketer Gary Sobers – 'a panther-like creature with ... the relaxation of the big cats' – exemplified the notion.)

He believed that craft became exceptional when combined with Zen: the effortless hitting of the target came out of contemplation and spontaneity. 'Zen, by its counsel of living in the moment, responding to it, with complete spontaneity, really is the philosophical background upon which all my creed of high definition is based.'

During the seventies, when Ken retreated somewhat from the public arena, high definition performance seemed all the more important to him. He returned not to his youthful espousal of art for art's sake, but rather to skill for pleasure's sake.

The part of him that admired spontaneity and playfulness, whether out of Zen or the hippies, looked kindly on the experimental theatre of the sixties, such as Jim Haynes' 'ramshackle, sweet-tempered and eclectic' Arts Lab. But the side of him that admired exceptional skill hated the random and slapdash work he sometimes found there – the improvisation and audience confrontation. It was all very well, he felt, for Walter Gropius to propose that the purpose of the modern playhouse was to 'abolish the separation between the "fictitious world" of the stage and the "real world" of the audience', but not when this dictum was taken literally. Ken did not participate at Off-Broadway productions like the Performance Group's *Dionysius in '69*, for example, where the audience was encouraged to make love to members of the cast.

When a naked actor approached him during a performance, in London, of Arrabal's *The Labyrinth* with an invitation to tango, Ken declined, resisting a momentary impulse 'to get out my cigarette lighter and give him a hot foot'. Of this encounter he wrote in Shouts and Murmurs, 'I believe in art ... as an activity that offers the results of perception to those who may be able to perceive them; but this belief is constantly being eroded by the new notion that there is no difference between the artist and his audience.' The argument for participation, he pointed out, had lately been pushed to its final and absolute extreme by Marshall McLuhan, who expected 'to see the coming decades transform the planet into an art form.... Man himself will become an organic art form.' In other words, Ken commented contemptuously, 'Whatever is is art.'

Whereas Ken had given up weekly drama criticism to write at length in a manner which did not compel him to grab his reader's attention, he had now chosen, at the *Observer*, to return to the short, eye-catching paragraph. I remember very clearly feeling concerned about this move, for the first time critical of Ken for taking what looked like an easy and unworthy course. He did, however, continue to write for American magazines at length, notably with a well-argued piece in defence of hard-core pornography, turned down by *Playboy* and eventually published by *Esquire*.

What he found in many anti-censorship tracts was an evasive, often hypocritical attitude to pornography: 'the special tone of veiled liberal distaste', the view that pornography was read merely in the line of duty, not for pleasure; and that it never provoked masturbation.

Ken wrote that hard-core pornography, orgasmic in intent 'and untouched by the ulterior motives of traditional art', served the admirable purpose of inducing erection. 'Contrary to popular myth,' he argued, 'it takes discipline and devotion to be a first-rate pornographer.'

He pointed out that though hard-core could 'vary or intensify the customary fun of sexual coupling', it was also designed for those less fortunate, offering the illusion of release to the aberrant, the lonely, the physically plain and the poor. He defended masturbation, just as he had thirty-five years before, when at the school debate he argued against the idea that 'the present generation had lost its ability to entertain itself'. He believed that language could be used in delicate ways to arouse, but that pornography was defensible in its own right: 'Freedom to write about sex must include the freedom to write about it badly.'

He took issue with George Steiner's essay 'Night Words', which contends that pornography is doomed to ultimate monotony because of the limitations of sexual activity. Ken replied, 'Dawn and sunset are likewise limited, but only a limited man would find them monotonous.' And he refuted the theory that sadistic pornography produces slaughter for fun, and declared that the really evil books on physical cruelty 'can be found among Catholic tracts of the Inquisition or contemporary military manuals. Ken concluded: 'One inalienable right binds all mankind together – the right to self-abuse. That – and not the abuse of others – is what distinguishes the true lover of pornography.'

A truncated version of this hymn to onanism was preceded, the week before, in the column, by a declaration of his retreat (aged forty) into privacy. The decision inspired a parody from the satirist John Wells. 'Mr. Kenneth Onan's retreat', he wrote, 'may induce a downright masochistic delight in being subjected to the immutable social realities of long, self-indulgent dinner parties, drinks with the nobs, clobber from Twitties or the Magic Pant Boutique, etc. etc.'

'Shouts and Murmurs', by its very nature, sensationalized Ken's views on sex and made the extracts he took from his journal on the powerlessness of the intellectual in the West, for example, seem merely trivial. His celebrity, and a reckless lack of concern for guarding his reputation, made him an easy subject for attack. In March the London press reported that Ken had been made a contributing editor of *Playboy*, to which, according to Hefner, he would devote the major part of his writing. The satirical magazine *Private Eye* produced a devastating cartoon by Gerald Scarfe, of Ken as a cavorting bunny, holding a cigarette in one hand and with the other pushing away a top-hatted skull.

Ken had resisted, some years before, being co-opted on to the *Playboy* masthead, a position which was purely nominal. He had told his agent that if he were included, 'I somehow become responsible for everything that goes into the magazine.' And why, he asked, should he be described as an editor when he did not edit? Several years later he agreed to be listed to please the editor he liked; when Spectorsky was no longer in charge, Ken requested that his name be withdrawn.

In 1969 the magazine published a long article on Vietnam, called 'Open Letter to an American Liberal', in which Ken provided an eyewitness report of the Sartre–Russell International War Crimes Tribunal, held in Stockholm. He concluded: 'Without international law we perish, and no other body seemed to be concerning itself with applying the rule of law to the bloody carnival of Vietnam.'

He proposed a war crimes tribunal in the United States, with a panel of American jurists sitting in judgement on their own political leaders. If the findings of the court cut no ice, he suggested that the young might wish to opt out of the system. 'But opting out need not mean giving up: form a political Third Force of tough mindedly leftish character. Alternatively they could join the hippies. . . . Ten years ago I used to attack the Beats for being nonpolitical; I told them to stay in the boat and rock it. Since then, the boat has grown steadily more unrockable. . . . None the less,' he argued, 'make bridges to political radicals and be patient.'

Vietnam appeared from time to time in 'Shouts and Murmurs': an attack on hawkish journalism; a defence of Susan Sontag's visit to North Vietnam. Meanwhile, Ken and I were marching and protesting against the war, and chalking up further accusations of radical chic: it was hard not to care and sometimes hard not to respond foolishly.

Early in February I saw Felix Greene's film *Inside North Vietnam* and, mightily affected, went to work to help organize the planned protest march on the American Embassy. Invited to dinner by the American Ambassador and his wife, I took along with me a handful of stickers advertising the march, handed a couple of these out and stuck a couple in the ladies' loo. This tentative gesture was picked up by the press and I was described as having covered priceless furniture with my handbills. Although Tariq Ali, the student leader, wrote to congratulate me on my 'very effective "guerrilla" work', nobody else seemed pleased. Nor could I deny the extent of my crime without looking craven.

Newsweek magazine reported the event and quoted Ken gushing in *Vogue* about his wife ('She finds where there are springs bubbling inside you and makes them flow'). William F. Buckley Jr wondered where I had learned my social manners. And Walter Winchell brought the matter to the attention of the FBI. (The FBI, with its genius for putting two and two together, came to the conclusion that this was not the Mrs Tynan from Great Neck, as the age of the woman in question 'would indicate that she would have been approximately 13 years of age at the time of her marriage'.)

While the great issues were being fought in the States, and students were rioting in Paris, we in England could at best exert only a mild influence on

US policy. For most of us, however strongly we felt, protesting against Vietnam could be done at a distance safe from personal peril; and solidarity with the student movement was often merely a fashionable gesture.

I remember very clearly at one of our parties somebody suggesting a Pee-In at Buckingham Palace. On another occasion, to emulate the students who had occupied the Beaux Arts, we planned to take over Covent Garden Opera House. An argument started among the prospective occupiers over what we would present on stage. Was it to be propaganda or art? Readings from Shelley or from Freud? And on that note of aesthetic discord the plan was dropped. Instead we wondered whether it would not be better to burn down the Old Vic.

All these plans were fun, as we sat around at Thurloe Square, dressed up in the latest beads and bobbles, eating my turbot *monégasque*, or lamb *Casa Botin*, and drinking wine we could not afford. There were evenings with political friends, like the television producer Tony Garnett, of the far left. An evening with Mike Nichols. John Lennon sitting on the stone stairs in a white suit, offering an idea for an *Oh! Calcutta!* sketch: 'You know the idea, four fellows wanking – giving each other images – descriptions – it should be ad-libbed anyway. They should even really wank, which would be great!' Sharon Tate, newly married to Roman Polanski, a gentle, raw-boned girl, cross-legged and doling out a hash brownie cake she'd just baked.

Close friends like Jonathan Miller saw that Ken ran his parties like pro-ductions (using his wife as stage manager). Miller recalls how Ken would bring together excitable people whose confrontation might provoke a lively row. 'His affection when it was on and when it was directed at you was charismatic. You actually felt the less if you weren't the subject of his attention or if you lost it.'

But if Ken was bored he could be awful. He never bothered to find out the first name of a wife he didn't consider interesting. And if someone whom he did not find amusing dropped in, he would either walk out or watch television. Beautiful and intelligent girls were welcome, as Marina Warner was. She in turn found Ken an erotic figure and rather alarming. 'I never felt very relaxed with him, I always felt slightly wobbly. He was so sharp and held very strong, uncomfortable views.' She describes our guests as 'golden *canailles*', a rabble where you might meet any kind of person. As master of ceremonies Ken 'wanted you to be very clever – which is actually something quite faded in English society now. He created an atmosphere where you didn't want to fall short; you always wanted to glitter and sparkle.'

I remember best over the years our social disasters, for they always provided the best post-mortems. The testy meeting of Mary McCarthy and Germaine Greer in the early seventies, after which Miss McCarthy complained of Miss Greer's 'auto-idolatry'. The time that we offered the house to Vanessa Red-grave to raise money for some anti-Vietnam GIs, filled a hat with contributions, and discovered at dawn that someone had gone off with its contents.

Or the evening, early in 1968, when Ken decided to show avant-garde films as after-dinner entertainment. The guests were the Snowdons, Harold Pinter and his then wife, Vivien Merchant, and Peter Cook and his wife. The evening started inauspiciously with Ken's failed attempt to introduce the Snowdons and Vivien Merchant. 'I put out my hand,' Princess Margaret recalls, 'which was refused. So I sort of drew it up as if it were meant for another direction.' At dinner the actress sat next to Tony Snowdon, who had just photographed her as Lady Macbeth at Stratford. 'Of course,' we heard her say, 'the only reason we *artistes* let you take our pictures is because you are married to her.' Whereat she stabbed a finger towards the Princess. Everyone began to drink steadily.

After dinner we viewed some short films by Bruce Conner, while the atmosphere among the group moved fom edgy to forced humorous; with Jean Genet's *Chant d'Amour*, it became merely glum. Here is Ken's report of what happened:

Genet's film is about convicts in love with one another and themselves, and it contains many quite unmistakable shots of cocks – cocks limp and stiff, cocks being waved, brandished, massaged or just waggled – intercut with lyrical fantasy sequences as the convicts imagine themselves frolicking in vernal undergrowth. Silence became gelid in the room. Suddenly the inspired Peter Cook came to the rescue. *Chant d'Amour* is a silent film, and he supplied a commentary, treating the movie as if it were a long commercial for Cadbury's Milk Flake Chocolate and brilliantly seizing on the similarity between Genet's woodland fantasies and the sylvan capering that inevitably accompanies, on TV, the sale of anything from cigarettes to Rolls-Royces. Within five minutes we were all helplessly rocking with laughter.

I do not know how we managed to entertain on such a scale on an annual income of around £10,000. I remember occasional sobering promises to each other of no more dinner parties, of plans to leave city life for simple wilds.

Ken was labelled a 'champagne socialist', and to this day that view of him sticks hard. The right objected, while the puritanical left, who in England like their spokesmen to be ascetic, were even more offended. 'Ken did seem to enjoy his life,' Tony Garnett points out. 'Now that's pretty well unforgivable.' About this time Garnett had instigated weekly educative meetings for the Trotskyite left to coincide with publication of the broadsheet *Black Dwarf*. At one of these a Workers' Revolutionary Party stalwart spotted Ken and asked, 'Who's the fuckin' antique dealer?'

Ken kept his head above the parapet: he never apologized and barely explained, while he continued to express his views, and to change them, working out his thoughts in public.

He believed in material well-being, though he did not approve of saving or of profiting from investment. He had a genuine and visceral dislike of inherited wealth, to the extent of being ashamed of his own small bequest. Earned income in his view was to be spent (and shared with friends) on food, books, wine and holidays. It had to be used up, just as the moment had to be consumed, and as dynamically as possible. He was positively hostile to extending the short lease on our house, or to putting any money aside. He would quake at the idea of an insurance policy.

The far left among Ken's friends had no problem with his politics. They did not bother Michael Foot nor Eric Hobsbawm. 'He *was* radical chic,' Hobsbawm says. 'But the point is he was also genuinely radical. In addition he never fell for the revolutionary romanticism of violence.' His friends in politics believe that Ken's convictions were deep but essentially romantic; that he was someone in touch with feeling, and able to put himself on stage without fear of the consequences. They also conceded that he may have been more interested in texture than in social structure; that for all his classlessness, no one was less egalitarian.

Ken's doctor had written to him in 1965 to report that tests showed he had a mild degree of emphysema, though the 'lung fields were otherwise clear'. (But I do not think Ken registered the implications of the word 'emphysema' until William Styron's jolting test on Martha's Vineyard, two years later.) On our return from the States, I tried to persuade him to take up exercise with Edward Bolton, with whom Olivier worked out. At the same time our general practitioner, John Henderson, wrote to Bolton to tell him that Ken had chronic emphysema and 'one of these nasty rigid chest walls that move all in one piece and a very little distance indeed'. Overworking, over-drinking and over-smoking, he added, did not help. He might also have noted the ill effects of amphetamines, which Ken had taken since 1952.

I do not recall that Ken ever went to Bolton's gym, but he had no serious trouble from his lungs until early in 1968 when he suffered from a series of asthma and bronchial attacks, culminating in New York with a bout of pneumonia. In March, he had an operation to clear his infected antra, and was described by a leading chest specialist as having a moderate degree of emphysema. He was told to give up smoking, take his chest seriously and obtain treatment in hospital.

Ken told *Playboy* that he had fallen behind in his work, and asked them to stop payments. He wrote to Spectorsky: 'I feel terrible finking out on you like this, but the accumulated carbon-monoxide-and-nicotine-poisoning of a lifetime has caught up with me like a runaway truck, and I've got to pay some kind of penalty. It seems that where most people exhale 80% of the air they breathe in, I exhale 29%.'

One of the penalties was a week's stay, in May, at Midhurst Hospital, Sussex, for remedial treatment and exercise. The food so upset him – 'foam rubber sprinkled with dried pus, going by the name of scrambled eggs' – that he called his secretary to tell her there was 'a smashing place for lunch in Haslemere', and asked her to come down by taxi and rescue him. A few days later he called her to say he had had enough. 'I'm getting out of here but we've got to do it secretly, so get a taxi.' 'To go where?' asked Rosemary Nibbs. 'Back to London.'

In the meantime I had been in France interviewing Katharine Hepburn for American *Vogue*. This thoughtful lady, on hearing of Ken's problems, wrote off to the doctor who had treated Spencer Tracy for emphysema, and he in turn put Ken in touch with the leading chest expert at the Hammersmith Hospital in London, Dr Charles Fletcher. With great effort Fletcher and I managed to get Ken to give up smoking and to start exercises to drain his lungs. We never managed to persuade him to work out and he always refused to walk when he could take a taxi.

With the warmer weather, Ken was again his ebullient self, and we speedily forgot about his illness. He had begun to prepare a BBC television programme, *One Pair of Eyes*, about his perceptions of Oxford. For this event Alan Beesley, the exemplar of spontaneity during Ken's time at Oxford, was tracked down and brought to our house to be interviewed. In walked a stocky man wearing a crumpled suit, with a slick of hair that fell over one eye and a little goatee.

Where had he been since Oxford? Searching for treasure, shark fishing, running a highly successful language school in Helsinki, so Ken heard. There had been a single Christmas card, unsigned and with the single word 'fuck' scrawled across it. Next Ken learned he was in Nigeria, running an educational radio programme for the Ford Foundation. And now after some sort of breakdown, and a second broken marriage, he was living in Ireland.

A microphone was placed before him and Ken began the interview. What did he think of contemporaries like Alan Brien or Kingsley Amis? He didn't. But he wondered who this 'implacably amiable' Ken could be, 'stalking around with stethoscope in a geriatric ward'. Ken pursued: Did he remember being very rude to Dylan Thomas? 'That was an extremely wrong thing,' said Beesley. What did he feel about his close Oxford friends? 'You sort of loomed and cavorted in a few dreams of mine. I always woke with a sense of deprivation, of something no longer there that was part of me. 'I like this word "flewed". I flowed. I was twenty-two, I hadn't had any life – school, air force – bing-bong – shuffled about like a parcel. Then okay, suddenly one had a tranquillity. One *was*. These little cells up here, there were no wayward ends in them, one was working at one's full capacity, one was happy.'

Soon after the interview, Alan came to stay. He slept in the ground-floor study and fell into the routine of the house. He would sit in the kitchen doing the au pair's homework; play with the baby; co-opt Ken's secretary to help him type out his latest scheme for commercial publishing; and show up promptly at drinks time. He'd strut fiercely into the drawing-room, hands deep in the pockets of trousers that hung somewhere around his hips, and announce himself: 'Beesley! Inter-galactic wanderer! Space poet!'

We each observed our houseguest from a different perspective. Ken saw him as a misfit, or rather a non-competitor in a competitive society.

I was more struck by his coruscating common sense, and his kindness. I knew also, as did Ken, that he was very desperate. But for a while we gave him some lightness. All he had to do was stick to the anti-depressant pills, he told us, and he would be all right. He didn't need any 'fucking people burrowing around' in his head. He would say to Ken, 'That's all it is, boy. That's all it is. Just a chemical imbalance. Give me another drink.'

One evening, early in June, we took Alan to Clive Goodwin's crowded party in honour of the Parisian student leader Daniel Cohn-Bendit. Ken liked the bright, undogmatic radical, but had qualms about his optimism. How could the revolution be won without 'strategic planning or military support'? Cohn-Bendit replied that it would be improvised. Nobody at the party pursued this argument because everyone was too busy debating whether it was correct to allow the uninvited reporter from *The Times* to stay or to kick him out. Beesley sat hunched at the back of the party in his crumpled suit, among the leather jerkins and bright prints, sucking demoniacally at a cigarette, his black eyes darting contemptuously around. He thought the whole student movement ludicrous.

The pages of Ken's engagement book for that summer and autumn were black with plans: a Vietnam march, work appointments and entertainment. Alan Beesley disappeared and we put an advertisement in *The Times* to try to find him. Roxana learned to crawl. I travelled on various journalistic forays. And at Thurloe Square our entertainments continued.

But I now felt the first cool winds of fear, money fears, health fears on Ken's behalf (we talked sporadically of moving out of England), and fears for Ken's reputation. The attacks on him in the press troubled me more than they did him. Though I was blindly loyal, I did consider that Ken put himself at unnecessary risk. I thought he was dangerously self-critical in private, yet dangerously combative in public. It seemed to me that retaliation against attack merely exhausted him and gained no advantage. I must have taxed him on this matter, and wounded him perhaps, for I wrote a note to him which reads: 'I'm shaking too. I can't bear to hurt you. And hurting you is an entirely new feeling since I've never loved anyone as I love you.'

In March 1969 we went back to Valencia for the winter feria of the *fallas*. The plan was to rest, to enjoy the corridas and fireworks and for Ken to collect material for an article about the city. In the line of duty, he set off one night to test a local nightclub while I took to my bed. I paraphrase his version of what happened: He buys drinks for himself and a fat little hostess with hair like steel wool. At 1.45, with no sign of a floorshow, he asks for his bill. This turns out to be hefty, and he complains to the manager. The manager calls three uniformed cops. He says the Englishman not only refused to pay his bill but vilified General Franco, abused the Spanish people and referred to the Valencia police as corrupt pigs. Ken is frisked, arrested and taken off to the local prison. His thoughts are of glowing cigar-ends and electrodes, mixed with panic at the prospect of English newspaper headlines. A posse of police, Ken in their midst, next moves to his hotel to retrieve his passport. I am woken; I dress, and in a taxi I follow my handcuffed husband, who is in a police car. At 5 a.m. Ken is taken to a fortress-like court house for his case to be heard. He is now very happy to turn over 1700 pesetas to the nightclub manager. Case dismissed. Prisoner is finally released.

I was by now more or less resigned to trouble, and with each new threat to Ken's security and well-being I would brace myself and try to figure out what was to be done. I went so far as to pay a visit to Olivier to beg him to keep Ken on at the National.

Two aspects of my husband's dramatic personality I could rely upon: he was a great wolf-crier, so that over the years I learned how to suspend my disbelief upon hearing his bad news from the field, to make my own assessment *before* I let myself panic. He had also an astonishing capacity for recovery: having declared that all was lost, he would in the next breath cast off his gloom and propose a celebration.

But during the spring of 1969 he faced a real battle – or rather an old one, now grown deadly serious. If Lord Chandos and his Board had wanted to rid themselves of their unruly employee two years before, they now had in hand the right weapon: Ken's request for four months' leave of absence.

The events leading up to this confrontation were as follows. 1968 and 1969 were years at the National of uneven quality. Ken brought in John Lennon's *In His Own Write* as part of a triple bill, and Charles Wood's *H*, about the Indian Mutiny. At his instigation, Clifford Williams came to direct Shaw's *Back to Methuselah*, and Michael Blakemore to direct a highly successful new play by Peter Nichols called *The National Health* (hated by Lord Chandos and loved by the critics). With the departure of John Dexter and William Gaskill, and Olivier weakened by ill health, Frank Dunlop was brought in to help run the theatre. He directed Somerset Maugham's *Home and Beauty* (a play which Ken rejected as 'an authentic whiff of Windsor rep'), and a year later a fine production of Webster's *The White Devil*.

Ken meanwhile was planning: corresponding with Mike Nichols about doing *Long Day's Journey into Night*; discussing new plays by Dennis Potter, David Rudkin, David Halliwell and Peter Shaffer; and trying to persuade Olivier to do *King Lear* in the scenic style of Eisenstein's *Ivan the Terrible*, Part II. Ken became enthused by this latter project, and worked out a plan of production, which he described to the Oliviers. Joan Plowright asked him, when Olivier was out of the room, 'Why don't you suggest that you want to direct it?' And Ken replied, 'I couldn't ask Larry. I fear his disdain.' Eventually he did broach the idea of co-direction, and Olivier appeared to be sympathetic.

If Ken had found a way to direct (tried out at another theatre) or had co-directed *King Lear*, the problem of his growing frustration at the National might have been solved, his talent authentically tested. His other colleagues remained unaware of this ambition, but, when asked recently whether he knew how much Ken wanted to direct, Olivier paused and then said, 'Why didn't I want him to? I wish I could dig out the truth root of that. I certainly didn't. I was probably jealous. Also, would it have gone down well with the company?'

Olivier might have added that Ken's influence at the National had been severely damaged by *Soldiers*. What Ken never knew was how hard and generously Olivier had fought to keep him in the job: 'The bitterest battles I had were on Ken's behalf. The Board knew that if they did fire him, they'd have fired me too, and there wouldn't be a National. They hated being in that weak position. It made them hate Ken more and finally made Chandos hate me – so angry that he'd bring his face close up to mine, purple with rage. But Ken was absolutely safe as long as I was there. It was the one decent thing I did for him.'

In October 1968, with the campaign for and against the play building up in expectation of the London opening, and on the tail of a hostile communication from Lord Chandos, the Director of the theatre wrote to his Chairman. In the contentious matter of Ken's consultations with various historians and political figures over the Sikorski incident, and the 'very open verdict' he had announced as a result of his researches, Olivier wrote:

It did not seem to me that he was given more than a very meagre opportunity to explain himself, and my own reading of this incident was that he was guilty more of over-stating his case than bare dishonesty.... But again I must say that I do not regard the conduct of any of us as being immaculate....

I think anyone in any such job as his, or indeed as mine, is entitled to slight ups and downs in the matter of bull's-eye-hitting.

He then pointed to the theatre's record to date (twenty-two hits out of thirty-eight productions), and listed in detail, year by year, Ken's large contribution to that success.

He concluded: 'Were Ken Tynan to be got rid of I should be not only extremely unhappy but most unlikely to find a replacement who could in any way compare to him in the way of theatrical brains, or provide the National Theatre with half his value. I would be quite stricken if a partnership such as this were to be dissolved.'

On 30 April of the following year Ken went to see the Chairman, seeking a sabbatical from the end of June in order to write a book. Lord Chandos again made known his displeasure partly over *Soldiers*, and partly due to the interviews Ken was giving at the time, in New York, on nudity and sexual intercourse on the stage, which did not consort well with his position as Literary Manager. The Chairman thought it was time for a change, a new mind in the job. Ken replied that he had hoped to retain his job until the opening of the theatre's new building.

He subsequently wrote to Chandos:

Since my work for the National Theatre is my main professional interest in life, and since I know that Sir Laurence is anxious for me to remain in the organisation, I, have decided to withdraw my application in its present form. Instead, I should like to ask for *three* months leave, bearing in mind that my contract with the National Theatre provides for free time to pursue 'authorship activities'....

I understand that exception was taken to my saying that my principal loyalty was to the National Theatre rather than to its Board. In my own defence, I can only say that this seems to me analogous to a Labour M.P. declaring complete loyalty to the Party while disagreeing with a specific Cabinet decision. I should imagine that even the Board might feel that its main loyalty was to the National Theatre rather than to itself.

During the next week Lord Chandos considerably modified his position with respect to Ken. Pressure had been brought to bear, certainly by Olivier, and a face-saving scheme had been arrived at: to allow Ken a six-month sabbatical and then to demote him while not actually firing him. On 10 June 1969 Chandos wrote to Ken to say that no one had suggested he be dismissed, that the Board had decided that his work in future should be done as a consultant, and that more than one consultant might be taken on. Such a post, with the same salary, was now on offer. On the whole, Ken replied, he should like to accept it.

It was not pleasant for Ken when, five months later, the change was made public and another man taken on to share the job. 'In making Tynan a literary consultant with Derek Granger,' Lord Chandos told the press, 'I had to tell him that he had been considerably under fire lately.' Might Tynan be ousted? 'I could give a schoolboy answer to that,' said the Chairman, 'and say it would help if he behaved himself.'

On reading this and other press reports, Ken was enraged. Olivier cabled him in Italy asking him to keep calm, and promising to deal with the situation. 'I beg you to stay with me ... and patiently abstain from any other most natural inclinations to explosion and remain firmly calmly and sweetly in Joanie's and my love Larry.'

Ken cabled back that he would make no comment 'provided Chairman keeps big mouth shut', and signed off, 'Yours in Abraham's bosom – Job.'

29

Oh! Calcutta!

On 11 June 1966, William Donaldson, producer of *Beyond the Fringe*, went to see Ken at Mount Street. He had in mind (as in fact had several others) a show based on sex, in the burlesque manner – a sort of English version of *La Plume de Ma Tante* – and, having read somewhere a statement by Ken to the effect that sex and blasphemy should be explored on the stage, had decided to approach him. 'I couldn't give an account at all of what it was I had in mind, except that I knew burlesque was important. Ken said, no, that wasn't on at all. He explained that it wouldn't work because English comedians were very puritanical. He wanted to do something much more classily erotic and to cut out the sort of comedy I was thinking about. In his mind the show was already taking shape.'

A few days later Donaldson wrote to say how exciting he found Ken's original idea, an Evening of Erotica, and that he hoped to produce it in the West End.

Meanwhile we went to Paris, Ken to write about the theatre for the *New Yorker*, and I to write an article on the surrealist painter Clovis Trouille, the book of whose erotic canvases, discovered by Ken, had inspired our election party. One of his works was a naked odalisque, lying on her side to reveal a spherical backside. The title was *Oh! Calcutta! Calcutta!*, and the subtitle, *La Conquête de la lune*.

While drinking an aperitif at the Dôme in Montparnasse, I suggested to Ken that he call his erotic revue *Oh! Calcutta!*, and make use of the painting he found so appealing. Would it not make an unforgettable title? I did not know at the time that it had the further advantage of being a French pun, *O quel cul t'as*.

When Ken returned from London he wrote a three-page letter to Donaldson. 'The idea is to use artistic means to achieve erotic stimulation. Nothing that is *merely* funny or *merely* beautiful should be admitted: it must also be sexy.'

He wanted an intimate theatre, and a variety licence so that the wordless items would not have to be submitted to the Lord Chamberlain. 'The show', he wrote, would be 'devised (or produced) by me, directed by some like-minded person (Jonathan Miller?), and choreographed by a non-queer.'

He suggested *Oh! Calcutta!* as a title, subtitled *An International Erotic Revue*; the cast to consist of eight to ten girls who could dance and sing, and about four men, all expert comics. Possible items: a double strip, with one stripper a woman and the other a female impersonator. A serial silent film, 'a sort of sexy Batman', each episode of which would leave the audience cliff-hanging, American burlesque and Parisian music-hall routines. Dance numbers to include a ballet based on the paintings of Clovis Trouille. 'His fantastic visions of begartered nuns, novices doing the splits, circus performers who are half-girl and half-horse, would make the ideal erotic ballet.' He also suggested a Beardsley ballet, and a homage to the Crazy Horse Saloon. If the owner of this famous Paris club gave permission, this would include 'the classic bath number in which a stripper is first seen in silhouette, projected on a downstage screen, and later perched on a black marble bath, meditatively soaping herself; and of course Bernardin's famous "La Veuve", in which a widow, sitting in a pew at her husband's funeral, devoutly strips as the organ plays.'

He suggested some semi-documentary items, one on the history of under-wear; another a series of tableaux representing national erotic obsessions, 'such as a nun being raped by her confessor (Italy), a middle-aged bank manager bound hand and foot by a Superwoman (U.S.A.) and a St. Trinian's sixth-former being birched (Great Britain)'.

Among the straightforward strip numbers he proposed one by Dailly Holli-day, a stripper from Guadeloupe (appearing at the time in Paris). 'She comes on pure black and brutally militant, snarling at the audience and shoving her arse and tits straight into the onlookers' faces ... Black Supremacy incarnate.'

In addition, there would be erotic sketches by well-known writers, whose names would be billed but not attached to a particular contribution. Among the names he put forward were Terry Southern, Jean Genet and John Osborne.

All these items, Ken concluded, would be 'shuffled and interspersed, so that a strip would be followed by a sketch, a sketch by a ballet, a ballet by a film excerpt'.

The first person he approached to direct the revue was Peter Brook. Brook said that the only erotic show that he would be interested in directing was a brothel; that just as the object of comedy was to create laughter, so that of an erotic show was to arouse. In August he wrote to Ken to confirm that he did not see how his interest in directing an orgiastic happening could possibly be done in public. He thought, however, that Ken's idea of a 'cool, witty and sophisticated tease' could be successful. He wondered whether Mike Nichols might not be the man.

Shortly after Brook had been consulted, Willie Donaldson disappeared. Since no deal had been formalized, Ken joined forces with the producer Michael White.

He next discussed the project with Harold Pinter, who seemed interested in directing. The décor, Ken suggested, should be minimal and elegant – David Hockney, Peter Blake and Allen Jones were possible candidates. He had no first choice for choreographer. The music was to be a small chamber ensemble, 'Strings plus horn, possibly spinet: as for "Eleanor Rigby", "For No One". George Martin? [Ray] Davies (The Kinks)? Paul McCartney?'

Pinter in turn demonstrated symbolically what *he* thought an erotic show should be: he put a table napkin over a glass and very slowly drew it off. He said that even if there were just a tiny whisper of Scotch in the glass, the slow revelation of the Scotch would be exciting to him. The discussion continued, though it was never recorded, as Ken hoped, by a nude stenographer.

By early January 1967 Ken was soliciting contributions from his writer friends on both sides of the Atlantic. There was to be 'no crap about art or redeeming literary merit: this show will be expressly designed to titillate, in the most elegant and outré way.' Sketches were to be of any length from a few seconds to twelve minutes: 'You can either (i) create on stage your own sexual fantasy or (ii) make a comment – satirical or ironic – on eroticism.' Male homosexuality was excluded, but all kinds of fetishes and sexual ambiguities were welcome. Payment would be the accepted scale for normal revue royalties.

He added that, for legal reasons, 'indecent exposure is out, and so are 4-letter words. However, female nudes are permissible so long as they don't move.'

By the end of January, Pinter had had second thoughts. He did not relish judging the sketches of fellow playwrights, nor the prospect of dictating how they should be directed. He also wondered practically 'how much time I can devote to other things, however worthwhile, outside my own fucking writing. I am', he concluded, 'in what is loosely called twosometwisomeness (James Joyce – doubt. ref. Fin. Wake).' Without Pinter, Ken continued to work at several sketches of his own, and to collect the erotic fantasies of his fellow writers.

In the summer of 1967, Joe Chaikin's Open Theater came to London with *America Hurrah*, part of which, including *Motel*, was directed by Jacques Levy. Ken liked its non-orgiastic style, its extreme cool, and persuaded Levy to direct *Oh! Calcutta!* 'We had one of those long talks', the director recalls, 'where both people are harbouring their own fantasies of what the show might be. But we got on well.'

At that stage Ken intended to mount the show in London, and was waiting for the end of the Lord Chamberlain's jurisdiction over plays. He had already in hand a short piece by Samuel Beckett; a homage to the Crazy Horse Saloon, and one based on the paintings of Clovis Trouille; an idea for two three-minute films, called 'The Voyeur', which Roman Polanski had devised and would direct; John Lennon's 'Liverpool Wank'; and top-quality sketches from David Mercer, Edna O'Brien, Joe Orton and Jules Feiffer. His own contributions included a sketch about sado-masochism, cerebral though not very intelligible, called 'Who Whom'; a sketch eventually titled 'Suite for Five Letters', based on the perverse letter column of *London Life*; a history of underwear; and a humorous homage to girls' schools in the manner of Angela Brazil.

There were promises of sketches from many other writers, and there were refusals. Tennessee Williams felt he was still too much of a romantic to write a parody of sex: 'I suppose there is a good deal of absurdity in the kind of sexual experience I'm mostly acquainted with. But when you love – the absurdity is obscured.' Eventually Williams sent in a sketch about a married couple who could only excite each other by fighting. This was filmed for the show but not used.

On 26 February 1968, Jacques Levy, Ken and I met at Sardi's. We were joined by Jacques's agent, Hillard Elkins, a fast-talking showbiz dandy from Brooklyn, who gave us his history (he had represented Steve McQueen and produced *Golden Boy*), and proceeded swiftly to explain that he was the one and only man to produce *Oh! Calcutta!* We were, I recall, totally charmed by this preposterous self-promoter, with his little goatee beard on the chin of an urgent, intelligent, city-coyote face. A few days later, since Ken was ill, we took up Elkins' offer to stay at his apartment. He would be out of town, he explained, though later we learned he had moved into the Plaza.

In the spring of that year David Merrick became involved as a possible producer for *Oh! Calcutta!*, should it open in New York, but the collaboration was short-lived. 'He wants to make too much of a creative contribution,' Ken explained.

In the early autumn the decision was made to open in New York, where the climate for the show seemed perfect, and with Hilly Elkins as producer. He and Levy brought in new writers and artists, among them Robert Benton and David Newman, with promises of material from Pat McCormick, Elaine May, Kurt Vonnegut and Sam Shepard. Godard and Fellini would provide short films. Michael Bennett would choreograph. (Bennett decided not to go ahead, and his dance captain from *Promises, Promises*, Margo Sappington, stepped in.)

Elkins was open to experiment, generous with money (the Off-Broadway show ended up costing $125,000) and ready to risk closure from the police. Above all he was a brilliant promoter.

In February 1969 Michael White turned over to Elkins certain rights in the show given to him by Ken – all the rights were by that time owned by a company to which Ken had sold his services, since he was fearful of police interference and badly in need of cash. Over the years Ken made around $250,000 out of the show. In other circumstances, and had the subsidiary deals been properly managed, he would have made millions.

But in March 1969 money was not the issue; nudity was. Though it had never been a priority for Ken, it was for Jacques Levy. There was already some exposure on the New York stage, but none within the context of pure sexuality.

Levy chose five men and five women who could sing, dance and act, none of whom had previously appeared nude on stage. Before rehearsals began on 30 March the director considered how to get his actors to undress. Put out the lights and ask them to take their clothes off? Hardly the answer. He had been impressed with Anna Halprin's modern dance troupe in which a naked cast, stranded in the orchestra pit, jumped up grasping at the stage, only to fall back. They conjured up images of prisons and death camps, rather than sexual union, but they gave Levy courage.

Using non-verbal improvisation techniques and sensitivity exercises which he had developed at the Open Theater, he worked towards getting his actors to the point where they could deal with any material that required nudity or simulated sexual contact (he was never intent on sexual intercourse). The object was to allow the actors to accomplish their task as professionals while at the same time creating a sense of erotic connection. 'I always wanted the feeling that the showing of the whole body was something special.'

With this in mind he created all sorts of rules. The actors could not fraternize outside the theatre – a ruling which came to be known as the NFL (No-Fucking Law). They were never to wear their own clothes at rehearsals; taking his cue from the world of sports, he provided each of his troupe with a locker with his or her name on, and two sets of outfits, a robe on which was written *Oh! Calcutta!* and a set of rehearsal clothes which could be used for dance and for working on scenes. The idea was that the cast was to come in, change clothes and do their warm-up exercises; that they were never to be naked, except when they were working on something that required nudity.

At one point during early rehearsal, while the actors were dancing, their director said, 'Take off your robes,' and everybody did so with a great sense of excitement and liberation. 'It was back to the Garden all of a sudden, a great high,' Jacques Levy recalls, 'but not an erotic one. Once they'd broken that barrier it was a lot easier.' That experience was adapted for the opening number of the show. The idea was to perform what appeared to be a burlesque tease – one that the audiences would except – and then finally, under total white light, for everyone to stand naked.

When Ken arrived in New York early in May to see a run-through he was appalled to find that the director had hardly begun to rehearse the sketches. Nudity was all very well, but wasn't it all a bit like a YMCA summer camp? The problem with Jacques, Ken announced, was that he was 'a straight fucker'. The problem with Ken, Jacques Levy felt, was how to bring him kicking and screaming out of the nineteenth century into the sixties.

On 12 May I arrived in New York to hold Ken's hand. He was on the verge of hysteria, desperately concerned about the quality of the revue. He told me that Jacques was a great teacher who loved improvisation, but had no sense of pace and no regard for the audience. He felt that somebody else should be brought in.

We settled into Elkins' back bedroom at $19\frac{1}{2}$ East 62nd Street and were momentarily diverted by our host. Hilly ran his life from a canopied bedroom permanently sealed from the light of day. From there he would emerge in a dapper outfit (which might include a leather jerkin, a sapphire-blue silk shirt, a jacket with six zips, or a pair of ornate patent pumps) and hold court, or work the telephone – any telephone – as he made his way from the bedroom to the dining-room on the floor below. This room, decorated with red velvet in the style of horror-movie baroque, was dominated by a glowering portrait of Napoleon. Hilly would answer Ken's complaints with 'See my analyst. I used to be just like you – tall, thin and Christian.' Once he had made us laugh, he could get back on the telephone: 'We've sold the wife-swapping sketch for a movie. I think I can get Burton and Taylor,' we'd hear him say, or to a backer, 'We're not into a royalty structure situation yet,' which roughly translated meant that Hilly did not have the money to open. He did, however, think there was enough material for two shows. Would it not be a good idea, Ken and he concluded, to do a late-night version called *The Black Hole*, using scabrous rejects?

Opposite the dining-room, a living-room had been recently, and incongruously, decorated in a floral print by Hilly's fiancée, Claire Bloom. There we would find the English beauty wandering around, teacup in hand, and there we would take refuge.

I was not the best person to back my husband, for my judgement, on my first visit to a dress rehearsal, was thrown by the astonishing business on stage. It didn't look like a YMCA camp to me, and the sight of the glorious body of Margo Sappington dancing the can-can wearing nothing but a carnation between her legs was amazing. Shortly after, a naked girl, bound, gagged and trussed in a net, was lowered over the stage. 'Fly her in very slowly,' a technician shouted, 'and see how she does on the electrics.'

The problem, Ken explained when he could get my attention, was the hitherto unexplained question of taste in sex. We knew what made us laugh or cry, but not what was sexually acceptable to an audience. As far as he was concerned Dan Greenburg's parody of a sex clinic experiment was 'crude beyond words'.

But as the previews built, and sketches, film and dance numbers were tried and rejected or polished and worked on, the real problem emerged, which had nothing to do with sex and all to do with the nature of the revue form.

The David Mercer piece about two lesbians, and Edna O'Brien's prison fantasy, had to be dropped. Although they filled Ken's requirements for sophisticated eroticism, they were both too downbeat; no slot in the show's running order made either of them work.

Ken gave notes at rehearsal, and in the evening he would type up long and precise instructions. On 19 May he left for London to try and salvage his job at the National Theatre, leaving me as a watchdog in New York.

It seemed that most of New York was going down to the Eden Theater on Second Avenue and Twelfth Street to attend one of the forty-one previews. Senator Javits thought it was 'Very interesting', Rudolf Nureyev declared that the bodies were beautiful, and Jerome Robbins described it as 'joyous, healthy and alive, a celebration'.

New York was ready for *Oh! Calcutta!* Norman Mailer was running for mayor, the magazine stalls were full of explicit images of the body's most hidden regions. The cast, now apparently liberated beyond recall, told stories of the dramatic changes in their private lives. Therapeutic sex clinics were burgeoning. Everybody was exploring sexuality, while I had not yet abandoned my bra. It seemed ironic that my sex-pedlar husband was far too concerned about his future career in London, and his reputation in New York, to leave much time for sex.

When Ken returned ten days later, Jacques Levy and his cast were improvising techniques for the closing number. By now *Calcutta* was very much a show within a show, the group numbers encompassing the sketches. The evening opened with a chorus line which strips. After the intermission, the nude cast appeared in a choreographed group grope, with short filmed biographies of each performer projected on the backcloth. At the end the cast again stepped forward, each as himself or herself, and voiced what the audience might be thinking: 'I mean what is the point, I mean what does it prove? ... Nudity is passé.... She really is a natural blonde.... That's my daughter up there.... If they're having fun, why don't they have erections?'

In rehearsal Jacques had said, 'Don't everybody keep shooting for the laugh. We don't want uptown values around here. Don't let yourself be seduced by the audience. Try to make whatever you want to happen happen.' 'You know,' said Ken sitting up in the balcony, 'the actors in this show, and the production staff, behave not like craftsmen but like people in a movie about a Broadway production.' No theatre historian since has pointed out that *Oh! Calcutta!* was the precursor of *A Chorus Line*.

Ken went back to London on 5 June and returned five days later. By the 12th he was preparing to take his name off the show. He wrote to Elkins:

Kathleen and I have been doing some checking. *Everybody* is (ludicrously) under the impression that *Calcutta* is my show.... In fact, of course, it is Jacques' show with your backing.... What we now have is not an *erotic* show – eroticism means sex plus psychological content – but a *flesh* show. There are ways of concealing this failure –

by means of running order and the restoration of items like 'You and I' [by David Mercer].... Unless my feelings about 'my' show are respected by Tuesday night's performance, I shall have to wield the club Jacques mentioned last night and pull out, not with a whimper but a resounding bang.

During the next few days matters were resolved. Ken resigned himself to the opening night, while agreeing without enthusiasm to give interviews to the press and the major television talk hosts.

The *New York Times* published an interview between Ken and an 'intelligent puritan' of his own invention. Was there not enough sex already in the theatre? 'There may be quite enough heavy-breathing, grimly perspiring, earnestly symbolic sex on the New York stage,' Ken replied, tacitly referring to *Che!* and the Performance Group's *Dionysus in '69*, 'but what about sex as play, nocturnal diversion, civilized pastime?'

Ken's own sexual preferences, he confided in another journal, were as follows: 'The slow revelation of the body, not immediate nudity ... certain voices and the combination and use of words ... Mirrors, bathrooms.... I don't like group sex, and, as a matter of fact, I haven't tried any.... For me the most unerotic garments ever invented are body stockings and tights.'

Although *Oh! Calcutta!* hardly resembled Ken's ideal, it had an exuberant and undeniable life of its own, and he recognized this. The New York Police Department vice squad, meanwhile, having visited the show on several occasions and objected to genital contact, agreed not to prosecute. As the Police Commissioner put it, 'The pillars of the guidelines are shaking every day.'

Opening night was 17 June 1969. Ken stood pale and sombre in a white suit at the back of the stalls. The celebrities took their seats (some going for the scalper's price of $45 a pair). At the end there was decent applause and some cheering.

Hilly had already seen the bad notice by Clive Barnes of the *New York Times* but kept it from his colleagues. Upstairs at Sardi's he ran the cast party in high spirits. Later a group of us climbed up to the press room to get the reviews. At 10.15 the first television critics came through with 'No wit', 'All the sophistication of a men's-room wall'. Shortly afterwards, the Barnes notice came in, in which he described the show as innocent and sophomoric. Hilly read it out to us: 'This is the kind of show to give pornography a dirty name. I have enormous respect for Ken Tynan, as critic, social observer and man of the theater. But what a nice dirty-minded boy like him is doing in a place like this I fail to understand.... To be honest, I think I can recommend the show with any vigor only to people who are extraordinarily under-privileged either sexually, socially or emotionally. Now is your chance to stand up and be counted –' 'I'll stand up and be counted,' interrupted Ken.

The *Daily News* critic found it 'hard-core pornography'. Emily Genauer of the *New York Post* hedged her bets. *Oh! Calcutta!* was 'the most pornographic, brutalizing, degrading, shocking, tedious, witless ... concoction' she had ever seen in the legitimate theatre. It was also 'the most shatteringly effective'.

In the days after the opening the euphoria of preview time dissolved. Friends who telephoned to commiserate sounded muffled. We heard that Diana Vreeland liked the show less the second time around.

But Elkins remained feistily optimistic. Seats were being sold, and good reviews were coming in: 'A dazzling entertainment with music', 'A unique experience.... So unlike anything else ever in the theatre that you're not quite sure how to judge it or what your reaction should be.' *Time* magazine gave it a minus on eroticism but 'two pluses for the laughter it evokes and its rousing celebration of the body beautiful'. Jack Kroll at *Newsweek* agreed. *Oh! Calcutta!* was not only revolutionary but salutary.

Yet Ken could not be cheered. Much of the criticism had been personal and his pride was wounded. The day after the opening we lunched at Trader Vic's with Michael White. 'It'll be off in two weeks,' Ken said. 'It's a disaster. I've wasted three years of my life.'

'You're wrong, Ken,' Michael White said, in his familiar laconic voice. 'It'll run for years.'

The boisterous theatrical changeling ran in New York until 1972 (and returned to Broadway in 1976, where it is still running). It has played in some 250 cities world-wide and has grossed, according to its New York producer, $360,000,000. Ken's simple little idea made fortunes for people other than himself.

Two other nude revues were mounted in *Calcutta*'s wake, *Let My People Come* and *The Dirtiest Show in Town*, but neither of them was a great success. *Calcutta*, it would seem, was influential in forms other than the revue. Jacques Levy believes it influenced not only *A Chorus Line* but also Bob Fosse's work in *Dancin'* and *All That Jazz*. Jules Feiffer's *Calcutta* sketch 'Dick and Jane' turned out to be an experiment for a longer piece which became *Carnal Knowledge*. When Gore Vidal put pen to paper to write a sketch for the original show, he told Ken that 'Myra B. came, as it were, into all our lives.'

Ken spent much of the next seven years trying to conquer *Oh! Calcutta!*, to achieve what he had originally intended, and had singularly failed at, first in London, with a revamped version of the original, later with a sequel called *Carte Blanche*, and finally in an erotic film script of his own to be directed by himself. Lack of financial backing, ill health, opposition from me and from friends finally prevented him from exploring his own sexual mythology on the screen.

30

Treading Water

Ten days after the disastrous opening of *Oh! Calcutta!*, drained and depressed by the hostile reaction of the New York critics, Ken lay on a bed in my mother's house in London (for our own house had been let), his will and energy spent. Even his faithful Sancho Panza no longer had heart for getting-on-with-it, and I moved among our trunks and papers and suitcases listlessly. We were not only poor, but dishonoured. What was to be done?

By dusk the following night, in Paris, as I recorded in the Prologue to this book, Ken was facing his condition with surprising equanimity. Within a day or two his spirits lifted high and stayed up more or less throughout those 'brooding and blissful halcyon days', during our sabbatical in Italy.

Perhaps he should not have returned to England but stayed in the sun in retreat. Perhaps a book about *Soldiers* and *Oh! Calcutta!* (his reason for a leave of absence) was not what he should have contracted to write, but rather the autobiography he had promised himself so many years before. In the event, Ken went back to his old life, and fell into the pattern of work that he had left – the National Theatre, journalism – while more and more of his time was used up and abused in punditry: in giving interviews, standing on platforms, and being a minor international celebrity. Yet at the same time he moved unsurely towards the goal he wanted: work on the inside, in the theatre and in film; to write and to direct a film, in particular, and to do so on his own terms.

In the middle of its last decade, Ken's life turned tragic. He sent up a series of distress signals, vital clues to his problems and neuroses, and pointed them out to himself and to others; he even acted them out. But he never managed fully to expose and exorcize these demons by means of an embracing and coherent analysis.

Meanwhile he made valiant, and even brutal, attempts to change direction. Time and his rapidly failing health were against him. Without those handicaps he might have unravelled himself, tapped the root deep enough to expose the guilt which would not permit him to forgive himself. Without his physical disability, he might at least have come up with further surprises or had a better time.

As I write this I hear a vast number of voices competing to explain Ken's shortcomings and failures, for Ken seemed to provoke the world to explain and dismiss him. Above these voices I hear Ken. He is behind me, having read my own comments, and as I turn I see him in a rage: 'Who the fuck do you think you are, you condescending bitch!' he screams, and having lashed out, his face collapses and is drained of colour, his eyes turn away from me, as he says quietly, 'My problem is that I know myself too well.'

Back to Italy, in the summer of 1969, before life caught up with our truancy. Snorkelling with Ken off the shores of Porto Ercole. Ken 'hovering like God on the waters' (he explained) blessing the fish, emitting hoots through his periscope tube 'to warn the wicked'. I, delighted by his playfulness, as he by my foolishness. Catching sight of me in a minidress with a silly hat he said, 'You're such a girl, you're really a girl, you really are my girl.'

At the Villa Serbelloni at Bellagio, our next port of call, by courtesy of the Rockefeller Foundation Ken wrote one long article and turned down requests for others. When asked to write about what was happening in the arts, he told his agent that he had escaped precisely not to have to consider or answer such a question. To another offer for a series on 'general ideas' he replied that he hated 'cooking up pieces to fit a prescribed gap.... I'd rather write about something that interests me *while* it interests me *and* at length.'

At Bellagio, when not at his typewriter, Ken led an unusually healthy life. I wrote to my mother to tell her that 'we actually play tennis, very fiercely, and I beat Ken while he beats me at croquet and chess'. Our companions at dinner were mostly American academics, some of whom had lost their posts during the student unrest.

Once installed at the Fattoria Mansi above Lucca we were entirely alone, with the exception of a happy visit from Tracy and a boyfriend. Ken temporarily broke his resolve not to write journalism with a short review for the *Observer* of Lillian Hellman's *An Unfinished Woman*, a work he admired, though he hoped that in future books Miss Hellman would 'direct the spotlight towards her public self, where nakedness can often be more sensitive than the private area of an artist's life'.

Of his own calm private life, he wrote to his editor at the *Observer*, on 28 September, 'A small cloud appeared in the eastern sky this morning and we are all panicking. Why should God single us out for his wrath in this way?'

Journeys: to Orvieto, to Volterra, to Florence, guidebook in hand. Journeys with Roxana, now three. She liked to sing with Ken, and she liked it when he cupped his mouth to make a noise like a trumpet.

Words for play, instead of for work. He taught me a song Phil Silvers used to sing. It goes:

Phil: A word a day
Sue: (A word a day)
Phil: Like résumé
Sue: (Like résumé)
Both: That's how we keep our fancy IQ
Phil: A word a day
Sue: (A word a day)
Phil: Like matinée
Sue: (Or cheese soufflé)
Both: Keeps us ved-dy Park Av-en-ue.

And the verses lasted along the shaded drive and up to our peach-white house. Time for a sunset drink. Time to inspect the slow exposure of a thousand horned snails on the terrace. Time even for a few words on paper. Here are some of Ken's: 'People who can share their minds and bodies with others and live happily together spend much of their time reverently obeying the orders and admiring the fantasies of people who cannot and who must find other ways to fulfil themselves. These latter are called politicians and artists. They are interesting but not inherently superior kinds of people.'

Time, of course, did not stand still. Like the snails on our terrace, I was slowly stretching my neck and the manner of doing so was in a soft-backed green exercise book, titled, in my spidery hand, 'One to One'. Here I set down my first thoughts and ideas for a novel: 'Once in a while I see time pass. A personality is changed at certain times and becomes someone different.... I am left treading water but with the sensation of drowning.'

I thought I was referring to Ken, but I suspect it was to myself. I was beginning to think, beginning to exercise a mind dulled by my good-wife role, by complacency, by narcissism.

I intended to write a novel about romantic love, which was all I knew about. But I had no ending. I saw that our constancy caused irritation, even anger in others, but that would not do for a plot. What was this conjoining about? A neurotic dependence? A fear of loneliness? I asked the set questions. I read Tolstoy's *Family Happiness* and commented, 'Where does the couple go wrong? When he asks her to marry him and she accepts.' I read *Anna Karenina*, and came to the conclusion that romantic novels were about unemancipated women: 'Books about strongly felt relationships between men and women are nearly always about the women's struggle for rights – for independence and self-expression.'

I tried on aphorisms: 'I believe if I were less happy, I'd be happier.' Or 'We danced for each other, until our steps became the same. And at that point we lost the feel of each other.' Or 'Betrayal stimulates a new lease on life. It frees you from the anxious state of constancy.' But I knew nothing of betrayal. So what to do with my characters?

One afternoon I asked Ken, 'What do you think of romantic love?' He was not excited by the question. 'I don't know,' he told me. 'Read Lionel Trilling – isn't it an attachment to something unattainable?'

'And love?' I asked.

'You order that mistress to be the perfect mother. Now will you let me read my book.'

'But what do you think about monogamy?'

'Monogamy is an anti-social activity.'

'But do you approve of infidelity?'

'You can only be unfaithful to that which you call faithful.' My husband, patient but glazed with boredom, returned to his book.

Why isn't he interested? Is there not some fallacy in the way he functions? Why is he so unself-protective? Why has he no reserve, by which I mean storage area, a place to keep bits and pieces of his past, of his childhood, a sort of makeshift sanctuary? I recall that when I first met Ken I would instruct him to clear an imaginary space somewhere in his chest for just such a purpose. I thought it might be comforting.

So began my first tentative flight from the nest. Less than four years later some of my questions on the nature of love and fidelity were answered.

31

Third Act: Curtain Up

In December 1969 we slipped back into our London life. Hardly had we returned than Ken was preparing for our traditional Christmas Eve party. His diary reads: 'Rehearse xmas dinner. Print menus.'

On New Year's Eve, as usual we went to the Snowdons' annual party – an event planned and carried out by the hosts with the same care and panache which Ken put into our entertainments. When the servants appeared at midnight to sing 'Auld Lang Syne', Ken used to make a rather awkward effort to join their group; and when asked to announce himself to the policeman at the gate of Kensington Palace he once answered, 'We're a new group called the Coup d'État.'

All too swiftly after our return the old work patterns closed Ken in, and the third act began without any warning. For *Playboy* he planned to write a piece on soccer's World Cup to be fought the following June in Mexico City. Would they also be interested in a profile of Victor Mature? he asked his agent, 'something of a legend because of his magnificent disenchantment'. Neither of these ideas was carried out. Meanwhile he began research for a *New Yorker* profile on the actor Nicol Williamson. With Olivier's approval Ken had, in January 1970, offered Williamson a succulent choice of parts at the National Theatre: Judge Brack in *Hedda Gabler*, to be directed by Ingmar Bergman; Danton in *Danton's Death*; Hildy Johnson in *The Front Page*; the title role in *Macbeth*; and the elder son in *Long Day's Journey into Night*. This wayward young actor, whom Ken had admired as the cynical, defeated lawyer in John Osborne's *Inadmissible Evidence*, turned down the National's offer. He did, however, agree to be interviewed by Ken.

Williamson interested Ken for his performance on and off stage – one that ranged from dazzling–belligerent to abject–vulnerable. Fascinated by men able to impose themselves effortlessly on their peers, Ken saw in this actor 'a sly but well-organized urge to dominate whatever group he finds himself in'.

It so happened that Harold Wilson had seen Williamson in Tony Richardson's production of *Hamlet*, and had praised the actor highly to Richard Nixon. In February 1970 a White House invitation was issued to Williamson to provide the President with an evening of Shakespeare. And, shortly after, he set off to plan and rehearse an entertainment which would include readings from Eliot, Beckett and Lardner, as well as from Shakespeare, along with some songs to be accompanied by a nine-man Dixieland band called The World's Greatest Jazz Band.

Ken described, in his article, the triumphant White House performance on 19 March, as well as the drunken, disaster-filled rehearsal period before Williamson, his agent, his band, and his Boswell arrived at the White House. 'Are you the entertainment?' asked a guard. Ken had in the meantime not only been advising on repertory and performance, but had been drinking for his friend: 'When he ordered wine, I would consume as much of it myself as I discreetly could, in order to keep his energies fresh for rehearsal. I do not know whether this unselfishness was of any real use to him. It nearly crippled me.'

In joining Williamson's bizarre progress to Washington, Ken executed a thorough, though not savage, undressing of the actor's psyche – one that he might have performed on any consummate actor, including himself.

Waiting to fly back to London, nursing his hangover, he described seeing Williamson on a television screen at Dulles Airport.

Dozens of Nicols float before my eyes: will the line stretch out to the crack of doom? He looks supremely buoyant; I, on the other hand, feel drained and enfeebled, a mere husk of a man. How much (I wonder) of Nicol's neurosis is a deliberate, expertly adopted pose? On the whole, actors are not the compulsive neurotics we take them for. Many of them come from idyllic and unbroken homes, where they were idolized by their parents. They seek (and will go to any lengths to obtain) the same central position, the same applause, the same devout attention in adult life. These things, to use behaviourist language, are their reinforcers. No, actors are not crazy, nor are they compensating for emotional neglect. They are simply reenacting golden childhoods. Remove the reinforcers, however, even temporarily, and what one gets is that other Nicol, sunk in accidie, of whom I've had so many glimpses this past week.

It is worth making the connection that, although Ken may have been damaged by the lie surrounding his birth, he was also at the idolized centre of a golden childhood.

Aged sixteen, he had written to his friend Julian Holland to tell him about hanging out at the Kardomah café in Birmingham, surrounded by his fans: 'Put on my best Welles leer and brusqueness, and succeeded in imposing myself very happily upon them.' Several decades later Ken swooped upon the French word *s'imposer*, claiming that it denoted the ability not just to impose one's will on others but also 'to dictate the conditions – social, moral, sexual, political – within which one can operate with maximum freedom'. (Such a creature, he declared, was Laurence Olivier, to which the actor replied, 'That is the pot calling the kettle quelque chose. More than anyone I know, Ken practises *s'imposer*. He's usually very subtle about it.') An imposer, Ken believed, 'is one about whom you worry whether his response to one's next remark will be a smile or a snarl. You shrink from his scorn and cherish his praise.' And this so-called quality, which Nicol Williamson had, Roman Polanski had in spades.

In spring 1970 the Polish director, who had been a friend for several years, asked Ken to co-adapt *Macbeth* for the screen. It would mark Polanski's return to the cinema after the grievous and brutal murder of his wife Sharon the previous year. Early in May they met in Polanski's West Eaton Place flat for the first script discussions. They agreed that the Macbeths should be young with more to win or lose by putting their future at risk. 'The point about the Macbeths', Ken recorded, as the work progressed,

is that they do not know they are in a tragedy. They think they are in a story that is going to have a triumphantly happy ending. When the witches prophesy that Macbeth will be king, he is filled with exhilaration, like a man who has come into an unexpected fortune. That is the dream. Rushing to fulfil it, the Macbeths encounter the reality of their own natures, which hitherto neither of them knew; and that is the tragedy. ...

There is plenty of evil in the play; and, though he denies it, I suspect that Roman believes in the existence of evil as an active force in the world. Certainly he takes a fairly low view of human motives. So does the script.

I'd expected that I would be mainly concerned with the verbal aspect, and Roman with the visuals. But not at all: he knows the text inside out, and many of the staging ideas are coming from me ... he has a polymath's appetite for knowledge.

When *Macbeth* opened it received excellent reviews in Britain and a mixed response in the States. This tactful, crafted film was not quite what the public had expected. Nudity, financial backing from Hugh Hefner, Ken's association with *Playboy* and Polanski's gory personal saga had led to a rash of salacious press. 'So much has been written and rumoured about the nudity and violence of Polanski's *Macbeth*,' wrote the critic of the *New York Times*, 'that it seems worth insisting that the film is neither especially nude nor unnecessarily violent.'

Ken insisted yet again that *Playboy* remove his name from the masthead. With his debt to the magazine finally cancelled, this misleading liaison was at last ended.

It was not merely Ken's association with *Playboy* which drew such unsavoury publicity upon him, but his connection with *Oh! Calcutta!*, and the promise of its production in London in July 1970. *Private Eye*, who referred to him as a 'bloated voluptuary', delivered themselves of the following parody:

> Now am I grown to Capitalist's estate!
> First did I swear upon the Public Box.
> Then *Oh! Calcutta!* Now I swim in gold.
> O Hefner, tremble, exploiter of bare flesh.
> A greater comes.

The build-up to the London production was even louder and more hysterical than the one that preceded the New York opening. Would the revue be prosecuted by the Attorney-General under the provisions of the Theatres Act of 1968, as depraving and corrupting? Might Ken, as deviser, Michael White, as producer, and Clifford Williams, as director, be arrested? John Mortimer was called in to give legal advice. He had no doubt that a production of *Oh! Calcutta!* would be at serious risk of prosecution, that the average jury might judge the repeated references to oral sex and sado-masochism to be depraving and corrupting; and that if a prosecution were to be launched, the chances of a conviction would be about fifty–fifty.

No theatre would agree to take the show except the manager of a disused railway shed called the Roundhouse, in North London. During rehearsals the vice squad was despatched to keep an eye on proceedings. Elsewhere a battalion of Grundys went to work: Mary Whitehouse, and her Viewers' and Listeners' Association; a moral rearmer called the Dowager Lady Birdwood; and a Tory GLC Councillor called Frank Smith.

Before the show opened, *The Times* published an attack on *Oh! Calcutta!* by Ronald Butt, as the 'sort of exhibition of sexual voyeurism that used to be available to the frustrated and the mentally warped in the side-turnings of a certain kind of sea-port'. Even the description of such a show, he argued, would affect and damage the minds of the young.

During previews and even on the opening night of the show the audience of specially invited influential persons (along with pop stars and other celebrities) were given questionnaires to fill out on whether they deemed the revue liable to 'corrupt and deprave'. Neither the public nor the critics felt threatened.

Four days after the opening, Sir Peter Rawlinson, the Attorney-General, decided on the evidence before him that there was 'no reasonable likelihood that a prosecution would be successful', and accordingly decided that no proceedings should be taken. Councillor Smith announced that the decision was 'a disaster for Britain', while the cast cracked a few bottles of champagne to celebrate.

It was not merely the legal aspect of the London *Oh! Calcutta!* that had caused Ken anxiety since his return to England but also the quality of the revue. He was determined to improve upon the original.

In March, I had written a wifely letter to Hilly Elkins reminding him how brutal to Ken's reputation had been the reception in New York of *Oh! Calcutta!*, and that since its première there had been at least four or five references to Ken and the show in every batch of newsprint that arrived on our doorstep.

I told him that Lord Chandos had let it be known that Ken had been demoted at the National Theatre as a sort of punishment for the sex show. All the more reason, I argued, to reassure Ken that the production standards would be maintained. 'After Italy,' I wrote, 'it looked as if he might get the peace and the self-confidence to start being himself. Now he's too low for it.' It was not beyond possibility, I added, that Ken might suffer a breakdown.

Before the opening night the press heralded the London production as 'the nudest, rudest, most scandalous revue in the world', and Ken's anxiety grew. *Oh! Calcutta!* was not a revolution, he insisted. 'Our attitude to sex is simply one of amusement – thanksgiving, if you like. It is completely traditional theatre.' At the same time he hoped that it would contribute towards the erosion of sexual shame.

Ken's friends believed his sponsorship of *Oh! Calcutta!* was merely naive, since they, needless to say, were already liberated. Jealous journalists saw him 'presiding affluently over a spectacular rape of the theatre by the box office'. The use of the word 'fuck' on television, Ken's campaign against the Lord Chamberlain: were these not merely steps in his nefarious campaign to install an international money-maker?

On 27 July, Clifford Williams' revamping of Jacques Levy's original opened. The 'deviser', looking rather fleshy around the jaw, wore a black shirt and a pale yellow tropical drill suit; his wife was turned out in Thea Porter shot silk.

Several members of the New York original had joined the extremely handsome London cast. Lighting and costumes were of the highest quality. Four new sketches, including one by Ken on the history of underwear, elegantly lit and designed by Allen Jones with costumes inspired by mail-order catalogues, and an outrageous piece by Joe Orton called 'Until She Screams', were added to the menu.

The critics were generally undepraved and uncorrupted. Here was 'a show of our times, and our times make a lot of people nervous'. 'I have seen better revues than *Oh! Calcutta!*,' wrote Irving Wardle of *The Times*, 'but none based on ideas that strike me as more sympathetic. Namely, that the ordinary human body is an object well worth attention: and that there is no reason why the public treatment of sex should not be extended to take in not only lyricism and personal emotion but also the rich harvest of bawdy jokes.' Most critics found the material inferior. Yet nearly everybody agreed that the revue had crashed the sex barrier once and for all: that it was a theatrical breakthrough.

As the show moved from one country to another, new experiments were tried in rehearsal, and more often than not the original model was restored. In the Paris production two excellent sketches by Ionesco were added – one a duel in which the participants slowly undress to reveal that one of them is a woman; the other an undressing by a maid of her mistress (set at the turn of the century) until she has removed glass eye, teeth and wig, while another maid prepares another old lady for youth.

In the States, in 1970, *Calcutta* was filmed and shown in some fifty closed-circuit cinemas. In 1972 the film went on general release. There seemed to be no end to the deals Elkins was making and no end to Ken's suspicions that he would be ripped off.

The stage show moved from Off-Broadway to Broadway, and in London, in the autumn of 1970, it transferred to the Royalty Theatre in the West End. Ken followed its progress like a vigilante, writing to the director and the producer, for example, with a complaint about a certain actor who was misreading and misplaying in 'Suite': 'The point of the number is to demonstrate to deviants that they are not alone and anyone who finds deviations disgusting and offensive certainly does not belong in the number and probably not in the show.'

A sketch called 'Was It Good For You Too?' he described as a shambles. 'Tony's latest contribution is to look at Brenda and say, "See nipples and die." I almost did. Jonathan plays the whole number with his cock hanging out and looked as if he was going to hit me when I suggested he might refrain. At the end he and Tony mimed the act of buggery; this is perhaps the lowest point of the whole evening.'

At the end of 1971 Ken turned to another sex project. The plan, initiated around the time of the opening of *Oh! Calcutta!* in New York, was to put together an anthology of masturbation fantasies by distinguished authors, to be called 'For Myself Alone'. A contract for this dubious idea was drawn up with Grove Press, for which Ken received a first payment of $7,500; and over the course of two years some twelve authors contributed sketches, while a further dozen – among them Alain Robbe-Grillet and Gore Vidal – agreed to take a shot. But the vast number of writers turned Ken down. From Samuel Beckett a curt refusal; from Vladimir Nabokov: 'I have no interest whatever in pornography and cannot imagine myself being titillated by what I write.' From Graham Greene: 'I'm afraid I don't feel like joining this children's game.' From W. H. Auden: 'there are a number of subjects which one does not put into a book, and pornography is one. If written at all, it should be written to amuse one's intimate friends. My objection to pornography in general is that, with very few exceptions, it is Manichaean and anti-sex.' And from Norman Mailer: 'I'd never write to arouse my own sexual impulse. I don't even know if I can wish you well on your book.'

Dominique Aury, the reputed author of *L'Histoire d'O*, wrote to say that the writer 'to whom you are addressing your request through me – if I understand rightly – is altogether out of this creative world. ... If she tried again, she would write trash. Better not.'

In July 1971 Ken wrote to Grove to explain that most of the authors who had agreed to contribute had failed to come through, and those 'few contributions that have actually arrived are lousy'.

Meanwhile, in his role as journalist Ken kept up his public campaign for a free and open attitude towards sex. When the editors of the underground magazine *Oz* were sentenced for obscenity, Ken spoke out: 'Battle has been joined between Judge Argyle's England and a free England. In this battle Richard Neville and his companions are the first prisoners of war.'

To the dozens of journalists who queued at his door, Ken doled out his views. He hoped that sex could be demystified. He deplored the 'no sex without love' nonsense that had caused 'so many generations of adolescents to associate simple physical pleasure with shame and self-disgust'. He told *Playboy* (in an unpublished interview) that whereas monogamy happened to work for him, for many of his friends it was sheer torture. He saw no reason why it should be eternal.

In declaring his political views Ken remained consistently, idiosyncratically himself, usually arriving at a position out of strong emotional response. His disillusion with the British two-party system did not stop him fighting hard against Britain's entry into the Common Market, which he viewed hysterically as the 'greatest historical vulgarity since Hitler's 1000-year Reich'.

In the underground magazine *Ink* he tackled the subject of the press and its Conservative bias, advising his youthful readers:

When everyone talks about life style, talk about life content. ... The British don't need coercion by secret police or torture chambers: in most cases the mere threat of disapproval is enough to deter them from anti-Establishment opinions or activities. ... What distinguishes the true Socialist from the true Tory? Answer: his *fury* when poor or underprivileged people are prevented from full enjoyment of their lives. No Tory feels this fury. Nurture it.

Since 1968 Ken had been keeping sporadic notes in the form of a journal. From 1970 until his death, he kept a more elaborately worked journal of his thoughts – less didactic and over-simplified than those offered to the public. Herein he recorded his theatre criticism and his political views, and explored metaphysical questions.

Here the retired drama critic set down his complicated and contradictory views on the work of Harold Pinter. 'Harold Pinter *has* a theme, I reflect. It is: The betrayal and spoliation of innocence and purity. *Vide:* the abduction of the hero in *The Birthday Party*, the electric shocks applied to Aston in *The Caretaker*, the erosion performed by time upon the pure romantic memories of the wife in *Landscape* and the husband in *Old Times.*'

But Pinter was also too involved with the minor emotional crises of the middle class. Ken wrote: 'Disturbed by sudden, widespread praise (in the narrative arts) of the smooth vis-à-vis the hairy. Discretion, tact, restraint, kid gloves, the snaffle and the bit with no sign of the bloody horse – these are the virtues presently being acclaimed.'

While Ken's public voice expressed a confident point of view, and an occasionally irritating rectitude, his private voice – recorded in the journals – was one of self-doubt and self-criticism. Writing became more difficult, as fringe activities pulled him apart. In 1971 he wrote: 'I used to take Dexamyl to give me enough confidence to start work. Now I take it to give me enough confidence not to.'

To his journal he committed the following:

I disbelieve in art because I no longer believe that there is a secret something inside me which, when properly expressed, will take on a higher reality and deserve the name of 'art'. What I do believe is simply that a good painting makes you see what I (the painter) saw; and a good book makes you experience what I (the author) experienced. The best books are works of personal testimony – letters, reportage, intimate biography, autobiography. But they are merely reflections of events, they do not express an 'inner reality'.

The journal was not only a place to argue with himself but a record of self-exploration. With his growing feeling for privacy, 'for string quartets, small jazz groups, dinner parties of no more than six people', he had become a committed chamber musician; just as in the public arena he was becoming a parlour politician rather than an activist. 'All the applause I need is supplied in my private life,' he wrote. But in his private life, he admitted, there were pitfalls. To have to debate the desirability of a work project with a spouse was strong counsel against matrimony. 'The decision to *do* must be singly taken.'

32

Change

Excavating the past by means of our separate journals, I pick up small signals of marital discord, as natural to an intense and lengthy union as our continued intense and romantic monogamy was unrealistic (I hesitate to say unnatural).

Observers entered our drawing-room and found a settled domestic scene. A three-year-old being read to. Chamber music. An Abyssinian kitten along with several grown cats. Tracy on a visit, her last year at school, slim and pretty, with straight brown hair, on her way to Sussex University to read social anthropology. 'Is she really interested in social work,' Ken wonders, 'or is that an escape?' 'Needs more confidence and clarity,' he notes, 'but she's marvellous all the same.'

Alan Beesley, our 'intergalactic hobo', tears in. He brings a new plan for a series of travel books called 'Before It's Too Late'. Spring 1970 turns into summer, friends turn up to drink and talk, and it is always the early hours of the morning before we bid the last guest farewell and go downstairs to call the cats in.

As Roxana grew older, Ken penned a series of poems for her in honour of the feline, one of which celebrated my corralling cry:

> If you were a cat, wouldn't you hasten
> To come to a call so wild and high,
> That woke the echoes, that rode the sky,
> That made you feel an important beast,
> As big as an elephant, at the least:
> Especially if you knew that she
> Loved you as much as herself – and me.

We were rarely apart. I went to Venice to write about the director Luchino Visconti; Ken to New York on a work mission, from where he cabled 'Terribly miss the touch of you my only love.'

We went with Roxana to Rome during the summer of 1970 (our seventh summer together) and on to the Costa Smeralda in Sardinia, to share a house with Joan Axelrod and her daughter Nina. I recall a visit to Corsica. I remember some harsh rows between us. I recall how mutually dependent we were, one upon the other. At one point during the summer, separated for the space of a day due to faulty travel plans, Ken scribbled inside the book he was reading: 'The sensation of vanishing. Nothing registers on me: I register nothing. Hunger wanes, thirst does not exist. A shadow, I sit in shadows. And wait. For her, my source, my current, my light, my darkness, my dear.' He tore out that note and kept it.

If my influence upon Ken was to turn this unlikely candidate into a monogamist, to turn him inwards and away from public life, his influence on me was to encourage – though hardly initiate – my taste in party-giving, an easy first step towards self-expression.

In March 1971 I gave a party for Jean-Louis Barrault, his wife Madeleine Renaud, the then French Ambassador the Baron de Courcel and his wife, Martine, Ingrid Bergman, Laurence Olivier and Joan Plowright, Ron Kitaj, Roman Polanski and assorted others.

'No more parties,' Ken now begged of me. 'Let's just have a few people to dinner.' Asked to dinner, one evening at George Weidenfeld's, he found himself sitting down with fifty others. 'A tiring rout,' Ken wrote in his journal, 'made doubly so by the additional hordes who poured in after dinner, making it necessary to talk standing up, a thing I hate to do after about 10.30. Seeing Cyril [Connolly] prompted me to rephrase his most famous aphorism: inside every Weidenfeld soirée a dinner party of 8 people is wildly signalling to be let out.'

Meanwhile, in the way of marriage, complaints were registered. Ken noted in his engagement book any evidence, however flimsy, of my disloyalty in an argument with a third party. He complained of my public *pudeur*, my reticence, my lack of enthusiasm. 'KH decides she can't go' (to a performance of *Macbeth*). 'After all,' he quotes me, 'it isn't anything serious – it's a *play!*' And in September 1970: 'On return from dinner – after rapturous pre-dinner fuck – KH forbids me to play my [word] game with [friends]. Me – the believer in *Homo Ludens* – forbidden to play games!!!! This is an encroachment I cannot bear!!' 'KH', whose character was stronger than she knew, had fallen, by way of wifely solidarity, into the role of mother–arbiter, personifying the twin evils of prohibition *and* encroachment.

A few days after this entry in his diary Ken records: 'K says "From now on I want to get up at 8.30 a.m. You must stop trampling on me." ' But on the same day this New Woman records, in *her* diary, the joys of walking hand in hand with her mate through Oxford's Botanical Gardens.

My wish to work, not merely to continue in freelance journalism but to try fiction, prompted the declaration that I would thereafter rise at 8.30 a.m. My wish to share in the ownership of our house caused a further confrontation. Prudence and property had intruded.

There was first the question of Ken's study, which he found uncongenial for work. Why had I not made available a better room? 'How could you fail to see that this was a matter of life and death for me? How could you hesitate and haggle and complain and shrug as if I was a Pakistani immigrant trying to rent an attic in Wolverhampton?' (This just complaint was written after I had failed to make the dining-room his.)

And not long after, I wrote to him – as was our custom when things were out of hand. We had been offered a fifty-five-year extension to the lease of our house, which had twelve years to go. I argued for extension, and for security; Ken for mobility and liquid money. He quoted Samuel Butler's line: 'A brigand demands your money *or* your life; a woman demands both.' While I insisted that I was a partner, Ken riposted that I was a kept woman. 'This shocks her to tears,' Ken recorded in his journal. 'She says she has never before realised that she was "kept" in the Victorian sense. I cannot believe that, as a supporter (like me) of Women's Lib, she is so naive.'

My letter, which evidently followed the tears, and our decision to go ahead and extend the lease, focused on Ken's refusal to put the house in our joint names. I argued that I had no desire to be involved in his finances, only in sharing the ownership of our house, and that my domestic services were of some worth. 'I believe', I told him, 'that maybe you have reacted this way because you feel under siege because you have been so constantly attacked these last few years. But that I should be the one that receives the burden of your reaction is just daft.' At which point my letter took a sharp turn to the subject of my head and heart that autumn: Germaine Greer.

Something of an Uncle Tom in the field of women's liberation, I was sympathetic though not engaged. I had read Betty Friedan, dropped in to a local women's lib group, protested dutifully, at parties, for equal pay. Then I read *The Female Eunuch* and my eyes were opened. Here was the explanation for my own half-realized discontent. Marriage, however privileged and protectionist, was turning me into that 'vain, demanding, servile bore' about whom Greer wrote with such fury. I heavily underscored the following: 'Woman must have room and scope to devise a morality which does not disqualify her from excellence, and a psychology which does not condemn her to the status of a spiritual cripple.' With a frisson of terror and delight I read that the penalties for such delinquency might be terrible, that I would be alone on this journey, and in the dark.

I went out and interviewed Germaine. What impressed me in this handsome, large, raucous woman was the patient pedagogue. I would hear her argue with Ken calmly and fearlessly; between them there was never a possibility of flirtation. They admired each other's intelligence (and possibly each other's celebrity), and they could make each other laugh. It was Germaine's tone of voice, her boldness, her sexual risk-taking that impressed me even more than her radical arguments, though the two aspects appeared indivisible. Was I circumscribed by the institution of marriage, or hypnotized by romantic love? Was there an alternative happiness? Perhaps not. But I had – we had – to 'retrieve our power of invention', unleash our particular female energy on a world badly in need of it.

Looking back, two aspects of Germaine still impress me: her insistence that reform was not good enough – that we needed not to imitate men but to effect a revolutionary change in our social structure. I was also moved by this earth mother with a mission *not* designed to please: here was the Miss Jean Brodie of the sexual revolution (she used to tell the girls whom she first taught: 'A teacher is yours to plunder').

The love that forms communities was what she prized, rather than my beloved *égoïsme à deux*. Years later I have still failed her, escaped not at all from the 'treadmill of sexual fantasy, voracious need of love, and obsessiveness in all its forms' which she so disparagingly condemned. Now re-reading *The Female Eunuch* – a 'free', self-supporting woman – I find it sadly inadequate. Yet I must thank her for raising my expectations and challenging me to explore. In some sense (and to explain this detour from my subject's story) Germaine and feminism helped me to move away from Ken. As for Ken's attitude to the movement, he approved in principle and in practice not at all.

He loathed to have to explain himself, as Germaine points out: 'He liked to keep his touch light.' She saw that he disliked falsification, that he liked to be clear and sharp, but his patience in argument would run out long before hers. 'I liked him very much. I liked him too much to play games with him. I thought he was one of the best minds of his time and I thought he frittered it away because he was seduced by his own loathing of tedium.'

Some time after my first encounter with Germaine Greer I backed a women's lib magazine called *Spare Rib*, and became casually involved in other women's projects. One evening, early in 1973, berated by his daughter Tracy and a leader of the women's movement, Ken retreated to write the following: 'After three hours of this strident nit-picking I slink off to bed. Their need to attack me is, of course, identical with the tribal assault traditionally launched by the sons of the chief: the king must die. What is sad is that new women should turn out to be no more than old Adams writ large. (But perhaps if I were not so prominent a figure, they would be gentler with me.)'

At the beginning of 1970, Ken returned to the National Theatre to share his old job with Derek Granger. He had been demoted, to placate the Chairman, to 'Literary Consultant', but in effect he continued with business as usual as if his kind and uncompetitive cohort did not exist.

Ken sought out new plays from Václav Havel, Tom Stoppard, Trevor

Griffiths, Peter Nichols, Michael Weller and Eugène Ionesco. He got Olivier enthused over a projected production of *Guys and Dolls*, which Garson Kanin would direct and in which Olivier would play Nathan Detroit. He also argued that whereas it was important to find enticing parts for valuable company members, 'We are getting into the habit of placing this aim above that of finding the plays we ought to be doing.'

The theatre overall was in good shape. The previous autumn Ken had been responsible for introducing Michael Blakemore, who came to direct Peter Nichols' *The National Health*. He had also persuaded Olivier to employ Jonathan Miller to direct *The Merchant of Venice*. Before the opening night Ken wrote to Olivier to thank him for giving 'by far the best performance of Shylock I've ever seen', and for the privilege of watching this performance take shape. 'The man at the beginning is a businessman first and foremost, only secondarily a Jew. When the Christians steal his daughter, he begins to realise what it means to be Jewish, and by the end of the trial he knows it through and through – so indelibly that no-one in the theatre will ever forget it.'

Other critically acclaimed productions that spring included Gaskill's *The Beaux' Stratagem* and Ingmar Bergman's *Hedda Gabler*. In both plays Maggie Smith gave great performances. But by the summer the theatre's good fortune changed. Olivier came down with pneumonia, and suffered a mild thrombosis; and his services as an actor were lost to the Cambridge Theatre, which had been taken to expand the company's work in preparation for the new building.

Both in his testy memos to Olivier and in his record of events in his journal, Ken was expressing a growing grievance with Olivier's leadership. He was not prepared to be 'one of a dozen planets circling round a dying sun', and he pushed with eventual success for Dexter and Blakemore to be made associate directors. On a small matter of a programme note about prostitution, contributed by Germaine Greer for Shaw's *Mrs Warren's Profession*, Ken complained in a memo about the censorship of four-letter words; and in his journal he wrote: '[Larry] calls Germaine and gets her to change "fucking" to "sexual intercourse". "I blamed myself, Kennie, I told her you had shouted at me. I said it was my fault." "Yes," I said, "but you employ me and I put up with it." G.G.'s reaction must be to think me a weakling. I can imagine her amused pity.'

If Olivier's usually strong leadership seemed unsteady, his illness offered a sympathetic excuse. During this winter he also had to put up with the singular antics of a young French–South American director called Victor Garcia, who had been brought in by Ken to direct Fernando Arrabal's *The Architect and the Emperor of Assyria*.

Olivier had gone through the text marking 200 passages that disturbed or offended him. On meeting Garcia he had said, 'Cher Maître, there are just a few things I'd like to ask you about the play ...' At that, the five-foot director with frizzy black hair and an ochre face stepped forward, took the script from

Olivier between thumb and forefinger, and dropped it into the wastepaper-basket. 'Sir Laurence,' he said, 'I detest literature. I abominate the theatre. I have a horror of culture. I am only interested in magic!' Patiently Olivier pursued his case: 'There's a scene towards the end where the Architect *eats* the Emperor. How do you intend to stage that?' 'Sir Laurence,' replied Garcia, 'I *could* tell you; but it would scare the shit out of you; so I will *not* tell you.'

The result of this near-disaster was a generally poor press. The play was followed by a popular production of Carl Zuckmayer's *The Captain of Kopenick*, with Paul Scofield, under the direction of Frank Dunlop; and an excellent ensemble version of Heywood's *A Woman Killed with Kindness* directed by John Dexter. Thereafter, however, and until the following December, the National mounted no major successes.

Of the less well received ventures, Ken was most closely associated with *Tyger* by Adrian Mitchell. This was a 'celebration' based on the life and work of William Blake, a story of his survival as a man and an artist 'in a festering society'. The author's idea was that Blake spoke to 'our world as clearly and radically as any man alive', and he tried to demonstrate this with songs, Blakean paintings and illuminations, in an episodic structure like a 'cranky panto'.

By May 1971, with the play in rehearsal under the joint direction of John Dexter and Michael Blakemore, Ken was already fighting against the censorship of seditious sentiment and randy references. When Olivier sought Lord Chandos' approval of the text, Ken argued fiercely that he had no need to do so. 'Nor will I let him intimidate and unnerve dear good-natured Adrian,' wrote Ken in his journal. 'Of course *all* the disputed lines are not *necessary*: but "reason not the *need*" – they are Adrian's, they are part of his play, and they must be included. The supreme irony is that the play deals precisely with the way in which England and the Establishment try to gag and castrate their revolutionary poets.'

On the 11th *Tyger* had its first musical read-through and Ken wept shamelessly at Mike Westbrook's setting of Mitchell's song 'The Children of Blake' and predicted a triumph. When *Tyger* opened, it was described as 'a mess', the music 'unmemorable', a 'sprawling hotch-potch', though also as 'a real celebration' and 'the most ground-breaking entertainment staged at the National since its inception'. The directors knew that the play would have done much better in a smaller theatre than the New, and with a less expensive and overloaded production.

During rehearsals of the next National production of Büchner's *Danton's Death*, directed by Jonathan Miller, neither Olivier nor Ken was hopeful of a success. 'Four flops in a row. Now they'll *have* to ask me to go,' Olivier declared. 'It was not entirely in jest,' Ken noted in his journal: 'Larry's torpid fatalism is exactly like Danton's: he ruminates and reminisces as the hatchet-men gather in the shadows. And always, at the back of his mind, is the unspoken thought which Danton actually utters: "They'll never *dare*." '

In the autumn of 1971, Lord Chandos was asked to step down from the position of Chairman of the Board. This was as a result of Olivier's complaints (to Lord Goodman of the Arts Council and to the Minister for the Arts, Jennie Lee) that they could no longer work together. Chandos was replaced by Sir Max Rayne, a businessman with a strong commitment to the arts. Olivier immediately offered to step down, to which Rayne replied that he hoped Olivier would stay long enough to lead the company into the new building.

During this time, Ken was busy fending off press criticism of the National. While admitting errors, he insisted that there was 'nothing wrong that a couple of hits would not cure'. Behind the scenes he was more troubled. On 9 December he wrote to Olivier complaining that, while willing to put up a public front, he was not enthusiastic about the play opening that very night, Goldsmith's *The Good-Natur'd Man*; that he had opposed *Cyrano, The Idiot, Mrs Warren's Profession, The Rules of the Game* and Olivier's interpretation of *Amphitryon 38*. He admitted, however, that he had supported two other flops of the recent past including the Arrabal play.

But the real burden of his letter was to complain urgently about the weakness of the company, which he felt could not succeed in any programme of plays. He suggested a cutback to about fifteen actors, and building from there. This missile fell into Olivier's lap on the first dress rehearsal of Eugene O'Neill's *Long Day's Journey into Night*, in which the Director had reluctantly agreed to play James Tyrone, after intense pressure from Ken (he thought the play boring and hated the idea of playing an actor – particularly a drunken actor). Not surprisingly under such pressure, and barely recovered from illness, Olivier exploded over Ken's insensitivity to his anxieties of the moment. Ken apologized for his timing. A week before the opening, he wrote of the Blakemore production: '*Long Day's Journey*, as all four of you are playing it, emerges as a masterpiece of so many kinds that I stopped counting. At various moments it looks like (a) the best American play, (b) the best Irish play, (c) the best *Greek* play, (d) the best family play, (e) the best Freudian play and (f) the best Marxist play ever written. Thanks forever for doing it.' And he added a postscript: 'What an irony that that poor devastated man spent 30 years writing grandiose pseudo-tragic plays when all the time the great play he had it in him to write was about how his family made him precisely the sort of poor, devastated man who would spend 30 years writing grandiose pseudo-tragic plays! (I *think* that's what I mean ...)'

In February 1972, misinterpreting the intent of Ken's original letter, Olivier wrote a long reply, providing a list of the theatre's repertoire to date, and giving credit where credit was due. But what Ken had asked for was not more status or more money but to have his job recognized for what it was. 'At present I am something betwixt and between [Literary Manager and Literary Consultant] which allows my enemies to attack me for holding a sinecure when the NT is doing well and to blame the whole of our artistic policy on me when the NT is doing badly.'

Olivier replied: 'No, I am sorry, there is nothing I can do until I have had a talk with the Chairman as he has refused any discussion on any such matter until I have a very long, as he calls it, relaxed talk with him. If that sentence doesn't bear with it the sound of an axe on the grinding stone I don't know what does.' On the whole Olivier did not think the Board would agree to a change: 'It was only by claiming that Consultants were within my gift, and not the Board's, that I managed to keep you on, and then only if I had another one besides yourself.'

Long Day's Journey into Night was a huge popular and critical success, badly needed after the previous season, during which the theatre had lost £80,791. The O'Neill was followed, by another successful production, Tom Stoppard's new play *Jumpers*, with Michael Hordern and Diana Rigg, a complicated, witty, intellectual whodunnit with a large cast. At the first preview the piece was in dire trouble. Ken went to work suggesting cuts and transpositions; questioning, clarifying and trying to keep the energy going. A couple of weeks after the opening Stoppard delivered a decanter to Ken with a generous note which read, 'It comes with love, thanks, and a sincere appreciation of your influence on *Jumpers* in those last days. It is s.r.o. [standing room only] and ... it would not have got there I think without your intervention.'

Four months later Ben Hecht's and Charles MacArthur's *The Front Page* opened in Blakemore's marvellous production. 'A gigantic hit,' Ken noted in his journal, 'following my earlier choices, *Long Day's Journey* and *Jumpers*, to make a Tynan grand slam. Larry sees me backstage after the curtain,' he added with pathetic gratitude, 'and proffers personal thanks.'

33

An Erotic Scenario

In 1970 Roman Polanski had suggested to Ken that he write an erotic movie for Polanski to direct. Ken took the idea to heart and began, during 1970 and 1971, to make notes and to sketch out scenarios. He consulted his own experience: loss of virginity at seventeen, elaborate sexual charade to avoid military call-up, girl seduced on the Pan Am jet, pornographic *Lehrstück* (a play he had composed in the manner of a sexual catechism), the need to masturbate before writing. But he soon abandoned personal experience and settled on fantasy: 'The main point', he wrote in a first outline, 'is the basic combination of characters in an isolated, enclosed setting – two girls and a man, a Mediterranean villa, an atmosphere of secrecy and slightly decadent sensuality – all of which I think works better if the girl is being "corrupted" in a period setting.' He introduced young girls, maids, strict governesses and a setting *circa* 1900. Next he worked on a drop-out scenario. A married man with children gives up his family, meets a girl and escapes to the suburbs of a city where he co-opts a second girl. 'They achieve a perfect trio. ... Film shd. act out every man's dream that if he had power over 2 girls life would be a painless process. ... He decides to reject everything that isn't part of the erotic life. His argument: he is mature enough now not to need to work, or to need power. Everything in his life has become a function of sex.' Does this bring happiness? Ken asked, and answered with an aphorism that has the ring of a personal confession: 'I know one thing. *Happiness* doesn't bring happiness. (He was happily married.)'

For a while the villa scenario was abandoned in favour of 'Skinflick in Ten Takes', a scenario of multiple choices, with a hero who is charming, blundering and romantic, and a heroine 'ideal for him'. 'We should desperately want them to end up together; and if they don't we should suffer.'

On the weekend of Friday 12 February 1971 we went to Hamburg with Joan and George Axelrod. There we ate *Hummer*, *Krabbe* and venison, and drank Rhine wine. And there Ken gave George and me (for Joan had wisely decided to keep out of the wind blowing off the Elbe) a guided tour of the Hagenbeck Zoo. So concentrated on his maps and guides was he, as he conducted us from one area to the next, describing the animals and throwing in 'occasional ad libs about their Latin names', as George recalls, that we had not the heart to tell him that there were no animals in the zoo; they had evidently been removed for the winter.

The Reeperbahn, however, was alive and populated with coupling couples – our first view of sex on stage. In one club Ken noted: 'A girl lies down naked, feet to the audience, and then raises her splayed legs over her head. She then inserts two lighted candles into her cunt and bumhole. Bagpipe music is then heard and a kilted Scot enters with a cigar which he proceeds to light at the vaginal candle. He then exits and the bagpipes fade. *Why is he Scots?'*

We were particularly impressed by the stamina of one beatific-looking young man and by the effort of an inventive girl, naked but for a pair of socks. Also impressed was our friend Warren Beatty, who happened to be shooting a film in Hamburg, and thought to check out the Reeperbahn. He had the temerity, or the charm, to go backstage and ask the girl in socks (who turned out to be Scots, like the bagpiper) whether she was ever excited by her work. 'The day I come,' answered this haughty professional in a broad Glaswegian accent, 'I quit!'

During our weekend, Ken found, in a local bookshop, an erotic novel of 'no redeeming literary merit' but useful to his purpose, a contemporary story about a man and wife who capture and sexually coerce two girls; and on our return to London he set to work to write a synopsis. Polanski was not overly enthusiastic about the result. He said he wanted to make a film about love as well as sex, and Ken decided thenceforth both to write and direct the script for a young producer called Andrew Braunsberg, and for an option of £500, the budget not to exceed £150,000.

My response to this new project was twofold. I liked not at all its subject, and was fearful that, if produced, the film – good or bad – would throw Ken back into another maelstrom of publicity. On the other hand, here was a chance for Ken to direct (in my view, what he most needed to do), to take the driver's seat and to leave the National, where his labour and influence were so frustratingly unrewarded.

That spring, however, this conflict hardly impinged upon me. I was heavily pregnant, and thereby protected against anxiety; no woman enjoyed being pregnant more than I. Late in March we rented Emma Tennant's thatched cottage called Teasel, near Salisbury, overlooking a quiet loop of the river .Avon. Roxana recovered there from chickenpox, and picked daffodils in the raw spring sunshine. Ken listened to his new recordings of Haydn's Prussian quartets. Only the sound of a Bartok piece, he noted, in this pigeon-cooing *douceur*, spoke 'distantly of conflict and unease'. I cooked shepherd's pie, steak and kidney pudding, sausages and mash: all the brown things that Ken liked, served with gravy and splashings of Lea and Perrin's Worcestershire sauce.

We lunched with Cecil Beaton, who lived nearby, and noted how well he had endured, how prepared he was, as a solitary homosexual – unlike married couples – for age. As we left he urged us to work, 'Tap, tap, tap, like woodpeckers.' A few days later he came to lunch with us, wearing a mouth-watering combination of velvets, corduroys and silks. Another guest was Edna O'Brien, who came to stay, walked to Stonehenge as on a pilgrimage, and there wrote a poem in honour of its ghosts.

On 4 April Ken wrote in his journal: 'Living a mile from Stonehenge, near the heart of Old Albion, and the places of Arthur, I again come across the books of C. S. Lewis – on sale in Salisbury Cathedral. I read *That Hideous Strength* and once more the old tug reasserts itself – a tug of genuine war with my recent self. How thrilling he makes goodness seem – how tangible and radiant! But what problems he raises! . . . the film Andy Braunsberg wants me to write and – greatest, most consummate of temptations – to *direct* has an erotic and anally sadistic theme. To do this work may well be a wicked act. Am I being tempted with sin, or tested with the chance of committing myself to responsible work?'

Back in London shades of C. S. Lewis, and sin, dissolved, and he decided to write the erotic screenplay. To work in peace, outside the cocoon of domestic life, he took off for a hotel, the Château de Meyrargues, some ten miles north of Aix-en-Provence. Here he completed the first half hour of his scenario. Two hitchhikers, Sally and Nicole, are picked up in southern France by an Englishman, Alex, driving a Mercedes. He recognizes them as cocaine smugglers wanted by the police, questions them about their lives and offers them refuge in his nineteenth-century château. Here they are welcomed by an Indochinese butler called Lee, and led to a book-lined room whose window is barred. Meanwhile we cut to Alex in the sumptuous bedroom of his wife Sophie, 'Attractive, in her mid-thirties, slight French accent'. On the walls are erotic paintings, and out of the stereo comes a Bach suite for unac-companied cello. Sophie is reading Cocteau. Alex tells his wife he has brought her two girls, 'ideal candidates, but in need of polish'. 'Shall I start them in the usual way?' asks Sophie.

Thereafter there is a lot of sexual tuition, some rewards, some mild pun-ishment, while Lee serves *toast de crevettes* and Montrachet '52. Jokes are occasionally cracked, the tone of the proceedings remains light, even while the dialogue sounds arch. Sophie, we are told, is a radical and an optimist who has sold out to the soft life; Alex, a pessimist and a conservative who is usually extremely happy. He tells his guests that he does not wish to fuck them; that he is interested in ownership and control: 'What I do is to practise in my private life what my father practised in business' (wherein one may recognize a personal confession).

Two quotations echo Ken's own voice: 'You see, there are sadists and sadists. I belong to the largest and commonest class – the ones who cannot bear the thought of bloodshed. We are to the guards of Auschwitz what the pot smoker is to the heroin addict. And in fact I have never heard of anyone graduating from the hair-brush and cane to the thumbscrew and rack.' Later on Alex tells one of his now willing victims: 'I find it's always safer to make people dislike me than let them hurt me.'

The two girls are offered the choice of staying, and submitting, or leaving and fending for themselves. They choose to stay. Quite soon this odd foursome are busy making a home movie of their antics.

Re-reading 'Alex and Sophie' (as it was eventually entitled), I am as unreliable a reporter now as I was all those years back: my evidence, my voice is suspect. I can argue that the sex is not particularly shocking, the antics not extreme, nor the scenario boring. In fact it is rich material, considered by some who read it to be brilliant. Is my profound dislike of it to do with my own dignity – or worse, vanity? Was I more sexually excited by it than I would admit; or did I simply feel guilty for having tried to suppress it? Forcing truth a little further, was the film merely a symptom, writ large, of unearthed dissatisfaction between us? These questions are relevant only because of the horrible consequences set off by this project in my life with Ken.

How can I unravel the puppet master who created Alex – himself a puppet pulled by his own compulsions – and the Ken whose voice comes to me so movingly in a letter from Meyrargues, while he was working on that very script? From Provence, in May, he asks: 'What am I doing here churning out pornography? It is very shaming. I shall try to do it with a will but truly I question whether I should do it at all. I look out over this still and God-bitten countryside and feel pampered and trivial. ... Should I not forget Andy Pandar? Advise me my darling, and take and hold all my love for ever.'

I wrote without addressing his question but rather with little pieces of domestic news and closed, 'I wait for your voice on the telephone, or a letter, and most of all for you, my love.'

A further letter from Ken read:

It is after dinner and the mistral once more rattles my roof; but I think it explains the fits of accidie that beset me so often when I should be working. Nathanael West once wrote: 'I need women and, because I can't buy or force them, I have to make poems'. ... But I do not. ...

Some gleanings from Auden's commonplace book: ... 'A tom will remain playful until he is quite old; but even in play his face never loses the gravity that is stamped on it' (Colette). And:

> Meekly smiling with her mouth,
> And merry in her lookes,
> Ever laughing for love –

from an anonymous mediaeval man who somehow glimpsed you.

I look out over the black valley and have gloomy night-thoughts about the soul. Perhaps those who die unbelieving really *do* die as atheists imagine it – like the switching off of a light – while only those who have achieved the hard miracle of belief achieve the greater miracle of resurrection? That seems fair to me, but I am just as far from belief. I type this letter however knowing that God may be watching and may give me a mark or two for trying, or at least caring, or at least seeming to care, or at least for being humble enough to confess to mere seeming. ...

Don't be surprised or censorious if I suddenly come home. Could we meet perhaps at Teazel Cottage – perhaps on Monday? I'm serious – call me – working in a total vacuum is airless work, bad for the spiritual lungs, literally uninspiring.

On 9 June 1971 at 3.30 in the afternoon I gave birth in Westminster Hospital to a son weighing 7 lb 3½ oz. He had a finely shaped head, and turned out to be a noticing, uncomplaining, altogether model baby. We called him Matthew, after my father, and Blake, after William Blake; and gave him Edna O'Brien, Pamela Harlech and Alan Beesley as godparents.

Ken brought to the hospital the gift of a cassette recording of one of Adrian Mitchell's songs from *Tyger*, then in rehearsal. In collusion with the National Theatre's stage manager, he had persuaded the actress, and the band, to record the song, thereby sending the director, John Dexter, into a caterwaul of professional rage; it was about the only time Ken ever took advantage of his post.

The words of the song, not Adrian's finest but moving nonetheless, went:

> The children of Blake dance in their thousands
> Over nursery meadows and through the sinister forests,
> Beyond the spikes of cities, over the breasts of mountains,
> The children of Blake dance in their thousands.
> They dance beyond logic, they dance beyond silence,
> They are dancers, they are only dancers,
> And every atom of their minds and hearts and their deep skins
> And every atom of their bowels and genitals and imaginations
> Dance to the music of William Blake.

Later that night Ken wrote in his journal: 'I had thought I could sire only girls and rather wanted a third. ... What I feared was a husky thug of a boy: I do not like male competition – in fact I am not all that crazy about men *per se* – so I was much relieved to find that Matthew is sensitive, resembles Roxana when she was born. ... K is positively glowing with earth-motherliness. She has always wanted a boy and now she *has* one. I begin to feel almost superfluous. The problem about this second child will not be that *Roxana* may feel overshadowed, but that *I* may – a situation of which Freud had omitted to warn me.'

34

End of Summer

Early in February 1972, Ken and I set off for Egypt, having ascertained that Luxor was the warmest place within striking distance of Europe: time in the sun would be a guarantee against the dread winter cold that, in England, inevitably struck, and lingered on Ken's chest for months. Our trip began with a swift visit to the pyramids near Cairo, before flying to Luxor to stay at the Old Winter Palace.

The dry pure air cleansed Ken's lungs and within days he was slim, brown and healthy. In the mornings he worked on his film script. In the afternoons we plunged into the temples of Karnak and the Valley of the Kings, Ken noting 'like the Frenchman Denon who came here with Napoleon's army in 1798, a terrible lack of theatres, arenas, *pleasure-domes*. It is a humourless, monolithically ceremonial civilisation. But of an ordered beauty, a hierarchical span linking peasant with sun-god, that casts a very deep spell.' He rejoiced in the wall paintings of the nobles' tombs, celebrations of materialism – of flesh, fish, fowl, sunlight and lotus blossom.

We hired a boatman, a young Nubian called Mukhta Ali, to pole us slowly up the Nile in his felucca, past date and banana groves, and women filling their water bottles at the river bank. We moored near his mud village, where Ali cooked for us pigeons stuffed with rice and herbs, and shared with us a pipe of hashish.

If he had to choose, Ken said, between this Nile-side life and that of a Lancashire factory worker, 'compensated as he is by more money, entertainment and mobility for the appalling weather', he would be hard-pressed. To our boatman he put the question, 'When you see a rich man, with a big house and two cars, are you angry?' Mukhta grinned and answered, 'Angry, yes. Very angry.' As a socialist Ken felt reassured, though he refrained from pointing out that he had a big house and two cars.

After this brief skirmish with his political conscience we skimmed slowly towards Luxor. The sunlight had turned white. A white ibis floated overhead, and a kingfisher arched, descending vertically on the river. All anxiety was vanquished and Ken was content. Luxor, he pronounced, would be the next sacrifice on the altar of tourism.

Back in Cairo we visited the great museum, still full of sandbags from the Six-Day War, and we installed ourselves at the Omar Khayyam, a dreadful hotel full of trip wires for its guests. Ken developed the theory of how a good *soi-disant* socialist country like Egypt had co-opted its hotels to disorient and finally purify the bourgeoisie: if we asked for tomato soup, pea soup turned up. Haut Brion 1949, advertised on the menu, turned out to be old malt. 'Take an Egyptian wine, sir,' said the wine waiter. 'It's fresher.'

One night we were taken to the desert by a rich young hippie and his friends for a party in a tent. Outside, the desert dogs howled; inside, a fat boy belly-danced while we sat cross-legged in the sand and tried to chew tough bits of charcoaled lamb. The guest list was made up of *le tout* Cairo, so we were told, and *le tout* Cairo was eager to know why the men in *Oh! Calcutta!* did not have erections. No answer was forthcoming and they looked at Ken suspiciously.

In the spring we were once more *en vacances*, embarked on a tour of the châteaux of the Loire, of Amboise, Azay-le-Rideau, Ussé, Villandry, Chambord and Talcy; and a week's *grande bouffe*. On 10 April, while dining with Pierre and Nicole Salinger at Montoire-sur-le-Loire, an emergency telephone call came through for Ken from his assistant Rozina Adler: someone had leaked to the *Observer* newspaper that Peter Hall had been appointed Olivier's successor. Ken at once telephoned Olivier, who told him that several weeks before he had been summoned by the Chairman, Sir Max Rayne, and told – for the first time – that the Board had decided on Hall. Olivier had been asked to keep quiet until the negotiations were complete. Ken expressed his chagrin that neither he nor his colleagues John Dexter and Michael Blakemore had been consulted. He had already put forward Blakemore as a possible successor to Olivier and did not welcome Peter Hall.

Having cut short his holiday and returned to London, he contacted one of the Board members, John Mortimer, who told him that he had been under the impression that the artistic directorate had been consulted. Next Ken tracked down Dexter and Blakemore, both abroad at the time, and both outraged by the news and the lack of consultation. Then he set to work to mount some sort of counter-offensive. But his almost lone battle was fought too late, and without sufficient ammunition, to change the day.

At the root of the matter was Olivier's refusal to solve – or even seriously consider – the problem of his succession. When he had addressed himself to it, he had always proposed an actor. Sounded out by Lord Chandos, he came up with Albert Finney and Richard Attenborough as possible contenders for his title. Joan Plowright recalls that at one dinner in Brighton, with Elizabeth

Taylor and Richard Burton, 'he offered the entire National Theatre to Richard between the soup and the fish. In his cups.'

Olivier argues that for the last five years of his reign he *was* concerned with the succession, and to this end he denied himself his dearest wish, which was to direct, in order that others might be tested for future leadership. The fledgling director he most passionately wished to succeed him was his wife. He still believes she would have made an excellent leader, in the tradition of other ladies of the theatre, like Lilian Baylis and Helene Weigel. Joan Plowright thinks otherwise. She was not Helene Weigel, and had no wish to take up her husband's mantle, nor had she the experience or the time for the job.

The background to Hall's appointment is as follows: in July 1971, with the National's fortunes at a low ebb, its sixty-four-year-old leader recovering from a thrombosis, without having provided a viable heir, Lord Goodman as head of the Arts Council made a highly secret approach to Peter Hall. He told him that although the directorship of the National was not within his gift, if an offer were made, would he accept? '[Hall] said, pretty quickly,' Goodman recalled, 'YES.' But he was not going to come in as Olivier's assistant and he wanted Olivier's approval. He was asked to keep quiet about the matter for the time being.

During this time, and particularly towards the end of 1971, Ken was strenuously trying to push the Artistic Director into decisions about future management. By early 1972 the company had been pared down, and elaborate plans for the move to the South Bank initiated. More important, they were on a roll of dazzling success. It was at this juncture that Ken lobbied for the appointment of Michael Blakemore as Deputy Director, to be schooled to take over the leadership from Olivier when he chose to retire.

It was on 24 March that Sir Max Rayne told Olivier that the Board favoured Peter Hall. Angry and humiliated, Olivier felt that the decision was a *fait accompli*, and he acquiesced with the new arrangements as gracefully as he could, while nursing (to this day) a sense of outrage at his treatment.

Two days after the news broke, Olivier called a company meeting to tell his colleagues that Peter Hall's appointment was not fixed, that he would be staying as Artistic Director until the move, and that nobody's job was in jeopardy. Ken leaked this to the press and recorded in his journal: 'At least a bombing pause has been gained.' On the 13th Ken spoke to Peter Hall by telephone to point out the lack of consultation about his appointment. Hall replied that he had no wish to go over the heads of Dexter, Dunlop and Blakemore, and he added that he was worried about the amount of power wielded by the Board. The day before Ken had seen Max Rayne to propose that the Board meet the artistic directorate to hear *their* ideas about the succession.

Ken wrote in his journal:

I hate the most important decision in the administrative history of the English theatre being taken by a property tycoon (Rayne) and a lawyer (Goodman), without full word from the people who planned, created and evolved the National Theatre. When I mentioned Michael Blakemore's name to Max [Rayne], he said: 'Alas, I've never met Mr. Blakemore.' He also regretted that I had not consulted him about the succession six months ago. I pointed out that he was the titular boss, and if he had wanted to know my opinion he had only to pick up the telephone.

But it was Olivier Ken blamed above all: 'By refusing to nominate a possible successor from his own colleagues, he has passed a vote of no confidence in us all. . . . He has hired us, stolen our kudos, and now shows no compunction about discarding us.' Olivier's defence was that Blakemore was not ready for the job of Director, to which Ken argued that if his boss had taken his colleagues into his confidence a year or more before, a joint decision might have been reached.

The 'disturbed party', as Lord Goodman referred to Ken, sat down to prepare his case, and that of his colleagues, for a meeting of the Board on 18 April. He would argue that in the best of the theatre's productions there was a 'flamboyance, a showmanship' – 'We are the Cavaliers, Stratford the Roundheads' – with the emphasis on analytical intelligence and textual clarity. Under Peter Hall the country would have two Roundhead theatres.

He would argue that the theatre was launched on one of the most successful seasons it had ever had, and that the Board had chosen at that very moment to 'send out an sos for a saviour. . . . It is not the National Theatre who should appear to be climbing on to Peter Hall's bandwagon. The National Theatre is the bandwagon now, and it is Mr. Hall who should be glad of a chance to join it.'

He would argue that theatre should develop organically, by evolution, 'as Mr. Hall evolved out of the previous Stratford regime, as Trevor Nunn evolved out of his. What is happening to the NT is a heart transplant on a perfectly healthy patient.' He would admit that the meeting was mere window-dressing, since Hall's contract was drawn up and the press announcement ready for release. Nonetheless he would propose on behalf of Blakemore, Dexter, Dunlop and himself that in future Associate Directors and the head of the Literary Department should attend Board meetings as a right. 'We do not demand the right to vote. . . . All we ask is consultation, participation in decision-making.' The current rift between the Board and the executive had come about as the result of a breakdown of communication.

Finally he would propose off his own bat that Michael Blakemore be given the post of Deputy Director – 'A claret who needs a year or two more in bottle, ready for drinking in mid-70s, so that in the event of PH's absence through illness, other engagements, it is clear who stands in for him.'

On 18 April Ken delivered a version of these notes to the theatre's Board. His words had no effect at all, although he did manage to persuade the Board to include in their press statement announcing the new appointment a clause which spelled out that Peter Hall would be joining the theatre in 1973 to work with Olivier 'and the artistic executive as Director Designate.

On the 20th, Ken wrote to Peter Hall to fill him in on the proposals he had made. He offered congratulations, told Hall that none of the executive had anything against him personally, and ended, 'I needn't warn as wary a bird as you to keep a sharp eye on the Board and its doings.'

Peter Hall has recorded in his Diaries that Ken wanted his contract extended for three years. That was not at all the case. Ken had asked the Board to guarantee the jobs of the artistic directorate for three years. Having attacked Hall's appointment, he knew he would not be invited to stay on after Olivier's departure. Hall, needless to say, wanted Ken out and was 'fed up with everyone pussyfooting round the subject'.

On 5 July, according to Ken's journals, Hall popped into his office:

He pays extravagant but (I think) sincere tribute to my part in creating the N.T. and adds (not 'but' adds – he is too much the diplomat even to imply 'but') that he hopes I don't envisage that I'm to be thrown out. Nevertheless, he's not entirely sure (and wants my views on) whether we shall get on, both being so good at politicking, both with such strong ideas. I disabuse him of the thought that I ever intended (even under Michael Blakemore) to stay on after the move to the new building, when I would like to be phased out. ...

He outlines some of his ideas for the new operation. ... Peter is far more the Man with a Plan [than Olivier]. He says he wants to do far fewer major productions and rehearse them longer, so that each when it appears is a model of 'the pursuit of excellence'. ... At the same time he wants far more experimental productions.

I feel, of course, a slight pang now that all has been said and the end of the chapter settled. It would be exciting to plan a new N.T. with a new policy. ... But enough of this vicarious living. I must go back to taking responsibility for what I do, which is write.'

He did not need the job at the National, indeed he knew that in many respects it was damaging to him, but his commitment and his enthusiasm were so passionate that it was hard to break off. 'The National was his way of participating in the theatre,' as Michael Blakemore points out. 'If he lost that, there was no other way he could participate, except possibly by starting something on his own.'

In the spring of 1972, in the knowledge that he would be leaving the National Theatre, and having had in May to find £7000 in damages and costs as a result of the successful libel action brought by the pilot in the Soldiers case, Ken negotiated two book contracts. For George Weidenfeld, he would write 'The 300 Plays That Stood the Test of Time'. He planned to start with a definition of the qualities that make a play last, then to devote a chapter to each of the great periods of theatrical history, isolating the survivors and the non-survivors. He felt equipped to write such a book since it mirrored some of the kind of work he had been doing for Olivier during the past decade. He did not, however, take an immediate advance, which suggests that he had little intention of proceeding.

Instead he began a long profile for the *New Yorker* on Wilhelm Reich. The idea for such a piece had been provoked the previous autumn, partly by Dusan Makavejev's film *WR – Mysteries of the Organism*, and by Ken's re-reading of Reich's 1927 study *The Sexual Revolution*. (He had first read this subversive text in New York in the mid fifties, having had to purchase it at an inflated price from a pornographic bookseller.) His initial plan was to concentrate on the analyst's last tragic years in America, culminating in his trial for fraud and his death in 1957. Reich claimed to be able to concentrate natural energy in 'orgone accumulators', and this among others of his experiments incurred, in 1956, the hostility of the American Medical Association and the Federal Food and Drug Administration. He was pronounced guilty and imprisoned. His books were burned, his research and scientific equipment destroyed.

'I don't know anyone into whom more of the complexities of the twentieth century were unhappily crammed,' Ken wrote to William Shawn, and in the same letter he asked for expenses to pursue his Reichian research. He explained that apart from his 'honorific job at the National Theatre', and a 'dwindling trickle of author's royalties from *Oh! Calcutta!*', he had no regular income.

With Reich's *The Function of the Orgasm*, Character Analysis and *The Mass Psychology of Fascism* more or less digested, Ken began to explore the life of this remarkable Austrian who had begun his career as one of Freud's outstanding young disciples, and who had tried to build a bridge between Freud's theories about psychology and Marx's about society. Reich's heresies led to his expulsion from both the International Psychoanalytical Association and the Communist Party. In exile from Nazi Germany he continued his search for the source of energy, dipping into biology, pathology, physics and meteorology, meanwhile polarizing his detractors (who considered him, in his later years, to be an insane scientific charlatan) and his followers (who believed him to be a prophet).

In late May Ken flew to Portland, Maine, and from there drove to Reich's estate called Orgonon, near the village of Rangeley. It was here that the 'mad' scientist had lived and worked after 1942, and where Ken was able to inspect the 'cloud-busters' designed to break up rain-clouds, and the orgone blankets made of alternate strata of organic and inorganic material which Reich believed attracted orgone energy.

Ken asked the caretaker if he had ever considered Dr Reich to be insane. 'Oh sure,' came the reply. 'I remember one time, 1947 I think it was, he was looking through a telescope and I said to him, "We ever going to get to the moon, doctor?" "Oh, yes," he said, without looking up, "and soon, Mr Ross, quite soon." '

In New York Ken stayed with Adolph and Phyllis Green, from whose apartment he made forays to Philadelphia and Washington in pursuit of Reich. He wrote to me with a few details of his research, mentioning briefly his therapy sessions 'of Gestapo intensity' with a Reichian therapist. But he gave me no details and instead complained that words on paper seemed a 'strained and unfamiliar means of communicating. We've *outgrown* them. I need looks and glances and sound and touches, the soft side of your elbow, and the underside of your foot. ... And the noise of you, so little and muted compared with all the blare of here.'

Back in London Ken told me, in passing, that his Reichian therapy had produced a violent dream about me in which I was evidently not that 'muted' creature to whom he had addressed his letter. He did not elaborate, while I was too complacent to question him further.

Recently, and for the first time, I read Ken's Reich manuscript (which was never published). Other than the announcement that the author was an 'emphysematic neurotic', there is no outright personal confession except for a brief description of the three 'sample sessions', as Ken described them, that he took with the therapist Elsworth F. Baker, President of the American Association for Medical Orgonomy, that summer of 1972, sessions that worked on the breakdown of muscular armour. Baker explained to Ken that what was revolutionary about Reichian therapy was its refusal to accept that neurosis is an exclusively psychological phenomenon, and its assumption that the purpose of treatment was to enable the patient to release 'blocked' energy through orgasm. The chest segment was crucial, since it locked in the deepest emotions; and the object of the therapy, Reich had emphasized, was to release not only muscular tension but also emotions. (Reich was the precursor of Esalen, the Primal Scream, and other ersatz therapies.)

Ken's experience, after he had stripped to his underpants and climbed on to a bed, he recorded as follows:

Baker's mouth is as tight as a trap. He leans over me and presses on my chest, forcing me to exhale every last gasp. Presses, prods, presses harder, prods deeper. He's stronger by far than he looks. I try not to yell: why? Finally, stoicism crumbles and I scream, long and loud. He tells me that in my wailing he hears hatred, fear, woe. ... He tells me to turn over and pummel the bed and scream with rage. The screams and the pummelling produce the rage. I hope the room is sound-proofed. ...

Baker encourages me by snarling and roaring himself. Tears begin to flow. He returns to the attack on my chest, probing until he finds the points of maximum vulnerability, until he releases the most heartfelt cry. This is shock treatment beyond anything I had imagined. I feel invaded and outraged. The whole thing is sadistic and paternal: there's no other phrase for it. But would I object so much if a woman were doing it? Just as I ask myself this question, an episode swims back into memory in which my father behaved sadistically towards me. And this reminds me of how much I preferred my mother's anger to his.

I pounce upon this revelation, but there is no elaboration. Ken continues, 'After the second of my three sessions with Dr. Baker, I had an appallingly vivid dream. ... In it, I was derided by someone I loved, and I launched on her a physical assault of such murderous savagery that I woke up shaking. Clearly, the Baker treatment had dislodged an emotional log-jam of whose existence I had previously been unaware.'

Did that assault on the unconscious simply reflect Ken's deep resentment over my opposition to his filmscript – and by association to his sexual nature? Or did it signpost some deeper, older battle of the sexes? Or was it merely a bad dream, as Ken might well have said if I had been able to quiz him, for he had a fastidious distaste for solemn probing.

In his final Reichian session, Dr Baker explained that the purpose of therapy was not cure. 'One doesn't basically change character structure. The patients just get closer to health than before. The best we can hope for is *functional* cure, where a person can function well without building up tension.' Ken left and did not return.

Instead he spent the years between 1971 and 1975 engaged in two very different writing projects: the biography of Reich, up to the point where the analyst arrived in the United States (thereby altering his original plan to write about the last years for the *New Yorker*); and the pornographic filmscript. One was the opposite of the other in style and attitude, though both were about sex. In each the authorial persona is largely curtained off from the action.

For the biography the work is scholarly, the research vast. The first half of the book exists; the second half is mapped out with notes and references. On one level Ken must have identified with Reich, who, as a radical moralist and nonconformist on sex and politics, ended up ostracized and rejected. 'He fought the Establishment,' as the educator A. S. Neill put it, 'and they killed him.'

To paraphrase Ken: Reich believed that Freud's energy-functioning principle, rather than his discovery of the unconscious, was the more truly radical part of his work. By introducing the energy principle into psychology, Reich claimed, 'He broke the barrier which separated the science of that day from that of today.' The connection made by Freud between the physical symptoms of anxiety neurosis and undischarged libido led to Reich's conclusions that a fulfilled sexual life rendered neurosis impossible. Freud's 'quantities of excitation' eventually led to Reich's research into the nature of physical energy, and to his conclusion that libido was one of the concrete forms (which for Freud remained a hypothesis) in which orgone energy manifested itself.

What caught Ken's interest was not so much the work on orgone energy as Reich's view that human nature is alterable and perfectible. 'Reich shared the moralist's distaste', Ken wrote, 'for the kind of sexuality that flourished in brothels. He distinguished between primary drives, which were natural and wholly benevolent, and unnatural or secondary drives, which came into being when primary drives were frustrated. ... Thus for Reich sadism and masochism, for example, were not biologically innate in man, as Freud was tending to believe; instead they were caused by the repression of basic desires that were inherently life-enhancing.' To a man as obsessed with secondary drives as was Ken, Reich's theories provided reassurance at least on the intellectual plane. And he fell upon the following words of the analyst:

Human beings live emotionally on the surface, with their surface appearance. ... In order to get to the core where the natural, the normal, the healthy is, you have to get through that middle layer. And in the middle layer there is terror. There is severe terror. Not only that, there is murder there. All that Freud tried to subsume under the death instinct is in that middle layer. He thought it was biological. It wasn't. It is an artifact of culture.

Ken went on to explain that where Reich declared that orgastic potency was a prerequisite of psychic and emotional balance, Freud put it the other way round: psychic and emotional health must come first, and orgastic potency might follow. Unfortunately Ken never let us know with whom he agreed, though it seems that he would *like* to have agreed with Reich, particularly when Reich declared that there is no biological urge towards suffering – a statement that 'opened up the possibility that social and political conditions (such as patriarchal authoritarianism) were responsible for perpetuating human misery'.

Ken described how Reich moved away from Freudian therapy, where he felt patients would hide behind verbal smoke-screens, to examine the patient's demeanour, his 'character armour' (which the analyst had summed up as 'frozen history'). 'A man's whole past, Reich said, lived on into the present, crystallised in the form of "character attitudes". His make-up was the "functional sum total of all his past experiences". ... in the late 20's and early 30's Reich came to the conclusion that there existed a muscular armour which precisely corresponded to the psychological character armour. ... might it not be possible to dissolve repressions by working directly on muscular tensions. ... Few neurotics, he noticed, could breathe properly. When he succeeded in removing respiratory tension, patients felt a sensation of deep emotional release.'

Ken recorded, explained in a noncommittal manner and then passed on – to Reich's politics, his exile and his scientific experiments.

Never again did he try out even a 'sample' session of Reichian therapy. Perhaps he had not the energy (for his health during this period was rapidly deteriorating). Perhaps Reich's appeal was only to his head and his heart – it certainly didn't coincide with the functioning of his own libido.

By the spring of 1972 the making of the erotic film had become a bone of contention between us. Instead of notes for my novel, my notebook is full of short, often irascible thoughts on Ken. One such: 'Why do I want to write? I thought it was to talk to myself. I think it's to be able to talk to my husband.' Was it exhibitionism or masochism that propelled him to want to make his pornographic film? What was the point to it? Where the pleasure? Was it an act of self-destruction? Or a need to be accepted, to think well of himself? Were his fantasies and obsessions formed in childhood more powerful than his love for me? From where came his sense of outrage, as if something nameless had been done to him?

Poor Ken. How I constrained him with my blinkered and censorious love. In October he went to see the producer of the film and gave him two false reasons for postponing the project indefinitely. He wrote in *his* notebook: 'Thus I erase my hope of becoming a film director. In the evening I tell K what I have done. Her immediate reaction: "And what forfeit do you expect me to pay?" The lack of understanding is chilling, so much so that I almost reconsider. Have I done right to deny myself a career to spare her feelings, since she seems so impervious to mine?'

Our problem, of course, was more complicated. The marriage needed air. Even I, with my consuming love of Ken, dreamed occasionally of adventure.

35

A Testing Time

In 1968, on the instructions of Dr Charles Fletcher at the Hammersmith Hospital, Ken had given up smoking. But he gave up too late, and the emphysemic lung condition from which he suffered grew worse each year. At my instigation he tried out new doctors, a number of physiotherapists, new broncho-inhalers, and various courses ranging from autogenous vaccine to a diet of potato and onion.

In May 1971 he asked Dr Fletcher if his illness might be explained by a hereditary enzyme deficiency about which he had recently heard. If he had such a condition, came the reply, it could not be corrected. The problem, Fletcher explained, was that a considerable part of the respiratory tissue in the lung was damaged, and the damage could not be repaired by any treatment 'other than grafting in new lungs, and this is not yet possible'. So the only line of defence was to avoid tobacco, to treat infections promptly with antibiotics, and to exercise as much as possible.

On our return to London in mid-September, after two healthful months in the sun, Ken caught a severe cold and developed bronchial repercussions that stayed with him well into the autumn. He went so far as to enlist Dr Fletcher's help in persuading me that we must leave England, at least for the winter months, to enable him to live in a warmer climate, where he would be less likely to pick up infections.

That autumn a different kind of chill settled on me. I was so used to Ken's colds that I no longer – as I should have done – took them seriously. I was concerned that no work was being done, that one holiday followed swiftly upon the other, that we were running out of money. If Ken was off course, I was nowhere. To try and ground myself, I read, made notes for my novel and, more important for myself, tried to figure out why our beautiful life was in jeopardy. If we were to survive, the party had to end. I began to stay at home, while Ken continued to accept invitations. At one such evening he met an out-of-work actress, who asked if he could help get her a job at the National. He took her out to lunch, and some time later that afternoon left a letter on my desk. The letter explained that the girl had claimed to have studied acting at RADA but on the occasion of the lunch had broken down in tears and confessed she had had no such schooling. Ken's letter ended:

Then I took her home and fucked her. Or at least that is what I would have tried to do if I had suddenly gone stark staring berserk. But I am not berserk, and I know that non-berserk people do not exchange coral lagoons in the sunshine for tin baths in the back kitchen; nor do they, when they have the key to the secret garden toss it into the canal in favour of a season ticket to the municipal baths. So, in the full glow of my sanity, and not regretting a split second of it, I wished her the best of luck, said goodbye on the pavement and set off to walk the half-mile to where I had parked the car. On the way I began to whistle to myself and to think of simple congenial everyday irreplaceable things like caviare and Diamant Bleu champagne and the *New Oxford Book of English Verse* and you.

I paid no heed to this sweet letter.

Early in November he made a visit to a leading chest expert at the Brompton Hospital, Dr John Batten, and on 11 November, with the first two chapters of his book on Wilhelm Reich in his luggage, he flew to Tunisia, to the sun, to try and cure his latest cold. I had declined to go with him. He stayed at the Hotel Amilcar in Sidi Bou Said, and wrote some dozen letters to me. 'I have a new moon (have you?) and made the usual wish,' he wrote on 12 November. 'I test my lungs every few minutes to see whether the rattle is subsiding. So far, not; but it's early days. Tomorrow, if they can produce a promised plug, I shall try to start work. I miss you lovingly, and wonder for the hundredth worried time why you cried the other night, and whether you will ever tell me.' He wrote of food and temperature, and of what he was reading. 'Proust said: "In matters of love, it is easier to overcome a deep feeling than to renounce a habit." I cannot renounce mine: if anything, it grows with the years, swelling as other interests recede.... My present theory is that I cough and laze because of insufficient hairbrush wielding – inhibitions in one area causing inhibitions in others.... Write truly and also comfortingly. I am in a maze and need your thread to lead me out.'

On Monday Ken wrote to say that every fifth breath produced a spasm:

You cannot imagine the yearning with which I look back to Luxor in the Spring: it seems ten years ago. I feel ten years older. Are you *sure* my last attack was last autumn? I can't recall being ill in Cuarton or [the hotel] Fuentebravia or Jerez. Surely it was the year *before*, when we stayed with the Axelrods in Sardinia? I seem to remember 2 good years, years when I did not have to take every breath as a conscious experiment that might lead to an explosion. O one, figure-toi how I feel....

Write, my love. There is no help anywhere else. At least teach me to stop self-dramatising. (I find it a sad proof of my mental decay that I can no longer find exact images in which to express it.)

On Tuesday: 'Today the same driver took me on a little tour of Sidi Bou and district. The blue-and-white village is beautiful. So, even more, is the La Marsa area beyond, with a really splendid sea-side hotel called the Baie des Singes. "Why don't you live here?" he said. I murmured about work, wife, children ... "What use are they without health?" he said. "Same use as food to a man without teeth." It would be nice to come back here WITH YOU. In the village I bought a photomagazine that has some pictures of women by Lartigue – one of them, incredibly sexy, shows his first wife, Bibi, sitting coyly on the loo in 1920 – "*Elle n'était pas très consentante et m'a dit: Tu exagères un peu...*".'

Thereafter there are comments on Craft's *Stravinsky*; and quotations from Graham Greene's movie reviews. 'Sorry I go on so. This is my conversation for the day. I try to imagine and anticipate your comments and get the illusion of contact. I do love you so.... The next letter will be wildly erotic. Full of what G. Greene calls "charming minor Middle European humiliations". ... A final word before licking this envelope: *please* on receiving this, send a cable employing the word "love".'

On Wednesday his letter ended:

Query: whom are you seeing? what doing? with whom laughing? into whose responsive eyes staring? beside whom sleeping? with whom bemoaning the sad decline of

Your loving

l. [One]

PS I don't actually feel as gloomy as that, it just seemed a neat way of ending the letter.

On Thursday the 16th, Ken cabled, 'dying of loneliness', and sent a long letter on the nature of erotic love: 'Without affection, humiliation cannot be justified. But humiliation can intensify affection. It is an offering to the beloved of that which is offered to no one else. A homage....'

On the same day I sat down to write to Ken. He had asked me to find the thread, to lead him out of a maze. I had been trying to find it, it seemed, for years. I did not manage to get my letter down as I wanted until Sunday.

The Friday letter from Tunis read:

Well, today is the *best*. High still heat, the sea so glassy and quiet that the little incoming ripples are up to a hundred yards long and still don't break.... I send you a sketch of the view from my balcony. Do you wonder I ask myself whether I should not go on to Luxor instead of back to Blighty?...

I will send you some Wit and Wisdom of Lord B[yron]. soon.... Odd how Victorian literature is sealed off at each end by an anal scandal – Wilde up Bosie's bum, Byron up Annabella's....

As health returns, guilt diminishes. I believe I could corrupt *you*, if you were here. ONE MUST LAUGH MORE. Byron again: 'I remember a Methodist preacher who, on perceiving a profane grin on the faces of part of his congregation, explained: *No hopes for them as laughs.*'

... WHY NOT COME HERE? NOW, AS YOU READ THIS. I HAVE A DOUBLE ROOM ANYWAY, SO THE ONLY COST WOULD BE AIR FARE.... IF YOU ARRIVED WEDNESDAY WE COULD HAVE THURS, FRI, SAT AND SUN, RETURNING MON. I CD. POSTPONE THE HOSPITAL FOR A COUPLE OF DAYS. ONE CAN POSTPONE *ANYTHING* A COUPLE OF DAYS EXCEPT SEEING EACH OTHER.

On Saturday his letter read: 'I wait all day for an affirmative answer to my cable, though I know all the objections: nanny problems, Requiem Canticles, Frecknessa ... but HOW IRRELEVANT AS YOU WOULD SEE IF YOU WERE HERE.' He had been to Tunis, to the souks and to the zoo.

Stars include a hippo who leaps and grimaces like a dolphin, teasing its keeper by playfully letting him sit in its mouth while pretending to bite off his balls. The thing weighs almost a ton and frolics like a kitten....

Before dinner, saw Bergman's *La Honte* and now want to see all the Bergmen we've missed. A terrifying fable about how war brutalizes: at one awful point when the leading couple, a husband and wife, are being submitted to some fearful moral humiliation, the wife says: 'I feel we are in someone else's dream, and when they wake up they will be ashamed.'

Tuesday's communiqué listed possible winter retreats. 'Best plan is for me to leave in November; and you to join me with the children in December when the school holidays have started. We all then stay abroad till mid-March or thereabouts.... Only four days now.'

Three days later my letter of Sunday reached Ken. I told him it would be mad for me to come to Tunis. That I had a cold; that I had to attend to my mother's plumbing; that there was no one to look after the babies. That I was invaded by 'creeps': 'They just come to the door, since I never answer the telephone. "Truly" as Roxana would say.' That the children were absolutely adorable and held hands solemnly to be photographed.

I then engaged on the task at hand. I began with the tears Ken had referred to in one of his letters.

I wept out of a kind of frustration, years of seeing you handle small everyday practicalities, puzzles, personality conflicts like a man from Mars, making everything insanely and pointlessly difficult for yourself – letting all these small failures build up to block you and what you are....

It seems to me you have become armoured against other people's reaction to you. Only natural, you say, after all those attacks? Yes, but why originally? You who react to and articulate other people like nobody I know, never seem to care what their reaction is to you. Blithe bravery, or fear on your part? I don't know.

You have all the virtues in the book. You are generous, kind. But you are without pity.... Pity is mundane, every day, muddling-together.... It is what one can feel about the awfullest people – not virtuous or distant, certainly. And above all it is noticing, a binding understanding.

To cut the sermon and get back to armouring [for Reich's influence had evidently had its effect on me], I believe you to be exceptionally armoured (pity is always 'naked') not with the kind of armour that protects while giving you the maximum freedom of movement, nor the usefully aggressive kind. . . .

I think you will climb out by writing a couple of books, making a film, directing a show – in each case, confined by the technique you will be released through it. . . . I'm getting awfully heavy-handed here, but I'll go on staunchly if not lightly. . . . You are not a politician, you are not somebody who can juggle a lot of different worlds at once.

. . . One reason you like to be Abroad is that you can control your environment. . . . You *are* aggressive and you do need to impose. But you've abused, subverted, submerged this crucial part of you. What a giveaway your letter was. Of course you aren't going to give up your sexual life. But that's only part of it. 'It grows with the years, swelling as other interests recede,' you write. Surely you're wrong. Your sexual habits appear to be more important as you cut off the other interests. . . . *More* sex and more everything else too.

Incidental thoughts on your quote from Proust:

1) There is sexual imprinting, indelible and unchangeable.

2) There is compulsive behaviour, which runs the risk of playing the same track relentlessly, the same fantasy, so that you miss out or cut off other sense pleasures. . . .

3) Habit, how you coat or dress the imprinting, can be changed, can't it? More filth, better fantasies, more touching. My problem is that I resent Proust even if he is right. Are you still reading? . . .

I don't know how to make all this sound the way I'd like. If it seems carping . . . or silly or badly put, then tear it up and wait till you see me. As you rightly say of me, I hate to offend, so if I have, take pity. I love you.

Ken kept this letter, as I kept his. He wrote on it, 'Pity for whom?' And he scribbled at the bottom: 'What a deeply unattractive and unappetising letter. Who *needs* that??'

On his return he told me that my letter was the most cold-blooded thing he had ever read, that receiving it had been like being hit in the mouth.

In despair, and some shame, I shut up. We never spoke about the letters again, but took up our everyday life together, rather edgily for sure, because my husband (though I did not know it) had started an affair. We went to Paris on our annual Christmas weekend and Ken complained that breathing was like 'painfully clenching and unclenching two vast stiff fists – the lungs'. We gave our usual attention to Christmas, which was lavishly planned and executed. But we were not extraordinarily pleased with each other.

36

Into the Labyrinth

Early in January 1973 we flew to Sri Lanka in search of a month's sun to fortify Ken's chest, and a peaceful place to work. He set up his typewriter in a large room at the Blue Lagoon Hotel, north of Colombo, and continued to stitch together the life of Wilhelm Reich.

The modern bungalow-style building faced a brackish lake on one side and the Indian Ocean on the other, and looked like Malmö on a hot day. Ken noted that for the first time since early childhood he had had twelve consecutive meals in the same room, and the hotel dining-room provided the kind of nursery menu – rice pudding, custard, steamed fish – that the British had inflicted on their colonies. We escaped on a number of sorties: to watch a Buddhist parade at Kelaniya, where the participants drummed and danced along a pile carpet of elephant shit. Driving home through a crowd of 200,000 brown people, nudging and jostling – even lifting up – our puny car, Ken halfheartedly shook a can opener (the only weapon at hand) at this smiling sea. Later he noted: 'The sight of wrathful whitey has some effect and one is thankful that the good old colonial reflex survives in these people.'

We went to Sigiriya, to the Buddhist rock-temple of Dambulla, and to the twelfth-century temple and ruins of Polonnaruwa. Ken was not much impressed with the architecture, 'the short, square, rough-hewn pillars (matchsticks after Greece or Egypt) and the dagoba or Buddhist relic–receptacle shaped like a giant inverted golf-tee'. But he was much taken by a huge reclining Enlightened Buddha. At sunset we sat for a long time regarding this serene figure, while Ken debated whether the contemplative life would be a voyage of fulfilment or a cop-out. At Wilpattu, the great gamepark in the south, we spied spoonbills weighing down the branches of a fragile tree, pewter-grey sambur, a sounder of wild boar, a mongoose, painted stork, finally a leopard. Not up to Kenya perhaps, but rich in our eyes.

In this nursery paradise we were content, and with each other chastely so.

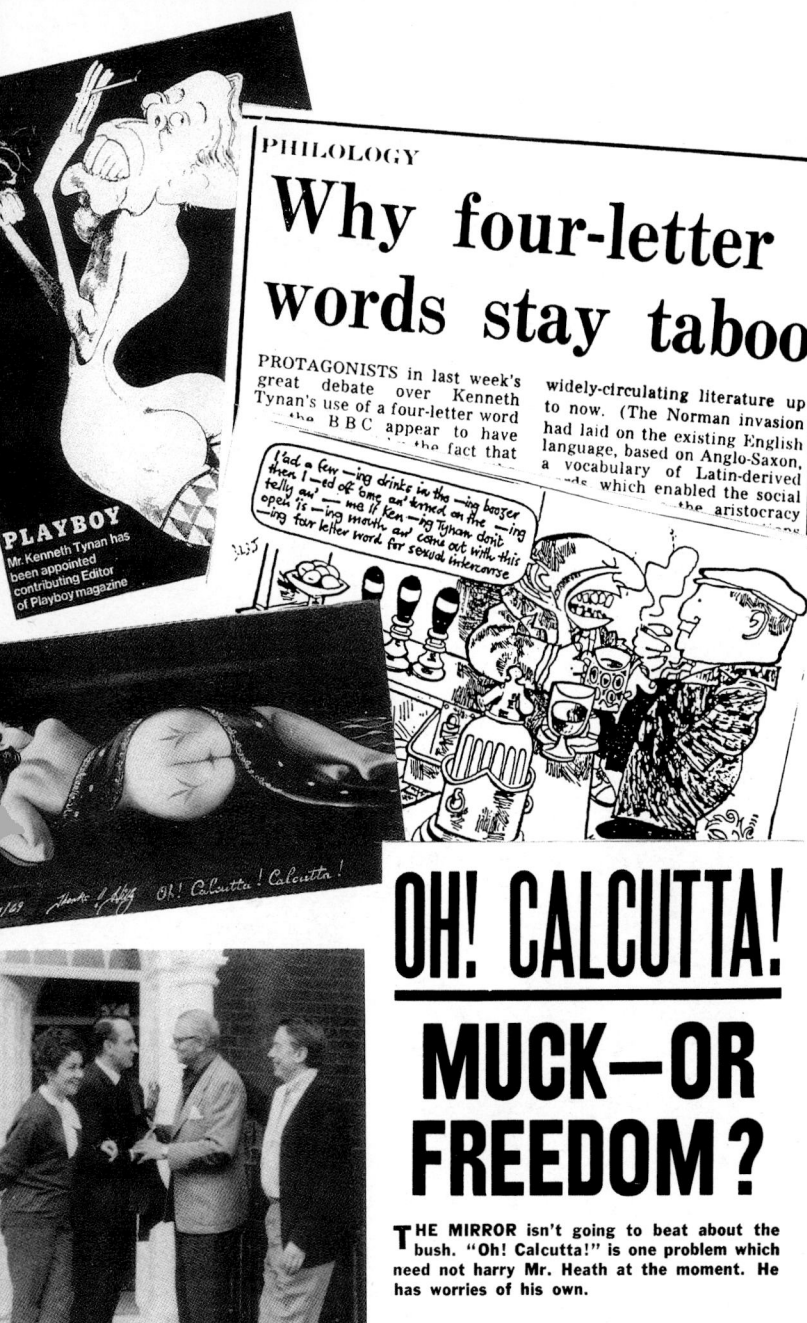

Joan Plowright, Rolf Hochhuth, Laurence Olivier and Ken, Brighton, April 1967

Wedding, 1967: Kathleen and Ken with Marlene Dietrich

Roxana and Ke

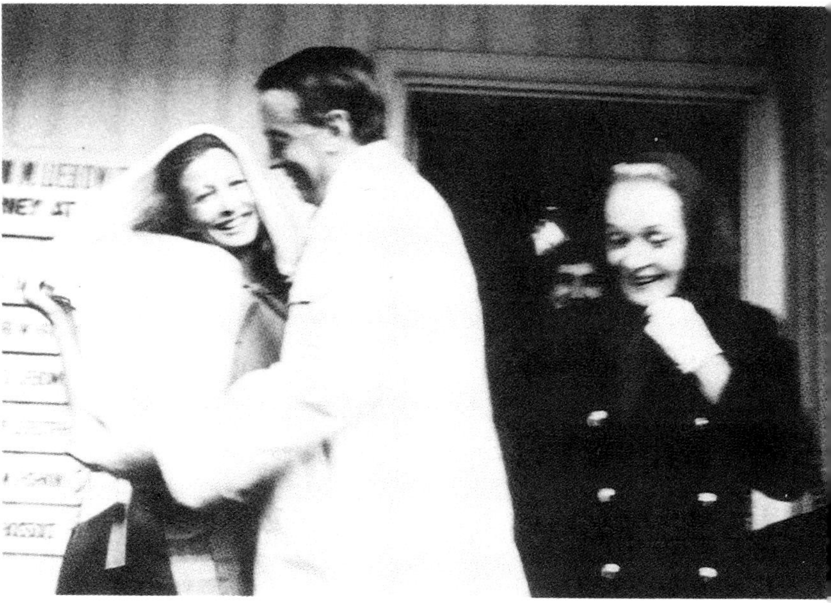

Ken and Kathleen in Italy

Edna O'Brien with Roxana
outside Thurloe Square

Kathleen, 1971

Tom Stoppard

Matthew and Ken

Mary McCarthy and Germaine
Greer, Thurloe Square

Ken with Elia Kazan, Sam
Spiegel, Budd Schulberg, 1972

FOR ROXANA

THE SONG OF RAT THE CAT
- -
I RATTY am,
And I do fight
Horribly by day and night.
Sometimes in the evening, too,
When I've nothing else to do.
Now I'll scrat ch, and now I'll nip,
Leaving scars upon your hip,
Or upon your rotten ear,

(Left and below) Part of a poem for Roxana; Ken
with Ratty; Ken by David Bailey

(Below right) Ken in Italy, 1969; Roxana and K
Lucca, 1969

Ken as Louise Brooks

Kathleen and Ken, Alsace, 1974

Matthew and Ken in Paris

(Centre) At home in Los Angeles

Roxana with Ken, Puerto
Vallarta, 1978

Ken in Havana

Tynans, Tony Richardson, Princess Margaret,
Gore Vidal and Jack Nicholson in Bel Air

Michael White, Tracy and Jim McBride

British films): but we all miss you like mad. If you get here
before mid-July we shall expect you under our roof.

I may go and live among the Calabashi Indians of
Ecuador, whom I invented last month to fool a tourist in
Puerto Vallarta. They live to be 106 years old in a high
mountain valley where nothing grows except forests of Caramba
trees. They eat the bark and carve canoes out of the rest. This
traditional craft has survived despite the fact that there has
been no water in the valley since the neolithic era. This of
course accounts for their longevity: nothing keeps you fitter
than paddling a canoe on dry land.

The Cromwell Road arrangement sounds ideal - please

I envy you the cottage in Suffolk.
show delights me: I had heard
e Tennants keep their word. As
showcase for it in L.A. would be
tiful middle-sized theatre run by
ight chap called Gordon Davidson.
transplant to Broadway and it
can help to make this connexion,

gs could not be more ominous
ent. You can't pick up a paper or

etch by Ken

uise Brooks

(Top) Letter to Adrian and Celia
Mitchell

Burial service in Oxford, 1980

Ken, Spain, 1978

Never bored with one another's company, it seemed we could play, whether at home or abroad, a multiplicity of parts from 'friendly neighbourhood philosopher', as Ken put it, to fellow accountant, businessman, consultant in child-rearing, companion-in-shorthand to each other's jokes and foibles. But we were no longer, as Ken noted, and as lovers must basically be, 'simple cock and cunt'. Was there not a vicious circle in the true companionship of marriage? he asked.

After several months without sex, and sensitive to my distress, Ken admitted that he had, since late November, been having an affair with the very girl he had rejected in October. He told me that she was twenty-eight, called Nicole, dark-haired, slim, not especially pretty, and extremely shy; that he had discovered that his anal–sadistic fantasy exactly matched hers. It was merely the guilt of concealment, he explained disingenuously, that kept the thing going, and that it posed no threat.

I received this information in silent, stunned disbelief, since no one had thought fit to reveal to me the great secret of married sexual love, which is that it comes to an end. During the next few months I remained in a state of profound shock. Ken took pains to explain to me that his occasional afternoon forays meant nothing, that if I had a similar predilection – needing, for example, to have my shoes licked – he would not deny me. He explained insistently that pain, for the sado-masochist, was not a source of pleasure, that it was the varied excitements of role-playing, and anticipation, that made it all such a sport. Even Wilhelm Reich, the self-regulating, healthful sexual guru, was co-opted, for he had declared that masochism was nothing to do with the death wish, as Freud had maintained.

None of these arguments at the time soothed me; indeed they hardly registered. I particularly minded that our complex bond was being replaced with a new arrangement, as pedestrian as a new diet, a change carried out so suddenly after such closeness.

'Everything's going to be all right,' Ken said. But 'Everything's changed somehow,' said the Noël Coward lyric from *Shadow Play*, which I listened to day after day:

> Here in the light of this unkind familiar now
> Every gesture is clear and cold for us,
> Even yesterday's growing old for us,
> Everything's changed somehow.

And with tears streaming I would listen to Gertrude Lawrence pick up from the plaintive voice of Coward to tell me:

> Then, we knew the best of it,
> Then our hearts stood the test of it.
> Now, the magic has flown,
> We face the unknown,
> Apart and alone.

We were not, however, apart and alone. As Ken confided to his journal, four months after his first confession of unfaithfulness: 'Part of our problem is that we have hardly any life outside our own relationship. Kathleen has no [full-time] job to give her a link with the outside world, and my own bridgehead, the National, disappears when I move out of my office in August. At home we live among children and servants: and we are both at home most of every day. Hence our one-to-one relationship, instead of being simply the most important in our lives, is virtually the *only* one. And whenever anything goes wrong in it, it is as if the whole of life was incurably poisoned.'

In March, while on a writing assignment in Rome, I sat alone in a cinema watching *Last Tango in Paris*, and cried some more. Its director, I read, had pronounced his film to be about solitude. 'Every sexual relationship is condemned. . . . history, reality are all but romantic.' I would not be persuaded.

Ken went on enjoying himself, setting out twice a week for lunch, while sometimes apologizing rather ruefully. 'It's rather pathetic, don't you think?' he would say, putting on a khaki Yves Saint Laurent suit in which he looked extremely well. 'A forty-six-year-old man dressing up.'

He told me I was suffering from an undue sense of loss, and should see an analyst. How about a Reichian? After some pressure I agreed to see a woman in Catford, and took the train, on half-a-dozen occasions, to a dingy semi-detached in South London. 'Your body is more angry than you know,' said this disciple of Reich. I told her I felt cold, that I felt there was an iceberg in my centre, and that if only I could break it up, the water would melt and flow. 'How curious', said the analyst, 'that you should imagine a block of ice. Reich referred to such a block as "frozen energy".' Apart from this sliver of enlightenment, I was not much helped.

'The more K is convinced that I love her, the more she suffers when I see N,' Ken wrote in his diary. 'But I *do* love her and cannot help acting lovingly.' Yet my grief could not be ignored: to lessen his guilt, he set about rationalizing his pleasure. What did he need? The sun, the company of people he loved and was loved by, good food and wine, a willing female slave. Admiration for his work and the company of intelligent people; fast cars and sunlit villas were secondary. Thoughts on the dark night of the soul were banished. Instead he devoted himself to planning his sexual theatre with Nicole, inventing quizzes and various forms of humiliation, ordering costumes and polaroid film, and seeking, as the months went by, willing third parties, or paid masseuses, to provide the vital missing element in the scenarios: the audience.

All of which would have been well enough had he not insisted on confiding in me, because he *still* wanted my approval; in that respect he was seriously irresponsible. He also wanted a scapegoat, and unfairly found one in Elaine. (His mother, Elaine and later me: the fault was always that of a woman. Odd that he never thought to blame his father.) He wrote in his journal that

'Nicole is really a tremendous reaction to ... feeling ashamed of my sexual preferences – being [reproached] ... with them by Elaine.... It is appalling that K, whom I love, should be suffering.... But I cannot allow myself to hate myself *again* – for whatever reason, even for causing K. pain.'

Ken did not wish to be condemned for what he described as the 'temporary, brief and unauthorised lodging once or twice a fortnight' of his sex. He wrote to me: 'Of course I would have been disturbed, indeed shattered, if you had taken a similar course. But for a good reason: because for you, a temporary loan of your cunt would undoubtedly have developed into a permanent gift of your whole being. So I would have had cause to fear that I might lose you. You know that – UNLESS A CRISIS IS FORCED BY EXTERNAL PRESSURES – you are in no danger at all of losing me.' I was suffering too keenly to notice how elaborately argued was Ken's double standard.

The Victorian still life, now a Victorian melodrama, was temporarily eclipsed by Tracy's twenty-first birthday dance. We took the Young Vic Theatre, cleared the central area, and kept the seating on three sides. We organized some complicated lighting, by way of decoration, set up a number of trolleys, serving hot curry and buck's fizz. We installed Shakin' Stevens with a rock group, and organized a cabaret with John Wells, Dudley Moore and the great comic Max Wall – whom Ken brought out of his recent obscurity. It was a good party with some 300 guests, about which all three of us were justly proud.

In May 1973 Ken was asked to return to the *Observer* as drama critic. He replied that he was 'flattered out of his trousers' by the offer, and would bear it in mind for the future. In December the *Evening Standard* tried to persuade Ken to write a weekly column. They did not, however, want something 'overtly political', nor anything that might be about sex and 'potentially libellous'. Ken decided against this offer too, and confined his inflammatory thoughts to his journal, and to an occasional letter on politics to *The Times*.

He believed that inflation was high by intention: 'A super-rich class is being built on top of the existing structure – an international conglomerate – business rich, drawing on the US and the Common Market – with the aim of keeping the insurgent and overweening middle classes in their place, and of decisively depressing the proletariat.... Only members of the super-rich – the new feudal class – will be able to keep their heads above the decline in the real value of money, because they are paid in perks, property, possessions and tax-exempt benefits. This is what will separate them from the rest of us, whose efforts will perforce be dedicated *not* to changing society but to keeping ourselves from drowning.' This was written in June 1973, almost a decade before the era of Thatcher and Reagan.

Ken's journal seemed to give him direct access to his thoughts and to his feelings; writing the book on Reich (under a contract signed with Cape in July 1973), he could not seem to find the right tone of voice. Instead he decided to reactivate his financial interest in his erotic film; and, in the summer of 1973, to plan a sequel to *Oh! Calcutta!* This time he would go further, and he set down some of the questions he would like to explore, if not to answer. What was sexy and why? Was it possible, or desirable, to stimulate the audience sexually? Should children observe their parents having intercourse? Was perversion what happens when primary sex drives are blocked? Should incest taboos, toilet-training, be examined? Was the word 'sado-masochism' a mode of alternating dictatorships, rather than a form of democratic sex? Was it possible for people to be sexually faithful, and contentedly so, in marriage? He added oxymoronically that he wanted his new revue to 'demystify and at the same time hypnotise' (which indicated that he wanted to demonstrate that sex was normal, safe and acceptable even while its 'sinful' or *outré* aspects took hypnotic hold). Just as wishfully he added that the revue would advance the argument at every stage with sketches, songs and dances: 'Not isolated pearls, but pearls on a string.'

To side-step the inorganic nature of this particular theatrical form, he came up with the idea of two stages, or acting areas. The first would be where the erotic show took place with about eight performers, most of whose work would be danced or mimed or sung, where costumes and décor should represent 'the acme of artificial sexuality'. On the second stage would be a group of four actors representing ordinary people – the audience's representatives on stage. They might interrupt to explain, for example, why they found certain parts of the show unstimulating. 'As time goes on, the foursome begin to act out their own private fantasies in their own acting area: thus we contrast real sexual fantasies with the glamourised ones in the Erotic Show.' They also ask where the line should be drawn. 'Finally, the two stages merge and become one. There is a happy coalition of fact and fantasy.'

With a view to creating such a show, with Michael White as producer and Clifford Williams directing, Ken approached Trevor Griffiths to discover whether the playwright would like to take on the project. In July, Ken and Griffiths made an exploratory trip to France and Germany. Ken's notes recorded: 'We must try to have at least one erect penis and visible fuck.... It's essential that the people in our sex show – especially if fucking or being fucked – should have sympathetic personalities that inspire affection.' This was written after a visit to the Salambo in Hamburg, where, he reported, 'Two nude girls make love and lick: then a short, disgruntled-looking man, chewing gum, naked except for a cloth cap and little ballet shoes, trudges on, patiently waits for one of the girls to lick him erect, and then, taking his time and with total unconcern, fucks both of them in every conceivable position. Trevor and I were very taken with Cloth-Cap and would like to use a similar character in our show.'

In Paris Ken and Griffiths saw *La Grande Eugène*, and Ken wrote that it was 'one of the most audacious and original shows I've ever seen. The [male] performers aren't camp or drag queens: they are like gods who are above mere matters of sex.... Conception, decor and costumes are by Franz Salieri.... Should we consider the possibility of inviting Salieri to "conceive" the sex-show part of "After Calcutta"?'

Griffiths was equally enthusiastic. *La Grande Eugène* had taste but was not tasteful: 'To be "tasteful" is, almost always, to stop well short of psychic or sexual disturbance in one's audience.' He found the Crazy Horse Saloon, on the other hand – another stop on their tourist map of sex – vapid.

On one occasion during this exploratory trip, these two intimate half-strangers were walking along a street on a hot night, when Trevor noticed that Ken was not with him. 'I turned around and saw him leaning against something, in spasm. He looked like death and I suddenly realized how sick he was. On the same trip I remember him telling me that he had lost his taste buds. He had ordered some very hot chili, something that would lift his palate's spirit a little. It occurred to me that he was embarked on that line of march, not just at the level of his taste buds, but with everything – so that sensation now had to be fairly extreme.'

In the autumn there were discussions with their respective agents, and a refusal by Griffiths to work with another writer, or to assign copyright: 'In your view,' he wrote to Ken, 'I'm a writer hired to "treat" an idea by you. In mine, I've been preparing to make a personal and hopefully powerful and *relevant* statement about contemporary sexuality.' And he added, 'There have been times when I've felt very queasy about the whole thing: at the power of the Big Money; at the way in which, if *Oh Calcutta* is anything to go by, you have not been especially successful in beating it.'

Now this was the kind of personal rebuff that hit Ken very hard. When the two men met, after the reception of the letter, Ken was emotionally upset, shaking and crying, because his honour had been impugned. Griffiths recalls: 'He got up and he said, "You don't seem to understand" – and he was weeping – "I am a totally trustworthy person." And he said it at the top of his voice. It was one of the most incredible psychic breakdowns that I've ever seen.'

Griffiths felt that Ken's real preoccupation at that point in his life was not with his list of general questions but with a fetishized and relatively narrow sliver of the sexual sensibility; whereas he himself wanted to examine a broader spectrum of sex – its roots in life, in history and in society. Nonetheless he went ahead with the two-stage conception. Ken thought the piece too earnest: 'As if we were saying: "Don't think we're trying to charm you or amuse you or win you over. This isn't an entertainment."'

In November 1974, Griffiths took back his half-finished script, declaring that Ken had failed to respond to its meanings. Ken had always wanted a

331

collaboration and, when he brought in the writer Barry Reckord, Trevor saw the writing on the wall.

'I dreamt a Shakespearean pun,' Ken said one morning. 'Man hath no solace, Madonna, for man is *solus*.' By July 1973 his private life was very troubled, with 'loss of interest in sex' (he recorded in his journal) 'due to guilt'.

Early in August he joined me, Roxana and Matthew, now aged two, at a cottage overlooking Cardigan Bay, in North Wales. It was not an unhappy time. We composed animal poems and went picnicking. At Llanberis Castle, Ken improvised the sad tale of the Fair Lady of Llanberis who, while her husband was away at the Crusades, rode off with the Black Baron of Barmouth. At one point in his story-telling a handsome young man in a black jerkin and black boots appeared on the ramparts. Pretending not to have seen this interloper, Ken persuaded Roxana that she had seen the ghost of the Black Baron.

In the middle of the month we moved to a farm in Wiltshire, where I worked on my novel and Ken on his conscience. He wrote in his journal: 'I am slowly developing the habit of indifference. I am learning how not to feel very strongly about anything. With this withdrawal of emotion goes a withdrawal of energy.' A few days later he added: 'There is one important way in which I need not be sorry for K. Never in her life has she experienced what for most people is the most powerful, savage, heart-rending and unforgettable experience in their lives – and one that is constantly and agonisingly repeated. . . . She is like a member of an exclusive club who has lost – for some inexplicable reason – her right to park anywhere for any length of time. 90% of the rest of us are pedestrians, and have been so since our teens.' Ken saw me as a beauty and, therefore, as unlikely to suffer the pain of rejection as a rich man hunger. That view must have reassured him, and he refused to look at me more closely, to observe that I was almost as much a victim of myself as was he, that I was as obsessively attached to dependence on romantic love as he on his perennial need to think well of himself. Ken was intent on exposing and demonstrating his sexual life, about which he felt a mixture of the deepest guilt and the deepest reverence; while his wife, who had refused this exploration – or so he believed – waited in hopeless hope for her old world to be made whole.

At the end of August we drove through France, eating at the Hostellerie de la Poste, at Avallon; Chez La Mère Charles, at Mionnay, near Lyon; La Pyramide, at Vienne – rich *grande cuisine* which delighted Ken, while it pushed me to the edge of nausea. I was that worst, and most self-absorbed, of companions: the spurned woman. What Ken wanted from me was reassurance and succour. What he got was the wan smile, or tears, expecially when the voice of Roberta Flack, singing 'Killing Me Softly', came whining out of cafés and car radios and funfairs, as it did all that summer. 'Your tactics are so poor,' Ken sensibly told me. But at the same time he asked me to lead him out of the labyrinth into the sun.

Ken insisted on sunbathing nude at the Escalet beach: it was a matter of principle. I went along with him, complaining that he was a 'Savonarola of sex', while all I wanted was sex.

In St Tropez Ken dreamed of a naked girl, covered with dust and excrement, her hair shaved off, with dozens of drawing-pins driven into her scalp. He later recorded: 'At this point I woke up filled with horror. And, at once dogs in the hotel grounds began to bark pointlessly, as they are said to do when the King of evil, invisible to men, passes by.'

On his return to London, he resumed his affair with Nicole, telling me he had to go ahead, 'although all commonsense and reason and kindness and even camaraderie are against it. . . . It is my choice, my thing, my need (to prove that I am separate). . . . It is fairly comic and slightly nasty. But it is shaking me like an infection and I cannot do anything but be shaken until it has passed. As it will. As it must.' He told me that he could not bear my belief in him, my faith in what he ought to be. He preferred the company of someone who had no ideals for him. Not only was he excited by his sexual life with Nicole but he could perform in a controlled environment with a controlled subject. 'Life in abasement', one of his good women friends told him ruefully, for it was in a basement that some of the affair was conducted. Then it moved from place to place: to a transsexual's flat, to hotels, and back to a basement. The girl was decent, and she was in love. She was also, as Ken's confidante explained to me, willing to execute any of Ken's demands while being dazzlingly unaware of repercussions.

Ken rationalized the situation by telling himself that he did not wish to be the non-stop 'chairman of a family' (choosing, of course, the one role he most feared and despised: that of those other chairmen, Sir Peter Peacock and Lord Chandos – both middle-of-the-road, middle men, no-sayers, whom Ken so violently resented).

Was he capable of being his own master, oblivious of the approval of women, for a change? Any pain was better than staying where he was, 'about 55 degrees below par'. But to sustain his life he had to abolish love. The word, he announced, was no longer useful. Friendship, affection, but not love.

While working, during this period, on his book about Wilhelm Reich, Ken took on a book review for the *New Statesman*, of Robert Melville's *Erotic Art of the West*, a personally revealing exercise in criticism. The trouble with the new anthology, he wrote, was that it would not encourage 'scrotal stirrings that herald tumescence' (the nearer Ken came to public confession, the more arch grew his English). 'If an agnostic is an atheist with aspirations to the Royal Enclosure, "erotic art" is pornography with aspirations to the coffee-table.' And this volume, he complained, paid scant attention to the female bottom. To which he added: 'Pygophilia may be, in Mr. Melville's phrase, "an infantile condition", but it is by several months less infantile that the curious obsession with breasts that plays so dominant a role in modern machismo.' Nor was there enough attention paid to soft flagellation. A humanist, Ken added, with wondrous lack of humanity, was someone 'who remembers the faces of the people he spanks'.

In his relationship with me Ken was secure: it represented an impregnable vault, the key to which he had thrown away. It could not be destroyed. But I nearly was. There was nothing very unusual in this story, except perhaps my innocence. I turned for help to Trevor Griffiths, looked into his kind blue eyes, and listened to his good sense. He was wise, and he was solid. And he was too responsible to become my lover, even had he wanted to. He explained that everything was converging upon me at once: that it was not a question of saving my children or my roof, but my wits; that Ken, whom I loved and desired, would hate me if I pulled him out; that my husband would not rescue me. 'You cannot', he told me severely, 'ask your adversary for help.' Finally he told me reassuringly. '*We* come through, you know.' I eventually 'came through'. In the process and over the years I discovered that Trevor had been wrong and that Ken, 'my adversary', had been my most vital and irreplaceable teacher.

Trevor's view was that Ken lived a fantasy of total freedom. 'Most men', he explained, 'believe that all they have to do to ratify something is to choose it, and that guilt is produced when responsibility or duty obfuscate their fantasy of total autonomy. Women don't grow up believing that all they are going to have to do to validate their behaviour is to choose to do it. They grow up with accommodations.' He felt that Ken didn't really like men very much, and certainly he had a lot of fear of them. He was fixated on women. 'I think he took his pleasure with women, and I think he felt guilty about taking his pleasure with women. There's nothing as powerful as the anger that one feels towards someone who makes you feel guilty.'

Years later Trevor reconsidered this painful saga and wondered whether Ken's mother had exquisitely betrayed him. 'She was the all girl, the all meeter of needs, but he blamed her for his ignorance of bastardy.'

When, after a year or so of domestic drama, I began a short affair – one that was circumspect and without resonance – Ken was outraged. He announced, 'Now you're soiled for me.' The accusation was unkind as well as a contradiction of his new dictum in favour of 'open' marriage. But at that stage I did not have the emotional musculature to fight back. Nor was I aware that this was the beginning of Ken's campaign (however unconscious) to test my loyalty with a series of escalating demands.

He wanted total fealty, yet he feared encroachment. When I repeated Trevor Griffiths' maxim, that 'we only die if we fail to take root in others', Ken described it as 'a prescription for parasitism. That which takes root in, draws sap from: it also invades, imposes itself. The cuckoo takes root in the nest of its unwilling host. . . . I do not want anybody else's roots embedded in my psyche. Trevor's little apothegm might be Dracula's family motto.'

But freedom, apparently, was not the solution. Ken wrote in his journal, during the autumn of 1973: 'Life is a bountiful murderer. It comes to us bearing an armful of gifts, of which the last is a knife to the heart.'

At a press conference in March 1973, it was announced that Laurence Olivier would be leaving the National Theatre earlier than planned, in December 1973; and that Peter Hall would join as co-Director in April and take over as Artistic Director the following November. Ken would be leaving in December, with Olivier (and earlier than planned).

The day before the press conference, Peter Hall had told Ken, 'As far as I'm concerned, you won't leave a minute earlier than you want to. No bull-shitting.' He explained that Olivier had insisted he take over the directorship earlier, and that he quite understood why: 'Larry wouldn't want to be kept hanging around waiting for the theatre to open.' Ken commented in his journal:

All this time I am squirming with embarrassment, wanting to say: 'But we are up to *here* in bullshit, Peter, and it isn't Larry who would have been kept waiting around, it's *you*. Why do you bother to put on this act?' . . . Peter – uniquely in the theatre – has no enemies and no friends. I don't know which is the more eloquent criticism. He does not seem to be made of flesh and blood but of some resilient gelatinous substance like a jelly fish. Behind that strange round face, boyishly puckered, ruefully grinning, is a . . . voluptuous love of power. . . . (Note on gamesmanship: as I entered his office, P. Hall said jocularly: 'Good afternoon, *sir*.' This mode of address indicated (a) *mock*-servility, plus (b) suggestion of deference due to *age*. You have to hand it to him; and, of course, people do, on a plate. The man's sub-fusc pomposity knows no bounds.

Some few weeks later Ken dined very affably with Hall at a Soho restaurant, and discovered that their views on how the National should be run were remarkably similar: that permanent companies had no future because television and film siphoned off actors; that the Olivier theatre should house big classical productions, a separate company should work the Lyttelton stage, with plays cast in pairs and not in repertory, while the studio should produce a continuous firework display of experimental work. Ken asked if he could direct Firbank's *The Princess Zoubaroff*. Subsequently Hall suggested that Ken should do a Theme Season, with the result that Ken proposed two alternatives. One of Mediterranean comedy: Eduardo de Filippo's *These Ghosts*, Giraudoux's *Intermezzo*, Molnar's *The Play's the Thing* and Firbank's *Zoubaroff*. 'Linking theme would be the Mediterranean as the cradle of escapism (set any of these plays in England or Germany and they would cease to exist).'

He proposed an alternative of 'artificial comedy': *Intermezzo*, *The Play's the Thing*, *Zoubaroff*, and an idea which Ken had concocted: 'A Week with Ring Lardner'. Lardner, he claimed, was the funniest of all American writers. (His short surrealist plays, written in the twenties and parodying the drama of the period, had been privately performed by Benchley, Woollcott and Thurber.)

In September Hall wrote to Ken to tell him that he would not be running seasons at the Lyttelton for some time, and that he would not be in a position to involve Ken until the end of 1975, or early 1976. And that, sadly, was the end of a promising project.

Though Ken was leaving shortly, his devotion to the National cause did not abate. During his last year he worked closely on three productions: Molière's *The Misanthrope* and Peter Shaffer's *Equus*, both directed by John Dexter, and *The Bacchae* of Euripides, directed by Roland Joffé.

The last two plays of the Olivier regime were both put on at Ken's suggestion. The first, by the great Neapolitan playwright and actor Eduardo de Filippo, was *Saturday, Sunday, Monday*, in which Franco Zeffirelli directed Laurence Olivier and Joan Plowright, a subtle and moving comedy about the lack of communication within a family. Needlessly fearful that the critics would complain of lack of 'contemporary relevance', a notion Ken loathed, he wrote: 'The de Filippo play is about Naples in the 50s; and to enjoy it we must assume that Naples in the 50s is as interesting as London in the 70s or Moscow in the 1980s. We go to plays to learn about others; if we learn about ourselves in the process, that is a bonus.'

The second production was of a new play by Trevor Griffiths, set in England during 1968, called *The Party*, and commissioned by Ken. It played on variations on the theme of left-wing commitment and the doubtful possibility of revolutionary change in Britain unless the working class creates its own leadership. Dexter was again directing, and Olivier proposed himself for the part of an intransigent, elderly, working-class Glaswegian Trotskyite called John Tagg. The performance on opening night was one of the purest and the most unforgettable of his career. It was, as the actor puts it, 'the most thrilling candlelight to go out on'. How ironic and splendid, Ken thought, that a call to revolution should be delivered by Olivier from the stage of the National.

The reviews of the play were largely virulent. As Milton Shulman wrote: 'There is nothing more likely to send an English audience into a deep sleep than a serious political play.' Ken noted: 'If – like Trevor – you are hoping to conquer a castle, you must not expect too much eager collaboration from those whose life-work is to guard the castle gates.'

Several nights after the opening of *The Party*, Olivier took Ken and me to supper at the Savoy Grill. Shortly after, he sent a scroll of signatures collected in Ken's honour, to mark his ten years with the Theatre. He also included some good wine. But Ken's valedictory was sad, and somewhat demeaning. He had to contend with the derisory views of William Gaskill and John

Osborne on his influence at the National (as reflected in a book by Logan Gourlay). He wrote to the *Sunday Times*: 'nowadays I feel rather like a good Samaritan who has crossed the road to be greeted by a kick in the face'.

In October he wrote to Olivier – having failed to make any headway with management – asking his help in the matter of severance pay. He pointed out that he had been working at the same salary at the National Theatre for ten years. What Ken wanted was a year's salary. 'I don't in the least mind being pushed out, but to be pushed out without proper compensation (granted readily to my assistant) leaves the permanent suggestion that I've failed in the job.' Olivier replied that he would approach Lord Rayne and, if necessary, the Board, and to this end he wrote to Rayne offering to present a 'full survey of Ken's record'. Eventually, and without a great deal of enthusiasm, some £2500 pounds was awarded, and Ken's career at the National came to an end.

37

Disaffection

The more disaffected Ken felt, the more rigid became his views. He had to get your vote and would twist facts to do so. He became dogmatic to the point of lunacy, without subtlety or lightness. He once declared that anyone who owned dogs must be an enemy of democracy and an upholder of the feudal system. Now that we no longer had slaves, or Victorian-type servants, and treated our children well, 'The only way left to command complete obedience and ownership was to have a dog.' Ken preferred cows and I once sighted him in a field, on a country weekend, wearing a cream silk dressing-gown, smoking a cigarette in a long holder, contemplating the herd.

The director Clifford Williams, who loved and trusted Ken, acknowledges that 'he was not very good at seeing that there could be another point of view that should be dealt with'. When Nicholas Tomalin dined with Ken, to interview him for a planned book on the National, he noted Ken's 'emotional need for complete rectitude, at the same time as being a controversialist by temperament'. And he added: 'Kathleen protectively anxious to justify Ken. Worried about his irascibility. He leaves with his arm warmly round [her].'

On one occasion, at a dinner of John Mortimer's, Ken started an argument with his old friend Jean Marsh. She recalls: 'He was going on about the bourgeoisie. He said, "I see the yellow press has got to you, the bourgeois press." I said, "What fucking bourgeois press? I don't even notice it on paper stands." Then I scraped my chair back and found myself saying in my old Cockney accent I hadn't used for years, "If you don't stop being so bleedin' condescending, I'm going to give you a fucking bunch of fives." John Mortimer took me to another room. I said, "I don't know why I'm doing this. Why am I so cross?"'

But Jean saw, too, that Ken was ill, that his looks had changed: 'It was difficult to explain to new people that inside that face, inside that body, was somebody so good-looking. When I first knew him he was startlingly beautiful,

338

and startlingly nice, a bringer out of people, a sun-shining person.'

Tony Garnett, who had traced Ken's fight for liberation since the mid-fifties and had seen how he influenced the changes in the sixties, observed that during the seventies Ken's enemies had their chance to get their own back. 'They could never stand him, and they bided their time and they were, on the whole, mean-spirited, which he never was.'

With many of the doors to his old life closed, Ken threw his energy, during 1974, into trying to set up his erotic film, an arduous, nerve-racking and ultimately unsuccessful campaign. With his private life in turmoil, and his work life unresolved, his behaviour was by turns unpredictable, hysterical, violent, craven. The odd friend who visited Thurloe Square during the day might hear Ken screaming and ranting at his wife over the matter of a pair of socks; or booting a group of children out of a room, which he suddenly and inexplicably had need of. 'It must be like living with a madman,' one terrified friend whispered to me. But Ken's madness had become normalcy to me.

I continued to function as best I could, to take the blows with my own improvised forms of self-defence, but without any liberating understanding of Ken's behaviour nor of my own. His moods would swing from adoring dependence upon me to heated verbal rage. My only aim was to keep myself and him as steady as I could, while protecting the children from our discord. But as a disturbed, reproachful and constant factor in his life, I was the very last thing he needed. Only in my notebook, or when talking to Trevor, did I begin to ask the questions which would eventually help me to see my commonplace condition in the larger context.

In the long run this weeping, impassioned woman who swamped Ken with guilt was tougher than he, more wilful and more manly. Had anyone told me so, I would have been aghast. Maybe he had sensed this, for in better times he once wrote me a poem in prose. It ended: 'There was never so straight a purpose yoked with so wavering and tremulous a physical vessel.'

Ken employed a new secretary, a small, trim girl who was absolutely unflappable. On her first day he swore in language she had never heard in her life. Dacia Mills asked whether he was swearing at *her*. She thought it wasn't quite necessary. It was one of Ken's tests and she came out with flying colours. He would from time to time dictate a letter with some impossible word that she couldn't spell, but, apart from the initial confrontation, he was kind and appreciative, as he was with all his secretaries. Dacia explains: 'I think he wondered, "Can I shock people more than I shocked them in the first place?" Just to sort of get everybody moving.' But as time went by she would watch him stir up a fuss with a letter here or an article there and then resent the outrage which ensued.

She recalled that he went to an Oxford reunion and returned disconsolate, saying that all his contemporaries had made it. She realized that he felt very lonely and let down at what had been done to him at the National, not knowing whether his old friends were worth having or were loyal; that he was looking for escape. Part of him still wanted the high life and to entertain, and part wanted simplicity and a cheap Indian restaurant. He could become obsessed with the making of a certain dish for dinner, or send back a new shirt from the boutique Deborah & Clare because one ruffle was not quite right, or demand within the hour – with childish petulance – a particular record. He could resent paying for the plumber or for his children's clothes. 'Yet he wanted to give you expensive gifts, and when you refused he became upset.'

'He needed to know where all the books were in the library,' Dacia continues. 'But when you got somebody to reorganize, he found that too much. His files were chaotic. He would ask me to create order, and then add, "Oh, what does it matter? It's all sort of so senseless." He wanted a secretary whom he could have rung up at three o'clock in the morning and said, "I suddenly feel like writing to the tax man." Yet part of him resented staff. I think he wanted you, as his wife, to be his cook, his housekeeper, his secretary and everything else. At the same time, he wanted you to work. He would go crashing out of the house saying, "I've got to go out," finding the intrusion of the children fairly difficult, and then come back again quite quickly, not knowing where he wanted to go.'

To accommodate the confusion in his private life, Ken 'out-theorized himself' (as Penelope Gilliatt put it) with the following decree: 'My solution to the problem of monogamy ... [is] to make marriage permanent and indissoluble, but at the same time, to make sexual infidelity compulsory for both partners who would be required to prove that in the course of each calendar year they had slept with a stated number of people other than their spouses.' He had forgotten that he had already accused me of being soiled for him because I'd been unfaithful. More thoughtfully he asked himself whether 'sex had filled the career vacuum'.

Ken wrote to me – as he did when he needed to think things out, or if he wanted my sanction: 'When I first met Tennessee Williams we got on very well and he said: "you're like me, you're a driven person." Well, my "drive" has driven me to this impasse up which I am now roaring at 100 mph.' In the cul de sac, 'on the fringe twilight', as he described it, he was safe, pleasured and in control.

Gradually Ken came to associate Nicole with his Birmingham life, comforting and comfortably ordinary and out of the light, unlike the world he had occupied since Oxford (and which he associated with me). On one occasion he went with Nicole to visit Bournemouth, where he had spent his childhood summers, had first learned about sex and had 'worshipped the concert party on Boscombe Pier'. He felt that the part of him that loved one world hated the other and vice versa. Once again he tentatively reopened his childhood (was perhaps Nicole a reflection of Rose?) and fumbled with the key to his past.

With Nicole he felt he did not have to prove himself, and was thereby eased. He could hide out with a girl he liked, without any demands being made. He did not much care for her interest in fatalism and astrology, nor for her acceptance of failure, but he liked her emotional honesty, her sweetness and her matching sexual tastes.

He made contact with Eileen Rabbinowitz, the Oxford girlfriend with whom he had had a sado-masochistic affair years before. Would she care to join him and Nicole? Eileen Rabbinowitz 'shied right away. It would certainly have been a bad emotional thing for me, and Ken was a person about whom it was impossible to be indifferent. This sounded potentially obsessive and disastrous. When I said no, he was very hurt that he should be rejected. He said very huffily, "I shan't trouble you again." What an unlike-Ken thing to say! Ken with his brilliant caustic wit and awareness of the absurd.'

He seemed to have lost his sense of the comic. He would attend London dinner parties and tell baffled guests that he now shaved his legs and wore women's underwear. He wanted to play as many sexual roles as possible, man–woman, master–slave, brother–sister. Failing to obtain my participation, he tried to get that of his one good woman friend. He asked her to visit him in a basement, and on another occasion to dine with a group where he was dressed in drag, in a shirt, long pink underpants, and stockings. Nicole was dressed as a man. 'He was deadly solemn. It was not the Ken I knew,' this friend recalls, 'and I had to go. I told him as I left, "I can't bear seeing this." He made a furious face and banged the door, but when we next saw each other we didn't talk about it. There were very few people who went on loving him and at the same time were capable of saying to him with great authority, "Look, don't do this." But I believe it was a minimal part of his life.'

At another time, when he was buoyant and younger, Ken's experiments might have been courageous adventures. But in the circumstances, and in the seventies, his sexual exploration – rather than being exclusively about passion, obsession or even curiosity – was also incited by ill health which he could not control but for which he was to some extent responsible. (With the pressures of trying to launch his film 'Alex and Sophie', he had begun smoking again for the first time in six years. He went on smoking until within a few months of his death.)

During these times, I was occasionally visited by spectres of death. It began around 1972, when a friend of ours gave us some honey hash ('from the virgin bees of Afghanistan'), which we spooned up together one evening while alone and watching television. The stuff barely registered on Ken, but I had a bad time. Somewhere during the course of an hour or two of hallucination I saw, between us, a rocking chair in which swayed an accusing skeleton.

Several years later, lying abed one night, I dreamed that I had succoured an old woman, brought her back to life with a transfusion of blood. The old woman was effusively grateful. As I lay beside Ken, in my dream, I said: 'We should think of the old woman, she's alone.' At which point my clothes and the blankets on the bed were swiftly and viciously torn off by an icy though unseen hand. My journal records: 'It is the old lady taking me away. She is death. I wake for comfort. The telephone rings and it is Nicole hysterical and full of suicidal threats. I tell K he'd better go and deal with her. Is she not a messenger of death? I'm so spooked that I pray. On my knees!'

For several years I treated these apprehensions as suspect, reflections of a suffering wife in a distorting mirror. Now I believe them to have had a more objective basis, as symptoms of Ken's real and central drama: his contest with mortality. He was not 'assenting to life even to the point of death', in Georges Bataille's famous definition of eroticism, so much as challenging life, and battling with it, in his endeavour to fend off the consequences.

Norman Mailer says Ken had 'impeccable logic from A to Z in any kind of system he was adopting, but these alphabets were stuck up there like dominoes and you could go in between them. If you're going to drive very close to the rim, then you've got to have a very coherent philosophy; otherwise, you don't know the parts of yourself that you're abusing. If you said, for example, "You're smoking too much," he would say, "Oh, go fuck yourself. The intellectual stimulation I get from smoking is quite worth the physical damage." I think Ken had a tendency to exorcise situations. He was not suicidal, he was self-destructive.'

In April 1974 Ken noted: 'I have now been working non-start since January.' He felt hopelessly blocked on his Reich book. In that month we went to Tunis for a gloomy week's holiday in the rain. Ken reported to his journal on our return that the last time he could remember feeling confident was two years before, when in Egypt. 'Were I to commit suicide, I would merely be killing someone who had already – to many intents and most purposes – ceased to exist. These grim reflections have had a markedly depressing effect on my libido. Sex in such a context seems as trivial as reading comics in a cancer ward.' He recorded that he could not find the necessary $150,000 to complete the new budget of $500,000 of 'Alex and Sophie', that even if he had the money he wondered whether he would have had the energy to direct.

In fact he proved throughout 1974 that he still had extraordinary energy and application: his engagement book is black with his continuous efforts to raise the money for the film and to find actors, locations and a production team. In June 1974 Ken recorded: 'If I could laugh at the situation, I would compare setting up a film to making a jigsaw out of quicksilver. But I am past laughing. I have only one basket and my one egg, and if that breaks, I can't survive.' But, despite this dramatic declaration, Ken went on fighting for the financing.

During the summer, Ken from time to time worked out of an office in Paris, interviewing actresses who might be suitable for the part of Sophie.

His producer, Christopher Neame, recalls that in Paris one night after dining with Thomas Quinn Curtiss, and discovering that Peter O'Toole was making a film (called *Rosebud*) in Curtiss's apartment below the Tour d'Argent restaurant, Ken decided to play a joke on his actor–friend. Since mirror writing had been a subject of conversation that evening, Ken hit upon the idea of leaving a letter in mirror writing for O'Toole, accusing the actor of being a renegade Irishman and a traitor to the IRA. He wrote that a bomb had been planted and that it would go off at a certain hour unless certain demands were met; and he signed it on behalf of the IRA. The note was found the following morning, the police called and the building cleared. O'Toole took his revenge by turning up at Ken's office with two members of the crew in attendance and beating him up.

This unhappy incident was, a month later, reconstructed by the magazine, *Private Eye*, which reported that Ken had appeared in a Chinese restaurant and removed his trousers to expose the O'Toole bruises before a table which included a twelve-year-old girl. *Private Eye* later conceded that Ken had not exposed 'the lower part of his anatomy'. Everybody giggled except Ken, who was piously though genuinely enraged: what if Roxana should hear of it?

Meanwhile the film situation remained only bearable, according to Ken, 'with constant recourse to pills and booze'.

In January 1975 Ken called upon a German porno-flick producer in Munich (who greeted him naked and in the midst of shaving). Nothing was forthcoming from the nude shaver, and although Ken continued during the next two years to fight for his project, it never took wing.

In September we were the guests of Ken's lawyer Oscar Beuselinck at a dinner dance in honour of the film *That's Entertainment*. His other guests were John Osborne and his then wife Jill Bennett. Ken and Osborne were uneasy with each other, could not perhaps remember whether they were on speaking terms or not. Osborne had attacked Ken for 'intellectual spivvery' at the National Theatre, whereas Ken had confided to his journal, after seeing *West of Suez* in 1971, that Osborne's opinion of the natives of a West Indian island – a mixture of 'lethargy and hysteria, brutality and sentimentalism – was not a bad description of J. O. himself'. He particularly objected to the snobbery of Osborne's appropriation of pain. He thought the play about as universal and Chekhovian as N. C. Hunter's *A Day by the Sea*, 'a Haymarket hit of the 1950's which it much resembles. Ironically it was from N. C. Hunter and his school that J. O. was alleged to have saved the English theatre.'

To break the ice, Jill Bennett asked me to dance (Ken did not, John would not). I accepted. 'I had a frock on,' she recalls, 'and you wore trousers. We were by far the most handsome couple in the room.' The ice was broken and it occurred to the two men that for all their mutual vituperation they were still worth each other's company. Within a week the Osbornes were dining *chez n*█████████████ *S*quare dinner' *à quatre*, Ken recorded in his journa█████████████████me sort of sexual prank. His signals to me, however, received no response, and after the Osbornes had left a huge fight broke out. Ken noted that by refusing to play the game I had 'made a very crucial psychological misjudgement, or a very ill-timed display of principled honesty'. But I doubt that the Osbornes, whose marriage was not in the finest shape, had any idea of their host's intentions. I sensed that what he really wanted was to co-opt me, rather than 'to corrupt' me, as he had put it more seductively several years before. I retained enough independent judgement to see that his proposal was preposterous, unerotic and ill judged. And I turned him down. But it gave me no comfort. A close friend, to whom I later confessed, saw my part less charitably. She said, 'You colluded with Ken all along.'

The day after our September rapprochement with the Osbornes, Ken and I set off on a week's eating tour across France into Alsace. We viewed Grünewald's great altarpiece at Colmar, between three-star restaurants. I paid for this *grande bouffe* by way of an article in a glossy magazine, and we were duly attacked for wicked indulgence by the left-wing press.

With the film in limbo Ken returned half-heartedly to his perennial biography of Reich. But he did not feel he could write well without a stance, 'without a cogent moral or political philosophy'. In addition, he asked himself, 'Could I have split myself if I had not already lost my entireness?'

Around this time he wrote a note to me from the drawing-room (where he now worked) and despatched it to wherever I was in the house. He reminded me that he was immobilized by anxiety. 'Also, I think, by the knowledge that your enormous grace will allow you to forgive me almost anything. You can forgive my sexual wandering; you will even forgive my idleness. And the knowledge that you will be merciful increases my guilt; and my anxiety. Thus the vicious circle is complete.' He added that of course he was self-dramatizing, and that his reason for writing was to postpone working – that he even preferred the pain of self-hatred to the drudgery of work. 'Is it guilt again – the feeling that I *ought* to suffer? Or is it fear that the book, even if finished, will not be any good? It is both these things; but more. Although I am tearing you apart,' he ended, 'please hold me together.' I do not recall how, or even if, I responded to this letter. It was hard to tell if Ken were dramatizing or not, while I was like some old campaigner punch-drunk with fatigue and unable to see the way ahead.

On 30 November Alan Beesley, aged fifty, killed himself, and a sharp reality broke into our murky drama. Alan had completed an autobiographical book called 'Breakdown', a moving and precise record of manic-depression for which Ken had written a foreword:

He does not write as we expect an English literary chap to write, since he has never learned the restraints, the decencies, the shocking decorum of what is called 'good taste'. If he had, his book would be a much more flattering self-portrait.... Hedda Gabler has the bad taste to shoot herself in the presence of her husband and his guests. 'People don't do things like that,' says the shocked Judge Brack. But they do. Alan ... (though I pray he won't) just might.

Alan was desperate, for all his wisdom and good sense, desperate because of his inability to control a cyclical depression and sickness, because of his fear of penury and of much else. He would say, 'I'd kill myself tomorrow if I didn't think hell was worse.' His mother, with whom at the end of his life he was living in a small house in Worthing, reported that he had put his head on her lap and said, 'Do you believe in hell? Do you think it's really bad?' And she had answered, 'Alan, I'm sure you've had your hell on earth.' Shortly afterwards he told her that he was going to take some new pills which would put him to sleep for thirty-six hours, and that he must not be disturbed.

In the grim funeral parlour Ken and I joined Alan's mother, his girlfriend, two of his three children and several Oxford contemporaries. It was a thin little service, and there were no flowers. Ken wept a great, heaving, tear-streaming boy's grief for his friend. How we wished we had offered more constant and loving care.

For all Alan's despair, Ken recorded, the words that sprang to mind when he thought of him were 'buoyancy, verve, resilience, and an insane indomitable optimism. "Don't worry, Ty-nan," I hear him braying with a convulsive flourish of his cigarette, "Next year is going to be our year." '

In February 1975 I took off for New York and Los Angeles for several weeks – a necessary step towards mind health and a rebuilding of self. It was now two years since our world had fallen apart. I was saner, and stronger, with an explosive appetite for lost life.

On Valentine's Day Ken sent me a cable with instructions to read Shakespeare's sonnet number 109 ('O, never say that I was false of heart'). He noted in his journal that, upon telephoning me in Beverly Hills, he had discovered I had not looked up the relevant sonnet. The following day he was felled by 'flu, 'my hoodlum ambusher, who always chooses low moments to step out of the shadows and zap me'. Meanwhile he recorded, with less than perfect accuracy, that a party was being given for me in Los Angeles, 'a poolside wing-ding with Tony Richardson, Warren Beatty, Billy Wilder and cast of surely hundreds. I don't wish I was there: but can she really wish she was here? Feel powerful need to fly to some sunny island, perhaps in the

Seychelles, and damn everything and everyone, including Kathleen and the expense.'

At the end of the month Ken set off for Taroudant, in southern Morocco (where I joined him), in an attempt to rid himself of the bronchial attack which he had endured for five weeks and for which he was taking antibiotics four times a day, along with salbutimol, cortisone, spandet, quinine and piriton. To this medication Ken added, to cheer himself up, a daily dose of one or two amphetamines, several glasses of hard liquor and a bottle of wine. (On reflection it is hardly surprising that his moods were dangerously quixotic.)

With the film moribund, two entrepreneurial projects remained: the sequel to *Oh! Calcutta!* and the production of a stage version of William Donaldson's so-called autobiography of an Etonian ponce, *Both the Ladies and the Gentlemen*, which Ken had described as worthy of comparison with the best of Evelyn Waugh. But in neither was he passionately involved. While reading an account of Hemingway in Spain, Ken saw in the writer's 'arid, despondent, written-out condition . . . a giant mirror-image of my own accidie'.

The journals record more of Ken's accidie than his fun and gaiety, an astonishing degree of which – until almost the end of his life – he could still muster. He was always surprising. No member of Ken's household knew how any particular day was going to go; whether he would finally decide to buy a Cadillac hearse *circa* 1955, costing £500, with beautiful brass knobs and baroque silver lamps; or whether we would buy a 170-foot Victorian gothic tower, known as May's Folly, near Tonbridge in Kent. After coming close to laying out £10,000 for the folly, it occurred to Ken that a tower, with its winding steps, might be hard for him to climb. With hearse and tower abandoned he settled on a Jaguar XJ-12, bought for some £8,000 on installment plan. He loved this 'silently lumbering giant', and the 'sense of cushioned escape'. he felt bowling along the motorway – protected yet truant and with the sensation, however illusory, of being in control of his life.

At home he dabbled; bought shirts or records, and persuaded John Wells to adapt *Both the Ladies and the Gentlemen* when Clive James had to drop out. (The project, in the stage and screen versions, was eventually abandoned.) In the meantime Ken wrote an introduction to Donaldson's second collection, *Letters to Emma Jane*, and there were other work doodles: an outline for an unusual television chat show with the working title 'At Home with Kenneth Tynan'. It would take place in a Tynan-type living-room, where a pianist would play and cats might stroll. In each of the proposed six programmes two 'resident' friends would make up the conversation piece: 'John Gross (lively editor of *Times Lit Supplement*), his beautiful wife Miriam, Benny Green, George Weidenfeld . . . Edna O'Brien'. There would also be one token celebrity and several oddballs per programme. Each session, conducted by Ken, might have a general theme – criminals, comedians, athletes. From time to time

Tynan would play games with his guests, such as betting an actor that he could not cry real tears in sixty seconds flat or challenging all present to converse exclusively in words of one syllable for five minutes, or playing the truth game, in which the participants had to deliver two truthful answers to one lie. There would be no studio audience, and Ken hoped that out of this loose group framework and domestic atmosphere would emerge something 'highly unpredictable (and often very un-cosy)'.

Nothing came of the television idea, nor of Ken's admirable notion for live cinema: a movie house devoted to film of the great live performers (excluding theatre, opera and ballet) but including great sportsmen, bullfighters, strippers, and stars of circus, music hall and cabaret.

That spring of 1975, however, he did write six talks on words for BBC radio, which were broadcast the following autumn. Ken talked about slang, surnames, the language of manipulation as practised by journalists and politicians; and adjectives coined from the names of the famous. He also talked about erotic language, and coined 'to palp', which might mean to squeeze a woman's breast gently. 'The obvious associations here are with "palpable", "pulp" and "pap", the old English word for "breast".' He had other suggestions: 'When a man and a woman of unorthodox sexual tastes make love, the man could be said to be introducing his "foible" into her "quirk".' He coined the word 'dislove' (which I have since stolen): 'It is what love becomes when a relationship has ended badly. It is how the ashes taste when the other person has put out the fire.' And he added a new verb, 'to tromp', as in 'he tromped (deceived) her'. He argued that what was needed, 'if we regard sex as a legitimate subject for literature, is a new, more neutral sexual vocabulary'.

In April 1975 my novel *The Summer Aeroplane* was published, and Ken had a copy set up in a rich leather binding marked 'From K to K'.

And in April we took Roxana to see *Henry v* at Stratford, to visit Shakespeare's tomb, and to show her Oxford, all of which, Ken hoped, would be deeply imprinted on the seven-year-old. In Stratford Ken found a copy of C. S. Lewis' *The Problem of Pain* and noted that 'As ever, I respond to his powerful suggestion that feelings of guilt and shame are not conditioned by the world in which we live but are real apprehensions of the standards obtaining in an eternal world.' A few months earlier he had assured himself, in a more recognizable Tynan voice, that the Judaeo-Christian God was 'the criminal who imported into civilisation the crippling notion of sin. Neither in pagan Rome nor in Buddhism (Zen or orthodox) is a man condemned because he behaves *badly*.'

Reading C. S. Lewis, who had such a potent (and mysterious) effect on him, Ken concluded that he should abandon his affair. But he asked himself whether he had not already undermined his wife's love to the point where he would lose her. 'Is it too late for me to unravel myself back to the first dropped stitch and knit the garment all over again? Signs and portents surround me.'

Ken had reminded himself how much he missed Spain, and the 'late-afternoon anguish of the corrida, without which holidays in other Mediterranean countries are like vegetarian diets'. So in May we went to Madrid for the festival of San Isidro, sat through two weeks of unexceptional bull-fighting, and toured the city. We were not ideal companions, made conscious of what we had lost by memories of so many other visits when we had been intimately and delightedly attached.

Ken reported to his literary agent that the city was 'buzzing with politics and on all sides one hears strong rumours that Franco is going to step down some time this Autumn. . . . If that happens it will transform the scene.' He wanted to hold off on the writing of a promised article to see what direction Spain might take.

I gave Ken a book on Goya, with a *catalogue raisonné* of the work. He was entirely delighted and decided to add the painter's name to his list of ideal dinner guests – which already included Shakespeare, Byron and Wilde. He recorded that it was nice to reflect that Bernard Berenson, 'the arch-mandarin', believed that modern anarchy began with Goya.

In August Ken joined me and the children *chez* the film producer Sam Spiegel, in his villa at St Tropez. The local doctor came by to prescribe various pills, and managed to silence a cough that had lasted months. Ken described his exorcism: 'a curious sensation in the left lung, "lair of the beast": as if three needles were being driven into it, one after the other. Like stakes into a vampire's heart. It's now mid-day on the following day: still no paroxysm. Begin to feel life is a rational possibility.'

We drove up into the hills above the coast to lunch with Tony Richardson in his converted peasant village. Ken felt a great envy for the unpretentious luxury of this wild, quiet place in the forest, and an even greater envy (and admiration) for Tony Richardson, who orchestrated a large extended family to the apparent happiness of all.

When we returned to London, he agreed to submit to a nature cure I had secured, by courtesy of a Dr Alan Moyle. An exclusive diet of onions and potatoes lasted all of a couple of days. He did, however, stick longer with a glutinous drink of boiled carrageen moss, brought up to his bedroom of a morning by a mountainous Spanish cleaning woman called Ofelia. This curious ritual was noted by the most recent secretary, an exceptionally pretty girl called Suki Dimpfl, who always arrived late for work, and quite often hung over too. On one such morning Ken gave Suki a monumental list of things to do, which included taking a new shirt back to Harrods and typing out letters to *The Times* and to the *New Statesman*. She said, 'I can't, Ken, I simply can't,' because she had a crackerjack of a hangover. And he said,

'Don't worry.' He went downstairs and got a bottle of Pouilly Fuissé and two glasses. He told her, 'I'm going to teach you the rudiments of cricket,' and with the white wine in hand he sat her down before the television set to watch a Test match.

On Thursdays, Suki had to hand out wages. Matthew, aged four, would watch her trying to make the sums balance. He wore a cowboy outfit at this time, with hat, a holster and gun. Suki asked him, 'Matthew, where's your horse?' He said, 'It's outside.'

When a child could talk and therefore entertain him, Ken became an excellent father: a father for occasions. Tracy, now twenty-three, came to stay with us and Ken noted how well she had survived, 'every horizon open to her sweetness and energy. Whatever my sins, I can certainly sire exquisite children.'

His womenfolk, he once proudly claimed, did not survive. In August he encountered Elaine Dundy at a party, the first time they had met since parting. She had spent several years at the Riggs psychiatric clinic in Stockbridge, Massachusetts. In 1974, while living in London, she published a novel called *The Injured Party*, in which – among much else – a wife murders her husband. Ken thought he detected a portrait of himself. He found the idea that he might be the model for the fictional sadist, who drew blood, 'wonderfully horrid'.

I had met Elaine on my own, in 1974, and had found her charming and lively. On the occasion of the summer party, over a year after my first meeting, I noticed that she had put on a considerable amount of weight, and that she shook. She was cordial, and that night sent us a little letter enclosing a report of Tracy's academic career (studying liberal arts at Sarah Lawrence College), of which she was pleased and proud. She added that with such a witty and brilliant father, no wonder Tracy had been doing well. It was a generous communication, and Ken wrote back, 'At least *something* worked!'

After this encounter I asked Ken whether he thought I might not be pointed along Elaine's unhappy route. Impossible, he said absently. 'But what *am* I to you?' I asked. 'You are my wife,' he said.

38

Tynanosaur

In September 1975 Laurence Olivier came to lunch with us before being interviewed by Ken for television. We had not seen him for a year or more and were shocked by the effect upon him of a muscular wasting disease called myositis. His glorious voice seemed caught in the thin higher registers, and he had the vegetable-healthy pink skin of an old man. He was still riveting to listen to, and unpredictable. Ken noted: 'His Rolex watch hangs loosely round his wrist; and he has unwisely grown a little suburban moustache which makes him look ... like a ... retired major in a Sunningdale saloon bar. He will never appear on the stage again.'

In October 1975 Ken went to East Berlin, for the *New York Times*, to take a look at the Berliner Ensemble, four years after Weigel's death and nineteen after Brecht's. What he found was 'a haunted house – part enslaved to, and part trying to break away from his great ghost'. He wrote in his journal: 'Trying to avoid rigid Brechtian procedures, it has plunged into a capricious electicism that is either no style at all or (at times – e.g. in the new production of *Die Mutter*) a strange throwback to Expressionism....' But he admitted that Brecht was still the major influence on European theatre.

While in Germany Ken reflected that 'politics is serious in Europe in a way that it never is in England.... Because Socialism as a political fact has never been nearer to us than – what? – 1,000 miles, we have never had to take it seriously, as a real and immediate possibility. Other Capitalist countries of Europe – France and Italy, for example – have adopted homeopathic remedies; they have inoculated themselves against the dreaded disease by tolerating strong Communist parties within their borders.... The presence of powerful Marxist parties provokes the Social Democrats and right-wingers to genuine thought. Lacking such provocation, our twin parties have no ideological foundations: they are like opposing attorneys playing a game in court, after which they will share a bottle of wine at their club.' Ken did not add that this state of affairs might provide a good argument for being in the Common Market – a club he could not stand.

On 27 November *The Sound of Two Hands Clapping*, a collection of journalism written since he had given up regular theatre criticism, was published, described by Ken in the preface as a collection of 'enthusiasms' for people, places and ideas that had excited him. His enthusiasm for bullfighting, masturbation and certain stars understandably offended those critics who viewed with horror killing animals, self-abuse and celebrity worship. A collection as diverse and as occasional as this came in for a degree of censure.

Germaine Greer, in the *New Statesman*, quoted Ken saying as a young man, 'When maturity overtakes me, I shall have a great many less important but weightier things to do than sit trembling in theatres,' and she concluded, on the evidence of *The Sound of Two Hands Clapping*, that maturity was 'as far off as ever'. But she added that Ken, though 'no more grown up than Peter Pan', was much more necessary and beloved than his repressive and disapproving opponents.

Greer argued that Ken was fascinated by supermales 'in a manner almost girlish' (while another critic, Russell Davies, described his celebration of the famous as 'boyish' – even while the writing was done with 'no apparent effort, and absolute hard-edged clarity of outline').

Accusations of contradictory thinking and disconnectedness were thrown out by the critic and scholar John Carey: 'Disillusioned, desperate and powerless, sustained only by the chance that there may yet be someone somewhere whom he can shock and outrage, the figure that emerges from the book is almost a blueprint of the disaffected English intellectual in later middle age.'

Ken's own relentless self-criticism made anyone else's sound paltry. A book on prehistoric animals that he happened to be reading prompted the following:

The fossilized remains of Tynanosaurus Thurloviesis (the so called 'pseudo-lizard of Thurloe Square') are unique survivals of the late pre-holocaust era. The penis, in retraction a paltry object, seems to have been capable of monstrous extension, and there has been speculation that it was used as an offensive weapon or as a 'truffling snout' to dig up tasty tubers. The thoracic cavities were thickly lined with the characteristic layers of nicotine and tar with which many vertebrates of this epoch armed themselves against anxiety. The arms (or 'wings', according to the eccentric and largely discredited hypothesis of Ricqwihr) are tenuous and brittle, scarcely capable of supporting any manual exercise more demanding than self-abuse. (Was the Tynanosaur *homo masturbans*, as Guddle posits?) The cerebral hemispheres, though relatively huge were filled with rust, used stamps and bird droppings, suggesting that the creature's brains had been 'picked' by members of his peer-group (a not uncommon feature of life in the *genus journalisticum*), or that they had somehow fallen out of his ears (*vide* Ricqwihr's curious monograph: 'Braindrop by Aural Seepage'), or that the Tynanosaur had fallen into such general atrophy and disuse that, by a process of accelerated natural selection, his brains had been eliminated altogether. All these features point to a remarkable conclusion: for the first time in the history of palae-ontology, we have here a creature which, long before physical death overtook it, had already become partially extinct.

Yet this 'partially extinct' monster could, without warning, celebrate life. On a golden weekend that autumn of 1975, we took the children to a hotel in the Cotswolds, and Ken recorded: 'Matthew's vocabulary grows apace and he now qualifies as a person with whom conversation is possible. Roxana long since passed that test. Both are simply breath-bereaving in their prettiness. Watching Matthew eating pâté (for which, at 4, he has developed a con-noisseur's fondness) and being asked by Roxana to explain the meaning of democracy, I caught K's eye across the lunch-table (roast beef and Burgundy) and felt for almost the first time that we were a family – i.e. that each had tough and durable wires of sympathy connecting him/her with the other three that he/she would never feel for any other person.'

In December, on the strength of my novel, I was asked to write some scenes for a troubled movie called *Trick or Treat*. (It featured Bianca Jagger in a lesbian love affair, with Michael Apted as director and David Puttnam and Sanford Lieberson producing.) My new scenes were approved and shot almost as I wrote them, a saga which became even more Walter-Mittyesque when I was asked to rewrite the whole film, followed by a further mad request to fly to Los Angeles to help with some complicated and preposterous negotiation. Fortunately for the honour of all, the film was cancelled. But out of this venture David Puttnam asked me to come up with an idea for an original. Early in 1976 I proposed writing a script about the strange eleven-day disappearance in 1926 of the mystery writer Agatha Christie. This idea was accepted, and I went to work.

I was thereafter fully occupied on one project or another; and earning money, which we needed. The effect on Ken of the partial emancipation of his wife was mixed: he both liked and resented my new status. He saw that I was still his woman, that he could try me and I would come running, but he felt that my new independence provided a further threat to the small control he held over his life and his satellites.

During the autumn and spring of 1975–6 he was engaged in putting together and appearing before camera in a series of twelve arts programmes for BBC television. His first programme for *Arena* had included the interview with Laurence Olivier. In a talk with Trevor Griffiths, Ken noted that the contemporary fringe theatre, instead of seeking to change the Establishment from within, stayed outside in permanent opposition. He would have preferred it to be more belligerent, more determined 'to conquer the commercial and subsidised citadels'.

It is not surprising that during the flowering of the fringe theatre in the early seventies, Ken gave his allegiance to those writers and groups who took a political position. He lauded David Hare's co-operative venture, *Fanshen*, about revolution in a Chinese village – the 'first offshoot of the Brecht tradition to stand comparison to the parent tree'. And he admired the work of John McGrath and his politically committed theatre, 7 : 84.

In another programme he suggested that the leadership of the National Theatre should be reappraised – because the task was too great for one man ('Preferable to appoint a triumvirate or quartet of directors with a chairman who would be first among equals, but who would not be creatively involved in theatre himself and could bear the huge burdens of administration, liaison with government and Arts Council, and committee work in the corridors of power, while the directors controlled artistic policy'). He argued that there was a 'crisis of criticism', and that the critics at work feared ideology, tended to sneer, were dogmatic only in their determination to be different, did not act as rallying-points, as beacons or even as signposts, and remained deadeningly in the middle of the road.

Late in 1975 Ken had been invited by Clay Felker of *New York* magazine to become their drama critic. He was gratified, but since his allegiance was to the *New Yorker*, he checked with William Shawn. He was not plotting to try to oust Brendan Gill, but he did not want to turn up as drama critic for another Manhattan magazine without first consulting a man he greatly honoured. Shawn proposed that, starting the following autumn, Ken write six profiles for the magazine a year, and that he be paid $44,000 plus expenses to transplant himself and family to New York, and Ken gratefully accepted. Shortly afterwards, at my suggestion, he decided to settle in California, where the climate would better guard his health.

In February 1976 he went to New York to see Shawn and to discuss the new job. He took Tracy and her boyfriend to dine at Sardi's and was reassured to find that after four years' absence he was still recognized and welcomed. He felt extremely lonely, despite the proximity of loving friends like the Sidney Lumets and the Adolph Greens, and called me in France (where I was taking a short holiday with my loyal friend Dirk Bogarde) to report on his condition and to tell me that he could not face the high spirits and spontaneity of those 'excellent, enviable people'.

He flew down to Miami to help publicize a revived production of *Oh! Calcutta!* and recorded that 'Even the weather, here, is falsified for money. As the palms bend outside my window in the gale, I turn on TV to hear that it's another "sweltering day for Miami Beach".... As posters remind the citizens: "Visitors are vital." '

While in Miami he read Martin Green's *Children of the Sun*, and fell upon an extract from the diary of the famous Oxford undergraduate and homosexual dandy Brian Howard: 'In a month I shall be 50. What has kept me from writing hitherto, was – first – too much self-criticism, perfectionism. Secondly, a swelling guilt: I have it as others have elephantiasis.... Once I had not only talent, but what English people call "character". By which they mean the power to refrain. Now I have neither – Will has left me, and the capacity truthfully to imagine – vision – is leaving. I consider myself damned.' Ken noted that but for the difference of a year this could be a self-description, of *'ce moi haïssable'*. He added that Howard killed himself shortly afterwards.

Ken's behaviour was polarized in a manner almost schizoid. He could be practical, life-loving and gaily pleasure-seeking even while he was self-hating and self-destructive. Sometimes 'the tripartite conspiracy between the sexual, the excretory and the cruel' (in Laurence Olivier's brilliant phrase) seemed to have consumed him, just as at other times he was all sweetness and exuberant sexuality.

Years before, in reviewing Mailer's *Advertisements for Myself*, he had written that in this writer's 'quest for Hip, he is in danger of losing the prime virtue of civilized man – the ability to shock oneself'. That virtue Ken never lost. But he had a small side too, as Edna O'Brien observed, 'which was of not letting you hide your own shame'.

In the autumn of 1974 I began an affair with Daniel Topolski, an athlete and writer. In his company and that of his family I found a sanctuary. I would sit in the kitchen of their Regent's Park house, and Marion Topolski, a black-haired intellectual beauty, would cook up something and complain about the state of the world or, from time to time, complain about Ken. 'He eats away deep into you,' she once said as she dished up shepherd's pie. But worst of all, according to Marion, he was betraying his talent.

I gradually regained spirit and confidence. One day I went with Daniel to visit his father's studio. Feliks, who was at work on a vast mural, came down off his ladder to greet us. He said he did not recognize me. 'You look so much younger and taller. Also I can see your feet' (which happened to be in sandals). 'When I knew you before, when you were a hostess, I never saw parts of you like that.' For some reason this comment cheered me enormously.

On one occasion after the beginning of the affair Ken wrote in his journal that, having made love to his wife, potency abruptly vanished 'after she spends another night with her lover Dan Topolski'. When I explained that this new affair would not break up our marriage, he asked me angrily why I could not choose an older man rather than someone in his twenties. He said he intended to write about Topolski for the *New Yorker*, as the perfect twentieth-century Englishman. On another occasion, suspecting that the self-same Englishman might have accompanied me on a trip to the north of England, he telephoned each member of the Topolski family to discover where I was.

He would say, 'I don't see why you have to have a lover just to spite me,' followed by, 'The trouble is I love you.' Then he would leave to see Nicole.

Dirk Bogarde saw that I was now stronger but concluded that I would not leave Ken. He told me, 'You love your foolish Oblomov husband, and you will do all you can to make it work. There's nothing to be done about it. At least you've got your children.'

The drama continued and we played it out. In March Ken noted in his journal that debts were mountainous and the telephone might soon be cut off for non-payment. 'Kathleen says we must put on merry faces and appear to enjoy ourselves. My comment: I don't enjoy *enjoying* myself any more.'

He described himself as a 'stricken, blotchy, corpse-pallid, double-chinned, river-veined wreck', and a narcissist to boot. He insisted, 'One can detest oneself intimately and still be a narcissist.' And he quoted Norman Mailer: 'It is not love of the self but dread of the world outside the self which is the seed of narcissism.'

On 30 January 1976 *The Times* ran a fierce editorial following the acquittal of Linda Lovelace's autobiography on charges of obscenity. The leader was headlined 'The Pornography of Hatred'. *The Times* decreed that the fact that the book was written 'in language a lorry driver would understand . . . should not be decisive against it'. It continued to ramble on and to suggest that there would be more of such books, 'books which illustrate and glorify sadistic practices' and 'the general hatred of mankind. . . . This is Nazi pornography, the pornography practised in the concentration camps. . . . Such pornography does deprave; indeed we can see that pornographers themselves have been depraved by just such an exposure to the pornography of cruelty. (In last week's *Times Literary Supplement* Mr. D. A. N. Jones analysed the development of Mr. Kenneth Tynan's acceptance of cruelty; the process of corruption in a talented writer was precisely that of pornography.)'

D. A. N. Jones had recently reviewed two Tynan collections, *A View of the English Stage* and *The Sound of Two Hands Clapping*, and had examined Ken's attitude to the productions of Peter Brook, in an effort to prove, with no great effect, that Ken had endorsed violence and cruelty in Brook's work.

Ken wrote to the editor of *The Times*, William Rees-Mogg: 'What you said about me, quite unequivocally, was that I had been "depraved and corrupted" by the pornography of cruelty. . . . This is such a stupefying charge that even to deny it is in part to legitimise it. It is like trying to answer the question: "When did you stop getting pleasure from seeing Jews gassed?" ' Ken had described the D. A. N. Jones review as 'transparently dotty', and he ran over the points. One example is as follows:

Writing in 1946 about Peter Brook's production of Sartre's *Huis Clos*, I said it ended with three people in Hell suffering 'the completest torture that malevolence could prescribe for them.' This is precisely accurate: but the torture involved is not physical:

it is simply – each other's company! Realising this, they burst into a 'frightful peal of laughter, exquisitely timed and protracted by Mr. Brook'. So they do: this is the laughter of the damned. Yet from this sentence Jones extracts two words, puts them together to form the phrase 'exquisitely frightful', and later cites the phrase (which I never used) as one of the milestones on my road to perdition!

After legal action, *The Times* published a brief apology on the leader page. But Ken had been stunned and deeply wounded by this attack. He told Daniel Farson in an interview: 'The connections that are made in the English minds are very, very subterranean and of great interest to psychoanalysts, I have no doubt, but they can be extremely painful and hurtful when they are applied to oneself.'

Two small incidents during the spring of 1976 serve to illustrate Ken's tendency to expose himself to ridicule. On 2 February, his beloved Shirley MacLaine opened at the Palladium in her one-woman show, a performance which he found 'staggering' and a triumph of high definition performance. Later that evening we gave a party in her honour, to which Ken invited a number of actors and writers. One playwright recalls that when Miss MacLaine eventually arrived from the Palladium, 'we stood in line to be presented to her, exactly like the Queen, and Ken slotted perfectly into place as the Queen's equerry, whispering into her ear the name of the person she was about to meet next.'

In May Ken decided to dress as his screen heroine Louise Brooks for a fancy-dress ball. To this end he wore a wig modelled after the hairstyle of the young Brooks, a feathered blue Lurex gown, sequinned underwear, a suspender belt and black stockings. He carried a handbag, and a six-inch ivory cigarette-holder. I was elected to make him up for this event, a procedure he submitted to with the utmost seriousness. He found the idea of dressing as a woman very appealing. 'This doesn't make me a transvestite,' he wrote in his journal. 'But it does mean that I enjoy exploring more sexual possibilities than those available to macho males in jeans and T-shirts.' And he added, 'I regard it as a gap in me that I've never been turned on by the sight, touch or thought of a man.'

Though he made a big effort to control his gestures and behave like a vamp, this was a performance which as his partner – dressed in the Garbo dress from *As You Desire Me* which Ken had copied for me in happier years – I found extremely depressing. But Ken eventually forgot the solemnity of the occasion. When asked who he was meant to be, he answered, 'Baden-Powell.'

Having abandoned the notion that the sequel to *Oh! Calcutta!* should be a journey of discovery conducted by one author, Ken and Clifford Williams returned to the original formula. Williams points out that there was only one way to follow the original show, to put sexual intercourse on stage. 'We knew that that was expected of us.' But it happened to be illegal, and they could not deliver.

Titles were tried and abandoned: 'After Calcutta', 'Queen Kelly's Secret Circus', 'Soft Anvil', 'The Blue Revue' were suggested. *Carte Blanche* – nobody's first choice and everybody's second – was finally chosen. Ken tried to give shape to the material at hand: visual erotica, sketches concerning soloists, or twosomes, or threesomes, group sex. Sex as practised by geriatrics. To this pot-pourri he contributed, amongst other sketches, a playlet called 'Triangle in Six Takes', in which a man and two women play out various fantasies, some of which include flagellation and incest. Neither the director nor the producers really liked 'Triangle'. The lighting adviser, Richard Pilbrow, declared it would drive people out of the theatre. Williams felt that Ken had an excellent visual imagination, but that he wrote dialogue by numbers, so that it was 'a bit constructed' – curious, in view of Ken's brilliance at mimicry.

Ken, on the other hand, was obsessed by this particular piece, and had taken care to write into his contract that the number could not be excluded. Williams – who loved Ken and respected him – was exceptionally irritated at not being able to communicate his point of view. 'I could not begin to sum up the aggravation which I felt for him during the rehearsals of "Triangle". He was so *mad*.'

On 30 September *Carte Blanche* opened in London, to generally poor critical response.

On 4 July 1976, Ken had gone, under his doctor's orders, into the Brompton Hospital once again. He wrote in his journal: 'I listen to the falsetto, gibberish moans that are the audible half of the dialogues in which old men take part while they sleep; the other speakers are heard only in their dreams.'

Ken was passed from doctor to doctor. His general practitioner, John Henderson, wrote to a colleague to explain that Ken had been seeking 'the Holy Grail of the easy cure from one doctor after another and finally has come back again to me. Considering that he is an intelligent man it seems amazing to me that having given up smoking for [so] long he has taken it up again now.'

On 26 September, a few days before setting out for Los Angeles, where Ken would join me and the children, I paid a visit to the chest specialist Dr John Batten, under whose care Ken had been for several years. Batten felt that despite the deterioration of Ken's lungs, and on the condition that he were able to avoid serious infection, he should have a life span of a further ten years – though with increasing debility. It had not occurred to me – rather it had not fully registered – that Ken's life was under sentence of death, and I left Dr Batten's office in great despair.

The summer had been a term of trial. I had gone to Los Angeles on an earlier visit to find a house for us; meanwhile Ken, according to his secretary Rosemary Nibbs – now back with us – sat in our dining-room (his latest workplace) and did not work. He was excessively depressed.

In August we went for a weekend to Cornwall, to a hotel on a bend of the River Tamar, and from there we visited the woolly monkey sanctuary, on the coast near Looe. It emerged that the preservationist in charge, Leonard Williams, was also a victim of emphysema. He asked Ken whether he had trouble putting on weight. Ken had believed that his weight, 147 pounds, was a tribute to diet. Now he wondered if he might not be wasting away. What he took as a source of pride now became a source of fear.

In London, we let our house and moved temporarily into the home of neighbours. The news that Ken was leaving England was received by several members of the press with xenophobic derision. How could any good Englishman dream of jumping ship? He would answer that 'for emotional openness and accessibility of ideas I'm very Americanized'. Of his fellow English intellectuals he said: 'They produce wasps but they don't make honey.' Ken told Daniel Farson that the horizons across the Atlantic looked bigger: 'People seem less concerned with picking on the petty, or tearing off old scabs. . . . When I did *Oh! Calcutta!*, somebody said, "He has queered his pitch for the rest of his career," the assumption being that one's career was the final, ultimate, encircling aim of one's life. . . . My aim has only been to do what I think I can do, as well or better than other people in the same field.' He told another journalist that in the States 'it doesn't surprise people that you want to review plays *and* write films. Here you're stuck with your one thing.' He was not concerned with writing something 'serious' or 'distinguished', as was expected of him. He wanted not only to accomplish what he and only he could do, but also and above all to get pleasure out of so doing. The erotic film would have filled the bill. A directorial post in the theatre would have pleased him. If he had been well he might have been able to make the change.

Now the *New Yorker* and life in America promised new hope. He wanted to get his life back, and he terribly badly wanted to stay alive.

Ken moved into a flat near his beloved Lord's cricket ground, while in early October I left for California. He gave a farewell party in the flat of Rosemary Nibbs. Nicole was there, and Jonathan Miller, and one or two other friends, like Michael Blakemore. The latter recalls that it was a nice party, but not the kind of ebullient celebration he associated with Ken.

Two days later, on 25 October, he attended the opening of the new National Theatre building, a gala affair presided over by the Queen. Laurence Olivier made a florid speech, and then fell asleep during the second half of the play – a production of Goldoni's *Il Campiello*. In the interval, the old but sprightly playwright Ben Travers told Ken that 'If they had to open the theatre with a thoroughly rotten play, why couldn't they choose a thoroughly rotten English play?' Ken thought the choice perverse to the point of madness, and the evening a disaster.

On 30 October 1976 he flew to California, and – but for the odd few weeks – never again lived in England.

39

Los Angeles

'Life in Santa Monica is very curious. Every morning a large golden orb appears in the sky. People remove their clothes and jump into pools of water. It is very strange for an Englishman.' So wrote Ken of his first few days in California. It was all very new to him, and surprisingly agreeable. I had rented a glorious, sprawling Spanish-style house at the end of Kingman Avenue, in the Santa Monica Canyon, for $2,200 a month. It was more than we could afford (our income from renting our London house, and from *Oh! Calcutta!* came to £10,200 a year, and Ken had not yet completed his first profile for the *New Yorker*), but it was a luxury I felt we needed to launch our new life. The place had thick-walled privacy, and silence, except for the cooing of pigeons and the sound of the children splashing and squealing in the swimming pool. We were close enough to the ocean to be free of smog, and the air smelled of eucalyptus and orange blossom, and at night of wood smoke from the open fire in the high-beamed living-room.

Very swiftly Ken's health, as a 'climatic émigré', improved. Every few days he would visit the local foreign newspaper shop or the Brentwood Mart to pick up some reading at the Book Nook. He looked very unusual, elegant and formally dressed, among the bland and bronzed, casually dressed crowd. He complained that the only way you could tell it was a weekend was when your neighbour wore shorts.

Hilary Champion had come from England to look after the children, and Sheila Weeks, a Canadian divorcée with a sharp sense of humour, moved in to act as a part-time cook in exchange for a room. After preparing her first meal, Sheila apologized for 'leaning on the spices'. 'In future, darling,' Ken told her, 'lean.'

I found a corner of the master bedroom where I laid out my notes and began my screenplay – a speculative fiction based on the disappearance of Agatha Christie. Ken occupied a study of his own. The children, Roxana then nine, Matthew, five, went to the local school. This institution deemed Roxana a 'specially gifted child', and told her to express herself by digging a hole in the playground, a kind of Orwellian pacification device for dangerously bright children, we concluded. Quite soon afterwards we transferred both children to a small private school.

One morning, a tall good-looking, blonde girl came to be interviewed for the job of part-time secretary. She found her prospective employer in the kitchen, dressed in a pumpkin-coloured shirt under a spotted mustard-coloured dressing-gown, his skinny legs resting in hand-made *gros point* slippers. Judy Harger had never in her life met anyone so eccentric-looking, nor so serious and apologetic. She could not match him with his wife. After a couple of weeks in his employ his reserve broke down and she discovered Ken's sense of humour. He would complain and cry wolf in a slightly martyred way. But he also made her laugh. One day she told him that she would like to have a child called 'Clarity' and this moved him to tears. He said that was the nicest name for a child, and he wished he had more of it himself.

He said he felt badly about Matthew, not being able to play with him in an active way; that he was reminded of his own bed-ridden father. He felt very close to his son, very like him. 'As for Roxana, he was fascinated with this female reproduction of himself. She had his features, his precociousness. She had his genes, and there she was – a woman, which was exciting to him. He felt an unspoken, undefined bond with her.' Though I appeared to be in charge, and more responsible than my husband, Judy saw that Ken had a great emotional hold over me, and could turn me quite swiftly into a tearful little girl. Roxana was never frightened by him. Nor did he ever try to humiliate her. He respected her and never played any tricks.

We explored Los Angeles with our usual passion for new cities: the beaches of Malibu and Venice, houses by Frank Lloyd Wright, and the architects Greene and Greene; the Norton Simon Museum, the County Museum, Art Deco movie houses, old movie lots, Disneyland, and the Tar Pits with their meagre display of prehistoric animals. We travelled in a leased new four-door Buick Riviera with seats which moved back and forth, up and down, by remote control and were covered in baby-blue crushed velvet. Here was the real selling point of the car, Ken concluded: all the German auto engineering encountered on the road, labelled Mercedes and Porsche, was merely a pathetic diversionary tactic to distract attention from a lack of upholstery such as ours.

Ken soon discovered the ceremony of the car wash, where you vacate your machine and watch it pass through a tunnel of 'spray, cascades and whirling brushes', followed by a 'shivery curtain of chamois leather'. He noticed that almost every car passing through this procedure was clean *to start with*, and concluded that the business had very little to do with the washing of cars. 'It is in fact a purification in which it is not so much the car that is purified as its owner. It is he who feels morally and spiritually cleansed, as his machine emerges gleaming from the assembly line. And for an extra dollar he can subject it to a further ordeal: an inundation of hot wax. This represents the annealing fire through which the soul must pass.'

Los Angeles was in other respects lush and worldly. The rats lived in palm trees, and the used-car salesman was 'into no grief'. Ken asked himself what he had done, and 'more ominously' what he was going to have to do, to deserve it all. At the same time he was disturbed to discover that California was the country's chief weapons arsenal and military research centre. Los Angeles also appeared to be a vast supermarket of sex. It was not *The Times* that Ken now read, but *The Fetishist Times*, a mind-bogglingly explicit and arcane tabloid. On one occasion he visited a sex clinic which advertised all sorts of erotic delights. 'The sweetheart assigned to me', he later reported, turned out to be a huge black woman 'built like a Watusi warrior with an Afro hairdo like a geodesic dome'. Ken got the impression that she wanted to wrestle with him ('about as enticing as taking on King Kong') and he fled the place as soon as he dared.

Quite soon after his arrival he discovered a local bullfight club, and a cricket club formed by some homesick English actors. But he had no need to look for entertainment: during our first years in Los Angeles, Ken was thoroughly and assiduously sought out by agents, movie stars and elderly socialites. He was wonderful company and was always asked back.

Ken noted that in London he wore a dinner jacket roughly once a year, whereas in Los Angeles, during the course of one week, he had worn black tie to the première of *The Last Tycoon*, to the wedding of Marisa Berenson in a tent; and to a dinner given by the agent Swifty Lazar and his wife Mary, where he encountered Jack Nicholson, Warren Beatty, Merle Oberon and Liza Minnelli. It was at this gathering that Sue Mengers, who planned to entertain a group of the same ilk on the following night, hissed into Ken's ear: 'I'll show the bastard. I'll get Streisand tomorrow, so help me.' And of course she got Streisand, and a supporting cast which included Steven Spielberg, Ray Stark and Tatum O'Neal. Ken later set down his conversation with Miss O'Neal, then aged thirteen:

KT: Is there any living person you'd specially like to meet?
TO'N: (After a brief shrug) No (Pause) Maybe Laurence Olivier. (Pause) But really – no.

We spent Thanksgiving *chez* Billy and Audrey Wilder, where Ken questioned George Burns about a legendary vaudeville act in which he had never quite believed, called Swain's Rats and Cats. 'The rats were dressed as jockeys, and rode round a little race track on the cats' backs,' Burns explained. Ken still didn't believe it.

By New Year's Eve we were back with the Wilders, followed by a party given by Peter Bogdanovich. Ken commented that the crowd was younger and in general less attentive, and took refuge with Gore Vidal. 'Have you noticed how, no matter what you say, no one ever listens?' his friend pointed out, and Ken replied, 'They don't even way-way huh *wait* for me to stop stammering.'

Los Angeles reinforced Ken's view that the United States was a country of success for its own sake, of timing for timing's sake (*vide* Johnny Carson), and of being cheered for its own sake (*vide A Chorus Line*). He could find no other motive, such as pleasure. He also discovered that 'dictatorship of good intentions', as Joan Didion has put it, 'a social contract in which actual and irreconcilable disagreement is as taboo as failure or bad teeth, a climate devoid of irony'.

But we did find an escape from these strictures, an oasis of friends living in the city: Tony Richardson, Robert Towne, Christopher Isherwood and Don Bachardy. Ken admired Isherwood's strict candour and classlessness (so unlike most other writers of his generation), and his enthusiasm, which was as pure as a child's. This blue-jeaned, crew-cut septuagenarian believed that in the eyes of eternity there was no such thing as good or bad. 'It is too important for that.' He would talk admiringly of E. M. Forster and Jean Cocteau, while Gore Vidal, Ken noticed, would listen with quiet respect. Having read *Christopher and His Kind*, Ken congratulated Isherwood on mastering the 'literature of testimony, or eye-witness accounts of significant events' which he suspected would prove to be the most lasting form of art. 'Christopher surprises and pleases me', Ken noted, 'by saying that he agreed.' Also in this oasis were the writers John Gregory Dunne and his wife Joan Didion, whom I had first met several years before, and who became good friends during our Californian sojourn. Dining with them promised inspired gossip and comment from John, and the sight of Joan's thin and neurasthenic body in a silk caftan, perhaps an orchid in her hair, preparing lunch in the kitchen, listening to John – for who could resist? – her bee-stung lips parted, as she devoured the odd, the particular, the preposterous details of some story, till she could stand it no longer and would break into peals of laughter, flapping her frail hands about her in helpless delight.

In November Ken and I drove to Las Vegas to stay with Shirley MacLaine and Pete Hamill, and to see Shirley's show at Caesar's Palace. He found Las Vegas a 'loutish, shameless, shattering, gargantuan folly' redeemed by the free-spirited Miss MacLaine.

We drove north that autumn, stopping at San Simeon; Hearst's greedy accumulation of artefacts from all over the world appealed to that vulgar side of Ken which preferred shock value and originality over good taste. Why not a musical on the place called 'The Folks who live on the Hill', or 'Simeon's Rainbow', or simply 'His and Hearst'? The visit was a lark, but it was also made in honour of *Citizen Kane*.

While settling down to serious work for the *New Yorker*, Ken agreed to co-write a script with Donald Cammell, adapting Stephen Knight's book on Jack the Ripper, *The Final Solution*. Though nothing came of the collaboration, Ken was edified by the Columbia executive in charge. This man, worried about falling attendance at movies, was considering employing Marshall McLuhan to give the top brass at the studio a seminar on how to select scripts and stars that would make both hemispheres of the brain react favourably: 'How about Streisand and O.J. Simpson in a film about the French Revolution?' was the idea, and McLuhan would then ordain what the hemisphere rating would be. Ken had the feeling that the situation at Columbia was like the last days of the Romanovs: suffering from haemophilia of the box office (the bleeding away of audiences), they send for McLuhan as their Rasputin. Next thing you know, he concluded, 'all the executive vice-presidents will be shuffled off to a disused garage in Burbank. A volley of machine-gun fire will ring out....'

Shortly after arriving in Los Angeles, he had made a brief trip to New York to see the actor Ralph Richardson (about whom he was writing for the *New Yorker*) in Harold Pinter's *No Man's Land*. His friend Ellen Holly, whom he took to the first night, was angered when she saw that Ken still smoked and was saddened that the boyish, wide-eyed aspect of his personality had been replaced by a pessimistic and complaining attitude.

To William Shawn of the *New Yorker*, however, Ken never showed his discontent or self-doubt. For Shawn he always wanted to 'perform' well. He knew that attention would be paid, that there was no need to exaggerate or be strident in his work because he already had the eye and ear of his editor, whom he regarded as, among other things, a sort of literary father-figure. When Ken asked why the magazine never published critical profiles, Shawn told him that he shrank from the idea of destroying people in print and would rather leave that to other magazines.

In February 1977 Ken's first profile for the *New Yorker*, on Richardson, appeared. More than six months before, Ken had visited the actor at his London house and had accepted a cocktail of gin, vermouth and vodka. His host opened with 'I don't know what we're going to talk about. After all, where did we come from? Did you ever have visions of the place you came from before you were born? I did.... It looked like Mexico.' Ken commented that the man was a poet: 'Who else could start a conversation like that? I barely knew him before entering the room; when I left, after listening to an hour of his fantastic musings (and ingesting a steady flow of that murderous cocktail) ... I felt I had known him all my life.'

Having read his profile, Sir Ralph wrote to thank Ken and to tell him that 'Fact, fiction and philosophy is neatly joined together, a bit flattering, and thanks for that, an absolutely true portrait would have been damn dull.'

Ken had reviewed, for the *New Yorker*, a biography of Noël Coward by his friend Cole Lesley. He wrote: 'I submit, in fact, that infantilism may be the essential cocoon within which certain kinds of talent need to flourish; that with Coward "The pipeline to infancy, and all the mischief and imaginative exuberance that go with it, is always open."' He further described the playwright–performer as 'a creature of impulse, who was tough-minded enough to resist the temptation to become what passes, in our society, for a "grown-up"'. (Nearly a quarter of a century before, Ken had written that, as a child, Coward was 'Slightly in *Peter Pan* and you might say that he has been wholly in *Peter Pan* ever since'.)

Early in January Tom Stoppard came to Santa Barbara and lectured to the state university. Ken went up to record the event, and to add Stoppard's performance to his already expansive dossier on the playwright.

The profile eventually appeared in December 1977, and focused on Stoppard's work, drawing a parallel with another playwright of Czech origin, the dissident Václav Havel. Havel's plays were 'distorting mirrors in which one recognized the truth. Stoppard belongs in precisely the same tradition, for which there is no Anglo-Saxon equivalent. Moreover, Havel shares Stoppard's passion for fantastic word-juggling.'

A notable difference, Ken argued, was that Havel was protesting against modern bureaucracy. He had been imprisoned as a leading signatory of Charter 77, the document demanding respect for the 1975 Helsinki Accords on human rights, and particularly those rights relating to free speech. He had a goal: the improvement of man's lot by the improvement of his institutions. Stoppard, on the other hand, had escaped such political pressures when his parents took him into exile, though Ken did concede that Stoppard's work evinced a growing involvement in human rights. When the profile appeared, the British playwright wrote to Ken that he felt he had taken something of a risk with its diversionary comparison, but had brought it off.

As usual, all 32,000 words had been processed by the *New Yorker* checking department. Ken told his checker that he felt 'like the hero of *Mata Hari*, blinded in the war, to whom Garbo murmured, "I weel be your eyes." (Don't check that statement, for God's sake. It will probably turn out to be Dietrich in *Morocco*.)'

Ken's next choice of subject was Johnny Carson, whose mien Ken described as that of 'a king-sized ventriloquist's dummy'. As part of his research on the talk-show host, he set off for Harvard to witness Carson's performance as a guest of the Hasty Pudding Club. Ken proceeded to New York, and then to London for several sessions with Laurence Olivier, about whom he also planned a profile. He wrote to the children of winds and torrential rain, and of missing them very much. 'I can't wait to hug you both and do my silly best to make you laugh.'

In London he was struck down with the 'flu, which stayed with him throughout a week's visit to Madrid, and made further research on his planned piece about the city almost impossible. Bed-ridden at the Hotel Victoria under the care of Spanish doctors, he reminded himself as he lay in the darkened room, barely able to eat, of the 'bankrupt's Howard Hughes' and was rather tempted by semi-invalid life.

When Ken first arrived in Los Angeles, I arranged for him to see a woman doctor of high repute called Elsie Giorgi. He walked into her surgery for his first appointment and said, 'Before we start, I want you to know that I do not like the idea of a woman doctor, and I don't like Beverly Hills fees.' Dr Giorgi said she was glad because she did not wish to take any new patients. She would refer him to a male doctor. She also pointed out that he hadn't even asked what she charged.

'Ken said, "Are you firing me?" or words to that effect, and I answered, "No, you fired me." He said, "Let's start over again." He was angry at his illness, and he directed this anger outward, because if he directed it at himself, he would hate himself more. I told him, "Kenneth, you don't tell yourself the truth. You're so bright, and I've never seen anyone with so much insight use it so little."' The doctor correctly deduced that he did not know how to postpone pleasure, that he needed instant gratification. And she felt that his manner was very superior. 'My job wasn't to probe. It was just to make him tick. At certain times, during those years, he had the highest carbon dioxide ever recorded by our hospitals, and the lowest oxygen. We didn't know why he was alive. He had the most remarkable buffer system.'

Dr Giorgi continues: 'I did tell him once, "It's hard on Kathleen, with the children and everything," and he said, "I know." Then later he said, "Do you think she cares?" I said, "I know she does. Look what she puts up with." He was afraid of losing you and that made him disparage you. He tested and he tested, but that way you wear the fabric thin.'

In Los Angeles Ken discovered that he had a rare enzyme deficiency. It was explained to him that he suffered from a genetic alpha$_1$ antitrypsin deficiency. Antitrypsin, it is thought, protects the lungs from destructive enzymes, in response to infection and other stimuli. Without the antitrypsin inhibiting factor, the elasticity of the lung tissue is destroyed, the airways narrow and life expectancy is inevitably reduced. A bronchitic all his life, and a heavy smoker from an early age, Ken inevitably developed extreme emphysema, or chronic obstruction of the airways.

Elsie Giorgi recalls that whereas most of her patients in similar straits ask how long they are likely to live, Ken never asked. 'He always felt that he was going to live.' But that did not stop him from dramatizing the possibility of his death to the extent that he marked down in his journal the music he wished to have played at his memorial service, which was to take place in London at the Inigo Jones church of St Paul's in Covent Garden.

Those close to Ken observed his illness from different perspectives. Some, more romantically inclined (and in my view wrongly so), declared that Ken wished to die as an ultimate diversion from self, that he could not face old age, that he would never have been able to navigate the 'third act' of life, that he could not express his talent. I believe that Ken might have surprised the world and himself had he not been ill.

In the spring of 1977 he noted in his journal that if he did not write, he would soon be broke – that he had $300 in the bank, and an overdraft in excess of £5000 in London. To write he had to smoke. 'So I opt for writing self-pitying, self-exonerating journal entries like this. (The fact that I *know* they are self-exonerating does not, of course, exonerate me.)'

He also noted a yellow discharge from his penis, after some months of sexual abstinence. 'Bankruptcy, emphysema, paralysis of the will – and now this! Feel that God is making his point with rather vulgar overstatement.'

In this frame of mind Ken picked up a biography of de Sade, and noted his view that 'An enjoyment that is shared is enfeebled.... if you try to give enjoyment to the object of your pleasures, you will soon have to recognize that you are doing so at your own expense; there is no passion more egoistic than lechery.' Or, as Ken put it, as winningly, 'A pleasure shared is a pleasure halved.' He went on to record in his journal that, at fifty, de Sade started an affair with an actress, aged thirty, named Marie-Constance Quesnet, and that this woman went to live with him in the mad house at Charenton, where he spent his last ten years. 'At 50,' Ken asked himself, 'who will join me in Charenton?' He did not speculate on the matter of Madame Quesnet's devotion. Ken himself turned fifty on 2 April 1977. 'ISN'T IT WONDERFUL,' cabled Gore Vidal from Rome.

Meanwhile, in California the golden orb was on daily view. Ken worked on his Carson profile, and in addition took part in a theatre and film symposium, under the direction of Gordon Davidson of the Mark Taper Forum. Beforehand he jotted down some generalizations: that film and most television are in the past tense, theatre in the present. That in television and cinema the audience is mobile – it moves when the camera moves. 'Theatre is an art seen in the permanent long-shot – which makes it the hardest of the three.' Theatre starts with nothing but an empty stage; film starts with landscape and architecture and interior decoration. 'Maddens me when critics say how brilliantly Antonioni evokes Milan or Tunisia or whatever, as if he designed, built or created it. He simply hired a cameraman to photograph it.' Film is the art that is hardest to be bored by. 'The camera is moving, the scenery is picturesque, the weather is usually first rate. Almost any dialogue sounds acceptable in a fast car on the corniche.' Ken also made a note that 'the first generation of Americans nourished on sound movies are now at an age where they rule the media – and it's frightening to see how deeply (in their behaviour as well as their work) the movies are imprinted on them'.

As a theatre guru *in situ*, Ken was often sought out to speak or give interviews. For a book on Harold Clurman, the unsnobbish boulevardier whom he loved and admired, Ken pointed out that it had been Clurman's dream to build a permanent company and lamented that he was not put in charge of a national theatre. He added: 'Eventually if you have no permanent base like a nationally subsidized theatre, you become a labourer and let yourself be hired out to whomever will pay the price. For most serious talents, this is not a good thing.'

It was not a good thing for Clurman, for Ken, nor for Orson Welles – both of the latter living at the time in southern California, like exiles from themselves: both qualified to be in charge of their own theatres. (Of his own career, Welles claimed, no one was prepared to cross the ballroom floor and say, 'Will you?')

In autumn 1978, Ken was invited by the American Film Institute to take part in a series of discussions on 'Working with Welles'. Peter Bogdanovich and Ken appeared on the platform, in a panel entitled 'From Theatre to Film'. On a subsequent evening Ken discussed the lost and unfinished film of the great director: he was able to make a small contribution, having once played the part of a journalist from Mars in the never completed *Don Quixote*.

Ken had not seen his old friend for some time and found him dressed in black and awesomely huge. Welles, who had no idea that Ken was ill, simply presumed, seeing him sweating and out of breath, that he was drunk. After this encounter the two rarely met. Welles believed Ken was living in San Francisco, 'ruling the place the way he ruled everywhere', while he himself, he explained, had lost touch with almost everybody.

During this time, Ken was corresponding with another sacred monster whom he had worshipped since his youth, Marlene Dietrich. She was living in Paris, hard up and struggling with her autobiography. She told Ken that she wished she could go back on the stage. 'How easy singing is (and there is involved companionship, musicians, lighting-men, and all the fun ...) compared with this loneliness.'

When she heard that Ken was ill she was terribly concerned, wondering why he had chosen to live in Los Angeles, and in a country founded on 'treachery, theft'. She recommended that, to cheer himself up, he eat at the Cock and Bull on Sunset, where the roast beef was 'BETTER than in England'.

He wrote to her to say how delighted he was that after her troubles – she had recently hurt her hip – she sounded as 'chipper and dauntless' as ever, and that the 'Bloody Book' was getting written. He reminded her to put in a story she used to tell about her funeral, which would take place in Notre Dame and be attended by all her lovers (Dietrich could not remember it). He gave her a list of possible titles and, having read the manuscript, sent her a helpful critique. He warned her not to start with 'I, personally, am not interested to tell about my life....'

Dear Marlene, please do not sound so grudging. You really cannot start out a book by saying you have no interest in writing it. The reader's reaction will be: 'So why should I be interested in reading it?'

You say you 'hate anecdotes'. Please don't. One's life is an extended anecdote. And you can tell good anecdotes very well. Later on, when you describe how you always did exactly what the dictator von Sternberg told you, and how the actor's job is to obey the supreme commander, people may draw a parallel between your *artistic* obedience and the *political* obedience the German nation gave to Hitler. I think you should be careful of this.

You tell me: 'Nobody of any stature ever related with whom they slept.' Well, Stendhal did; and so did Boswell and Samuel Pepys and Jean-Jacques Rousseau.... You will help us to understand you if we know the kind of men who attracted you physically as well as intellectually. You will also help us to *like* you.... I remember one evening when you told me the depth of your feeling for [Jean] Gabin and how much you agonised over his demand that, if you were to stay together, your career must come second to his. It was a very moving story. Your book needs it.

Ken counselled her to give facts, and not to make generalizations. 'If you are frank with us, we will trust you. If not – if we feel you are holding us at arm's length – we may suspect that you don't trust *us*.' It was a long letter, and very typical of the pains – most particularly in matters of their work – which Ken would take to help friends.

When I finished a second draft of my screenplay in the spring of 1977, I presented Ken with a list of problems. How was I to cut ten pages? Should Agatha be more of a winner? Did I have to spell out how the whole episode of her traumatic disappearance changed her, and that she went on to remarry and to make a success of her life? Ken, as always, was prepared to give generous help, though he was less intrigued by questions of character than by problems of pace and energy, of the logic of events.

We would work all day and go to parties, more often than either of us really cared to, in the evening. When things were not well between us, it helped to practise civility in public. We went to a dance where Ken pointed out that the caviare was served out of a milk-churn with a soup-ladle, 'chuckwagon style'. We went, one night in April, to Sue Mengers', in honour of Truman Capote.

On arrival Capote informed his hostess that the two people he hated most in the world – Ken and Sammy Davis Jr – were present, and that he had not spoken to Tynan since their altercation over *In Cold Blood* more than a decade before. Towards the end of the evening a glazed rapprochement took place between Ken and his erstwhile friend, and we drove him back to his hotel. At the Beverly Wilshire, he insisted on asking us in for a drink. Ken later recorded:

Either Truman is on a mind-paralysing drug or he has fallen prey to some form of sleeping sickness. The vivacity of old has gone completely. His voice is a sluggish whine, and his gestures now move at a pace that would make a slow loris look like a bush baby. For an hour he treats us to a repetitive and barely audible aria of narcissism: it seems that he has been having an affair with a banker, but has lately transferred his affections to the banker's daughter. 'You mean you actually *fuck* her?' I ask with [amphetamine-]induced candour. 'Yes', he snarls torpidly (and incredibly). Our quarrel, it seems, is made up.

When I returned some of the hospitality we had received, by giving a large dinner, Ken defaulted. He said he hadn't been consulted, and that we could not afford to entertain, which was true. He proceeded to spend several hours sitting in the car, tuning into his citizens' band radio, then he slunk into our bedroom, where he began to ensnare some of the guests.

That April Ken's eye was caught, while reading the *Los Angeles Times*, by an advertisement for a jazz cruise to Cuba. On 14 May we flew down to New Orleans and on the following day boarded the *Daphne*, a Greek cruiseship which had been given permission to land briefly in Havana, and which carried the first Americans (since 1961) directly from the United States to Cuba.

On the morning of the 17th we sailed into Havana harbour, the shimmering water full of little boats come out to meet us, and the Malecon crowded with onlookers. The greeting at the port was clamorous and euphoric, especially between the North American and the Cuban musicians, and that night we sat in on a four-hour concert at the Teatro Mella, at which Americans were joined on stage by the locals in a cacophonous impromptu collaboration.

Ken had not been back since the beginning of the revolution in 1959, and was deeply impressed with what he saw – the housing developments, the obvious well-being of the people, the lack of racial discrimination, the impressive evidence of health and education. He took me outside Havana to visit Hemingway's old house at San Francisco de Paula, a little hunting lodge, kept as it had been left by its owner. He also took me to the Floridita bar, where we drank Papadobles and ate spicy shrimps. It was as it used to be, Ken noted, except for the clientele: 'The man next to me at the bar is an assistant electrician from a local theatre ... not uncritical of Fidel Castro.... no nervous side-long glances one associates with a police state.' On this little visit Ken could not see any evidence for complaint that the lifting of the embargo would not cure. And nor could I.

When the boat and its passengers departed, thirty-six hours after arrival, I alone managed (with my Canadian passport, and without need of a visa) to jump ship. I moved into the Havana Riviera, Meyer Lansky's old hotel, and set about making contact with the poet Pablo Armando Fernandez and some members of the film community. It was a heady time for me, as I prepared to write about my experience, and on my return I resisted all accusations that, as a 'tourist of the revolution', I had been gulled. As so often in my life with Ken he had opened yet another door, which I would otherwise not have discovered.

We stayed in Los Angeles through the summer, and Ken made valiant efforts to give up smoking. We took the children to the island of Catalina, and did not leave our hearts in the tourist-ridden Avalon – though Ken continued to play the old Al Jolson recording of the song. We drove down to Tijuana, just across the Mexican border, for a bullfight, taking with us Tracy – now living in West Hollywood and working in film. Ken was still working on his Carson piece and beginning to prepare a profile on Mel Brooks.

Brooks had made Ken laugh since he first heard his routine at Moss Hart's birthday party in 1959. He tracked him to Pasadena, where the actor–comedian–director was shooting a Hitchcock parody, *High Anxiety*. Brooks told Ken he would never think of making a film that wasn't a comedy: 'With me it's "Shoemaker, stick to your lathe."' Ken felt great affection and admiration for him and on several occasions – with his secretary Judy Harger in charge of the tape recorder – listened to a very full version of the comedian's life. Brooks provided some excellent vintage wine, and by the end of the longest session Ken was quite drunk. Alone with Judy, who was a stalwart friend, he became suddenly depressed, as if 'the thorns from his past were really pricking him', she recalls. 'He stood in the dining-room, holding on to the back of a chair, and he said, "Do you know what it's like to be described by the newspapers in your own country as a purveyor of violence?"' Judy did not know that Ken was referring to *The Times* editorial of 1976, but she had never seen him show such anger. He implied that that accusation alone had made him leave England.

In August I was in London for two weeks working on the script of *Agatha* with its director Michael Apted, while our producer David Puttnam put together the financing. By the end of August the English backing had fallen through, and Puttnam showed the script to Dustin Hoffman, then in search of a movie to complete his contract with First Artists. Hoffman read it on 31 August and decided the same day to back the film, and to play the part of a tall, blond, English aristocrat who works as a gossip columnist. While the actor's enthusiasm for the project was flattering, he did not seem ideal casting for the part, which was a secondary one, and I set to turning the tall, blond Englishman (at Ken's suggestion) into a short American journalist. We would start shooting in October, and Hoffman gave a dinner to celebrate. Ken described him as incredibly observant: 'feral might be the word if he weren't so obviously nice'. He thought that he should play Mozart in a film based on the theory that the 'wee Salzburger was poisoned by his rival operatic composer Salieri' – an idea which anteceded *Amadeus* by two years.

Ken's reaction to my good fortune was at first enthusiastic, though he admitted to a pang of envy that he had not had similar luck with his own film project. For me this intimidating work meant financial freedom.

After returning from one of my short visits to London, Ken wrote in his journal, 'No matter what happens, we are the centre of each other's lives. In her absence, I am Saturn without its rings, a planet of leaden melancholy.' I, in turn, continued to love Ken and only Ken; my few affairs were conducted in affection and out of need as life with him grew increasingly difficult. He worried about money, but half resented that I worked. 'He was the bread-winner and you were off in your room doing he knew not what. Certainly not making his breakfast nor pressing his shirts,' Judy Harger remembers. He exercised his control, his authority, by antagonizing me, by criticizing me at every turn. He knew he could upset me emotionally, catch me off guard, make me weep, but at the same time I was stubbornly determined to do my work and to keep our family on some sort of course. I functioned in this manner not out of generosity of spirit, nor merely out of love, but in order to survive.

It grew so bad between us, during the autumn of 1977, that even I, intent on patching up our life and keeping it whole, gave up, concluding that Ken really needed to part from me, that he should go and live with Nicole in England, that life outside the family, life with more ease, was what he required. I feared, more than anything else, the quarrels of non-love, the rage that seemed to provide more satisfaction than amity.

A series of soft-hearted au pairs (in particular Michele Winebrenner) helped me keep the children cocooned from their parents' discord. We never fought in public, though occasionally a close friend, like Joan Axelrod, would be privy to some argument about my failure to provide the right kind of wine, for example; on one occasion Ken's eyes bulged and his face became so red that Joan was persuaded he was having an epileptic attack. 'I was very concerned for both of you as I watched him, full of self-loathing and getting angry at the person he loved.'

I reversed the gender of Hazlitt's marvellous line from *Liber Amoris* so that it read: 'He has robbed me of himself: shall he also rob me of my love for him?'

On 26 September I had to fly to London to write the new part for Dustin Hoffman. I was provided with a small flat in Knightsbridge, and there I worked, when I wasn't exploring locations or sitting in on casting.

While I was in England Ken called me frequently to complain of my desertion; to complain that the children were suffering; to complain that I was seeing Daniel Topolski and that, as a result, he was going to divorce me. He told me that he wanted money from me, that he had detectives on me, that he would stay in Spain (where he planned to spend several weeks in November) and kill himself. Halfway through one particular week, with new scenes to write overnight and a sink full of dirty soup plates, I almost gave up. I couldn't think of anything to write, and suspected that my scenes, even if they miraculously appeared on the page, would not be used. I combed through my occasional book looking for ideas and found John Osborne's lines from *Look Back in Anger*: 'It's no good trying to fool yourself about love. You can't fall into it like a soft job without dirtying your hands. It takes muscle and guts.' But I'd run out of both.

The next time Ken telephoned me, I told him I believed that he wanted nothing less than my blood. He was very shocked. A few hours later he wrote me a letter to tell me that he was drinking a large Scotch 'to quiet some of the terrors'. He told me he could feel whole only if he was accepted whole. 'You have convinced me that I am without value. You are sleeping with a man with enviable attributes ... who acts only on the noblest motives. How do you think this knowledge makes me feel? I will tell you ... like a house in which you once lived that you hate to quit because you don't want to be held responsible for the fact that it has dry rot and no roof and smashed windows. To put it more bluntly, you feel too guilty to move out.' He continued:

Nobody will hold it against you that you are having an affair in the place where we met and fell in love, in the midst of everyone we know, surrounded by journalists who know they can print anything about me with impunity. They will agree with you that it is monstrous and characteristic of me to spend a few weeks in Spain with a friend [Nicole] who is so much less than perfect.

I am stopped in my tracks, wakeful, trapped at a fork in the road, knowing that if I move forward I shall split on it, as if it were a circular saw.... Counted the faithful pink pills. Only 22 and a half. Not enough. Is this your doing – saving me from myself? Or saving you from myself? Or saving me for yourself?

He went on to explain that he felt no self-pity.

You have to like yourself to do that. Interesting symptom: a journal is the last refuge of whatever ego one has, and I have made no entries in mine for months. Everything has been said. Everything is an effort. Self-dislike so marked that even masturbation, once the work of a moment, has become impossible; I fall asleep achieving it, like a senile opossum no longer able to climb its own tail. God knows ... you are under pressure, but it is a pressure you care about, with something precious to you at stake.... Your future is wonderfully open-ended.... Mine, too, is open-ended, but rather horribly so. As [Osric] says in *Hamlet*, just before the envenomed point goes in: 'Nothing neither way'.

I was terribly affected, and only mildly consoled to receive a letter from Judy Harger to assure me that the children were in splendid shape, and to remind me that Ken had one set of rules for me and another 'more malleable' for himself.

Ken spent the month of November in Madrid and its constellation of towns, taking up his affair with Nicole, doing further research on the city for a *New*

Yorker profile. He wrote to his friend Bill Davis that he was amazed to find himself treated as a cultural hero because of the success of *Oh! Calcutta!* 'It seems that they read political implications into the nudity. One reporter asked me whether I saw myself as leading a heterosexual revolution in Spain, to which I replied that most of the nightclub shows I had attended were inclined to be homosexual. The result of this was a headline the next day: "Kenneth Tynan says all Spanish Men are Homosexuals". The concierge at the Suecia was very frosty with me after that and positively threw my key across the desk.

Ken told his friend that another journalist had declared that he represented 'might'. 'I told him I did not believe in might, but he persisted and it took me nearly half an hour to discover that he meant that, to him, I was a "myth".'

On this trip Ken filled several notebooks with his thoughts: his memories of Hemingway in Madrid and Luis Miguel Dominguín's comment on same: 'I hate Madrid. Hemingway brought the wrong kind of tourist.' Ken added: 'Hemingway lived by laws that make no sense in drawingrooms. He was a literary man of a kind very rare in the Anglo-Saxon world, a species of sensitive tank, heavily armoured yet equipped with moral antennae as delicate as radar.... In Madrid, which has no salons of any consequence, he felt at home, and it was Goya's Madrid that he specially loved, a city of bars and classless taverns.' In Goya's work, which Ken hunted down throughout the city, he observed 'content tearing at and distorting form (as it always does in revolutionary times), the subconscious wrestling with the super-ego (as in Bosch)'.

He saw as many of Carlos Saura's films as he could and liked best *Elsa Vida Mia*, in which an elderly man, who long before had walked out on family life, meets his daughter again. 'Their late-blooming love for each other keeps reminding me of my present relationship in L.A. with Tracy.'

In Spain Ken's relationship with Nicole did not thrive. Nicole complained that she was supposed to pity 'Lord and Lady Tynan', but instead felt resentful and embittered. Meanwhile Ken noted his loss of interest in 'advanced sex'.

Agatha started shooting on 31 October. After a certain number of days on the set in Harrogate, I discovered the basic condition of the screenwriter, which is that he or she becomes the least important person on the film. Hoffman, knowing I was a beginner, explained this to me as gently as he could. He had seen how hard I'd worked, and he had sensed my domestic turmoil. He asked me out of the blue: 'Do you think you could fall in love with Ken again?' I did not know how to answer. I believed I *was* in love with my husband.

In November my agent negotiated a large advance for the novelization of *Agatha*. This allowed me to return to Los Angeles and to turn my little entertainment into something entirely my own.

Ken met me and the children (they had joined me briefly in London) at the airport early in December, and all was well between us for a while. We went down to Mexicali for a bullfight, and stopped for lunch at the health farm, La Costa, where Gore Vidal was working on a new novel. Ken noted that Vidal's conversation on Perrier was quite as vivacious as his own on two vodka martinis and white wine.

We missed England at Christmas and celebrated as best we could among the fake reindeers and coloured lights and, worse of ironies, the rain. Ken sent his Johnny Carson profile to the *New Yorker*, and received praise and a cheque for $15,000 – 'like a benediction' – he told Shawn. But the proofs marked up by the *New Yorker* staff, full of questions on accuracy, were more in the nature of 'an artillery bombardment'. When the piece finally appeared in print Ken wrote in his journal that he feared the editing process had ironed out 'much that might have made it identifiably mine; also, when writing for the magazine, one automatically censors audacious phrases lest they should be demolished by the inquisitorial logicians on 43rd St.' He felt (as with every piece) that he had done too much research and not enough analysis and interpretation.

When Ken heard that Carson might be quitting the *Tonight* show to do specials, he wrote to him suggesting he reconsider: 'Carson scriptbound would be Carson strait-jacketed. . . . I cannot tell you how many bad days you have saved, and good days you have improved, by simply being there on Channel 4, doing what nobody else can do anything like as well.'

But nightly Carson, evidently, was not sufficient nourishment, and he marked down, out of Dr Johnson's *Prayers and Meditations* of 1764, the following: 'A kind of strange oblivion has overspread me, so that I know not what has become of the last year; and perceived that incidents and intelligence pass over me without leaving any impression.'

40

Louise Brooks

On Sunday morning 8 January 1978, while flipping through the television guide, Ken saw that at 1 p.m., on Channel 28, Louise Brooks would be appearing in a 1929 silent movie by G. W. Pabst, called *Pandora's Box*, based on the Wedekind play, a film he had seen twice before and would eagerly watch again. In his journal he 'wondered how many of my Southern Californian neighbours would be tempted to forgo their poolside champagne brunches, their bicycle jaunts along Ocean Front Walk, their health-food picnics in Topanga Canyon, or their surf-board battles with the breakers of Malibu in order to watch a silent picture, shot in Berlin just fifty years earlier, about an artless young hedonist who, meaning no harm, rewards her lovers – and eventually herself – with the prize of violent death.'

The film brought back all his infatuation for Miss Brooks, and he wrote in his journal: 'She runs through my life like a magnetic thread, this shameless urchin tomboy, this unbroken, and unbreakable porcelain colt. This Prairie Princess, equally at home in a slum pub or the royal suite at Neuschwanstein, creature of impulse, unpretentious temptress capable of dissolving into a fit of giggles at a romantic climax, amoral but selfless, Lesbian and hetero, with that sleek black cloche of hair that rings so many bells in my memory . . . the only star actress I can imagine either being enslaved to or wanting to enslave.'

A few days later he wrote to William Shawn to ask if the name Louise Brooks meant anything to him. He explained that she was a silent movie star, first in the States and later in Germany, 'where she made a couple of classic films for Pabst (*Pandora's Box* and *Diary of a Lost Girl*)'. Ken added that he had always thought of her as the most beautiful woman, with the possible exception of Garbo, who had ever 'illuminated the screen; and – with no exceptions at all – the most sexually attractive'. He told Shawn that he had discovered she was living alone in modest circumstances in Rochester, New York, that she was in her early seventies and that she wrote occasional articles for specialist movie magazines. By all accounts she seemed to be a woman 'of strong opinions and total recall'. Would the magazine be interested? They would indeed.

Ken sent a formal letter to Louise Brooks early in February. His letter began, 'You probably don't know me, but I am an English writer and author who used to be a drama critic for the London *Observer*.' He asked if he might meet her in Rochester and write about her life and work. If she agreed, he would want to see her films in the archive of the Eastman Institute in the same city.

Miss Brooks responded that Ken's letter 'positively tickled me pink – making me think I am worthy of a Tynan *New Yorker* profile – because I have written some film articles and found it easy to dispatch most celebrities with a thousand words'. And she added that the only people she knew who inhabited 'unique, fascinating worlds were Martha Graham, Gershwin, Chaplin, G. W. Pabst and Mr Hearst'. It was typical of Louise Brooks that her immediate response to Ken was to believe that he had possibly found her of some *intellectual* interest – that was the route to her real talent, and to her heart. She told Ken that he put words together better than anyone she had read since Shaw. And she declined to be interviewed.

Her excuse was that she was not well enough. Her real reason was that she might offend the Paley Foundation, and more particularly William Paley, who since 1954 had provided her with a small monthly stipend of some $400, on which she depended for survival. In the late 1920s he had had an affair with her, adored her independent spirit and, when Louise eventually deserted Hollywood and fell upon hard times, he offered to help. It was a strange anomaly that Brooks had sabotaged a life of financial security, both in Hollywood – where she could not be directed, nor bedded, against her will – and in her marriages and affairs, and had ended up a penniless recluse but for her one concession to outside help, the Paley Foundation. In every other respect she had elected to live on her own terms, alone with her books and her writing, from which, by virtue of her history, as a great beauty, a movie star, a feckless vamp, she had been unnaturally cut off.

Ken would not accept her refusal, and having discovered the true reason for her reticence he sent her a formal letter assuring her that he would undertake not to question anyone about her private life, and that she would see the manuscript. Louise Brooks replied that 'As a lawyer's daughter I am bound to regard your cleanly written agreement as your finest work'. If the representatives of the Paley Foundation were not averse, she would agree to be interviewed. She added: 'Reading your great Carson Profile I began to laugh thinking the same writer who wrote about Carson with an audience of 17 million and a yearly income of $2½ million also wanted to write about an unknown old actress sitting in bed with a weekly audience of the milkman and the cleaning woman, and an income of $435 a month. How you would have pleased Herman Mankiewicz who always found me unaccountably funny.'

After further toing and froing an agreement was struck. 'What a relief to be able to write you without fear of seepage,' Brooks wrote to Ken. 'Deceit enrages me – it destroys the freedom and grace of my mind – and that's about all that's in it.' It would be a revelation to meet him: 'Because on the phone you are 6' 2" without a face, and your telephone personality is strange, mystifying, damnable. Most of the time you do not react at *all* to what I say. You listen, pay attention, you understand – There is a pause – Then you go on talking about what's on your mind.'

This was the first of many letters and telephone calls from Brooks in which she tried to unravel her inquisitor. The touching, insistent sub-text of all their exchanges and conversations (which he never revealed in his brilliant profile of her) was Louise Brooks' search for Ken. She declared before she met him that she had been suddenly overpowered by the feeling of love – a sensation I have never experienced with any other man. Are you a variation of Jack the Ripper who finally brings me love which I am prevented from accepting, not by the knife but by old age?' She added: 'It is true that I have never been in love. If I had loved a man would I have been faithful to him? Could he have trusted me beyond a closed door? And how did Pabst know without meeting me that I possessed this tramp essence of Lulu? That he could toss me in front of a camera to behave in this perfectly natural way?' She also told Ken that she had always needed to be alone a great deal, which was why she had made an impossible wife and mistress.

'Why do I ask you questions?' she asked him. 'You don't even answer. But I'll get the answer when we meet. No man has ever denied me face to face truth. And no woman has ever told me the truth. In fact they condemn me as a traitor for telling.' She added: 'I don't know you and forget that Tynan on the phone is not Tynan at the typewriter.'

For herself Brooks made notes on Ken's criticism, copied out certain passages, queried his attitude to women, noted his trick of putting his own lines in others' mouths. She told him that she had read all of Ruskin's works: 'Sometimes I would slam a book shut hollering, "What the hell do I care about a lot of damned rocks." Then I would go on for the beauty of his prose and all I learned. That is how I read you ... you are the only critic who understands, who sees the movement of actors. Ethel Merman stalking back and forth out of time. And you caught me blind with Cagney, his movement was so integrated with his being that I didn't see it until you wrote: "He released his compact energy quite without effort." '

She made a list of questions to ask him when they met: 'Who do you write for? Is it possible to write about me as if I were dead? How are conceptions formed? Education, experience, reading, travel?' She wanted to find out about Ken, and she wanted to ask him about writing. Before his arrival in Rochester she was stricken by stage fright: 'There is nothing I can do about a face 50 years older than the one you have in mind.'

On 2 May, wearing a long leather coat, and with a briefcase full of notes on the subject in hand, as well as some expensive Burgundy, Ken pressed the doorbell of Louise Brooks' two-room apartment. 'After a long pause, there was a loud snapping of locks,' he later wrote. 'The door slowly opened to reveal a petite woman of fragile build, wearing a woollen bed jacket over a pink nightgown, and holding herself defiantly upright by means of a sturdy metal cane with four rubber-tipped prongs. She had salt and pepper hair combed back into a ponytail that hung down well below her shoulders, and she was barefoot.... She was seventy-one years old, and until a few months earlier I had thought she was dead.'

'You're doing a terrible thing to me,' Brooks said. 'I've been killing myself off for twenty years, and you're going to bring me back to life.' They talked for three days very candidly: about her life and work, about their sex lives, about books and ideas, with Brooks announcing in her youthful, delighted and delightful voice that she was 'probably one of the best-read idiots in the world'. They talked unguardedly, cutting in, forgetting the point, showing off, like twins who had somehow been mysteriously cut off from each other since birth.

Because severe arthritis prevented the 'ravishing hermit of Rochester' from sitting upright for long without discomfort, she reclined on her bed in the neat little room with the statue of the Virgin on the chest of drawers, and Ken pulled up a chair beside her, so that they could talk and examine the photographs and mementos that burst out of the bedroom wardrobe.

At one point Ken told her that he thought *Pandora's Box* should have ended on her. 'One wants to see your lovely face again, darling.' 'As a matter of fact,' he continued randomly, 'the film takes the play and turns it upside down. It doesn't make her a destroyer of men.' 'She was just the same slob I am,' said Louise and changed the subject. 'Shall I tell you this story which I've never told anyone? If Paley throws me out, it's on your head. *Don't* give me that false smile!'

'I'll be full of pity,' Ken teased.

'Oh you bastard!'

'I shall write you such nice letters,' he went on.

'Well, in the first place Pabst was a man who never loved anyone, not his wife, no one in his whole life ...'

Some time later Louise asked: 'Have you ever given a marvellous performance in bed and think you can't go back?' 'Of course,' said Ken, and sidetracked her question: 'One fails all the time. What does it matter?'

Another still was produced from the cupboard, and Brooks explained that for that particular shot she was 'stewed'. 'I wondered why you were so radiant in that scene,' said her confidant. 'Yes, I was drunk again.' Ken picked up a photograph of a group in Zelli's, the Paris nightclub. He said it had more of the twenties than any other photograph he had ever seen: 'Shady, sleazy people', he pointed out to Louise, 'with this angel whore in the middle of them'.

Louise Brooks had indeed been an 'angel whore' until that repressed part of her, the natural writer, a lover of words and a truth-seeker, walked out of her early life for good: unsimply wrecked it. 'I was a trial,' she explained. 'You were a judge, and a witness, and an ideal,' Ken replied.

On 12 May Brooks telephoned Ken to tell him that for three months she had been living on his voice and then his presence. 'Now on the last glass of red wine I'm sinking into the grave again.' She told him that her 'loveliest time was listening to your perfect reading of Precious Lillie'. (She liked Ken's line about the comedienne Bea Lillie: 'She is uniquely alone. The audience, like Alice, is just a thing in her dream.')

She still could not figure out Ken's silences. 'During your visit those damned Tynan intervals never indicated whether you were pleased or bored with my routines.' She liked it when he 'got mad and showed me that spoiled little boy through a crack in the Tynan façade'. She read Curtains again and wrote to tell him that, like Shaw, his lines were 'so smooth, your starts and stops so right, it is dangerously easy to arrive at the end of a piece not knowing where I've been. I love you first because you make me laugh with the truth.' In June she told him: 'When I think of all the precious time I wasted when you were here, jabber, jabber, jabber, never getting my questions answered.' A few weeks later a letter from her began: 'Three days in May there was a tall strange blond man here. Dressed in a great shiny black coat, like a Wagner figure he stood in the lobby doorway, looking down at me with a mysterious questioning expression – maybe I shouldn't have let him in. Sometimes he would talk to me, sometimes he would listen to me, but I never knew what he was thinking about. He said he was going to write a story about me. Wouldn't it be wonderful if he told me what I have been running away from for 71 years? And more baffling still, what I was running to? I understand he is very good at penetrating fairy tales.'

After leaving Louise Brooks in Rochester, Ken embarked on a summer of disasters. His plane to New York was cancelled, and claiming to be expiring from fearful illnesses, he was transferred to a plane to Buffalo. That too was cancelled. Another airline got him to Toronto, where he lost his luggage. A Polish couple named Szynanski were also on the Buffalo flight, and the similarity of names caused all his luggage to be sent to Warsaw (including all his manuscripts of books and articles).

He wrote to me about these events, and to explain that he had eventually been flown to Paris, via Amsterdam, where his luggage was returned to him from Warsaw after forty-eight hours ('Fall to my knees and pray to C.S.

380

Lewis'). In Paris, he told me, he was met by Nicole, who was going to spend time with him in the south of Spain, and by his secretary Dacia, who had brought the Jaguar from London. The Jaguar broke down. After several days the desired part was found and he rushed out to meet the mechanic: 'By blue, the fellow has reason. The machine marches! I pay through the little grey nose and zoom out of town toward Lyon, only three days late. Am bowling along autoroute at 100 mph about two days afterwards with no ill effects except screaming migraine ... when SCRUNGE-UPPITY-SCRUNGE-UPPITY-CRANG-CRANG-CRANG-PHUT. The car bumps, shudders, rocks, stops and won't start. Some unidentified jagged metal object has torn front left tyre to shreds... Spare tyre contains about as much air as my left lung.'

Several days later Ken arrived in the south-eastern Spanish village of Mojácar. Here, in this parched and uninviting place, he had rented a villa, some 100 yards from the sea, surrounded by untended scrub. He told me that there was a seaside café within walking distance, which served sausage and bacon and chilli con carne. He also told me that the price for this find – where he intended me and the children to join him – was exactly twice what he had expected, the equivalent of £133 a month. What he wanted to know was whether we could still afford our planned pilgrimage north to Santiago de Compostela. 'Ought we to consider abandoning the northern trip for another year and spend the whole month in Mojácar? How would the children feel? The weather down here would certainly be better and they'd be saved the problem of car-sickness. You and I would certainly be deprived.' Would I be prepared to make an extra financial contribution? Ken ended, 'Please drop everything and ponder hard and write or cable urgently.'

I wrote back to tell him I had tried to let our London house and had returned to Los Angeles. I told him that I was walking regularly on the Malibu beach with Shirley MacLaine, and that Roxana and I were taking yoga classes. I told him that Tracy was back from Texas, where she had been shooting a documentary on the Dallas Cowboy cheerleaders. And I asked him in the midst of this account of my life not to go to Valencia before I arrived in Spain. I did not mention how angered I was that he had left us in Los Angeles so short of money, nor how angry I was in general. The lease had expired and we had moved out of Kingman Avenue and put our belongings in storage. I made a temporary arrangement with the Axelrods to take their house in the autumn, until we should find some permanent rental. Then I flew to London with the children and eventually on to Spain.

Ken and I had been away from each other for two months – the longest separation of our married life. In the meantime I received his description of disasters with a pursed indifference, while Louise Brooks told him more generously that 'the crazy horror of your trip to Almería reads like a day in the Mexican letters of Malcolm Lowry. Unfortunately your style makes me laugh my head off.... But will you stop crying – you'll rust up your typewriter.' She couldn't make it to Spain because she was afraid to travel alone. 'Bill Paley should have me flown to Almería in the company plane. He would too if I could see him and bring back laughter, for he has a screwy sense of humor. . . . And if I cannot come to Almería I can imagine what fun it would be – you snorting in B^b over the typewriter while I practice Zen with a goodly supply of bottles in the tower room, letting down my hair and howling "Bull shit" out the window.'

Anyway, Louise pointed out, Ken had Nicole to look after him. Years later, after Ken's death, Nicole told me how she remembered Ken's face in the villa at Mojácar, as he sat before the typewriter, just staring straight ahead. 'He hated writing, didn't he? He loved doing things with other people. He really wanted to direct.' She collected pebbles from the beach and laid them out on his desk; she cooked for him. But it was hard to keep his spirits up. He talked about how he would like to have known his father, 'to have talked to him about everything. He was incredibly guilty about his mother's death, absolutely tormented by it. That's what he used to harp on, that he hadn't looked after her, that he'd been too busy because of his career, because of his unhappiness with Elaine. He loved getting his own way, and very good at it he was too. He seemed totally unaware that he was causing all this hurt. He never told me you and the kids were coming to Spain. It was horrible. When you arrived and I wasn't able to get a plane out, I was sent up the hill, out of the way. One was supposed to sit back and say OK, which I always did.'

Ken wrote to Louise Brooks to tell her that after the dreadful journey he had managed to get some work done, but that in his role as Nicole's lover he had begun to miss his other life, which led to 'extreme depressions'.

Ken later set down, in his journal, the events that followed. Suffering from bouts of extreme lassitude, he decided to take sleeping pills and go to bed for three days. In the afternoon of the first day, while Nicole was at the beach, Ken woke up to find his handbag had been stolen, with a gold pen, nearly a thousand dollars in pesetas, his passport with the HI visa that allowed him to work in the States, driving licences, credit cards, air tickets and travellers' cheques.

Am assured by neighbours that I am lucky: woman in nearby house woke up while burglars were in her room some weeks ago, and had her kneecaps shot off. Now begins horrendous routine of reports to police, to traveller-cheque companies, to banks, to embassies, to travel agencies, all complicated by the fact that the villa has no telephone ... and nearest point of contact with outside world is public phone in village 7 miles away. American Express refuse to refund a cent unless I travel 200 miles to their office in Granada to swear affidavit that report of theft is authentic. . . . Meanwhile a lorry, passing too close on a mountain road, nearly tore off lefthand side of Jaguar, which goes into garage looking like Al Capone's jowl. Finally (or so I thought) a prolonged paroxysm of coughing caused by a piece of meat stuck in my throat produces ... my first hernia unpleasantly close to scrotum on left side. Local doctor advises immediate surgery and prescribes truss, which turns out to be medieval contraption as effectively anti-aphrodisiac as a chastity belt. Sexual activity now ceases completely. Emotionally there is turmoil...

In addition, Ken's lungs were troubling him, the emphysema made worse by the extreme heat. Late in the evening of 1 July, I arrived with the children at Almería. Ken met us at the airport. He was painfully thin, and had grown a spiky, grey moustache and beard. His voice and manner were fragile, and he seemed pathetically grateful for our arrival. We moved into the simple villa at Mojácar, and after two days Ken and I were mysteriously restored as of old to each other. We sat, one night, hands entwined, under the stars, blessedly happy to be together. The planned 'pilgrimage' to Santiago, which we had sworn to make a year before, now seemed imperative, for the pleasure of it and to give some sort of thanks. We would celebrate the day of the disciple San Jaime, whose remains were said to have been brought to the coast of Galicia and conveniently discovered, in the ninth century, at a place which became known as Compostela. From all over Europe the pilgrims came, among them El Cid in 1064, and St Francis in 1241.

In Mojácar, the children swam and got brown for two weeks. Ken remained frail, and in need of sleep – which I did not recognize as a symptom of carbon-dioxide narcosis: he was simply not getting enough oxygen.

On 17 July we set off, in intolerable heat, driving eastwards through Alicante and Murcia, through ugly camel-grey landscape, a husk-dry land of high-rise and tourist development, the air full of stale fish and petrol fumes. By evening we reached the green ricefields south of Valencia, and skirting the city, drove to the Monte Picayo at Puzol. Here Ken collapsed, unable to enjoy one of his favourite hotels, a hugh kitsch palace of wrought iron and red velvet, where he used to take friends as part of the elaborate joke which was Valencia.

The next day I again climbed into the driver's seat, and we set off north east, through Teruel, with its famous pair of stone lovers. We slept at Soria and joined the pilgrims' route at Logroño. We reached Burgos by lunch on 20 July, where the Jaguar (our mode of pilgrimage travel) began to overheat dangerously.

We continued through high and winding hills. Behind me the children idly argued. In the front seat Ken was dying. He was simply unable to wake up. A yellow spittle had formed around his lips, and he made no sense. When we finally reached the cathedral city of León, and the Hotel San Marcos, he was talking gibberish. He was carried to our rooms. A local doctor came and injected him with cortisone, and the drug revived him. Two hours later he insisted on ordering champagne and supper in our bedroom. He described himself with his new beard as a romanesque saint struck by lightning.

He was now keen to explore the converted seventeenth-century monastery in which we were staying. But not until he had rested for two days was he able to leave the hotel room, and we set off on the 23rd, the last lap of our curious journey, reaching Santiago later in the day. Ken considered the lovely city second only in beauty to Salamanca; and the Plaza de las Platerias the most exquisite Renaissance square he had ever seen. It was already exploding with pilgrims, most of whom were in fact young political activists. They marched and they sang and they waved banners. On that particular holiday of San Jaime, the cathedral doors – for fear of riot – were firmly shut for the first time in a millennium. At night we stood in the square and watched the fireworks.

Our holiday ended on a small island off the Galician coast, the Isla de Toja, and in the Grand Hotel, where Ken drank champagne out of a foot-high glass, still looking saintly, but at peace.

In Madrid we parted. I flew with the children to the South of France, where I left them with friends, and continued to New York to begin a promotional tour for my novel.

A couple from Mojácar, one of whom had agreed to drive the Jaguar back to England, joined Ken in Madrid. On his first evening in the city Ken took them to dine at Valentin's. As they left the restaurant, around midnight, a young Spaniard, sprinting at full speed, dashed past Ken and snatched his new handbag. He gave chase but tripped over a kerb, badly cutting both knees. Inside the handbag were his new travellers' cheques, his new passport, his money and his diary. Once more he was forced into a bureaucratic nightmare, with the added disadvantage, as he noted in his journal, that 'many of the people to whom I now apply for refunds and replacements are frankly reluctant to believe that lightning could have struck twice within such a short time. . . . I recall what a Madrid friend told me just before Franco died: "You will be able to tell when Spain has democracy because at the same time Spain will have crime."'

Louise Brooks cabled Ken to come and finish his article on Mel Brooks in Rochester. She told him that out of the disasters at least one good thing had emerged: he was back with his wife. 'You are a writer not an actor. You can't pile mess upon mess and expect to have sense enough to write.'

Early in August Ken arrived in Los Angeles and was taken off the aeroplane by wheelchair. He moved into a temporary apartment on Sunset Boulevard, while he waited for the Axelrods' house in Beverley Hills to be vacated. I was still on tour, however, and he complained to our nanny how badly he felt about being left alone.

On 6 September he entered St John's Hospital in Santa Monica for a prostate operation. During his hospitalization he underwent further pulmonary-function tests which showed 'markedly severe obstructive ventilatory' disease and 'profound gas abnormalities'. He was discharged twelve days later and told to use an oxygen tank at night. He continued to smoke between eight and twelve cigarettes a day, and was readmitted to the hospital in December in a state of collapse.

The children, particularly Tracy, found it very difficult to see Ken hooked up to an oxygen tank, and I had to explain to them, as best I could, the extent to which his illness had progressed. Though protected by their parents, we could not entirely cocoon them, and they suffered accordingly. Matthew, a wise and compassionate little boy, tried to draw upon himself the burden of responsibility. Roxana, an optimist and extrovert, put on a brave face and endeavoured to make us smile. That autumn she wore a pink uniform and started at the Marlborough School. For her birthday Ken penned a poem which began:

> Lift your glasses high as Heaven –
> Miss Roxana is eleven!
> Bright as a button, gay as bee,
> Most nice things a girl should be;
> Pretty as a pot of paint,
> She says 'isn't', never 'ain't';
> Works with dedicated zeal,
> Dives as sleekly as a seal;
> Yes, I wouldn't be surprised
> If she grew up civilised.

Louise Brooks wrote to cheer Ken up. She told him she should have been a writer's moll. Once she proposed: 'Maybe my life *has* had some meaning; ...''Seeking a reconciliation [she quoted from Goethe] between interiority (beauty) and reality''.' She praised *Agatha* ('Kathleen wrote a lot about my condition.... She has another story going there'). She wanted to know who was the 'gloomy Dane' I had quoted saying, 'He who does not really feel himself lost is without remission.' Ortega y Gasset, she said, wrote the same thing. But Ortega and the 'gloomy Dane' had no remedy for people 'who don't *get* lost, who are *born* lost'. Ken replied: 'My wife, who is bowled over with delight by your reaction to *Agatha*, has released from her private collection the enclosed rather seedy pictures of me.' And he asked her to visit us in California.

By October Louise sensed a renewed gloom and complaint in Ken's voice. She wondered whether 'to keep yourself in operation you have to wear life like an itchy suit of underwear'. She admitted she really did not know 'one damned thing about you'. She read him to search out the 'mysterious person moving behind a transparency of words'.

But Louise would not come to visit nor to 'talk and look and laugh at Hollywood again'.

In December I returned to Cuba, ostensibly to write some articles, but in fact to explore an idea I had for a filmscript. It was not the right time to leave my family, with Ken sick and depressed, and the children – despite the nanny's valiant efforts – in need of me. At the same time it was a necessary venture both financially and for my sanity.

I returned on Christmas Eve just in time to eat a huge dinner, orchestrated by Ken and cooked by our nanny Michele. For New Year's we drove to Death Valley with the children and stayed at Furnace Creek, with a mobile oxygen tank at hand. Ken pointed out that the Valley had '*less* of anything than any tourist resort in the world – less of everything attractive to the civilised mind except heat'.

With his profile of Mel Brooks published in October, and his work on Louise Brooks well under way, he had begun to research, for the *New Yorker*, a portrait of Laurence Olivier. In July 1977 he had lunched with Olivier at the Bel Air Hotel, during the shooting of *The Betsy*. The actor's energy in spite of his illnesses continued to impress Ken. On instructions from the project's producer, Ken offered Olivier $500,000 to play Sir William Gull in *Jack the Ripper*. But the money was not acceptable. Ken was dispirited to hear him nonetheless complain of financial straits and of the cost of educating his children.

In September 1977 Olivier wrote to Ken with details of his career and activities since leaving the National Theatre. Over a year later Ken wrote back to explain that the profile was late, first because of his chest disease, and second because the piece looked as if it would be longer than expected: 'So long, in fact, that I hope to publish it – in expanded form, of course – as a book when the *New Yorker* have finished with it. There's nothing I'd rather write, and although it won't be the authorized biography or anything as impressive as that it might be quite a nice little monument.' He hoped to see Olivier the following April in England.

It happened that Ken's agent, Irving Lazar, had negotiated a deal with Simon and Schuster for Ken to write a book on Olivier, and to be paid $360,000, a contract which was eventually signed in January 1979. It was put about in publishing circles that Ken would be writing of his homosexual relationship with Olivier and it took years to kill the rumour. There were certain indisputable facts one could count on, like the earth going round the sun; one of these facts was that Laurence Olivier and Kenneth Tynan had never laid lascivious hands on each other.

Two cheques were paid out to Ken early in 1979, a $60,000 advance, and another of $30,000 for research. At the same time Lazar negotiated a sale to Simon and Schuster of Ken's profiles for the *New Yorker*, which produced three advances of $1900 each.

Despite the promise of financial ease, and the assurance that I would be contributing with a new screenplay, Ken became more and more concerned about money. He wanted to sell our London house, which we jointly owned, and he made many a threat to persuade me to comply. I resisted. Since it was Ken's policy to spend everything we earned, the house was all we had with which to protect the children's future.

He continued making efforts to stop smoking. He took a course, for five days, which involved being strapped into a chair while wired up with electrodes and facing a mountain of cigarette butts. The effect was to bring out his stubborn side: he was not going to develop another conditioned reflex, he decided, since he already had quite enough of those. It also occurred to him that as soon as he returned home he could smoke without being attached to electrodes. Hypnosis was equally ineffectual. For a time he sucked on a dummy cigarette, and then he returned to the real thing.

In February we moved once again, this time to a clapboard house deep in Stone Canyon, Bel Air. There was a small pool and a wendy house, which Matthew liked. At night the raccoons would crouch on the low roof, their eyes glinting, waiting for the right moment to grab and devour our cat – a dim-witted marmalade neuter, soon lost to us.

On 5 April Ken sent the *New Yorker* his long profile of Louise Brooks with a letter pointing out that there were one or two passages 'more explicit than the magazine may care for. In their defence, I can only say that Miss B made her name in erotic roles and that she talks about sex as openly as you or I might talk about the weather.' The piece, which 'bowled over' the editor, was entitled 'The Girl in the Black Helmet', and was published in June. Louise Brooks told Ken that she took it for granted he would cut her off with the end of 'Black Helmet'. 'Your note therefore made me happy because a little piece of me and a little piece of you will always belong together.'

Early that spring Ken realized that Olivier's co-operation on the biography was uncertain. Gore Vidal asked the actor at a Hollywood party why he was making it so difficult and Olivier replied: 'I owe Ken a great deal but not my life.' He had in fact decided to write his own book, a very reasonable decision, but his manner of refusing was less than kind. After Ken's death he conceded that he had caused hurt and added, 'I didn't do much to relieve it either, as I remember.'

Olivier had been much vexed by an interview in the *New York Times Magazine* which had quoted him talking intimately about a violent episode in his marriage to Vivien Leigh. Hearing from Olivier's agent that he was upset, Ken wrote on 2 April asking him not to allow that unpleasant experience to 'poison your mind against *all* attempts to capture you in print'. He hoped that Olivier was in no doubt about his good intentions. Ken went on to say that seeing him in the famous Old Vic season at the end of the war had convinced him that he wanted nothing more passionately than to write about the theatre. 'The book I have in mind will be a belated act of thanksgiving.' He did not want to write an authorized biography. Rather pathetically he added that his health had 'not been exactly radiant in these past few years', and that he doubted he had the stamina left for more than one full-length book. He pointed out that if he failed to deliver 'an *acceptable* manuscript within three years, the entire advance must be repaid.' He apologized for his appeal to sympathy and asked to meet and talk with the actor, in Los Angeles (where Olivier was presented that April with a lifetime achievement award at the annual Academy ceremonies) or in London.

Still hopeful that all would be well and that he could accept the large advance, Ken and his accountant explored a complicated system of avoiding US tax on his world-wide income. He set about getting an I visa, and becoming a resident of Mexico as a 'retired income holder'. To this end we travelled to Mazatlán and San Blas, ending up at Puerto Vallarta on the Pacific coast, a tourist village in lush tropical vegetation, with easy access by air to Los Angeles where the children would continue, the following autumn, to be schooled. We chose a house overlooking the bay; and spent several pleasant, unthinking days at the local hotel, drinking margeritas and eating shrimp. Had I allowed myself to think, my anxiety would have been unbearable, because the whole new life plan was crazy.

On 16 May Ken flew to England armed with a huge supply of medication. On the plane to London he collapsed and had to be given oxygen. He was put temporarily into a clinic and later – after fainting in a bank – admitted to Brompton Hospital. Here, on fourteen hours of oxygen per day and ranting and raving at all the nurses, Ken improved, though he had begun to suffer from a severe tremor.

When not in the hospital in London he stayed with Nicole, but this did not work out. Ken was now fighting for his life and had no time for drama. He told me by telephone that he felt as if he were being pulled to pieces by a dog, that it was like struggling in a strong sea and knowing you were drowning.

His spirits had not been improved by Olivier contacting his friends and associates to tell them not to talk to Tynan. The situation was made worse by a gossip columnist of the *Evening News* who had bumped into me in a London nightclub and reported me as saying that Olivier was keen Ken should tell the truth about his relationship with Vivien Leigh. I eventually extracted an apology for this inaccurate piece of reporting, but it managed to antagonize the actor further and to provoke a number of letters between the three of us, letters which led nowhere, because the matter had already been decided. In one letter Ken enclosed a retraction published by the paper which had misquoted me, adding that Olivier's attitude had dismayed him 'because it seemed to violate some quite basic rules about civilised behaviour between friends'. He cabled his agent to stop the deal. He would do a profile for the *New Yorker*, but not the biography, and he returned the advance to the publishers.

Some months later, when Ken eventually returned to Los Angeles, his doctor, Elsie Georgi felt that he had lost heart: 'For the first time, I saw him give up. I said, "Write your own memoirs, and bring in everything. And don't be kinky!" And he laughed. But he got hurt. He thought the man was his friend, and it was another rejection.'

I arrived in London with the children in mid-June, to find Ken remarkably recovered. We drove to the country to visit our Abyssinian cat, and we spent a lovely weekend with Diana Phipps at Buscot, south of Oxford, on a sleepy bend of the Thames. Diana was upset to see Ken hitched to an oxygen machine (which he passed off with mock solemnity as diving equipment). We lunched in Oxford with my novelist friend Angela Huth and her husband James Howard Johnson. It was a sunny day and Angela didn't recognize Ken when, thin and aged, he walked into her house. He put out, with as much energy as he could muster, Angela recalls, 'But I was shocked to see him leaning on the piano after lunch, and then saying, "Would you mind if I went and had a sleep?"'

We flew to Paris with the children, took them to Les Deux Magots and to La Coupole, climbed the Eiffel Tower, and viewed the Unicorn tapestries at the Musée de Cluny. We made our usual pilgrimage to the Tour d'Argent. And there, in a light and silly mood, Ken scribbled on the back of the restaurant's postcard of the original owner 'préparant son célèbre canard': 'Ibsen in the act of tackling a roast duck "on the wing" as he put it. Note doggy bag under Ibsen's right arm. The handlebars of the great playwright's tricycle can be seen on the right of the picture slightly spattered with gravy.'

Ken discovered that an old hero of his, Bud Freeman, was playing tenor sax in the Caveau de la Huchette, and we went along to listen to this elegant and moustachioed musician from Chicago, playing 'I Cover the Waterfront' and 'Tea for Two'. With Ken feeling well, and declaring his love for me, the evening was curiously reminiscent of our first night together in Paris sixteen years before.

41

Endgame

On 12 July 1979, I flew to Madrid with the children *en route* to Cuba – where I would continue to gather material for my screenplay, while the children would stay for the month in an international camp. On the same day Ken flew to New York, where I arranged for a friend of Tracy's to care for him. In the city Ken renewed his annual contract with the *New Yorker* and began negotiations for publishing his autobiography. He returned to Los Angeles, and shortly after flew down to Puerto Vallarta with our secretary Nancy Sundquist, and the friend of Tracy's who had offered him hospitality in New York.

A young local doctor and playboy, Alfonso Curiel, heard that this famous Englishman was living in Vallarta – though he did not quite know what he was famous for – and gave a party for him. Curiel was well known for his parties, at which the town's architects, Texan tourists and pretty single girls on packaged holidays were welcomed. At the party in his honour, Ken met a handsome young American couple called Tom and Toody Competello. Tom had worked at the Actors Studio as a director but had exchanged New York for Vallarta, supporting himself as a professional backgammon player; his wife Toody took on a number of jobs, secretary, teacher of English, to underpin the times when Tom's luck was out. The Competellos and Ken became, over the next months, a little unit: Ken would entertain them with his jokes and his stories and Tom would compete with Ken over who played what and when in which B movie. They played blackjack for matchsticks. Occasionally they would take a boat and go down to John Huston's place, a cluster of huts in the lush jungle south of Vallarta, and there the great director would take on the professional backgammon player with elaborate deference and good manners, and only a soupçon of irony, because he usually won.

Ken's day would begin at nine, when an elderly Mexican maid would arrive at the large two-level house and serve him coffee and eggs on the terrace outside his bedroom. When Nancy Sundquist returned to Los Angeles, Toody took on the job of part-time secretary and Ken would dictate the odd letter to her (still hooked to his oxygen tank), or ask her help in organizing his notes on Laurence Olivier (whose profile he intended to write before starting on his own book). During the six months spent on and off in Puerto Vallarta, Ken wrote one sentence. He thought about work, Toody recalls, but he did not have the health or the energy for it.

By 1 p.m. Ken would be dressed, usually in sarong, shirt and wide-brimmed straw hat, his leather handbag with money, spectacles and inhaler slung over one shoulder, and he and Toody would climb into a taxi and drive to the El Dorado restaurant to meet Tom, picking up on the way a copy of the local English paper, *Vallarta Today*. (The only other reading matter on sale was *Backgammon for Beginners*, *Wilcome to Port Vallarta!* and the collected works of Agatha Christie.)

At the El Dorado, a large, thatched Mexican–Indian-style restaurant on the edge of the ocean, Ken would order the Copa de Nada, a giant tequila concoction, followed, on his instructions, by fish soup served in two cups, the liquid separate from the meat; or the *sopa de chile 'estilo Ken'*, as it came to be called, because he demanded that it be inhumanly spicy. Or, if he was feeling particularly frail, the cheese soup. After lunch Ken always took a siesta. He would say, 'It's amazing how well I sleep,' which did not surprise Toody, who knew that half a bottle of tequila had gone into the Copa de Nada.

In the evening the Competellos would pick Ken up and take him to Tony's place, or the Red Onion, or the Fonda del Sol, where almost always raw-boned, red-faced tourists, mostly from the States, would be roaring at the next table in competition with a relentless *mariachi* band.

Those *mariachi* bands, tinny, high-pitched, dispiriting, would play all over town until around three or even four in the morning, and when sleep was finally possible up in the house in Calle Mine, the roosters would start – 85,000 of them, Ken believed, and most of them living just below his bedroom window. It seemed likely that they were blind, he guessed, since they began to herald the dawn around three in the morning and continued until lunchtime. Cotton wool and rubber plugs were useless.

Some time in August a telegram arrived at the Riviera Hotel in Havana, which I was using as a base to explore the island. It read: 'This is my last summer and I took this house for us to spend it in. Come with children by end week or I shall not live longer.' Several days later the children and I arrived in Puerto Vallarta by way of Mexico City. We were, all four, awfully pleased to see each other. The children laid out all their trophies in their bedroom – flags and buttons, letters and photographs, addresses they had collected in their holiday camp from Vietnamese, Bolivian, Bahamian, Soviet, Angolan and ghetto children from the United States sponsored by the

Venceremos Brigades. The experience had been pleasant and easy going, in the Cuban manner. I, in turn, was full of my own stories, of hearing Fidel Castro speak on 26 July at Holguin, in the company of the Sandinista leaders – one week after their victory against Somoza. I was evidently affected by my transitory brush with the revolution. The life-giving, life-enthusing nature of the people I had met was precisely what I craved after years of Ken's negativism and illness. But our stories did not seem to excite him.

The day after our arrival, as the four of us sat on the terrace watching the sunset, Ken proposed playing a certain game for the benefit of the children: 'On Monday I went to Navarre and spent two days with John before continuing to Houston, where ... Now can you tell me ...?' It was a familiar game. I had played it many times, and the answers were based on a trick to do with words that ended in vowels or consonants. On this occasion I went blank and forgot the rules. Ken said, 'It's my fucking passion, and you can't fucking remember how to play.' The children laughed nervously.

'I'm not good at games,' I told him.

'Life's a game.'

'No, it's not,' I mumbled.

'It's a game of survival,' Ken said. 'Now let's try once more.'

Then I began to laugh, giggling first, then laughing loudly. My face went red and I began to cry hysterically, trying at the same time to regain my composure, but laughing more loudly. I knew the children were upset and embarrassed but I couldn't stop. I asked Ken: 'What if I give you the point, so that you win?'

Later in the evening Ken said to me: 'I don't think we'll ever be able to trust each other again. Not quite completely. Don't you think?'

A few days later we attended a dinner that was supremely boring. Ken was later able to reconstruct it for me so that, as we lay in the damp heat on our bed, I laughed until I cried. He took me in his arms and said that he truly loved me. He said that I made him want to be alive. A fierce tropical storm came up and I went to check the children in their room across from ours, and then we fell asleep despite the *mariachi* bands and the roosters that paid, I presume, no heed to the storm.

We went swimming most days, and lunched at the El Dorado. And the weeks went by. A month after our arrival, trying hard in the heat and humidity to work on my screenplay, I made a note in my journal: 'It is just possible that the lies I live by and dignify will grow so unbearable I shall become a guerrilla against my life.' I could not share this shocking thought with Ken. One morning when he woke up, and struggled to sit upright, he said, 'Life itself is my enemy.'

I fell, as secretly as I could, into a leaden depression, listening to Ken's complaints: that he had made all the wrong decisions; that he'd been too dependent on other people's good opinion of him; that he should have followed the escape route of Gauguin; that he was only ever happy working as a director; that he'd never had a moment's pleasure from writing. Depression in the tropics can be savage. It accumulates undramatically. Our clothes, within days, were covered with mildew and the air in the house stank of tropical plants. With all the dampness and the water, the place felt to me as arid as a dust bowl. I tried to think of cities in autumn, and bright hopeful endeavours, and all that came to mind were past grievances and betrayals. If I woke early and went to work, Ken would complain that my briskness was offensive. So I would lie there and listen to the roosters until I could surreptitiously and safely rise.

I took the children back to Los Angeles to put them into school, completed some journalism and returned to Vallarta. Ken hated being there alone.

He continued to dicker with his Olivier notes, and persuaded Shawn, along with the London *Observer*, to help finance a winter trip to Australia so that he might write about the English–Australian cricket Test matches. He worried about money and having to run two households. He knew he was mortally ill, but thought it would be a long and lingering business. Ideally he would like to have had his children educated in England, and he would like to have lived in Spain. Nothing was in place.

On 17 October Ken flew back to Los Angeles in order to extend his visa and finalize negotiations on his autobiography. Three days later he entered St John's Hospital for a week's treatment. He said to me, with a degree of desperation: 'I just need things not to happen to me.' Baffled and befuddled, he announced: 'I am not myself.' He gave himself the illusion of life by demanding of me every kind of service. I had to make his breakfast (no one else was allowed to substitute), deal with his accountant and pack his things for the return to Vallarta. When the Mexican airline refused to take him because of his oxygen unit, he returned to Los Angeles. That night I dreamed of a number of plots set up by Ken, which I was compelled to enter and solve. By daylight I was enraged that he should have to suffer so. When I slacked in my work on his behalf, as I often did, Ken told me, 'You're like one of those heroines in a John Marquand novel who think they should be treated as royalty.' I did not feel royal.

At the beginning of December Ken managed to return to Puerto Vallarta. He had finalized the contracts for his autobiography, with Lippincott and Crowell in the States and with Weidenfeld and Nicolson for the rest of the world. His advances would amount to £250,000. But the prospect of writing the book was as daunting as ever. Instead, with Toody Competello's co-operation, he planned our Christmas in Vallarta. He went in search of a charro suit for Matthew. He explained that the hat had to be big because his son had the same kind of large, long, English head as he had. He told Toody that he was pleased that Matthew was so good-looking and sensitive.

Thinking about, though not writing, his autobiography (while advertising for information about himself in literary magazines), Ken committed to his journal a quotation from Somerset Maugham's *The Summing Up*: 'There is a sort of man who pays no attention to his good actions, but is tormented by his bad ones.... He leaves out his redeeming qualities and so appears only weak, unprincipled and vicious. Shall I fall into this trap?' Ken wondered.

He wrote to Adrian and Celia Mitchell of the 80° daily temperature, the otter-coloured drinking water and dysentery. 'It's hard to type in the toilet all day.... I lost weight and now resemble a bronzed but bloodless vampire. Women flock to me and hang their coats on me.... The children and I miss England more than Kathleen does (she wants to write more films and there are no British films): but we all miss you like mad.'

By 24 January 1980 Ken had decided to abandon Vallarta for good, and together we returned to Los Angeles.

The new plan was for me to take the children to New York and get them into schools, and for Ken to spend the winter months in the Caribbean. I wrote to Dirk Bogarde to tell him that I thought it was 'Time to Move On. A small voice keeps telling me that I'm losing all sense of what's right and what's wrong and what it's all about. And the children, who've maintained standards all along, tell me it *really* is time to move on. So what about New York?'

In February Ken's health rapidly worsened. Peter Cook and Dudley Moore came to lunch with a group of friends, which was the last time we entertained. The host gallantly played his part, gave a spectacular imitation of John Huston, and retired, before his guests had left, to his bed and his oxygen tank.

To the few old friends who visited him in Stone Canyon he seemed rather sad and withdrawn, but welcoming. When Jonathan Miller visited he felt that Ken was like a fish that had been landed on a bank: 'He was simply choking for air in this awful exile, this community that he really despised. And I think that he longed for London, although he felt that he'd been repudiated there.'

Ken had noted in his journal that he had read a 'sickening clipping' from a London gossip column which said that he was dangerously ill and living on oxygen, 'that one shred of one lung is all that remains to me.... These grotesque exaggerations and lies are couched in terms of praise for my pluck in "fighting back". The damage to me professionally is incalculable: what publisher or editor would commission a work from a dying man? And – worst of all – suppose Matthew or Roxana had happened to read the piece? I shall have to take legal action.' And legal action he took, though his solicitors understandably did not move swiftly to his defence.

Around this time the editor of a London newspaper called to say that an interview with Ken had been submitted to him, which he did not want to use. Did Ken know about it, since it seemed rather personal? It turned out to have been taped by a woman with whom Ken had fallen out violently when she refused (as he had insisted) to allow him to correct the transcript. Ken had done the interview as a favour, and claimed that at the time he had been drinking heavily. When he was eventually shown the transcript, he was horrified. It was not only rambling and inaccurate, full of oft repeated stories, but in it he talked freely about his sexual life with Nicole. 'What would she [Nicole] do with her life now?' he had been asked. 'Remember,' he had answered dismissively. When asked why he had married for the second time, he replied, 'I don't know.... I can't remember why we got married.'

The damage in my eyes was irreversible. Something snapped and broke. What affected me was Ken's betrayal of our past, or more precisely his casual forgetfulness. His was no more than a minor treason, objectively viewed, but it triggered my sentimental vanity and caused me for the first time to freeze on him. I was not aware that by testing me beyond my toleration Ken had provided me with the dispensation I needed. Nor was I fully sensitive to his central battle, which was to stay alive.

Some years later I read Lillian Hellman's *An Unfinished Woman*, and felt remorse and guilt in retrospect, when I read how she had been so often 'silent angry' with Dashiel Hammett, while his lungs were giving out, angry for 'making the situation hard for me, not knowing then that the dying do not, should not be asked to think about anything but their one minute of running time'.

On 2 March Ken flew to New York to help publicize a collection of his *New Yorker* profiles. He had doubts about the title, *Show People*, which sounded to him 'like a gossipy history of vaudeville', and suggested to Michael Korda at Simon and Schuster that perhaps 'Party of Five', 'Special Faces' or 'Above the Crowd' might be preferable. Eventually *Show People* was settled on – and his five subjects were yoked together somewhat to the disadvantage of each portrait. In these long essays (middle-distance writing, as Ken described them) he delved into politics and religion and much else besides show business. In the introduction, he over-modestly conceded that among great essay writers he could 'go a couple of rounds' with Charles Lamb.

Ken put himself through the usual gruelling publicity. On the Dick Cavett Show he appeared in his habitual summer clothes – striped shirt and white suit on this occasion – looking frail and equine and old, so that his ears seemed extremely large, lowering his eyes a good deal as he leaned forward to draw breath, but at the same time giving a thoroughly winning performance. Of Hollywood movie talk on social occasions he expressed reservation: 'It's depressing for someone like me who likes to have a laugh before pottering off to bed.' Asked by his host how he would define sexual decadence, he replied: 'It is whatever makes a man who thinks his ideas of sexuality are liberal, wince.'

On his last night in New York, an old friend, Jean Stein, asked Ken to dinner with Norman Mailer, his new wife Norris Church and Milos Forman. Mailer recalls that despite Ken's emphysema, he was more magnetic that night than he had ever seen him. 'I think he knew that he was near to his end. He told a story as well as I've ever heard a story told. He played all the parts. One just had to lay down one's arms and listen. It was incredibly funny, and it was funny because he was able to contain more details in each instant, and they all were relevant and they all were spicy and juicy and pointed and hilarious and tricky and terrific. Well, it was one of the best little dinners I think I've ever had. But I've noticed something about truly wonderful stories: you never do remember what the story was. Which is perfect. Because if it's good enough, you shouldn't have a photograph of the damn thing. You don't want a tape recording of a great evening because then you start to hear the sub-text and the sub-text will kill anything on earth if it's a real event.' Less than a fortnight after this dinner Ken was admitted to St John's Hospital in Santa Monica.

That spring letters began to arrive in response to Ken's request for auto-biographical material. He was very touched to hear from his Birmingham girlfriend Pauline, who wrote fondly of their love affair, and sent photographs of the two of them in Bournemouth. Ken wondered if she would care to help him research the book, and he apologized for the paltry salary he'd be able to offer. Pauline said she would not need to be paid for doing research.

On 1 April Ken went into the intensive care unit at Cedars-Sinai Hospital in West Hollywood. On Easter Sunday the children and I spent the day at Tony Richardson's in the company of Laurence Olivier and his family. Olivier reiterated that he wished to do his own book, which was why he had been so tough on Ken. Ken was very bitter. From his bed in intensive care he told me: 'Larry complains, but he can move, and breathe, and earn $1 million a picture, and get up at 5 a.m. I have to ask help to get to the lavatory.'

He came back to Stone Canyon but collapsed a few days later, and was rushed to St Johns. He had to be immediately intubated, a procedure of aerating the lungs by connecting them, via the nose and throat, with a tube which effectively prevents the patient from talking. Unable to speak, Ken panicked. I produced a hospital pad and encouraged him to write down what he wanted and what worried him. Where was the urinal bell so that he could summon the nurse? Would he have to endure the awful tubes through the night? Did I remember when he had once had his nose operated on in London and had panicked with pain – with every breath, with every swallow? Would the nurses fool him, and not remove the tubing for several days, telling him they would have to wait upon the doctor's orders?

I calmed him as best I could.

By 24 April he weighed 117 pounds, down from 146 pounds the previous year, and was terribly worried about the hospital bill. He had received a note from Louise Brooks congratulating him on his Cavett performance in New

York. 'As for the fabulous Louise Brooks whom you have invented, don't you think you should hold me down a bit?' She told him that she had recently been hospitalized, and that she too had emphysema. Could Ken advise? Ken wrote back to tell her not to get into a panic, that there were hundreds and thousands of people suffering from the disease. 'Since physical exercise is not your speciality, try learning some breathing exercises. . . . The important thing is to keep your lungs as flexible as possible. Everything follows from that. Since worry will make them tense, don't worry. Just relax and write.' Louise replied some weeks later, to tell Ken that she loved him and that she felt 'subhuman not to have understood when I first met you that you were very ill'. She had fallen apart with sickness 'just lying here'.

From hospital Ken asked me to get the latest Michelin guide for France, and made plans for our summer holiday, booking two double bedrooms at Talloires on Lake Annecy in France for mid-July.

Several days before being discharged he made the following note in his diary: 'Must have someone to share equally the depths of my life – 24 hours a day.' That very day he had told me, when I visited him, 'If you don't come down to the bottom with me, I don't want to go anywhere with you.' I recall very clearly his look of rage and fear, and even more sharply my own shifty, evasive response, my awful absence of feeling. I had brought him some Indian food and a bottle of wine, and I tidied his hospital room, which smelled of antiseptic and stale food; I fussed around and I made idle chat while all I wanted was to get out. I said, 'Would you like my thoughts?' And Ken answered, 'I don't want your thoughts, I want your instincts and your emotions.' I remember that I mumbled defensively about loss of honour, of betrayals. I could tell he knew that I had withdrawn. He said testily, 'I thought one had to honour one's father and mother. After that I don't see why one should have to honour anyone else.'

I came in the next day and Ken announced, 'There are no jokes.' I had no answer, and no jokes, so I busied around his room as I usually did. He said after a time, 'I have no life line.' I said, 'You have me.' 'But I don't feel it,' he answered.

Ken returned to our house in Stone Canyon. He worried about money, jotted down a reminder to make his will. He asked me to buy him protein powder in order to bolster his weight, a supply of champagne and a biography of George Orwell. He contacted a doctor at the Pritikin Longevity Center, on the insistent advice of a friend, and told him that he was taking the following medication: theo-dur, bronkosol inhaled through a machine, Prednisone, Digoxin and tetracycline.

He made a note in his diary in his now shaky hand: 'Ask Gore re lending me $25,000 in trust in case I'm too ill to finish book.'

Through the night of 7 May his sleep was laced with broken sentences: 'A small talent for brilliance'; 'He took his child and shot his ...'; 'Aunt Millie it was'. No amount of oxygen cleared the delirium. In the early hours of the morning he woke and asked, 'Darling, are you there? I'm terribly frightened.' I calmed him until he fell asleep again, and then I crept off to Matthew's room. When I returned in the early morning, Ken was howling, unable to get out the right words. He gnashed his teeth and forced out 'gleary' and 'luggish'. But from the terror on his face it was evident that he realized they were not correct. The day nurse arrived, and registered his high blood gases. We called the ambulance, and we waited. Unannounced there walked into our bedroom, which gave on to the garden, a young man in a seersucker blazer, with a clean almost transparent complexion that you see in babies or the very old. This young man announced that he was from the Pritikin Clinic. He had come to help. If only Ken would change his diet he'd be fine. While the smiling lecture was in progress Ken lay deathly still. 'Are you hearing me, Mr Tynan?' asked the visitor. I saw Ken open one eye, then the other. Quite deliberately he started to sing. I don't remember the words, they were of no importance, though they made perfect sense. The man from Pritikin had acted, unintentionally, as an ideal circuit breaker. Only somebody with such a wrong-headed solution for survival could have shocked Ken into an appalled consciousness. The ambulance arrived and the patient was removed to yet another hospital for yet another intubation.

(Two years before this loss of control over speech Ken had once woken having dreamed all night of words. He wrote in his journal: 'Why do all words that juxtapose the letters "b" and "l" (in that order) have connotations of clownish clumsiness? "Bl" people dribble when they drink; their stomachs rumble after meals which they gobble. Rather than walk, they amble, stumble, hobble, shamble, or tumble; they are bloated and bleary-eyed; vocally they babble, bleat, burble, bluster, and mumble; physically they are feeble.... Many of them are Russian: Oblomov is the classic example.... In a word, they are bumblers, for the most part humble, and although impossible to live with, they may in good time be blessed. (In many ways I am their double).

Ken remained in hospital for two weeks. He told me, 'I'd like to go to sleep. The only thing that prevents me is my fear of death.' I made solicitous, evasive, uncomprehending noises. 'It's up to you to look after me all the time,' Ken said. 'And to make me want to live.'

He managed to dictate some letters. He wrote to Elaine Dundy, who had sent him a beautiful letter recalling their time in Paris. He had been given a copy of Elaine's biography of Peter Finch and told her that he had read her book in 'one munch'. 'It wasn't until I'd finished that I realized what an enormous amount of research you'd done, and how lightly you carried it off.' He ended, 'It was very nice to feel, after so many years, that something like a normal relationship was being resumed. Love and thanksgiving.'

On 23 May Ken transferred to the Brotman Hospital for a pulmonary rehabilitation programme devised by Dr Kenneth Fisher, an attempt to increase the endurance of the respiratory muscles and to improve the patient's ability to ventilate on his own. Ken wrote to William Shawn to tell him of this programme, which would delay the Olivier profile. He had the research, he explained. All he needed was a 'period of peace in which to finish off the writing'. He hoped the *New Yorker* would renew his contract for another year. Shawn, who knew how sick Ken was, replied that the agreement had been extended and that he was happy Ken was beginning to recover. 'The writing will follow,' he gently added.

For a few weeks in the Brotman Ken's ability to ventilate increased, but he was unable to improve the effective gas exchange system – nor did his diet help. He had me bring in the usual Indian food, and drank at least half a bottle of wine in the evening. He spent his time watching television, and he discouraged visitors. When friends appeared, he would not accept that they had come to see him simply because they cared about him. As usual he wished to be reassured that there was good reason to live and that he was sufficiently loved. He told me: 'I used to pretend to my mother I was going to kill myself: "You don't love me enough." I did that to Elaine, and I'm doing that to you.'

The most reassuring life-line thrown to him was by his three children, whose visits made him smile. For Matthew's birthday, on 9 June, he wrote his last birthday poem, exhorting his son to start his tenth year on earth:

> With a wild jungle yell
> And a kiss for Michele.

During this time he made efforts to put his affairs in order, trying to work out his debts, his assets and his obligations, and to make peace. He wrote to Nicole: 'We need to mend our friendship and there may not be all that much time.' Harold Hobson wrote to wish Ken better health and to tell of the recent death of his wife: 'The great days when you and I did weekly battle over new plays – generally, indeed almost always ending in your victory – now seem a part of some legendary Homeric past.' Ken was very touched by this and at the same time very upset to hear of Elizabeth Hobson's death. 'I certainly miss our duelling days,' he responded. 'The trouble with our successors is that nothing seems *at stake* for them.'

At the Brotman Ken was visited by a psychiatrist who listened to his tale of woe and then said he'd never heard a better argument in favour of suicide. 'This was not quite the advice I'd been expecting,' Ken observed to a friend.

During June I packed up our Stone Canyon house and stored our belongings, having found another and less expensive house, in Brentwood, which we planned to occupy early in July. I wrote to the New York schools where the children had been entered for the autumn, and cancelled. I juggled with our chaotic accounts. (A week's visit to the intensive care unit at Cedars Sinai had cost $11,436. And although Ken's *New Yorker* insurance policy paid 80 per cent, there were huge sums outstanding as a result of his different hospital visits.) On 22 June I took the children and went to London to install new tenants in our house, and to deal – on Ken's instructions and as best I could – with his finances.

Two days after our arrival his doctor telephoned to say that he had become suddenly worse, his carbon-dioxide levels rising to unprecedented levels. Dr Fisher could find no explanation, except that Ken had possibly caught an infection. Undoubtedly the amount of alcohol he had had smuggled into the hospital had done him no good. He transferred Ken to a special unit and asked him if he were prepared to be intubated. Fisher told him that his life depended on it and Ken agreed. On the night of the 29th Ken's lungs were vigorously suctioned. On the 30th the doctor and his colleagues managed a lengthy and horrific intubation, during which Ken struggled and fought and had to be held down. Once the tubes were inserted, Ken, in his delirium, thought he had swallowed his teeth. The nurses tied down his hands and freed him only momentarily so that he could write down terrified messages on a clipboard.

On 3 July the fearful procedure had restored his life and the tube was removed. By the date of his discharge, on 16 July, Ken's lung function was slightly worse than it had been when he had entered the hospital.

Adjacent to our new house in South Westgate Avenue was a large studio room with a beamed ceiling and red-tiled floor. There was a bathroom and cooking facilities. Here I installed a hospital bed for Ken and a couch for myself, three different kinds of oxygen tanks, a breathing machine called a nebulizer, and a refrigerator full of cans of protein powder and fruit juice. We put down a Mexican carpet and pinned up a favourite poster of Ken's, a railway engine named 'Exactitude'. Outside the studio was a little terrace where Ken would sit in the afternoons.

The children returned from England, moved into new rooms, and made their sober visits to their father. Sometimes Roxana sat outside the studio and sewed, while Matthew played ball or went in search of his cats.

Ken was very fragile. He relied upon the routines of illness, and each day selected his television programmes. His stomach grew large with food substitute. He could no longer, by the evening of 25 July, be wheeled up to the house to pick at his plate while we dined. For the first time he refused a glass of champagne. He said, 'I don't understand, darling. It's strange, the end of the day. Will it bring a dark conclusion?'

That night he talked disjointedly in his sleep: 'I'll go in a moment.' He began to sing:

Why did we forgo
All those little pleasures
That we loved so long ago
Why did we say no?
We have to complete our ... our transaction.

He woke up and I crossed the room to sit beside him. 'Not very happy,' he said. 'Don't rush.'

In the morning the nurse said Ken was too weak to stand up and be weighed. Around mid-day he became extremely animated. He sat up and showed me the television programming for the day. He said he had figured out why he went into intensive care only on a weekend. His collapse never had anything to do with his chemical or medical condition. It was simply due to the dearth of anything of quality on Saturdays and Sundays, and an excess of children's entertainment and sports. Stock-car racing, he pointed out in disgust. *Tarzan* at twelve followed by *Tarzan and Super Seven* at twelve-thirty! Open golf! I held his hand. I told him that I was going to take the children for a short run on the beach. 'Please come back soon,' he said.

The children and I ordered hamburgers at the Brentwood market, and then we went down to the Santa Monica beach. The fog had rolled in and we ambled along for half an hour, then we drove home. On the way back into South Westgate, our Buick passed an ambulance. 'It's Daddy,' Matthew said, 'I saw the nurse.' I deposited the children at the house and drove to St John's Hospital. Dr Giorgi was already there. She explained that Ken had been brought in unconscious with ventricular tachycardia, a chaotic action of the heart which prevents the necessary ejection of blood. 'Blood can't get to the brain,' she said.

In the emergency room, an army of doctors and nurses were working frantically on Ken like a swarm of Lilliputians over Gulliver. They had intubated him in the vein and begun to massage the heart to get the blood up to the head. There was a strip of normal rhythm and then it flattened out. Three times they brought him back from cardiac arrest, but after an hour his vital signs were no longer obtainable. His heart finally stopped.

A nurse pushed me angrily away from where I stood, and drew the curtains. Elsie explained that Ken's brain had gone before his heart gave out. She knew that Ken lived in his head, and had hoped that the medical team would give up. 'Every time they revived him it was cruel. But I couldn't say, "No code blue".'

Our doctor went back to pick up Roxana. She told her, 'It's not a pretty sight. You don't have to come to the hospital if you don't want to.' Roxana said she would like to be with her mother. A little later Tracy and Matthew joined us.

I went into a small room surrounded by curtains where Ken now lay, his long body shorn of all the tubes and machinery. I closed his eyes and rested my hand on his bird-thin white shoulder. I placed his hands under the sheet, muttered to him, kissed his brow and left. Then the four of us, with Elsie Giorgi, drove home. Elsie took Matthew aside. (She had spoken to Roxana on the way to the hospital, and knew that she would be all right.) She said to him, 'You must have some questions.' 'No,' Matthew replied. 'I have some answers.'

Elsie Giorgi left, then Tracy. I wept throughout the night. The next morning I sat at my little desk and tried to work out what had to be done. Matthew came in and leaned over the table. He gathered a handful of paper clips and, making sure that I was watching, spelled out LIFE, then LOVE, then I LOVE YOU. He walked away as casually as he could.

On Tuesday 29 July Joan and John Dunne went with me to All Saints Episcopal Church on Santa Monica Boulevard to organize the funeral. I explained to the minister that Ken was not a parishioner, and he said it did not matter: 'We like to think we can reach out into the community.' John told me later that they had done a lot of 'star turns' at that chapel.

On Wednesday Tracy and I went to the Cunningham and O'Connor funeral parlour on Melrose. We put my dozen red roses on to the cardboard box serving as a coffin, on which Ken's name was scrawled in large letters. I added a posy from the children. Waiting to set off for the mortuary, I glanced at Roxana's note. It read: 'In accordance with the death of my father (who had many enemies) I wish this to go with the remains of the man I admired and loved more than any other in the world (his enemies admired him too).' Beside her signature Matthew had added his. I drove behind the hearse, and Tracy followed me in her car.

Rosedale mortuary has been on West Washington Boulevard since the late nineteenth century, a handsome, tree-shaded cemetery. Ken's body, in its makeshift cardboard box, was driven up to the white crematorium. I got out of my car and took a rose from the wilting bouquet. An official said, 'You can't go further, you know.' She said the job took two and a half hours and there was no point in waiting. Tracy left. I sat on a stone wall under a tree, watching the Chinese employees in hard hats disappear into the crematorium. There was no one about. I clutched my rose, and grinned insanely. Who would want to burn alone? The least I could do was sit it through. It seemed very odd that Ken had ended up in Rosedale, Culver City.

Telegrams and flowers came in, and telephone calls. Someone in London told me that the first announcement of Ken's death on the BBC merely mentioned that he was notorious for saying a four-letter word on television and had been responsible for the obscene revue *Oh! Calcutta!* An actress whom I'd never met called to ask me, 'Are you very, very bereft?'

My brother arrived from Canada, and Penelope Gilliatt came from New York. She told me that William Shawn had come into her office to tell her the news of Ken's death. 'I cried, and looked out of the window. Bill said, "He was just a boy."'

The little chapel filled up with about seventy people on the afternoon of the 31st. There was some organ music, and a short service conducted by the Reverend M.G. Richards. Three friends spoke. First, Christopher Isherwood quoted a paragraph from Ken's profile on Louise Brooks, and then read a passage from the Quaker William Penn's *Some Fruits of Solitude*. Shirley MacLaine stood up next. 'Ken, there are some things I didn't get to tell you ...,' she began. She said everyone in the room would help look after his family, and that the thought of his smile lit up her heart. It was about 95° in the chapel, and the atmosphere – as at all funerals – mixed tears, embarrassment and slight hysteria. The third speaker was Penelope Gilliatt, who spoke about Ken's courage.

Roxana had picked out and read a particularly lugubrious psalm, number 6, 'O Lord, rebuke me not in Thine anger, neither chasten me in Thy hot displeasure.' The lesson was delivered, the organ played and we walked out into the sunlight.

Throughout August I stayed in Los Angeles, trying to make some sense of the chaos, the logistical mess that had been left, and kept my feelings under lock and key. I made a list of Ken's considerable debts. I began arranging his burial at Oxford and preparing the memorial service in London.

Having decided that Oxford would be a fitting place for Ken's ashes to be buried, I wrote to the President of Magdalen asking if there were any facilities on the grounds of Ken's old college. Keith Griffin wrote back to explain that they used to be able to bury people in the chapel but this was now illegal. He told me, however, that successful approaches had been made to St Cross Church, that here was a quiet almost rural cemetery near the college where many Oxford people like Sir Maurice Bowra, Charles Williams and Kenneth Grahame were buried. This suggestion pleased me and the matter was decided.

Letters of condolence came in. Adrian Mitchell was reminded of how, at a rehearsal of his play *Tyger*, 'the cast were all singing: "For everything that lives is Holy", and when I looked at him, [Ken's] face was scarlet and the tears were coming down like Niagara and he wasn't hiding them at all and he was smiling that very long smile.' John Marquand wrote to say that he had been playing some Spanish flamenco music and had been reminded of his times in Spain with Ken. 'That night I had a dream: Sue [John's wife] and I were in Spain, at a fun fair ... at a booth where people lined up to throw hard balls at shelves of crockery. No prizes for marksmanship, just the satisfaction of smashing plates. Kenneth appeared in this dream in the role of counselor–supervisor; he had something to do with the fun fair management and he cautioned us against doing too much damage. What the dream meant, I do not know. But the next morning ... I bought the *N.Y. Times* and saw Kenneth's photograph and read that he had died.... He was about the most brilliant friend I ever had, certainly the brightest, the *funniest*. I shall miss him all my days.'

The obituaries came in. A few stood out. Gore Vidal wrote that the last time he had seen Ken he had noticed 'that when he mentioned his illness, there was a sudden gelid glare in those gooseberry eyes: rage, pure rage'. The critic John Simon hoped that his 'perturbing spirit' would never rest. Harold Hobson said that 'like Latimer and Ridley' Ken 'would have been proud to be called a heretic'.

I continued to clear up. I emptied Ken's handbag. In the big pocket were various scraps of paper that must have been there for months: a letter from Matthew, an old prescription, a poem I'd written for him six years before, on which he had scribbled some addresses. It read:

> All my life
> Dream-Haunted by loss
> Till you
> When I didn't dream
> But closed my eyes.
> Now alone
> I am pursued again

On 17 September my mother, Tracy, Roxana, Matthew, Penelope Gilliatt and I climbed into Ken's old Jaguar (having put his ashes in the boot) and drove to Oxford. We were followed by Adrian and Celia Mitchell, and Christopher Logue. At Angela Huth's house, at the top of Headington Hill, we were joined by Diana Phipps, the Rev. Brian Findlay, Dean of Divinity from Magdalen College, who had agreed to perform the service, and Karl Leyser, representing the college. We drove to St Cross Cemetery.

The undertaker took charge of the copper box (he was clearly offended that it lacked handles). We attached our notes to the flowers. Then we walked between the cedar trees through the long grass, the rambling roses and the unkempt graves to the burial site, which was next to a sapling oak. The Reverend Findlay committed the ashes. Adrian read a love poem he had written, part of Blake's 'Vala or the Four Zoas', whose refrain is 'For everything that lives is holy', and an excerpt from a letter of Ken's. Then Christopher delivered a short poem. Finally Roxana read a passage from C.S. Lewis' *Screwtape Proposes a Toast*. It ends: 'These things – the beauty, the memory of our own past – are good images of what we really desire: but if they are mistaken for the thing itself they turn into dumb idols, breaking the hearts of their worshippers. For they are not the thing itself; they are only the scent of a flower we have not found, the echo of a tune we have not heard, news from a country we have never visited.'

Epilogue

With the words of Ken's tutor, the short service ended. Later that afternoon, with Penelope Gilliatt, I drove to a stonemason's yard outside Oxford and chose Hornton Blue Oxfordshire granite for a headstone. The stone reads: Kenneth Tynan 1927–1980.

The memorial service, on the following day, began at 12 p.m. in St Paul's Church, Covent Garden. There was an opening prayer, after which Albert Finney read part of a preface to a collection of Ken's work about being a critic. The words seemed right for the actors' church. They ended: 'I admire actors; but I worship the theatre. Serving the end, I must occasionally injure the means.'

Tom Stoppard spoke last and most movingly: 'Because he was about the wittiest person one could hope to meet and because he had a good figure, it was possible to make the mistake that Ken was a dandy ... but without the toughness of mind, and the intellectual sense that history could be nudged and the politician's sense of how to nudge it, and above all the hard work which made the rest of it possible, one would only have that part of Ken which caught the light.'

Stoppard spoke about the writing: 'His paragraphs – paragraphs were the units of his prose, not sentences – were written to outlast the witness.'

Then he turned to Ken's children and said: 'For those of us who were working in the English-speaking theatre during those years, for those of us who shared his time, your father was part of the luck we had.'

Since Ken's death his literary reputation has been more or less in limbo: his published collections of theatre reviews, essays and journalism are out of print. Millions of words of his writing in newspapers and periodicals are not reprinted in book form. His letters and journals have not yet appeared.

From time to time someone still takes a shot at him. Was his a fine mind going nowhere? Was he 'an anti-intellectual', as the academic George Steiner states, 'to the tip of his brilliant, histrionic fingers'?

Admirers of his theatre reviews describe him as a prophet, 'the greatest evocative critic in history, and also the greatest visionary of what theatre could be'; while for others he is merely uncanny in his talent as a great recorder of the exceptional performer.

Some saw Ken as a 'war correspondent', an outstanding journalist consuming the moment. Others point out that this very definition of journalism (and of Ken's work) is pejorative and imperfect, that the bias in favour of academic criticism has blinded us to the much wider contribution to our literary past by the journalist.

A young critic has recently written of Edmund Wilson that the characteristic virtues of his writing, 'the qualities that make readers return to his essays even after their arguments seem to have been superseded, are journalistic virtues: the commitment to the language of the general, rather than the specialist; intelligence; the sophisticated curiosity that confronts the high and the popular, the new and the outré, with equal poise; and most of all the ability ... to give ideas the quality of actions.' What Ken prized about sophistication was 'precisely its ability to perceive and mock irrational excesses, whether committed in the service of Calvin or Mao. (When told once by a fan, 'I read you religiously,' he answered: 'Please read me agnostically.')

No one was more adept at giving 'ideas the quality of actions', at presenting them with their marching orders. Art and ideology had to 'stand guard against chaos'. The task of drama was not simply to reflect calamity but to show us how to survive it. The aim of propaganda in the theatre was to start the audience talking. Art was for 'our sake', truth was concrete. Satire was 'protest against the notion that there is anything more important than the fact that all men must die'. But effortlessly squeezed between that imperative was always a proviso: satire had to be 'couched in wit'.

As for the critic crying these maxims abroad, what counted was not the opinion but the art with which it is expressed: the critic's job, Ken believed, is to write for posterity.

I believe that I was wrong ever to argue that Ken was a performer who happened to write. He was a magician with 'the magic innovation of our species'. He could make words perform for him, 'skip, leap and gyrate', in the service of order, wit and beauty. At his best his prose is natural and immaculate. Here he was in his element, at home, in a place where his lungs never failed him.

As a man he was an oddity always; he didn't set out to be anything else. Restless, energetic, vivid, inspired, *sui generis*.

Like his hero of the English revolution, the Puritan John Lilburne, Ken felt contempt for the dutiful citizen. He was not easy to deal with in public or in private. Nor was he easy on himself: unresolved, even undone by 'nature's livery, or fortune's star'. Unlike John Lilburne, who established the principle that no man should be compelled to bear witness against himself, Ken was self-incriminating. He was also without vanity or pretension regarding his reputation.

Now that he has 'eluded the idiot snowman hurling white powder at his temples', as Deacon Lindsay wrote to me after Ken's death, he 'remains ever a traveller'.

I do not think of him so much these days; I've moved on. But even without him, a subterranean part of me still plays the rescuer, is still stubbornly, preposterously determined to hold on to our love.

Part of me also wishes the traveller with whom I lived for a while the peace that he wanted. A few months before the hospital claimed him for good, he wrote to me:

I used to quote what follows as if it were addressed to you. It now goes to what Tommy Lasorda calls the Big Dodger in the Sky, and I still do not know its origins. *'A l'heure de ma mort, soyez le refuge de mon âme étonnée, et recevez-la dans le sein de votre miséricorde.'* ['At the hour of my death, may You be the refuge of my astonished soul, and receive it into Your merciful breast.'] This comes to you from the desk of

Your husband
Ken

Acknowledgements

I would like to thank the following people for their generous contribution to this book:

Maggie Abbott; Eileen and Larry Adler; Richard Adler; Rozina Adler; Ivan Alderman; Tariq Ali; Jay Presson Allen; Lewis Allen; Ted Allen, Kingsley Amis; Lindsay Anderson; Lord Annan; The Hon. David Astor; Maxine Audley; George and Joan Axelrod; Lady Baker; Michael Balcon; Michael Balfour; Michael Banton; William Becker; Sally Belfrage; Hercules Bellville; Jill Bennett; Eric Bentley; John Berger; Ballard Berkeley; Burton Bernstein; Oscar Beuselinck; Drusilla Beyfus; Theodore Bikel; Michael Billington; Graham Binns; Yolande Bird; Kitty Black; Vera Blackwell; Robin Blackburn; Michael Blakemore; Diana Boddington; Robert Bolt; Charles and Mary Bolté; Peggy (Boyesen) Brooks; Bernard Braden; Barbara Brecht; The Berliner Ensemble; Patricia Brewer (Feeney); Alan Brien; Nancy Brien; Lord Briggs; Maria Britneva (Lady St Just); Peter Brook; Dinah Brooke; Brigid Brophy; Georgia Brown; Richard Buckle; Peter Buckley; Trevor Buckley; Peter Bull; Sybil Burton (Christopher); Brenda Bury; John Calder; Gerald Campion; Rosemary Carvil; Ruth Cashmore; Ronnie Cass; Hilary Champion; Tsai Chin; Barbara Clegg; Reginald Colin; George Colouris; Betty Comden; Tom and Toody Competello; Angela Conner; Peter Cook; Irwin Corey; Peter Cotes; Heather Couper; Jill Craigie; Quentin Crewe; Michael Croft; Ruth Cropper (Lupton); John Crosby; Rosalie Crutchley; Constance Cummings; Thomas Quinn Curtiss; Robert Cushman; Su Dalgliesh; Geoffrey Darby; Annie and Bill Davis; James Dawson; Sir Robin Day; David de Keyser; John Dexter; Joan Didion; Marlene Dietrich; Suki Dimpfl; Jarvis Doctorow; William Donaldson; Frank Dunlop; John Gregory Dunne; Anthony Easterbrook; Hillard Elkins; John Elsom; Russell Enoch (William Russell); Martin Esslin; Peter Eyre; Bernard Fairbrother; Ellen Fairbrother; Daniel Farson; Andrew Faulds; Trader Faulkner; Judy (Sheftel) Feiffer; Lawrence Ferlinghetti; José Ferrer; Dr Kenneth Fisher; Michael Foot; Milos Forman; Barry Foster; Clement Freud; Lee Fox; Richard Gale; Tony Garnett; Bamber Gascoigne; William Gaskill; Jack Gelber; Penelope Gilliatt; Prof. Roger Gilliatt; Hermione Gingold; Dr Elsie Giorgi; Michael Godley; Milton Goldman; Walter Gotell; Dr Sydney Gottlieb; Michael Gough; Alex Grahame; Derek Granger; John Grant; Roger Gray; Adolph Green; Germaine Greer; Trevor Griffiths; Miriam Gross; Sir Alec Guinness; Shusha Guppy;

Geoffrey Hackett; Edith Haggard; Kenneth Haigh; Michael Halifax; Alice Hall; John Hale; Jean Halton; Paul Hardwick; Earl and Countess of Harewood; Judy Harger (Gideon); Barry Harmer; Kenneth Harris; Kitty Carlisle Hart; Ronald Harwood; Richard Hatton; Frank Hauser; Jim Haynes; Ann Head; Lillian Hellman; Dr John Henderson; Katharine Hepburn; Addie Herder; Eric Hobsbawm; Sir Harold Hobson; Betsy Holland (Gehman); Julian Holland; Ellen Holly; Father Walter Hooper; Jo Hopkin; Elly Horowitz (Miller); A. E. Hotchner; Penelope Houston; Elizabeth Jane Howard; Trevor Howard; Angela Huth; Eugène Ionesco; David Irving; Christopher Isherwood; Derek Jacobi; Emilie Jacobson; Henry and Sylvia James; Conrad Janis; Helen Jay; Lionel Jefferies; Belita Jettson Turner; Derek Jewell; Gloria Jones, Mervyn Jones; Bettina Jonic; Garson Kanin; Austen Kark; Mirian Karlin; Barbara Kelly; Gene Kelly; Bryan Kent; Terence and Joanna Kilmartin; Peter Kneebone; Arthur Kopit; Michael Kustow; Gavin Lambert; J. W. Lambert; Verity Lambert; Michael Law; Betty Lawley (Peacock); Sylvia Stratford Lawrence; Dilys Laye; Irving Lazar; Nydia Leaf; Simon Lee; Daphne Levens; Bernard Levin; Jacques Levy; Karl Leyser; Derek Lindsay; Vera Lindsay (Russell); Joan Littlewood; Marguerite Littman; Joshua Logan; Christopher Logue; Nicholas Luard; James Lund; Rupert Lycett-Green; Alexander Mackendrick; Hilary Mackendrick; Diana Mahony (Sinden); Norman Mailer; Raymond Mander; Hugh Manning; Linda Marlowe; John P. Marquand Jr; Mary Martin; Betty Marsden; Jean Marsh; Jack May; Mary McCarthy; Allen McClelland; Vanessa McConnell; John McCormick; John McGrath; Alan Jackson Mee; George Melly; Sue Mengers; John Metcalf; Michael Meyer; Margaret Michael; Hugh Millais; Joan Miller; Jonathan Miller; Dacia Mills; Adrian and Celia Mitchell;

Joe Mitchenson; Lord Montagu; Charles Monteith; Royston Morley; Sheridan Morley; Lord Morris; John Mortimer; Stanley Myers; David Nathan; Christopher Neame; Rosemary Nibbs; Peter Noble; Patricia Nye; Ken O'Bank; Edna O'Brien; Roman O'Casey; Lord Olivier; Alun Owen; Sir Peter Parker; Bertha Peacock; G. W. Peacock; George Perry; Diana Phipps; David Pierce; Richard Pilbrow; George Plimpton; Joan Plowright (Lady Olivier); Roman Polanski; Ellen Pollock; Derek Prouse; Roy Purcell; Oscar Quitak; Eileen Rabbinowitz; Jennifer Ramage; Rupert Rhymes; Tony Richardson; Stella Richman; Joan Rodker; Robin Rook; Annie Ross; Gillian Rowe-Dutton (Lady Parker); Gladys Ruddle; Lady Rumbold; D. D. Ryan; Mort Sahl; Anthony Sampson; Carol Saroyan (Matthau); Philip Saville; John Schlesinger; Anthony Schooling; George Scott; Judy Scott-Fox; Irwin Shaw; William Shawn; Ned Sherrin; Bill Shine; Maurice Shock; Milton Shulman; Barbara Siggs (Simon); Alan and Ruth Sillitoe; Phil Silvers; Joe Simon; Frank Singuineau; Carole Skelton; Godfrey Smith; Maggie Smith; R. D. Smith; Virginia Smith; Terry Southern; Victor Spinetti; Heather Standring (Smythe); Gillian Staynes; Robert Stephens; Tom Stoppard; John Stride; Michael Strutt; Nancy Sundquist; Donald Swann; Peter Symcox; Georgia Tennant; Brian Tesler; Rev. Frank Thewlis; Elizabeth Thorndike; Trevor Tolley; Harry Towb; John Trevelyan; Ossia Trilling; Kieran Tunney; Warren Tute; Dorothy Tutin; Peter Ustinov; Gloria Vanderbilt; Joan van Poznak; John Veale; Pamela Vezey; Gore Vidal; Beata von Schine; John Wain; Hazel Vincent Wallace; Irving Wardle; Marina Warner; Harry Watt; Sheila Weeks; Pat Welch; Orson Welles; John Wells; Arnold Wesker; Michael White; Sam White; Gordon and Jane Whiting; Pauline Whittle (Shirley); Michael and Penny Wigram; Peter Wildeblood; Sir Hugh

ACKNOWLEDGEMENTS

Willatt; Clifford Williams; Sandy Wilson; Michele Winebrenner; Digby Wolfe; Marie Woolf; Dora and Stan Wright; Alix Wyatt (Coleman); Hazel Young (Holt); Wayland Young (Lord Kennet); Elisabeth Zaiman (Harris).

With grateful thanks to: Arts Council Archives; BBC Programme Index; Birmingham Central Library; The Bodleian Library; The British Library; British Theatre Association; The London Library; The Louise Brooks Estate for use of quotation from her letters to KPT, and other material; The Chandos Papers, Churchill College, Cambridge; *Cherwell*; the *Evening Standard*; The Tyrone Guthrie Foundation; *Isis* magazine; King Edward's School, Birmingham; Magdalen College, (Oxford) Archives; the *New Yorker*; the *Observer*; the Oxford Union Society; University of London Senate House Library; Victoria and Albert Museum Theatre Collection; Warrington Museum and Library; and the many other publications to which Ken contributed, which are credited in the notes and sources.

I would particularly like to thank Ernie Eban for putting together a comprehensive bibliography – an indispensable guide to Ken's life. I would also like to thank the following, who at various stages in the preparation of this book provided me with valuable research: Owen Hale, John Mason, Celia Mitchell, Patty Pigott, Jesse Schulman and Ann Wilson.

I am indebted to the following itinerant secretarial labourers: Arlene Chapman, Kathleen D'arcy, Maureen Hossbacher, Molly Pawley and Helen Swift.

I am also deeply indebted to my editors at Weidenfeld & Nicolson, John Curtis and Alex MacCormick.

During my long, arduous and sometimes painful sleuthing, Leon Wieseltier was my most diligent friend. I thank him for his wise help, sweetness and wit.

I also thank my children Roxana and Matthew, who unselfishly guarded me. And Barbet Schroeder, always.

Books by Kenneth Tynan

(excluding contributions to collections)

He That Plays the King, London: Longmans, Green, 1950.
Persona Grata, London: Allan Wingate, 1953; New York: G. P. Putman's Sons, 1954.
Alec Guinness, London: Rockliff, 1953, 1961; New York: Macmillan, 1955.
Bull Fever, London: Longmans, Green, 1955, 1966; New York: Harper Bros., 1955; New York: Atheneum, 1966.
Quest For Corbett (radio play), London: Gaberbocchus, 1960.
Curtains, London: Longmans, Green, 1961; New York: Atheneum, 1961.
Tynan on Theatre (paper version of *Curtains*), London: Penguin Books, 1964.
Tynan Right and Left, London: Longmans, Green, 1967; New York: Atheneum, 1967.
A View of the English Stage, London: Davis-Poynter, 1975; London: Paladin Books, 1976.
The Sound of Two Hands Clapping, London: Jonathan Cape, 1975; New York: Holt, Rinehart and Winston, 1975; New York: Berkley Books, N.Y., 1981.
Show People, London: Weidenfeld & Nicolson, 1980; New York: Simon & Schuster, 1980; New York: Da Capo Press, 1981; London: Virgin Books (paper), 1981.

Source Notes

KEY

KPT	Kenneth Peacock Tynan
KHT	Kathleen Halton Tynan
D	Diary
EB	Engagement Book (sometimes referred to as 'diary')
EJs	KPT Early Journals 1967–1970
J	KPT Journal 1961
	KPT Journals 1970–1980
Int	Interview
L	Letter
[ ]	Additional Information

In almost every case the KPT published work is referred to in its original publication, and not in the collected books.

Those quotations not attributed in my sources are from interviews (90% of which were taped), of people listed in the acknowledgements.

PROLOGUE

Page

3 'Rouse tempers, goad': KPT, *He That Plays The King* (London: Longmans, Green, 1950), p. 23.

3 'He was the sort': Alan Brien, 'Down Memory Lane', *New Statesman*, 7 June 1968.

4 he capered, he had eyes: *Merry Wives of Windsor*, III, ii.

4 'grievously thin': Godfrey Smith, 'Kenneth Peacock Tynan', *Sunday Times Magazine*, 25 Aug. 1963.

4 'What could a Beardsley': Alan Brien, 'The Boy Wonder', *Truth*, 1 Oct. 1954.

6 'theatre of fantasy': KPT, *Curtains*, (New York: Atheneum, 1960), preface, p. viii.

7 Kierkegaard says: 'Repetition', *Kierkegaard's Writings*, Vol 6 (Princeton, 1983), p. 293

8 *The Rack*: A. E. Ellis [alias Derek Lindsay] (London: Heinemann, 1958).

9 'Soleil, soleil!': Paul Valéry, 'Ébauche d'un Serpent', *Paul Valéry An Anthology*, (London: Routledge and Kegan, 1977), p. 242.

9 But Akhenaten: C. S. Lewis, *Reflections on the Psalms* (London: Collins Fontana, 1974), p. 73.

10 'Gentlemen, many things': Int. of KPT, 'The Critic Comes Full Circle', *Theatre Quarterly*, Apr./June 1971, p. 40.

10 'I am for the intricacy': David Pryce-Jones, *Cyril Connolly, Journal and Memoir* (Collins, 1983), p. 238.

1. PEACOCKS AND TYNANS

12 'In any real sense': David

Woolcombe, Int. of KPT, *Nouslit*, Spring 1973.

12 'that cemetery without': Eleanor Hoover, int. of KPT, 1978.

12 'because [Birmingham] bored': Susan Barnes, 'The Hidden Shallows of Kenneth Tynan', *Sunday Times Magazine*, Aug. 1972.

12 'We got on': Godfrey Smith, 'Kenneth Peacock Tynan', *Sunday Times Magazine*, 25 Aug. 1963.

12 Samuel Johnson: KPT J, 8 Mar. 1978.

13 'heart-transplant': KPT, 'One Pair of Eyes', BBC 2, 31 Aug. 1968.

14 four stalls: Market returns, Warrington Market.

14 [Peacocks] There still exist 67 branches of Peacocks in Wales and the West Country.

14 At fourteen he: *Warrington Guardian*, 4 Feb. 1914.

15 Around 1896: *Warrington Guardian Yearbook*, 1914.

15 'working man's friend': *Warrington Guardian*, 12 Dec. 1903.

15 In 1912 Peter: Ibid., 16 Oct. 1912.

15 Chairman of boards: Ibid., 21 Jan. 1913.

15 [take charge]: Sir Peter's motto (with regard to civic improvements) was 'Do it now.'

15 [family business]: In 1919 the Peacock drapery business motto was 'Quick Returns – Small Profits.'

15 'When I walk': *Warrington Guardian*, 27 Feb. 1915.

15 [justices of the peace] Peter Peacock was Justice of the Peace, Warrington Borough bench, from 14 Nov. 1916 to 18 April 1947.

15 Peacock's Bazaar: *Examiner*, 8 June 1918.

15 'get soured': *Warrington Guardian*, 1 Jan. 1919.

16 that by 1921: *Kelly's Street Directory*, and *Local Electoral Register*.

16 Samuel Tynan: 1 June 1846,

Abbeyleix in Queens County, now County Laois: parish baptismal records.

16 [an army private]: Samuel Tynan was enlisted 24 June 1863, 21st Regiment of Foot, and transferred in 1867 to 2nd Battalion 8th of Foot, part of the King's (Liverpool) Regiment.

17 his sister Annie: Annie Peacock.

2. CHILDHOOD

19 From 1921: *Kelly's Street Directory*.

20 'At these moments': Godfrey Smith, 'Kenneth Peacock Tynan', *Sunday Times Magazine*, 25 Aug. 1963.

20 'When I was': Margaret Fishley, *Woman's Journal With Flair*, Nov. 1976.

20 [bungalow called Kenrose]: 9 Brightland's Ave., Southbourne. Sir Peter would take Ken and his cousins to restaurants for braised golden plover and steak and kidney pie. On the chauffeur's day off he would ride home with them on the streetcar. Every afternoon they went to a beach of their choice – Peacock owned two beach huts. They would play in the pines at Branksome, and watch the ships come in at Southampton. At Christmas there were parties in the big stores, the pantomime at the Pavilion, and lighting the candlelamps in the Winter Gardens.

21 Auntie Annie: Annie Corradine.

21 *Hatter's Castle*: account drawn fro KPT, 'Shouts and Murmurs', *Observer*, 3 Mar. 1968, and EJs.

22 Portland Road: No. 229, *Kelly's*, 1936.

22 'Mother is going': KPT D., 1 May 1939.

22 '... skeletons in the cupboard': F. W. Bebbington to KHT, 1984.

24 Stumpz: KPT D., 11 June 1941.

24 [Foundation Scholar]: Ken received £8 a term.
24 The city endured: *History of Birmingham*, Vol. III, Anthony Sutcliffe and Roger Smith (Oxford University Press, 1974), pp. 25–31.
24 favourite films: KPT D., 1941.
25 Laurence Olivier: Ibid., 5 Sept 1941.
25 Mary Martin: Ibid., 1941.
25 Charlie Chaplin: Ibid.
25 Brenda Joyce: Ibid.
25 James Thurber: Ibid.
25 'Meditations on Basic Baroque': KPT, *King*, Sept. 1966.
25 mother's dress: KPT D., 6 Apr. 1941.
26 'The Unilateral Triangle': Ibid., 26 Dec. 1941.
26 Gilbert and Sullivan: KPT, *Observer*, 11 Feb. 1962.
26 'scared to death': William Foster, 'Critic in the Crow's Nest', *The Scotsman*, 11 Nov. 1967.
26 *Rookery Nook*: KPT D., 12 Jul. 1941.
26 *The Man Who Came to Dinner*: Ibid., 20 Nov. 1941.
26 *Dear Brutus*: Ibid., 13 Sept., 1941.
26 Jewell and Warriss: Ibid., 18 Feb. 1941.
26 Jimmy James: Ibid., 30 Apr. 1941.
26 'He would incline': KPT, *He That Plays the King*, (London: Longmans, Green 1950), p. 168–169.
26 'Have decided': KPT D., 16 Mar. 1941.
26 sham-Harrovian: description by James Agate from S. A. Moseley, *Who's Who in Broadcasting* (London, Pitman 1933) p. 116.
27 Winston Churchill: Winston Churchill L to KPT, 25 May 1939.
27 Lord Beaverbrook: Lord Beaverbrook L to KPT, 23 Aug. 1940.
27 Joseph Kennedy: Joseph Kennedy L to KPT, 4 Apr. 1940.

27 'A chap': KPT D., 16 Nov. 1941.
27 'Insignificance': KPT, *King Edward's School Chronicle*, Dec. 1941.
27 'I spoke about sex': KPT D., 3 Dec. 1941.

3. THE YOUNG DANDY

28 'nice bit of surrealism' KPT L to Julian Holland, 10 Feb. 1944.
28 ('My stock garment'): Ibid., 2–4 Nov. 1943.
28 'abominable brazilian': Ibid., 5 Nov. 1943.
28 red silk ribbon: Ibid., 23 Jan. 1944.
29 'I saw KPT': James Dawson D., 17 Jan. 1944.
29 'for I have': Ibid.
29 'As long as I'm': KPT L to Holland, 20 Feb. 1944.
30 'if you go to ealing': Ibid., 29 Oct. 1943.
30 'I am wondering': Ibid., 10 Feb. 1944.
30 'In tears': Ibid., 1 Mar. 1944.
30 'dazzled by': KPT, 'Orson Welles', *Show*, Oct. 1961.
30 [Jed Leland]: Drama critic of *New York Inquirer* in the movie.
30 'Believing all I read': KPT J., Apr. 1971.
31 'the opening sequences': KPT L to Holland, 5 Nov. 1943.
31 'The New Playboy': KPT, *KES Chronicle*, Dec. 1943.
31 'I like whores': KPT L to Holland, 30 Jan. 1944.
31 'Entered Gaumont': Ibid., 4 Mar. 1944.
31 ['L'oeil était dans la caverne, et regardait Ken']: 'The original of the Hugo line,' Ken added at the end of his letter, 'ends "Cain".'
32 'I am thinking not so much of *Macbeth*': KPT, 'Orson Welles', *Show*, Oct. 1961.
32 'Write heresy': Dawson D., 18 Jan., 1944.
33 'the platinum': KPT, 'Alexander

Woollcott', *KES Chronicle*, Jul. 1943.

33 'Otherwise I shall': KPT L to Holland, 13 Sept. 1943.

33 'Film as Graphic': King Edward's Literary Society minutes, 16 Feb. 1944.

33 'unwilling to provoke': KPT L to Holland, 26 Jan. 1943.

33 'TRY AND BE': Ibid., 14 May, 15 May 1944.

33 'This House considers': King Edward's Literary Society minutes, 27 Mar. 1944.

33 'Tynan was at': Dawson D., 18 Feb. 1944.

33 'I made certainly': KPT L to Holland, 1 Apr. 1944.

34 'Independent Confucian': Ibid., 4 Mar. 1944.

34 ['Contemplative Leisure']: In the autumn of 1963 Ken wrote to Richard Crossman, Labour MP, proposing a Ministry of Leisure.

34 JDC [the history master]: KPT L to Holland, 4 Mar. 1944.

34 anarchism: KPT L to Holland, 29 Nov. 1944.

34 Fabian socialism: Ibid., 2 Nov. 1944.

34 the ideal: Ibid., 23 Jan. 1944.

34 'Whipwords': Ibid., 30 Jan. 1944.

35 'Worry about words': Ibid., 22 Jan. 1945.

35 'What is the characteristic': KPT L to Holland, 9 Dec. 1943. Quote found in Sergei Eisenstein, *The Film Sense*, (London: Faber Faber 1943), refers to 'The Case of Wagner', *The Works of Friedrich Nietzsche* Vol. XI, (London: Macmillan, 1896) pp. 24–25.

35 'Beware of half-tones': KPT, occasional book, 1943.

35 'Johnson is marvellous': KPT L to Holland, 30 Jan. 1944.

35 'Dreamt of a KPT': Ibid., 23 Jan. 1944.

35 literary quiz: Ibid., 9 Mar. 1944.

36 disturbing news: Ibid., 11 Dec. 1943.

36 On jazz: Ibid., 30 Jan. 1944.

36 'Read Edmund Blunden's': Ibid., 15 May 1944.

36 'you may have guessed': Ibid., 15 Aug. 1944.

4. QUAND MEME

37 'Shaw's plays': KPT L to Holland, 1 Sept. 1945.

37 essays and criticism: Ibid., 27 Apr. 1944.

37 *Macbeth*: Ibid., 12 Dec. 1944.

37 *Richard III*: Ibid., 4 Mar. 1944.

37 Volpone: Ibid., 12 Dec. 1944.

38 'stubby dane': Ibid.

38 [*Peer Gynt*]: It seems very likely that on 3 Jan. 1945 Ken saw Olivier for the first time on stage in the small part of the Button Moulder in Ibsen's *Peer Gynt*.

38 'From a sombre': KPT, *He That Plays the King* (London: Longmans, Green, 1950), pp. 32, 34.

38 'like a dirty penny': KPT L to Holland, 17 Dec. 1943.

38 [state scholarship]: worth approx. £200 a year. (Between arrival and departure at King Edward's School Ken acquired twelve major school prizes. He was secretary to the debating and literary societies, sub-editor and editor of the school magazine, member of school First Eleven cricket team, secretary to his school house, prefect, president of the Foundation Conference of 1945).

38 'So he's done it': James Dawson D, 8 Dec. 1944.

38 Higher School Certificate: KPT L to Magdalen Tutorial Board, 4 May 1945.
[Higher School Certificate 1944]. 'Distinction': English Lit and History. Over 95% scholarship papers in English and History.

'Good': French.

39 'Mother found': KPT L to Holland, 9 Dec. 1943.

39 'My father': Ibid., 27 Dec. 1943.

39 'My Tynans': KPT L to Hazel Young [Holt] and Barbara Siggs [Simon] 8 Mar. 1945.

39 Charles Morris: KPT L to Holland, 1 Apr. 1944.

40 'All you need': King Edward's School, Prefects Minutes, 1945.

40 Pat Martin: KPT L to Holland, 13 Sept. 1943.

40 'the Girl of': Ibid., 10 Oct. 1943.

40 'first time in': Ibid., 29 Oct. 1943.

40 named Joy: Ibid., 5 Nov. 1943.

40 meets Kathleen: Ibid. 26 Dec. 1943.

40 ['Whirlaway']: According to James Dawson, this could refer to 'a fairground machine.' Julian Holland suggests 'a whirlaway spray' or 'might be made-up word for "whirling spray", an old-fashioned contraceptive.'

40 'When in their': Dawson D, 10 Dec. 1944.

40 'if only *you'd*': KPT L to Holland, 11 Feb. 1944.

40 'I am now': Ibid., 20 Feb. 1945.

40 'she stripped': Ibid., 4 Mar. 1945.

40 perform in a doorway: Dawson D, 1 Mar. 1945.

40 'Only she can': KPT L to Holland, 20 Mar. 1945.

41 'I shall never write': KPT L to Hazel Young and Barbara Siggs [Simon], 8 Mar. 1945.

42 'preserved their poetic': KPT L to Holland, 31 Jan. 1945.

42 'Only in his actions': Ibid., 13 Mar. 1944.

42 'since they knew': Ibid., 11 Jan. 1945.

42 'Towards a New *Hamlet*': King Edward's School Literary Society minutes, 9 Feb. 1945.

42 '[not] a psychologist': KPT L to Holland, 22 Jan. 1945.
[Of his proposed production of *Hamlet* he said: 'What I aim at is to bewilder the illiterate and impress the cultured'] KPT L to Holland, 4 May 1945.

42 making appearances: Ibid., 20 Feb. 1945.

43 'Throughout he tends': T. C. Kemp, *Birmingham Post*, 14 June 1945.

43 At the close: F. L. Kay L to KHT, 1981.

43 up to London: Pauline Whittle L to KHT, 16 Mar. 1982.

43 'I wept then': Ibid., 5 Jan. 1980.

43 'This is about the end': KPT L to Holland, 10 May 1945.

44 'Ken, for the last six': Ibid., 3 June 1945.

44 'I am so instinct': KPT L to Whittle, 25 May 1945.

44 'fast, loose': KPT L to Holland, 3 June 1945.

44 'Joy so brilliantly': Ibid., 6 June 1945.

44 'I was quite': Whittle L to KHT, 25 May 1983.

44 'Believe me, J': KPT L to Holland, 3 June 1945.

44 'The tousled': KPT L to Whittle, 5 June 1945.

45 original contributions: KPT L to Holland, 1 Dec. 1943.

45 'Little Poem': KPT, *KES Chronicle*, July 1945.

45 'a butcher boy': KPT, *Observer*, 20 Aug. 1961.

46 'My Dear Hamlet': James Agate, *Ego 8*, 20 July 1945, (London: George G. Harrap, 1947) p. 172.

46 ['Verlaine was always chasing Rimbauds'] was stolen by Ken from Dorothy Parker.

46 'I SHALL': James Agate, *Ego 8*, 21 July 1945, p. 173.

46 'I have, as you must know': James Agate, *Ego 8*, 27 July 1945, p. 185.

46 A further letter: James Agate, *Ego 8*, 28 July 1945, p. 188.

46 Hamlet replied: James Agate, *Ego 8*, 31 July 1945, p. 194.

47 'Lunch with Hamlet': James Agate, *Ego 8*, 4 Aug. 1945, p. 205.

47 Balkan Sobranie: KPT L to Holland, 18 Aug. 1945.

47 swing seat: Whittle L to KPT, 5 Jan. 1980.

47 He wrote off to: KPT L to Magdalen College, 18 Aug. 1945.

47 The college wrote: Magdalen College L to KPT, 22 Aug. 1945.

5. GANGSTER IN THE GROVES OF ACADEME

49 'Your extroverted KPT': KPT L to Julian Holland, 14 Oct. 1945.

49 'worried about knives': John Dugdale, 'Tynan 25 Years On', *Isis*, 2 Nov. 1973.

49 'my clique': KPT L to Holland, 30 Oct. 1945.

49 *Huis Clos*: Ibid., 4 Dec. 1945.

49 Taj Mahal: Ibid., 23 Nov. 1945.

49 'Lying flat': Ibid., 5 Nov. 1945.

49 'except for his voice': *Isis*, 28 Nov. 1945.

50 'It's typical': Evelyn Waugh, *Brideshead Revisited* (London: Chapman and Hall, 1945), p. 93.

50 less robust: Dugdale, *Isis*, 2 Nov. 1973.

50 'We could pass': James Morris, *Oxford Book of Oxford*, (London: Oxford University Press, 1978), p. 186.

50 'trying to live': KPT MS, Unpubl. Int. for 'One Pair of Eyes', 1968.

50 'I never liked': KPT J., 28 Oct. 1974.

50 'He was the epitome': Alan Brien, 'Down Memory Lane', *New Statesman*, 7 June 1968.

51 'a gangster': KPT, 'Tynan's Oxford', *Listener*, 17 Oct. 1968.

52 'Fiat Luxicar': Briget Brophy L to KHT, 2 Apr. 1983.

52 [£20]: Ken said that he received £5 a week from his father during his Oxford career (slightly less than a man's average weekly earnings).

Evidence suggests he received double this amount. Either way his family paid his bills.

52 a girlfriend recalls: Gillian Staynes L to KHT 10 Apr. 1983.

52 'unalterably foreign': KPT L to Pauline Whittle, 21 Dec. 1945.

52 'Richardson never rollicked': KPT, *He That Plays the King* (London: Longman, Green, 1950), p. 49.

53 'There was a sharp': Ibid., p. 51.

53 'This Shallow': Ibid., p. 52.

53 'mordant burlesque': KPT L to Holland, 20 Mar. 1946.

53 'a glossy': Ibid.

53 'inconstant consort': Ibid.

53 [Prince of Wales]: More precisely, KPT occupied the rooms of the Prince's bodyguard, Cloisters 5.

53 'a superbly extravagant': *Oxford Magazine*, 21 Feb. 1946.

53 'an absolute masterpiece': Sir Edward Boyle, BBC, quoted in Int. for KPT unpubl. MS 'One Pair of Eyes', 1968.

53 'licensed shocker': Sir Robin Day L to KHT, 18 Jan. 1983.

53 Lamb and Gibbon: KPT L to Holland, 5 Feb. 1946.

54 'Occasionally': KPT, *The Canadian C.S. Lewis Journal*, Jan. 1979.

54 'Keep a strict': C. S. Lewis note on KPT essay *Early Drama*.

54 'too many of his': KPT, *Persona Grata* (London: Allan Wingate, 1953), p. 69.

54 compared his old tutor: KPT *The Canadian C. S. Lewis Journal*, Jan. 1979.

55 *Isis* 'Idol': KPT, *Isis*, 12 Feb. 1947.

55 'For Christ's sake': BBC, Int. for KPT unpubl. MS 'One Pair of Eyes', 1968.

55 'a tightly packed': George Scott, *Time and Place* (London: Staples Press, 1956), p. 146.

56 'The great object': KPT back of EB, 1947.

56 'Eat, drink, toil': KPT L to Whittle,

1 Jan. 1946.

56 'To my plans': Ibid., 29 Nov. 1946.

56 'I will tell you': *Oxford Guardian*, 3 Mar. 1947.

57 'Ken Ty Nan': *Oxford Guardian*, 25 Apr. 1947.

57 'And here I': KPT, *Isis*, 12 June 1946.

58 'Did you know': KPT L to Elisabeth Zaiman, 24 May 1946.

58 'I have received': Ibid., 27 May 1946.

58 'All right': Ibid.

59 'I used a balletic': KPT L to Holland, 9 Sept. 1946

59 'With a sprawling': Ibid., 17 Sept. 1946.

59 The lodge at Magdalen: Paul Johnson, Int. for *Reputations*, BBC2 1982.

60 'ingenuous claqueurs': KPT, *Cherwell*, 18 Oct. 1946.

60 'For until the bores': Alan Beesley, *Cherwell*, 29 Nov. 1946.

60 'a drunken Gingold': KPT, *Cherwell*, 29 Nov. 1946 [reference to Hermione Gingold].

60 'the grey evil': KPT, 'Si Non E Vero ... Ben Travato', Ibid.

60 'an exquisitely bored': *Isis*, 20 Nov. 1946.

61 'Cervillism': KPT, *Cherwell* 23 Jan. 1967.

61 'If unmarried': *Oxford Mail*, 31 Jan. 1947.

61 'Idol' of Alan: KPT, *Isis*, 12 Feb. 1947.

61 '(1) The wild': Skunk, *Oxford Guardian*, 3 Mar. 1947.

61 'Irvingesque': *The Times*, 26 Feb. 1947.

6. THE MARVELLOUS BOY

63 [John Godley]: Godley is the journalist and author Lord Kilbracken.

64 minor journalist: *Oxford Mail*, 25 June 1942.

64 'He was, of course': Stanley Parker, 'Cage Me a Tynan', *Cherwell*, 14 June 1948.

64 'He took me home': Pauline Whittle L to KHT, 25 May 1983.

64 'My thoughts': Gillian Rowe-Dutton L to KPT, Good Friday 1947.

65 'I'm living with Jill': KPT L to Holland, 30 Apr. 1947.

65 'he will go apart': Alan Beesley, 'Idol', *Isis*, 14 May 1947.

65 'the authentic': KPT, 'Paradise Regained and Samson Agonistes', unpub. essay for C. S. Lewis.

65 'This sad age': KPT, 'An Oxford Production', *Mandrake*, Jul. 1948.

66 [The production]: advertised with billboards which read: 'This Space is Reserved for Ken Tynan'.

66 'Even with the resources': Nevill Coghill L to KPT, 1 June 1947.

67 'I nearly had': KPT L to Holland, 17 Sept. 1946.

67 'I have seen': James Agate, *Ego* 9 (London: George G. Harrap, 1948), p. 309.

67 'Doddering, precious': Derek Jewell, *Isis*, 15 Oct. 1947.

67 'This is a gift': Shakespeare, *Love's Labour's Lost*, IV, ii.

68 'Jill has left me': KPT L to Holland, 24 Sept. 1947.

68 'Please *see* me': KPT L (undelivered) to Gillian Rowe-Dutton.

68 Wilde's old rooms: Gillian Staynes L to KHT 10 Apr. 1983.

68 'He cavorted round': Gillian Staynes L to KHT, 26 Jan. 1984.

68 'Without noticing': Gillian Staynes L to KHT, 10 Apr. 1983.

69 ['Let's get engaged']: Ken would say, or: 'Any altar I might lead you to would be purely sacrificial.'

69 'Is there anything': David Woolcombe MS *Nouslit*, Spring 1973.

69 'Ken Tynan ... arrived': Mary Bolté, D., 2 Nov. 1947.

70 'Oh Orson, yes': KPT, 'Bits and Pieces', unpub. MS. c.1947.

70 Martyrs' Memorial: KPT 'Afterword' to Alan Beesley's unpub. autobiography, 'Breakdown', 1974.

70 'In a very real': KPT unpub. MS for 'This House Believes Sincerely to Be the Refuge of Fools'.

70 'I want to protest': KPT, 'Attack', Isis, 19 Nov. 1947.

71 'frisking around': Ludovic Kennedy, Isis, 4 Feb. 1948.

71 'Catarrh can strike': KPT, 'The Invincible Must, II', Oxford Viewpoint, Feb. 1948.

71 C. S. Lewis: KPT L to C. S. Lewis, Jan. 1948.

71 For this wildly: Isis, 2 Feb. 1948. [Ken was president of ETC, 1947–1948.]

71 'Now Roger': KPT unpub. 'Production Number' MS, 1948.

71 'breath-taking': Cherwell, 25 Feb. 1948.

71 'My God': Brigid Brophy L to KHT, 2 Apr. 1983.

71 [Winterset]: Judge Gaunt – KPT; Herman – Michael Croft; Mio – Simon Lee; Hobo – Peter Parker; Garth – Sandy Wilson.

71 [sound man]: Jarvis Doctorow.

72 Wilde and Ruskin: Le Monde, 24 June 1948.

72 'What sets Oxford': KPT, 'Oxford Now', Vogue, Mar. 1948.

72 'Few of us': Alan Brien 'In Defence of Oxford', Isis, 5 May 1948.

72 'He knew that': Alan Brien, KPT memorial service, 18 Sept. 1980.

73 Ken was seen to hobble: Judge J. A. Baker L to KHT, Nov. 1983.

73 'virilescent': Isis, 26 May 1948.

73 [As the term drew]: On 25 May 1948, Ken played Fear in a royal masque devised by Nevill Coghill and performed for Princess Elizabeth. He declared: 'Of all lands, my favourite and pet is ENGLAND blitzed and starving and in debt.'

73 'a judicious blending': KPT, 'The Stratford Hamlet', Oxford Viewpoint, June 1948.

73 'a political tragedy': Programme Note, Hamlet, Oxford University Players, Civic Playhouse, Cheltenham, 7–14 Aug. 1948. [Hamlet – Peter Parker; Horatio – Lindsay Anderson; Ghost – Ken Peacock Tynan; Corambis – Jack May; Fortinbras – Robert Hardy.]

74 'We thought you'd': Matthew Coady, Daily Mirror, 12 Mar. 1969.

74 'uprooting toy soldiers': KPT L to Whittle, 22 July 1948.

75 'Do you have a block': Sunday Times Magazine, 6 Aug. 1972.

76 'I like your slant': KPT L to Eileen Rabbinowitz, Aug. 1948.

76 university magazine: KPT, Varsity Supplement, 6 Nov. 1948.

76 'I wish my mum': Sandy Wilson, I Could Be Happy, I, i.

77 'Peter Brook': Gillian Staynes L to KHT, 10 Apr. 1983.

77 'His general psychological': Dr Edward Glover, 16 Nov. 1948.

78 'authorities of the': C. S. Lewis L to KPT, 23 Feb. 1949.

78 'Not excluding': Sir Robin Day L to KHT, 18 Jan. 1983.

78 'The Golden Age': Lois Stockley, Isis, 19 Jan. 1949.

78 'legend': Robert Kee, Picture Post, 25 Nov. 1950.

78 'prophet': Cherwell, 6 Nov. 1950.

78 not a legend: KPT, 'One Man's Oxford', L to Picture Post, 16 Dec. 1950.

78 'with all those gramophone': KPT, Cherwell, 6 Nov. 1950.

78 'Oxford was': Alan Beesley, Unpub. Int. for 'One Pair of Eyes', 1968.

78 'Like all the best': KPT, 'One Man's Oxford', Picture Post, 16 Dec. 1950.

79 'Removed something': KPT, 'Tynan's Oxford', Listener, 17 Oct. 1968.

7. A LEAPING SALMON

80 *The Times: The Times*, 4 Jan. 1949.

80 'You are clearly': Michael Redgrave L to KPT, 2 Feb. 1949.

80 'I now pretend': KPT, '... Nor am I out of it', *Isis*, 18 Jan. 1950.

81 'Lichfield All-sorts': *Illustrated London News*, 9 July 1949.

81 ['D-d-don't you e-e-ver']: Ken apologized to Grant the next day and explained, 'It's only beause I'd given such a shocking performance.'

81 'Instead of becoming': KPT L to Henry James, 17 Aug. 1949.

82 Ken wrote: KPT L to Patricia Brewer, Oct. 1949.

82 'A Citizen of the World': Also known as Man of the World.

82 ['leading part']: KPT: 'I hate group theatre. I like big actors in big parts', *News Review*, 2 Mar. 1950.

83 [11 December]: With Stella Richman and Theodore Bikel.

83 'a bit of Kafka': Peter Brook, *Harper's Bazaar* (U.K.) Oct. 1954.

83 speed and fire: Harold Hobson, *Sunday Times*, 26 Feb. 1950.

83 [*Desire Caught by the Tail*]: Trans. Roland Penrose.

83 Lady Macbeth: KPT unpub. notes on text, 1950.

83 'leapt salmonwise': KPT, *Isis*, 18 Jan. 1950.

83 'It is difficult': Georgina Willoughby, 'Portrait of a Prodigy', *Contact*, May/June 1950.

83 'hotly pressed': KPT L to Brewer, Oct. 1949.

84 French diplomat: Thérèse Mayer L to KHT, 24 Jan. 1983.

85 'In that case': Pauline Whittle L to KHT, 16 Mar. 1982.

85 [first person]: Ken knew about Brecht before meeting Bentley. In notes begun in January 1950 on theatre production styles (notes recycled and published in 'We Await the Messiah', *Vista*, June/Jul. 1950, and 'Styles and Producers', BBC Third Programme, 21 Sept. 1950), he wrote the following: 'On the theatre of the future. Brecht? The acting will tend to develop into a kind of stylised shorthand ...' In notes written on theatrical trends in the autumn of 1950 (recycled and published in 'Around London's Theatres', *Panorama*, Winter 1950/1951), Ken wrote: 'trend is an ugly refrigerating word ... all we can say is that Brecht is taking his theatre in [a certain] direction, and Brecht is very powerful indeed. But Brecht is German and Communist, and thus a little inaccessible to us nowadays.' In 'Prompt Corner' *Theatre Newsletter* 17 Feb. 1951, Ken recommended: 'any of the writings of Bertolt Brecht (not yet translated and published in book form over here). The wisest modern writing on the unimportance of the actor'.

85 ['I told him']: Eric Bentley: 'Within a few years *Ken* was Helene Weigel's hero and *I* was her villain.'

85 'There was much': Tyrone Guthrie L to Charles Landstone, 9 Dec. 1950.

85 'maestri': KPT, *Vista*, June/July 1950.

86 'posturing butterfly': KPT, *Vista*, June/Jul. 1950.

86 tradition of playcraft: KPT, 'Where Are the Playwrights', *Theatre Newsletter*, 16 Sept. 1950.

86 Brecht: Ibid., KPT's first published reference to Bertolt Brecht.

86 'we have produced': KPT, 'Styles and Producers', BBC Radio 3, 21 Sept. 1950.

86 [*He That Plays the King*]: Ken drew upon and rewrote published and unpublished writings from his school days. A single-page essay

which he penned at Oxford (and quoted in a Cambridge debate of 1948 'The Economist is a Menace to Society') is rewritten for the Epilogue: the short essay is an early declaration of his stance as a critic: 'I am an embalmer of nuance, a champion in unimperilled lists.... I mummify transience.... My business is to accustom every sight, or sound, or smell to the companionship of good words. I may even persuade myself that this grace, this balance, this constellated equipoise, exists in my own life ...'

86 'almost limitless': KPT, *He That Plays the King* (London: Longmans, Green, 1950), Preface, p. 17.

86 Finlay Welles: KPT, *Isis*, 18 Jan. 1950.

86 'this witty': Redgrave, *Times Literary Supplement*, 27 June 1951.

86 'devastated': Roy Walker, *Theatre Newsletter*, 6 Jan. 1951.

88 'I saw a tall': Elaine Dundy, *The Dud Avocado* (London: Pan Books, 1984) p. 237.

88 Polish-born: Obit., *New York Times*, 14 June 1963.

88 Heyman Rosenberg: Obit., *New York Herald Tribune*, 1 Mar. 1952.

89 'He was a terror': Terence Anderson to Howard Senzel, 16 Oct. 1983.

89 Signal Corps: Civilian Personnel Records Center.

89 '1-Yank girl': KPT EB, 14 Dec. 1950.

89 'At one of': Elaine Dundy, *Reputations*, BBC 2, 25 July 1982.

89 'scary': Peggy Boyesen L to KPT, 11 June 1980.

90 'If you hadn't': Elaine Dundy, *The Dud Avocado* (London: Pan Books, 1984), p. 271.

90 'He would screw up': KPT, 'Toby Jug and Bottle', *Sight and Sound*, Feb. 1951.

90 'spring-heeled walk': KPT, 'Cagney and the Mob', *Sight and Sound*, May 1951.

90 'it unbends': KPT, 'One Another's Best', *Vogue*, Mar. 1951.

8. BOTH SIDES OF THE FOOTLIGHTS

91 'are not good or evil': KPT, working notes for production.

91 'When Clunes': KPT J 5 Feb. 1971.

92 [Guinness had had a dream]: Alec Guinness to KHT: 'Almost every single member of the cast of *Hamlet* became a star of some sort.'

92 'as skinny as a willow': Godfrey Smith, *Sunday Times Magazine*, 25 Aug. 1963.

92 'As the murderer': KPT, *Alec Guinness* (London: Rockliff, 1953), p. 98.

93 'The Worst Hamlet': Beverley Baxter, *Evening Standard*, 18 May 1951.

93 'merciless volubility': 'The Monstrous Regiment of Critics', *Panorama*, Spring/Summer 1951.

93 open letter: KPT L to *Evening Standard*, 22 May 1951.

93 he lunched with Ken: KPT EB, 17 May 1951.

93 'I have invited': Percy Elland L to Lord Beaverbrook, 18 May 1951.

94 'Is He Great': KPT, *Evening Standard*, 29 May 1951.

94 'It has particularly': Elland L to Beaverbrook, 1 June 1951.

94 'Overpraise in the end': KPT, *Evening Standard*, 9 July 1951.

95 'His Hal was': KPT 'The Young Lions of 1951', *Panorama*, Spring 1952.

95 'After supper': Peggy Boyesen D, 19 Aug. 1951.

95 a polo party: KPT EB, 25 Aug. 1951.

95 'Christ fuck': KPT J 25 Nov. 1972.

96 'An average of two': KPT, *Embassy*, 8 Dec. 1951.

9. STAR QUALITY

97 'A curious young': *The Noël Coward Diaries*, (London: Weidenfeld and Nicolson, 1982), p. 177.

97 'I don't know': KPT, *Panorama*, Spring 1952.

98 'comedy gone flabby': KPT, *Bandwagon*, Oct. 1952.

98 'No doubt about it': KPT, *Evening Standard*, 19 Oct. 1951.

98 'hunching his blubber': KPT, *Sketch*, 24 Oct. 1951.

98 'that three months': KPT, *Evening Standard*, 24 July 1953.

98 Claire Bloom's: KPT, *Daily Sketch*, 26 Feb. 1954.

98 'their steady marble': KPT, *Panorama*, Spring 1952.

98 Frankie Laine's performance: KPT, *Evening Standard*, 22 Aug. 1952.

99 *South Pacific*: KPT, *Spectator*, 9 Nov. 1951.

99 'like a matron's': KPT L to Peter Wildeblood, Dec. 1951.

99 To the visitor: KPT, *Spectator*, 11 Jan. 1952.

100 *Guys and Dolls*: KPT, *Spectator*, 1 Feb. 1952.

100 *Pal Joey*: Ibid.

100 Ethel Merman's: Ibid.

100 Phil Silvers: Ibid.

100 In his first article: KPT, *New York Times*, 20 Jan. 1952.

100 'Expose yourself': KPT EB, 11 May 1952.

101 [Martine]: 'flawless', according to Maurice Wiggin, *Sunday Times*, 18 May 1952, He complimented the 'brilliant young Mr. Tynan' on his combination of 'tact and passion.'

101 'glittered like': KPT, *Evening Standard*, 27 June 1952.

101 'I hope in future': Beaverbrook L to Elland, 15 Apr. 1952.

101 'Drama criticism': KPT unpub. note for Foyles speech, 21 Nov. 1952.

102 'It is not': Orson Welles, introductory letter, *He That Plays the King* (London: Longmans, Green and Co. 1950), p. 14.

102 'nobility, more grace': KPT, *Theatre Newsletter*, 8 Dec. 1951.

102 'But now the bullfight': KPT, *Bull Fever* (London: Longmans, 1955), p. vii.

102 The Seven Year Itch: KPT, *Americana*, May, 1953.

102 'What a possession': KPT L to Cecil Beaton, May 1952.

103 'got some honies': Beaton L to KPT, 29 Dec. 1952.

103 'She was very upset': Charles Higham L to KPT, 3 May, 1980.

103 'First she acts': KPT, *Evening Standard*, 6 Mar. 1953.

104 'thick white line': Ibid., 10 Apr. 1953.

104 'When oh when': *Evening Standard*, 15 May 1953.

104 'Since I'd made': KPT L to *Evening Standard*, 20 May 1977.

104 Ken wrote to: Elland L to Beaverbrook, 24 July 1953.

105 'If you want': Charles Curran L to KPT, 26 July 1953.

105 'The older generation': KPT, *Evening Standard*, 7 Aug. 1953.

106 'Then we saw [her] stand': John P. Marquand Jr L to KHT, 25 Aug. 1980.

107 A Bunch of Comics: KPT, *Observer*, 20 Sept. 1953.

108 'with a decent amount': KPT L to David Astor, 19 Dec. 1953.

10. A FLEET STREET BISHOPRIC

109 'new Bernard Shaw': Hannen Swaffer, *World's Press News*, 8 Jan. 1954.

109 'It looks like': *Time*, 7 June 1954.

109 Insider's view: Peter Brook, *Harper's Bazaar* (U.K.). Oct. 1954.

109 'exclusive': *People*, 10 Jan. 1954.

109 'like exiguous': Alan Brien, 'The Boy Wonder', *Truth*, 1 Oct. 1954.

109 went on trial: Jeffrey Weeks, *Coming Out* (London: Quartet Books, 1977) p. 161.

110 homosexuals; Elland L to Lord Beaverbrook, 15 Jan. 1954.

110 'discard the mask': Peter Wildeblood, *Against the Law*, (Harmondsworth: Penguin Books, 1957) p. 188.

110 'In retrospect': KPT J., 4 Apr. 1976.

110 'a sophisticated': KPT, *Observer*, 27 Dec. 1959.

110 most unmistakable: KPT, Ibid.

111 'bruised individual': KPT, 'American Blues', *Encounter*, May 1954.

111 'ignoble': KPT, Ibid.

111 'Flew out': KPT, 'Days in the Dream Factory', *Punch*, 12 May, 1954.

111 Buster Keaton: KPT J., 4 July 1977.

111 'People either': KPT, *Punch*, 12 May 1954.

111 'playing one-eyed: KPT, *Punch*, 19 May 1954.

112 'thunderous face': KPT EB, 5 Apr. 1954.

112 'subpoena envy': KPT, 'Shouts and Murmurs', *Observer*, 31 May, 1968.

112 'dismayingly': KPT, *Punch*, 12 May, 1954.

112 *faux-naïf* wit: KPT J., 25 July 1977.

113 autobiography: KPT EB, 20 Apr. 1954.

113 'snappish': Betsy Holland L to KHT, 26 Apr. 1983.

113 'On the plane': KPT, unpub. MS, *All-Girl Elephant Hunt*, 1954.

113 Perelman to drinks: Holland L to KHT, 26 April 1983.

113 'fabrication': KPT, 'Garbo', *Sight and Sound*, Apr. 1954.

114 lipstick: KPT, *Persona Grata* (London: Allan Wingate, 1953), p. 49.

114 'What, when drunk': '*Sight and Sound*, Apr. 1954.

114 'She has sex': KPT, *Persona Grata* (London: Allan Wingate, 1953), p. 38.

114 rhinestone sheath: Leslie Frewin, *Blonde Venus* (London: MacGibbon and Kee, 1955), p. 134.

115 'curled up': KPT, *Everybody*, 10 July 1954.

115 altruistic activities: KPT, 'Some Notes on Drama Criticism', *The Writer*, July 1954. [He added that theatre reviews should be letters addressed to the future, to people twenty years hence who may 'want to know what it is like to be in a certain theatre, on a certain distant night.']

115 the second-rate: KPT, *Observer*, 19 Sept. 1954.

115 *Separate Tables*: KPT, *Observer*, 26 Sept. 1954.

115 actors performing: KPT, *Observer*, 24 Oct. 1954.

116 *Saint's Day*: KPT, *Lilliput*, Oct./Nov. 1951.

116 'Loamshire': KPT, *Observer*, 31 Oct. 1954.

116 apathy: KPT, 'British Cultural Apathy', *Atlantic*, Nov. 1954.

116 Irish, that conspiracy: KPT, *Observer*, 12 Dec. 1954.

116 'put on flesh': KPT, *Observer*, 21 Nov. 1954.

11. NEW BLOOD

117 vital as politics: KPT, *Observer*, 2 Jan. 1955.

117 'international in scope': KPT, *Observer*, 9 Jan. 1955.

117 *Mother Courage*: KPT EB, 1 Jan. 1955.

117 'a glorious': KPT, *Observer*, 9 Jan. 1955.

117 'I have seen': Elaine Dundy, '*Reputations*', BBC 2, 1982.

117 *The Caucasian*: KPT, *Observer*, 26 June 1955.

118 'ovally built': KPT, 'The Theatre Abroad: Germany', *The New*

Yorker, 12 Sept. 1959.

118 English premiere: KPT, *Observer*, 3 July 1955.

118 point of view: Ibid., 22 Jan. 1956.

118 'genius-watching': KPT L to Longmans, 3 July 1955.

118 'pure theatrical': KPT, *Observer*, 19 June 1955.

118 'The final decision': KPT, 'Profile', *Observer*, 20 Nov. 1955.

118 Welles replied: Orson Welles L to KPT, 20 Apr. 1956.

119 'Last night': KPT, *Observer*, 12 June 1955.

119 'more niminy-piminy': Ibid.

119 'receives the news': Ibid., 21 Aug. 1955.

120 'Those minds': KPT, note at back of EB, 1955.

120 'Save me': Ibid., 1955.

120 'women wished': KPT, 'What Men Hate Most About Women', *Picture Post*, 4 Sept. 1954.

120 'Discovered that': KPT, note in EB, 25 Sept. 1955.

120 loved him: KPT EB, 22 July 1955.

120 fed up with: Tennessee Williams L to KPT, 12 July 1955.

121 soft-fleshed: KPT, 'Valentine for Tennessee', *Mademoiselle*, Feb. 1956.

121 candlelight: KPT, 'The Judicious Observer Will Be Disgusted', *The New Yorker*, 25 July 1970.

121 a plague: KPT, 'The Other Face of Spain', *Jerusalem Post*, 18 Apr. 1958.

121 social untouchables: KPT, 'Prose and the Playwright', *Atlantic*, Dec. 1954.

121 'passionate desire': KPT, *Observer*, 22 Jan. 1956.

121 'We just don't': Williams L to KPT, undated, 1955.

122 'frankly jettisons': KPT, *Observer*, 7 Aug. 1955.

122 'godotista': Ibid., [The only other notable British critic to praise *Waiting for Godot* was Harold Hobson.]

122 'Not visionary': KPT, note, unpub. MS. 1955.

122 Moscow Arts: KPT, 'Curtain Time in Moscow', *Harper's*, Mar. 1956.

122 'symbol of': KPT, *Observer*, 20 Nov. 1955.

122 'pizzicato of the Spirit': KPT, *Observer*, 4 Dec. 1955.

122 *Nekrassov*: KPT, *Observer*, 8 Jan. 1956.

122 Jean-Louis Barrault's: KPT, *Observer*, 15 Jan. 1956.

123 'art for our': Ibid., 22 Jan. 1956.

123 *The Threepenny Opera*: Ibid., 12 Feb. 1956.

123 'far from dragging': Robert Hewison, *In Anger* (London: Weidenfeld and Nicolson, 1981), p. 110.

123 as Brecht said: *Brecht on Theatre*, trans. John Willett (London: Methuen, 1964), p. 23.

123 'hoarse with rage': KPT, *Observer*, 1 Apr. 1956.

123 'drama of individual': Ibid.

123 *The Mulberry Bush*: Ibid., 2 Oct. 1955.

124 'It seems to me': Lindsay Anderson L to KPT, Apr. 1956.

124 *The Crucible*: KPT, *Observer*, 15 Apr. 1956.

124 'The Voice of': Ibid., 13 May 1956.

125 'exasperating': *Daily Sketch*, 9 May 1956.

125 'self-pitying': *Evening Standard*, 9 May 1956.

125 'ducked in a horse pond': *Evening News*, 9 May 1956.

125 'wearing his colours': John Russell Taylor, *Look Back in Anger Casebook* (London: Macmillan, 1968), p. 153.

125 'I am ashamed': John Osborne, *A Better Class Of Person* (New York: Dutton, 1981), p. 271.

125 lean and driven: KPT, 'Men of Anger', *Holiday*, Apr. 1958.

125 'the most hedging': John Osborne, Int. for '*Reputations*', BBC 2, 1982.

126 a new play: KPT, *Observer*, 27 May, 1956.

12. INVOLVED, COMMITTED, ENGAGED

127 'then a long': Elaine Dundy, '*Reputations*', BBC2, 1982.

127 [La Goulue]: dancer; painted by Toulouse-Lautrec.

128 'Dear Mrs T': KPT J, 30 Mar. 1973.

128 'What counts is': KPT, *Observer*, 24 June 1956.

128 no such thing: KPT, *Observer*, 1 July 1956.

128 'who cleared': KPT, 'The Demolition Expert', *Observer*, 22 July 1956.

128 'Come on, Jebby': Julian Jebb L to KPT, undated, 1980.

128 new records: *Desert Island Discs*, 1 Oct. 1956.

129 'slairtly': KPT L to Patrick Dixon, 12 Oct. 1955.

130 'the true function', Cyril Connolly, *The Unquiet Grave*, (London: Horizon, 1944), p. 1.

131 'pink child's face': KPT, 'An Inner View of Cyril Connolly', *Harper's Bazaar* (U.K.), Mar. 1954.

131 'Miss Gardner': KPT L to Connolly, 22 May, 1955.

131 'Did you read': KPT J. 5 Sept. 1971.

131 'So our playing': *Brecht on Theatre*, trans. John Willett (London: Methuen 1964), p. 283.

131 'There speaks': KPT, *Observer*, 2 Sept. 1956.

132 'the most drastic': KPT, *Observer*, 7 Oct. 1956.

132 'I know my dear': KPT, 'The Theatre Abroad: Germany', *The New Yorker*, 12 Sept. 1959.

132 *The Good Woman of Setzuan*: KPT, *Observer*, 4 Nov. 1956.

133 *The Life of Galileo*: Ibid., 20 Jan. 1957.

133 *A View from the Bridge*: Ibid., 14 Oct. 1956.

133 'stern, Ibsenite': KPT, 'Profile', *Observer*, 14 Oct. 1956.

133 ['Cause Without a Rebel']: Second *Encore* Symposium: 'Cause Without a Rebel', Royal Court, 18 Nov. 1956, Chairman: KPT; Panel: Benn W. Levy, Wolf Mankowitz, Arthur Miller, John Whitney, Colin Wilson.

133 [committed]: see Eric Bentley, *The Theatre of Commitment*, 1966 (New York: Atheneum, 1967).

134 *Sight and Sound* interviewed: 'Replies to a Questionnaire', *Sight and Sound*, Spring 1957; KPT: 'I am in fact committed to myself, which is much harder (and lonelier) than being committed to any creed.'

134 'Steel stood': KPT, *Observer*, 31 Mar. 1957.

134 *Fin de partie*: Ibid., 7 Apr. 1957.

135 'Slamm's Last': KPT, Ibid., 2 Nov. 1958.

135 'a grand purpose': Ibid., 14 July 1957.

135 *The Entertainer*: Ibid., 14 Apr. 1957.

135 *Long Day's*: Ibid., 26 May, 1957.

135 Titus Andronicus: Ibid., 7 July 1957.

135 'Apart from lending': David Astor L to KPT, 24 Aug. 1957.

135 'in spite of': KPT L to Astor, 28 Aug. 1957.

13. RAISED VOICES

139 pangs of guilt: KPT J., 30 July 1977.

140 perfect paragraphs: KPT J., 13 Feb. 1976.

140 article: KPT 'Tight Little Studio', *Harper's* (U.S.), Aug. 1955.

140 'to act as a pipeline': KPT L to Michael Balcon, undated, 1958.

140 'offers a crime': Charles Barr, *Ealing Studios*, (New York: Overlook Press, 1982) p. 178.

141 play competition: KPT, 'The Play Competition', *Observer*, 18 Aug. 1957.

141 cloakrooms: KPT, *Observer*, 19 Jan. 1958.

141 Littlewood's actors: KPT, *Observer*, 13 Oct. 1957.

141 He was photographed: *Encore*, Jan./Feb. 1958.

141 personal essay: KPT, *Declaration*, Edited by Tom Maschler (London: MacGibbon and Kee, 1957), pp. 109–29.

141 He wrote: Robert Knittel L to KPT, 29 Oct. 1957.

142 five thousand: John Minnion, Philip Bolsover, *The CND Story* (London: Allison and Busby, 1983).

142 'We shall go': KPT L to *Tribune*, 7 Mar. 1958.

142 *Uncle Vanya*: KPT, *Observer*, 18 May 1958, 25 May 1958.

143 [Stanislavsky]: Ken made a 90-minute programme for Associated Television on The Method, broadcast 20 June 1958.

143 'Ionesco: Man of': KPT, *Observer*, 22 June 1958.

143 The following week: Eugène Ionesco, 'The Playwright's Role', *Observer*, 29 June 1958.

143 Back came: KPT, *Observer*, 6 July 1958.

143 [human activity]: 'I am not advocating a revolution: merely a return to the ancient idea that drama concerns all of us, that it is an extension and an illumination of our own experiences, not something different and "artistic" and relaxingly apart.' KPT, The Artist, the Critic and the Teacher Forum, National Film Institute, 30 Mar. 1958.

144 Philip Toynbee: Philip Toynbee, 'An Attitude to Life', *Observer*, 6 July 1958.

144 George Devine: George Devine, *Observer*, 6 July 1958.

144 Orson Welles: Orson Welles, 'The Artist and the Critic', *Observer*, 13 July 1958.

144 Lindsay Anderson: Lindsay Anderson, *Observer*, 13 July 1958.

144 'courteous enemy': Eugène Ionesco, 'Notes and Counter-notes' (Calder, Winter 1959), p. 105.

144 'higher order': Eugène Ionesco, *Paris Review*, Fall 1984.

144 'Being as schizophrenic': Richard Roud, 'The Theatre on Trial', *Encounter*, June/July 1958.

144 *Rhinoceros*: KPT, *Observer*, 12 June 1960. [In his EB of 1 July 1960, Ken wrote: 'Ionesco: no room for doubt, as in Brecht who was torn between individualism and credos'.]

14. ROSE ABANDONED

145 'We despise': KPT, *He That Plays the King* p. 106.

146 'If she had': KPT, J., 20 Jan. 1976.

146 'old Gibbs has cooled': Alan Brien L to KPT 5 Mar. 1975.

147 'a small, round': KPT, 'The Time of My Life', *Punch*, 16 Apr. 1975.

147 publisher: Simon Michael Bessie L to KPT, 4 Feb. 1957.

147 'I longed to': Ibid.

148 'Jazz, beat, Mort Sahl': KPT EB, 2 Nov. 1958.

15. THE TOAST OF NEW YORK

149 'carnival of concrete': KPT, 'A Memoir of Manhattan', *Holiday*, Dec. 1960.

149 'They say': *Sunday Times*, 2 Nov. 1958.

149 'bright, blind': KPT, *Declaration* (London: MacGibbon and Kee, 1957), p. 127.

149 criticize his friend: KPT, *Observer*, 28 June 1959.

149 'I don't have': James Thurber L to KPT, 18 Dec. 1958.

149 'What I want': John Steinbeck L to KPT, 12 Dec. 1958.

150 *La Plume:* KPT, *The New Yorker*, 22 Nov. 1958.

150 *The Shadow:* Ibid., 6 Dec. 1958.

150 *Flower Drum:* Ibid., 13 Dec. 1958.

150 sober thoughts: Ibid., 20 Dec. 1958.

150 *Sweet Bird:* Ibid., 21 March 1959.

150 Elia Kazan: KPT, 'The Dilemma of the Theater', *Holiday*, Oct. 1959.

150 He explained: KPT L to David Astor, 25 Feb. 1959, 20 Mar. 1959.

150 William Shawn: KPT, *Punch*, 16 Apr. 1975.

151 'Write play': KPT EB, 26 Jan. 1959, 29 May 1959.

152 Mort Sahl: KPT, 'Broadway Babies', 27 Apr. 1958.

152 'Lean and pallid': KPT, *Observer*, 29 Apr. 1962.

152 Pope John: Lenny Bruce, *How to Talk Dirty and Influence People* (London: Granada, 1975), introduction.

152 Irwin Corey: KPT J, 18 Nov. 1973.

152 'Nothing that Peter': KPT J, 10 Nov. 1974.

153 'as acute as': KPT, Jules Feiffer, *Sick, Sick, Sick* (London: Collins, 1959), introduction.

153 'wider than any': KPT, *Village Voice*, 18 Nov. 1959.

153 'It was pre-radical': Jules Feiffer, TS, *Reputations*, BBC2, 1982.

154 'functionalism': KPT, 'Mañana or Tomorrow?' *Observer*, 8 Mar. 1959.

155 Elaine to write: Elaine Dundy, 'The Sound of Marriage', *Queen*, 13 Apr. 1960.

16. TRAVELLERS' TALES

156 'We should be': Ernest Hemingway L to KPT, 1 Mar. 1959.

156 Of Havana: KPT, 'A Visit to Havana', *Holiday*, Feb. 1960.

156 'In manner': Ibid.

157 Two days later: KPT, 'Papa and the Playwright', *Playboy*, May 1964.

159 The storytelling: George Plimpton, *Shadow Box* (New York: G. P. Putnam's Sons, 1977), pp. 142–7.

160 letter marked: Tennessee Williams L to KPT, 12 May 1959.

160 'distorted by': KPT, 'The Dilemma of the Theater', *Holiday*, Oct. 1959.

160 *A Raisin:* KPT, *The New Yorker*, 21 Mar. 1959.

161 'infant Dalai': Alistair Cook, *Manchester Guardian*, 9 Apr. 1959.

161 *Desert Incident:* KPT, *The New Yorker*, 4 Apr. 1959.

161 *Gypsy:* KPT, *The New Yorker*, 30 May 1959.

161 In May 1959: KPT L to William Shawn, 11 May 1959.

163 'versatility': KPT, *The New Yorker*, 12 Sept. 1959.

163 'green, water–girt beauty': Ibid.

163 'a bitter attempt': KPT, *Curtains*, (London: Longmans, Green, 1961), p. 458.

163 *The Theatre of Bertolt Brecht:* trans. John Willett, (London: Methuen, 1959).

163 *Brecht: A Choice of Evils:* (London: Eyre and Spottiswoode, 1959).

163 'one of the most': KPT, *The New Yorker*, 12 Sept. 1959.

163 'Now and then': Williams L to KPT, undated, 1959.

164 *The Long:* KPT, *The New Yorker*, 26 Sept. 1959.

164 *Roots:* KPT, *Observer*, 3 July 1960, 31 July 1960.

164 West End: KPT, *The New Yorker*, 26 Sept. 1959.

164 'Olivier's': KPT L to Shawn, 14 July 1959.

164 two toreros: Ibid., undated, 1959.

164 *mano-a-mano:* KPT, *Bull Fever* (New York: Atheneum, 1966), p. 158.

165 Hemingway apologized: KPT, 'Eclipse of the Fun', *Esquire*, May 1963.

166 'inability': KPT EB, 8 Nov. 1959, 29 Sept. 1959.

17. BACK TO BROADWAY

168 San Francisco: KPT, 'San Francisco: The Rebels', *Holiday*, Apr. 1960.

168 'direct elliptical': KPT EB, 20 Sept. 1957.

168 'more precise': KPT, 'Bearding the Beats', *Observer*, 1 Nov. 1959.

169 'What a city!': KPT L to William Shawn, 30 Aug. 1959.

169 *The Sound of Music:* KPT, *The New Yorker*, 28 Nov. 1959.

169 *Fiorello:* Ibid., 5 Dec. 1959.

169 *A Loss of Roses:* Ibid., 12 Dec. 1959.

169 *Act One:* 'Miles and Miles and Miles of Hart', 28 Nov. 1959.

170 'the most memorable': KPT, *Observer*, 17 Jan. 1960.

170 he wrote to: KPT L to Shawn, undated, 1959.

171 documentary: *We Dissent*, ATV, 27 Jan. 1960.

171 'discredit American': KPT FBI file, 28 Aug. 1959.

171 'appropriate congressional': Ibid., 30 Aug. 1959.

171 told his subcommittee: Congressional Record, 5 May 1960.

172 'My first response': KPT, 'Command Performance', *Harper's*, Oct. 1960.

172 J. G. Sourwine: Frank J. Donner, *The Age of Surveillance* (New York: Knopf, 1980), pp. 408–409.

172 'How did it': Congressional Record, 5 May 1960.

173 'I respectfully suggest': KPT, *Harper's*, Oct. 1960.

173 'If I say that': KPT J, 20 Apr. 1971.

173 wrote to say: Edmund Wilson L to KPT, 21 May, 1960.

173 'intricate, stunningly': KPT, *Observer*, 26 Mar. 1961.

18. THEATRICAL BATTLES AND POLITICAL STAGES

175 [Tom Stoppard]: Stoppard said, 'He made it worthwhile trying to be good', *Reputations*, BBC2, 1982.

176 Magda: Hermann Sudermann, *Die Hermat*, 1893.

176 [cross-fertilizing]: 'Indicative of a generation without strong roots, socially and intellectually mobile, striving to create a unity of the disparate parts of its inheritance.' Clive Baker L to KHT, 24 Jan. 1985.

176 Robert Bolt: KPT, *Observer*, 10 July 1960.

176 Sartre's *Altona:* Ibid., 23 Apr. 1961.

176 Mother Courage: Ibid., 29 Jan, 1961.

176 Stockholm: Ibid., 8 Jan. 1961.

176 Warsaw: Ibid., 15 Jan. 1961.

177 'What I look for': Ibid., 1 Oct. 1961.

177 Zeffirelli: Ibid., 9 Oct. 1960.

177 *The Caretaker:* Ibid., 5 June 1960.

177 *The Birthday Party:* Ibid.

177 *A Night Out:* Ibid., 8 Oct. 1961.

177 'a whole School': KPT, *Tynan Right and Left*, (London: Longmans, Green, 1967), p. 75.

178 [Obscene Publications Act]: Robert Hewison, *In Anger* (London: Weidenfeld and Nicolson), p. 194.

178 'that rock among': KPT *Observer*, 6 Nov. 1960.

178 recent article: Lord Altrincham, 'Lady Chatterley's Trial', the *Guardian*, 22 June 1961.

178 'The Hero': KPT 'The Plainest of Dames', *Observer*, 25 June 1961.

178 Altrincham wrote to: Lord Altrincham L to *Observer*, 2 July 1961.

178 'Lord Altrincham': KPT L to *Observer*, 2 July 1961.

178 'better red': KPT, 'The Price of Berlin', *Time and Tide*, 3 Aug. 1961. ['He would rather live on his knees than die on his feet': Ronald Reagan angrily referring to 'The English commentator Tynan' in a TV speech on behalf of Barry Goldwater's bid for the presidency, 27 Oct. 1964.]

179 'alarm': KPT, note in back of EB 1961.

179 'gibberingly': Noël Coward, *Diaries* (New York: Little, Brown, 1982), 12 Jan. 1963.

179 time to protest: KPT L to *New Statesman*, 4 Apr. 1961.

179 Bay of Pigs: KPT L to *The Times*, 19 Apr. 1961.

179 political cabaret: KPT, *Observer*, 23 Oct. 1960.

179 *Beyond the Fringe*: Ibid., 14 May 1961.

179 'But immeasurably further': KPT, 'Quartet with a Touch of Brass', *Holiday*, Nov. 1962.

180 'Kenneth Tynan': Roger Wilmut, *From Fringe to Flying Circus* (London: Methuen, 1982), p. 17.

180 'engaged more': KPT, *Observer*, 2 Sept. 1962.

180 'Mr Bruce drawls': Ibid., 29 Apr. 1962.

180 'Satire is protest': Ibid.

180 *The Death of Tragedy*: Ibid., 22 Oct. 1961.

180 *Heartbreak House*: Ibid., 5 Nov. 1961.

181 *The Theatre of the Absurd*: Ibid., 3 June 1962.

181 'Nature has chastised': Ibid., 26 Aug. 1962.

182 'One effect': KPT J, 9 July 1961.

183 [father died]: 12 June 1963.

183 'the courteous': KPT J, 13 Aug. 1961.

184 facile parodist: Mary McCarthy, *Observer*, 22 Oct. 1961.

184 *Sights and Spectacles*: KPT, *Observer*, 10 May 1959.

184 further attack: A. Alvarez, *Beyond All This Fiddle* (London: Allen Lane 1968), p. 243.

184 'God knows': *John Whiting on Theatre* (London Magazine editions 1966), p. 49.

184 'Distinguish erotic art': KPT EB, Summer 1961.

184 Of the fifteen editions: KPT, 'Tempo Fugit', *Encounter*, June 1962.

185 Court of Protection: KPT L to Dr. Tibbetts, 18 Sept. 1958.

185 [hospital noted]: Records, St. Andrew's Hospital, Northampton.

185 'I am sending': KPT L to Dr. T. G. Tennent, 13 Feb. 1961.

185 number of visits: KPT L to St. Andrew's, 26 June 1961.

185 'appallingly': KPT J, 20 Jan. 1976.

186 [Mind blitz]: No doubt exacerbated by amphetamines, 'emblem of the insecure', as Ken described them 'and saviour of the shaken.'

186 'With Elaine': KPT notes on scraps of paper and theatre programmes, 1962.

187 'Mind your eyes': KPT EB, 26 July 1958, 1 Sept. 1958.

188 'A neurosis': KPT J, 9 July 1961.

188 '[It's] about the tensions': Francis Wyndham, *Queen*, 17 Jan. 1962.

190 'What happens when': Elaine Dundy, *The Dud Avocado* (London: Pan Books 1984), p. 213.

190 *Happy Days*: KPT, *Observer*, 4 Nov. 1962.

190 'prophet who': Ibid.

190 *King Lear*: Ibid., 16 Dec. 1962.

190 'Instead of assuming': Ibid.

190 *The Wars of the Roses*: Ibid., 21 July 1963.

190 *Comedy of Errors*: Ibid., 16 Sept. 1962.

191 *The Physicists*: Ibid., 13 Jan. 1963.

191 *Afore Night Come*: Ibid., 10 June 1962.

191 *Oh What a Lovely War*: Ibid., 24 Mar. 1963.

191 *Who's Afraid*: Ibid., 31 Mar. 1963.

191 *Mother Courage*: Ibid., 21 Apr. 1963.

INTERLUDE

192 'Work of seeing': Rilke, "*Wendung*" (Turning Point, 1914), *An Unofficial Rilke* (London: Anvil Press Poetry, 1981).

193 postwar Spanish plot: KPT 'The Other Face of Spain', *Jerusalem Post* 18 Apr. 1958.

193 'Bullfighting': KPT, 'Beatle in the Bullring', *Playboy*, Jan. 1965.

193 *garbo*: KPT, *Bull Fever* (New York: Atheneum, 1966), p. 47.

193 'as though': Ernest Hemingway, *The Dangerous Summer* (New York: Charles Scribner's Sons, 1985), p. 192.

194 'Gertrude Stein': *Letters of F. Scott Fitzgerald* (London: Bodley Head, 1963), p. 592.

195 [Patricia Harewood]: Patricia Tuckwell, not yet married to the Earl of Harewood.

195 'My ultimate': KPT L to Jocelyn Baines, 29 Nov. 1954.

195 'the wart': KPT, 'The Judicious Observer will Be Disgusted', *The New Yorker*, 25 July 1970.

196 'prolonged spasms': Ibid.

20. THE NEW GIRL

198 *Make voyages!* from *Four Plays* by Tennessee Williams (London: Secker and Warburg, 1957), p. 279.

200 'coarse-grained': KPT, *He That Plays the King* (London: Longmans, Green, 1950) p. 41.

200 'probably establish': KPT, 'Tragedy, Masque and Myth' *Lilliput*, Aug./Sept. 1951.

202 [*Epitaph for George Dillon*]: Commercial Road Hall, Oxford, 26 Feb. 1957.

202 'Who would have': Marion Shapiro L to KHT, 25 Feb. 1957.

202 Too much use: Felix Frankfurter L to KHT, 21 May 1961.

203 'drive toward': Ibid., 10 Mar. 1962.

21. WOOING

204 'At the last': KPT, 9 May 1977.

204 'Say we've': KPT EB, 11 Aug. 1963.

204 'to fill in': John Calder, programme note, The Purpose of the Drama Conference, McEwan Hall, 27 Sept. 1963.

205 [my editor]: Mark Boxer, *Sunday Times Magazine*.

206 2000 strong: Jack Gelber, 'Edinburgh Happening', *Evergreen Review Reader*, 1964, p. 593.

206 He picked up: KPT, Dramatists in Perspective, *Observer*, 15 Sept. 1963.

206 future of the theatre: Ibid.

206 Happening: Charles Marowitz, 'Happenings at Edinburgh', *Encore*, Nov. 1963.

206 Kenneth Dewey: Magnus Magnusson, *The Scotsman*, 9 Sept. 1963.

206 'to discuss experimental': KPT, 'Dramatists in Perspective', *Observer*, 15 Sept. 1963.

206 pile of tyres: Jan Kott 'Happenings in Edinburgh', *Theatre Notebook 1947–1967* (London: Methuen, 1968) p. 215.

206 Lady Chatterley: Bernard Levin, *New Statesman*, 20 Dec. 1963.

207 'Big chin': KPT J, 9 May 1977.

208 'This is after': KPT L to KHT, undated, Sept. 1963.

208 'It's midnight of': Ibid., 4 Oct. 1963.

209 'Today *Private Eye*': KPT L to Elaine Dundy, 18 Oct. 1963.

210 'DARLING WHAT': KPT Telegram, 9 Dec. 1963.

210 Elaine replied: Dundy L to KPT, 12 Jan. 1964.

210 'in the very': KPT, *Observer*, 31 May 1964.

210 Erwin Piscator: KPT, 'The Antic Acts', *Holiday*, Oct. 1964.

211 'He showed me': Pauline Whittle L to KHT, 2 Aug. 1980.

211 'I'm thirty-six': Ibid., 16 Mar. 1982.

211 She wrote: Dundy L to KPT, 22 Mar. 1964.

211 Ken telephoned: Whittle L to KHT,

27 May 1983.

212 'Tax their brains': KPT J, 15 Nov. 1978.

213 'two generations': Orson Welles L to KPT, 15 May 1964.

22. THE PARTNERSHIP WITH OLIVIER

215 'what other': KPT, *Daily Sketch*, 1 Jan. 1954.

215 [campaign]: Main texts: KPT: *Observer*, 1 Jan. 1956, 30 Sept. 1956, 22 Dec. 1957; 'Replies to a Questionnaire', *Sight and Sound*, Spring 1957; *Encore* Jan./Feb. 1958; *Observer*, 27 July 1958, 11 Mar. 1962, 8 July 1962, 22 July 1962; 'To Divorce Art from Money-making', *New York Times*, 1 Dec. 1963; 'On the National Theatre', lecture, Royal Society of Arts, 18 Mar. 1964.

215 proposed in 1848: John Elsom and Nicholas Tomalin, *The History of the National Theatre* (London: Jonathan Cape, 1978), pp. 6–52.

215 'had forgotten': KPT, *Observer*, 1 Jan. 1956.

215 'not for the theatre': Sir Anthony Quayle L to KPT 6 Feb. 1956.

215 Artistic Director: Laurence Olivier, *Confessions of an Actor* (London: Weidenfeld and Nicolson, 1982), p. 179.

215 best man: Elsom and Tomalin, *History of the National Theatre*, (London: Cape, 1978), pp. 113–114.

216 'nothing is more likely': KPT, *Observer*, 8 July 1962.

216 endorsed the idea: KPT, *Observer*, 11 Mar. 1962.

216 'If Laurence Olivier': KPT, *Observer*, 8 July 1962.

216 *The Broken Heart*: KPT, *Observer*, 15 July 1962.

216 'Undaunted he bowed': Virginia Fairweather, *Cry God for Larry* (London: Calder and Boyars, 1969), p. 70.

217 'It will probably': Olivier L to KPT, 21 Aug. 1962.

217 'Anti-Fuddy-Duddy': Elsom and Tomalin, *History of the National Theatre*, p. 151.

217 '*Everything* imaginably': Olivier L to KPT, 31 Jan. 1963.

217 press conference: 6 Aug. 1963.

217 'spectrum': KPT, 'The Dilemma of the Theatre', *Holiday*, Oct. 1959.

218 [opened its doors]: Peter Hall, then running the Royal Shakespeare Company, wrote to Ken to say that his good wishes were genuine and full of self interest: 'I believe that if you thrive, we all have a chance of thriving.' (1 Sept. 1963.)

218 established itself: KPT, 'Making of the National Theatre', *Playbill*, Apr. 1965.

218 Jan Kott's idea: Jan Kott, 'Shakespeare's Bitter Arcadia', *Shakespeare Our Contemporary* (New York: Anchor, 1966), p. 287.

219 'Good repertory': KPT, 'The National Theatre' *Royal Society of Arts Journal*, Aug. 1964.

219 'was partly tailored': KPT J, 5 July 1972.

219 blueprint: *Charles Marowitz*, 'Talk With Tynan', *Encore*, July 1963; Paul Neuberg, int. of KPT 'Behind the Scenes', *Transatlantic Review* 1965 (London: Putnam, 1971), p. 155.; Ralph Allison, int. of KPT, *England's National Theatre*, 1970.

219 [forty plays]: KPT: 'I don't think it's possible to get more than, say, twenty plays into orbit at the same time.' *The Role of National Theatre*, BBC Radio 3, 11 Dec. 1963.

220 subsidy offered: KPT, *Tynan Right and Left* (London: Longmans, Green, 1967), p. 165. Original text: 'The National Theatre', *RSA Journal*, Aug. 1964.

220 'the hot breath of unity': KPT, int.

of Laurence Olivier, *Great Acting*, BBC, 26 Feb. 1966.

220 not impose a veto: Donald Carroll, *Interviews* (London: Talmy Franklin, 1972), p. 3.

221 'in a breakneck': KPT L to George Devine, 31 Mar. 1964.

221 angry response: Devine L to KPT, 9 Apr. 1964.

221 'a theatre of': KPT L to Devine, 10 Apr. 1964.

221 'It is obvious': Olivier L to KPT, 12 Apr. 1964.

221 'Sir Laurence's': William Foster, 'Critic in the Crow's Nest', *The Scotsman*, 11 Nov. 1967.

221 'backseat driver': Mike Bygrave int. of KPT, *Men Only*, 1973.

221 unpredictable: Carroll, *Interviews*, (London: Talmy Franklin, 1972), p. 17.

222 'passive feminine': KPT J, 13 Apr. 1972.

222 'Technical things': KPT, note at back of EB, 1964.

223 '[He is a] man': KPT, note on a book,

224 'It is agreed': KPT, programme note, *Black Comedy*, 27 July 1965.

224 If John Dexter: KPT memo to artistic directorate, 26 Aug. 1964.

225 He pointed out: Ibid., 'Reflections on Year One', 1964.

225 Olivier and Dexter: Ibid., 20 Oct. 1965.

225 Bob Dylan: Ibid., undated, Sept. 1965.

225 Tyrone Guthrie: Ibid., 10 June 1966.

225 Roger Planchon: Ibid., 6 Oct. 1966.

225 Seneca *Oedipus*: Ibid., 10 Mar. 1967.

225 *The Bacchae*: Ibid., 13 July 1967.

226 'He was so much': Jonathan Miller, *Reputations*, BBC 2, 1982.

226 inhuman capacity: Tom Stoppard, *Reputations*, BBC 2, 1982.

227 'Olivier's conception': KPT, *The Recruiting Officer – the National Theatre Production*, (London: Rupert Hart-Davis, 1965), p. 14.

227 *Othello*: KPT, *Othello – the National Theatre Production* (London: Rupert Hart-Davis, 1966).

227 'dead similes': KPT L to Robert Graves, 25 Aug. 1964.

227 [elegant programmes]: The design modeled on the Berliner Ensemble programmes.

227 'a perfectly designed': National Theatre Building Committee minutes, 7 Oct. 1964.

228 'the L. C. doesn't': KPT, memo to artistic directorate, 11 Feb. 1965.

228 Ken immediately cabled: KPT cable to John Dexter, undated, 1964.

228 Dexter cabled: Dexter cable to KPT, 12 Nov. 1964.

228 A drama committee: Yolande Bird (Asst. Sec. to the Board), L to KHT, 18 Aug. 1983.

228 differences of opinion: Sir Kenneth Clark L to Olivier, 16 June 1966.

229 [Board Chairman]: Lord Rayne L to KHT, 21 Sept. 1982. 'Since I became chairman ... the policy has been to leave artistic decisions to the Director, on the understanding that the Board is consulted by him if and when issues of obscenity, blasphemy, lèse majesté and suchlike might arise in relation to any individual production.'

229 'to become': Paul Neuberg, *Transatlantic Review*, Autumn 1965.

23. LIVING WITH KEN

234 Humes began: KPT J, 30 Jan. 1977.

24. A FOUR-LETTER WORD

236 [first time]: The journalist Peregrine Worsthorne claims to be the second man to have used the word on television (outside TV drama).

236 'McCarthy could visualize': Ned

Sherrin, *A Small Thing Like an Earthquake: Memoirs* (London: Weidenfeld and Nicolson, 1983), p. 206.

236 'Oh I think so': KPT, BBC Radio 3, 13 Nov. 1965.

237 In subsequent years: KPT, unpub. *Playboy* int., 1970; KPT, *The Sound of Two Hands Clapping* (London: Jonathan Cape, 1975), pp. 144–145.

237 'I used an': KPT, *Daily Sketch*, 16 Nov. 1965.

237 'bloodiest outrage': William Barkley, *Daily Express*, 16 Nov. 1965.

237 'that one simple': Stanley Reynolds, *Guardian*, 17 Nov. 1965.

238 Wedgwood Benn: Hansard, 8 Dec. 1965, col. 422.

238 'The only generalization': Int. of KPT Humanist Society, London University, 1966.

239 [Jim]: James West, Mary McCarthy's husband.

239 'limit and decorum': *The Times*, 15 Nov. 1965.

239 impassioned plea: Laurence Olivier L to *Observer*, 21 Nov. 1965.

239 'What the image': KPT L to *New Statesman*, 24 Dec. 1965.

239 'rational cohesive': Lindsay Anderson L to KPT, 11 Apr. 1966.

240 'with the sort': John Mortimer, *Clinging to the Wreckage* (London: Weidenfeld and Nicolson, 1982), p. 173.

240 'When it actually': KPT J, 21 Apr. 1972.

240 'creates order': Johan Huizinga, *Homo Ludens* (Boston: Beacon Press, 1955), p. 10.

241 'no one speaks': KPT, *Observer*, 8 Nov. 1964.

241 'Wilful, aimless': Ibid., 5 Sept. 1965.

241 *Masculin-Féminin*: Ibid., 15 May 1966.

242 'more serious criticism': KPT,

Observer, 7 Mar. 1965.

242 *Courage for Everyday:* Ibid.

242 *The Return of the Prodigal:* KPT, *The New Yorker*, 1 Apr. 1967.

242 *A Blonde in Love:* KPT, *Observer*, 29 Aug. 1965.

242 *Repulsion:* Ibid., 13 June 1965.

242 *Help!:* KPT, Ibid., 1 Aug. 1965.

242 *The War Game:* Ibid., 13 Feb. 1966.

242 director cult: Ibid., 22 Nov. 1964.

242 boring film: KPT, *Observer*, 23 Jan. 1966.

242 'consensus without': KPT EB, 12 Nov. 1964.

242 female critics: KPT, *Observer*, 29 Nov. 1964.

25. IT WAS ALWAYS SPRING

244 'looking grave': KPT J, 2 July 1975.

244 'I write to become': KPT EB, 7 Jan. 1966.

244 'It seems to us': A. C. Spectorsky L to Emilie Jacobson, 23 Nov. 1965.

244 'a fairly light-hearted': KPT L to Jacobson, 22 Dec. 1967.

244 'We hoped that': *Playboy* L to Jacobson, 21 Oct. 1968.

245 'scared stiff': KPT L to Jacobson, 22 Nov. 1965.

245 long review: KPT, *Observer*, 13 Mar. 1966.

245 'Something to scent': Truman Capote L to KPT, undated, 1965.

245 'We are talking': KPT, *Observer*, 13 Mar. 1966.

245 'the morals': Capote L to *Observer*, 27 Mar. 1966.

246 party piece: George Plimpton, *Shadow Box* (New York: G. P. Putnam's Sons, 1977), pp. 148–9.

246 'a strong claim': KPT, 'The Theater Abroad: Prague', *The New Yorker*, 1 Apr. 1967.

26. SOLDIERS

249 'More sustained': KPT note,

undated 1968.

249 *Shadow of Heroes*: KPT, *Observer*, 12 Oct. 1958.

250 'like Victorian': KPT L to Laurence Olivier, 23 Aug. 1966.

250 'might endanger': Sally Beauman, *The Royal Shakespeare Company* (Oxford: Oxford University Press, 1982), p. 284.

250 'Are we keeping': KPT 'The Theater Abroad: London', *The New Yorker*, 9 Nov. 1968.

250 'Our own deaths': Rolf Hochhuth *Soldiers*, souvenir programme note, 1969.

250 'Once it had been demonstrated': *Die Zeit*, 7 Oct. 1967.

251 [circumstantial evidence]: David Irving, *Accident* (London: William Kimber, 1967).

251 Ken wrote: KPT memo to Olivier, 23 Dec. 1966.

251 'Subsidy gives us': Ibid., 3 Jan. 1967.

251 'The same decisions': John Dexter L to KPT, 3 Jan. 1967.

251 expressed the view: Lord Goodman L to KPT, 9 Jan. 1967.

252 to make a serious: Lovell, White and King legal report, 5 Jan. 1967.

252 smear on Churchill: Sir Arthur Harris L to Lord Chandos, 24 Apr. 1967, Chandos papers, Churchill College.

252 quizzed Hochhuth: KPT L to Hochhuth, 16 Dec. 1966.

252 how much or: Hochhuth L to KPT, undated, 1966.

252 [Historians and military advisers]: Among those consulted: Sir Isaiah Berlin, A. J. P. Taylor, Alan Bullock, John Ehrman, Hugh Trevor-Roper, Kingsley Martin, Hugh Thomas, Michael Howard, David Irving, General Sir Colin Gubbins, M. R. D. Foot.

252 'in the bad sense': Ken added: 'A theatre can survive without a first-rate chairman; but it cannot survive without playwrights.' Lord Chandos underlined this section of his copy of the memo and wrote 'Impudent!' in the margin. (KPT, memo to the Board, 7 Jan. 1967.)

153 'Crew-cut and jackbooted': KPT, *The New Yorker*, 9 Nov. 1968.

254 'the doctrine' KPT, memo to the Board, 'Three Aspects of the Hochhuth Situation', Mar. 1967.

254 'Nothing would induce *me*': Chandos L to Robert Blake, 3 Feb. 1967, Chandos papers, Churchill College.

254 'private and informal': Lord Cobbold L to Chandos, 12 Jan. 1967, Chandos papers, Churchill College.

254 Lord Chamberlain's: Assistant Comptroller L to KPT, 19 Jan. 1967.

254 [final script]: 'I think the thing will be turned down unanimously.' Chandos L to Cobbold, 5 Apr. 1967, Chandos papers, Churchill College.

254 foundation grants: KPT L to Emilie Jacobson, 29 March 1967, 10 Apr. 1967.

255 retaining his salary: *Sunday Times*, 30 Apr. 1967.

255 'It would indeed': KPT L to *Sunday Times*, 7 May 1967.

27. SEX AND POLITICS

256 24 January: Joint Committee on Censorship of the Theatre Report, 19 June 1967, pp. 79–87.

256 signed an advertisement: *The Times*, 24 July 1967.

256 turned him down: Paul McCartney L to KPT, undated, 1966.

257 wrote about her: KPT, 'One or Two Things I Know About ...', *Playbill*, Oct. 1967.

257 'did *not* know': Marlene Dietrich L to KPT, undated, 1967.

258 Inscrutable black servants: Mike Bygrave, int. of KPT, *Men Only*, 1973.

258 discovered Chicago: KPT, 'Shouts and Murmurs', *Observer*, 11 Feb. 1968.

258 New York was fetid: KPT L to A.C. Spectorsky, 27 June 1967.

258 In Englewood: KPT J, 9 Apr. 1973.

259 'He's an Englishman': John P. Marquand, Jr., L to KHT, 25 Aug. 1980.

260 Café Cino: KPT, EJ 1967.

260 'a Catholic spy': Ibid.

261 'The size and quality': John Raymond, *Sunday Times*, 5 Nov. 1969.

261 'Like George Orwell': Richard Boston, *New York Times*, 10 Dec. 1967.

262 'It would be': John Mortimer, *Observer*, 22 Oct. 1967.

262 'Tynan's Doppelgänger': unpub. MS Harold Clurman, 15 Oct. 1967.

262 'championed': Olivier L to William Gaskill, 25 Sept. 1967.

262 implored Chandos: Olivier, *Confessions of an Actor* (London: Weidenfeld and Nicolson, 1982), Appendix A, pp. 262–83.

262 'You should, however': Lord Chandos L to Olivier, 10 May 1967.

263 Lord Chamberlain: Assistant Comptroller L to KPT, 14 Aug. 1967.

263 'makes Churchill guilty': Herbert Whittaker, 'Hochhuth Soldiers, restores stage to greatness', *Globe and Mail*, 1 Mar. 1968.

28. END OF THE DECADE

265 'high definition performance': KPT, 'Shouts and Murmurs', *Observer*, 7 Apr. 1968.

265 'an extension and an illumination': KPT, 'Making Connections', *Theatre World*, 30 Mar. 1958.

266 'ramshackle': KPT, 'Shouts and Murmurs', *Observer*, 28 Apr. 1968.

266 *The Labyrinth*: KPT, *Theatre Quarterly*, Apr./June 1971.

266 'I believe in art': KPT, 'Shouts and Murmurs', *Observer*, 30 Mar. 1969

266 defence of hardcore: KPT, 'Dirty Books Can Stay', *Esquire*, Oct. 1968.

267 A truncated version: KPT, 'Shouts and Murmurs', *Observer*, 28 June 1968.

267 'Mr Kenneth Onan's': John Wells, *Spectator*, 2 Feb. 1968.

267 cartoon: Gerald Scarfe, *Private Eye*, 15 Mar. 1968.

267 'I somehow become': KPT L to Emilie Jacobson, 28 June 1966.

268 'But opting out': KPT, 'Open Letter to an American Liberal', *Playboy*, Mar. 1968.

268 not the Mrs. Tynan: KPT FBI file, 10 Sept. 1968.

269 On another occasion: Christopher Logue L to KHT, 15 July 1982.

269 'His affection': Jonathan Miller, *Reputations*, BBC 2 1982.

270 'Genet's film': KPT J, 17 Dec. 1971.

271 'lung fields': Dr. John Henderson L to KPT, 13 Dec. 1965.

271 'one of these': Henderson L to Edward Bolton, 26 July 1967.

271 'I feel terrible': KPT L to A.C. Spectorsky, 4 Apr. 1968.

271 'It seems that': Ibid., 20 May 1968.

272 'implacably amiable': KPT, int. of Alan Beesley, 'One Pair of Eyes', BBC 2, 1968.

273 He buys drinks: KPT, 'The Judicious Observer Will Be Disgusted', *The New Yorker*, 25 July 1970.

274 *King Lear*: KPT memo to Laurence Olivier, 31 Mar. 1969.

275 'It did not seem to me': Olivier L to Lord Chandos, 24 Oct. 1968.

276 'Since my work': KPT L to Chandos, 28 May 1969.

276 Chandos wrote: Chandos L to KPT, 10 June 1969.

276 Ken replied: KPT L to Chandos, 18 June 1969.

276 'In making Tynan': *Daily Telegraph*,

3 Nov. 1969.
276 'I BEG YOU': Olivier cable to KPT,
5 Nov. 1969.

29. OH! CALCUTTA!

277 Evening of Erotica: William
Donaldson L to KPT, 13 June
1966.
277 'The idea is': KPT L to Donaldson,
28 June 1966.
278 'cool, witty': Peter Brook L to KPT,
25 Aug. 1966.
279 The décor, Ken suggested: KPT
notes for show, autumn 1966.
279 Pinter in turn demonstrated: Alan
Coren, unpub. *Playboy* int. of KPT,
1970; KPT, *The Sound of Two Hands
Clapping* (London: Jonathan Cape,
1975), p. 146.
279 'no crap': KPT, sample letter to
contributors, 12 Dec. 1966.
279 Pinter had had second: Harold
Pinter L to KPT, 23 Jan. 1967.
279 non-orgiastic style: KPT EB, 2 Aug.
1967.
280 'I suppose there': Tennessee
Williams L to KPT, undated, 1968.
283 'joyous, healthy': Jerome Robbins L
to KPT, 19 June 1969.
283 'Kathleen and I': KPT L to Hillard
Elkins, undated, 1969.
284 'intelligent puritan': KPT,
'Pornography? And Is That Bad?',
New York Times, 5 June 1969.
284 sexual preferences: KPT,
Mademoiselle, July 1969.
284 Barnes notice came in: Clive
Barnes, *New York Times*, 18 June
1969.
284 'the most pornographic': Emily
Genauer, *New York Post*, 2 June
1969.
285 Not only revolutionary: Jack Knoll,
Newsweek, 30 June 1969.
285 [first in London]: Ken asked Jacques
Levy to direct the London version.
When Levy would not, Clifford
Williams stepped in.

30. TREADING WATER

286 'brooding and blissful': Walt
Whitman, Halcyon Days', *Complete
Poetry*, (London: The Nonesuch
Press, 1938), p. 458.
287 happening in the arts: KPT L to
Emilie Jacobson, 6 Sept. 1969.
287 'cooking up pieces': Ibid., 14 Oct.
1969.
287 'we actually': KHT L to Jean Halton,
31 Aug. 1969.
287 *An Unfinished Woman*: KPT,
Observer, 19 Oct. 1969.
287 'A small cloud': KPT L to Terence
Kilmartin, 28 Sept. 1969.
288 A Word a Day: KPT truncated
version of words by Johnny Mercer
© 1951.
288 'People who can share': KPT, misc.
note 1969.

31. THIRD ACT: CURTAIN UP

290 'Rehearse xmas': KPT EB, 9 Dec.
1969.
290 'something of a': KPT L to Emilie
Jacobson, 26 Jan. 1970.
290 In February 1970: KPT, 'Are You
the Entertainment?', *The New
Yorker*, 15 Jan. 1972.
291 'Put on my best': KPT L to Julian
Holland, 1 Apr. 1944.
291 'to dictate the': KPT, 'The Polish
Imposition', *Esquire*, Sept. 1971.
292 'is one about whom': Ibid.
292 'The point about the Macbeths':
KPT, notes for production of
Macbeth, 1970.
292 'So much has': Roger Greenspan,
New York Times, 21 Dec. 1971.
293 John Mortimer: Michael White,
Empty Seats (London: Hamish
Hamilton, 1984) p. 128.
293 'sort of exhibition': Ronald Butt, *The
Times*, 23 July 1970.
294 'After Italy': KHT L to Hillard Elkins,
10 Mar. 1970.
294 'the nudest': *News of the World*, 23

Aug. 1970.

294 'Our attitude': Quentin Crewe, int. of KPT, *Sunday Mirror*, 26 July 1970.

294 'a show of our': Herbert Kretzmer, *Daily Express*, 28 July 1970.

294 'I have seen': Irving Wardle, *The Times*, 28 July 1970.

295 'The point of': KPT memo to Michael White and Clifford Williams, 21 Sept. 1970.

295 'I have no interest': Vladimir Nabokov L to KPT, 12 July 1969.

295 'I'm afraid': Graham Greene L to KPT, 30 June 1969.

295 'there are a': W. H. Auden L to KPT, 30 June 1969.

295 'I'd never write': Norman Mailer L to KPT, 8 July 1969.

295 'to whom you are': Dominique Aury L to KPT, 15 Mar. 1970.

295 'few contributions': KPT L to Elkins, 30 July 1971.

296 'battle has been joined': Int of KPT, *Daily Mail*, 6 Aug. 1971.

296 'no sex without': KPT L to *Sunday Times*, 9 May 1971.

296 He told *Playboy:* Alan Coren unpub. *Playboy* int. of KPT, 1970; KPT, *The Sound of Two Hands Clapping* (London: Jonathan Cape, 1975), p. 150.

296 'greatest historical': KPT J, 13 May 1971.

296 'When everyone talks': KPT, 'Afterword', *Ink*, 1 Sept 1971.

296 'Harold Pinter': KPT J, Aug. 1971, 3 Aug. 1971, 6 July 1971, 1 Oct, 1971.

296 'Disturbed by': Ibid., 6 July 1971.

297 'I used to take': Ibid., undated, June 1971.

297 'I disbelieve in': Ibid., 21 Oct. 1971.

297 growing feeling for privacy: Ibid., 11 Jan. 1971.

297 'The decision to do': Ibid., 20 Sept. 1971.

32 · CHANGE

299 'After all,': KPT EB, 24 June 1970.

299 'On return from': Ibid., 5 Sept. 1970.

299 'K says': Ibid., 27 Sept. 1970.

300 'How could you': KPT L to KHT, undated, 1970.

300 'A brigand': KPT J, 24 Jan. 1971.

300 'I believe': KHT L to KPT, undated, 1970.

300 'vain, demanding': Germaine Greer, *The Female Eunuch.* (London: Grafton, 1971), p. 95.

301 'treadmill': Ibid., p. 97.

301 'After three hours': KPT J, 26 Mar. 1973.

302 'we are getting': KPT memo to Laurence Olivier, 23 Apr. 1970.

302 'by far the best': KPT L to Olivier, 28 April 1970.

302 'one of a dozen': KPT J, 11 Dec. 1970.

302 *Mrs. Warren's Profession:* Ibid., 9 Dec. 1970.

302 Ken complained: KPT memo to Olivier, 4 Dec. 1970.

302 Olivier had gone: KPT J, 20 Jan. 1971.

303 Blake spoke to: Adrian Mitchell synopsis for his play *Tyger, The Times,* 21 July 1971.

303 'Nor will I let': KPT J, 3 May 1971.

303 'Four flops in a row': KPT J, 3 Aug. 1971.

304 result of Olivier's: Olivier, *Confessions of an Actor,* (London: Weidenfeld and Nicolson, 1982), p. 240.

304 Rayne replied: Lord Rayne L to *Sunday Telegraph,* 3 Oct. 1982.

304 'nothing wrong': Int. of KPT, *Sunday Times,* 11 Dec. 1971.

304 Behind the scenes: KPT L to Olivier, 9 Dec. 1971.

304 *Long Day's Journey:* KPT L to Olivier, 14 Dec. 1971.

304 Olivier wrote: Olivier L to KPT, 16 Feb. 1972.

304 'At present I': KPT L to Olivier, 9 Mar. 1972.

305 'No, I am sorry': Olivier L to KPT, 10 Mar. 1972.

305 previous season: John Elsom and Nicholas Tomalin, *The History of the National Theatre* (London: Jonathan Cape, 1978), p. 229.

305 'It comes with': Tom Stoppard L to KPT, 20 Feb. 1972.

305 'following my earlier': KPT J, 8 July 1972.

33. AN EROTIC SCENARIO

306 'The main point': KPT, 'story idea A', notes for erotic film.

306 drop-out scenario: KPT, 'The Siege', notes for erotic film.

306 a scenario of multiple: KPT, notes on 'Skinflint in Ten Takes', erotic film.

307 'A girl lies down': KPT J, 12 Feb. 1971.

307 'distantly of conflict': Ibid., 26 Mar. 1971.

308 'Living a mile': Ibid., 4 Apr. 1971.

308 first half hour: KPT, 'Our Life with Alex and Florence', first draft screenplay, 1971.

309 'What am I doing': KPT L to KHT, 9 May 1971.

309 'I wait for': KHT L for KPT, 20 May, 1970.

309 'It is after dinner': KPT L to KHT, 21 May 1971.

310 'I had thought': KPT J, 9 June 1971.

34. END OF SUMMER

313 'At least a': KPT J, 11 Apr. 1972.

314 I hate the most: Ibid., 12 Apr. 1972.

314 'By refusing to nominate': KPT misc. note, 13 Apr. 1972.

314 He would argue: KPT, draft memo for Board, undated, 1972.

315 On the 20th: KPT L to Peter Hall, 20 Apr. 1972.

315 'fed up with': Hall, *Diaries* (London:

Hamish Hamilton, 1983), p. 11.

315 'he pays extravagant': KPT J, 5 July 1972.

316 His initial plan: KPT L to William Shawn, 20 Dec. 1971.

316 'I don't know anyone': Ibid., 29 Mar. 1972.

316 'Cloud-busters': KPT, unpub. MS.

317 'of Gestapo': KPT L to KHT, 5 June 1972.

317 'Baker's mouth': KPT notes for book on Wilhelm Reich, 1972.

320 'Thus I erase': KPT J, 1 Oct 1972.

35. A TESTING TIME

321 'other than grafting': Dr. Charles Fletcher L to KPT, 10 May 1971.

322 'Then I took her': KPT L to KHT, undated, 1972.

322 'I have a new moon': KPT L to KHT 12 Nov. 1972.

322 'You cannot imagine': Ibid., 13 Nov. 1972.

323 'Today the same': Ibid., 14 Nov. 1972.

323 'Query: whom are': Ibid., 15 Nov. 1972.

323 'DYING OF LONELINESS': Ibid., 16 Nov. 1972.

323 'Well, today is': Ibid., 17 Nov. 1972.

324 'I wait all day': Ibid., 18 Nov. 1972. [Frecknessa]: Our friends Freck Vreeland and Vanessa McConnell.

324 'Best plan is': KPT L to KHT, 21 Nov. 1972.

324 my letter: KHT L to KPT, 19 Nov. 1972.

325 'Painfully clenching': KPT J, Dec. 1972.

36. INTO THE LABYRINTH

326 'The sight of': KPT J, 18 Jan. 1972.

326 'the short, square': Ibid., 20 Jan. 1972.

327 'friendly neighbourhood': Ibid., undated, Dec. 1972.

328 'Part of our problem': Ibid., 25 June 1973.
328 'The more K': Ibid., 22 May, 1973.
328 What did he need?: Ibid., 5 June 1973.
329 'Nicole is really': Ibid., 20 June 1973.
329 'temporary, brief': KPT L to KHT, 28 May 1973.
329 In May 1973: David Astor L to KPT, L to KPT, 15 May 1973.
329 He replied: KPT L to Astor, 22 May 1973.
329 *Evening Standard:* Charles Wintour L to KPT, 18 Dec. 1973.
329 'A super-rich': KPT J, 4 June 1973.
330 sequel to *Oh! Calcutta!*: KPT, unpub. notes for sequel: 'Thoughts on Calcutta Two', 1973.
330 'the acme of': KPT, outline for 'After Calcutta', 18 May 1973.
330 Salambo: KPT, notes on trip with Trevor Griffiths, July 1973.
331 'To be "tasteful" ': Trevor Griffiths, unpub. notes on trip to Paris, July 1973, for 'After Calcutta', 1973.
331 'there have been times': Griffiths L to KPT, undated, Nov. 1973.
331 'As if we': KPT note on 'Come', by Griffiths.
332 'I dreamt': KPT J, 15 Mar. 1973.
332 'loss of interest': Ibid., 1 July 1973.
332 Ken improvised: Ibid., 17 Aug. 1973.
332 'I am slowly': Ibid., 10 Aug. 1973.
332 'There is one': Ibid., 25 Aug. 1973.
333 'At this point': Ibid., 10 Sept. 1973.
333 'although all commonsense': KPT L to KHT, undated, Aug. 1973.
333 *Erotic Art of the West:* KPT, *New Statesman*, 17 Feb. 1974.
335 'Life is a': KPT J, 16 Oct. 1973.
335 'As far as I'm': Ibid., 13 Mar. 1973.
335 Ken dined: Ibid., 5 Apr. 1973.
336 In September: Peter Hall L to KPT, 26 Sept. 1973.
336 'The de Filippo': KPT J, 31 Oct. 1973. [Ken would have been enraged by the post-modernist

trend in the arts to pacify, to emasculate, and to level the past by reducing it to nostalgic kitsch.]
336 How ironic: KPT J., 6 Nov. 1973.
336 'There is nothing': Milton Shulman, *Evening Standard*, 21 Dec. 1973.
336 'If – like Trevor': KPT J, 21 Dec. 1973.
336 derisory views: Logan Gourlay, *Olivier* (London: Weidenfeld and Nicolson, 1973).
337 'nowadays': KPT L to *Sunday Times*, 11 Nov. 1973.
337 In October: KPT L to Laurence Olivier, 1 Oct. 1973.
337 Olivier replied: Olivier L to KPT, 23 Nov. 1973.
337 'full survey': Olivier L to Lord Rayne, 6 Nov. 1973.

37 · DISAFFECTION

338 'emotional need': Nicholas Tomalin research note, Mar. 1973.
340 'My solution': KPT J, 6 Apr. 1974.
340 'sex had filled': Ibid., 9 Jan. 1974.
340 'When I first': KPT L to KHT, undated, 1974.
340 'worshipped the concert': KPT J, 23 Feb. 1974.
342 'I have now been': Ibid., 4 Apr. 1974.
342 'Were I to commit': Ibid., 7 May 1974.
342 'If I could laugh': Ibid., 11 June 1974.
343 *Private Eye: Private Eye,* 23 Aug. 1974.
343 later conceded: Ibid., 20 Sept. 1974.
343 'with constant recourse': KPT J, 23 July 1974.
343 'intellectual spivvery': Logan Gourlay, *Olivier* (London: Weidenfeld and Nicolson, 1973), p. 152.
343 'lethargy and hysteria': KPT J, 13 Aug. 1971.
344 'A superb Thurloe': Ibid., 10 Nov. 1974.

344 'without a cogent': Ibid., 6 Dec.
1974.

344 'Also, I think': KPT L to KHT,
undated, 1974.

345 'He does not': KPT, foreword to
'Breakdown', unpub. by Alan
Beesley.

345 'buoyancy, verve': KPT J, 2 Dec.
1974.

345 'my hoodlum ambusher': Ibid., 17
Feb. 1975.

346 'arid, despondent': Ibid., 23 Mar.
1975.

346 'silently lumbering': Ibid., 14 Jan.
1975.

346 television chat show: KPT, unpub.
outline, 4 Jan. 1974.

347 erotic language: BBC Radio 3,
recorded 14 May 1975.

347 'As ever': KPT J, 3 May 1975.

347 'the criminal who': Ibid., 21 Jan.
1975.

348 'Is it too late': Ibid., 5 May 1975.

348 'late-afternoon': Ibid., 25 Mar.
1975.

348 'buzzing with politics': KPT L to
Emilie Jacobson, 25 Sept. 1975.

348 'the arch-mandarin': KPT J, 11
June 1975.

348 'a curious sensation': Ibid., 19 Aug.
1975.

349 'vicious and vengeful': Ibid., 12 Jan.
1974.

349 'At least *something*': KPT L to Elaine
Dundy, 28 Aug. 1975.

38. TYNANOSAUR

350 'His Rolex watch': KPT J, 12 Sept.
1975.

350 'a haunted house': KPT J, 8 Oct.
1975 *New York Times*, 11 Jan.
1976.

350 'politics is serious': KPT J, 12 Oct.
1975.

351 'as far off as': Germaine Greer, *New
Statesman*, 5 Dec. 1975.

351 'boyish': Russell Davies, *Observer*,
30 Nov. 1975.

351 'Disillusioned': John Carey, *New
Review*, Vol. 2, Feb. 1976.

351 prehistoric animals: KPT J, 31 Dec.
1975.

352 'Matthew's vocabulary': Ibid., 3
Nov. 1975.

352 'to conquer the commercial': KPT,
'One Man's Week', *Sunday Times*, 9
Nov. 1975.

353 *Fanshen:* KPT J, 24 Apr. 1975.

353 In another programme: KPT,
'Three Wishes', *Arena*, BBC Jan.
1976.

353 not plotting: KPT L to William
Shawn, 2 Dec. 1975.

353 'Even the weather': KPT J, 4 Mar.
1976.

353 'In a month': Ibid.

354 'the tripartite': Laurence Olivier L
to *Observer*, 21 Nov. 1965.

354 'quest for Hip': KPT, *Village Voice*,
18 Nov. 1959.

354 'after she spends': KPT J, 15 Mar.
1976.

355 'Kathleen says': Ibid., 27 Mar. 1976.

355 'stricken, blotchy': Ibid., 6 Apr.
1976.

355 Ken wrote: KPT L to William Rees-
Mogg, 24 Feb. 1976.

356 'staggering': KPT J, 2 Feb. 1976.

356 'This doesn't make': Ibid., 20 May
1976.

357 Titles were tried: Ibid., 25 July
1976.

357 'I listen to the falsetto': Ibid., 4 July
1976.

357 'the Holy Grail': Dr. John
Henderson L to Dr. Peter Healy, 24
Feb. 1976.

358 'People seem less': Daniel Farson,
unpub. int. of KPT, 1976.

358 'If they had': KPT J, 25 Oct. 1976.

39. LOS ANGELES

360 'Life in Santa Monica': KPT L to
Marlene Dietrich, 28 June 1977.

361 'spray, cascades': KPT, unpub. MS,
1977.

362 'more ominously': KPT J, 4 Nov. 1976.
362 'The sweetheart': Ibid., 28 Dec. 1976.
362 'I'll show': Ibid., 23 Nov. 1976.
362 'The rats were': Ibid., 25 Nov. 1976.
363 'Have you noticed': Gore Vidal, 'Fond Farewell to a Youthful Prodigy', Observer, 3 Aug. 1980.
363 Los Angeles, reinforced: KPT, misc. note.
363 'dictatorship of good intentions': Joan Didion, The White Album (New York; Simon and Schuster, 1979), pp. 86–7.
363 'It is too important': KPT J, 21 Aug. 1977.
363 'literature of testimony': Ibid., 21 Dec. 1976.
363 'loutish, shameless': Ibid., 13 Nov. 1976.
363 'The Folks who live on the Hill': Ibid., 13 Dec. 1976.
364 Columbia executive: Ibid., 9 June 1977.
364 Shawn told him: Ibid., 14 Mar. 1976.
364 His host opened: Ibid., 14 June 1976.
364 'Fact, fiction': Sir Ralph Richardson L to KPT, 6 Mar. 1977.
365 'I submit': KPT, The New Yorker, 24 Jan. 1977.
365 The profile: KPT, 'Withdrawing in Style from the Chaos', The New Yorker, 19 Dec. 1977.
365 Ken told his: KPT L to Sara Spencer, 18 July 1977.
365 'a king-sized': KPT, 'Fifteen Years of the Salto Mortale', The New Yorker, 20 Feb. 1978.
365 'I can't wait': KPT L to Roxana and Matthew Tynan, 16 Mar. 1977.
366 'bankrupt's Howard Hughes': KPT J, 30 Mar. 1977.
366 [lung tissue is destroyed]: 'The lack of oxygen and the elevated carbon dioxide also affects the brain in all aspects, cognitive and mood components', Dr Elsie Giorgi L to KHT, 8 Feb. 1987.
367 In the spring: KPT J, 30 May 1977.
367 a yellow discharge: Ibid., 29 May 1977.
367 'An enjoyment': Ibid., 18 Apr., 19 Apr., 22 Apr. 1977.
367 some generalizations: KPT, notes for theatre and film symposium, Mack Taper Forum, Los Angeles, Apr. 1977.
368 'Eventually if you': KPT, 'A Conversation with Kenneth Tynan' for a proposed book on Harold Clurman, Summer 1977.
368 'How easy singing': Marlene Dietrich L to KPT, undated, June 1977.
368 Cock and Bull: Ibid., 22 July 1977.
368 He wrote to her: KPT L to Dietrich, 28 June 1977.
368 'I, personally': Ibid., 13 Jan. 1978.
369 'chuckwagon style': KPT J, 1 Apr. 1978.
369 'Sue Mengers': Ibid., 30 Apr. 1977.
370 housing developments: Ibid., 17 May 1977.
370 'The man next to me':Ibid.
371 'feral might be': Ibid., 27 Aug. 1977.
372 'No matter what': Ibid., 13 Aug. 1977.
373 a large Scotch: KPT L to KHT, undated, Oct. 1977.
373 mildly consoled: Judy Harger L to KHT, 13 Oct. 1977.
374 'It seems that': KPT L to Bill Davis, 7 Dec. 1977.
374 Elsa Vida Mia: KPT J, 18 Nov. 1977.
374 Ken noted: KPT J, 14 Dec. 1977.
375 'like a benediction': KPT L to William Shawn, 30 Jan. 1978.
375 'much that might have': KPT J, 17 Feb. 1978.
375 'Carson scriptbound': KPT L to Johnny Carson, 22 Apr. 1979.
375 Prayers and Meditations: KPT J, 17 Feb. 1978.

40. LOUISE BROOKS

376 'wondered how many': KPT, 'The Girl in the Black Helmet', *The New Yorker*, 11 June 1979.

376 'She runs through': KPT J, 8 Jan. 1978.

376 name Louise Brooks: KPT L to William Shawn, 16 Jan. 1978.

377 'You probably don't': KPT L to Louise Brooks, 6 Feb. 1978.

377 'positively tickled me': Louise Brooks L to KPT, 16 Feb. 1978.

377 'as a lawyer's daughter': Brooks L to KPT, 25 Feb. 1978.

378 'What a relief': Ibid., 25 Mar. 1978.

379 'After a long pause': KPT, 'The Girl in the Black Helmet', *The New Yorker*, 11 June 1979.

380 'so smooth, your starts': Brooks L to KPT, 3 June 1978.

380 'Three days in May': Ibid., 8 July 1978.

380 ('Fall to my knees'): KPT L to KHT, 21 May 1978.

381 I wrote back: KHT L to KPT, 22 May 1978.

382 Ken wrote: KPT L to Brooks, 1 Aug. 1978.

382 Ken later set down: KPT J, undated, May–Sept. 1978.

384 Ken considered the lovely: Ibid.

384 On his first: Ibid.

384 'markedly severe': Dr. John Dalton, St. John's Hospital, Santa Monica, 15 Dec. 1978.

385 'Maybe my life': Brooks L to KPT, 3 Sept. 1978.

386 '*less* of anything': KPT J, 3 Jan. 1979.

386 Mel Brooks: KPT, 'Frolics and Detours of a Short Hebrew Man', *The New Yorker*, 30 Oct. 1978.

386 Olivier wrote: Laurence Olivier L to KPT, 9 Sept. 1977.

386 'So long, in fact': KPT L to Olivier, 3 Nov. 1978.

387 'more explicit': KPT L to Shawn, 5 Apr. 1979.

387 'bowled over': Shawn L to KPT, 12 Apr. 1979.

387 'I owe Ken': Gore Vidal, *Reputations*, BBC 2, 1982.

387 Ken wrote: KPT L to Olivier, 2 Apr. 1979.

388 The situation was made: *Evening Standard*, 2 May 1979.

388 'because it seemed': KPT L to Olivier, 15 June 1979.

41. ENDGAME

391 'THIS IS MY LAST': KPT cable to KHT, Aug. 1979.

393 persuaded Shawn: KPT L to William Shawn, undated, 1979.

394 'There is a sort': KPT J, 29 Jan. 1980.

394 'It's hard to type': KPT L to Adrian and Celia Mitchell, 2 Feb. 1980.

394 'Time to Move On': KHT L to Dirk Bogarde, 3 Dec. 1979.

394 'sickening clipping': KPT J, 29 Jan. 1980.

395 'making the situation': Lillian Hellman, *An Unfinished Woman* (London; Macmillan, 1969).

395 'like a gossipy': KPT L to Michael Korda, 25 July 1979.

397 'As for the fabulous': Louise Brooks L to KPT, 10 Apr. 1980.

397 Ken wrote back: KPT L to Brooks, 23 Apr. 1980.

397 Louise replied: Brooks L to KPT, 27 May 1980.

397 'Must have someone': KPT EB, 28 Apr. 1980.

397 'Ask Gore re': KPT EB, 8 May 1980.

398 'Why do all words': KPT J, 8 June 1978.

398 wrote to Elaine: KPT L to Elaine Dundy, 20 May 1980.

399 delay the Olivier: KPT L to Shawn, 9 June 1980.

399 'We need to mend': KPT L to Nicole, 4 June 1980.

399 Harold Hobson wrote: Sir Harold Hobson L to KPT, 29 May 1980.

399 'The trouble with': KPT L to
    Hobson, 5 June 1980.

400 ['Exactitude']: reproduction of
    1929 gouache by Pierre Fix-
    Masseau.

403 successful approaches: Keith Griffin
    L to KHT, 21 Aug. 1980.

403 'the cast were': Adrian Mitchell L to
    Tynans, 4 Aug. 1980.

403 'That night I': John P. Marquand,
    Jr., L to KHT, 25 Aug. 1980.

404 Gore Vidal wrote: Gore Vidal,
    Observer, 3 Aug. 1980.

404 'perturbing spirit': John Simon, The
    New Yorker, 18 Aug. 1980.

404 'like Latimer': Hobson, Drama, Oct.
    1980.

404 'These things': C. S. Lewis,
    Screwtape Proposes a Toast (London:
    Fontaine, 1979), p. 95.

EPILOGUE

405 'I admire actors': KPT, Tynan on
    Theatre (London: Penguin Books,
    1964), p. 113.

405 'Because he was': Memorial Booklet
    (printed privately through the
    kindness of Lord Bernstein.)

405 'an anti-intellectual': George
    Steiner L to KHT, 4 Feb. 1983.

406 'the greatest evocative': Penelope
    Gilliatt, to KHT.

406 A young critic: Louis Menand, The
    New Republic, 1 Dec. 1986.

406 'precisely its ability': KPT, 'Shouts
    and Murmurs', Observer, 8 Dec.
    1968.

406 'I read you religiously': KPT, Tynan
    Right and Left (New York:
    Atheneum, 1967), p. viii.

406 'skip, leap and gyrate': KPT, He That
    Plays the King (London: Longmans,
    Green, 1950), p. 164.

406 dutiful citizen: KPT J, 21 Apr. 1976.

407 'eluded the idiot': Derek Lindsay L
    to KHT, 9 Jan. 1981.

Index

Note: Plays and films appear under title; published works under the author.

Abbot, Maggie, 233
Abraham Lincoln
    (Drinkwater), 38
Absurd, Theatre of, 181
Acte sans paroles
    (Beckett), 134
Act One (Hart), 169–170
Acton, Harold, 50
Actors' Studio, 132, 143
Adamov, Arthur, 162,
    181, 205
Addams, Charles, 68,
    173
Adler, Larry and Eileen,
    106
Adler, Richard, 99
Adler, Rozina, 224, 312
Adrian, Max, 76
Advertisements for Myself
    (Mailer), 153, 354
Afore Night Come
    (Rudkin), 191
African Genesis (Ardrey),
    222
African Queen, The (film),
    101
Agate, James, 37, 45–7,
    67, 105, 110
Agatha (film), 371–2,
    374, 385
Akhenaten, 9–10, 86
Albee, Edward, 152, 191

Alexander, Shana, 99
'Alex and Sophie'
    (Tynan), 308–9, 341–
    3
Ali, Tariq, 268
All-Girl Elephant Hunt
    (Perelman), 113
All That Jazz (musical),
    285
Allen, Lewis and Jay
    Presson, 120–1, 138
Altona (Sartre), 176
Altrincham, John Grigg,
    2nd Viscount, 178
Alvarez, A., 184
Amadeus (P. Shaffer),
    371
America Hurrah (revue),
    279
Amis, Kingsley, 51, 56,
    75, 116, 134, 184,
    272
Anderson, Judith, 205
Anderson, Lindsay, 51,
    59, 73, 124, 140,
    144, 164, 239
Anderson, Maxwell, 71–
    2, 88
Anderson, Terence, 88–
    9
Anna Christie (Eugene
    O'Neill), 81

Anna Lucasta (Philip
    Yordan), 69, 72
Annan, Noel, Baron,
    239
Anouilh, Jean, 86, 103
Antonioni,
    Michelangelo, 244,
    367
Antony and Cleopatra
    (Shakespeare), 92, 94
Apted, Michael, 371
Archer, William, 215,
    217, 219
*Architect and the Emperor
    of Assyria, The*
    (Arrabal), 302–3
Arden, John, 110
Ardrey, Robert, 222,
    249
Arena (TV series), 352
Arnold, Matthew, 215
Arrabal, Fernando, 10,
    266, 302, 304
Arsenic and Old Lace
    (Kesselring), 81
Art of Zen, The, (Watts),
    168
Arts Council, 85, 141,
    251, 254, 304, 313
Arts Lab, 266
Arts Theatre Club,
    London, 84, 91, 121

Astor, David, 106–8, 135, 150, 178, 219
Atkinson, Brooks, 161
Atlantic Monthly (journal), 116
Attenborough, Richard, 312
Auden, W. H., 295, 309
Audley, Maxine, 87, 98, 119
Aury, Dominique, 295
Author-Critic Club, Oxford, 54, 56
Avedon, Richard, 173, 182
Axelrod, George, 102, 306–7, 381
Axelrod, Joan, 299, 306, 372, 381
Axelrod, Nina, 299
Ayliff, H. K. 37

Bacall, Lauren, 173
Bacchae, The (Euripides), 336
Bachardy, Don, 129, 363
Back to Methuseleh (Shaw), 274
Baddeley, Hermione, 49, 76, 95
Báez Litri, Miguel, 102, 121, 213
Baker, Elsworth F., 317–18
Baker, Stanley, 87
Balcon, Sir Michael, 140
Baldwin, James, 153, 172–3
'Ballet Shame' (revue), 76
Bamburger, Freddy, 26
Bande à part (film), 241
Bandwagon (magazine), 91
Bandwagon (radio programme), 26
Barcelona, 120, 130; *see also* Spain
Barkley, William, 237
Barnes, Clive, 284

Barnes, Susan, 75
Barr, Charles, 140
Barrault, Jean-Louis, 76, 117, 122, 162, 220, 299
Barry, Sir Gerald, 101
Barton, John, 190
Bateson, Timothy, 59
Bataille, Georges, 342
Batten, Dr John, 322, 357
Battleship Potemkin (film), 33
Baxter, Beverley, 93–4, 101, 104
Baylis, Lilian, 313
BBC, 29, 86, 89, 101, 180, 230, 235, 236–8, 272, 347, 352, 402
beat generation, 168–9, 268
Beaton, Cecil, 101–3, 107, 110, 113, 308
Beatty, Warren, 307, 345, 362
Beaulieu, Lord *see* Montagu of Beaulieu, 3rd Baron
Beauvoir, Simone de, 172
Beaux' Stratagem, The (Farquhar), 81, 302
Beaverbrook, William Maxwell Aitken, 1st Baron, 27, 93, 101, 104–5, 106, 110
Bebbington, Gladys, 74
Beck, Julian, 170
Becker, William, 85, 165–6
Beckett, Samuel, 110, 121–2, 134–5, 143–4, 152, 180–1, 190, 218, 221; *Oh! Calcutta!* sketch, 279; declines KT's proposal for contribution, 295
Bedford Theatre, Camden Town, 83–4
Beerbohm, Max, 40, 45, 46, 64, 105, 151, 173

Beesley, Alan: friendship with KT at Oxford, 54–7, 60–1; marriage, 62–4; visits Lindsay in Switzerland, 78; child, 78; resumes friendship with KT, 272–3, 298; as godfather to Matthew, 310; suicide, 344–5; *Breakdown*, 345
Beesley, Marie (*née* Woolf), 62–4, 78
Behan, Brendan, 126, 164, 177, 180
Beiderbecke, Bix, 47, 92, 128, 265
Belafonte, Harry, 173
Belfrage, Cedric, 137
Belfrage, Sally, 137, 139
Belle et la bête, La (film), 76
Bells, The (adapt. by Leopold Lewis), 84, 127
Benn, Anthony Wedgwood, 51, 56, 72, 78, 179, 238
Bennett, Alan, 179, 184
Bennett, Jill, 120, 343–4
Bennett, Michael, 280
Benny, Jack, 26
Benthall, Michael, 85
Bentley, Eric, 85, 118, 150, 227
Benton, Robert, 280
Berens, Harold, 26
Berger, John, 10, 123, 134, 144, 239
Bergman, Ingmar, 176, 302, 324
Bergman, Ingrid, 299
Berkeley Square (Balderstone), 42
Berlin: KT visits, 132–3, 163, 176, 186, 210, 350
Berliner Ensemble, 110, 117, 131–3, 163, 210, 350

Bernard, Jean-Jacques, 101
Bernhardt, Sarah, 41, 45
Bernstein, Burton, 151
Bernstein, Leonard, 112
Bessie, Michael Simon, 118, 147
Betjeman, John, 179–80
Betsy, The (film), 386
Beuselinck, Oscar, 343
Bevin, Ernest, 39
Beyfus, Drusilla, 100
Beyond the Fringe (revue), 179–80, 277
Bigger, Duff, 195
Billington, Michael, 175
Birch, Patricia (Mrs William Becker), 166
Bird, David, 43
Birdwood, Dowager Lady, 293
Birmingham, 12, 17, 22, 24, 37, 41; *see also* King Edward's School
Birmingham Post, 38
Birthday Party, The (Pinter), 177
Black Dwarf (journal), 270
Black Comedy (P. Shaffer), 224
Black Peter (film), 242
Blair, Betsy, 112
Blake, William, 303, 310, 404
Blakely, Colin, 220
Blakemore, Michael, 274; directs at National, 302–5; KT proposes to succeed Olivier, 312–15; and KT's departure for California, 358
Blonde in Love, A (film), 242
Bloom, Claire, 98, 103, 282
Blow-Up (film), 244
Blunden, Edmund: *Cricket Country*, 36

Bogarde, Dirk, 355, 394
Bogart, Humphrey, 24, 95, 231, 244
Bogdanovich, Peter, 368
Bolt, Robert, 176
Bolté, Charles and Mary, 69
Bolton, Edward, 271
Bosch, Hieronymus: *Garden of Earthly Delights* (painting), 68
Boston, Richard, 261
Boswell, James, 2, 29, 369
Both the Ladies and the Gentlemen (William Donaldson), 346
Boty, Pauline, 235
Boudin, Leonard, 173
Bowles, Paul, 160
Bowra, Maurice, Sir, 201, 403
Boy Friend, The (musical play), 87
Boyesen, Hjalmar, 89, 95
Boyle, Sir Edward, 51, 53
'Boy Wonder, The' (Brien), 109
Braden, Bernard, 95
Braine, John, 87
Braithwaite, Dame Lilian, 35
Brando, Marlon, 2, 243
Braunsberg, Andrew, 307–8
Brecht Bertolt, 6, 176, 179, 220, 228, 350; KT admires, 85, 86, 110, 117–8, 121, 122–3, 131–3, 134, 135, 144, 163, 184, 190, 210, 353; *see also* individual plays
Brewer, Patricia, 44, 80–2
Brideshead Revisited (Waugh), 50
Brien, Alan, 50, 72, 75, 109, 146–7, 272

Brien, Nancy, 146
Brimberg family, 88, 99; *see also* Dundy, Elaine
British Broadcasting Corporation, 101
British Cuba Committee, 179
Britneva, Maria (Lady St Just), 95–6
Britten, Benjamin, 110
Broken Heart, The (John Ford), 216
Brook, Peter, at 1962 Edinburgh Festival, 204; declines *Oh! Calcutta!*, 278; directs *King Lear*, 190; directs minor Shakespeare, 135; directs *The Physicists*, 191; directs *Venice Preserv'd*, 103; early productions, 37, 59–60, 77, 85; friendship with KT, 231; KT's attitude to, 355–6; on *A Citizen of the World*, 83
Brooke, Dinah, 201
Brooks, Louise, 356, 376–82, 384–7, 396–7
Brooks, Mel, 170, 231, 371, 384, 386
Brooks, Peggy (Boyesen), 89–90, 95
Brown, Georgia, 183, 188–9
Brown, Ivor, 70, 106–7, 109
Bruce, Lenny, 152, 179–80, 260
Bryden, Ronald, 224
Büchner, Georg, 225, 303–4
Buck, Pearl, 161
Buckley, William F., 268
Buckstone Club, London, 87, 89
Bull Fever (Tynan), 102, 156
bullfighting, 68, 102,

bullfighting – *contd.*
121, 164, 193, 195,
213, 273, 348, 375
Bunch of Comics, A
(Tynan), 107
Burroughs, William,
168
Burrows, Abe, 103, 179
Burton, Richard, 2, 95,
98, 110, 251, 263,
313
Burton, Sybil
(Christopher), 95
Bury, Brenda, 188–9
Butler, Samuel, 300
Butt, Ronald, 293
Byron, George Gordon,
Lord, 2, 3, 56, 323
Byron, John, 37

cabaret, 179–80
Caesar and Cleopatra
(Shaw), 94
Cagney, James, 90, 378
Calder, John, 204–5,
207
California, 353, 358–75
Cambridge University,
50
Camino Real (Tennessee
Williams), 111, 198
Cammell, Donald, 364
Campaign for Nuclear
Disarmament, 142
Campiello, Il (Goldoni),
358
Campion, Gerald, 87
Canada, 257–8
Capote, Truman, 70,
146, 163, 172, 245–
6, 369–70; *In Cold
Blood*, 245–6, 369
Capron, Marion, 166
Captain of Köpenick, The
(Zuckmeyer), 303
Caretaker, The (Pinter),
177, 296
Carey, John, 351
Carnal Knowledge
(Feiffer), 285
Carr, Raymond, 202

Carson, Johnny, 363,
365, 367, 375, 377
Carte Blanche (revue),
285, 357
Cashmore, Ruth (KT's
cousin), 20, 22–4, 29,
52, 145, 186
Cassady, Neal, 169
*Castle of Perseverance,
The*, 59
Castro, Fidel, 156, 158,
172–3, 177, 179,
370, 392
Cat on a Hot Tin Roof
(Tennessee Williams),
121
Caucasian Chalk Circle
(Brecht), 117, 131
'Cause Without A
Rebel', 133
Cavett, Dick, 395, 397
Cazalet, Victor, 263
censorship, 87, 103,
116, 228, 236–241,
256, 302, 303
Chaikin, Joe, 279
Chairs, The (Ionesco), 143
Chamberlain, Neville,
24, 27
Champion, Hilary, 360
Chances, The (Beaumont
and Fletcher), 216
Chandos, Oliver
Lyttelton, Viscount;
attitude to KT, 262–3,
274–6, 294; National
Theatre, 215, 217,
228, 304; Olivier
opposes, 253–4, 263,
275; on *Soldiers*, 252–
4, 276; on *US*, 250
Chant d'amour (Genet),
270
Chaplin, Charlie, 25,
234
Chaplin, Oona O'Neill,
139
Charon, Jacques, 218
'Chass', 69–70
Chataway, Christopher,
51

Chekhov, Anton, 7,
142–3, 216
Chemins de la Liberté, Les
(Sartre), 56
Cherry Orchard, The
(Chekhov), 142
Cherwell (magazine), 56,
60–1
Chicago, 258
Chichester Festival, 184,
216
Chicken Soup with Barley
(Wesker), 125
Children of the Sun
(Green), 353–4
Chimes at Midnight (film),
213
Chin, Tsai, 189, 194,
210, 212
Chorus Line, A (musical),
283, 285, 363
Christie, Agatha, 352,
360, 369
Christmas Garland, A
(Beerbohm), 40
Church, Norris, 396
Churchill, Winston S.,
27, 249–53, 263–4
Cid, Le (Corneille), 117
Cilento, Diane, 186
Citizen Kane (film), 12, 30,
45, 98, 214, 262, 363
Citizen Kane Book, The
(Kael), 30–1
Citizen of the World, A
(Webber), 82–3
Civic Playhouse,
Cheltenham, 73
Clark, Sir Kenneth, 228,
255
Clarke, Shirley (*née*
Brimberg), 88
Classics and Commercials
(Wilson), 184
Clements, John, 253
Clunes, Alec, 91, 264
Clurman, Harold, 99,
107, 143, 150, 160,
183, 262, 368
Cobbold, Cameron F., 1st
Baron, 254

Cocteau, Jean, 8, 76, 91, 363
Coghill, Nevill, 66, 70, 201
Cohn-Bendit, Daniel, 273
Cold Comfort Farm (Gibbons), 84, 87
Colicos, John, 264
College Road School, 20, 21
Comden, Betty, 102, 111, 169, 179
Comédie Française, 117, 141
Comedy of Errors, The (Shakespeare), 190
Compagnie Renaud-Barrault, 117
Competello, Tom and Toody, 390–1, 393
Compton, Fay, 91
Connection, The (Gelber), 170
Conner, Angela, 257
Conner, Bruce, 270
Connery, Sean, 87
Connolly, Cyril, 10, 130–1, 139, 143, 202, 299
Conrad, Barnaby, 168
Contact (magazine), 83
Cooch Behar, Maharajah of, 95
Cook, Peter, 179–80, 184, 270, 394
Cooke, Alistair, 161
Cooper, Douglas, 184
Cooper, Tommy, 107
Cordobés, El, 213
Corneille, Pierre, 117
Corporate Club, Oxford, 72
Corso, Gregory, 168
Cory, Irwin, 152
Courage for Everyday (film), 242
Courcel, Baron and Baronne de, 299
Cousins, Norman, 171
Coward, Noël, 35, 43,

97–8, 114, 179, 218, 227, 364–5
Cowlishaw, Joan, 80, 82
Craig, Edward Gordon, 184
Craigie, Jill, 185
Craven House (from novel by Patrick Hamilton), 84
Crazy Horse Saloon, Paris, 278–9, 331
cricket, 3, 12, 20, 21, 24, 36, 41, 349
Cripps, Sir Stafford, 72
Cronin, A. J.: Hatter's Castle, 21
Cropper, Ruth, 73
Crosland, Anthony, 56
Crucible, The (Arthur Miller), 124
Cuba: KT visits, 156–60, 172–3, 177, 179, 370; Kathleen visits, 385–6, 390–2
Cukor, George, 111–12
Cul de Sac (film), 242
Curiel, Alfonso, 390
Curran, Charles, 93, 104–5
Curtiss, Thomas Quinn, 161, 343
Cushman, Robert, 175
Cybulski, Zbigniew, 205, 207
Czechoslovakia, 246–7

Daily Mail (newspaper), 87
Daily Sketch (newspaper), 98, 107–8
Dalgleish, Su, 182–3
Dance of Death, The (Strindberg), 253
Dancin' (revue), 285
Danton's Death (Büchner), 225, 303
Darby, Geoffrey, 33, 43, 45
David Garrick theatre, Lichfield, 80–2
Davidson, Gordon, 367

Davies, Russell, 351
Davis, Bill and Annie, 130, 139, 165, 374
Davis, Sammy, Jr, 369
Dawson, James, 29–30, 33, 38–40
Day by the Sea, A (N. C. Hunter), 343
Day, Sir Robin, 51, 53
Dean, James, 126
Delaney, Shelagh, 164–177
Dear Brutus (Barrie), 26
Death of a Salesman (Arthur Miller), 83, 85
Death of Tragedy, The (Steiner), 180
Declaration (essays), 141
Deep Blue Sea, The (Rattigan), 103
de Filippo, Eduardo, 336
Dennis, Nigel, 180
Desert Incident (Pearl Buck), 161
Desire Caught by the Tail (Picasso), 83
Desmond, Paul, 168
Devine, George, 123, 132, 144, 221
Dewey, Kenneth, 206
Dexter, John, 188; and National Theatre, 217, 220, 222, 224–8, 274, 302–3, 306, 312–4; and Soldiers, 251; and Tyger, 310
Dhéry, Robert, 150
Diares (Hall), 315
Diary of a Lost Girl (film), 376
Diary of Anne Frank, The (play), 132
Dickson, Rache Lovat, 203
Didion, Joan (Dunne), 363, 402
Dietrich, Marlene, 4, 64, 94, 113–15, 257–9, 368–9
Dietz, Howard, 170

Dimpfl, Suki, 348–9
Dingo (Charles Wood), 228
Dionysus in '69, 266, 284
Dirtiest Show in Town, The (revue), 285
Doctor Knock (Romain), 38
Dodd, Thomas J., 171–2
Dominguín, Luis Miguel, 164–5, 374
Don Quixote (film; unfinished), 368
Donaldson, William, 277, 279
Doors of Perception, The (Huxley), 122
Dors, Diana, 83
Driberg, Tom, 238
Drinkwater, John, 38
Duncan, Ronald, 83, 87
Dundy, Elaine (*née* Brimberg; KT's first wife): 88–90, 95, 145, 161, 233, 328, 398; separation and divorce off, 186, 188–90, 204, 208, 209, 210–1; on Tynan, 117; Tynan's married life with, 89–90, 99–101, 104–6, 111–4, 119–20, 127–9, 137–40, 147, 149, 153–5, 159, 165–6, 182–3, 185; writing career of, 88, 90, 139–40, 153, 155, 182, 188, 209, 349; WORKS: *The Dud Avocado*, 88, 90, 139–40, 153, 190; *The Injured Party*, 349; *My Place* (play), 188; 'The Sound of a Marriage' (short story), 155; biography of Peter Finch, 398
Dunlop, Frank, 274, 303, 313–14

Dunne, John Gregory, 363, 402
Dürrenmatt, Friedrich, 191

Ealing Studios, 140
Eden, Sir Anthony (1st Earl of Avon), 133
Edinburgh Festival, 1962: Writers' Conference, 204–7
Egypt, 311–12
Eisenstein, Sergei, 29, 33
Eliot, T. S., 57, 103, 177
Elkins, Hillard, 280, 282–3, 285, 293, 295
Elland, Percy, 93–4, 104
Ellington, Duke, 26, 59, 231
Elsa Vida Mia (film), 374
Elwes, Dominic, 195
Encounter (magazine), 111, 144, 203
Endgame (Beckett), 134, 180
End of St. Petersburg, The, 33
English Stage Company (Royal Court Theatre, London), 110, 123–4, 132, 134–5, 164, 177, 190
Entertainer, The (Osborne), 135
Epitaph for George Dillon (Osborne), 202
Erotic Art of the West (Melville), 333
Equus (P. Shaffer), 336
Esher, Oliver Sylvain Balliol Brett, 3rd Viscount, 215
Esquire (magazine), 266
Esslin, Martin: *Brecht*, 163; *The Theatre of the Absurd*, 181
Establishment Club, London, 180
Evans, Dame Edith, 60

Evening Standard (newspaper), 93–4, 101, 104–5, 329
Evening with, Beatrice Lillie, An (revue), 102
Experimental Theatre Club, Oxford (ETC), 49, 57, 60, 71, 201

Fairbrother, Nellie, 17–18
Fair Play for Cuba Committee, 172
Fanshen (play), 353
Farquhar, George, 81, 116, 131
Farson, Daniel, 356, 358
Faulkner, William, 157
Fausses Confidences, Les (Marivaux), 76
Faust (Goethe), 163
Feiffer, Judy (*née* Sheftel), 89, 153
Feiffer, Jules, 153, 171, 280, 285
Felker, Clay, 353
Fellini, Federico, 280
Ferlinghetti, Lawrence, 169, 171
Fernandez, Pablo Armando, 370
Fetishist Times, The, 362
Field, Sid, 26, 60, 92, 107
Fields, W. C., 89, 90, 107
Film Pictorial, 24, 25
Fin de partie (Beckett), 134–5
Final Solution, The, (Knight), 364
Finch, Peter, 87, 398
Findlater, Richard, 265
Findlay, Rev. Brian, 404
Finlay, Frank, 227
Fings Aint' Wot They Used T'Be (musical), 177
Finney, Albert, 77, 231, 312, 405

Fiorello (musical), 169
Firbank, Ronald, 87,
199, 335
Fisher, Dr Kenneth,
399–400
Fitzgerald, F. Scott, 111,
157, 194
Flack, Roberta, 332
Flanagan and Allen, 26
Flanner, Janet, 162, 212
Flea in Her Ear, A
(Feydeau), 226
Fletcher, Dr Charles,
272, 321
Flower Drum Song
(Rodgers and
Hammerstein), 150
Foot, Sir Dingle, 107
Foot, Michael, 179, 238,
271
Ford, John, 216
Forman, Miloš, 242,
396
Fosse, Bob, 285
Franco, General
Francisco, 348
Frankfurter, Felix, 202–3
Franklin, Sidney, 154
Freeman, Bud, 26, 389
Freeman, John, 179
French Club, London, 94
Frieda (Ronald Millar),
53
Friedrich, Otto, 259
Front Page, The (Hecht
and MacArthur), 305
Frosch, Aaron R., 246
Fry, Christopher, 86,
101, 103
Fugs, The, 260
*Funny Thing Happened on
the Way to the Forum,
A* (musical), 191

Galbraith, John Kenneth,
171
Garbo, Greta, 113–14,
376
García, Victor, 302–3
Garden Party, The
(Havel), 246

Gardiner, Gerald, 178
Gardner, Ava, 131,
194–5
Garland, Judy, 103, 112
Garnett, Tony, 269–70,
339
Gascoigne, Bamber, 175
Gaskill, William: at
National Theatre,
217–18, 220, 222,
225, 227; and
Soldiers,
255; leaves National,
274; on KT at
National, 336
Gates, Oliver Kathleen's
first husband), 202–
4, 207–8, 210–13,
233
Gates, Pauline, 202,
213
Gates, Sylvester, 202,
212–13
Gelber, Jack, 152, 170,
205, 207
Genauer, Emily, 284
Genet, Jean, 152, 181,
270, 278
Geneva Club, 134
Geraldo (dance-band
leader), 36
Germany: theatre in,
162–3; *see also* Berlin
Ghosts (Ibsen), 60
Gibbs, Wolcott, 146–7
Gielgud, Sir John, 26,
38, 43, 86, 102–3,
109
Gigi (Colette), 100
Gill, Brendan, 353
Gilliatt, Penelope, 164–
5, 179, 197, 258,
262, 340, 402–5
Gilliatt, Roger, 164
Gingold, Hermione, 43,
76, 99, 104
Ginsberg, Allen, 153,
168, 171, 247; *Howl*,
169
Giorgi, Dr Elsie, 366,
388–9, 401–2

Glass Menagerie, The
(Tennessee Williams),
145
Glorious Days, The, 103
Glover, Edward, 77
Godard, Jean-Luc, 241–
2, 280
Godley, John (3rd Baron
Kilbracken), 63, 68
Goldberg, Bertrand, 258
*Good Woman of Setzuan,
The* (Brecht), 132
Goodman, Arnold,
Baron, 216, 240, 251,
304, 313–14
Goodwin, Clive, 212,
235, 273
Gosling, Nigel, 197
Gough, Michael, 92
Gourlay, Logan, 337
Graham, Sheilah, 111
Grande Eugène, La
(revue), 331
Granger, Derek, 226,
276, 301
Granger, Stewart, 111
Grant, John, 81
Grant, Lee, 100
Granville Barker, Harley,
215, 217, 219
Graves, Beryl, 233–4
Graves, Robert, 60, 213,
227, 233
Green, Adolph, 102,
111–12, 169, 170,
179, 317, 353
Green, Benny, 346
Green, Martin: *Children
of the Sun*, 353
Green, Phyllis
(Newman), 317, 353
Greenburg, Dan, 282
Greene, Graham, 295,
323
Greene, Sir Hugh
Carleton, 238
Greer, Germaine, 269,
300–1, 302, 351
Griffin, Keith, 403
Griffith-Jones, Mervyn,
178

Griffiths, Trevor, 175, 330–2, 334–5, 336, 352
Gropius, Walter, 266
Gross, John and Miriam, 346
Grossman, Jan, 246
Grove, Press, 295
Gründjens, Gustav, 163
Guinness, Alec, (Sir), 92, 107
Guthrie, Tyrone, 85
Guys and Dolls (musical), 100, 302
Gypsy (musical), 161

H. (Charles Wood), 274
Hackett, Geoffrey, 23, 27
Hagen, Uta, 100
Haggard, Edith, 147
Haigh, Kenneth, 126, 154
Halifax, Michael, 225
Hall, Alice, 195
Hall, Peter: 121, 135, 164, 190, 229, 254–5, 312–5, 335
Hall, Willis, 180
Halliwell, David, 274
Halprin, Anna, 281
Halton, Jean Joslin (*née* Campbell; Kathleen's Mother), 199, 212–13, 260, 286, 287, 404
Halton, Matthew (Kathleen's father), 199–201, 310
Hamburg, 306–7
Hamill, Pete, 363
Hamlet (Shakespeare), 37–8, 43; KT plays, 42–3, 45–6; First Quarto production, 73–4, 80; Olivier's film of, 76; Guinness plays, 92–3; Brook's Moscow production of, 122; National Theatre's first production, 218

Hammerstein, Oscar, II, 150
Hammett, Dashiell, 395
Hammond, Kay, 253
Handley, Tommy, 27
Hands Across The Sea (Woollcott), 33
Hansberry, Lorraine, 160–1
Happenings, 206
Happy Days (Beckett), 190
Hare, David, 352
Hare, Robertson, 26
Harewood, George Lascelles, 7th Earl of, 123, 184, 187, 194–5, 204, 206
Harewood, Patricia, Countess of, 187, 194–5
Harger, Judy, 361, 371–3
Harlech, Pamela, Lady, 310
Harper's magazine, 170
Harris, Sir Arthur, 252
Harris, Julie, 100
Harris, Kenneth, 53
Harris, Richard, 243
Harrison, George, 256
Hart, Kitty Carlisle, 169–70
Hart, Moss, 86, 169–70
Harvey, Laurence, 95–6
Hastings, Michael, 126
Hathaway, Henry, 83
Hatter's Castle (Cronin), 21
Hauser, Frank, 92
Havel, Václav, 246, 301, 365
Hawkins, Coleman, 63
Hayes, George, 37
Haynes, Jim, 266
Hayworth, Rita, 70
Hazlitt, William, 37, 50; 77, 86, *Liber Amoris*, 372
Head, Ann, 137
Heartbreak House (Shaw), 180–1

Hedda Gabler (Ibsen), 302
Hefner, Hugh, 244, 257–8, 267, 292
Heiress, The (John Burgoyne), 87
Heller, Joseph, 259
Hellman, Lillian, 173, 205, 259–60; *An Unfinished Woman*, 287, 395
Hellzapoppin (film), 35, 206
Help! (film), 242
Helpmann, Robert, 71, 73
Hemingway, Ernest, 2, 156–9, 164–5, 374
Hemingway, Mary, 156
Hemingway, Pauline, 158
Henderson, Dr John, 271, 357
Henry IV (Shakespeare), 52–3, 95, 117
Henry VI (Shakespeare), 190
Hentschel, Irene, 107
Hepburn, Audrey, 100
Hepburn, Katharine, 90, 101, 234, 272
Herder, Addie, 161–3
Hi, Gang! (radio programme), 26
Hickock, Richard, 246
Higham, Charles, 103
Hiller, Wendy, 87
him (e.e. cummings), 85
Hiss, Alger, 171
Hitchcock, Alfred, 94
Hobsbawn, Eric J., 179, 271
Hobson, Elizabeth, 399
Hobson, Sir Harold, 70, 77, 83, 115, 125, 399, 404
Hochhuth, Rolf *see Soldiers*
Hoffman, Dustin, 371–2, 374
Hoggart, Richard, 178

Holland, Betsy, 113
Holland, Julian:
   friendship with KT,
   28–31, 33–40; and
   Hamlet, 42; and KT's
   girls, 43–4; meets
   Agate, 47; Oxford
   letters from KT, 49,
   53, 59, 65, 67–9;
   and death of KT's
   father, 75; and KT's
   dominance, 291
Holliday, Dailly, 278
Holliday, Judy, 100
Holloway, Stanley, 92
Holly, Ellen, 166, 364
Holt, Seth, 140
Home and Beauty
   (Maugham), 274
Honte, La (film), 324
Hope, Bob, 26
Hopkins, Anthony, 220
Hordern, Michael, 305
Horne, Lena, 2, 112,
   115
Horowitz, Elly (Miller),
   72–3
Hostage, The (Behan),
   164
Hotchner, A. E., 165
Houston, Penelope, 35
Howard, Brian, 50, 353–
   4
Howard, Elizabeth Jane,
   129
Howard, Trevor, 69
Howerd, Frankie, 107
Huis clos (Sartre), 49, 85,
   355
Huizinga, Johan: *Homo
   Ludens*, 240
Humes, H. L. ('Doc'),
   234–5
Hungary: 1956 rising,
   133–4
Huntley, Raymond, 264
Huston, John, 95, 390,
   394
Huth, Angela, 234–5,
   389, 404
Huxley, Aldous, 56, 121;

The Doors of Perception,
   122

I Am a Camera
   (Isherwood/John van
   Druten), 100
Ibsen, Henrik, 41, 60,
   61, 129
Illustrated London News,
   81
In Cold Blood (Capote),
   245–6
In His Own Write
   (Lennon), 274
Inge, William, 169
Ink (magazine), 296
Inside North Vietnam
   (film), 268
Intermezzo (Giraudoux),
   335–6
International War
   Crimes Tribunal,
   Stockholm, 268
Intimate Relations
   (Cocteau; transl. of *Les
   Parents Terribles*), 91
Ionesco, Eugène, 110,
   143–4, 180–1, 190,
   206, 294
Irving, David, 250
Isherwood, Christopher,
   129, 363, 403
Isis (magazine), 35, 49,
   53, 55, 61, 65, 67,
   70, 72, 78, 83
Italy, 256, 286–7, 299

J.B. (MacLeish), 150,
   161
Jackley, Nat, 26
Jackson, Sir Barry, 37
Jacobi, Derek, 224
Jacobs, Nacomi, 129
Jacobson, Emilie, 244
Jagger, Mick, 256
James, Clive, 346
James, Harry, 41, 81
James, Jimmy, 26
Janis, Conrad, 195
Javits, Senator, 283
Jeans, Ursula, 83

Jebb, Julian, 128
Jellicoe, Anne, 144
Jenkins, Hugh, 238
Jenkins, Joseph P., 246
Jewell and Warriss, 26
Johnson, James Howard,
   389
Johnson, Paul, 51, 59
Johnson, Samuel, 3, 12,
   35, 54, 375
Jones, Allen, 294
Jones, D. A. N., 355–6
Jones, Sir Elwyn, 238
Jones, James and Gloria,
   161–2, 204, 207
Jonic, Bettina, 205
Joy (Davies), 43–4
Jumpers (Stoppard), 305
Juno and the Paycock
   (O'Casey), 82

Kael, Pauline: *The Citizen
   Kane Book*, 30–1
Kanin, Garson, 112,
   302
Kaprow, Allan, 206
Kaye, Danny, 29, 77,
   93–4
Kazan, Elia, 85, 107,
   110, 121, 150, 191
Kazin, Alfred, 183
Kean (Dumas), 83
Keaton, Buster, 111
Kelly, Barbara, 95
Kelly, Gene, 112
Kemp, T. C., 43
Kennedy, Joseph, 27
Kennedy, Ludovic, 51
Kenway and Young, 26
Kerouac, Jack, 168: *On
   the Road*, 169
Kerr, Walter, 161
Kilmartin, Terence, 107,
   115, 135–6, 197
*King Edward's School
   Chronicle* (magazine),
   27, 45
King Edward's School,
   Birmingham: KT
   attends, 24, 27, 29,
   32–4, 45; Literary

King Edward's School –
contd.
   Society, 33–4, 42;
   Sixth Form
   conference, 45
King, Martin Luther Jnr,
   173
King Lear (Shakespeare),
   60, 134, 190, 274–5
King's Row, 36
Knight, Stephen: The
   Final Solution, 364
Knittel, Robert, 141
Kopit, Arthur, 152, 207
Korda, Michael, 395
Kott, Jan, 180–1, 204,
   218
Krapp's Last Tape
   (Beckett), 135
Krejča, Otomar, 246
Kroll, Jack, 285
Kurnitz, Harry, 198

Labyrinth, The (Arrabal),
   266
Lady Chatterley's Lover
   (Lawrence) trial, 177–
   8
Laine, Frankie, 98
Laing, R. D., 235
Lamantia, Philip, 169
Lambert, Gavin, 93
Lang, Harold, 85, 87,
   129, 179
Langton, Basil, 37
Lardner, Ring, 336
Lasdun, Denys, 227
Last Tango in Paris (film),
   328
Lawrence, D. H., 34;
   Lady Chatterley's Lover,
   177–8
Lawley, Betty (KT's
   Peacock cousin), 21–3
Lawrence, Gertrude, 77,
   327
Lazar, Irving, 169, 362,
   386
Leaf, Nydia, 154
Lee, Jennie, Baroness,
   304

Lehrstück (Tynan), 306
Leigh, Vivien, 25, 86,
   94, 119, 173, 176,
   253, 387–8
Leishman, J. B., 201
Lennon, John, 2, 269,
   274, 280
Lerman, Leo, 233
Lesley, Cole, 365
Lessing, Doris, 141–2,
   179, 227
Lessing, Gotthold
   Ephraim, 217
Lesson, The (Ionesco),
   143
Lester, Richard, 242
Let My People Come
   (revue), 285
Levant, Oscar, 25, 111–
   12
Levens, Daphne, 49–50,
   61
Levens, Robert, 49
Levin, Bernard, 206
Levy, Benn, 141
Levy, Jacques, 279–8,
   285, 294
Lewenstein, Oscar, 123
Lewis, C. S.: tutors KT at
   Oxford, 38, 47, 52–4,
   71; on KT's degree,
   78, 105; on Protestant
   conversion, 141; The
   Problem of Pain, 347;
   Screwtape Proposes a
   Toast, 404; That
   Hideous Strength, 308
Leyser, Karl, 404
Lichfield see David
   Garrick Theatre
Liehm, Antonin, 247
Life of Galileo, The
   (Brecht), 133, 163,
   180
Lilburne, John, 406–7
Lillie, Beatrice, 102, 173,
   380
Lilliput (magazine), 25, 91
Lincoln Center for the
   Performing Arts, New
   York, 160, 191, 217

Linden Tree, The
   (Priestley), 80
Lindsay, Derek (Deacon):
   on KT at Oxford, 54,
   58; on Beesley, 55;
   character, 55–6; life at
   Oxford, 56–7; writes
   for Cherwell, 60; meets
   Jill Rowe-Dutton and
   Marie Woolf, 63; in
   Swiss sanatorium, 78;
   and KT's death, 407;
   The Rack, 8, 56
Lindsay, Vera (formerly
   Lady Barry), 101, 106
'Litri', Miguel see Báez, M.
'Little Poem in Prose:
   L'Art pour l'art'
   (Tynan), 45–6
Littlewood, Joan, 100,
   118, 126, 164, 177,
   191, 205, 207
Livesey, Roger, 83
Living Theater, 170
Lloyd George, David, 15,
   75
'Loamshire' plays, 116
Logan, Joshua, 99, 150
Logue, Christopher, 133,
   142, 147, 212, 234,
   240, 404
London Life, 25
Long and the Short and the
   Tall, The (Willis Hall),
   164
Long Day's Journey into
   Night (O'Neill), 135,
   227, 274, 304–5
Longman, Mark, 77,
   118
Look Back in Anger
   (Osborne), 110, 123–
   6, 133, 226, 373
Lord Chamberlain, 228,
   256, 263, 279
Lorenz, Konrad, 261
Los Angeles, 111, 345,
   357, 360–75, 381,
   393–4
Loss of Roses, A (William
   Inge), 169

Lovelace, Linda, 355
Love's Labour's Lost
  (Shakespeare), 67,
  181
Luard, Nicholas, 180,
  195
Lumet, Sidney, 173, 353
Luther (Osborne), 180
Luxor, 311–12
Lynn, Ralph, 26

Macbeth (Shakespeare),
  26, 37, 83; film of,
  107, 119, 292
McCarty William, 257
McCarthy, Senator
  Joseph, 111, 124,
  137, 172
McCarthy, Mary, 125,
  183–4, 236, 238–9,
  269
McCartney, Paul, 256
McCormick, Pat, 280
Macdonald, Dwight, 173
MacDonald, Robert
  David, 250
McGrath, John, 175,
  185, 353
Mackendrick, Sandy,
  140
MacLaine, Shirley, 356,
  363, 381, 403
MacLeish, Archibald,
  150, 161
McLuhan, Marshall,
  260, 266, 364
MacNeice, Louis, 83–4,
  184
Madrid, 366, 373–4; see
  also Spain
Maeterlinck, Maurice,
  57
Magdalen College,
  Oxford, 38; see also
  Oxford
*Magnificent Ambersons,
  The* (film), 31–2
Mahagonny (Brecht),
  210
Mahony, Diana (Mrs
  Donald Sinden), 80

Mailer, Adele, 166
Mailer, Norman, 153,
  166, 170–2, 184,
  231, 259, 283, 295,
  342, 354–5, 396
Málaga, 130, 161, 164–
  5, 183, 189
Malina, Judith, 170
Mallarmé Stéphane, 34
Malraux, André, 162
Man and Superman
  (Shaw), 37
Man for All Seasons, A
  (Bolt), 176
*Man Who Came to Dinner,
  The* (Hart and
  Kaufman), 26, 57
Mander, Raymond, 84
Mandrake (magazine), 53
Mankiewicz, Herman J.,
  31, 378
Manning, Hugh, 41–3,
  47
Margaret, Princess, 212–
  13, 270, 290
Marks, Captain, 159–60
Marowitz, Charles, 206
Marquand, John and
  Sue, 106, 130, 259,
  403
Marsh, Jean, 154, 167,
  338
Martin, Kingsley, 45
Martin, Mary, 99
Martin, Pat, 40
Martine (Jean-Jacques
  Bernard), 101
Marxism, 173, 181, 242
Mary Stuart (Schiller),
  163
Masculin-Féminin (film),
  241
Mason, James and
  Pamela, 111
Master Builder, The
  (Ibsen), 227
Matthews, Jessie, 26
Mature, Victor, 290
Maugham, William
  Somerset, 124; *The
  Summing Up*, 394

May, Elaine, 152, 179,
  280
Medea (Euripides), 59,
  66, 76
Mee, Alan Jackson, 21,
  23–4
Melly, George, 179, 234
Melody Maker, 25, 27
Melville, Robert; *Erotic
  Art of the West*, 333–4
Memorandum, The
  (Havel), 246
Mengers, Sue, 362, 369
Mercer, David, 280, 282,
  284
Merchant of Venice, The
  (Shakespeare), 210,
  227, 302
Merchant, Vivien, 270
Mermaid Theatre,
  London, 164
Merman, Ethel, 100,
  161, 378
Merrick, David, 280
*Messingkauf (Dialogues,
  The)* (Brecht), 210
Mexico, 154–5, 388,
  390–3
Midlander, The, 29, 149
Miles, Bernard, 164
Millais, Hugh, 195
Millar, Ronald, 53
Miller, Arthur, 110–11,
  121, 123, 133, 143,
  144, 160
Miller, Jonathan, 179–
  80, 184, 186, 226,
  269, 302–3, 358,
  394
Millionairess, The (Shaw),
  101
Mills, C. Wright, 171
Mills, Dacia, 339–40,
  381
Milton, John, 65–7
Misanthrope, The
  (Molière), 336
Mrs Warren's Profession
  (Shaw), 302
Mitchell, Adrian, 303,
  310, 394, 403–4

Mitchell, Celia, 394, 404
Mitchenson, Joe, 84
Moby Dick (Welles's adaptation), 118
Molina, Judith, 170
Monde, Caris, 82
Monde, Le (newspaper), 72
Monroe, Marilyn, 112, 133
Montagu of Beaulieu, Edward, 3rd Baron, 109–10
Montero, Germaine, 117
Moore, Dudley, 179, 184, 201, 329, 394
Moore, Henry, 228
Moreno, Rita, 211–12
Morley, Robert, 26
Morley, Sheridan, 175
Morris, Charles, Baron, 32, 39
Mortimer, John, 218, 240, 243, 261, 293, 312, 338
Moscow, 122
Moscow Arts Theatre, 142
Mosley, Sir Oswald, 72
Mostel, Zero, 191
Motel (play), 279
Mother, The, 163
Mother Courage (Brecht), 117–18, 131–2, 191, 228
Mount Street, Mayfair, 127–9, 137–9, 182, 230–3
Mountbatten, Philip, Prince 200
Mourning Becomes Electra (O'Neill), 186
Moyle, Dr Alan, 348
Muggeridge, Malcolm, 107
Mulberry Bush, The (Angus Wilson), 123
Muni, Paul, 83
Murdoch, Iris, 136
Murray and Mooney, 26
Murrow, Edward R., 111–12

Music Hall (radio programme), 26
Mutter, Die, 350
My Place (Dundy), 186
Myers, Peter, 84, 96

Nabokov, Vladimir, 295
Nader, George, 140
Naked Lunch, The (Burroughs), 168
Nasser, Gamal Abdel, 133
Nathan, George Jean, 99, 173
National Health, The (Peter Nichols), 274, 302
National Theatre: delays in building, 141; KT joins, 175; campaign for, 191, 204, 215; Olivier appointed Director, 216–23; KT appointed Literary Manager, 216–23, 226; early productions, 218; character and repertoire, 225–8; rehearsal logbooks, 226; programmes, 227; Board and administration conflicts, 228–9, 253–5, 262, 305; censorship at, 228–9; docudramas, 249–50; production of *Soldiers*, 250–4, 262, 275; KT's declining influence at, 275–6, 337; KT asks to leave, 276; KT shares post with Granger, 301; failures and successes, 303–5; Rayne replaces Chandos as Chairman, 304; Hall succeeds Olivier, as Director, 312–15, 335; KT

leaves, 336–7; KT's severance pay, 337; new building opened, 358
Neagle, Anna, 103–4
Neame, Christopher, 343
Neher, Caspar, 133
Neill, A. S., 318
Nekrassov (Sartre), 122–3
Neville, Richard, 296
New Commercial Club, 77
New Dramatic Company, Birmingham (NDC), 41–3, 45–6, 59, 81
New Statesman (weekly journal), 45, 134, 179, 184, 333
New York, 99–100, 102, 110, 148
New York (magazine), 353
New York Drama Critics Circle, 161, 173
New York Times (newspaper), 100, 244, 284, 292
New York Times Magazine, 387
New Yorker (magazine): KT appointed drama critic, 146–9, 164; language, 150–1; KT writes on world theatre for, 244, 256; KT's profiles for, 290, 316, 318, 353, 358, 360, 364–5, 373–5, 386–8, 390, 399; collection of KT's profiles published, 395
Newman, David, 280
Newton, Robert, 202
Nibbs, Rosemary, 262, 272, 358
Nichols, Mike, 152–3, 179, 182, 259, 269, 274, 278
Nichols, Peter, 256, 274, 302

Nicole (KT's lover), 327–9, 333, 340–1, 355, 372–4, 381–2, 388, 399

Nietzsche, Friedrich, 35

Night Out, A (Printer), 177

'Night Words' (Steiner), 267

Nineteen Eighty-Four (Orwell), 92

Nixon, Richard, 291

No Man's Land (Pinter), 364

Norman, Frank, 180

Not So Much a Programme More a Way of Life (TV programme), 230

Nothing Up My Sleeve (Ronald Duncan), 87

Novello, Ivor, 26, 35

Nowhere to Go (film), 140

Nunn, Trevor, 314

Nureyev, Rudolf, 283

Nye, Pat, 83–4

O'Brien, Edna, 280, 283, 308, 310, 346, 354

Observer (newspaper): KT appointed drama critic on, 106–9; KT reviews for, 115–16; renews KT's contract, 135; play competition, 141; and KT's *New Yorker* appointment, 150–1; KT contributes to from New York, 151–2; KT returns to, 174–5, 184; activities and people at, 197; Kathleen at, 197–8, 203; KT as film critic for, 241; KT gives up film criticisms, 244; and Capote's *In Cold Blood*, 245; 'Shouts and Murmurs' (KT's column), 265–8; KT renews reviewing for, 287; offers to re-engage KT as drama critic, 329

O'Casey, Sean, 116, 150

Oh! Calcutta! (revue): sketch 'Suite for Five Letters', 25, 280, 295; KT devises, 249, 277–80, 282–4; title, 277–8; contributors, 280; financial returns, 280–1, 285; nudity in, 281, 374; in New York, 283–5; reception, 284–5; London production, 292–5; world-wide productions, 294–5, 353; filmed, 295

Oh What a Lovely War (musical), 191

Olivier, Laurence, Baron: in Birmingham, 37; plays Richard III, 38; as Shallow, 53, 60; as Lear, 60; *Hamlet* film, 76; KT criticises as director, 86; KT advises, 91; plays with Vivien Leigh, 94; KT meets, 119; in *The Entertainer*, 135; plays Coriolanus, 164; as Director of National Theatre, 175, 215–22, 225–6, 250; Harewood interviews, 184; at 1962 Edinburgh Festival conference, 204; relations with KT, 219, 221–3, 302, 305, 336, 386; personality, 222–3; at work, 227; and censorship, 228–9, 239; and *Soldiers*, 251–6, 262, 275; and *Strindberg's Dance of Death*, 253; conflict with Chandos, 253–5, 263, 275; health, 262–3, 274, 302; and KT's proposed *Lear*, 274–5; defends KT at National, 275–6; and imposing self, 292; at Tynans' party, 299; and *Guys and Dolls*, 302; plays Shylock, 302; and Garcia, 302–3; and National failures, 303; in *Long Day's Journey into Night*, 304; Hall succeeds at National, 313–15; leaves National, 335–7; in *The Party*, 336; and KT's National severance pay, 337; myosotis, 350; visits Tynans, 350; KT's television interview with, 352; describes KT 354; KT plans profile of, 365; KT meets in California, 386, 396; KT's proposed biography of, 386–7, 391, 393, 396, 399; and Vivien Leigh, 387–8

O'Neal, Tatum, 362

O'Neill, Eugene, 81, 86, 135, 186, 191, 304–5

One Pair of Eyes (TV programme), 272

Ono, Yoko, 256

'On Social Plays' (Miller), 123

'Open Letter to an American Liberal' (Tynan), 268

Open Theater, 279, 281

Ordóñez, Antonio, 158, 164–5, 183, 193

Orton, Joe, 256, 280, 294

Osborne, John: KT praises, 125–6; and social commitment, 134, 143; *Declaration* essay, 141; and KT's *Tempo* ideas, 184; adapts Lope de Vega play, 227; proposed as *Oh! Calcutta!* contributor, 278; on KT at National, 337; relations with KT, 343–4

Ostos, Jaime, 165

Othello (Shakespeare), 67, 85, 98, 227

O'Toole, Peter, 164, 218, 244, 343

Owen, Alun, 84, 241

Oxford: KT at University, 12, 38, 47–51; effect on KT, 13, 50, 78–9; Union debating society, 53, 61, 70, 73; Kathleen at, 201–2; KT's ashes buried in, 403–5

Oxford Circus (revue), 76

Oxford Magazine, 53, 61

Oxford University Dramatic Society, 38, 67, 201

Oxford Viewpoint, 67, 71

Oz (magazine), 296

Pabst, G. W., 376, 378–9

Pal Joey (O'Hare, Rogers and Hart), 100, 107

Paley, William, 377, 379, 382

Pandora's Box (film), 376, 379

Panorama (magazine), 91, 93

Parents terribles, Les (Cocteau) *see Intimate Relations*

Paris, 117, 389

Paris Review, 106, 153, 165–6

Parker, Gillian *see* Rowe-Dutton, Gillian

Parker, Sir Peter, 56–7, 73, 78

Parker, Stanley, 63–4, 72

Party, The (Griffiths), 336

Peacock, Albert (KT's uncle), 14, 17

Peacock, Annie (*née* Timmins; Sir Peter's first wife), 14, 21

Peacock, Bertha, 15, 74

Peacock, Douglas (Sir Peter's son), 17

Peacock, George (Sir Peter's nephew), 17, 74, 84

Peacock, Jesse and Susan (*née* Grummitt; Sir Peter's parents), 14

Peacock, Maria, Lady (*née* Timmins; Sir Peter's second wife), 15, 17–18, 74

Peacock, Marian (Sir Peter's daughter), 15, 17

Peacock, Sir Peter (KT's father): relations with KT, 12, 20–1, 23, 25, 32, 39; effect of death on KT, 13; life and career, 13–15, 17–18; knighted, 15; relations with Rose Tynan, 16–18, 22–3; character, 18, 21; holidays with family, 20; theatrical influence on KT, 25–6; death, 73–5; in KT's psychoanalysis, 186–7

Peacock, Peter (son of Sir Peter), 14, 17

Peacock, Reginald (Sir Peter's son), 17

Peacock, Stanley (Sir Peter's son), 17

Peer Gynt (Ibsen), 38, 117

Peking Opera, 117

Pelléas et Melisande (Maeterlinck), 57

Penrose, John, 83

Perelman, S. J.: *All-Girl Elephant Hunt*, 113

Philippe, Gérard, 117

Phillips, William, 153

Phipps, Diana, 261, 389, 404

Physicists, The (Dürrenmatt), 191

Picture Post (magazine), 25, 120

Pierrot le Fou (film), 241

Pilbrow, Richard, 257, 357

Pinter, Harold, 177, 180, 206, 256, 270, 279, 296

Piscator, Erwin, 210

Pitt-Rivers, Michael, 109

Play (Beckett), 218, 221, 225

Playboy (magazine), 244–5, 266–7, 271, 290, 292, 296

Play's the Thing, The (Molnar), 335–6

Plimpton, George, 106, 153–4, 159; *Shadow Box*, 159

Plowright, Joan (Lady Olivier), and KT's proposed *Lear*, 274; and National Theatre, 216–7, 220, 222–3; at Tynan's party, 299; defends KT, 263; life with Olivier, 253; on Peter Hall, 312–3

Plume de ma tante, La (Dhéry), 150, 277

Poel, William, 66

Poitier, Sidney, 160

Polanski, Roman, 2, 91, 269, 280, 292, 299, 306–7

Pollock, Ellen, 96

Pope, Virginia, 200
Portman, Eric, 118
Potter, Dennis, 274
Potter, Gillie, 26
Pratt, John, 119
Praz, Mario: *The Romantic Agony*, 56
Prchal, Edward, 263
Prendergast, Tessa, 90
Present Laughter (Coward), 81
Pretenders, The (Ibsen), 61
Priestley, J. B., 80
Princess Zoubaroff, The (Firbank), 87, 199, 335–6
Pringle, Bryan, 164
Private Eye (magazine), 209, 267, 292–3, 343
Problem of Pain, The (Lewis), 347
Prouse, Derek, 85, 129
Pryce-Jones, Alan, 184
Puerto Vallarta, Mexico, 388, 390–4
Punch (magazine), 107
Puttnam, David, 352, 371
Pygmalion (Shaw), 82

Quadrille (Coward), 98
Quare Fellow, The (Behan), 126
Quayle, Anthony, Sir, 215
Quennell, Peter, 45
Quesnet, Marie-Constance, 367
Quest for Corbett, The (KT and Harold Lang), 129
Quintero, José, 135
Quitak, Oscar, 82

Rabbinowitz, Eileen, 74–6, 341
Rack, The (Lindsay), 8, 56
Rafter, Georgina (*née* Tynan; KT's aunt), 16–17

Raisin in the Sun, A (Lorraine Hansberry), 160–1
Rattigan, Terence, 103, 107, 115
Rawlinson, Sir Peter, 293
Ray, Johnnie, 102
Raymond, John, 261
Rayne, Sir Max (later Baron), 304, 312–14, 337
Reckord, Barry, 332
Recruiting Officer, The (Farquhar), 227
Redgrave, Sir Michael, 80, 86
Redgrave, Vanessa, 269–70
Rees-Mogg, Sir William, 51, 355
Reich, Wilhelm, 173, 258; KT writes on and studies, 316–19, 322, 325, 333, 342, 344; on masochism, 327; *The Sexual Revolution*, 316
Renaud, Madeleine, 299
Report on the Party and the Guests, A (film), 242
Repulsion (film), 242
Resistible Rise of Arturo Ui (Brecht), 163
Return of the Prodigal Son, The (film), 242
Rexroth, Kenneth, 168
Reynolds, Stanley, 237
Rhinoceros (Ionesco), 144
Richard III (Shakespeare), 37–8, 190
Richards, Lloyd, 160
Richards, Rev. M. G., 403
Richardson, Jack, 152
Richardson, Maurice, 197

Richardson, Sir Ralph, 37–8, 52–3, 60, 364
Richardson, Samuel, 42
Richardson, Tony, 51, 73, 123–4, 348, 363, 396
Richman, Stella, 87, 89
Rigg, Diana, 305
Ritzy, Regal and Super (revue), 71
Rivera, Diego, 154
Robbe-Grillet, Alain, 295
Robbins, Jerome, 161, 191, 283
Robinson, Robert, 236
Robinson, Sugar Ray, 103
Rodgers, Richard, 150
Romain, Jules, 38
Romantic Agony, The (Praz), 56
Romeo and Juliet (Shakespeare), 177
Rookery Nook (Ben Travers), 26, 82
Room At The Top (Braine), 87
Roots (Wesker), 164
Rosenberg, Heyman, 88, 99
Rosencrantz and Guildenstern Are Dead (Stoppard), 218
Ross, Annie, 128
Ross, Harold, 149
Roud, Richard, 144
Roundhouse, London, 293
Rowe-Dutton, Gillian (Lady Parker), 50, 62–5, 67–8, 78, 186
Royal Court Theatre *see* English Stage Company
Royal Dramatic Theatre (Sweden), 177, 219
Royal Hunt of the Sun, The (Shaffer), 218
Royal Shakespeare Company, 190–1
Ruark, Robert, 130

Rudkin, David, 274
Runyon, Damon, 25
Russell, Bertrand, 186, 268
Russell, Nipsey, 171
Russell, Rosalind, 102

Sacher-Masoch, Leopold von, 60
Sade, Marquis de, 6, 46, 367
Sagan, Françoise, 162, 184
Sagner, Alan, 172
Sahl, Mort, 148, 152, 179
St Joan of the Stockyards (Brecht), 163
St Just, Maria, Lady, 95–6, 138, 183
Saint's Day (Whiting), 116
Salieri, Franz, 331
Salinger, Pierre and Nicole, 312
Salome (Wilde), 64
Salzburg, 85
Sampson, Anthony, 203
Samson Agonistes (Milton), 65–7, 96
San Francisco, 168–9
Sane Nuclear Policy (USA), 171, 173
Sappington, Margo, 280, 282
Saroyan, Carol (Matthau), 112–13, 139, 166
Sarraute, Nathalie, 184
Sartre, Jean-Paul, 49, 56, 103, 122–3, 143, 172, 176, 190, 268
Saturday, Sunday, Monday (de Filippo), 336
Saundby, Air Marshal Sir Robert, 252
Saura, Carlos, 374
Saved (Bond), 239
Scarfe, Gerald, 267
Schall, Ekkehard, 163

Schlesinger, John, 51
Schorm, Evald, 242
Schwartz, Arthur, 170
Scofield, Paul, 37, 73, 122, 190, 303
Scott, George, 67
Scott-Fox, Judy, 189
Screwtape Proposes a Toast (Lewis), 404
Segal, Clancy, 249
Sellers, Peter, 152
Senft, Paul, 186–8
Separate Tables (Rattigan), 115
Seven Year Itch, The (George Axelrod), 102
Shadow Box (Plimpton), 159
Shadow of a Gunman, The (O'Casey), 150
Shadow of Heroes (Ardrey), 249
Shadow Play (Coward), 327
Shaffer, Peter, 218, 224, 274
Shaw, George Bernard, 128, 184
Shaw, Robert, 92, 164
Shaw, Irwin and Marion, 106, 113
Shawn, William: at New Yorker, 146–7, 149–51, 161, 164, 170, 316, 353, 364, 375–6, 399; and KT's death, 402–3
Sheftel, Judy *see* Feiffer, Judy
Shepard, Sam, 280
Sherrin, Ned, 236–7
Shock, Maurice, 28, 33–4
Shop on Main Street, The (film), 241
'Shouts and Murmurs' (Tynan), 265–8
Shrimpton, Jean, 256
Shulman, Milton, 93, 104–5, 336
Sick Sick Sick (Feiffer), 153

Siggs, Barbara (Simon), 41
Sigh No More (Coward), 43
Sight and Sound (magazine), 90–1, 124, 134
Sights and Spectacles (McCarthy), 184
Sikorski, General Wladyslaw, 251–3, 263
Silvers, Phil, 100, 103, 170, 231, 288
Simon, Joe, 41
Simon, John, 404
Simpson, N.F., 110, 144, 180
Sinden, Donald, 80
Six Characters in Search of an Author (Pirandello), 82
Sketch, The (journal), 98
Skin of Our Teeth, The (Wilder), 94
Slight Ache, A (Pinter), 177
Smith, Frank, 293
Smith, Godfrey, 20
Smith, Harold, 15
Smith, Maggie, 140, 220, 302
Smith, Perry, 246
Smith, Roger, 175, 249
Snow, Carmel, 99
Snowdon, Antony Armstong Jones, Earl of, 201, 212–13, 270, 290
Sobers, Sir Garfield, 265
Sokolsky, George E., 171
Soldiers (Hochhuth), 228; controversy over, 249–54, 262–3; produced, 263–4, 275; libel writ, 264, 315
Sondheim, Stephen, 161
Song of Songs, The, 60
Sontag, Susan, 268

Sound of Music, The (musical), 169

Sourwine, J. G., 172

South Pacific (musical), 99

Southern, Terry, 152–3, 165, 198, 222, 278

Spain: KT visits, 120–1, 130, 139, 164–5, 183, 204, 213, 246, 348, 366, 381–4; KT's liking for, 192–6; *see also* bull-fighting

Spanish Tragedy, The (Kyd), 70

Spare Rib (magazine), 301

Spectator (weekly journal), 91, 99

Spectorsky, A. C., 258, 268, 271

Spiegel, Sam, 349

Spring Awakening (Wedekind), 228

Sri Lanka, 326–7

Stamp, Terence, 256

Stanislavsky, Konstantin, 66, 143

Stapleton, Maureen, 100

Staynes, Gillian, 68

Stein, Jean, 395

Steinbeck, John, 149

Steiner, George, 405; *The Death of Tragedy*, 267; 'Night Words', 267

Steiner, Rudolf, 92

Stephens, Robert, 220

Stern, Isaac, 185

Stevenson, Adlai, 103

Stewart, Desmond, 72

Stewart, Donald Ogden, 209, 234

Stewart, Donald Ogden, Jnr., 151, 209

Stockholm, 176

Stoppard, Tom, 2, 175, 218, 226, 262, 301, 306, 365, 405

Strange Interlude (O'Neill), 191

Strasberg, Lee, 132, 143

Stratford-upon-Avon, 37

Streetcar Named Desire, A (Tennessee Williams), 86

Stride, John, 223

Strindberg, August, 225, 253

Styne, Jule, 161, 258

Styron, Rose and William, 260, 271

Suez War, 1956, 133–4

'Suite for Five Letters' (Tynan), 25, 280, 295

Suites d'un course, Les, 122

Summer Aeroplane, The (Kathleen Tynan), 347

Sundquist, Nancy, 390–11

Sutherland, Graham, 185

Sweeney Agonistes (T. S. Eliot), 57, 66

Sweet and Low (revue), 43

Sweet Bird of Youth (Tennessee Williams), 150, 161

Sweetest and Lowest (revue), 76

Taber, Robert, 172

Taming of the Shrew, The (Shakespeare), 37, 69, 82, 92

Taste of Honey, A (Shelagh Delaney), 164

Tate, Sharon, 269, 292

Tati, Jacques, 107, 150

Taylor, Elizabeth, 263, 313

Tempo (TV programme), 184–6

Tennant, Emma, 307

Tennent, H. M., 83

Tesler, Brian, 185

That Hideous Strength (Lewis), 308

That's Entertainment (film), 343

Theatre Act, 1970, 256

Théâtre de l'Epée du Bois, Le, 10

Théâtre National Populaire, Paris, 117

Theatre Newsletter, 86

Theatre of Bertolt Brecht, The (Willett), 163

Theatre of the Absurd, The (Esslin), 181

Theatre Workshop, London, 110, 118, 177, 180, 191

These Ghosts (de Filippo), 335

Thewlis, Rev. Frank and Edna, 145–6

Thomas, Dylan, 69, 76, 112–3, 272

Thomas, Norman, 171

Thorndike, Elizabeth, 85

Threepenny Opera (Brecht/Weill), 85, 117, 123, 163

Thurber, James, 2, 25, 149, 173

Thurloe Square, South Kensington: Tynans' home in, 247, 257, 260; parties at, 269–70, 273, 344; lease extended, 300

Time magazine, 30, 109, 268

Time and Tide (journal), 178

Times, The (newspaper): on KT's Oxford theatricals, 61, 80; on *Oh! Calcutta!*, 293–4; KT writes to, 329; accuses KT of accepting pornography, 355–6, 371

Titus Andronicus (Shakespeare), 96, 119, 135

Toland, Gregg, 31

Tolkin, Mel, 170
Tolstoy, Count Lev, 288
Tomalin, Nicholas, 338
Top Banana (musical), 100, 103, 231
Topol, Josef, 246
Topolski, Feliks, 354
Topolski, Daniel, 354, 372
Topolski, Marion, 354
Towne, Robert, 363
Toy in Blood, A (adaptation of Hamlet scene), 60, 66
Toynbee, Philip, 144, 197
Tracy, Spencer, 90, 272
Travers, Ben, 82, 358
Treasure Island (film), 214
Tribune (journal), 142
Trick or Treat (film), 352
Trilling, Lionel, 289
Trouille, Camille Clovis, 243, 277–8, 280
Trumpets and Drums (Brecht adaptation of Farquhar), 131
Tsai Chin, *see* Chin, Tsai
Tucci, Niccolo, 151
Tunisia, 322–4
Tyger (Adrian Mitchell), 303, 310, 403
Tynan, Bill (Rose's nephew), 16
Tynan, Georgina (aunt), 16
Tynan, Kathleen (*née* Halton; KT's second wife): childhood of, 199–201; children of, *see* Tynan, Matthew Blake; Tynan, Roxana Nell; cooking of, 8, 269, 307–8; diaries of, 199–200, 202, 260, 299; divorce of, 233, 247; education of, 200–2; first book of, 347; first marriage of, *see* Gates, Oliver;

political protests of, 268–9; pregnancies of, 247, 257–260, 307; Tynan's love for, 247–8, 298–9, 309, 328–9, 392; Tynan's marriage to, 199, 258–9; Tynan's relationship with, 5, 193–6, 197–9, 204–14, 230–5, 243–4, 247–8, 257–61, 262, 288–9, 298–300, 320–9, 339, 372; writing career of, 197–8, 203, 204, 205, 231, 272, 277, 298, 328, 332, 347, 352, 369, 371–2, 385–6
Tynan, Ken (Kenneth Peacock Tynan): acting career of, 12, 20, 21, 38, 42–3, 49, 53, 57, 59, 60, 61, 67, 70, 81, 85, 92–3; actors' reactions to, 95, 98, 104, 109, 223–4; aesthetic standards of, 10, 86, 265–6; aloofness of, 223–4; America attractive to, 20, 71, 89, 90, 110, 173; anti-authoritarianism of, 25, 32, 39, 126, 240–1; arrogance of, 84, 366; articles by, 71, 85–6, 93–4, 141, 244–5, 268, 287; autobiography planned by, 2–3, 113, 118, 141, 151, 198, 286, 390, 393–4; birth of, 13, 19; 'black book' kept by, 35; breakdown of, 182–3; brilliance of, 2, 29, 404; bullfighting passion of, 68, 102, 164–5, 193, 195–6,

348, 351; causes championed by, 109–11, 177–9, 181, 215, 230, 232, 240, 251–5, 256; celebrities entertained by, 49, 69–70, 77, 231, 343–4, 269–70, 299; celebrity profiles by, 97, 98, 121, 130–1, 133, 183–4, 244, 257, 290–1, 316, 353, 364–5; censorship and, 87, 103, 116, 228–9, 236–41, 256, 302, 303 childhood illnesses of, 21 childhood of, 4, 12–13, 19–27, 291; childishness seen in, 52, 58, 351; children of, *see* Tynan, Matthew Blake; Tynan, Roxana Nell; Tynan, Tracy Peacock; clothing tastes of, 4, 7, 28–9, 41, 49, 51, 84, 88, 104, 109, 111, 194, 243, 361; college allowance of, 52, 75; college scholarship of, 38, 52; congenital illness of, 5, 71, 271–2; contradictions in personality of, 6, 25; controversial label attached to, 3; cricket enjoyed by, 3, 12, 20, 21, 24, 36, 41, 349; Cuban trips of, 156–60, 370; death feared by, 8, 71; death of, 2, 3, 401–4; debating skills of, 27, 33–4, 53, 61, 70, 73, 78; descriptions of, 50, 54–5, 59, 62, 64, 106, 162; diaries of, 23–5, 35, 120, 148, 299; directing career of, 6, 57, 59–60, 65–

7, 71–2, 73, 80–4, 96, 101; drama criticism of, 2, 26, 35, 52–3, 91–4, 97–102, 103–5, 109–11, 118–9; *see also individual publications and list of works*; early criticism by, 26, 36, 37–8; early death foreseen by, 71, 89; early education of, 20–22, 23–45; early literary efforts of, 35–6, 45–6, 53–7, 59–61, 65–7, 70; early theatrical interests of, 20, 21, 25–6, 29, 35–6, 37–8, 41–3; earnings of, 100, 108, 147, 183, 217, 270, 281, 316, 337, 353, 360, 375, 386; at Edinburgh drama conference, 204–7; engagements of, 40, 44–5, 52, 58, 64–5, 68–9, 80–1; 84–5, 89, 198; erotic projects of, 277–85, 306–10, 320, 330–2, 339, 356–7; failing health of, 285, 286–7, 321, 331, 338, 341, 345–6, 348, 357, 366–7, 383, 394–401; family relationships of, 39; as a father, 352, 361, 365, 374; favourite films of, 24–5, 30–1; film criticism of, 90, 91, 241–2; film festival organized by, 212–3; film lectures and symposia of, 33, 367–8; as film script advisor, 140; film writing of, 140, 308–9, 341–3 first book of, 26, 86; first marriage of, *see* Dundy, Elaine;

first published piece of, 27; four-letter words and, 3, 178, 236–41, 279, 302; game playing of, 3, 41, 58, 81, 154, 240, 299, 392; generosity of, 52, 58, 87, 129, 189; high definition performance defined by, 26, 265–6, 356; holidays of, 7–11, 106, 111–12, 113, 122, 130–1, 132–3, 154–67, 168–9, 182, 183, 246–7, 311–12, 326–7; homosexuality and, 32, 46, 57, 77, 109–10, 116, 223, 244, 279; hospitalization of, 271, 357, 384–5, 388, 396–7, 398–400, 401; House of Commons attack on, 238, 240; humour of, 4, 78, 136, 231, 241, 290; illegitimacy of, 6, 13, 19, 39, 73–5, 89, 187; illnesses of, 3, 5, 119, 189, *see* congenital illness of, inheritance of, 186, 247; journals of, 3, 20, 24, 25–6, 27, 30, 76, 139, 207, 296–7, 299–300, 310, 315, 329–30, 335, 346; lefthandedness of, 20, 36; libel suits against, 104, 264, 315; masturbation and, 12, 25, 27, 306, 351; military deferment of, 38–9, 77, 306; money problems of, 52, 84, 90, 262, 355, 367, 403; on monogamy, 232, 289, 296, 340; moral beliefs of, 261; mother of, *see* Tynan,

Letitia Rose; musical tastes of, 26, 36, 307; New York visits of, 99–100, 102, 146–154; obituaries on, 5, 236, 404; permissiveness espoused by, 57, 232, 239–40, 266–7; philosophy of, 56, 61, 71; playwrights admired by, 100, 103, 110–1, 117, 121–2; on playwrights and directors, 85–6, 135, 142–4, 150, 176–7, 180–1, 206; poetry of, 36, 45–6, 210, 234, 298, 385; political convictions of, 5, 34, 56–7, 103, 117–8, 122–3, 133–5, 141–2, 153, 161, 170–3, 177–9, 249–51, 261, 270–1, 296; pornography and, 127–8, 151, 184, 231–2, 244–5, 266–7, 284, 295, 306–9, 330–1, 355; on propaganda in theatre, 123, 143–4, 161, 249; psychoanalysis of, 13, 19, 119, 186–7, 211; Reichian research by, 316–9; on repertory theatre, 219–20; repertory theatre run by, 80–2; second marriage of, *see* Tynan, Kathleen Halton; self-image of, 2, 12, 66, 120, 121, 182–3, 232, 261, 297, 351–2, 355 sexual attitudes of, 25, 57–8, 76, 162, 236–41, 244–5, 266–7, 277, 294, 309; sexual development of, 25, 40, 306; sexual tastes

Tynan, Ken – *contd*
of, 5, 6, 188, 232,
284, 331, 332, 333;
shock and surprise
used by, 27, 52, 53,
96, 339, 351;
smoking habit of, 5,
47, 341, 367, 371,
387; snobbishness of,
2, 23; social relations
of, 57–8, 84, 87, 94–
5, 99, 166–7, 234–5,
269; Spanish trips of,
192–6, 213–4, 273–
4, 348, 373–4, 381–
4; stammering of, 19–
20, 49–50, 53, 59,
66, 80, 86, 99, 109,
146, 223, 363;
suicidal thoughts of, 3,
22, 186, 372–3;
television work of,
184–5, 186, 230,
272, 352–3; on
theatre criticism, 115,
128, 134, 353;
theatrical investments
of, 83–4; theatrical
manifesto by, 65–6;
twenty-first birthday
of, 72; vulnerability of,
58–9, 93, 109; words
respected by, 34–5,
54, 67, 260, 347;
writing style of, 20,
26, 35–6, 97–9, 103–
4; young professionals
inspired by, 175–6;
youthful friends of, 23,
28–36; youthful
reputation of, 41, 44
SOME WORKS: 'Art for Our
Sake', 121; *Bull Fever*,
102, 156; *Curtains*,
183–4, 380; *He That
Plays the King*, 26, 38,
52, 86, 102; 'The
Invincible Must'
(article), 70–1;
'Meditations on Basic
Baroque' (article), 25;

'Oxford Now' (article),
72; *Persona Grata*,
107; 'Production
Number' (revue
sketch), 71, 76, 82;
The Quest for Corbett
(with H. Lang), 129;
Show People, 395; *The
Sound of Two Hands
Clapping*, 351, 355;
Tynan Right and Left,
261; 'Valentine to
Tennessee', 121; *A
View of the English
Stage*, 355; 'Where
are the Playwrights?',
86
Tynan, Matthew Blake
(KT's son): 310, 332,
349, 352, 361, 385,
392–3, 394, 399,
400–2, 404
Tynan, Peter, *see*
Peacock, Peter
Tynan, Rose (Letitia Rose
Tynan; KT's mother):
birth of, 16; cooking
of, 24, 47; courtship
of, 16, 17; death of,
13, 185–6, 382;
description of, 16;
mental illness of, 13,
145–6, 185; Peter
Peacock's relationship
with, 13, 16, 18, 22,
74; religious
background of, 13, 16;
shame felt by, 13, 19,
22, 23, 74; Tynan
helped financially by,
75, 84, 90; Tynan's
affection for, 12, 22,
47, 146; Tynan's
neglect of, 145–6,
185, 382; Tynan's
relationship with, 19,
20, 21, 22, 39, 44,
48, 74, 90, 125, 145–
6
Tynan, Roxana Nell
(KT's daughter): 4, 7,

10, 260, 273, 287,
298, 299, 307, 310,
332, 343, 347, 352,
360–1, 381, 385,
392–3, 400–3, 404
Tynan, Samuel and
Anne Rebecca (*née*
Mitchell; Rose's
parents), 16
Tynan, Tracy Peacock
(KT's daughter): 101,
103, 105, 127, 137,
138, 145, 149, 161,
246, 401–2, 404;
childhood of, 166,
182, 183, 189, 204,
210, 233, 234;
education of, 204,
298, 349; film work
of, 371, 381; 21st
birthday party of, 329;
Tynan's relationship
with, 105, 154, 208,
209, 233, 234, 260,
301, 349, 353, 374,
385, 390

Uncle Vanya (Chekhov),
142–3, 216
Under Milk Wood (Dylan
Thomas), 113, 202
Under-Thirty Theatre
Group, 82, 85, 87
Unfinished Woman, An
(Hellman), 287
'Unilateral Triangle, The'
(Tynan), 26
Unquiet Grave, The
(Connolly), 130
US (docudrama), 250
Ustinov, Peter, 83, 90,
101, 111

Vadim, Roger, 184
Valencia, 195–6, 213,
273, 382–3
Valk, Frederick, 67, 81,
84, 102
Van Damm, Vivian, 82
Vanderbilt, Gloria, 139,
154

Venice Preserv'd (Otway), 103

Vidal, Gore, 144, 160, 173, 184, 204, 243, 260, 285, 295, 363, 367, 375, 404

Vietnam, 250, 268–9

View from the Bridge, A (Arthur Miller), 123, 133

Vilar, Jean, 117

Vinaver, Steve, 234, 258

Visconti, Luchino, 298

Vitti, Monica, 207

Vogue (magazine), 72, 99, 268, 272

Vonnegut, Kurt, Jr., 280

Vreeland, Diana, 285

WR – Mysteries of the Organism (film), 316

Wain, John, 51, 60, 75

Waiting for Godot (Beckett), 121–2, 134, 206

Wajda, Andrzej, 205

Walker, Roy, 86

Wall, Max, 329

Wallace, Hazel Vincent, 82, 89

Wanamaker, Sam, 123

Wandering Jew, The (E. Temple Thurston), 104

War Game, The (film), 242

Wardle, Irving, 175–6, 294

Warner, Marina, 269

Warrington, Lancashire, 13–14

Wars of the Roses, The (adaptation, Shakespeare), 190

Warsaw, 176

Watergate theatre, London, 87

Waterhouse, Keith, 180

Watts, Alan, 168

Watts, Richard, Jr., 99, 101, 151

Waugh, Evelyn: *Brideshead Revisited*, 50, 116

We Dissent (TV documentary), 170–3

Webb, Alan, 92

Webber, C. E., 82–3

Webster, John, 45, 274

Wedekind, Frank, 228, 376

Weeks, Sheila, 360

Weidenfeld, George, Baron, 299, 315, 346

Weigel, Helene, 132, 176, 313, 350

Weill, Kurt, 179, 195

Weldon, Huw, 237

Welles, Finlay, 86

Welles, Orson: on English children, 19; influence on KT, 30–2, 214; KT writes on, 31, 98, 118, 183; Capote on, 70; KT proposes for *A Citizen of the World*, 82–3; writes introduction to *He that Plays the King*, 86; KT criticises *Othello*, 98; influence, 110; in Spain, 183, 189, 213; in KT's *Tempo* programme, 184; Kathleen meets, 213–14; on Falstaff, 214; KT interviews for *Playboy*, 244; declines *Soldiers*, 263; in California, 368

Welles, Paula, 189

Wells, John, 267, 329, 346

Wesker, Arnold, 110, 125, 164

Wesley, David, 171

West of Suez (Osborne), 343

West Rebecca, 103

Westbrook, Mike, 303

White Devil, The (Webster), 274

White, Michael, 9, 263–4, 279–80, 285, 293, 330

Whitehead, Robert, 160, 191

Whitehouse, Mary, 237, 293

Whiting, John, 115, 184–5

Whittle, Pauline, 42–3, 44, 47–8, 52, 56, 58, 64, 74, 84, 211

'Who Killed Kennedy?' campaign, 231

Who's Afraid of Virginia Woolf? (Albee), 191

Wiene, Robert, 33

Wigram, Michael, 195

Wild Duck, The (Ibsen), 129, 136

Wilde, Oscar, 25, 49, 50, 64, 68, 72, 116

Wildeblood, Peter, 70, 76, 84, 87, 90, 109–10, 120, 179

Wilder, Billy and Audrey, 362

Wilder, Thornton, 100, 110, 227

Willett, John: *The Theatre of Bertolt Brecht*, 163

Williams, Charles, 403

Williams, Clifford, 190, 263–4, 274, 293–4, 330, 338, 356–7

Williams, Emlyn, 87, 227

Williams, Leonard, 358

Williams, Shirley Catlin, 51

Williams, Tennessee: friendship with KT, 83, 95–6, 100, 340; influence, 110–11; with KT in Spain, 120–1; meets Hemingway, 157–8; in Cuba, 157–9; praises KT on Brecht, 163; sketch for *Oh! Calcutta!*, 280

Williamson, Nicol, 290–2

Wilson, Angus, 123

Wilson, Edmund, 173, 406; *Classics and Commercials*, 184

Willson, Effingham, 215

Wilson, Harold, 238, 291

Wilson, Sandy, 71, 76, 87, 103, 138, 140

Winchell, Walter, 268

Windmill Theatre, London, 82

Winebrenner, Michele, 372, 386

Winter, Ella, 234

Winterset (Maxwell Anderson), 71–2, 84

Wodehouse, P. G., 3, 24

Wolfe, Digby, 122

Wolfit, Donald, 26, 37–8, 47, 52, 67, 73, 104, 200

Woman Killed with Kindness, A (Heywood), 303

Wonderful Town (musical), 102

Wood, Charles, 256

Wooldridge, May (*née* Tynan; KT's aunt), 16–17, 19, 90, 185

Woolf, Marie *see* Beesley, Marie

Woollcott, Alexander, 26, 33

Workers' Film Association, 33

World of Suzie Wong, The (play adapt. by Paul Osborne), 150

Wyatt, Alix (Colman), 105

Wyatt, Woodrow, 105

Wyler, William, 110

X, Malcolm, 173

You Can't Take It With You (Kaufman and Hart), 42

Young, Hazel (Holt), 41

Young, Wayland (2nd Baron Kennet), 142

Zaiman, Elisabeth (Harris), 58, 69

Zeffirelli, Franco, 176, 204, 218, 336

Zen Buddhism, 168, 261, 265–6, 347

Zetterling, Mai, 83

Zuckmayer, Carl, 303